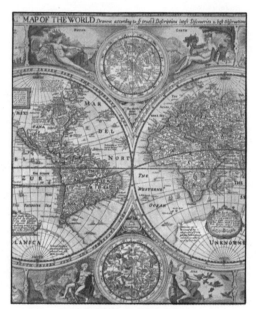

An Intellectual History of Modern Europe

second edition

Roland N. Stromberg
University of Wisconsin—Milwaukee

Prentice-Hall, Inc., Englewood Cliffs, New Jersey

Library of Congress Cataloging in Publication Data

STROMBERG, ROLAND N
    An intellectual history of modern Europe.

    Bibliography: p.
    Includes index.
    1. Philosophy, Modern—History. 2. Europe—
Intellectual life—History. I. Title.
B791.S84   1975   190   74-22388
ISBN 0-13-469106-7

Printed in the United States of America

10 9 8 7 6 5 4 3 2 1

Prentice-Hall International, Inc., *London*

Prentice-Hall of Australia, Pty., Ltd., *Sydney*

Prentice-Hall of Canada, Ltd., *Toronto*

Prentice-Hall of India Private Limited, *New Delhi*

Prentice-Hall of Japan, Inc., *Tokyo*

One cannot live without ideas; every step one takes
is directed, if not by a conscious, at least
by an unconscious or sub-conscious idea.

    ARNOLD HOTTINGER

All human history is fundamentally a history of ideas.

    H. G. WELLS

The narrowest life is the one into which there
enter the fewest ideas.

    VERNON LEE

There is but one thing more interesting than the
intellectual history of a man, and that is the
intellectual history of a nation.

    MOSES COIT TYLER

Contents

14

Preface

The reception accorded the first edition of this book (1966) was pleasant indeed. The publisher and I received many favorable comments from those teaching and writing in this field at colleges and universities small and large (and a few secondary schools too). I would like to thank all those who encouraged me by these comments, and would do so by name here, were it not that the list is a very long one. Many—students as well as teachers—offered helpful criticisms and corrections, and for these I am grateful.

The book evidently has served usefully in a large number of courses in modern history. On the basis of this reception one might feel justified in making few changes. Yet I have felt a need to do more than that, chiefly because I think the subject is one in which rapid development has taken place during the last few years: a great deal of interest, a great many more intellectual history courses taught, a considerable amount of new research, and a growing sophistication about the subject. Some alterations of fact or stress have been dictated by additions to knowledge coming from recent books, or by an improvement in my own education derived from greater study of certain areas. In general, though, I have not so much changed as added. This is especially true of the more recent period, where a fair number of readers requested fuller treatment, a request that seems especially valid in view of present intense interest in contemporary ideas, and to which I am the more sympathetic since I have lately tended to teach and work in the 19th–20th centuries rather than the earlier periods.

The bibliography, of course, has been updated, a large task in view of the quantity of recent writing. Many found this an especially valuable feature of the book; I have tried to make it as full as a necessarily selective listing in a huge area can be.

The preface to the first edition spoke of the need for a basic textbook in modern European intellectual history, combining adequate coverage with relative brevity, a nucleus around which one might build a course by adding source readings and other supplementary reading. Such a book "should be fairly concise, well-informed, attractively written, well-organized . . . full enough to raise the issues and introduce the topics that need to be introduced, above all able to stimulate the student to more exact investigations, and supply him with the references he needs to carry on these; yet not so long as to become tedious, and to drown the beginning student in detail." This goal has not been basically altered.

The earlier preface made the obvious point that this book rests on the labors of many other scholars working in the history of ideas who must supply the building blocks for any such synthesis. This battery of inquirers now has greatly increased. All academic fields have grown; but it is hardly in doubt that intellectual history appeals more to the newer generations of students and professors than most other branches of history. This is true in the United States and also in other countries. "The average citizen wants to know about his heritage of civilization, which is contained in a fabric of thought so old and complex that guides are urgently needed," the first preface observed. The citizen wants to know about the world in which he lives, we might add, a confused and churning world concerning which one observation at least would not be challenged: ideas are in ferment. And some of them, alive and vital today, are very old ideas. Radical youth, for all its "nowism", seems to thrive on the thoughts of those early Victorian thinkers, Marx and Kierkegaard, while neoconservatives resurrect Burke and Tocqueville. Debates about the role of science in cultural life are as fresh in the era of Snow and Leavis as they were in the time of Huxley and Arnold, or Newton and Swift. In brief, ideas which were born one or two or even three centuries ago are highly relevant to our present situation.

Whether or not it is true, as H. G. Wells urged, that all history at bottom is a history of ideas, certainly there are those to whom intellectual history is the most exciting kind of history, combining as it does, or should do, the special excitement of Man Thinking with an attempt to show this thinking in its connections with the realm of fact and action and as part of a larger cultural unity. Comments on the nature and status of intellectual history are best expressed elsewhere. A preface is a place to acknowledge debts; these, in addition to those mentioned, include (in this as in the first edition) the author's students, who over the years have given him knowledge and inspiration as well as satisfaction.

Roland N. Stromberg

1

The Age of Science and Enlightenment:
1590-1789

To "trace the history of the human mind," said Hume, is the task of the historian, as distinct from the chronicler. Voltaire added that "it is better to know how men thought in former times than how they acted." A great deal of intellectual history has crept, willy-nilly, into history, it being impossible to keep out the men of ideas. A current collection of readings offered to students of the beginning college course in Western civilization includes selections from Plato, Aristotle, the Bible, Cicero, Augustine, Aquinas, Machiavelli, Rabelais, Luther, Calvin, Bodin, Descartes, Locke, Bossuet, Rousseau, Burke, Tocqueville, Marx, Nietzsche, Sartre, and Camus. Obviously it would be difficult to justify their exclusion from such a course. One wonders, though, to what extent most freshmen are equipped to grapple with these formidable adversaries.

We no longer restrict history to politics or public events, if for no other reason than that these cannot be "understood" without reference to the climate of opinion in which they took place. The deeds of Charlemagne cannot be understood apart from the peculiar mixture of ideas and values that made up the mind of his age, a mind quite different from ours. Nor, to come closer to home in both space and time, can the deeds of Thomas Jefferson be understood except in the context of the Enlightenment—a "lost world," as one Jefferson student has cogently argued. Some men of ideas "made history" directly—Luther, for example. Others, who did not, contributed so much to those who did that we cannot leave them out: Robespierre had his Rousseau, Lenin his Marx. "If ideas in politics more than elsewhere are the children of practical needs," J. N. Figgis has written, "none the less is it true, that the actual world is the result of men's thought. The existing arrangement of political forces is dependent at least as much upon ideas, as it is upon men's perceptions of their interests." "Not ideas, but material and ideal interests directly govern man's conduct," Max Weber held, but he added "Yet very frequently the world images which have been created by ideas have, like switchmen, determined the tracks along which action has been pushed by the dynamics of interest." Nothing is falser than the view, often associated with a kind of vulgar Marxism (Marx never held it), that ideas are merely the mechanical reflection of some supposedly nonintellectual material interest. There is nothing mechanical about an idea. Created in the mysterious ways of individual genius, it will then be acted upon in the realm of social reality and can partly decide the nature of that reality. Or, as Lord Acton observed, if men are stimulated by the hope of material gain, they can also be stimulated to action "by political or religious motives with no hope of material profit, and a certainty of material loss." Nothing is greater than the power of an idea; if greatest "when its time has come," i.e. when it agrees with the direction of social evolution, the idea yet remains an indispensable part of the recipe for meaningful action; even if it runs against the main flow of social evolution, an idea can be important.

Here is not the place to go into the troublesome question of just how *ideas* and *interests* act together in history. It is enough to observe that they do interact, that they are the "two faces of reality," in Jean Lhomme's expression, which one sees in all the great issues of mankind. Ideas are quite commonly found first in the mind of some unworldly person, a recluse like Bentham, an obscure pauper like Marx, a poor vagabond like Rousseau; then they are taken up by men of affairs, who, as John Maynard Keynes observed, snatch them from the air perhaps without knowing that they came from some scribbler of yesterday.

The interaction of historically important ideas with the social milieu from which they emerge and which they in turn influence—this is, broadly, the domain of intellectual history. The separate disciplines, such as philosophy, the sciences, or political theory, insofar as they study their past ideas tend to do so unhistorically, treating them substantively and as if they arose in a vacuum. It must remain for the intellectual historian to show how these ideas interacted with social reality, with past ideas, and with each other. At any particular time and place there is a specific set of influences on the human mind, which includes (1) the legacy of past ideas available to men at that time, (2) a social context, consisting of all sorts of phenomena prominent in the environment of the times, political, economic, etc., and (3) other contemporary strains of thought and expression. If, for example, we wish to grasp the thought of Nietzsche, we have to know the older thinkers who influenced him (a great many reaching back to the Greeks); some more than others, such as his immediate predecessor Schopenhauer, also his social atmosphere, of nineteenth-century bourgeois culture, together with such events as the Franco-Prussian War and the Bismarckian supremacy; and finally other significant intellectual movements of his time, among them French estheticism, Darwinism, socialism, etc. A recent European scholar has remarked, "There is room for a discipline whose aim is to assess the factors which influence the human mind in one period or in one region," this being his definition of the realm of intellectual history.

What validates or testifies to the importance of intellectual systems? Few of them, if any, can stand the test of absolute logic: the great philosophies have all turned out to be postulates at bottom, mere assertions, fiats, resting on something assumed to be true without proof. This is quite as true of allegedly "scientific" structures such as Marxism, Newtonian physics, or logical positivism as it is of more patently "metaphysical" ones. The reason they appear and are adopted, become popular and influential, is related to factors other than the merely immanent laws of thought. These factors, it may be suggested, are historical and social; historical, in that ideas evolve in time as one generation hands down its thoughts to others who take them up and use them as a point of departure—the endless dialectic of intellectual history; social, in that the selection of some ideas rather than others for emphasis and discussion has to do with the structure of social reality at a given time—the issues, atmosphere, and great events of the day. Even genius must create with reference to the external social world it finds to hand; it cannot create in a vacuum.

Intellectual history as an academic discipline is fairly new and probably has yet to complete the task of clarifying its scope, methods, and content. Clearly the subject matter is intensely interesting, for those with a flair for ideas. Some do not have this taste and should probably avoid the subject. Indeed, other historians, fact-minded, often lack it, which is perhaps a reason why they suspect intellectual history. Defined as the study of the role of *ideas* in historical events and processes, intellectual history is admittedly a difficult art. In this connection a recent student observes that historical writing of the usual sort "often fails to apprehend the slow subterranean movements which minds inclined to be too matter-of-fact find intangible"[1]–those movements of the mind, of ideas and ideologies and tides of taste, which never appear overtly in history until one day, perchance, they explode in a French Revolution. While the details of politics and administrations and wars are studied in the most minute detail, because they are neatly documented in archives and can be grasped by the matter-of-fact mind, the role of ideas may be dismissed in a vague phrase or two. The need for careful and precise studies in intellectual history is now recognized and is being met.[2] But much work remains to be done.

Writing some years ago, that philosopher so celebrated in the "history of ideas," Arthur O. Lovejoy, noted the unnatural fragmentation of the study of ideas, apportioned out among at least twelve "disciplines."[3] While students of literature, of the arts, of science, theology, education, social thought, etc., each cart away a portion of the body of Western thought, to dissect it minutely in the privacy of their chambers in isolation from each other, the whole organism perishes of this process, and there is no one to restore it to life unless a discipline called "history of ideas" can do so. The specialist work done by the various departments of learning is extensive and valuable, but badly needs to be collated. And a service may be rendered to these various departments themselves, for Milton's poetry cannot be understood apart from the poet's store of general ideas, nor can Darwin's science be fully grasped without this context. That sometimes disparaged entity, the *Zeitgeist*, the "spirit of the age," assuredly does exist. Coleridge, perhaps, put it best: "Such as is the existing spirit of speculation, during any given period, such will be the spirit and tone of the religion and morals, nay even of the fine arts, the manners, and the fashions." (Nor is this the less true, he added, "because the great majority of men live like bats, but in twilight, and know and feel the philosophy of their age only by its reflections and refractions.") Later culture historians have attached much importance to the *generation* as a key to the discovery of that mysterious but omnipresently real set of the mind which permeates all aspects of the thought and expression of an era.

As an introductory textbook, in a difficult domain of study still far from mature, this volume need offer no apology for its defects.

[1]Henri Peyre, "The Influence of Eighteenth-Century Ideas on the French Revolution," *Journal of the History of Ideas*, January, 1949.

[2]See some apposite remarks in the introduction to Walter M. Simon, *European Positivism in the Nineteenth Century*, 1963.

[3]"The Historiography of Ideas," in *Essays in the History of Ideas*, 1948.

Introductory textbooks are intended for the important function of introducing the as yet fairly unsophisticated student to fields which it is hoped he will further explore, with the aid of the suggestions for additional reading supplied. This book should of course also be supplemented by outside readings in the sources of intellectual history. Asked what to read, Walter Pater advised students to "read the great authors whole; read Plato whole; read Kant whole; read Mill whole." Excellent advice, but a little impractical for many students. This textbook is not meant to substitute for the reading of the great thinkers, but rather to prepare for or supplement that task. It is, indeed, not meant to be more than a serviceable text for college courses. It has arisen from a number of years of experience in teaching such a course in Modern European intellectual history. Intellectual history, as it seems to us, should provide an introduction to the most important—from a general cultural viewpoint[4]—"ideas" (intellectual systems, movements of the mind) in the cultural heritage; it should relate these ideas to the social and political background so far as possible; it should show the continuity and lineage of thought; it should indicate the relevance of the ideas to general culture.

Most especially, perhaps, as a *history* of ideas, a presentation of this sort should provide a sense of history. That means a sense of the living context of reality, and it means a sense of the flow and movement of things. Too often the great thinkers and the great ideas are drained of life by being presented as disembodied abstractions. The historian wants to see Kepler in his classroom at the moment when he stumbled upon what seemed to him a great truth, and which really was not, but which launched him on a lifelong quest destined to alter the mind of the West. He wants Kepler's unhappy childhood and restless adolescence. (Arthur Koestler, that great contemporary writer, has done this in *The Sleepwalkers*.) He wants Voltaire's misspent youth and Rousseau's neuroticism and Marx's proud poverty; Locke's bourgeois prudence and Nietzsche's madness—all the human story of the great thinkers.

---

[4]Philosophy students, attuned to the analytical mood, often do not find the intellectual history course satisfying because it is not much interested in the truth or falsity, consistency or inconsistency, of intellectual systems or philosophies and is therefore prone to linger over some not interesting from this point of view, while ignoring others that are. Rousseau and Marx are not great philosophers and the essentially analytical mind soon grows impatient with their cloudy terms and vague ideas; they are historically and existentially of the highest importance, that is, they posed questions relevant to their age and of deepest significance for the human situation of modern times. It has been noted that specialists in whatever field, from economics to theology, will choose figures different from those selected by historians for their general cultural interest.

Nor should they, intellectual historians feel, deal only with the great thinkers, for Croce was right in observing that the spirit of an age is sometimes better found in the second-rate thinkers, and the spirit of the age must always be close to what the historian of ideas seeks. It is the general direction of the movement of thought that concerns him. From earliest times to the present, the great army of thought has marched—some individuals ahead, some in the rear, a large straggling army—steadily past one milestone after another, leaving behind some ideas, fashioning new ones, transforming old ones. We do not know the ultimate destination of the long trek, if it has any. But where we have been and what we have learned is worth knowing, for each of us is a part of the army, anxiously searching for signposts and wondering where, in the endless chaos of things, we are. History orients us.

It also equips us to live. To understand the past is to be able to live fully in the present. To be acquainted with the intellectual heritage of our long and rich Western civilization is to be a civilized person and to be prepared for constructive thinking. The object of this book is to present the most important general ideas in modern European history, not in isolation but as part of the stream of history. As Dr. Johnson said, "There is no part of history so generally useful as that which relates to the progress [?] of the human mind, the successive advances of science, the vicissitudes of learning and ignorance, the extension and resuscitation of arts and the revolution of the intellectual world."[5]

[5]Some additional references on the definition and methodology of intellectual history: Franklin L. Baumer, "Intellectual History and Its Problems," *Journal of Modern History*, September, 1949 (reprinted in pamphlet form by Bobbs-Merrill, their Reprint Series in History); John C. Greene, "Objectives and Methods in Intellectual History," *Mississippi Valley Historical Review*, June, 1957 (also reprinted by Bobbs-Merrill); Peter Burke, "Ideas Have a History," *The Listener*, February 9 and 16, 1967; Sir Isaiah Berlin, "Introduction" to Marc Raeff, *Russian Intellectual History: An Anthology* (New York: Harcourt, Brace & World, 1966).

1

The Great Tradition
and Its Decadence

*The Middle Ages formed one long training of the
intellect of Western Europe in the sense of order.*

ALFRED NORTH WHITEHEAD

*In the sixteenth century the collaboration of reason,
revelation and custom broke down. . . .*

GARRETT MATTINGLY

The Inheritance of Rationalism and Humanism

It is generally agreed that the specifically modern era of the European mind began in the seventeenth century, or at least that there
happened at that time a cultural and intellectual "revolution" of the
most profound significance, which we shall be describing. It is connected
with the great "scientific revolution," chiefly in physics and astronomy,
embracing the achievements of Galileo and Newton, names almost without equal in the Western tradition, and it is connected also with the
philosopher-scientists, Francis Bacon and René Descartes among them,
who illuminated the "century of genius" with their bold exertions toward a wholly new method in thought. This movement led on into the
eighteenth-century Enlightenment, which represented in some respects
a shift of emphasis from, yet built solidly on, the seventeenth-century
background—a period commonly thought of as the dawn of the modern
age.

There is less of revolution and more of continuity in intellectual history than we think. Let us begin by paying an all-too-brief tribute to the splendid heritage which Europe possessed before the seventeenth century—lest we make the egregious mistake of imagining that serious thought only began at that time. Think of the Greek scientists and philosophers of the ancient world, from Thales to Plato (600–370 B.C.), and then Aristotle, the Stoics, and the Neoplatonists (350 B.C.–350 A.D.), also the great Hellenistic scientists, Euclid, Eratosthenes, Galen, Ptolemy —a mother lode of pure intellectual treasure bequeathed to all the world, never lost in Europe though diminished after the barbarian intrusions caused a loss of contact with the Mediterranean world from the sixth to the eleventh centuries A.D. The Greeks, with that open-minded search for intellectual truth that characterized them, produced such an astonishing profusion of ideas that Europe lived off them for centuries. The history of Europe through the Middle Ages can be looked upon as a gradual absorption of the Greek heritage, not completed until the sixteenth century. St. Augustine, near the end of the Roman Empire (fourth century A.D.), mixed his devout Christian religion with small quantities of Neoplatonism and a few of the more edifying discourses of the Latin writers. Then in the "medieval renaissance" of the twelfth century, some of Aristotle comes in together with a little more humanistic literature, and some of the science (Euclid, Galen, and Ptolemy) is rediscovered. The thirteenth century brings back the full corpus of Aristotle, that one-man encyclopedia of the Greek mind. Finally the great Italian Renaissance of the fourteenth to fifteenth century intoxicated Europe as it quenched its thirst at all the springs of classical antiquity, now fully opened. As is well known, this Renaissance still looked back to antiquity as the source of all truth. The Renaissance humanists' literal worship of the ancients sometimes puzzles modern students, who want to think of them as daringly modern yet find them enslaved to ancient authority. The puzzle is solved when we remember the dazzling riches of classical thought, contained in golden prose and poetry. To be the adoring slaves of antiquity was liberation enough, so late as ten centuries after the collapse of ancient civilization.

The great philosophers of the Middle Ages, long since rescued from the prejudices against them and the charges that they were trivial or obscure—men like Anselm and Aquinas—labored to assimilate Greek philosophy into Christianity, to plant in barbarian Europe the rational outlook, seeking to shape one great tradition out of the Greeks, Romans, and Christian Fathers. They struggled to reconcile opposing-ideas. In a brief summary of the European intellectual tradition, one general characteristic to be first noted is its dynamism. Other civilizations have vegetated without discernible movement for centuries, caught in the web of custom, or have moved with glacial slowness. No other civilization (and Arnold J. Toynbee, the modern historian who has sought a morphology of civilizations, thinks he can find twenty-one or perhaps twenty-four in human history) has ever possessed the capacity for change that ours has shown. This was probably the result of its complex inheritance, which came to it from several sources. As Nietzsche pointed out, the Dionysian and Apollonian spirits had striven together in the soul of Greece at the very dawn of the West's civilized traditions —the result of Greece's role as a bridge between East and West, no doubt, and of her blending of peoples (Ionian and Dorian). In Christianity, the Hebraic element met and blended with Greek philosophy and other strains encountered during the epoch of the Macedonian and Roman world states. Then, in the Middle Ages, the multiple heritage of all the ancient world—Greek philosophy and science, Oriental religion —was poured into the mold of Germanic society, a barbarian world of intense physical energies. It was a case of old wines in new bottles or potent brew in young bodies. Europe was forced to integrate different systems of ideas and values and so push constantly on to ever-new syntheses. In the creative polarity of opposites, many have seen the recurrent theme of its history.

Dialectical movement has manifested itself abundantly in Western history. In Greek philosophy, Thales was matched against Pythagoras, Plato against Aristotle, the materialists and skeptics against both; Christianity fused with Greek philosophy in a higher synthesis. In the Middle Ages, Peter Abelard ranged his rational philosophy against St. Bernard's mighty existential faith, while Aquinas, who synthesized these two, was in turn negated by Ockham. We come to the time when Protestantism reacted against Catholicism, and when the revival of numerous ancient philosophies during the Renaissance gave to modern European man a fantastically rich menu of intellectual dishes.

If we can discern one basic tension or polarity beneath all the others, it would be one that opposed the scientific, rationally oriented, and intellectually sophisticated tradition of Greek philosophical thought to the fervent, "committed," ethically-oriented faith of Christianity. "Hebraism and Hellenism—between these two points of influence moves our world," Matthew Arnold wrote only a century or so ago. He defined the essence of the latter as "to see things as they really are," and of the former as "conduct and obedience." The thirst for truth, the unclouded mind, the keen insight, the penetrating judgment—here was the daemon of Greece, whereas the Hebrew pined after righteousness, demanded moral perfection, insisted on finding the rules by which men must act. The two could be at war, never more so than when Puritanism arose in the sixteenth century to rebuke the Renaissance humanists' speculative daring and sensuality alike. They might be held together, and the great intellectual systems from Augustine to Aquinas and on to Erasmus and Loyola did precisely that. They might take turns prevailing one over the other, or appear in different geographical areas in varying guises. But both were there, and still are though no longer so recognizable or so exclusive.

To medieval philosophers, these two realms, of divine and natural truth, each had its place and they were complementary to each other, different but not contradictory. The light of Christ and of the ancient philosophers each illuminated an avenue of human activity, the former no doubt loftier but the latter equally necessary. Reason and faith were partners and equals, in the thought of Saint Thomas Aquinas. Both were based on authority—the Church, and Aristotle. If these two mighty fountains of truth sometimes seemed to clash, they had enough in common to permit Aquinas the appearance of success in his attempt to harmonize them. They had much in common.

A chief general characteristic, of the utmost significance, was what may be called an optimistic rationalism, that is, the belief that the external world has a logical order which the human mind can apprehend; further, that conceptual language can almost exactly express this order. We must remember—perhaps, in view of this very heritage that we possess as children of the Greeks and Hebrews, we find it hard to—that the universe may well be seen as a chaos without plan or pattern. Many have believed so, including among the Greek philosophers the Epicureans as well as the earlier Heraclitus, the "dark philosopher"; but these voices were submerged beneath the counter view of a rational world order found in Plato and the Stoics. Or, again, it is possible to conclude that whatever the universe is like, our human minds, imprisoned within the senses and utterly incapable of encountering reality directly, cannot possibly know it. This skeptical position was also found among some of the Greeks, such as Pyrrho of Elis or that predecessor of Plato, Cratylus, of whom we are told that he had philosophized himself into complete silence (he only wagged his finger) believing that no statement about anything could be true. (An important contemporary philosopher once reached a rather similar impasse.) But Cratylus gave place to the exuberant Socrates, who never stopped talking until the Athenians closed his mouth with hemlock, and to Plato, who though aware of the shadows in which most men lived affirmed the existence of a reason higher than the senses, through which the wise man could ascertain true knowledge. If Pyrrho and the later teachers in Plato's Academy reverted to skepticism, it was not this which survived in the West, but rather, via Platonism or Stoicism (absorbed into Christianity), the faith in a rational objective order, knowable at least in part by man. (Ancient skepticism was rediscovered in the later Renaissance, but was submerged for many centuries before that.)

We should not overlook this rational strain in Christianity, which was of course an offshoot of Jewish religious thought. There was a cosmic order, guaranteed by the existence of God as a transcendent principle. A distinguished Israelite of our time, Abba Eban, has written that the Jewish mind was dominated by the belief that "the universe is not a chaos of wild, uncontrollable, mysterious forces but that it is a pattern of order and progress guided by an articulate intelligence and law." "It would seem," remarks Henri Frankfort (*Before Philosophy*) "that the Hebrews, no less than the Greeks, broke with the mode of speculation which had prevailed up to this time," that is, the generally nonrational and unordered view of nature characteristic of earlier peoples. "A universe peopled by miscellaneous gods and demons, or even a dualism as in Iranian religion, is a universe of chance and caprice. The omnipotent God of the Hebrews was a guarantor of order and law in the world, as well as of its ultimately benevolent purpose."

It remained for the Greek philosophers, reacting against the language of poetic metaphor and seeking a more precise terminology, to invent *rationalism* as the West was to know it. Greek philosophical rationalism was abstract and metaphysical. It was dominated by the Platonic mistrust of the sensory world—the world we touch, feel, see— as chaotic and unknowable, the saving principle of order being found only through resolutely overriding the sensory in favor of pure reason, of which the model was mathematics or deductive logic. Newton taught modern man that observation and reason can work together. But as late as the seventeenth century the feeling was that the former contaminates the latter. Nevertheless, Plato was not without interest in the sensible world and his disciple the great Aristotle insisted on beginning there. It is not true that either the Greeks or the medieval philosophers scorned careful observation, but there is something in the charge that they preferred abstract reasoning. We should at any rate appreciate that science must begin in the postulate of rational order in things, a condition which if lacking would make observation futile; and that to this faith the major stream of Western thought held fast against irrationalism or skepticism—held fast with a Socratic zest, a Platonic vision, a Christian faith. "Man is a rational animal," began Aristotle. This is so because he is part of a rational world. "Perfect rationality resides in the inmost depths of our own nature," Cicero declared. We believe this much less today, in the age of Darwin and Freud, than the ancients did. But all our modern sciences rest on it. It also permeated traditional thought about man in society.

The European tradition affirmed both the possibility and the high value of attaining genuine knowledge, "wisdom," via contemplation, speculation, "philosophy," that is, the love of wisdom. Plato and St. Augustine agreed that though man on earth is so encumbered with the muddy vesture of decay, so earthbound and imperfect, that he can only with the greatest difficulty see truth clearly, yet by the same token he is privileged to glimpse a portion of it and always to strive for it. His soul, according to Plato, came from the realm of pure knowledge and will return there, giving him an unbreakable linkage to that realm. And, as Aristotle said, the contemplative life is the life of greatest value, higher than the life of mere action. Later, some held that this bias toward pure contemplation robbed the great Western tradition of much valuable practical knowledge that it might have learned from humble sources. This was true of the medieval universities. Nevertheless it was a magnificent affirmation of the potentiality of thought.

There was tension, of course, between the pagan-classical and the Christian modes of wisdom, but Augustine at least partly resolved them, holding that the ideal of wisdom held up by the Greek philosophers is a positive good—only there is another and higher wisdom, to which the truly wise man will proceed after he has mastered the other. The Middle Ages, heir to both Aristotle and Augustine, exhibited this tension in the conflicting figures of Abelard, founder of medieval speculative thought, the rational analyst who used Aristotle's tools of logic, and St. Bernard, who preached the mystic way of knowing God not by logic but by Christian contemplation. But such figures as Hugh of St. Victor and John of Salisbury in the twelfth century, and the great Thomas Aquinas in the thirteenth, sought to mediate between these opposites, recognizing value in both. To repeat: the dominant theme in medieval thought is this search for a reconciliation between two modes of thought which did agree, after all, in the possibility of man understanding objective truth.

Another closely related point may be mentioned. The Western tradition rejected those tendencies to scorn the material world and view man's spirit as a stranger to it that are found in certain portions of Eastern philosophy and that indeed made an appearance now and then in the West. Early in its career, Christianity faced a penetration by what was known as Gnosticism, which probably went back to Persian dualistic roots. Gnosticism had some attraction for Christianity, which is also dualistic as between spirit and matter, though not so drastically as this Oriental creed. Eventually the Gnostics were treated as heretics. Something similar cropped up in southern France in the Middle Ages as Catharism, but was ferociously put down in one of the more celebrated episodes of medieval European history. Those Gnostics and Cathars shared with Hindu fakirs a complete contempt for the body. They believed that the spark of light within man which is his soul is trapped as a prisoner in the flesh, to which it is completely alien and from which it must try to escape. They often became complete ascetics, seeking death at the earliest opportunity, or else they expressed their disdain for the physical world by defying all moral laws and becoming libertines. Within Christianity, they denied that Christ was ever really made flesh, he only seemed so; to them the realms of spirit and body were absolutely divorced.

Orthodox Christianity, holding to the Incarnation, had to have more respect for the flesh than this. The world of brute matter and the flesh is, to the Christian, a good though a lesser one; this life is not to be treated with disrespect even though it is but a way station en route to another and purer one. Man is not a stranger on earth; rather the earth is given to him to have dominion over, to shape and create.[1]

The greater humanism of the West as compared to the East was evident early. In the eighth century, a violent controversy broke out between the Western and Eastern Christian Churches (Rome and Constantinople) concerning iconoclasm, or the prohibition of all depictions of Christ as a human figure in religious art decreed in Byzantine Christianity (it is also to be found in Islamic church art). Whereas the West loved to contemplate Jesus as a man, living and dying as a mortal being, the East thought this degrading.

Certainly naturalism and rationalism were always powerful ingredients in medieval thought, even as it adjusted itself to the imperious claims of faith. As soon as systematic thought revived in Europe in the eleventh century, we find Anselm trying to prove the existence of God by rational arguments and Abelard testing the consistency of Holy Scripture against logical scrutiny. The High Middle Ages, which saw the establishment of universities, leaned on Aristotle and were saturated with the idea of law, in the sense of necessary objective relationships governing all things.[2]

Medieval Thought and its Breakdown

If, contrary to a view once widely held, the Middle Ages were a seedbed for modern scientific rationalism, they were also technologically fruitful. And they can seem surprisingly modern in other respects, re-

---

[1] This Christian humanism, it need hardly be said, derives ultimately from Judaism with its prophets who "communicated with God in history" (Israel Epstein) rather than in a timeless dimension, who found deep cosmic significance in the events that befall men and nations from day to day.

[2] The greatest medieval glory, the mighty Gothic cathedrals once popularly looked upon as tributes to mysticism or disorder, are now recognized to have been geometrically rational, a deeply intellectual achievement based on Platonic notions of cosmic harmony. See Otto G. Von Simson's "The Gothic Cathedral: Design and Meaning," in Sylvia L. Thrupp, ed., *Change in Medieval Society*, 1964.

minding us of the essential continuity of Western thought. Popular thought often revealed a "chiliastic" or millenarian theme very like modern revolutionary ideologies. The followers of Joachim of Flores in the High Middle Ages found in the Biblical books of Daniel and Revalations the materials with which to construct a vision of the poor rising up against the rich and inaugurating an earthly utopia of justice, plenty, and equality. The course of history was to culminate in this apocalyptic event, a mighty revolution followed by the Kingdom of God on earth. Contemporary followers of Karl Marx have gotten little farther; the ideas of progress and of revolution were all here in germinal form. Such movements never succeeded but they testify to the rich diversity of medieval thought and to the fact that—again contrary to old clichés—it was not all embraced in the orthodoxy of the official Church.

From Medieval to Modern

Once sadly misunderstood, the Middle Ages now stand forth as the time of the most significant intellectual revival in European history, a revival which underlies and made possible everything that followed. By the thirteenth century the universities had come of age, and a good deal of ancient science, mathematics, and philosophy already was known, chiefly through the Arabs in Spain. In the thirteenth century even more flowed into Europe, usually embedded in Arabian or Jewish commentary, fruit of the East's long digestion of Greek thought. The main influence was that of Aristotle. It is now clear that there was not only Aristotelianism, but also Neoplatonism, the two sometimes fused, sometimes seen through their interpreters. The complex story of medieval philosophy cannot be unravelled here. It is enough to note that the great universities of Paris and Oxford were scenes of tremendous intellectual activity in the thirteenth century, out of which emerged, as simply the top peak in a range of mountains, the achievement of Thomas Aquinas.

Thomism represented a daring advance for European thought in that it made the naturalistic philosophy of Aristotle possible for Christians. Aristotle was a scientist and philosopher in whose all-embracing system no element of "faith" intruded; one observed, reasoned, accepted nothing that could not pass the test of the most rigorous analysis. Aristotle, later scientists were to find, was more often wrong than right, but he was not wrong because of any rejection of scientific inquiry. He had been mistrusted by men of the Church; Aquinas risked his career and reputation in a battle to win acceptance for the view that no Christian need fear Aristotle and reason, for reason and faith are in substantial harmony.

Aristotle was the author of a far-ranging, encyclopedic system of thought which seemed to sum up all the wisdom of antiquity. His was the great oracular voice in virtually every field. The historian of science A. C. Crombie sees him as "a sort of tragic figure striding through medieval science," holding the center of the stage until finally overthrown by the weapons he himself had forged. He can be seen in this light in fields other than physical science—in politics, in biological science, or in esthetics, not forgetting of course metaphysics or the pure theory of truth and knowledge. He prevailed in physics and astronomy until Galileo began the attack joined by other great seventeenth-century scientists, resulting in Aristotle's defeat at point after point—arrangement and structure of the heavenly bodies, the theories of motion, falling bodies, gravity, the vacuum, hydraulics. His substantially static outlook prevailed in natural science in basic ways until Darwin in the nineteenth century; his four elements were axiomatic in chemistry until the eighteenth-century revolution in that science. Metaphysically, the Aristotelian vision of a universe marked by the purposeful striving of things, each combining form and matter, in a great "chain of being" stretching upward to God, who stood as the ultimate cause of it all but had not created, nor could concern himself with, the universe—this vision permeated men's outlook until the seventeenth-century philosophical revolution, a counterpart of the scientific revolution. Aristotle's logic, though Renaissance humanists resented it and it lost the prestige it held in medieval times, could never be rendered entirely obsolete. Neither could his Poetics. His Politics, once again, made up the medieval background against which there was to be a seventeenth-century rebellion.

It seems best to leave details of the Aristotelian system until the revolt against it in the various fields of thought is dealt with. A general point worth repeating is that Aristotle's method was basically scientific and rational, whatever its errors. Nor did his conclusions agree with Christianity on a number of significant points (nature of God, divine providence, nature of the soul, creation of the world). But the Aristotelian system is not our world today, and it seems strange and even irrational to most of us. Apart from its factual mistakes such as the immobile earth, what are we to make of its explanations in terms of purpose of striving (teleology)? Or its evident endowing of inanimate objects with vitalistic traits? *Essence* and *accident*, *potency* and *act*, *formal* and *material principles* are terms crucial to the Aristotelian philosophy which have lost the meaning they once had; they belong to the terminology of medieval scholasticism. It would be well only to remember that this much-despised school taught the West to think in an orderly fashion, to classify, to criticize, and to observe. If Aquinas's great harmonization of the two systems, so characteristic of the thir-

teenth century, did not long survive, what did survive was his liberation of large realms of knowledge for pure reason or philosophy.
Science, politics, economics, and other realms now could be approached
as autonomous inquiries, not shaped immediately by the requirements
of religious orthodoxy or scriptural authority.

At the end of the thirteenth century, the Thomistic marriage of
theology and philosophy, of the realms of faith and reason, began to
break up not in divorce but in amicable separation; each tended to go
its own way. The two realms became distinct. Their paths might cross
and clash, but there was no question, normally, of one controlling and
dominating the other. Rational thought had been set free to travel its
long journey.

The fourteenth and fifteenth centuries were very bold ones; it was
a time of transition and deep change in basic Western institutions, with
the papacy in decline and the modern secular state beginning to appear.
This boldness appears in the thought of William of Ockham, probably
the most penetrating intellect of his age. For one thing, the thirteenth-
century synthesis of reason and faith was no more. The truths of religion, beginning with the existence of God, are not subject to rational
proofs at all, but must be accepted on faith, Ockham held. So, to a
lesser extent, did Scotus. Ockham who, as Gordon Leff writes, "for
sheer destructive capacity" may have been unequalled in European intellectual history, seems surprisingly modern in many respects. He and
his great Franciscan rival, Duns Scotus, bring us to the close of medieval scholasticism, though they carried on its methods; their conclusions, often radically skeptical, closed doors to "reason" in the older
sense, opened others. There is no point in trying to reason about God,
or the substances and essences of things, or any of the abstract concepts medieval schoolmen loved to explore. To Ockham this was a
game of words. All we can know is immediate experience; only the experienced, phenomenal properties of things are real. Ockham represented a shift of interest from metaphysics to science, from the abstract
and general to the concrete and particular. Some of his followers made
significant pioneer contributions to modern science.[3]

It is common to mark the late scholastics as a crucial turning point
in the history of thought. The overrefinement of scholastic methods,
made a reproach against the Subtle Doctor, Duns Scotus, was as much
a sign of decadence, perhaps, as the ending of its quest for metaphysical truth in skepticism. With the death of Ockham (1350), writes David
Knowles, "a great fabric of thought, and an ancient outlook on philosophy . . . gradually disappeared, and gave place, after two centuries in
which pure philosophy was in eclipse, to the new outlook and varied

[3]Oresme, Buridan, Albert of Saxony; see further below, page 32.

ways of the modern world." In the interlude, in those two centuries between the death of Ockham and the birth of Galileo, epochal movements not in the realm of "pure philosophy" swept through Europe: Renaissance humanism, religious mysticism, the Protestant Reformation. Among founders of the modern mind no one would neglect to include Erasmus and Luther and Calvin, though in some ways they were far from modern. The revolt that shook Europe in the first years of the sixteenth century belongs to history, not just intellectual history; it is the classical episode of Western civilization, comparable only to the fall of the Roman Empire and the French Revolution. It was, among other things, a movement of the mind.

The Renaissance

As scholasticism broke up into contending factions, *via moderna* (Ockhamism) versus the *via antiqua* or perhaps Scotism, the humanists of the Renaissance arrived to challenge the very disciplines of logic and metaphysics in favor of poetry and philology. Humanists and scholastics engaged in bitter strife, of which the most famous case was the German dispute between the Schoolmen of Cologne and the humanist followers of Jacob Reuchlin, a battle of books that produced the searingly satirical *Letters of Obscure Men*. From 1500 to 1520, on the eve of the Reformation explosion, this debate plus the writings of Machiavelli, Erasmus, Thomas More, and other great humanists throughout Europe marked the exciting high tide of the humanist movement. To understand it, one must think of it as a revolt against the aridity of an "age of reason"; for the humanists turned to literature as an antidote to the severely unimaginative intellectualism of scholasticism. But one must think also of the delights to be found in the classics of the ancient world. Perhaps these have now somewhat dried up for us, but they appeared during the Renaissance as a treasury of wisdom cast in the perfection of style. In an age when what was once a truism is increasingly forgotten, we should be reminded of the long, pervasive influence of the classical writers and their *grand style*. The humanistic educational ideal of enriching and ennobling the mind by contact with Greek and Roman literature lasted well into the nineteenth century and is still not quite dead; perhaps it never will be so long as Western civilization survives.[4] One found, in these writers, not only supreme wisdom ex-

---

[4]The eminent contemporary Swiss philosopher-historian Karl Jaspers has written that "we owe to the classical world the foundation of what, in the West, makes man all he can be. . . . In the West, each great uplift of selfhood has been brought about by a fresh contact with the classical world," *Man in the Modern Age*, 1963.

pressed in exquisitely molded words; one found also, in the totality of their impact, that enduring effect on the character which only the greatest works of art can exert. That the classics of antiquity could never be equalled, much less surpassed, remained almost unquestioned until the end of the seventeenth century, when even the questioning of it (see page 99) aroused the scornful amusement of the greatest critic of that day. This was because of the perfection of the ancient tongues, especially Greek, since corrupted but then incomparable in their range, grace, and precision. It was also because of the ancient's natural dignity —the Roman *gravitas,* the Homeric simplicity—which becomes impossible in more "decadent" times. Here in the youth of mankind words could be spoken as never again, in a style unpretentious, not "literary" but natural. There is a golden moment in the life of a civilization, as of a person, when the spontaneity of youth fuses with the wisdom of maturity to produce the highest powers of thought and expression. So it had been in ancient Greece and Rome. Something like this was the view widely held in early modern Europe.

The humanists turned also to history, as well as to the plastic arts; they advanced the study of human affairs by a realism that began to penetrate the genuine texture of human experience. But what essentially the humanists aimed at, the goal of this broad historical and literary education, was a unity of culture and of the intellectual personality—the Whole Man who possesses *sapienta* or wisdom. He is civilized by tradition and rendered articulate by literature. By no means like the modern alienated poet, he takes full part in society, functioning as political and civic leader. He shares the heritage of civilization with others, is aware of its corporate character and how little any individual can add to it. For the Renaissance humanists were classicists, in all senses of that word.

They also humanized theology. Martin Luther felt the influence not only of the humanists but of Ockhamism and its religious counterpart, the nonrational or mystical approach to God. And as Luther rejected scholastic theology with its pallid intellectualism, setting forth against it the claims of the inner emotional life, and bringing on an upheaval without precedent among the common folk of central Europe, we catch a glimpse of Henry VIII's agents burning the books of Scotus at Oxford; the Act of Supremacy which severed the English Church from the papacy was accompanied among other things by injunctions designed to alter education. "The study of canon law was suppressed, but classical Greek and Latin, Hebrew, mathematics, and medicine were to be encouraged. The standard medieval compendium of Christian doctrine, the *Sentences* of Peter Lombard, was abolished in favour of direct reading of the Bible. . . . Aristotle and logic were to be studied with the help of humanist writers, putting aside 'the frivolous questions and obscure glosses' of the schoolmen" (A. R. Myers, *England in the Late Middle Ages*).

It may be still necessary to dispel what historians call the myth of the Renaissance, "still living, despite so many criticisms," as a recent scholar remarks. This is the myth that the Middle Ages was a time of almost unrelieved blackness whose sole intellectual activity was a small amount of sterile and frivolous deduction and that the Renaissance of the fifteenth century came as a miraculous deliverance from ignorance in all fields, bringing freshness, light, science, and invention to Europe. The myth contains the least truth so far as concerns science and technology; Renaissance humanists contributed almost nothing to either. The more fruitful tradition for modern physics was that of the late medieval Parisian Schoolmen, such as Jean Buridan, Nicole Oresme, and Albert of Saxony. The humanists were addicted to the ancient books; they followed Aristotle and Galen slavishly, on the whole. There are some startling examples of their refusal to modify classical ideas in the light of new experience. As for technology, the artisans who built the medieval cathedrals and clocks kept alive a mechanical genius that was ignored by medieval and Renaissance scholars alike, but which modern science drew upon.[5] Modern science begins toward the end of the sixteenth century under the guidance of men who represent a different line from that of the humanists, and if we are to make them part of "the Renaissance," we must at least explain that this was not the same movement as that which produced Michelangelo and Machiavelli, Erasmus and St. Thomas More.

The humanists accomplished enough without attributing to them further and later horizons of which they never dreamed. To begin with, the so-called Renaissance accomplished a considerable widening of the European range of ideas. This sheer quantitative factor was, indeed, the most celebrated of Renaissance intellectual changes. Far more of the anicent literary heritage came back, exhumed from its hiding places, translated from Greek or Hebrew (substantially new linguistic horizons for most of Europe), edited, and published. The recovery included, naturally and significantly, that which had been repressed or forgotten because not in sympathy with the dominant modes of thought. The interesting off-beat Greek philosophers, the rejected (but as it happened more nearly right) scientists; Lucretius and the Epicureans; the Stoics; the skeptics; occult philosophies from the rich variety

[5]The technological fruitfulness of the medieval period should be stressed; "the later Middle Ages," as Lynn White, Jr. shows, "is the period of decisive development in the history of the effort to use the forces of nature mechanically for human purposes" (*Medieval Technology and Social Change*, 1962). In this respect the ancients had been astonishingly deficient, while the so-called Dark Ages had made decisive first steps.

of Hellenistic civilization, such as the Hermetic philosophy and the Jewish Kabbala were among the items that became available. The Italian humanists liked to dig, too, and gained a sense of historical insight into the ancient world, partly through archaeology, another familiar trait of this renowned school.

A sophisticated skepticism is the product of a wide range of knowledge and ideas, for it becomes difficult to suppose that just one of these is right, and also is the product of a historical sense, for it becomes possible to imagine other words and other ways. The Italian humanists pursued as an ideal, not one creed or ideology, but a *manner* of living, marked by elegance and "style"—"life as a work of art." One tried to cultivate the personality, by developing all the facets of human nature and harmonizing them through a sense of style that was essentially literary and a sense of harmony essentially classical. In effect, men made a synthesis of many ideas, eschewing dogmatism—an eclecticism of thought, held together by esthetic principles. The feeling for art and the sense of beauty, those famous Renaissance features, were in part the result of a sophisticated intellectual situation, replacing a simpler one. No new dogma or predominant line of inquiry had appeared; one luxuriated in a profusion of interesting old ideas.

From one point of view, Renaissance man was a highly sophisticated creature—skeptical, linguistically subtle, aware of a great variety of views and ways of expressing these views. From another point of view, he now seems amazingly quaint and simple-minded. He still held to the traditional cosmology and physics, and to the traditional physiology and psychology as well. He not only believed the earth to be motionless and the stars made of a translucent nothingness, but he believed in the four elements and the four "humours," blood, choler, phlegm, and melancholy, the mixture of which in the body determined temperament or personality. He believed, further, that there were correspondences between the macrocosm of physical nature and the microcosm of the human soul, so that emeralds protected virginity, for example, and the rumble of the bowels related to the thunder in the sky. He more than half believed in the alchemist's dream of transmuting stones into precious metals, or the magic power of the mystic letters and numbers in the Kabbala. Magic and witchcraft surrounded Renaissance philosophy, with the boundaries between the two blurred. Medicine had scarcely advanced since ancient times.

In brief, as it seems to us, the Scientific Revolution was overdue. But numerous historians have reminded us that this old-fashioned world of man was "existentially" more satisfying than the modern one. Its explanations were unfortunately not accurate, as subsequently became apparent, but they were in many ways delightfully agreeable to human nature. We need not dwell on this. The "discarded image," as C. S.

Lewis has called it, the "little world of man" (J. B. Bamborough) had more unity, more kinship between man and nature, more sense of man being the hub and center of the cosmos—these are familiar points. It was, arguably, a world of greater ontological security and esthetic inspiration. But it had to give way to another world less grossly in error on matters of scientific fact.

The Reformation

Whatever may be said about philosophers in the universities and rich connoisseurs of literature, it was Christianity which throughout the century had entered most deeply into the common life of the people. It saturated every aspect of life, determining the very rhythm of time with its holy days (holidays—the contemporary meaning of this term furnishes an ironic commentary on the changes that have come over Western civilization), determining too the forms of architecture and art, as well as the structure of the popular mind. Think of the sheer physical dominance of the churches, the abbeys, the cathedrals, the processions, the bells—those bells whose tolling so overhung the medieval community, as J. Huizinga has written in an evocative passage of his celebrated book *The Waning of the Middle Ages*. In some ways the trite image of the Middle Ages as an "age of faith" is irritatingly wrong, if we summon up a picture of universal piety and prayer. This was a time when the fierce energies of a barbarian people threatened to overturn all order; piety was driven to the monasteries, and even there had a hard time surviving, as the periodical need for reform testifies. The church was feudalized, the papacy intermittently degraded. A vigorous lower class produced from time to time loudly heterodox spokesmen, while folk songs and poems made fun of the clergy and celebrated the joys of the flesh. The most popular writer of the later thirteenth century, Jean de Meun, in his *Romance of the Rose*, was both sardonically critical of the clergy and utterly hedonistic and amoral in his attitude toward sexual love—these, we may assume, were typical attitudes of the day among the literary classes.[6] But even in protest it was impossible to escape the universal religion, for it embraced the whole of culture and it could scarcely even occur to anyone to move outside it.[7] The common belief, the common loyalty, was

[6]The first part of this famous book reflects the chaster tradition of "courtly love"; the second, longer part, written by Meun, assails this spiritual love in the name of a highly physical type.

[7]The one great example of an alien ideology with significant popular roots was the Catharist heresy among the Albigensians in southern France; this was ferociously stamped out in the most famous manifestation of medieval intolerance.

Christian. One might be this or that color of Christian and assail other Christians, but to be *anti-*or *non-*Christian was virtually inconceivable.

The Renaissance widened the outlook of educated Europeans, exposing them to certain ancient perspectives (e.g., Epicureanism) alien to the dogmas of the medieval church. But this affected the very few and was decidedly *recherché.* And the amount of downright anti-Christianism among the humanists has often been exaggerated; it was not really very great. No real intellectual foundations for an anti-Christian position existed until the seventeenth century. There was some vague dreaming of a synthetic or universal religion that would embody the essential truths of all religions, Judaism and Islam being the others known at this time, in a nondogmatic structure: foreshadowings of later deism. A few bold "atheists" did exist, especially in Machiavelli's Florence—Epicurean and Stoic denials of a personal and transcendent diety. Mostly, however, the humanists, Erasmus of Rotterdam leading the way, offered their own version of Christianity, not the less pious for being in revolt against the rationalistic theology of the Schoolmen and the cloistered spirit of the monks.

From 1520 to about 1540, the "German drama" held the attention of Europe: Luther's blows against the papal church were heard from one end of the continent to the other and resulted in a stir of excitement. Without pausing here to examine what has so often been described and analyzed, we may note the hardening of Protestantism into an equally intolerant dogma by the 1540s, the beginnings of religious warfare between Calvinism and the Counter Reformation, and a consequent disillusionment with religion among many of the intellectuals. Deeply excited by Luther's incomparable gesture of revolt, European intellectuals soon came to believe that it was sterile of all except new dogmatism and persecution of heretics. Protestant destruction of art and hysterical "papomania," along with outbursts of weird sectarianism among the lower classes, disgusted many of the humanists who had initially sympathized with the attack on corruption and insincerity in the church. Yet no one can deny the magnificence of the spiritual discipline that carried Calvinist or Jesuit to the heights of ardor, a discipline especially notable in its effects on the common folk.

The great Reformation movement did many things, in addition to arousing a more fervent and intolerant faith. Itself a manifestation of the growing maturity of the state and the rising strength of nationalism, it ultimately strengthened the sovereign national state by removing a check on the royal power, as it also strengthened nationalism by removing the rival loyalty to the international Catholic church. By throwing countries into internal strife and confusion, it forced the secular state to keep order and determine the requirements of faith. Thus the Reformation is of enormous political significance. In the world of ideas, it accompanies the emergence of sovereignty and the divine right of kings, as opposed to theories of the right of rebellion emerging from Calvinists or Jesuits. Determined to impose their views of right religion on society, the contending religious factions affirmed a power to dominate the secular arm of government and make it carry out the edicts of pope or presbyters. They unleashed grim civil strife in France in the last decades of the sixteenth century. Though a particularly un-lovely set of monarchical tyrants manipulated the situation to their own advantage and to the detriment of freedom, it is difficult not to have more sympathy with them than with the clerics who made Europe hideous with their bloody intolerance. So, in these several ways, the modern state was born of the bankruptcy of the church.

The explosion of the Reformation blew apart the religious unity of Europe, threw the continent into turmoil, and ultimately induced a skepticism born of disgust with theological fanaticism. "It is rating one's conjectures at a very high price to roast a man on the strength of them," Montaigne observed dryly. Europe edged crabwise toward toleration (a theme discussed in a subsequent chapter). It was some time before men fully accepted skepticism as the foundation of the political order. But ways of accommodation were worked out, and with the surprising discovery that two or more clashing ideologies could inhabit the same body politic without disaster, Western civilization had turned its most important political corner since ancient times.

The Beginnings of Modern Political Thought

A most significant thinker of the later sixteenth century was the political theorist Jean Bodin. His belief in sorcery and witchcraft, along with the wild disarray in which he presented his thoughts, reminds us of how far we are from the Enlightenment; but one of his tracts antic-ipated the economic theories of two centuries later, and he also joined Montaigne in arguing that debate about religion is futile, toleration is the only possible way (*Paradoxon*, published posthumously 1596). Bodin is most famous for his conception of sovereignty. No man, he said with but slight exaggeration, had understood the state before him-self. He attacked Aristotle, the classic source of political theory, though he used many of Aristotle's categories. Bodin laid hold of the idea that somewhere in a political body resides an "absolute and perpetual power," indivisible, unlimited, permanent, which a particular monarch may exercise but which survives him, an indestructible abstraction vested in the State. Bodin had been impressed by the disorders of the

French government in his day. Amid some confusion and lack of direction he arrived at ideas extremely important for the future.[8]

A new state was to emerge from the chaos of the sixteenth century: stronger, often absolutist, but more and more tolerant of diverse religious creeds and capable of furthering order and economic development over large areas. In the year before Bodin's death Henry of Navarre restored the unified French monarchy and healed the strife of religious factions, subsequently issuing the great Edict of Nantes in 1598; before his assassination in 1614, this able though dissipated king laid foundations for the powerful French state of the future. Thus as the seventeenth century dawned, Europe stood on the threshold of significant changes, which minds such as Bodin's dimly foresaw. The sovereign state under strong monarchical leadership was not the least of these. In Bodin's mind (and those of the *politiques*, as they were called, the school to which Bodin stood in close relation) the strong secular state and religious toleration were linked. Together, they could restore national unity, end the civil wars of religion. It is about this same time that a Heidelberg doctor, called Erastus, gave his name to a significant doctrine: *Erastianism* is the word long used to mean the supremacy of the secular power in matters of faith.

Bodin's thought is also remarkable for its attempt to arrive at a science of jurisprudence by the method of collecting, comparing, and analyzing laws. Resembling Aristotle's great synthesis of the ancient world, it began, with a new confidence, the modern search for a science of human institutions. So Bodin stands as a dim forerunner of the Enlightenment. One sees the dawn of a new era breaking through, but still mingled with old shadows.

Thus the humanism of the Renaissance combined with the Protestant assault on traditional religious authority to undermine traditional modes of thinking, at any rate in those countries that went Protestant; even in the others, things could not be as before, a fact which is reflected in the outlook of the new Society of Jesus, arm of the Catholic reply to the Reformation. One of the notable features in common between those arch foes, the Jesuits and the Calvinists, was an urge to repair the breach between the active and contemplative life. Plato and the Greeks had announced the superiority of the latter over the former,

---

[8]Bodin also wrote on historical method, conceiving the study of history to be much more important than did most of the seventeenth-century philosophers who soon fell under the sway of Descartes; in this respect too he anticipates the Enlightenment. Several other Frenchmen, including François Baudouin and La Popelinière, wrote tracts on historical method and philosophy at this time. See J. Franklin, *Jean Bodin and the Sixteenth-Century Revolution in the Methodology of Law and History*, 1963, and Donald R. Kelley, *Foundations of Modern Historical Scholarship*, 1970.

with a tendency to divorce the two, and medieval monasticism further extended this distinction. The thirteenth-century universities were staffed by friars who had broken away from the cloister, but they were still inclined to elevate metaphysics and theology over anything practical (law was a leading subject, but the mechanical arts remained outside altogether and laboratory science scarcely existed). Late medieval mysticism stressed quietism. The humanists themselves often reflected an aristocratic ideal of esthetic enjoyment for its own sake, but an important theme in the Italian Renaissance was a vindication of the active life, of the value of such careers as politics and business.

We can perhaps find in this revolt of activism a common denominator in the various revolutions of the age. They all held that the schoolmen had become bloodless and petty, and reproached them for having become divorced from reality. Monastic orders were castigated and abolished, even in Catholic countries. John Calvin is frequently credited with having elevated (secular) work to a dignity it had never had before. Soon Francis Bacon issued his call for an infusion of vitality from the mechanical arts and a break with sterile scholasticism in the sciences. The Jesuits, men of the world, counsellors to kings and travellers to far corners of the globe, burned to make their religious zeal emerge in works, to fuse theory with practice, action with contemplation. Machiavelli, Erasmus, and More made of politics an autonomous study.

The Age of The Baroque

Thus wherever we look we find at the end of the sixteenth century the signs of the decay of a great tradition. It is not that any of the rebels rejected it entirely. Recent scholarship has strongly asserted the traditional sources of Luther's thought, from St. Paul to St. Bernard and the late medieval mystics and Ockhamites; and if Calvin was more iconoclastic he was a fine classical scholar who of course sought to base Christian theology on the Bible. The humanists were worshipful to the point of idolatry of what they conceived to be the great classical tradition. As we shall note, the scientific revolution owed something to the past, though it broke fresh ground; most of its great pioneers, such as Kepler, Galileo, Bacon, Descartes, greatly admired Plato if not Aristotle. Be that as it may, in the sixteenth century there is scant respect for the great tradition as purveyed in most of the universities, there is a revolt against what is conceived to be the typical methods of scholasticism, there is discontent with Aristotelian philosophy, regnant since the Middle Ages, and there is a searching after some new synthesis.

A great figure of this sixteenth-century *fin de siècle* was the French essayist and skeptic Montaigne. With Shakespeare, whom he influenced, Montaigne shared a tremendous range of interests and curiosity about human nature for its own sake, a freedom from narrowness and dogma, a delight in the paradoxical and a dislike of pedantry—the fruit of a ripe Renaissance humanism. Steeped in the classics, Montaigne was not their slave, but used them in his own original ways. Philosophically he was a skeptic, drawing on such ancient philosophers as Pyrrho. At one stage in his evolution the recently rediscovered ancient philosophy or religion of Stoicism, as revealed in Seneca the dramatist, appealed to him. He did not stay long in one position. Deep within this great writer, whose wise essays have charmed so many readers, there lies a considerable cynicism about human nature and the human situation. It is possible to hold that Montaigne's onslaughts on the follies and delusions of mankind represent the highest wisdom, but it is hardly possible to deny that he was a pessimist. Though fortified with a Stoical faith in the philosopher's salvation through understanding and detachment, he does not radiate much hope and encouragement for mankind in general. No one would ever put him down as an apostle of the Idea of Progress. Montaigne was disgusted with the behavior of his fellows, who, he thought, killed each other for opinions they did not even hold sincerely: they were not merely cruel but hypocritical. "Is it possible to imagine anything so ridiculous as this miserable and wretched creature?" he wonders about man. The root of his pessimism is this skepticism. With only their hopelessly inadequate senses to guide them, men are cut off from all "communication with being" and if they think they are rational this is one of their absurd self-delusions. The wisest men know that all their learning only· reveals their profound ignorance. If, as suggested, the great tradition of Western thought was optimistically rational, it is hard not to think that with Montaigne it had temporarily played out.

If Montaigne though a professed Catholic really "strangles religion with a silken cord," if he was more a Stoic than a Christian and "acclimatized pagan morality in France,"[9] he perhaps foreshadowed the Enlightenment. The "libertinism" which circulated surreptitiously in seventeenth-century France and led on to eighteenth-century "deism" and atheism owed a good deal to him. But his skepticism and attacks on reason, his low estimate of human nature, is not in accord with what was to follow in the Age of Reason. Redeemed by the discovery of order in nature, the later seventeenth and eighteenth centuries recover their faith, though it is not exactly the old faith. Montaigne's genera-

[9]H. Daniel-Rops, *The Catholic Reformation*, 1962.

tion was one that lay between a dying age and one struggling to be born.

Montaigne had witnessed the horrors of religious war and turned for relief to Stoicism and the classics; his urbane skepticism conceals a spirit shocked to the depths of its being at the violence and apparent stupidity of his fellows. What assurance could they have that their beliefs were true? He ridiculed the Protestants for supposing that agreement was possible on the basis of Scripture. No, that contentious and ignorant species, man, would quarrel over every line of it. It was an argument the devout Bishop Bossuet would later use against Protestantism. But Montaigne sided with those Catholics who were *politiques* or realists prepared to tolerate as widely as possible and with the Protestant Henry of Navarre who was willing to give up his Protestantism for civil peace. (Montaigne visited Henry IV and may have influenced him.)

Montaigne has been seen as a typical baroque writer. The term *baroque* as applied to a style in the arts (painting, architecture, sculpture, also music) and then to literature has also been extended to embrace the whole mind of this age in Europe, the one that coincided with this post-Renaissance and in a sense post-Reformation interlude—from about 1570 to perhaps 1650. Dates given for the baroque period by scholars vary a few years, which is hardly surprising given the complexity of the phenomena covered. We have here, after all, a question of many different countries and many cultural areas. But there is broad agreement on the validity of the concept. It is at least a key to the mind and mood of this epoch, as good a key as we have. The baroque was a rebellion against pure classicism, with some wild and even disorderly aspects, somewhat foreshadowing nineteenth-century romanticism. It was a wonderfully creative movement in the arts, giving full vent to the esthetic imagination, but in its partial rejection of classicism and its mood of revolt it may be seen as a sign of the crisis in thought and feeling that came over Europe at this time. With the victory of science and rationalism, it would yield to a return of classicism beginning about the middle of the seventeenth century. The baroque was a disturbed style for a disturbed age—disturbed by religious intolerance and civil war, by skepticism and Renaissance complexity, and before long by the first impact of the new astronomy.

Before leaving Montaigne, the baroque characteristics of his writing may be noted. There is the disorder, or at least apparent disorder, of his style—no neat classical symmetry, no rules. There is the stress on change and movement: neither in his life nor writings did Montaigne stand still, and he is fascinated by the process rather than the result. "I do not depict being, but transformation," he wrote. This is a facet, of course, of his skepticism: no truth exists surely except this mind of mine, ever changing and becoming.[10] And here the premodern skepticism of Montaigne parallels very recent developments in Western thought, just as contemporary art forms have much in common with the baroque. But Montaigne was sure that human nature is the same, man is one, and therefore that in understanding his own mind he understood man in general. Modern existentialism, so drastically skeptical of everything else, seems to make this same assumption.

There is also the nervous, paradoxical style, which seeks to jolt and shock. There is, finally, a certain fascination with the grotesque and even the cruel. For all his genuine disgust at the barbarities men inflict on each other, he rather liked to dwell on the gory details, we feel. Montaigne had been a soldier, and liked it; the baroque was toughminded, on the whole, compared to nineteenth-century romanticism.

Beginning about 1560, the baroque dominated the south of Europe architecturally and spread to some extent into the north. Its supreme genius was Bernini, the Neapolitan whose titanic energy created so much of the new Rome begun around the turn of the seventeenth century, including many of the *piazze* and fountains at which tourists gape today. This association of baroque architecture with Rome, and generally with Catholic Church architecture of the period, especially with the Jesuits, the new and most dynamic of the Orders, has led to its being linked spiritually to the Catholic Counter Reformation. The desire for distortion in the striking painting of El Greco may be compared: an intense religiosity, straining at the barriers of objective reality, which wished, somewhat in the manner of nineteenth-century romanticism, to transform and distort—a divine madness, far from the cool rationality of the classical style.

Frequently also the term *baroque* is applied to the great post-Renaissance painters Rubens, Tintoretto, Rembrandt, and Velasquez. Of these, Tintoretto and Rubens seem the most typically baroque. Wherever we find it, baroque appears exuberant and unrestrained, seeking grand effects, admiring the asymmetrical rather than the symmetrical, things in motion rather than in repose, the unlimited rather than the neatly bounded. In literature, one can see the baroque spirit at work in the elaborate conceits and paradoxes of the "metaphysical" poets or, again, in the wilder features of Jacobean drama, with its themes of murder, incest, black magic, and thunderous world-conquering heroes. In France the theater showed the same taste for flamboyance and violence, the imported Spanish tragi-comedy being a case in

[10]Cf. John Donne, the English poet, on Inconstancy, in his *Paradoxes and Problems*: everything changes, and things are the better in proportion as they change the most.

point. "A grandeur without restraint, a wild extravagance, and a luxury of detail that would have been distasteful to Michelangelo" (Nikolaus Pevsner) appears in some of the more extreme art forms of the post-Renaissance period. ("Mannerism" preceded and foreshadowed baroque.)

The key idea in the baroque was movement and change. Nothing is constant, everything shifts as in a kaleidoscope. Jean Rousset, author of a perceptive study of French baroque literature, subtitled his book *Circe et la Paon*, Circe and the peacock—finding in the Greek goddess a symbol of change and magic, in the bird the decorative and ostentatious, both glorified by the baroque artists and playwrights. The complex rather than the simple, transformation rather than stability, multiplicity rather than unity—these were constant baroque themes, and it will be noted they are the opposite of classical ones. Classical paintings, as for example some of Poussin's in the neoclassical reaction of the later seventeenth century, freeze their subjects into timeless immobility and strive for perfect unity and symmetry. Classical painters also dislike curves. Baroque paintings, in contrast, notably exhibit curved and swirling lines, as do the great fountains of Bernini. The baroque "flees the straight line as a capital sin" (Jean Rousset). Frequently regarded as the most typical baroque creations, therefore, are the Rubens and Tintoretto paintings that are all circles and swirling lines, or those Bernini fountains that twist, contort, and gyrate. In addition, the baroque showed a preference for lower-class characters (the pastoral flourished), against classicism's demand for dignified heroes.

Colossal size and massiveness are frequently called baroque, too. It does not appear that all baroque need be large, or all that is large need be baroque, but the striving for spectacular effect as well as the love of illusion could lead to "giganticism." Bernini's huge piazza at St. Peter's and his massive fountains are baroque by general agreement, while some find baroque elements in the great palace of King Louis XIV at Versailles, despite a preponderance of classical modes. The same taste for colossal art appeared during the Hellenistic age of the ancient world, during which there was a reaction against the pure, severe classicism of city-state Greece. To throw off restraint and strive to reach the utmost limits obviously might lead to giganticism.

One should not make the mistake of disparaging the baroque. That once was the fashion, but the twentieth century appreciates this art much more than did the nineteenth, doubtless because of certain cultural affinities. It was, writes Professor Wittkower (a high authority), an "almost unbelievably strong generation," this baroque one. Bernini, Borromini, Velazquez, Rembrandt, Rubens, Hals are some of the giants of the arts in this period. It would seem permissible to add Tintoretto and the young Poussin. If we try to extend the concept of the baroque to literature, we might be able to embrace Shakespeare and the Jacobean dramatists, among others. In architecture, it produced perhaps the last truly original and vigorous European style, at least until the twentieth century. Eighteenth- and nineteenth-century eclecticism went back to it time and again, as also to the other great European styles, Gothic, Renaissance, neoclassical.

The baroque had many facets, and we must beware of the trap of overly pat definitions (just as in the case of romanticism, later). But the combination of adventurousness with confusion in the baroque fits well the image of an age in rapid transition, unsure of its balance as it pulled up ancient moorings to begin a voyage on seas still strange, heading toward unknown destinations. The stress on movement and instability is the essence of the baroque. Man most resembles himself when in motion, Bernini declared. "Whirl is king," the men of the baroque held with Heraclitus the ancient philosopher. This was an age of insecurity—insecurity political (the wars of religion, leading to internal as well as external strife) and intellectual. Beginning with the terrible collision of the Reformation and Counter Reformation, Europe then moved forward into the age when Kepler and Galileo were calling all the cosmos into question as they advanced toward a new order of physical science, an order not reached until Newton, near the end of the century. Small wonder that men of the later sixteenth and earlier seventeenth century could not abide the serenity of the classical. Nothing, for these generations, could be tame and balanced. They were the finders of fabulous, terrifying things. As a vision of reality two thousand years old shattered into fragments, the shimmering and uncertain contours of the modern world view danced before the eyes of seventeenth-century man, alternately inspiring him and scaring him.

It was a time of witchcraft and magic, but also of the birth of modern science and philosophy; a time of great art and architecture which lacked composure and soon fragmented; a time of wars and revolutions, famine and suffering, through which the modern state and economic society can be discerned in embryo. This was the marvelous Age of the Baroque. While the years from about 1580 to 1630 will always be associated with Shakespeare, Montaigne, and Rubens, they are also the years of Kepler, Brahe, and Galileo. It was the Scientific Revolution that ultimately gave shape and new direction to the century.

2

The Scientific
and Intellectual Revolution
of the Seventeenth Century

*The history of thought knows many barren truths and
fertile errors.*

ARTHUR KOESTLER

*The Hellenic ideal of science as a rational inquiry into
nature seemed to be the foundation of the distinctive
intellectual traits of Western civilization.*

MORRIS COHEN

Medieval Science

The Scientific Revolution, in reality, had deep roots in the past.
Medieval science was far from being as contemptible as was formerly
taken for granted and is still (since myths die hard) sometimes asserted.
The recovery of Greek and Arabic mathematics along with Aristotle's
logic and his treatise of scientfic methodology (*Posterior Analytics*)
dates from the twelfth century. Medieval mathematicians such as
Leonard of Pisa and Jordanus made real contributions and if the mathematical-deductive method of scientific analysis flourished, so to some
extent did the empirical approach, of observation and experimentation.
In practice, it is true, medieval universities hardly featured laboratory
techniques, but the dominant philosophical outlook, Aristotelianism,
was actually in a sense strongly empirical. Such great medieval doctors
as Albertus Magnus and Roger Bacon held strong scientific interests,
though the greatest of them, Thomas Aquinas, cared less for the physical and natural sciences than for ethical, political, and metaphysical

thought. First things must come first, and the twelfth and thirteenth centuries laid a solid foundation of logical thought on which later science could build. Thus it is perverse to ridicule Aristotle and the medieval schoolmen for their errors while forgetting the essential truths they established. Nevertheless they were unable to bring to birth a scientific renaissance; they were the prisoners of old error and could not break out.

The fourteenth century seemed about to make the breakthrough that actually did not come until the end of the sixteenth. Such late schoolmen as Nicholas of Oresme, Jean Buridan, and Albert of Saxony were playing with motional concepts such as Kepler and Galileo gained greater fame for attacking two hundred years or more later. This was an abortive scientific revolution, however. Historians have conceded that the promising beginnings made by these northern schoolmen played out: "towards the end of the fourteenth century the brilliant period of scholastic originality came to an end" (A. C. Crombie) and Paris and Oxford ceased to be creative in science. The whole period from about 1350 to 1660 is in almost every field a curiously ambivalent one; it was subject to the general disruption that accompanied the Hundred Years' War followed by the Reformation struggles. These disruptive forces attacked the north of Europe more than the south and help explain why Italy sprang to the front during this "Renaissance" era. The University of Padua in northern Italy became the chief residence of late medieval science; it has been accorded pride of place in the scientific revolution. Copernicus studied there, Galileo later lectured there, and Padua was also the home of the anatomist Vesalius, under whom studied the Englishman William Harvey, the Galileo of physiology. Padua preserved a degree of continuity with the medieval past.

The philosophic tradition at Padua actually was left-wing Aristotelanism, or Averroist (after the famous Arabian commentator), which retained the Aristotelian interest in experimentation without the dogmatism its medieval Christian adherents often exhibited. A long tradition of interest in the physical sciences existed at Padua and, in general, in Crombie's words, "the leading scientists of the 16th and 17th centuries both knew and used the writings of their medieval predecessors," Every great achievement in thought builds on the past. Ignorant history with an irrational prejudice against the Middle Ages used to perpetuate the view that they made no scientific contribution, and this view is still popularly prevalent. This is not so. Nevertheless, in the sixteenth century only a few places and a few men kept alive the scientific tradition, and they will always be honored as among the immortals of human intellectual achievement.

The Renaissance Italians themselves, insofar as concerned the dominant humanist group, tended to neglect science for literature. Some of the humanists, like the immortal artist-scientist Leonardo da Vinci, had scientific interests but on the whole their major stress was esthetic rather than scientific. (In any case Leonardo's prowess as a scientist has been exaggerated.) By its worship of the classics, humanism often exerted a reactionary influence on the sciences, for bookishness and respect for ancient authority were obstacles that science had to overcome. Still, humanists introduced Platonism and by thus making known rival theories to the Aristotelian, they indirectly stimulated scientific inquiry. While Plato was much less a scientist than Aristotle, he was a mathematician; few who know anything at all about the great Athenian are ignorant of the fact that he placed mathematics foremost in education, for it teaches us the basic principles of all advanced thought. Platonists (and Pythagoreans, closely related) had, because of this, developed views different from the Aristotelians on such significant matters as space, gravity, the nature of matter and of the celestial bodies. As background for the epochal work of Copernicus, this ancient school of science, rediscovered, is most important.

The Copernican Revolution

In 1543 the Polish-German astronomer Nicholas Copernicus published his book, *The Revolutions of the Heavenly Bodies*, suggesting the hypothesis of heliocentrism, with earth and planets in motion around the sun rather than the accepted doctrine of a motionless earth around which all celestial bodies revolved in a series of spheres. (The work had circulated in manuscript among a few scholars quite a few years earlier.) A more than usual number of myths exist concerning this epochal work. Two may here be mentioned. First, Copernicus was not the first to suggest heliocentrism, for in ancient times several notable scientists had done so; the most important was Aristarchus of Samos, third-century B.C. Alexandrian Greek, the "ancient Copernicus." Platonists had strenuously debated with the Aristotelians on just this issue, and the revival of Platonism and Neoplatonism during the Renaissance exerted a strong influence on such key figures as Copernicus, Kepler, and Galileo. (Even Francis Bacon appealed from Aristotle to Plato.) Before Copernicus, the fifteenth-century German churchman Nicholas of Cusa had speculated that the earth is in motion in an infinite universe, an idea immersed in his religious mysticism and which he derived from Platonism.

Secondly, the earth-centered theory, which had long prevailed, was not based on mere superstition or theological bias, but on what seemed the best evidence. The cosmogony which medieval scholars accepted was derived from Aristotle and from Ptolemy, the Egyptian astronomer of the Hellenistic period, who had suggested certain variants of the Aristotelian system while agreeing with it on basic features. The world stood motionless in the center of the universe, because it did not seem possible that a body known to be so heavy could be in motion, without anything to move it. The law of inertia was what the ancients did not grasp, a failure that should be easy enough to understand, for the notion of large bodies whirling along in space and keeping in their orbits without anything to move and guide them *is* a little remarkable. It took a great amount of work by scientific genius to arrive at this conclusion. Nor was this a conclusion readily to be reached by observation. Galileo praised Copernicus for having the *imagination* to conceive what the senses tell us is impossible. Experience seems to show that when we throw an object it does not continue indefinitely in motion, but soon falls to earth.

Aristotelian physics explained the impetus by air rushing to fill the vacuum at the rear of the thrown object. It believed that gravity was the force that impelled all material bodies to seek their natural abode at the center of the earth. The Aristotelian theory of motion assumed that the natural state of bodies is at rest, and except for living things, which have a "natural" movement, and things falling from a height, a mover is required to impart motion to anything. Objects dropped from a height would fall at a speed proportionate to their mass divided by the resistance of the air. In a vacuum, they would fall with infinite speed; but Aristotelians insisted on the impossibility of a vacuum.

Immediately beyond the earth lay the domains of water, air, and fire, explaining why these elements ascend, as it was assumed they did. Then came the celestial ether with the celestial bodies revolving around the earth in a series of spheres, first the moon, then Mercury, Venus, Sun, Mars, Jupiter, Saturn, and finally the stars. (The moon was a great divide, all above it being pure, incorruptible, immutable, divine, while all beneath it was imperfect, changeable, and impure.) The "primum mobile" was the sphere which turned the others by means of a sort of flywheel arrangement. Beyond the spheres lay "the abode of God and all the Elect," in the empyrean heaven, as it was customary to state on the celestial maps, but this had nothing to do with the system directly.

There were some difficulties with this picture; in particular, Aristotle and Ptolemy did not exactly agree and the observations of heavenly bodies had forced, in the Ptolemaic system, the awkward device of "epicycles" or small circles described by the planets on their spheres, as well as eccentric circles, that is, the earth not exactly at the center of the various orbits. As more accurate observations became possible, these devices to "save the appearances" increased. Still, it does not seem to be true that the Copernican hypothesis simplified the model, though this used to be a common view. It may be worth reiterating that the prime objections to any hypothesis which put the earth in motion were physical ones. The arguments in favor of a motionless earth were impressive, most especially in the area of dynamics: how could so heavy a body as the earth possibly be in motion, without a mover? And what would prevent it from falling? One had first to arrive at modern theories of gravity and inertial motion before one could believe in an earth spinning through space. Common sense and experimentation seemed to uphold the view that bodies do not remain in motion without a physical moving force being applied to them; the thrown ball soon falls to earth after leaving the hand though it clearly receives some temporary motion, which Aristotelian physics explained in terms of air currents. It also supported the view that, since objects fall toward the center of the earth, gravity must draw everything in the universe in that direction. Copernicus himself was aware of the many difficulties in the way of his hypothesis and did not dream that he had proved it; he offered it merely as a suggestion for future scientific examination.

A final fallacy is that there was some sort of conspiracy to suppress Copernicus's truth. When propounded it was neither self-evidently true—on the contrary, almost self-evidently absurd to most educated men—nor was it so startlingly new as has often been suggested. True it is that the accepted cosmology had been integrated into Christian theology and to abandon it was to involve many a wrench for the men of faith. Still, the Church made no objection to Copernicus's work. Luther called him a fool,[1] but so did many learned scientists. It has long been established that the reluctance to accept Copernicus was largely due to other factors than a reactionary conspiracy; to the absence of convincing evidence, principally. Through most of Europe, men's minds were still turned toward other studies, whether theological or humanistic, as the Reformation and the Renaissance continued to hold sway.

The arguments that Copernicus offered to meet the physical objections of the earth's motion were feeble and quite scholastic, that is,

---

[1]Calvin, contrary to what has been sometimes stated, apparently did not know of Copernicus at all. Had he known, the chances are he would have accepted his views readily, for Calvin's main point in his discussions on such questions was that the wondrous contrivances of nature testify to the glory of God; the more amazing the phenomena, the greater the tribute to Deity. Calvinists had no difficulty adjusting to the new astronomy. See Edward Rosen, "Calvin's Attitude toward Copernicus," *Journal of the History of Ideas*, July-September, 1960.

arguments in terms of the nature and purposes of things.[2] Thus he says simply that mobility might be considered as nobler and more divine than immobility, rather than vice versa; while gravity is "a natural inclination, bestowed on the parts of bodies by the Creator so as to combine the parts in the form of a sphere and thus contribute to their unity and wholeness." The reluctance of Copernicus to publish his theory (he did not do so until just before his death, and then at the insistent promptings of his young disciple, the German Protestant Rheticus) is to be attributed not to fear of ecclesiastical displeasure, for the pope himself seems to have urged Copernicus to publish, but rather to fear of ridicule, since he did not have the answers to objections certain to be lodged against it. Copernicus's secretiveness could be defended on the grounds that exposure of his theory at this time would have discredited and set back the whole scientific revolution. Premature publicity to a startling innovation may be bad policy; one should not announce it until it can be proved. The timidity of Copernicus might have been higher wisdom. At any rate the failure of Copernicus to make his hypothesis convincing is not in doubt. His contemporaries could not be blamed for receiving his cosmology with skepticism.

Kepler and Galileo

Yet gradually the whole Aristotelian science became discredited. Of considerable importance were the observations of a nova (new star) in 1572, and of a comet in 1577, for these phenomena could not be fitted into the Ptolemaic framework. (The comet went crashing through all the crystalline spheres!) Galileo assumed that the Aristotelians were dunces, as he directed a devastating fire at one position after another of the schoolmen. Wrong in their astronomy, they were also wrong in their dynamics, and elsewhere, for example, hydraulics, where the Aristotelian belief that objects sink or float because of something to do with their shape gave way to Galileo's specific gravity. What had once been a most estimable and satisfying scientific system collapsed all at once

---

[2]Of Aristotle's famous four kinds of causes, the material, formal, efficient, and final, the latter was often accorded the highest place and given the most emphasis. To understand an object we must know its physical components, its form or configuration, its shaping agent, but also, and most notably, its *purpose*. A window, for example, is made of glass, has the shape of a window, was built by an artisan, and these all contributed to making it what it is; but clearly there would not have been any window unless there was a use for it. The ultimate explanation of a window is that it exists for the purpose of seeing out of. This is impeccable logic; but it later seemed ridiculous, a sort of mental laziness, to keep explaining things by reference to what in fact they are. The revolution against teleology was a vital part of the scientific revolution.

in the early seventeenth century. But until Galileo the dynamics of any system that put the heavy earth in motion were most bewildering. The problem was not entirely cleared up until Newton.

If Padua assumed the lead in the solution of the Copernican conundrum, southern Germay also played a distinguished role in the early years of the revolution in cosmology. In fact, men of genius from all over Europe pooled their talents. Johannes Kepler, a Swabian of humble birth, encountered Copernicanism at the University of Tübingen (near Stuttgart in southern Germany), went to Prague in Bohemia to work under the colorful Danish astronomical observer Tycho Brahe, and later became official astronomer to the Hapsburg Emperor. Brahe had been welcomed by the German city of Augsburg at a time when he heard only jeers in his native Denmark. The tireless Brahe gradually accumulated evidence that made the old astronomy increasingly untenable, while Kepler, subject to all kinds of difficulties, and later working in the troubled atmosphere of the Thirty Years' War (1618-1648), broke the "tyranny of the circle" and managed to discover the true laws of planetary motion. He also explored the idea of inertial movement which Galileo was so brilliantly to demonstrate. The genius of Kepler was magnificent but he remained semimedieval, searching for the harmony of the spheres, combining mysticism with science in a way that illustrates the in-between status of thought. Withal he maintained an unshakeable faith in the geometrical foundations of the universe ("Geometry existed before the creation, is coeternal with the mind of God, *is God himself* . . ."). Buried in his speculations are the three laws of planetary movement together with other insights which had he been able to put them together, might have led Kepler to discover the law of gravity nearly a century before Newton.[3] One feels that the enormous labors and extraordinary creativity of Kepler marked the decisive breakthrough to the new physics and astronomy, but also that the synthesis of the new knowledge lay behind the grasp of this low-born German. As, in his time, it had to be.

"A Pythagorean synthesis of mysticism and science," as Arthur Koestler describes Kepler, he was a man of surpassing faith and surpassing energy, who fought his way through difficulties both physical and mental to reach the threshold of modern science, though he could not quite cross it. Ill-paid by the German Emperor who had much more

---

[3]The first law is the elliptical orbit of the planets; the second, that equal geometric areas are swept out in equal times when lines are drawn from the planet to the sun; the third, that the square of the period of a planet (that is, time of orbit around the sun) equals the cube of the planet's mean distance from the sun. It is the third law which suggests to us Newton's law of gravitation (an attraction inversely proportionate to the square of the distance between bodies).

important outlets for his limited funds, such as waging war, Kepler earned money by telling the fortune of eminent men, star-gazers being still hired more for astrology than astronomy, and died a penniless wanderer. Lacking sufficient mathematical tools, he had to resort to immensely laborious calculations. He never ceased his search for the harmony and law he believed to exist in the universe. His final misfortune was that almost no one would accept the most important of his discoveries, because men could not abandon the notion that circular motion was the ideal and perfect form. Only slowly did this view retreat. Kepler's ellipses seemed as awkward as the man himself, and he died in obscurity. Since then his reputation has constantly risen until today he is hailed as one of history's greatest figures.

From England William Gilbert, court physician to Queen Elizabeth, contributed his fruitful tract on the magnet in 1600 (carrying on, again, an investigation begun in medieval times), and John Napier introduced an important new tool in mathematics. Earlier, too, England had given support to Copernicus through Leonard and Thomas Digges and John Dee. France, before the arrival of Descartes, produced the great mathematician Pierre Fermat. In Germany, the city of Nuremberg can claim to have been the site of the earliest significant astronomical observations, and remained prominent in the scientific revolution. Yet it was Italy that held the center of the stage during the lifetime of the great Galileo. In 1610 his observations through the telescope (which he did not invent, but considerably improved), and his spectacular report on his observations, called Europe's attention to the collapse of the Ptolemaic system and aroused such widespread interest as the world has seldom known.

The genius and flair of Galileo took charge of the Scientific Revolution at this point. The great Italian was by no means always on the right track,[4] yet his stimulating prose as well as his powerful scientific imagination led him to establish the Copernican "hypothesis" beyond reasonable doubt in the minds of educated men. Not only had he made the observations that convincingly discredited the old cosmology, but he succeeded in refuting many of the stock arguments against the earth's movement, such as that centrifugal force would whirl it to pieces, or that a body thrown into the air would come down in a different spot. Then he found the law of acceleration of falling bodies, working with superb genius on a problem that had been discussed for a long time. Most crucial of all was his virtual discovery of the law of inertia: that objects, contrary to the old and apparently common-

---

[4]For one thing, he never accepted Kepler's important laws of the elliptical course of the planets and indeed always displayed toward his great German contemporary an ungenerous, jealous attitude.

sense view, need not have a constant mover to be in motion but will continue in motion by their own momentum once started.

Well known is the story of Galileo's clash with clerical authority. His trial, forced recantation, and subsequent confinement to his farm (which did not end his scientific writings) occurred in 1633, late in his career. The position of the Roman Church is sometimes misunderstood: it was prepared to tolerate the Copernican theory if presented as a mere "hypothesis" not a fact, and indeed did so.[5] But Galileo, though a genuinely pious man by all accounts, with no desire to flout religious authority or discredit the faith, argued powerfully, and prophetically, that the Bible was not intended to be a textbook of physics and that religion would be discredited if this view prevailed. The Church, dominated by the spirit of the Council of Trent, would not accept the facticity of Copernicus's and Galileo's universe in the teeth of certain Biblical passages to the contrary. Protestants sometimes reacted similarly. However deplorable, this ecclesiastical obscurantism was not effective, for in Catholic countries as well as Protestant the scientific revolution went ahead. Borelli and Torricelli in Italy, Descartes and Pascal in France, are outstanding proofs of this. These men did accept the convention of presenting some of their scientific work as "hypothesis" rather than fact. Descartes withheld some of his work from publication during his lifetime. Delay, rather than defeat, of the scientific revolution was the only result of persecution of scientists.

The tendency of much recent scholarship has been to conclude that the old story of clerical intolerance and obscurantism arrayed against scientific truth represents a considerable exaggeration. There is something in it, but not as much as one sort of popular history would have it, and a good many "rationalist myths" need to be disposed of. Kepler, though nominally a Lutheran, worked in Catholic countries honored and undisturbed for the most part. Galileo's dramatic clash with the Church is subject to the reservations already indicated, that is, that the latter never objected to Copernicanism if put forward as a hypothesis (which it perhaps in fact was, rather than absolute truth). Galileo himself has occasionally been seen as a rather pugnacious and difficult person; the arrogance that often goes with genius seems to have been his in full measure. The Jesuits were quick to accept and contribute to the new astronomy, for example, Scheiner at Ingolstadt, who was probably the first to spy the spots on the sun. (However, they hoped to gain support for Tycho's rather than Copernicus's theory. Tycho held that the planets revolve around the sun, but all of these

---

[5]In Roman Catholic Spain, as Christopher Hill points out, "The Copernican revolution was accepted without difficulty," was being taught at Salamanca in 1594, and Philip III invited Galileo to Madrid.

around the immobile earth, a variation designed to accommodate the new observations while retaining the spirit of the old system.) Conservative, hidebound opposition to the new theories did exist, of course, but more typically it was found in the universities and academies, its basis being what Arthur Koestler has called "professionals with a vested interest in tradition and in the monopoly of learning . . . pedantic mediocrities."

In our times, opposition to Freud, to modern painting, to the novels of Joyce and Lawrence might be a rough approximation. This opposition has not all been "religious," nor has it all been unintelligent. Conservatives of various sorts, and those who cannot make the mental adjustment to a startling new vision of reality, have joined it, while some perceptive clericals on the other hand have been among the avant garde. Conservatism and clericalism are hardly the same thing. The Church was more powerful in Galileo's time but a substantial element in it was eager to avoid using this power to constrain scientific inquiry. The higher clergy was more liberal than the lower, who were provincial in outlook. In brief, the deplorable disciplining of Galileo must not be thought of as simply an ignorant rejection of science by the whole Church.

Galileo had dedicated his career to disposing of the numerous classical objections to a theory of the earth's movement. Frequently called the greatest of experimental scientists, the Italian actually excelled in scientific imagination: in the conception of hypotheses, in knowing *what* experiments should be performed. (It is more than doubtful that he ever actually performed the celebrated experiment attributed to him of dropping the two objects of different weights from the tower of Pisa; the whole story seems to have been thoroughly garbled.) He thought of his method as mathematical rather than (primarily) experimental. A leading historian of the scientific revolution has observed that "the modern law of inertia was hardly a thing which the human mind would ever reach by experiment." Galileo's Platonism was a decisive influence, his central idea—one may say faith—being that "the universe is a book written in mathematical language." We here return to that old and central belief of the Western tradition, elaborated in the books of Job and of Plato, that there *is* an order in the universe, that things will come out even. Of course there was much more to it than this; Galileo's method was a sophisticated one involving hypothesis, the testing of that hypothesis under strictly controlled conditions, the use of that result for further hypotheses, and so on. But at the root of it lay a Platonic faith that the intelligible structure of nature would be revealed in mathematical formulae. The ability of Galileo to "mathematicize" physical problems, that is, to find a mathematical regularity rather than conceive the problem in purely sensory or kinetic terms, made possible such essential discoveries as inertial motion. It was actually a break with "empiricism," which Galileo considered Aristotelianism to be. This was the fruitful path that led to Newton.

The Continuing Scientific Revolution

At any rate the experiments Galileo's genius conceived struck Europe's imagination. His forceful prose and his clash with the papacy in 1633 contributed to establishing his reputation as pioneer of a new era in man's picture of his world. Few men have ever so combined power of intellect with a daring imagination. Meanwhile the cause of science obtained a martyr when Giordano Bruno was burnt at the stake in 1600. Mystic and heretic, Bruno was not really much of a scientist. (But many leading figures in the twilight-zone area between medieval and modern, men like Nicholas of Cusa or Paracelsus the physician, had combined genuine scientific genius with visionary, mystic, or occult philosophies; Brahe and Kepler did so too.) Though the exuberant Bruno fathered many unorthodoxies, the most disturbing one was the plurality of worlds. When the earth ceased to be unique, the only body possessing weight, as had been the case before, there opened up the possibility of there being many earths, many human species, hence many Christs. Modern Christians such as Alice Meynell may find no difficulty in conceiving of

The million forms of God those stars unroll

but most sixteenth-century Christians definitely did.

Even the dazzling genius, Pascal, confessed that the empty spaces of the new universe frightened him; he meant not only that the cosmos had been vastly enlarged but also that the old-world view had known no "empty spaces," since the conception was of a plenum in which no gaps or spaces existed. Plainly, the cosmological revolution involved large changes in the entire outlook of men. This matter of the "world view" is one that interests and concerns the intellectual historian more so than the strictly scientific questions, which he may leave to the scientists themselves. It has been declared, frequently, that "The modern world, as far as mental outlook is concerned, begins in the seventeenth century" (Bertrand Russell); that this change in mental outlook brought about by the sciences in the seventeenth century "outshines everything since the rise of Christianity" (Herbert Butterfield); that "the vision of reality that had supported the rational consciousness of men for a thousand years was fading" and being replaced by a new one (Meyrick Carré).

To describe this big change is to pass from the scientist to the philosophers of the seventeenth century, or rather to the scientist-philosophers, like Francis Bacon, René Descartes, Pierre Gassendi, Thomas Hobbes. This will be the theme of the next section. Here we may summarily describe the continuing course of the scientific revolution after Galileo, in the middle years of the century.

A major necessity was to develop mathematics so that it could carry out the grand mission set for it by Galileo, to be nothing less than "the language of nature." Galileo was limited to geometrical methods. The next step lay in the application of algebra to physical science; Galileo's own disciple, Cavalieri, made contributions here but the main steps were taken in France by Fermat and then by the great Descartes. To be able to express geometrical relationships in the symbols of algebra was an enormous gain for scientific method. From there, the road led on through Pascal to Newton and Leibniz, the founders of calculus.

Meanwhile another Galileo pupil, Torricelli, conducted an experiment in atmospheric pressure in 1643 which interested all the eager young scientists of Europe. It was publicized in France by the Abbé Mersenne, whose convent was a center of the scientific movement (another indication that the Church was by no means always an enemy to science), and developed in a series of classic experiments by the brilliant Blaise Pascal. Pascal climbed a mountain to see if the mercury level in a barometer fell as the weight of the air diminished. The result was a triumph this time for the experimental method, the development by Pascal of pneumatics, and another defeat for Aristotelianism. For, as we know, one of the most insistent dogmas of the old school was the impossibility of a vacuum. But Pascal had shown that a vacuum could exist! Experiments with the air pump became to the seventeenth century what electricity was to the eighteenth—the favorite demonstration performed by amateur scientists at parties, or exhibited in public to a gaping populace.

Robert Boyle, the English experimenter, found the laws of the expansion of gases through pressure and heat. Experiments in optics, begun in the Middle Ages, fascinated the seventeenth century, such great men as Descartes and the mighty Newton perfecting the analysis of light and its refraction into the colors of the spectrum. How to explain this phenomenon of light became a major scientific question giving rise to controversies.

With better microscopes and more careful observational techniques, scientists also subjected living things to closer scrutiny, and there were a few notable discoveries though in general the day of "biology" did not come until later. Outstanding here was William Harvey's work. Disciple of the great Italian experimental anatomist Vesalius, it was he, wrote his fellow Englishman Thomas Hobbes, who first made known "the science of man's body"; though in fact all Harvey did was describe correctly the action of the heart and the blood circulatory system, it was enough to excite general admiration and restore keen interest in anatomy. Descartes lent his great authority to the mechanistic approach: the bodies of animals and men are nothing but machines. This was an effort to drag organic phenomena into the same system as physics and was only partially successful because the two realms are not the same. Still, the new approach stimulated research and provided new insights. Another sensation came when Dutch observers sighted microorganisms; indeed, through the microscope a wealth of previously unknown data about living things became available.

By the 1660s, the time of the great scientific societies had arrived: the Royal Society in England, the Academy of Sciences in France. Earlier, scientific work owed much to the patronage of kings toward individual scientists—Tycho was subsidized by the King of Denmark, Kepler by the German Emperor—or to the activities of certain "virtuosi," amateur patrons of the sciences such as the Abbé Mersenne or in England, Henry Oldenburg. Scientific research became better organized and synchronized, so that much greater resources of knowledge were available. Isaac Newton arrived at the moment when enough scientific data and mathematical techniques had accumulated to make possible his great synthesis of it all. It took his stupendous genius to perform this act of synthesis, yet before 1687 even the greatest could not do so.

It may be said in general that until Newton came along, the many exciting scientific frontiers exerted a disturbing as well as a stimulating influence; no one knew quite whither they were going to lead, or how they might fit together. One only knew that the older vision of the universe, which had stood largely unimpaired since ancient times, no longer compelled assent:

> The Sun is lost, and th' Earth, and no man's wit
> Can well direct him where to look for it.
> *John Donne*

The New World View

The men whose work we have just been considering—Copernicus, Kepler, Galileo—were not philosophers, but their ideas had important philosophical results. They had overturned the medieval cosmology and much of the Aristotelian physics; at the same time they were inclined to disparage the Aristotelian explanation in terms of "final cause," purpose, teleology. Teleology came under attack in the seventeenth century. Francis Bacon remarked that it is like a virgin consecrated to the service of God—inspiring, but barren. In one of Molière's plays an Aristotelian is held up to ridicule for solemnly explaining that opium causes sleep because it is possessed of dormitive virtues, which by Molière's time seemed no explanation at all. Nor does it to us. Fashions in explanations change; Aristotle's had long satisfied most men, but the Bacons and Galileos of the scientific revolution impatiently rejected it. Unless one abandoned the effort to find final causes, one could get nowhere. To classify and measure the observable properties, forgetting about ultimate purposes, was less ambitious an aim but more fruitful. For the ultimate purposes are unknowable, while careful study of the efficient causes can give us power over nature.

Likewise under attack was the Aristotelian concept of the unity of all being. Galileo, with his drive to make physical nature subject to mathematical, quantitative treatment, suggested a division between "primary" and "secondary" qualities of things. Only the former should be regarded as real, or at any rate as meaningful for science, and all others could be reduced to these. These were the measurable qualities, size, shape, motion, mass, number. Physical nature should be reduced to a mechanical proposition, exactly calculable; it should be purged of all animistic features, that is, those that seemed to endow it with soul, life, or conscious will. Today we take it for granted that physical nature is this way, dead and not at all alive; so completely did seventeenth-century thinking permeate the Western world. (Very recently, philosophies have arisen again which suggest a "pan-psychism" but these have scarcely yet gained wide acceptance.) To attribute some degree of life to, say, water or a rock would strike us as strange. But in a sense Aristotle had done so. All things are a combination of form and matter, he had taught, and all are links in the single great "chain of being" that stretches from the most inert matter at the bottom to the purest angelic essence at the top. (At least such a view, incorporating perhaps some Neoplatonist elements, was widely shared in the Middle Ages.) The sharp dualism between matter (extended substance) and mind or soul (thinking substance) which Descartes built into his philosophy brought him into conflict with the Aristotelians, who regarded the soul as the form of the body, inseparable from it, body and soul being just two aspects of the same thing. The new outlook thought otherwise. The primary and secondary qualities, and the mind-matter dualism of Descartes, were most congenial to it. It may further be noted that the hierarchical or "chain of being" character of the Aristotelian universe gave way to one in which things are all alike, qualitatively—subject to the same laws, differing only in quantitative ways.

A mechanistic picture of the world replaced an organic one. "The body of the world is a whole body . . . of which the bodies of all animals are the parts. . . . The whole body of the world lives." Thus a leading Florentine Platonist of the Renaissance had written; it was a typical view of the Greek philosophers, whether Platonic, Aristotelian, or Stoic. We have learned to think of the world as a machine, essentially—at least for two centuries after Newton few educated men thought of it as otherwise than as a dynamic system of physical bodies in motion. Perhaps because they had not had much experience with machines, the ancient philosophers had tended to visualize the universe on the analogy of a living organism. One of the consequences of such an outlook which seems strangest to the modern mind was the idea of correspondences or affinities between man and the universe, microcosm and macrocosm. In Shakespeare's time, as the imagery of his plays often reveals, people assumed that a cloud in the sky or a thunderclap foreboded something ill in human affairs. This was not altogether idle superstition, but a permissible inference from philosophies which stressed the interrelationship of all things. Learned men seriously searched for the philosopher's stone and practiced all kinds of black magic during the Renaissance, because it seemed to them that nature was bursting with unrealized potentialities which might somehow be drawn from it.

But seventeenth-century science and philosophy was to detach man from physical nature, making it a machine and him something quite other—a separation of nature from mind quite new and revolutionary in Western thought. Nature, as Alfred North Whitehead has written, became "a dull affair . . . merely the hurrying of material, endlessly, meaninglessly"—"hard, cold, colorless, silent, dead." One no longer tried to understand stars, stones, or rainbows in terms of their purpose, or to link their submerged souls with the human soul, as had formerly been done. But the physical world had measurable relationships which could be discovered, and in grasping its laws man could make it serve him. Some penetrating critics have urged that in many ways the old universe was psychologically more satisfying, and that the new one represented a "dissociation," an estrangement between man and nature, which could have untoward effects. It was this that frightened Pascal and sent him back to religion. It is not likely that many reacted in this way, though. After Galileo no one could restore the old view, and philosophers like the great Descartes began to draw the inferences of the new one.

The "world picture" men were accustomed to see certainly underwent a sharp change. How strange to us, Professor Tillyard comments in regard to Shakespeare's world, are such notions as "that God put the element of air, which was hot and moist, between fire, which was hot and dry, and water, which was cold and moist, in order to stop them fighting, and that while angels take their visible shapes from the ether devils take theirs from the sublunary air. . . ." We recognize here the Aristotelian chemical theory of the four elements, which in truth was not entirely displaced until the end of the eighteenth century. But the teleological feature, that is, the explaining of things by their purposes, would cease to interest men of science, as would the possible shapes of angels and devils (though Newton devoted much time to alchemy and more than one seventeenth-century scientist still held to witchcraft). It took time for one whole mental framework to vanish and be replaced by another, but this was being done in the seventeenth century.

It may be well to repeat the key points: people would learn to think of the natural world as consisting of inert physical matter in mechanical relationships, rather than as a great organism analogous to a living thing; they would make a sharp separation between the world of mind and of matter, a dualism which contrasts with the monism of Aristotle, who thought that all objects had the same essential psychophysical features if in differing degrees. They would cease to seek the intangible "essence" of an object but instead would concentrate on its observable properties. Men would also greatly expand the "closed world" of medieval man into an "infinite universe," sometimes with the added difference that the former was conceived as a plenum in which there were no gaps while the latter was filled with vast empty spaces. This, it has been urged, was the most important psychological consequence of the scientific revolution: the change from "the conception of the world as a finite, closed, and hierarchically ordered whole" to "an indefinite and even infinite universe which is bound together by an identity of its fundamental components and laws . . ." (A. Koyré).[6] Men would perhaps no longer feel the same kinship and closeness to nature, of which under the old order man was an integral part. But the new knowledge brought power.

It will hardly do to assume unquestioningly that the new view, the Galilean-Cartesian-Newtonian, was the right one, the old wrong. We now know that in fact the universe is *not* like a machine; and the

---

[6]But, as R. G. Collingwood pointed out, the change was not primarily a quantitative one, but qualitative—not just the larger size of the universe, but the different position of the earth, entailing a loss of the organic character of the universe.

picture that men made of it in the seventeenth and eighteenth centuries, while it lasted down into our era and may still be unconsciously taken for granted by most people (not, in the age of Einstein and Planck, by the best educated), was an arbitrary one, a set of mental constructs not necessarily corresponding to any objective reality though it might prove useful as a tool. And to be sure it did prove mightily useful—the most fruitful error, someone has said, in all history.

Francis Bacon

Bacon, from the vantage point of a man of the world who had had a position in the Elizabethan power elite, boldly attacked traditional schools of thought and called for a new deal in the realm of knowledge, demanding new terms, new methods, new institutions, a new education.[7] He wielded a sharp pen, and is endlessly quotable. Indeed, his famous *Novum Organum* (1620) is almost a series of aphorisms. Bacon's most insistent message was "renounce notions, and begin to form an acquaintance with things"; turn to the mechanic for fresh knowledge; lay aside received opinion; reexamine terms; above all observe, experiment. He was ferocious in his attacks on all the ancients: the Greeks, he wrote, have not given us a single useful experiment. This cantankerous Englishman, in whom we sometimes detect too much of the "practical man" who will stand for no nonsense from the scribes, made the mistake of scorning Galileo, too: his judgment on scientific matters was most fallible. No great scientist though his dedication to observed knowledge was sincere, he failed to understand the importance of mathematical analysis, in his passion for experiment. But what he wrote was always stimulating and frequently penetrating, and it had a mighty influence. Hailed as "the modern Aristotle," the "secretary of nature" (a title also bestowed on his French contemporary, Descartes), Bacon was to be quoted in seventeenth-century England more than any other philosophical writer and was also widely known abroad. The founding of the Royal Society and the whole scientific renaissance in England, which produced a Boyle and a Newton, owed a great deal to his original inspiration. In later times Englishmen were inclined to attribute their national leadership in science and industry to Lord Bacon, "the father of inductive science."

Despite his flaws and inconsistencies, Bacon's insistent skepticism (in the sense of a refusal to take anything on authority, a questioning

[7]Bacon's fellow Elizabethan lord, Walter Ralegh, was also a bold assailer of traditional learning: "The first," thought Francis Osborn in 1656, "that ventured to tack about and sail aloof from the beaten track of the Schools."

of all received notions) was healthy, a fresh breeze blowing through the dead Aristotelian leaves. He hit not only the theologians, whom he rather brusquely warned to keep out of scientific matters, and school-men, but also the humanists, whose preoccupation with mere style irritated him. Nor had he any more patience with the foibles of magic and astrology which persisted into the seventeenth century, even in scientific circles. We feel we have entered the new age with Bacon. At the same time he did not fully succeed in defining the method to come. Pouring scorn on the mere theoreticians, Baconism in England often led to a chaos of unguided empiricism; "apothecaries and gardeners, cranks and tinkerers," Hobbes later wrote, were aimlessly experimenting in the Royal Society. Bacon is a less systematic thinker than Descartes, who must always overshadow him, and less of a scientist, too, than the Frenchman. Above all in his relative failure to take mathematics into account he missed the leading theme of the age. Though he was aware of some of the dangers of a crude empiricism, he may be criticized for overlooking that we cannot just heap up facts and expect to get far by merely arranging them in tables; we must first frame a question, a hypothesis, and test it against the facts. On the other hand it is no bad idea to plunge a while into the ocean of fact after too long a stay on the desert of mere speculation, and at this stage of development Bacon's suggestion may well have been strategically sound.

Most celebrated of Baconian passages is that portion of the *Novum Organum* where he expatiates on the Idols or errors to which men are prone—an attempt to classify fallacies, hardly definitive, but most stimulating. The four sorts of Idols are those of the Tribe, the Cave, the Theater, and the Market-place, he says. Tribal fallacies are those common to man as a species, and Bacon finds him above all too prone to fall in love with a dogma; we might call this the familiar fallacy of the hardridden thesis, or reluctance to keep an open mind. The Cave relates to individual idiosyncrasies, which lead people to attach excessive importance to a personal perspective or experience: one must rise above personal bias. Especially interesting is Bacon on the Market-place, for this is none other than his favorite point about words. Men are the victims of what has been more recently called labelitis; they attach words to things and then are misled by their own categories. It is the fallacy of the catchword, or the unexamined vocabulary.

The Theater fallacy turns out to be the familiar one of system-making; theorists have spun large webs from small substance and have trapped their followers in their plausible but fictitious systems. A large dose of Bacon's Idols would rescue us still from most of the errors of thought commonly made; they can slay hosts of facile journalists, fanatical ideologists, slipshod thinkers—and students writing poor examination papers. They are perhaps more useful as an elementary guide to clear thinking in everyday life, or in politics, than as scientific method strictly speaking. They reveal the basically iconoclastic trait of Bacon's mind, its skeptical inclination to insist that we dismiss the "idols" of the past and examine everything afresh—words, systems, dogmas. Once again, one can only comment that at this particular moment in European history no advice was more pertinent.

The whole seventeenth-century scientific renaissance can be viewed as a debate between the experimenters and the mathematicians, in which each side scored some points and lost some—until Newton arrived to explain that the proper mixture of both methods yielded the best results. Aimless experimentation could be quite barren; perhaps the best examples of this are in the natural sciences and in chemistry; no one exceeded the alchemists in enthusiasm for the laboratory. The Royal Society under Baconian influence frequently merited Hobbes's scorn. But out of this welter of crankish puttering emerged Robert Boyle with his laws of the expansion of gases, laws which could not have been found except by experimentation. The exciting discovery of barometric pressure by Torricelli and Pascal was another triumph for experiment, a discovery which overthrew the cherished Aristotelian principle that nature abhors a vacuum, thus modifying theory at the very top.

In the other camp, the purely mathematical-deductive method of Descartes (to a large extent it was also that of Galileo) earned its high rating in this century by many a sensational breakthrough, but ultimately was discredited when the scientific blunders of the great Frenchman were found to be as numerous as his successes. We shall turn next to the remarkable Frenchman, whose sway over seventeenth-century science was even stronger than Bacon's. Between them, they represented the seeming opposites of deduction and induction, though in practice neither school was quite consistent. That is, the Baconians did not altogether leave out theory nor the Cartesians observation and experiment. But Bacon, no mathematician, encouraged the view that by extensive factual researches, followed by the arranging of the results in tables, noting resemblances and variations, one could inductively arrive at a real understanding of the properties of nature. He was aware that hypothesis based on these results could prove a useful tool to further experimentation. He shared with Descartes a scorn for scholastic final causes, an urge to reduce physical phenomena to quantitative, mechanical ones ("matter and motion"), and a concern with power over nature—practical results rather than speculative wisdom.

Like Descartes, he wished to separate science from metaphysics. There were important similarities, then, as well as differences, between the two great seventeenth-century "secretaries of nature."

René Descartes

René Descartes was born in Touraine and educated at the celebrated Jesuit school of La Flèche. Though he always respected his learned teachers, he felt the traditional knowledge unsatisfactory as did Bacon and others of his generation. Only mathematics pleased him, because it seemed to display the quality of certainty, lacking in other studies. Serving in the Thirty Years' War, he experienced, according to his own later account, a sudden revelation, on the night of November 10, 1619, pointing out his road to the reconstruction of the sciences. Not until the 1630s was he able to complete and publish this work; when he did, it made an immediate sensation. The condemnation of Galileo persuaded him to hold up publication of his World System, but in 1637 his famous *Discourse on Method* (*Discourse on the Method of Rightly Conducting the Reason and Seeking Truth in the Sciences*) was published. There followed such writings as the *Meditations on First Philosophy* (1641), and *Principles of Philosophy* (1644). He died in 1650, only fifty-four, after a visit to Sweden. Subsequently his system of celestial mechanics, fully presented after his death, enjoyed wide popularity for a half century at least, until Isaac Newton dealt it fatal blows. A great mathematician, Descartes is credited with first publishing the important discovery of coordinate or analytical geometry, and also with developing the science of optics (laws of refraction of light). But above all else his methodology and his philosophy attracted attention. Cartesianism was a method, a philosophy, and a physical science. In all three guises it profoundly affected the mind of the seventeenth century and indeed the whole of the modern age.

The Cartesian philosophy became dominant in Europe at mid-century. Descartes seemed the perfect philosopher of the new science, for unlike Galileo he was a systematic philosopher and unlike Bacon he was much more than an amateur as a scientist. In addition, his literary gifts were of a high order, rivalling if not equalling Galileo's and Bacon's. All these writers formed a contrast to the crabbed pedantry of the schoolmen, who disdained the devices of rhetoric. Where Bacon tends to ramble, Descartes possesses that clarity long a special mark of the French intellect; though some say that Descartes himself invented it (and indeed there was nothing very orderly about his immediate predecessors, Rabelais, Bodin, and Montaigne), it may have been a legacy from Parisian scholasticism. Descartes received a thorough education from the Jesuits and certainly had read widely and deeply in the classics. But no less than Bacon he announced a break with the past and a new method.

Eventually Descartes was somewhat discredited as a scientist, his theory of gravitation and cosmic motion through vortices or whirlpools being supplanted by Newton's, though no one could deprive him of a number of scientific glories. Even in his own time, Pascal detected his weakness in experimentation and observation. And as philosopher, too, the Enlightenment of the eighteenth century turned away in the direction indicated by John Locke, not without a tribute to him as the great pioneer. His place in history nevertheless remains secure as one of the three or four most influential thinkers of modern times.

The "dream of Descartes," or rather the three dreams of 1619, was of a "universal science," a science of sciences or basic methodology which could be applied to everything. Making a fresh start, basing itself on self-evident first principles and building on them with inescapable logic, this method would be infallible. This meant that it must be mathematical, for Descartes had long believed that no other kind of knowledge possesses certainty. He had fallen under the spell of geometry. "Those long chains of reasoning, simple and easy as they are, of which geometricians make use in order to arrive at the most difficult demonstrations, had caused me to imagine that all those things which fall under the cognizance of man might very well be mutually related in the same fashion. . . ." Be sure only to *start* soundly, and to reason step by step, with problems broken down into their simplest components, and what may not be possible? The proper *order* of reasoning is everything. This was the same insight Bacon had, in a way, when he said that one must not leap too rapidly but must ascend the ladder of truth step by step. The differences between Bacon and Descartes include the mathematical cast of the latter, and his relative neglect of experimentation, as well as his great systematization; all we really need, Descartes sometimes implies, is a starting place in fact, and geometry will carry us the rest of the way.

He agreed with his English compeer (whom he had read) in beginning with systematic doubt, accepting nothing as true but what can prove itself beyond the possibility of error. He shared with Galileo and Kepler the belief in a world of which mathematics is the language— if with less of their Platonic mysticism, with an even greater determination and dogmatism. Descartes believed that logic, and particularly postulational reasoning of the geometrical type, is an infallible tool when properly employed and can be applied to nature to deduce physical laws from self-evident propositions. He had been struck particularly by his discovery of analytical or coordinate geometry, apparently revealing an exact relationship between algebra and geometry, the spheres of number and of space. The experience was similar to Pythagoras's amazement at how musical notes reveal a mathematical symmetry, which began the Platonic stream of thought. A further important idea of Descartes was analysis, that is, in order to reduce a problem to rationally manageable components we need to break it down—a plan doubtless suggested to him by his specialty, optics. Then, when we have solved the problems separately, we can reassemble the pieces to get the whole answer.

Descartes reduced all substances to *res extensa* and *res cogitans*, physical matter being identified with "extension." The basic nature of a body does not consist in it being hard or heavy or colored, etcetera, he asserted, but in having length, breadth, and depth, that is, "extension." The former are the "secondary qualities" of Galileo, and later of Locke, which are subjective; the "primary qualities" are the measurable ones. He became celebrated for this dualism. Cartesian dualism is between the physical and spiritual worlds; in his terms, extended substance and thinking substance. In order to handle the physical world, Descartes made it mechanical, exactly subject to laws; he purged it of the last remnants of Aristotelian vitalism. Everything that is physical, including the bodies of living things, must be subject to this realm of physical law. Over against this, the knowing mind of man participates in the other realm, that of mind or spirit. To make it "scientific," Descartes had to make the world of nature inanimate; he even held, in a famous and controversial proposition, that animals, having no souls, have no feelings, are merely machines. His dualism created some severe problems. We must evidently assume that the bodies of men have no relationship to their minds except an accidental one. The picture of "the ghost in the machine" has undergone severe modern criticism, though the exact nature of the body-mind relationship remains a mystery. Be that as it may, Descartes made of the material world a perfect machine, rigidly deterministic and thus reducible to exact laws.

There is no reason to believe that Descartes would have approved of the materialism some of his followers drew from him. If extended matter exists in an autonomous realm, so does thinking substance, and the latter was indispensable to Descartes's system. His famous starting place of certainty was our intuitive knowledge of our own thinking self, which we cannot possibly doubt. "Cogito ergo sum"—I think, therefore I am. From this alleged certainty Descartes inferred the existence of God, using arguments reminiscent of the medieval proofs of God's existence as found in Anselm and Aquinas, which Ockham had rejected and Kant would later reject. It was absolutely necessary to establish God's existence as proof of a rational world order. Even if

I exist, and have clear ideas, Descartes pointed out, these might be in error; the method of "hyperbolic doubt" allows us to entertain the suggestion that an evil God might have endowed me with such a nature that I am deceived. It is necessary to show that a perfect, benevolent Deity exists and I cannot do this from external objects (the method of doubt prohibits this; they might be illusions), only from my own existence. Descartes argues that I have clear and distinct ideas of perfection and infinitude, which could not possibly come from my own experience, hence must have come from God, and that I cannot derive my existence from myself, otherwise I would be perfect.

The *cogito ergo sum* followed by the argument from my own existence and thought to that of God, and thence back to the certainty of the objective world of nature, has failed to convince many and seems to involve circularity. We are told that even a clear idea is no proof because an evil demon might have put deception into my head; but a clear idea of perfection is brought forward as proof of God. The only reason for believing that God exists is that I have a clear and distinct idea of him, in effect; but the only reason I have clear and distinct ideas is that God exists. At least one of Descartes's arguments for God's existence is involved here; against all of them, telling arguments may be directed. What seems significant for the historian is the fact that Descartes was so anxious to set his science on a firm foundation. Like Copernicus and Galileo, he pursued certainty, not probability. He felt it absolutely necessary that there be a God, as guarantor of order, a principle which ensures that our science is not just an arbitrary set of symbols we make up, but in truth the language of nature, by means of which we are permitted to glimpse its secrets.

God was necessary, too, as the prime mover in Descartes's system of the universe. But no more than that, for the world-machine runs itself thereafter. Each particle in the circular stream pushes forward the next one, after one initial push from God, because nature abhors a vacuum. An elaborate set of these vortices or whirlpools scattered throughout space thus accounted for all movement, God being necessary only as the prime mover. In his desire to avoid empty spaces and his hostility to cosmic voids and vacuums, Descartes was closer to the old physics than the new. But his apparently ingenious system provided a mechanical explanation for the movements of the heavenly bodies. He was on the wrong track here; the right one was Newton's pursuit of the law of gravitational force. And the English genius was soon to show that even on its own terms Descartes's whirlpools would not account for the observed movements. But the Cartesian system won a large following for a time. "Beautiful romance" though it was, it took some time for Newtonianism to supplant it, even in England, let alone France where it continued to reign long after 1687.

It was not Descartes's only mistake; perhaps the most celebrated, after the denial of sensitivity to animals, was his confident locating of the soul (or, more specifically, the point of contact between mind and body) in the pineal gland. He believed, in fact, that an entire *a priori* medicine was possible, deduced from first principles! Obviously the deductive method could go awry. But it worked brilliantly in Descartes's analytical perfection of the theory of inertia and in his favorite subject of optics. His all-embracing universal scientific method was an illusion, we may be sure; there is no such magic key to unlock all the sciences. But like Bacon he gave a bracing stimulus to all thought. The tonic of his confident rationalism roused Europe and did more than anything else to make the seventeenth century an Age of Reason. The excellently written tracts of this nonacademic philosopher made good propaganda; Descartes wrote for a fairly popular audience, and indeed it has been suggested that his philosophy should be considered chiefly in this light. It may be most significant that the seventeenth and eighteenth centuries from Bacon and Descartes through Locke to Montesquieu, Voltaire, and Rousseau were dominated by thinkers who were not drawn as formerly from the universities.

Descartes made physical nature a machine, and man the reasoning mind capable of grasping its principles. Seventeenth-century "rationalism" found in him its primary prophet. He was sure that all men possess an innate and natural ability to perceive certain things, such as the proposition that "things equal to the same thing are equal to each other." We may recall Socrates and the slave-boy: even the untaught mind can understand a logical proposition. If we find an idea that is both clear and distinct, the chances are it is one of these *a priori* truths—truths not learned from experience. Therefore we can rethink philosophy from the beginning, if only we use the right method; our minds are capable of it. At the end of the century Locke's empiricism attacked the Cartesian "innate ideas"[8] but actually preserved much of his rationalism. Descartes opted for the rational universe, and to a large extent he carried the next two centuries with him. He was the real founder of the Age of Reason.

Other Seventeenth-Century Philosophers

Descartes was easily the strongest single force working on seventeenth-century thought, and he left behind him many ripples and waves

[8]Strictly speaking Descartes did not believe in "innate ideas," a definite content of the mind, but rather in an inherent faculty of thinking, an ability to recognize certain things as true without having been taught this or found it in experience. In this he would seem to have been correct, though he carried too far his belief that anything the mind intuitively sees as a "clear and distinct" idea must be true.

of controversy. There were disciples, foes, revisionists. Placed on the Index of prohibited works by the Church in 1663, his books were notably opposed by the Jesuits; but some of the Orders were more sympathetic, the Oratorians and Jansenists in particular seeing value in a modified Cartesianism. These were the repositories of an Augustinian-Platonic tradition, opposed to Aristotelianism, its dualism of ideas and matter resembling Descartes. The Oratorian father, N. Malebranche, was an especially famous proponent of a revised Cartesianism. In fact, Malebranche's philosophy may be regarded as an original synthesis of Cartesian and Augustinian elements, a new scholasticism harmonizing Christianity with Cartesianism as once Aristotle had been harmonized.

Father Malebranche wished to make the new scientific philosophy safe for traditional Christianity; he was not alone in this desire. In England, the group known as the Cambridge Platonists, including Henry More, Ralph Cudworth, and Benjamin Whichcote, sought to mediate between science and religion. Nature to them was thoroughly spiritual, the human mind furnished by Deity with a sacred lamp of reason, and so in exploring nature one performed an act of piety. John Ray's *The Wisdom of God in the Works of Creation* suggested their outlook. The Cambridge group helped create a climate of opinion in England in which religion and science were close companions. They were also known abroad, Leibniz being one example of an important Continental thinker who respected them. Robert Boyle, the great English scientist, endowed a well-known series of lectures against atheism, delivering the first one himself; into this pattern of scientific theism Isaac Newton, too, was to be drawn. One could well speak of a "union of the altar and the laboratory" at this time in England.

Yet it was in England that the most radically unorthodox offshoot of the scientific philosophy appeared, in the person of the doughty Thomas Hobbes. His chief rival for that title was the equally unorthodox Baruch (Benedict) Spinoza, the Jewish lens-grinder of Amsterdam, Holland. Hobbes proclaimed himself a materialist, doing away with the awkward Cartesian dualism by simply reducing mind to a "motion in the head." Deeply influenced by Descartes so far as concerned the geometrical mode of reasoning, Hobbes owed a great deal to his friend Pierre Gassendi, a French priest, who had revived ancient Epicurean atomism. Descartes was not an atomist, and he denied the vacuum; in his world there was no "void" or empty space, but rather each corpuscle impinged on the next. Gassendi's view that all that exists are "atoms and the void," with the atoms combining in different ways to make the objects we know, sounds more modern than the Cartesian plenum filled with linked corpuscles.

Hobbes, whom we shall meet again later in connection with his great treatise on politics, *The Leviathan* (1651), was a natural and aggressive radical. He was considered to be an atheist, and perhaps was, though he denied it and once spoke of God as being a "corporeal spirit" (on Hobbes's view, Deity would have to exist materially if at all; this had been the Epicurean position in ancient times). He denied free will, thus pushing to the forefront the deterministic element in the new scientific philosophy. As a scientist, Hobbes left no mark, receiving a severe drubbing in a debate with Cambridge professor John Wallis when he laid claim to mathematical prowess. It is as political theorist that he is principally known; but his atheistic materialism constituted a scandal to the orthodox, indeed to almost everyone in his day.

So left-wing Cartesianism could lead in highly subversive directions. Malebranche, laboring to make Cartesianism respectable, found himself under suspicion because of Spinoza, who discredited Cartesianism by making it appear atheistic. For the great Jewish philosopher, who died young in 1677, was so unorthodox that his synagogue in Amsterdam excommunicated him. (Hence his abandonment of his Jewish name, Baruch.) He was Cartesian in his firm belief that clear and distinct ideas cannot err, because the universe is rational and man is a part of it, likewise in his concern with efficient rather than final causes, and his quest for a single scientific method. But like Hobbes he departed from the Cartesian dualism to adopt a monism: all is of the same substance. He perceived the circularity of Descartes's argument and pointed out that the Frenchman had really started with God, not his own existence. That is where Spinoza started—and finished. The single substance that exists in all things he called God and identified it with nature. With a startling simplicity he inquired whether, if God is infinite, he can be transcendent, that is, separate and apart from the world.

This "pantheism" resembled ancient Stoicism; pantheistic creeds had reappeared in the Italian Renaissance, the martyred Bruno having had this charge laid against him. Now it returned in the wake of Descartes. Spinoza married it to the new scientific mechanism. Other minds and bodies, Spinoza held, are simply modes of the single divine substance. This pantheistic view led him necessarily to affirm a deterministic universe: free will is an illusion of our limited perspective. The toe, we might say, could imagine it has free will when it wiggles, but we know that the brain and in a sense the whole organism willed it. So it is with any of our actions, which really come from God's thoughts and are part of the great organism which is all that is. If everything is one, the modes or parts cannot have any freedom of their own. Determinism was Spinoza's central insight. This coincided with the new science, for it left no place for "final causes." Since all is as it must be, there is no point in asking for any further explanation of it except to describe its operations exactly as they are.

But Spinoza was more interested in ethics than in physics. The implications of his ethical system were much debated. When we understand the necessity of all, we accept all that is as inevitable and just, however apparently evil. Not a little of Spinoza's repute in the eighteenth century rested on his having supplied at least a consistent answer to the problem that almost obsessed the Enlightenment, the problem of evil. What we call evil is only something the ultimate purpose of which in the cosmic scheme of things we cannot see. The toenail, if it could think, would doubtless feel it an injustice that it must be cut off. Similarly it is only our human bias that makes us think anything is evil. In this calm philosophical detachment which Spinoza set forth as the ethical ideal, he resembled the Stoics, and beyond any doubt Spinoza received strong direct influences from that quarter.

He added an analysis of our misguided judgments about good and bad, tracing them to our passions. We call things good because we desire them, not vice versa. Our passions, tied to our senses, deceive us. But reason can disclose the true philosophy and prevail over the passions. (It is not clear why, in Spinoza's necessary world, the emotions are an exception.) Spinoza was in mood and manner very much the detached rationalist; it is necessary to point this out because romantic pantheists later tended to read into him a mystic nature worship which in fact he scarcely knew. He is still frequently presented in the guise of the "God-intoxicated man," but intoxication of any sort was alien to Spinoza. "Not to laugh or to cry but to understand" was his classic plea. Quietly dogmatic—"I do not presume to have found the best philosophy, I know that I understand the true philosophy"— Spinoza's modest, retiring ways concealed a placid certainty.

He was not perhaps the greatest of philosophers, but he added much zest to the already heady seventeenth-century philosophical brew. This was the classic rationalism; no other philosopher except the Stoics earlier and perhaps Hegel later have ever been so sure that all that is real is rational. The wholly unorthodox monism of Spinoza made him a byword for heresy among Christians and Jews alike. In this he surpassed Descartes: pantheism was felt to be a greater foe than Cartesian dualism, which could be reconciled with Christianity.

The materialism of Hobbes, the monism of Spinoza, and the atomism of Gassendi gave the speculatively inclined person of the years from about 1650 to 1700 abundant opportunity to depart widely from conventional paths of thought and chase after strange gods, or no gods at all. This despite the tendencies toward accommodation represented by Malebranche and the Cambridge Platonists. In some ways the most striking symbol of this era was the divided allegiance of Blaise Pascal. Born in 1623, Pascal was the mathematical and scientific prodigy who published an important contribution to geometry at the age of sixteen, invented an adding machine two years later, and went on to pioneer in calculus, which Leibniz and Newton would develop, as well as to make basic discoveries in probabilities. Excited by Torricelli's experiments with the vacuum tube and barometric pressure, he performed the experiments previously mentioned and formulated the law of hydraulic pressures which bears his name. He met and argued with the older Descartes on one occasion, though a mere stripling, and all in all he seemed destined for the most brilliant scientific career of all. But he lived only thirty-nine years, and after 1654, the date of one of the most famous religious conversions in history, he devoted a major portion of his talents to moral and theological questions. It is wrong, however, to say that he dropped science for religion, for he shared the view of the Cambridge Platonists that true science is the service of God.

Pascal did get drawn into the Jansenist controversy, destined to a long and stormy life in France, and wrote, in defense of the Jansenists against their antagonists the Jesuits, a great work of literature, the *Provincial Letters*. Jansenism was an Augustinian theology stressing, somewhat in the manner of Luther, the helplessness of natural man to attain salvation, and the all-sufficiency of Divine Grace. Pascal was not entirely a Jensenist, perhaps, but members of his family were, and he defended the Jansenists against efforts to secure their condemnation.

Unlike Descartes, Pascal recognized the limitations of the mathematical method. It is infallible within its own domain, but it cannot be applied to the natural sciences in the same way; there, experimentation is necessary, and probability, not certainty, is all that can be expected. In metaphysics, as well as in religion, we are in a different realm, that of faith, of the heart—which, in Pascal's immortal phrase, has its reasons that reason knows not of. "The God of the Christians is not simply the author of geometrical truth," cried Pascal from the bottom of his heart. "I cannot forgive Descartes" for making God only the great watchmaker or prime mover, he declared.

In fact, Pascal believed in *three* separate orders or realms of human activity. To the scientific and religious, the domains respectively of the brain and the heart (reason and will), he added the political, evidently the region of the muscles (force prevails there). Each of these realms is autonomous and ought not to be confused with the others. Pascal would not approve of scientists trying to be politicians, any more than *vice versa*, nor should the church meddle in either politics or science. This idea runs counter to much of Western thought and practice in modern times, especially in the Anglo-Saxon world. Hobbes was even then trying to reduce politics as well as religion to science, and the Enlightenment pursued this quest. Puritans moralized politics, a trend that carried on into modern political and social reform. But Pascal thought that the mathematician, for example, is as absurd when he tries to geometrize either God or the state as a politician would be who thought he could solve a scientific problem by waging war. Each of these areas has its own skills, its own modes, its own genius. Pascal would have us keep them in separate compartments.

In seeking to withdraw religion and indeed much of philosophy from the embrace of scientific reason, Pascal was running contrary to his age, and the whole century to come; even the Cambridge Platonists moved close to a deism in which one proves God by the works of nature. In the eighteenth century, Voltaire, who recognized his greatness, could not understand how Pascal could be so deeply a Christian. Pascal was a lonely titan who belonged to no school. In our time he has occasionally been seen as a forerunner of Christian existentialism. He felt deeply disturbed by the prevalence of a scientism that would destroy spiritual values if unchecked. Today, we can understand this better than some of his contemporaries. What is this mighty new force, to which I myself have contributed? we hear Pascal asking. What will it do to man? Three centuries later, along the road of a scientific civilization, we are still asking the same question. Pascal was the first who faced it squarely.

For all his forebodings, this was the Age of Descartes, the Age of Reason, the Age of Science. To silence what remaining doubts there were, in 1687 came a still greater man, Isaac Newton, from a Lincolnshire farm, to give the European world the final scientific synthesis for which it yearned.

The Newtonian Revolution

The intellectual revolution begun by Galileo, Bacon, and Descartes was enthusiastically carried on by a number of others in the latter half of the century. The interest in matters scientific and mathematical became a passion few could resist; excitement mounted with each discovery, from one end of Europe to the other. Physics and mathematics led the way, but with Harvey's discovery of the way in which the blood circulates, and Malpighi's subsequent additions, with Leeuwenhoek's penetration of the microscopic subworld of "little animals," and John Ray's great work in botany, the biological sciences, too, came into the picture. Whatever theological prejudice there had been against the new science mostly dissolved under the pressure of this success, and with such deeply religious men as Pascal and Boyle being numbered among the greatest scientists, there was a strong tendency toward accommodation. On the other hand, Cartesianism stirred up a debate in which some left-wing Cartesians moved toward materialism and atheism. And until Newton cleared the air in 1687, there was much uncertainty about the outcome of the scientific movement. With all the excitement, there was no agreed synthesis until Newton made it: general theories of motion and gravity were lacking, and the new world view was just being digested. A writer in 1672 observed that there was a choice of four different theories of the cosmos; others said seven. There was, for example, Brahe's theory that the planets revolve around the sun, but the sun around the earth. On the basis of observation, it was all but impossible to choose between them; different models satisfied the data equally well. Only the solution of the problems of motion and gravitation could settle the question.

It should be reiterated that, to many, Descartes was the "emancipator of philosophy from theology," breaker of the alliance between science, metaphysics, and theology so long upheld by the Peripatetics (that is, Aristotelians), the author of a mechanistic physics in which God was needed only for giving the first push in some remote past eon —dangerously untheistic notions even if Descartes leaned heavily on God as the warrantor of an orderly universe. Many great minds, such as Pascal and Leibniz, found this disturbing. The famous example of Pascal's retreat (if we may call it that) to mystical religion, in terror of the godless world machine, springs to mind. Though Cambridge Platonists and Malebrancheans sought an accommodation, many men remained uncertain about it all. There was need for a convincing demonstration that the new science would not undercut the foundations of moral and social order.

Despite the arrival of the pioneers of modern scientific rationalism, the great bulk of people, even educated people, were far from having been converted to or submerged in the universe of orderly scientific law it assumed. Belief in witchcraft and sorcery continued to flourish. The last of the judicial sentences against sorcerers or witches occurred in most European countries early in the eighteenth century; they persisted through the seventeenth though with some diminution. The celebrated outburst of witchcraft hysteria in Massachusetts at the end of the century cannot be written off as the eccentricity of a benighted part of Western civilization, for the Puritans were far from that, and educated circles in England and the Continent believed the same. Perhaps the greatest English writer of his day, Sir Thomas Browne, was an enthusiastic believer. Among other manifestations of a highly irrationalist spirit in the seventeenth century, mention might be made of

the secret societies dedicated to arcane knowledge, of which Rosicru-
cians were the best known. The "climate of opinion" was on the whole
not yet that of the Age of Reason and did not become so until after
Newton had given his convincing demonstration of the rule of law
in the cosmos.

With the great synthesis and summation made of the laws of
motion and of gravity by Isaac Newton in 1687, all obscurities seemed
cleared up; the pieces fell into place, nature revealed its secret of
secrets, and Europe prepared to enter into its optimistic Enlightenment.
Moreover, Newton lent his support to theism, and between religion
and science all was right again for a long season, as Hobbes and Spinoza became mere eccentric curiosities. "The most stupendous single
achievement of the human mind"—with such praise the Cambridge
giant has been freely showered, from his own time, when he was almost
immediately hailed as a demigod, to ours. On the Continent, some
Cartesians objected to his system, but with diminishing success; on the
other wing, a few grumbled at pantheistic tendencies. But not until
Bishop Berkeley was even one major voice raised against Newton's
world-machine as Pascal's had been against Descartes's. "God said,
Let Newton be, and all was light." Laplace paid tribute to the *Principia
Mathematica* as "preeminent among all products of human genius."
The contours of the cosmos as summed up in Newton's formula for
gravitational attraction formed the foundation for all physics until our
own age of Einsteinian revolution.

Newton was mathematician, physicist, and, perhaps less successfully, theologian and philosopher—also alchemist, as a hobby. Formu-
lator of the law of universal gravitation, and of the decomposition of
light, also with Leibniz of the differential calculus which enabled him
to make those calculations successfully, there is no doubt about his
genius. But he came along a broad highway prepared for him by others,
as he himself well knew and said; his was a task of synthesis, putting
together an immense amount of material coming in from various directions and all manner of scientists and mathematicians for a century.
The herculean pioneer labors of Kepler and Galileo, the mathematical
contributions of Descartes and Pascal, the various insights of Gilbert,
Torricelli, Boyle are only the most obvious; there were many more that
a brief general history cannot even mention.[9] It may simply be worth

[9]Among these others, one could note the Danish Roemer's work on the
velocity of light and stellar observations; the Frenchman Picard's geodesy, and the
Dutchman Huygens's numerous attacks on the same problems with which Newton
was concerned. The Italian Borelli and Newton's own fellow countryman and constant rival, Robert Hooke, came close to anticipating his law of gravitation. Hooke
always believed he had done so.

noting that Newton did not *invent* the theory of universal gravitation but merely gave it rigorous formulation and exact proof, and that the fact that he and Leibniz arrived simultaneously and independently at the calculus, subsequently engaging in a rather unseemly quarrel over the honor, indicates how much it was a cumulative product, in the air, its constituent elements having been introduced by the evolution of mathematics over a long stretch. Pascal had found some of it, for example. This is not to deprive Newton of any credit, but to put his achievements in perspective in view of the adulation with which he has been covered. It is a truism of oversimplified history that the man who turns out the last piece on an invention gets the credit; but invention is always a social product.

The fabulous ability of Isaac Newton is nevertheless not in doubt. Newton was a strange and moody genius, and the book destined to become perhaps the most important one in European history almost failed to be printed at all. A poor farm boy, Newton got to Cambridge University and became Professor of Mathematics there in due time, his mathematical talents being obvious. He returned from Cambridge to his native Lincolnshire in the plague year of 1665–1666, and apparently at that time, a young man of twenty-three, did the intensive thinking which laid the foundations for his later great discoveries in motion and gravitation. The old legend of the falling apple was based on the bucolic atmosphere in which the youthful Newton contemplated. The problems he was considering were hardly simple ones. It occurred to Newton that the force that drew a falling body to the earth might be the same force that kept the moon in its orbit, and, arriving at his inverse square law, he found, as he said, that the two forces were "pretty nearly" equal. Every particle attracts every other with a force obtained by multiplying the masses together and dividing by the square of the distance between them.

At Woolsthorpe, too, Newton began to work on the differential and integral calculus. This is the branch of mathematics that deals with varying quantities and with things in motion, as for example calculating the rate of change in a curving line. But upon his return to Cambridge, Newton busied himself with other fascinating scientific and mathematical games, ecpecially optics, that is, breaking up white color through a prism into the different colors of the spectrum. His optical experiments and analysis are a classic of scientific method. In 1672 Newton published them. For this he was admitted to the Royal Society. His theory of light, which he considered to be primarily corpuscular, that is, made of tiny particles, got him into some controversies, which he hated. (In the nineteenth century scientists discarded corpuscular theories of light in favor of the wave theory, which fitted the experimental data; but with the Einstein revolution in recent times they have recognized that light at least part of the time may be viewed as something like Newton's corpuscles—Einstein's photons, or light bullets.) His epochal work on gravitation was evidently published owing to a chance conversation at the Royal Society with Edmund Halley, known for his discovery of the comet that bears his name. Halley urged Newton to work out the details and to get them into print and undertook to bear the expense of publication. Thus stimulated, the secretive Newton went to work on the great book that he titled *Philosophiae Naturalis Principia Mathematica* (The Mathematical Principles of Natural Philosophy).

The *Principia*, published in 1687, accomplished not one but a number of things with surpassing genius. It demonstrated the exact law of gravitation, as is well known; it showed that this law applies to all bodies alike, whether earthly or cosmic, something not heretofore accepted. (Thus, Galileo had assumed that gravity on the earth is a different force from that which controls the movements of the heavenly bodies.) Newton had been able to unite Galileo's laws of the motion of falling bodies with Kepler's laws of planetary motion. Given the velocity of the planets, the laws of gravitation sufficed to account for their behavior. It is important to note that in solving the problem of universal dynamics Newton decisively resolved the debate about the relative motion of sun and earth. "He showed that it was dynamically impossible for the enormous sun to turn around the diminutive earth, but that a central body and its satellite must revolve around their common center of gravity, which in the solar system was inside the surface of the sun" (A. C. Crombie).

By precise and careful calculations, too, Newton disposed of Descartes's vortices, heretofore often accepted as the explanation for the motion of the heavenly bodies. Turning from the mechanics of the cosmos to its structure, he gave the masses of the suns and planets. His deduction that the earth was slightly flattened at the poles sent skeptical geometers of the next century as far as Peru and Lapland to confirm him. Another remarkable calculation was that of the precession of the equinoxes, the result of a slow change in the angle of the earth's axis back and forth, comparable to a slight wobble. Newton showed exactly how the slight bulge in the earth due to the flattening at the poles would have the observed effect on its axis. Nor was this quite all, for the *Principia* solved the problem of tides and comets, explaining these phenomena which had heretofore eluded satisfactory explanation. The tides are caused by the moon's gravitational attraction.

In brief, all the pieces in the puzzle suddenly fell into place. Newton had found the key. It was rather like a cipher or code which once cracked yields the whole meaning at once. It is important, then, to realize the significance of Newton's *method*. Like Pascal, he understood the importance of experimental verification and thus while using mathematics as a tool of research corrected Descartes's exaggerated belief in the deductive method. He accepted, of course, the basic postulate of Galileo and Descartes that science deals with the "primary" qualities, the measurable ones of motion and extension, and he expressed his famous equation for the force of gravity in mathematical terms, without which he could not have arrived at it. But Newton insisted that mere "hypothesis," by which he meant a theory uncorroborated by experiment, has no place in science. However logically attractive, theories are not to be accepted unless proved in experiment; their clarity or beauty is no proof of their validity. The "beautiful theory slain by an ugly fact" was a possibility well understood by Newton, less so by Descartes. "Dreams and vain fictions of our own devising" must be shunned. His was a sophisticated method which employed provisional hypothesis and made use of mathematics but was basically empirical. Newton's "rules of reasoning" included the principle of economy of explanation: do not use more of an explanation than is necessary to account for the phenomena. In Newton's words, "We are to admit no more causes of natural things than are both true and sufficient to explain their appearance."

In addition to his scientific triumph[10] and his fruitful methodology, Newton becomes important to the historian of ideas because of his sanctioning of a theism which made a place for God, presenting Him, as it were, as an active upholder of the plan on which the universe works. It must be stressed (because it is sometimes disregarded) that Newtonianism was an improvement over Cartesianism from the theistic point of view. Descartes had allowed to God a passive role as a kind of guarantee of the olderliness and rationality of the universe and had permitted him to start the machine, but thereafter it was considered to be perfectly self-running. Newton's world-machine, if it can be called that, required God to tend it. "He endures forever, and is everywhere present; and by existing always and everywhere, he constitutes duration and space," Newton declared. In his 1692 letter to Richard Bentley, who had solicited Newton's views on this subject, Newton wrote that "I do not think explicable by merely natural causes" the

---

[10]For some limitations of Newtonian physics (the assumption of absolute space and an absolute observer), see pages 386 ff. Newton was not entirely unaware of possible difficulties in this regard. They had not in his time or for two centuries afterward reached the stage of practical problems, and Newton was true to his own principle of not allowing theory to outrun observational data.

state of the heavenly bodies, "but am forced to ascribe it to the counsel and contrivance of a voluntary agent." "Such a Wonderful Uniformity in the Planetary system must be allowed [considered] the effect of choice." He explicitly rejected Cartesianism, that is, "deriving the frame of the world by mechanical principles from matter evenly spread through the heavens." The very principle of economy Newton espoused helped his theism; for in regard to gravity, he pointed out that "I do not pretend to know" its cause; he had only described how it worked. The Cartesians attacked him for this very reason, urging that Newton had not really given an explanation of gravity, such as Descartes had provided with his vortices, which was true. Newton rested content with having produced a perfectly accurate descriptive formula, all that is needed for practical purposes. To seek farther would be to ask unanswerable questions as the ancients had done. Gravity remained a mysterious force, an action-at-a-distance which could not be explained, but merely described. Newton left the impression that this mystery, among others, could be accounted for only by recourse to "the Author of the system." Accused by some of a materialism which would attribute inherent powers of motion and attraction to matter, Newtonians denied they held any such doctrine.

With Newton's law of universal gravitation and laws of motion the century of scientific genius which began with Copernicus reached, not its end, but its triumphant vindication and the end of the search for basic foundations. For another century little more would be done in the area of physics and cosmology than writing the footnotes to Newton. But men were mightily encouraged to think that the application of similar methods would lead to similar triumphs in all other areas. Descartes's dream of a universal scientific method died hard, and one could hardly resist believing that Newton's method had much wider applications though he did not specifically endorse such a belief. A modest man, Newton was aware of how little men can know, but his conquest of nature induced an almost overweening pride and confidence. All nature's secrets would soon be unlocked with the same key, men felt. Thus Newtonianism led on into the Enlightenment.

So far as concerns the seventeenth-century path, many a thoughtful historian has concluded that we do wrong to think of it as a sort of triumph of common sense over superstition. The grossest of fallacies is that which thinks something must have been easy to learn because we know it now. It took genius to reveal things we now take for granted, and the path of genius was more often than not *not* the path of common sense. Galileo was struck with wonder that Copernicus "allowed reason to commit such a rape on his senses" as to visualize a heliocentric universe: a view which, to repeat, *did* then constitute an almost unimaginable fantasy. A great scientist of our own age, Sigmund Freud, once wrote that it is an attribute of the scientific genius to assume that nothing is as it seems. From Copernicus to Newton, seventeenth-century scientific genius was marked more by visionary dreams, imagination, daring theory than by "common sense." It all ended in a simple formula and an apparently simple recipe for success, but we should not be deluded. Just as the seemingly effortless swing of a master golfer represents years of practice along with singular athletic ability, so the apparently simple Newtonian formula had behind it more than a century of genius.

So began the age of Newton. It took a few years for the word to spread. Several years after the appearance of Newton's book, the Cartesian system was still being taught at Newton's own university! Newton was not readily accepted in Europe, the Cartesian tradition being well entrenched and the imposing weight of both the Dutch scientist Huygens and the German genius Leibniz thrown against him. In 1690 Huygens, who had himself anticipated much of Newton's law of gravitation earlier, offered a revised version of Descartes's vortex theory, designed to meet Newton's criticisms. He did not doubt the validity of Newton's inverse square law, but he did not see that Newton had at all explained what gravity is (which was true). Fontenelle, the celebrated French popularizer of science and secretary of the French Academy of Sciences, an amiable courtier and graceful writer who anticipated the eighteenth-century *philosophes*, never was converted from the Cartesianism of his youth and in 1752, at the age of ninety-five, was still defending the *tourbillons* of Descartes.[11] It remained for Voltaire to undertake the conversion of France to Newtonianism as late as the 1730s, and even then Voltaire complained that to be a patriotic Frenchman one seemingly had to believe in the vortices. The Dutch mathematician s'Gravesande also played a key role in introducing Newtonianism to the French.

In addition to the Cartesians, who generally complained that Newton had not really explained anything, powerful if unavailing foes of Newtonianism appeared in Leibniz and in Bishop Berkeley (see pages 157–60). In particular Leibniz objected to the absolute space and time postulated by Newton's system. Space and time, he pointed out, do not really exist as entities but are relational terms; they are like "on" or "between," expressing only some relations between things. We deceive

---

[11]An American, Cadwallader Colden, produced a theory of cosmic motion in 1751 which tried to supplement and revise Newton with another kinetic image. The Cartesian quest died hard. Colden's ingenious system was soon shown to be nonsense.

ourselves if we endow them with objective existence. Newton conceived of space as a sort of empty box into which particles of matter are put, to act on each other according to certain mechanical laws. The German sage also ridiculed Newton's view of God, as a sort of bungling workman who is kept around to repair his own errors! His acute brain anticipated some very modern, Einsteinian conclusions, but they were premature in the early eighteenth century. Newton's long reign over the mind of Western man was just beginning.

3

The Seventeenth-Century Revolution in Political Thought

In the first place, I put for a generall inclination of all mankind, a perpetuall and restless desire of Power, after Power, that ceaseth only in Death.

THOMAS HOBBES

A people may let a king fall, yet still remain a people; but if a king let his people slip from him, he is no longer king.

THE MARQUIS OF HALIFAX

Throughout the seventeenth century, Europe, including England, had been involved in a political revolution not less significant than the intellectual and scientific one. The manifestations of this revolution were sometimes violent. In the 1640s the great Puritan revolution and civil war convulsed England, with the upshot being the virtual military dictatorship of Oliver Cromwell, followed by a reversion to the Stuart monarchy. On the Continent, the terrible Thirty Years' War (1618–1648) shattered Germany and brought down Spain and Italy, elevating France to the top of the European power structure. Climaxing the long French journey to unification, Cardinal Richelieu ruthlessly crushed opposition to the monarchy and established a uniquely powerful central state (1624–1640) which reached its apogee during the earlier part of the long reign of Louis XIV (1661–1715). Throughout these turmoils several things were evident: the rise of the sovereign state out of feudal pluralism; the search for a pattern of religious accommodation to end the strife of rival sects and churches; the rise of individualism to replace the group and corporate personalities of the Middle Ages; and the problem of individual liberty versus the sovereign authority of the new state.

New political ideas were produced in profusion, ideas relating to sovereignty, religious toleration, liberty, and authority. Men searched for the formula that would alchemize the perfect state. The scientific revolution spilled over into the political one: Descartes's universal scientific method, it was felt, might unlock the doors to political and social science, too; "reason" should now prevail in human affairs as well as in physical nature. (Christopher Hill finds significance in a conception of the king as the sun, or as the heart, metaphors derived from scientific discoveries. The English Puritans and Whigs talk about equilibria and balances of forces. Clearly the realm of science at least supplied an abundance of metaphors for the political debate.)

John Locke's distillation of the final English political verdict after a century of experimentation, published in 1690 just after the Glorious Revolution of 1688, was in some respects the political equivalent of his friend Newton's synthesis in physics. The eighteenth-century Enlightenment was the age of Newton and of Locke. To understand this Lockean political revolution, it is necessary to return and trace the adventures of political thought in the seventeenth century—here, too, veritably a "century of genius."

The Medieval Heritage

Once again, it was Aristotle who was the main source for traditional European political thought prior to the seventeenth century. His *Politics* was no insignificant part of the vast Aristotelian corpus of thought. A leading feature was the view that the state is something *natural* to man; it rises in response to human need; man is a "political animal." The *polis*, or Greek city-state, grew in an evolutionary manner out of the family and then the village. To regard the state as conventional or artificial, something men originally did without, was a seventeenth-century innovation. Combined with the teleological bent always present in Aristotle, this stress on the state's omnipresent and essential activity brought about what modern liberalism rejected as too statist or communitarian. The purpose of the state is to promote the good life, the common welfare. It must strive to do this in active ways, and this mission takes precedence over individual rights, on which Greek political thought placed little stress. Only through the state, the ordered community, is the good life attained; the state has the right or duty to suppress deviant opinions as well as individual selfishness if this conflicts with the common purpose. It may be remembered that the *polis* was a very small society by modern standards—Aristotle did not think any ordered state could be larger than this—and that in the small, closely-knit community, group feeling naturally predominates and individualism hardly arises.

Plato held even more extreme views in this respect, as is well known, subordinating the individual completely to a planned, ordered community with a hierarchial structure (*The Republic*). But it would be wrong to equate this with a ruthless totalitarianism. Greek political thought was suffused with the sense of *law*. The standards of political society are to be found in a structure of reason existing independently of man. Obedience is owed to properly constituted authority, when this agrees with reason, but tyranny, departing from the rule of law, is abhorrent and should be resisted. Aristotle left a formalistic classification of government, divided into the good and the bad forms.

	Good	*Bad*
Rule of One	monarchy (1)	tyranny (6)
Rule of Few	aristocracy (2)	oligarchy (5)
Rule of Many	polity (3)	democracy (4)

The numerals indicate the ranking, from best to worst. Monarchy, thus, is the best form of government, but tyranny is the worst. "Goodness" is conformity to reason and law and is more important than the specific kind of government. The rule of the many *could* be infinitely better than the rule of one, it may be noted, though Aristotelianism has seldom been considered friendly to democracy.

Medieval political thought, of course, owed its greatest debt to Aristotle with an admixture of Christian themes. St. Thomas Aquinas agreed that the state is a natural institution, for men must live together, life on earth is a positive good though not the highest one, and living together requires government. In contrast to some earlier medieval assertions that the "city of man" is unimportant in view of the corruption of this life, Aquinas, the great medieval synthesizer of knowledge, went far toward reviving an autonomous political theory, which is still a source of inspiration to some modern political writers of importance. With his natural moderation, Aquinas sought middle ground and stressed the rule of law. Man is not perfect and cannot be here below, hence he must be constrained by authority; yet neither is he naturally totally depraved, but has in him a saving remnant of reason enabling him to contrive a political order with some liberty. In political theory as in other matters Aquinas followed Aristotle rather closely. There must be authority, but tyranny should be held in check by popular will; government must seek the general good, and if it does not it ceases to be legitimate, with resistance to it permissible or even obligatory under certain conditions. It is a myth that the right of revolution had to await the Puritans or John Locke. One of the chief themes of medieval history was the rivalry of Church and emperor (or king), and in this strife each took much occasion to find reasons why people might overthrow the rule of the other. Manegold of Lautenbach, a medieval writer, comparing the king to a swineherd, said that he might be dismissed if he failed to do his job properly, and John of Salisbury, an important medieval political commentator, went farther than Aquinas when he conceded a possible right of tyrannicide.[1]

The stress of much medieval political thought was on a limited constitutional monarchy; modern constitutionalism, as in the British parliamentary system, is an outgrowth of medievalism. The study of law filled a large place in the medieval universities and medieval life. But several medieval notions were to be rejected, or at least challenged, in the seventeenth century. First is the unquestioning acceptance of a realm of eternal value which is the source of law. Law was not made in the Middle Ages, it was *found*. All human law was believed to take its origin and validity from a higher law. In Aquinas's theory there were three laws above positive human law, culminating in the eternal law and including the *natural law*, which is to guide human law and overrule it in case of conflict. None of this was made institutionally very concrete and specific in the Middle Ages, but the idea was deeply rooted, resting on Christian belief as well as on Greek and Roman (Stoic) philosophy. While the idea of a higher law continued to exert influence in the seventeenth century, it was challenged by Hobbes and Spinoza and underwent some change even in John Locke, who is usually regarded as a "natural law" philosopher. But its deep implantation is one of the most significant features of the Western heritage. It was Cicero who perhaps gave it classical expression, in long-remembered and much-quoted phrases: there is not "one rule at Rome and another at Athens . . . one rule today and another tomorrow," but rather "one law, eternal and unchangeable, binding at all times and upon all peoples," because this law has "one common master and ruler of men, namely God, who is the author of this law." It was a "pagan" Roman who had said this, before Christianity arrived, and the concept of natural law owed most to the ancient world's experience of universal empire and common citizenship in a world state. It is a familiar historical fact that this ideal of a world state, a single

[1] Within the Church itself rebellion against the supreme powers of the pope culminated in the decree of the Council of Constance, 1415—"the most revolutionary document in the history of the world," J. N. Figgis once enthusiastically called it. It would appear that this Conciliarist placing of power in the legislature of the Church rather than the executive was both strongly medieval and productive of influence on the later German Lutheran, French Huguenot, and English Puritan revolutions.

"Christian Republic," remained alive in the Middle Ages, revived temporarily by a Charlemagne or Otto the Great, even when fragmentation
rather than unity was the actual political situation.

These ancient concepts lingered on in the modern world, despite
basic alterations in some of them during the seventeenth and eighteenth
centuries. Natural law was slow to die and indeed has never quite died;
it was certainly still vigorously alive at the time of the French Revolution and American Revolution, when Thomas Jefferson will cite Aristotle
and Cicero as the foundations of sound political philosophy. The Aristotelian view of the forms of government and the dangers of tyranny,
too, remained a truism at least well into the eighteenth century. Jonathan Swift, for example, remarks, as an axiom, that "In all free states
the evil to be avoided is *Tyranny*, that is to say, the *Summa Imperii*, or
unlimited power solely in the hands of the *One*, or the *Few*, or the *Many*."
Montesquieu's famous *Spirit of the Laws* teaches a similar doctrine (see
below, pages 135–37).

Medieval political thought likewise agreed with Aristotle that the
state exists to further the good life in positive ways. Thus stated the
idea sounds innocuous; but it meant that the state should have the sort
of moral and ideological functions liberalism came to regard as repugnant in modern Europe. If asked, a present-day Englishman or American
would probably say that the state should not attempt to direct people's
religious life, or supervise their beliefs, or even concern itself with their
morals beyond what is necessary to keep the public peace. At least this
is what a nineteenth-century liberal would have said. It may almost be
said that individual "right" against society and the state did not exist in
ancient and medieval thought. Aristotle and Aquinas allow a limited
right of private property but insist that it is always subject to sacrifice
to the needs of the community. There is very little stress on individual
rights. As is well known, medieval feudalism saw property as communal
rather than personal.

The organic as opposed to the conventional view of the state, the
communal as against the individual, implied also an inequalitarianism
repugnant to modern liberalism. Like the universe, society was considered hierarchical. A body has different parts with different functions: it
would seem strange if the foot asserted a right to be just like the head.
Thomists define equality as treating persons according to their (different)
natures, not treating them all alike. The latter proposition is modern and
appears first in the seventeenth century.

Thus, in brief, medieval political thought resembles modern in some
ways but in some ways it does not and may puzzle us. Popular sovereignty, the supremacy of law, and the right to depose a tyrant may perhaps please us, while a hierarchy of classes, absence of individual rights,
and inquisitorial governments probably do not. It can only be said that

in politics as in philosophy and science the medieval heritage suffered a sea change in the seventeenth century, which while making use of some of its ideas greatly transformed the whole structure and abandoned much of it. Here also the new thinkers were more systematic. Medieval political ideas were rather chaotic. Society was then fragmentized, customs varied; thought seldom matched practice.

One thing lacking was the conception of sovereignty in the state. On the whole, medieval man felt so strongly that there was a structure of objective law governing even governments, and that there was a hierarchy of duties and responsibilities diffused through society, that he could hardly entertain the notion of a power centered in one place and issuing commands to everybody. If society is conceived of as an organism, there is no place for a sovereign power in the modern sense. During the Middle Ages there was no such thing as a sovereign state, but rather a division of powers, especially between the temporal and the spiritual "swords," the ecclesiastical and secular rulers. It is significant, however, that the important late-medieval theorist Marsiglio of Padua (*Defensor Pacis*, 1324) tried to resolve this division in favor of the temporal state, eliminating the Church entirely from the governance of this world.

The Italian city-states of the fifteenth century first broke through medieval pluralism to develop something like a unitary, sovereign state, though on a smaller scale than the nation-states of the north were to achieve. Machiavelli's brilliant beginnings in political science formed the backdrop for later thought. The great Venetian oligarchic republic was a model for some, a horrible example to others, but on any reckoning a technically more advanced state than anything north of the Alps until the seventeenth century.[2] (Consider the skill and thoroughness of the Venetian diplomatic reports, from which we gain much of the accurate knowledge we have of sixteenth-century affairs of state all over Europe.) Only in the seventeenth century did the major states of Europe begin to achieve this sort of political maturity. They could and did draw on the ideas as well as the practical experience of Renaissance Italy. They could also use the familiar body of political theory represented by the natural-law school, but they would have to modify it to meet new conditions. A political revolution was going on in seventeenth-century Europe.

Religious Toleration

In the sixteenth century, the great Protestant Revolt or Reformation had broken through all the premises of the old political thought and

[2]It may be worth recalling that Padua, whose university played so prominent a part in the scientific revolution, lay within the Venetian state, profiting by its thoroughly secular spirit as well as its efficient organization.

practice. The belief that the state must enforce a single faith and morality became intolerable when states were divided into two or more contending religions. The bloodshed of civil war and persecution of dissenters filled Europe with agony for a time but resulted eventually in a profound reaction against it and against many of the ideas underlying it. It became clear that only the secularized state, conceived of on a new foundation, could restore order to Europe. The secular state in any event profited from the destruction of the unity of the church. It is true that both Protestants and Roman Catholics tried to dominate the secular governments in order to destroy the other: Calvinists as well as Jesuits held to the old view that no temporal ruler had rightful authority unless he conformed to God's (that is, their) law. But in the long run this religious license to rebellion encountered the deep-seated opposition of peoples longing for peace and surcease from religious fanaticism. So when the frenzy of the religious wars had passed, Europe was the more ready for a new deal in politics. Banishing political churches, it hoped for peace from the strong secular monarchy, which could keep order, and it hoped for principles which would with dignity permit religious toleration. Toleration and the sovereign state march together through much of seventeenth-century history.

The toleration controversy began almost as early as the Reformation; Sebastian Castellion, of Basel, debated memorably with John Calvin himself on this issue. Castellion did not carry the day in the climate of the Reformation. The telling argument used against him by Calvin and Calvin's colleague, Theodore Beza, was this: Can it be that our faith is uncertain? Castellion had argued that these points of theology cannot be worth killing a man about, for they are so much in doubt. But if they are in doubt then Christ has deceived us and our faith does not exist, replied Calvin. It must be conceded that when men believe strongly— and belief is natural to men of character—they are not likely to be tolerant of opposing views; one does not tolerate egregious error. Does not toleration almost demand a degree of skepticism? "It is rating one's conjectures at a very high price to roast a man on the strength of them," as Montaigne wrote. Indeed it is, and the modern mind responds affirmatively to Montaigne's thrust. The word *conjectures* may be noted. If one's beliefs are only that, then to be sure it is folly to impose them by the sword. But if one really believes them to be God's truth, the case may be different. Few men in the sixteenth or even the seventeenth century were prepared to admit indifference in matters of religion.

Toleration was at first not so much a virtue as a necessity. The element of stark necessity meets us time and again in its voluminous literature, which began in the sixteenth century and swelled to a torrent in the seventeenth. Paradoxically, toleration owes its greatest debt to the fanaticism of religious believers, courageous dissenters whom persecution could not force to give up their beliefs—intolerant men themselves, for scarcely any of the Reformation sects would have failed to be exclusivist, we may surmise, if it had the sole possession of the state. But when numbers of different creeds shared the political society, it became necessary to invent some theory of the state to permit them to exist together without cutting each other's throats.

While it probably cannot be said that most of the smaller Protestant sects were naturally tolerant, they were in the position of wanting an extension of the range of toleration to include themselves and could hardly expect ever to control the state themselves. From their ranks occasionally emerged a real advocate of toleration. Among the heirs of Castellion should be mentioned the important Dutch anti-Calvinist, Arminius, of the University of Leyden, who attacked the Calvinist doctrines of predestination and natural depravity, producing a milder theology which, under the name of Arminianism, became well known in England as well as on the continent in the seventeenth century. By 1630 the Calvinist theocrats in Holland were no longer dominant, and the Dutch Republic became celebrated as a land which flourished impressively while harboring more than one creed. In France, the agony of the Huguenot civil wars stimulated the *politique* program which included religious toleration. The Edict of Nantes, 1598, marked Europe's first halting step toward toleration in a large state.

But it was probably in England that the debate about toleration went forward with the most vigor, encouraged by the atmosphere of the Puritan revolt and the long controversy that preceded it. The earliest English tract advocating toleration is said to have been written by a Baptist (Thomas Helwys) in 1612. But scattered support for toleration can certainly be found before that. Sir Walter Ralegh pleaded for toleration for the unpopular Brownists in Parliament in 1593, for example. The debate picked up speed and steam with the Puritan Revolution. Anglicans as well as Dissenters contributed to it, along with some laymen. Among the Anglicans, a notable group arguing for a measure of toleration were the "Latitudinarians," of whom Bishop Chillingworth was an early leader. Influenced by Arminianism, as well as by Christian humanism (they were close to the Cambridge Platonists, previously referred to in connection with science), this group warred against sectarian narrowness, regarding forms, ritual, or dogmatic quibbling as narrow. They stressed Christian conduct and tried to play down theology; indeed, their basic formula may be said to have been the effort to reduce the items of faith to a few "essentials." Dryden caught their spirit:

> Faith is not based on disquisitions vain.
> The things we must believe are few and plain.

These "men of latitude" who would later be identified with the "Low Church" group within the Church of England talked about "reason" as an antidote to intolerant dogmatism and in certain ways anticipated the deism of the eighteenth century; but they were not without religious fervor. If they would allow, in the title of a famous tract by Jeremy Taylor (1646), a "liberty of prophesying," they expected that all Christians might agree on the few essentials of faith and on that basis practice true religion without disunity. They held to a remarkable faith that "reason" could find these religious essentials. It was in practice not so easy to winnow the wheat from the chaff of Christian doctrine. Some Christians accused the Latitudinarians of abandoning too much. John Locke, who though a layman received considerable Latitudinarian influence, at the end of the century pared Christianity down to acceptance of two things: that God exists; that Christ lived and taught.

Not all Anglicans were so tolerant, needless to say. The Latitudinarians themselves never were tolerant of Roman Catholics or, it almost goes without saying, non-Christians. Few of the Puritans were, either. The Westminster Assembly of 1643 found the Brownists and Congregationalists more tolerant than the dominant sect among the Puritans, the Presbyterians. Richard Baxter, the eminent Presbyterian, said that when he disputed with the sectaries in the New Model Army, he found that "their most frequent and vehement disputes were for liberty of conscience, as they called it; that is that the civil magistrate had nothing to do to determine of anything in matters of religion . . . ; that the civil magistrate had nothing to do but with civil things to keep the peace and to protect the church's liberties." This distinction between the civil power and the spiritual was typical of the Puritan approach and reminds us of Roger Williams's famous tract of 1644 (written in England with reference to an English context, though often regarded as an American document). The path to toleration explored here was not that of reducing the requirements of faith; the Anglican men of latitude were likely to be accused by Puritans of lacking religious zeal. Rather, one should separate spiritual and civil matters. The function of the civil government is only to preserve the peace; its interests extend no farther than the prevention of violence. Spiritual matters must be handled in a spiritual way, with the weapons of the mind and soul only. The state, as Williams put it in a famous metaphor, is like a ship carrying a number of passengers to various destinations; its concern is to get them there safely, not to determine their destination. Let church and state be disentangled, and each religious sect might practice its own creed, without harm to others.

The multiplicity of sects did gradually force toleration. The laymen who entered the debate were inclined to argue practically. If England was to go forward successfully there was nothing for it but to recognize the facts of the situation and terminate the bootless, costly effort to enforce a single orthodoxy. During the civil war, each side persecuted the other, and the Presbyterians showed themselves as intolerant at the Westminster Assembly as Archbishop Laud's Anglicanism had been. Richard Baxter believed that toleration was all very well but we can "tolerate only the tolerable"! But Cromwell's protectorate practiced a degree of toleration in the interests of peace, drawing the line at Roman Catholics. The Agreement of the People resolution presented to Parliament by officers of the Army in 1649, which has been called "the first effective demand for toleration in England," exempted from toleration "papacy and prelacy," but in fact pious Anglicans were seldom bothered under the Puritan rule. With the passing of Cromwell and the restoration of Charles II, there was some vindictiveness against the regicide sectarians, expressed in Five Mile Act and Test Act. But the mood of the times also registered a reaction against dogmatism and theology—even against religion, conceived as anything other than a genteel code of good conduct.

Toleration in England won its final victory when James II tried to Catholicize the country 1685–1688. Erstwhile foes, the Anglicans and the Dissenters joined forces against the common threat of Romanism. The Glorious Revolution of 1688 cemented their alliance. Ironically, the victory of "toleration" rested on a most intolerant attitude toward Catholicism; but the largest breach in the ranks of English clergy, that between Puritan and Anglican, was healed in this way and the road was clear for a substantial degree of toleration. Far from completed by the Act of 1689, full religious liberty would steadily grow thereafter.

Various arguments used in the course of the long toleration debate are interesting. (*a*) It was urged that toleration is not Biblical, hence not Christian. Dissenters as well as Anglican Latitudinarians rested their religion on the Bible: "the Bible, and the Bible only, is the religion of Protestantism," said Chillingworth. To this it was added that the primitive (early) church had not persecuted and had required only a few simple items of creed. (But it might have been noted that before it became the official church, Christianity could not afford internal schism, being in the position of a persecuted minority itself.) (*b*) The futility of persecution, it was asserted, had been demonstrated in the terrible wars of religion, which had not succeeded in converting by force. Locke in his *Letter on Toleration* made the point that coercion can make hypocrites, but it cannot really alter belief. An outward conformity can no doubt be compelled by the sword but it is not worth anything. (*c*) Milton's great statement of faith, in the *Areopagitica* (1644), that all Truth needs is a fair field and no favors and she will prevail, might be dubious but was a magnificent affirmation. It was the counterpart of (*b*): If one can never really convince by compulsion, one *can* by rational argument, conducted in a climate of freedom. Milton believed that religious liberty would not lead to moral decay and intellectual anarchy, as some feared, but to an England where all men reached the level of saints. (*d*) Finally, to turn from the loftiest idealism to the most practical of arguments, men of affairs frequently declared that where conscience is free, commerce flourishes. They pointed to Holland as a demonstration of this. It did not make sense to them to drive away customers or workers because of their religion. The money of a Quaker is as good as that of an Anglican, and if a heretic be industrious he is still a useful citizen. This argument became more prominent after 1660. It was close to the position known as Erastianism: religion, in its public forms as regulated by the state, should be a matter of convenience to society; the criterion should be social utility, not ideal truth. Shocking at one time, this position was in actuality close to the one accepted by many of the triumphant Whigs after the revolution of 1688.

Absolutism and the Sovereign State

Against civil strife, also, was the reaction in favor of a strong state. In his *Political Testament*, Cardinal Richelieu assumes without question the goal of making the king unquestioned master of his realm.[3] Between 1624 and 1642 he carried out policies which struck down internal revolt, tamed the nobility, built up a large standing army, and strengthened the machinery of central government. Richelieu held up high standards for the monarch, who was supposed to rule justly and honestly; he selected servants of the state with care for their integrity and ability, despising corruption and self-seeking in public officials; and he patronized the arts and sciences, establishing the famous French Academy. But Richelieu wanted his king to be feared as well as loved, in line with the Machiavellian formula for princely success, and he was quite ruthless in crushing opposition, whether of nobility, of courts and parliaments, or of peasants desperate beneath the weight of taxation. He destroyed the independent military power of the Huguenots (Protestants), though willing to extend them religious toleration when they were no longer a political danger. This was a revolution quite as sweeping, and almost as violent, as that which took place in England at the same time but in a different direction.

When the Stuart kings tried to move toward royal absolutism in England, they lacked the finesse of a Richelieu and encountered an opposition from parliament and common law that finally broke them. But

[3]The essential authenticity of this document, doubted by Voltaire and others, seems established; see the discussion by Henry Bertam Hill in his edition of the work (1961).

most of Europe assumed during the seventeenth century that France not England was on the right path. While England was weak and divided, France moved into the lead in power, glory, and culture during the reign of Louis XIV (1661–1715). England's success with her adaptation of medieval constitutionalism was not evident until after 1688. For most Europeans sweeping away medieval relics in the state seemed like a counterpart to the revolution in science and philosophy; Richelieu and Descartes were both rationalists and reformers, replacing the medieval chaos with clarity and efficiency. (This is not to assert any direct influence, only that both shared a spirit of the age.) Royal despotism was the new movement. Kings were seeking powers not previously known, while Parliaments and (in England) the common law represented the medieval heritage.

The argument that monarchy is the best form of government was not new; Aristotle held it, as we have seen, and Dante was one who supported it fervently in the Middle Ages. But Aristotle and the main tradition did not favor an unlimited monarchy, rather a limited, constitutional one. Kings had long been granted a "divine right," but the term had not meant the equivalent of absolutism: that they received their powers from God did not mean in medieval times that they could do as they liked. But beginning with Bodin a new note is struck. We have already mentioned that pioneer of sovereignty (pp. 23–24). The author of the *Six Books of the Republic* (1576) might conceivably have a claim to be the Copernicus or Kepler of the political revolution. A mixed-up writer, still semimedieval, he criticized Aristotle and fought his way toward a new conception of the state. His leading insight was of that *puissance souveraine* that exists in every state, "the absolute and perpetual power of a republic" which cannot be limited or divided.

Bodin's influence was felt in England, and was partly responsible for a tendency in late Tudor times to "see in monarchy the one form of government that is 'natural' and approved by God, and . . . to suggest or even positively assert that the rights of the sovereign monarch are unlimited by human law or institution" (J. W. Allen). As is well known in English history, a really blunt statement to that effect came from the pen of the first Stuart king, the inept James I, who himself wrote a book, *The Trew Law of Free Monarchies* (1598), expressing ideas he ultimately endeavored to carry out with disastrous results. It was a crude tract, but it did certainly present vigorously the view that "Kings are justly called Gods," for they have the same awesome powers. And other writers of greater intellectual distinction argued similarly. The great writer John Donne was one of those who defended King James's sovereign powers in a battle of pamphlets when the Jesuits, Suarez and Bellarmine, along with Scottish Calvinists, argued for a right to depose kings.

The new concept of "sovereignty" tended to bolster the argument for monarchical absolutism. This idea stressed that there is in the state in one place, indivisible, a right and a power to command. Sir John Hayward (1603) drew the obvious inference when he observed that, while a single will might conceivably be expressed by many together, this is unlikely, and one sovereignty must normally mean one ruler. "Reason," wrote Sir Thomas Craig, "which governs in men, aims always at monarchy, as the most certain form of government." So many American students seem to think of monarchy as a kind of ancient superstition that this point needs to be stressed: absolute monarchy was a new idea which arrived in the seventeenth century supported by "reason" and (typically) by the same avant garde forces that stood for the new rationalism in science and philosophy. It accompanied the discovery of sovereignty, which was the main triumph of the political rationalists in this era, the political law of universal gravitation, one might say.

French royalists of the sixteenth century, and English ones later, went so far as to declare that rebellion against the worst of kings is unjustifiable, for even tyranny is better than anarchy. They wrote under the influence of civil war with all the horrors it caused, and they blamed this witches' broth of disorders on there being too many cooks in the kitchens of state. How can you have orderly government when many people, certain to disagree, are trying to rule? Two or more men can hardly drive a car at the same time; a state, like an army, must have a unified command. Better one poor general than two good ones, an old saying ran. Modern governments have learned techniques of delegating power and have learned also to enshrine sovereignty in an abstract national will, but in the infancy of the modern nation it was not unnatural to personify the sovereign will. The argument in some respects coincided with the rationalism of the scientists, who were simplifying, abolishing confusion, seeking clarity, and finding concise formulae to sum up nature and subdue it to principles of order.

Most of these defenders of absolute rule did not really mean that the king should have totally unlimited power. They often said so, because they wished him to have great power, and they wished an end to rebellion and civil disorder. But if pressed they certainly would have backpedalled somewhat. It is as difficult rationally to sustain unlimited authority as it is to uphold unlimited liberty. At this phase of European history, particularly in France, and on the Continent generally, the stress was on authority because anarchy and civil war had been the recent experience. The later sixteenth and seventeenth century produced a succession of theorists (Barclay, Hobbes, Bossuet, Filmer) who stressed authority rather than liberty, the sovereign state rather than the rights of the individual. They tried to support authority and sovereignty by the use of rational arguments, and usually they were compelled at some stage of their argument to admit qualifications.

Taking the transplanted Scotsman, William Barclay, who wrote in France at the end of the sixteenth century, as our example, we find among his arguments these: that authority is derived from God; that sovereignty is not divisible; that divided sovereignty leads to anarchy; that society urgently needs order; that the Bible supports monarchy; that by history as well as logic the king, not the parliament (Estates), is properly the sovereign; and similarly that the state is properly superior to the church. Barclay employs traditional arguments along with new ones, it will be observed, a mixture like Kepler of the medieval and the modern; he brings in the Bible and divine law, showing reliance also on the later medieval Imperialists who had backed the claims of the secular power against the church. But there are some new rational arguments, especially the idea of sovereignty, along with the utilitarian argument based on an urgently felt need for order during the religious turmoils of the times. Whether he relies on religious or utilitarian arguments, Barclay finds it difficult to escape a right of rebellion, much as he desires to minimize this right.

If the king is sovereign by God's will, then what if he should break the laws of God? There must always be a potential appeal to a "higher law" in the religious sanction, a fact which the antimonarchical activities of both Calvinists and Jesuits abundantly proved at this very time. And if the debate be placed on practical, utilitarian grounds solely, and the king be said to be sovereign just because this suits the interests of society, then the king may presumably be deposed should he fail to govern in the interests of society. So one could not destroy liberty altogether by rational argument, much as some of the seventeenth-century theorists tried. It is significant for the mood of the age that the greatest of political theorists tried the hardest to do so, but that, in combining philosophical radicalism with political conservatism, they fell into contradictions. This generalization applies above all to the English genius, Thomas Hobbes.

The Puritan Revolution

When England erupted into revolution in 1641, passing thereafter stormily through civil war, the execution of King Charles by Parliament (or by a military junta controlling that body), and several different experiments in alternatives to royal despotism, she also sent up showers of political theorizing. There was naturally an effort on the side of Parliament to justify its challenge to and overthrow of royal authority; this vein, of which Henry Parker may be taken as a sample, revived old justifications of revolt, with perhaps some new twists. Parker's argument that the king is less than the kingdom and may be deposed if he does not do his job of serving it, seems hardly to go beyond Manegold of Lautenbach's medieval remarks about swineherds; but Parker went on boldly to deposit sovereign power in Parliament. Nevertheless the Parliament leaders were loath to seem radical, and Parker was for some time well ahead of his party. Parliament represented the wealthy squirearchy, a conservative class defending its own self-interest as well as traditional concepts of English government against the new absolutism of kings who wished to tax them without their consent and overrule the common-law courts by more recently created royal courts. Parliament men claimed that the "ancient constitution" of England, reaching far back into Saxon times, reaffirmed by Magna Carta (1215) and embodied in the common law, was one of the limitations on monarchical power. Their foes ridiculed these arguments, but there was much substance in them. At any rate they were deeply and sincerely held. So in the beginning, at least, it was Parliament that posed as the conservative party.

The Puritan revolt, as it is often called, included a religious element, based on the rise and growth of Puritanism along with criticism of Charles's toleration of "papists" at Court and his laxity in enforcing the anti-Catholic laws. Puritanism was on the upswing in England. Though we customarily think of it in terms of John Calvin's continental theology of Divine omnipotence, predestination, and election of the saints, along with his extreme regulation of conduct, some students of English Puritanism have insisted on a partly native provenance. It was at any rate clearly a mood that transcended the boundaries of sect and could operate on "the Separatist, the Seeker, the Ranter, and even the Quaker, as well as the Presbyterian or the Congregationalist" (Alan Simpson). Whatever its exact limitations, Puritanism included a strong activism, a desire to do more than just criticize the remnants of the old unreformed way in church liturgy, organization, or doctrine. Puritans found it hard to understand that, more than a half-century after Good Queen Bess's stabilizing of the Church of England, the godly message had gotten to so few people. Their fervent zeal to reform the Church and preach the Word naturally spilled over into politics; most of them were not preachers of individual liberty of judgment, but of Calvin's reformed church in which the civil magistrates carried out the decrees of the clergy, purging the old, installing the new, and scourging the sinners. They had already proved themselves the most formidable revolutionaries in history, in France, Holland, and Scotland. And, as one of them remarked during the Revolution, "Without settling Religion, you shall never settle the common-wealth." Godliness was the foundation of politics.

The king and his adviser Archbishop Laud had embarked on a campaign to purge the Puritans from the Church of England. Puritanism, with its strong criticism of a dissolute age, represented a moral impulse as well as a religious one, perhaps chiefly a moral one. Not matters of doctrinal theology, but questions of theaters and maypole dancing, of Sabbath breaking and too elaborate church ceremonies, came to the front. While Sir Toby Belch complained indignantly that these people wished to abolish cakes and ale, Puritanism spread because it appealed to strength of character and high seriousness, the characteristic Calvinist ethic. For some time, of course—*vide* the French Huguenot "monarcho-machs" of the sixteenth century, and the last edition of Calvin's own *Institutes*—Calvinism had preached right of resistance to kings of the wrong religious faith. The Huguenot writings certainly were known to the English Puritans. However, there was little talk of revolution at first. The clash was between rival political bodies both possessing long traditions and great legal dignity.

While the king's rather simple mind clung to the logic of royal sovereignty (a king should be a king, not a "doge of Venice," and must decide policy for his people, though he might *consult* with Parliament), Parliament gradually moved, amid a flurry of pamphlets, from hazy views about its rights to share government with the king, to distinctions between the *office* of the king and his person, finally to bold claims that in Parliament, "this high court of law and counsel," the supreme power of the nation was deposited. Sovereignty having been discovered, the old vague acceptance of both king and Parliament as sharing in the governance of the realm no longer passed muster; one *or* the other must be sovereign. If two men ride a horse one must ride in front, as Hobbes observed. The lion and the unicorn would fight for the crown.

Once started, revolutions get out of hand, and before long even more daring theories appeared. Among other things, the interesting army debates produced an encounter between the democratic view that almost every man should have a vote and the conservative view that "no person hath a right to an interest or a share in the disposing of the affairs of this kingdom . . . that hath not a permanent fixed interest in this kingdom," that is, the vote should go with property ownership. Victory in practice, if not in theory, went to the latter. But the Puritan Revolution brought forward, in the Leveller movement, perhaps the first significant body of democratic thought in European history.[4] The engaging if somewhat irresponsible John Lilburne, along with such other Leveller pamphleteers as Richard Overton and William Walwyn, shows the influence of rationalist and scientific currents of the times. Overton, apparently an amateur student of the sciences, was of a vaguely Hobbean turn of

---

[4]The Levellers were not in favor of a completely democratic voting franchise since it seems clear they would have excluded some, including beggars and servants. Still, their support of what amounted to household suffrage put them more than two centuries in advance of their times.

mind in metaphysics. The Levellers rejected tradition and sought a reconstruction of the ideal society on grounds of reason, which makes them
somewhat utopian as politicians. Science and reason, we feel, were invoked to support what these plain people already wanted in their bones:
equality with haughty gentlemen, representation in Parliament, changes
in the law to aid poor men (for example, abolition of imprisonment for
debt), free education and medical care, an end to land monopoly. Rationalism was an ideological weapon which gave them grounds for rejecting the past and beginning anew. As theory, the Leveller pamphlets
can hardly be called very imposing, but of course they are tremendously
significant social documents. They look ahead to much later developments; the time was scarcely ripe for a democratic movement in the
seventeenth century, but its dim stirrings are heard. It is especially interesting to the student of intellectual history that what precipitated this
abortive democracy was not only the English revolutionary upheaval,
but also the currents of rationalist thought then in the air. If Descartes
can start all over again on the basis of reason, we almost hear Overton
asking, why can't we do the same in society and government? The age of
reason was to breed other political utopias in the next hundred and fifty
years.

At the same time an influence on the radicals of the Puritan Revolution also came from Christian millenarianism and messianism. During
the Reformation ferment, especially in Germany, such flowers had
bloomed in profusion. All students of history probably know how Martin Luther's defiance of Rome helped induce a great peasant uprising, of
which the Protestant reformer himself did not approve; and how such
strange radical outcroppings as the Commune of Münster emerged from
the left wing of the Protestant revolt. This popular revolutionary millenarianism had appeared in the Middle Ages, too. Poor men, reading the
Bible for the first time and encouraged by Luther's apparent teaching
that they might construe it in their own way, conceived some unusual
versions of Christian theology, which showed a remarkable tendency to
suit the interests of poor men against rich. The Book of the Revelation,
along with Chapter 7 of the Book of Daniel, in particular, proved a
happy hunting ground for visions of a final utopia. At the millennium
institutions like private property and private marriage would disappear,
and all brethren would be equal, as Christ returned to earth to rule as
king for a thousand years before the final reckoning. The Puritan Revolution throbbed with Biblical pronouncements cast in the haunting
imagery of the Old and New Testament. The Fifth Monarchy men, a
significant group for a time during the Revolution, expressed this scriptural vision of a social revolution in the name of holiness.

On the extreme left of the Revolution, Gerrard Winstanley, whom

some modern Communists have hailed as a forerunner, asked why economic democracy should not supplement political democracy, and why,
if lords of manor can rebel against the king, poor men might not rebel
against lords of manor? His "Diggers," who were landless agricultural
workers, did not attempt violent revolution, but did try to occupy the
common lands of the agricultural villages. The movement was a tiny one,
but Winstanley's thought has been regarded, not exclusively by socialists
and communists, as a significant contribution to social and political
theory. He has considerable importance as a forerunner of modern socialism, just as Lilburne does as a pioneer of democracy.

Harrington and Hobbes

Thus the period from 1640 to 1660 in England produced a host of
pamphleteers and political tracts. Among them was the poet John Milton,
who defended the execution of King Charles (1649) in a tract of 1650.
Of all these political theorists of the Puritan Revolution, the greatest
perhaps, next to Thomas Hobbes, was the republican, James Harrington,
author of the celebrated *Oceana* (1656). Like so many of the seventeenth-
century political thinkers Harrington wished to be scientific, and the evidence of a mechanical model is strong in his work: things are balanced
against each other; an equilibrium of forces is sought; a state can be
designed so as to run forever if only these principles are followed. But
Harrington, who knew Machiavelli and Hobbes well, was also a student
of ancient history, like those two; and his rationally designed state machine turns out to look much like the precepts of ancient writers. Polybius
being the great example, who stressed the balance of forces in a state.
And he considered it his task to recover the wisdom of classical antiquity
in this regard. Harrington seems more original in stressing the importance of economic power, though this too can be culled from the ancient
historians. Property holds the key to the political affairs of a community, he believed; a democracy or "commonwealth" can only work where
property is widely dispersed. He explained the coming of the English
Revolution as the result of an economic revolution which had ended the
monopoly of wealth by the king and a few nobles and had given it to
the "middle people." The economic structure having changed, the political superstructure was bound to follow. This is a striking analysis,
though the facts do not altogether bear it out (it works better on the
French Revolution); we can readily see its influence on Marx and other
economic determinists. But Harrington also exerted a great influence on
John Adams and the American Federalists—an influence aided by the
antiimperialism to be found in the *Oceana*, where colonies are regarded

as both burdensome and futile since they are bound to gain their independence eventually. He was no radical revolutionary; a member of the landed class himself, he found a place for it in his balance of forces. The lower class should be represented, but it should not dominate; the aristocrats would serve as a check on it and would prove invaluable to the state because of their leisure to study and serve as political leaders.

Nevertheless Harrington believed there should be laws keeping down the size of an estate, so that the rich might not become too rich. The wealthy class no less than the popular one is a danger if allowed too much power. Only power can check power, and no individual or class is to be trusted with too much of it. One could draw from him the grounds of opposition to a pure democracy, which would be a violation of this maxim because it gives power to one class only, which would use its power to dispossess the upper class and ruin the community. Yet he pursued his scheme of an agrarian law setting upward limits on the amount of land any one person could hold, against the considerable opposition to be expected. Harrington's "republic" is a state wherein not any one segment, but the whole people, expressing the common interest or general will, makes the laws. As a republican, incidentally, he was of course quite prepared to get along without a king, as England did between 1649 and 1660. With the restoration of Charles II, Harrington fell under a cloud; but his writings were not forgotten by everyone in England.

Somewhat visionary and utopian, dazzled like so many men of this age by the illusion of a perfect formula "scientifically" arrived at, Harrington yet remains as important a political writer as ever tackled that thorny subject, and his influence on such great successors as Montesquieu seems clear. The author of *Oceana* belongs among the pioneer immortals of modern political theory. In this fruitful season of political theorizing, only one excelled him, and that one was the great Thomas Hobbes.

The Puritan Revolution, from which he fled to Paris, directed Hobbes's thinking toward politics, and as he fell simultaneously under the spell of mathematical studies and the rationalist philosophy of Descartes, he determined to bring this area under the sway of scientific method— to become, we may well say, the first social scientist in the modern sense of that term. Karl Marx called Hobbes "the father of us all." Hobbes presented to the world in 1651 his most celebrated work, *The Leviathan*, an inquiry into "the matter, form, and power of a Commonwealth." Earlier, in 1640, the first year of the Revolution, Hobbes had written a shorter treatise which circulated in manuscript, and which, since it sustained absolutism against government by Parliament, was the cause of his flight from England (for he "doubted how they would use him.") It grew into *The Leviathan* during his years of exile. This work has been called the greatest treatise on political theory ever produced by an Englishman, though large numbers of Englishmen have dedicated their time and talents to demolishing it. Hobbes was, as we already know, an extremely bold thinker, and a corollary of his mechanistic materialism was the effort to bring human affairs within the purview of physical science. He tried to exclude everything except "bodies" subject to mechanical principles; mind and society must be considered in exactly the same way as other "bodies." This attempt to transpose human and social phenomena into the framework of physics appears to us today as an elementary error, confusing what are different categories; but it was natural for the seventeenth century to think there was a single scientific method and to attempt to apply elsewhere what worked so well in physical science.

Laboring on a scientific theory of politics, Hobbes sought like Descartes to begin with an unchallengeable truth and from that deduce the rest. He found his truth in his analysis of human nature, an analysis stressing the egoistic drives of power, pride, and envy. Selfishness and, between men, mistrust are the basic facts of political life. Consequently the original "state of nature" in which men found themselves was a state of war. We can see this even now, says Hobbes, in relations between states, which are brutal and amoral, marked by spying, deceit, even when not by actual violence. Formerly, he asserts, it was the same between individuals. Hobbes had much to say of a striking nature concerning the role of power in human affairs, a "perpetual and restless desire of power after power that ceases only in death." This is not, he observed acutely, just because men have an unlimited greed for power, but because they must always have more to protect what they have. The states whose power is greatest are the ones who seek it the most. Without much question Hobbes is right about this, and his penetrating realism seems a cool, clean wind, telling us something real rather than fanciful about human affairs. No doubt it is exaggerated: selfishness and power are not quite the whole of the matter, as Hobbes seems to imply. But they exist and it is good to have attention drawn to them.

When Hobbes turns next to his social contract, we are apt to wonder where the realist went. The idea of a social contract was not a new one. It can be traced far back into history (it "has haunted the generations," wrote Sir Ernest Barker) and had been freely used in the years before Hobbes's work, notably by French Huguenots and English Parliamentarians; it was a standby of the natural-law school. It is true that Hobbes gave it a new and startling twist. It had been used previously to justify resistance to government, a device to limit the powers of the state by asserting it could not exceed the bounds of an imagined agreement with the people. Thus the Huguenot tract, *Vindiciae contra Tyran-*

nos (1576): God alone commands unlimited obedience; the king is bound by God's laws; he has a contract with God to rule justly and maintain true religion. If he does not, the people are absolved from obedience to the king, for there is also a contract between king and people.

Hobbes turned the social contract into an argument for the unlimited authority of the sovereign state. But, in the first place, it seems strangely unhistorical to imagine that savage men, in a "state of nature" before there was any government or any civilization, solemnly met like a group of bourgeois lawyers and made a contract. David Hume, who subjected the social contract idea to searching criticism in the next century, was among those who noted that this procedure assumes not only a sophistication and rationality impossible to imagine in prehistoric man, but also a knowledge of the law—you must know what a contract is before you can make one! Hobbes's answer to this would have been that he was not really interested in the historicity of the contract. He was engaged in an exercise in Cartesian analysis. This is what rationally should have happened, or did happen in effect, not actually like this but logically like this. Scientific laws represent abstractions from nature.

In any case Hobbes made use of the social contract. To escape from their intolerable condition, their lives "solitary, mean, nasty, brutish, and short," the people came together and agreed to assign sovereign power to a despot, who is to see to it that they do not cut each other's throats as they are prone to do. *Salus populi suprema lex*. Hobbes's contract, be it noted, is between all the people, not between the people collectively and a sovereign. The people agree with each other to accept a sovereign; they do not bargain with that sovereign. They thus create a Leviathan state, a "mortal god" against which there can be no right of resistance nor any appeal to a higher law. Higher laws do not exist. The one law of nature was and is the law of self-preservation. From this one, Hobbes deduced others, such as the keeping of covenants: it is in our self-interest to do so. But all of these go back to the law of selfishness.

Having agreed, for selfish reasons, to surrender their liberty to the state, men must accept its fiat as law. Law is the command of the sovereign. It may be noted that Hobbes indicates we obey the law because we know it is in our interest to do so. I know that if I disobey it, others will too, and so there will be no security for me. Hobbes's rationalism is much in evidence here: we have people reasoning their way to their civic duties in a way, perhaps, that few of them do or ever have done. But this, he would reply, is the logic of the law.

The people, then, made the government initially, and they did so as equals, and individuals; then they chose to hand over power to an autocrat. Hobbes, it has been said, is an unusual combination, an equalitarian autocrat.

He did not opt necessarily for a monarchical absolutism. The "sovereign" might be a body of men, acting with a single will. He did argue that monarchy is the best form of government: its will is undivided; it can keep policy secrets; there must always be one man to decide even in a so-called democracy. Hobbes would doubtless have relished Bernard Shaw's quip that ambitious kings envy the president of the United States. But this is not a necessity; Hobbes left the way open for a group sovereign. In any case, he was far from supporting a "divine right" monarch. Divine right was something Hobbes would have no part of. Government must be justified by scientific, naturalistic reasoning, not by supernaturalism and superstition. A goodly portion of *The Leviathan* is given over to sharp attacks on the priesthood, who are told to keep out of politics with their nonsense. If the church exists, it must be under the control of the state, a thoroughly "Erastian" solution. The English royalists did not like Hobbes, any more than did the parliamentarians. Their case rested on custom, tradition, and religious sanction, all of which Hobbes severely denied. Some thought that he offered a rationale or apology for Cromwell the dictator, a *parvenu* strong man who owed his power to no hereditary right. This is doubtful, but at any rate Hobbes's case for monarchy was a thoroughly unorthodox one. He did not even argue for hereditary monarchy.

At the same time, it *was* a case for authority against liberty. Thoroughly frightened by the anarchy of the civil war, he wished to nail down the lid of sovereign power tightly, so that no glib rebel could slip through it. John Locke later remarked that Hobbes had been frightened by polecats and so delivered himself over to the lion. The worst tyrant is better than no government, Hobbes believed, adding that any right of rebellion will lead to anarchy. Hobbes's was an unusual combination of political conservatism and general philosophical radicalism. Perhaps that helps explain some of the contradictions in his thought. He hoped to bolster the authority of the state, but by depriving it of tradition and sanctity he may have weakened it; when all is said and done, Hobbes's sovereign is only justified by its usefulness and can surely be unmade by the same people that made it. The grandeur of *The Leviathan* rests in good part on the rigorous logic with which Hobbes pursues his argument; and yet, such is the irrational nature of politics, the whole thing is full of the most illogical assumptions. (Harrington believed Hobbes too lacking in practical political experience to be a sound guide in politics.)

Hobbes had current social development on his side in his basic assumptions, whether or not he had science. His state is sovereign, and is made up of individuals, who are equal in rights. The medieval world which lacked a sovereign power and consisted of corporate groups does not appear here, and Hobbes's political man is strictly rational, knowing exactly what he is and where his interest lies. He has ceased to root his political authority in the divine law working through nature; he makes his own laws. Hobbes's bourgeois rationalism, and his atomistic individualism, were both of his day and of the future rather than of the past. And, indeed, so was his authoritarianism, if we remember that his age was in search of a remedy against civil strife and ideological dissension.

But most Englishmen were outraged at Hobbes, some because he seemed to attack liberty, others because of the church and religion, still others because he made short work of tradition and sentiment. Royalists liked him as little as Parliament men, "Tories" as "Whigs" (in the terminology that came into use in the 1670s). So the "hunting of Leviathan" became a national sport; Hobbes's book received as many replies as did Rousseau's a century later or Marx's two centuries later. And debate about exactly what he meant still goes on. If each of our modern centuries has had its great political iconoclast, Hobbes can well claim to have played that part in the seventeenth century.

The Glorious Revolution and John Locke

Between the political *chefs d'oeuvres* of Hobbes and Locke lay the restored monarchy of Charles II, an uneasy time during which the issues raised by the Puritan Revolution were not resolved but only shelved. The limits of monarchical power, the rights of Parliament, the question of hereditary succession, all remained substantially undetermined until 1688. As a specific issue, the Exclusion Bill of 1680 divided England into Whigs and Tories. The alarums and excursions attending Titus Oates's imagined plots and the Rye House plot kept political temperatures high. Then in 1685 James II ascended the throne and determined to put an end to uncertainty. His headlong drive to absolutize and Catholicize England along the lines of the French monarchy soon led to a revolution of virtually the entire country against him, from which he fled in 1688, as the Dutch husband of his daughter, Mary, accepted the crown (jointly with her) upon the invitation of both Whigs and Tories in Parliament. The particular circumstances of this Glorious (and bloodless) Revolution had something to do with Locke's political theory, which came out soon afterward.

But Locke had been working on his political treatises for some years before that. The first of the *Two Treatises of Government* is a polemic against Sir Robert Filmer, an extreme royalist defender of absolutism. Sir Robert's *Patriarcha* had been written much earlier and was read in manuscript, but not printed until 1680. Sir Robert sought justification for absolute monarchy in a way that few Englishmen (except perhaps

Hobbes) ever had done. For the typical English royalist or Tory did not deny that Parliament had *some* share in government. Influenced by Bodin as well as Hobbes, Filmer held that the sovereign power must not be divided, for if it is there will be no government and anarchy will destroy society—a familiar argument. He sought to buttress monarchical authority by arguing that it stemmed ultimately from the father's role in the family, obedience to the king being an outgrowth of, and an analogy to, the natural obedience children owe to their parents. This patriarchal argument was an old one, too. It customarily traced the origin of familial authority to Adam, the first man, to whom God had given "dominion over all creatures"—the first monarch. Filmer gave it a somewhat more sophisticated statement. He was more cogent in rejecting the social contract as a myth, something that never happened or could happen.

Locke successfully ridiculed the weak links in Filmer's argument— a fairly easy task. Then in the much more celebrated second treatise he went on to set forth his own views, as against Filmer and (indirectly) Hobbes. Though Locke does not mention Hobbes in this work, there can be little doubt that he had in mind the well-known *Leviathan*, which many others had assaulted before him, for example, George Lawson, Bishop Bramhall, John Eachard: the "hunting of Leviathan" was a popular sport. Locke would not have been at all original in refuting Hobbes, who for one reason or another offended practically everybody. Much of what Locke has to say in this tract was far from original, it may be noted to begin with. He himself acknowledged considerable indebtedness to "the judicious Hooker"—Richard Hooker, Elizabethan divine and natural-law thinker—as well as to the German, Samuel Pufendorf, a contemporary writer on political theory then of much renown. Numerous other Whig pamphleteers had spoken up for liberty against royal tyranny, some more boldly than Locke, for instance, Algernon Sidney, martyred in 1684 for allegedly taking part in the Rye House Plot, probably in actuality because of his *Discourses concerning Government*. Locke was discreetly silent until the battle was won. It must be acknowledged, however, that none of them had written a treatise at once so eloquent, dignified, and closely reasoned. Coinciding with and seeming to speak for the Glorious Revolution, it quickly took its place as a political classic and long remained so. So much so that more than a century later James Madison and Thomas Jefferson, in the United States, took for granted that Locke had spoken the last and probably the only word on matters of government.

Locke had some practical experience of politics (secretary to the great Whig noble Lord Shaftesbury; Commissioner for Trade; Secretary to the Council of Trade; diplomatic special agent) and his broader philosophical outlook, as expressed in the important *Essay concerning Human*

Understanding (see below pages 110–17), was empirical, that is, based on sense experience rather than innate or abstract ideas. As a disciple of Robert Boyle, member of the Royal Society, and a part-time physician of the empirical school, he came honestly by his empiricism, though in his youth Descartes and Hobbes, too, had stimulated him. As will be seen, his philosophical empiricism was actually tinged not a little with rationalism. His political theory does not appear to be especially empirical; by comparison with Montesquieu, Hume, Burke, or Tocqueville later it is abstract-rational, closer to Hobbes than to them. It is, however, touched at various points by that "large, sound, roundabout sense" which is Locke's trademark. And his great genius for making fairly abstruse ideas seem clear is in evidence here as in his other works.

In the beginning men were free and equal, and living in a "state of nature" without civil government. Thus far, Locke is with Hobbes. He soon parts company with him. This state of nature was not one of constant war between men. Men have in them enough natural reason to teach them not to harm one another "in life, health, liberty, or possessions." There is a natural moral law, a law "intelligible and plain" to every human being in possession of his reason. In the hypothetical state of nature (Locke no more than Hobbes seemed very interested in whether it actually ever existed. Examples can be found, he thinks, and the existing relations between nations are of this sort, but even if it never existed, it is a logical necessity to assume it.) men had a natural right to their life, liberty, and property (property being that with which a person has "mixed his labor"). Men found life tolerable in this state, yet not convenient. The lack of an accepted arbiter to make judgments in matters concerning property, especially, rendered "the enjoyment of property very unsafe, very insecure . . . full of fears and continual dangers." Locke apparently meant that without government men would not murder each other, or even blatantly steal from each other, but disputes would arise and it would be most inconvenient to have no orderly means of settling them.

But, since they did not *have* to have government, men could drive a bargain with it; they did not have to give up all their rights to it. To set up a tyrant with unlimited power would be absurd, for having established government to protect their rights, if that government took them away it would defeat the very purpose for which government was established. In entering society, I give up only some of my liberties, the better to enjoy others. And these I give up only with my consent. "Men being by nature free, equal, independent, no one can be put out of his estate and subjected to another without his own consent." Only limited powers are surrendered to the government, one of the limits being that "the supreme power cannot take away from any man any part of this property without his own consent."

Then, once the specific agreement or constitution of government is decided upon by the majority, this government must not exceed its just powers. If any agent or government behaves in an illegal way, either by violating natural rights or in any other way exceeding the bounds of power granted to him by the constitution, he "ceases to be magistrate" and he may be resisted. Should a legislature not properly elected make laws, or should the executive fail its duties, the government is dissolved and power reverts to the people. Government cannot pass laws aimed at individuals, levy taxes without the consent of the people, or transfer legislative power to any other body without the consent of the people. The famous 1689 Declaration of Rights, imposed by Parliament on the new monarchs, had spelled this out; Locke would seem to be placing a bill of rights to some extent against the Parliament, too. Though he says that the legislative is the "supreme power," he also indicates that it too is responsible to the basic moral law. Some things it, too, cannot do, or "the people" have a "supreme power to remove or alter the legislative." (The British Constitution did not follow Locke's teaching in this respect.)

With much eloquence Locke urged that the danger of rebellion is far less than the danger of tyranny. The people do not rebel easily, but are more apt to suffer injustice than revolt. If you tell the men in power that they need fear no resistance to tyranny you invite worse mischief. To the classic Tory logic that (1) right of rebellion equals anarchy and (2) anarchy is worse than tyranny, Locke replied by denying both premises, but especially the first.

All this being so, liberty's debt to Locke is clear. But it is necessary to point out some limitations. The initial contract (Locke seems to assume two, which was usual in social-contract thought)[5] demanded the consent of everyone; thereby a society was made, men agreeing to belong to the same community and to accept the will of the majority. But this "social" contract happened once, in the remote past, and today we give tacit consent only, by accepting the laws of the country. Our only alternative is to go to some other country. This is really to say no more than that we are born into a political community.

But the second contract (or some sort of agreement), by which a specific government was established, also happened only once, it seems. By majority vote, a constitution was agreed upon; after that, it presumably remains in effect unless an illegal action by prince or legislative "dissolves" the government—a revolutionary situation, which Locke is at pains to insist rarely if ever happens. And this specific form of government, while it cannot be a despotism, can certainly be something other than a democracy. Locke clearly admired the aristocratic system under

---

[5]One does not find it in Hobbes, or in Rousseau later; it is a device of the natural-law school.

which England lived after the Glorious Revolution, with political power substantially in the hands of a small, landed upper class, the only group actually represented in Parliament. It is true that Locke wrote of the need for parliamentary reform from time to time. But it is far from evident that he wished a democratic electorate, and it is not easy to see that his theory leaves any place for popular control of the governing class under normal conditions.[6] One has the impression that he was content to justify and to perpetuate the Revolution of 1688, a revolution that may be said to have resulted in the parliamentary dictatorship of an oligarchy. Locke's other writings indicate no great sympathy for the "labouring poor" or other elements outside the Whig establishment. There is even, startlingly, a partial justification of slavery (and Locke drew money from West Indian sugar plantations).

Locke can be accused of producing little more than rhetoric, too, on such questions, which he claimed to have solved, as individual liberties and rights against the state. Does it mean much to say that "the state cannot take away property without consent" unless one defines the terms? (Would Locke have approved of an income tax, or eminent domain, or alien expropriation in time of war?) Whether or not it is absurd, as Locke says it is, suppose a majority approves of a basic law taking away an individual's property or any rights of a minority? Is it possible to distinguish by any general rules between rightful defense of liberty and unjustifiable rebellion against authority? In the United States, between 1830 and 1860, it was impossible for people who swore by the principles of Locke to agree on this point.

This is only to suggest that politics can never be a strict science and few binding general laws can be found. It does not take away from Locke the honor of having written superbly on the side of liberty at a time when it was needful to do so. As he said, there had been too much written about the evils that spring from rebellion and too little about the equally mischievous "rulers' insolence and endeavours to get and exercise an arbitrary power over the people." The liberty he defended meant to him, probably, the liberty of affluent Englishmen of his own class (and Locke was, by adoption at least, decidedly a member of the *haute bourgeoisie*), but it could not be without application to anyone who suffered unjust actions at the hands of government authority. Few if any treatises on government have been so lucid, so thorough, and on the

---

[6]"When the society hath placed the legislative in any assembly of men to continue in them and their successors, with direction and authority for providing such successors, the legislative can never revert to the people whilst that government lasts. . . ." It should be further noted that the right of revolution certainly may not be exercised (as some seem to think Locke said) just because the people happen to be discontented with a government. The government must have violated natural law or the constitution in specific ways.

whole so sensible. The *Treatises on Government* were a fitting introduction to the political Enlightenment.

There were other political thinkers worthy of attention we cannot give them. Locke regarded the German, Samuel Pufendorf, as one of the best of all writers on political theory, comparing him to Cicero, Aristotle, and the New Testament and naming two of his books among the five Locke recommended on this subject. And along with the Saxon sage one thinks of the Dutchman Grotius, often honored as "the founder of international law," in the modern sense of that term at least. Grotius was the natural-law theorist par excellence: he seems to return to Aristotle in positing a social instinct which, in direct opposition to Hobbes, makes government natural and not artificial. Grotius, however, fully accepted the *fait accompli* of the sovereign state; writing amid the horrors of the Thirty Years' War, his principal goal was to lay foundations for some cooperation and agreement between these Leviathan monsters. The eighteenth century deplored his baroque disorder—enormous erudition but no "liaison of ideas," as Condillac would say. Pufendorf, for his part, was a scholar of the next generation who attempted to draw together the ideas of Bodin, Hobbes, Grotius, into a coherent and, again, scientific philosophy of the state. To posterity he has usually seemed a less original mind than others of his era, however—scarcely a Locke. The Germans showed a strong liking for natural-law thought, perhaps as a result of their political structure, the Empire, which was not a sovereign state but a sort of federation within which many lesser units existed. Leibniz defended natural law against Spinoza and Hobbes.

Spinoza also dabbled in political theory; though a realist like Hobbes, as his monistic philosophy required him to be, Spinoza did not exalt authority and minimize liberty like the Englishman, but talked about the value of rational discussion, conducted in an atmosphere of freedom. Though he believed in the necessity of all things, this did not lead Spinoza to deny the need for liberty. The universe is rational, our minds are a part of that rational order, therefore no restraint should be placed in the way of the mind when it thinks rationally. Religious toleration and democracy were a part of Spinoza's outlook.

But Locke exerted the greatest influence, doubtless because the Glorious Revolution led England on to success in the eighteenth century. She came out of the long War of the Spanish Succession ahead of the monolithic monarchy of Louis XIV and waxed rich and strong through the eighteenth century. Ordered liberty seemed her secret; no all-powerful sovereign was needed to shape a strong, secure nation. England had managed after much turmoil to adapt her medieval constitution to the modern state, securing ancient liberties and new efficiency. It remains the most impressive political achievement of modern times. Writing well along in the twentieth century, one might still defend the proposition that no large modern state has managed to make parliamentary democracy work except England and those systems of government derived from hers. To this monumental achievement the pamphleteers of the Puritan Revolution, as well as all the giants of political thought—Harrington, Hobbes, Locke—had contributed something.

4

The Transition
to the Enlightenment
at the End
of the Seventeenth Century

'Tis well an old age is out, and time to begin a new.

JOHN DRYDEN

*The strongest intellectual forces of the Enlightenment
do not lie in its rejection of belief but rather in
the new form of faith which it proclaims, and
in the new form of religion which it embodies.*

ERNST CASSIRER

The Age of Louis XIV

The Thirty Years' War (1618–1648) nearly ruined Germany, while England was undergoing revolution and civil war. Spain, leading center of Counter Reformation and baroque, sank rapidly from the top to become a decadent, despondent, and second-rate power at this time. Italy, divided like Germany into numerous small states, lost its commercial prosperity and the glories of the Renaissance faded into a gentle glow. When Louis XIV came into his royal inheritance in 1661 he could note with satisfaction that France had no rival in Europe. United under a strong state, it found in Louis a magnificent actor capable of playing the part of Grand Monarch. Until checked by an unprecedented coalition of all the other states of Europe in the world struggle of 1689–1713, the Sun King's mighty machine of power dominated Europe politically, expanding France's borders and insisting upon recognition of her primacy. It so happened that at the same time French literature, science, philosophy, art, and architecture burst into glorious boom, too. So that, all in all, it is not strange that Voltaire looked back to this as the great age. Most Frenchmen always have.

It was at the age of Racine and Molière, whose drama is still "classic" for the French in the way Shakespeare and Jonson are for the English or Goethe and Schiller for the Germans; in general it was a time of the flowering of the French language, as English had suddenly realized its possibilities as an instrument of literature in Elizabethan times. Classicism was the rubric of this literature. With the establishment of political order and stability, it is tempting to suggest, the troubled and disordered baroque faded into a bad dream. It does appear that "absolutism and classicism have unmistakeable affinities" (R. W. Meyer): order, authority, unity. Certainly they met and blended in the era of the Grand Monarchy. Actually the rise of classicism began before Louis XIV, in the Richelieu years. Its principal prophet was Malherbe, a pedantic little man who won the day by imposing order on the chaos of the republic of letters. The language was to be purified, the canons of correctness laid down. Harmony, unity, order were the watchwords. Drama and poetry were required to obey the "rules." The era began when in 1636 Corneille had to defend his Spanish tragedy *The Cid* against the charge that it ignored the Aristotelian "unities" by not taking place within a single place and a single day. Thereafter Corneille kept within the rules. Racine, who followed him, gloried in them, and became the oracle of French literature. Richelieu created the *Académie Française* as official guardian of the proprieties as well as rewarder of respectable literary greatness. Louis XIV continued to encourage the arts and to use them in the glory of France (a kind of "cultural diplomacy").

Did he really understand them? The Sun King was a most unusual man, much as courtiers may have exaggerated his qualities. He possessed taste and intellect, was the friend as well as patron of Racine, Boileau, and Molière, helped Lully with his operas and made possible the great Versailles buildings with their gardens and sculpture. France was ready to burst into bloom, but Louis XIV did something more than preside with heavy dignity over this show. Whatever his faults, he stands in refreshing contrast to so many heads of powerful states who have been esthetic illiterates. He knew his art and literature and considered these among the foremost of his responsibilities. His taste, if severely classical, takes one of the first prizes among the politicians of history, at least this side of the Italian Renaissance.

In the time of Louis XIV, in the last third of the century, the great critic Boileau, the great dramatist Molière, and many painters and architects were foremost among those who showed that classicism could combine grace and decorum with wit, dignity, range. The orthodoxy of

Bishop Bossuet, expounder of royal absolutism, suited a court presided over by the king who above all other qualities had dignity and a sense of measure. Versailles was built; the great palace has a touch of the baroque, it has been claimed, in its attempt to overwhelm by sheer size and such effects as the giant staircase and the hall of mirrors. But its plan is severely rational in the classical manner. The gardens of Le Notre and the buildings of Mansart agree with the later paintings of Poussin in their severe simplicity, their studied rationality—the embodiment of harmony, dignity, grandeur.

Boileau was "the Newton of the arts." Reason gives us the science of art; there are proper rules for each genre. To the famous Aristotelian unities were added other precepts, all in the direction of clarity, economy, propriety, and objectivity. The mathematical interests of the period carried over into the arts; natural beauty, it was frequently explained, is geometrical, the irregular ugly. On the whole this esthetic attitude appreciated no novelties, was suspicious of innovations. The basic principles on which all art ought to proceed had been found out long ago. "The ancient Greek and Roman architecture answer all the perfections required in a faultless and accomplished building," thought John Evelyn, the English classicist; this truth had been corrupted by the barbarous Goths with their "congestions of heavy, dark, melancholy, and monkish piles," which was all that classical taste could see in the magnificent Gothic cathedrals. Now, through the work of such restorers of classical glory as Palladio (Italian late-Renaissance architect whose style was formal in the extreme), men were back on the right track. "An architect ought to be jealous of novelties," Sir Christopher Wren declared. Daring in its philosophy, the Age of Reason was to be conservative in its art. But both were based alike on reason and mathematics, law and order.

Indicative of this conservative spirit in the arts was the celebrated Quarrel of the Ancients and Moderns which broke out in 1687 when Charles Perrault (a brother of the famous architect) inquired poetically whether the writers of modern times were not as good as the ancients. This excited the scorn of the great critic Boileau, who found it scarcely believable that a Parisian in his right mind could disparage Homer and Virgil. Eventually Boileau admitted that the moderns were superior in some things; it was generally conceded that they had to lead in the sciences; but the victory lay with classicism and the "ancients" in regard to literature. An English "battle of the books," which drew in Jonathan Swift, paralleled this dispute, which dragged on for some years. While the Quarrel may have helped introduce portions of the Idea of Progress, it clearly revealed the deep respect for ancient models, and the belief that no new principles could be discovered for the arts.

As the quotations from Wren and Evelyn indicate, French classicism spread all over Europe, aided by French leadership in power and wealth. Charles II, the English monarch restored in 1660 following the civil war and Cromwellian dictatorship, had lived at the French court and molded his tastes there; he continued to be Francophile. The Restoration era represents almost the only time the English have ever taken their manners, morals, and canons of taste from a foreign country. The courts of the small German states became French cultural satellites. This cultural supremacy, unaffected by the wars the rest of Europe waged with France, extended into the eighteenth century when it was even more pronounced on the Continent, extending as it did into Prussia and Russia. Italian and German artists often came to France because the money and prestige were there. Paris was again, as in the epoch of Abelard and Aquinas, the intellectual capital of Europe; it was also the esthetic and social capital, the modern Rome and Athens put together. Visitors came there from all over Europe to gawk and, if lucky, mingle with the most civilized people of the continent in the *salons*.

Begun by the Marquise de Rambouillet earlier in the century, that unique French institution the *salon* provided a forum for writers, who mingled with the flower of French society in an atmosphere that encouraged good talk and good manners. The French aristocracy learned here to value a well-turned phrase more than a successful duel. This was at Paris more than at the court of Versailles, where the king was the center of an elaborate ceremonial cult that became pompous and stuffy. Dazzling ladies became the great hostesses at whose homes the *literati* mingled with the European aristocracy. (Because of the marriages of royalty and nobility, it was quite an international world.) Voltaire, in his memorable account of this era, declared that the greatest gift of the age of Louis XIV was "l'esprit de société": "a high and charming ideal of social intercourse and manners," as Matthew Arnold called it. "France is the country," Arnold added, "where the people, as distinguished from a wealthy refined class, most lives what we call a humane life, the life of civilized man."

Talk in some of the salons might secretly be bold: there were "libertines" who mocked at religion and perhaps even whispered against the king. But as yet this was not public. An old courtier of the next century recalled that they were silent under Louis XIV, they whispered under Louis XV, and under Louis XVI they talked out loud. Actually, there were a few whisperings under Louis XIV, but these did not disturb the outward spectacle of decorum and piety. Among Molière's delightful comedies many are rather ribald and a few pointedly satirical; *Tartuffe*, which makes fun of religious hypocrites, was suppressed for a time by Jesuit influence but finally allowed. A clandestine literature of pornographic sex circulated. But Molière also ridiculed excessively learned ladies (*Les femmes savantes*) and people who go too far in defying the conventions of society (*Le misanthrope*).

Compared to that of the eighteenth century, the Louis XIV taste was formal, grave, stately, even a bit ponderous. The court was pious, and by comparison with that of Louis XV, moral. (Louis XIV's mistresses were ladies of some distinction; in 1675 he dismissed one at the instigation of Bishop Bossuet; subsequently he married another.) The elaborate public ceremonies surrounding the king, from *lever to coucher*, reflected the delight in punctilious ceremony as well as the cult of sovereign power. "Centralized control of every sphere of life was characteristic of the rule of Louis XIV." And everyone knows that Louis XIV said, or was believed to have said, "I am the state." (The story is probably apocryphal.) Even literature and the arts were subject to official regulation. Here was an attempt to shape the entire cultural and intellectual life of a great nation into a single mold.

But we would be quite wrong to think of the Grand Monarchy in the image of an arbitrary despotism or a modern totalitarian dictatorship. In his Memoirs or *Instructions*, Louis and his councillors expressed their view of the monarchy: like Richelieu, they held up high standards for the king while assigning him unusual qualities because he stands at the pinnacle of society. Much of the rationale of Louis's state was drawn from the classical ideal, which was one of perfect symmetry, with everything in its place and no loose ends. The nation was conceived as a pyramid of which the king is the pinnacle; but he was a part of the whole order and in a significant sense subject to the laws which governed it. "Divine right" was mentioned, but the really vital ideas in the new absolutism derived from rationalist philosophy, that source of practically every political ideology in this age. We have seen that democrats, republicans, and authoritarians all elaborated theories based on "reason"; Overton, Harrington, Hobbes, Spinoza all thought they had founded their political opinions on science. So too in Louis XIV's state the influence of Cartesian rationalism was strong. It was pressed into the service of monarchical absolutism. What is more agreeable to reason than the stately pyramid, or that the state must have a head, one glorious sovereign to speak for its sovereignty?

Orthodoxy and Criticism

Most celebrated of the political theorists of this state was Jacques Bossuet, the bishop of Meaux. This very pious man agreed with the atheist Hobbes that only the yielding of full authority to a sovereign can end the anarchy which is man's natural condition. Monarchy is not the only possible legitimate form of government; but it is both the most natural and the most agreeable to God, thus the most rational. Bossuet distinguished between absolute government and arbitrary government. The latter is barbarous, the former civilized; arbitrary government is capricious and irrational, absolute is bound by reason. Thus it appears to Bossuet the king was bound by law, though not against his will, for by the very nature of his being the monarch of a civilized land in an age of reason he would use that power in a manner agreeable to reason. He was also bound by custom and respect for tradition. It would seem that "Bossuet's *Lieutenant de Dieu* is no Leviathan, whose power extends in terrifying uniformity over a mass of isolated individuals; his authority extends over the State and a complex hierarchy of subjects, to whom he is bound by a common respect for ancient customs and well-tried institutions" (Stephen Skalweit). Though Richelieu and Louis XIV greatly increased the power of the French monarchy, they never entirely breached the ancient structure of local rights and vested interests inherited from the Middle Ages; in theory absolute, the king was in practice limited by many ancient customs "as imperious in their operation as any laws" (Jacques Boulenger).

Bossuet's political writings were rather lacking in rigor and consistency, but he was a great stylist, author of numerous other works including a universal history,[1] and his position as almost the official apologist for Louis makes his writing significant. Tutor to the Grand Dauphin (heir to the throne), he exercised a personal influence on the king and though only a bishop was in fact the head of the church in France. He wrote against Protestantism and against quietism in the French Catholic Church, a prevalent form of Pietism preached by Mme. Guyon, and also against the Biblical criticism of the Oratorian, Father Richard Simon. In brief, Bossuet was the voice of orthodoxy. His eloquence (his favorite genre was the oration) impressed his contemporaries as dazzling. His political credo, that kings are answerable only to God, from whom they directly derive their power, put him at odds with *papal* orthodoxy. Bossuet was a Gallican, that is, one who would limit the pope's power both temporal and spiritual within France, placing that power in the French clergy whose overlord was the king. This was a leading issue in Louis XIV's reign. It was Bossuet who drew up the Gallican articles of 1682, a sharp attack on papal powers (the pope was declared to be not infallible; a general council of the Church was above him;

---

[1]Bossuet's *Discourse on Universal History* depicts the human past as the arena in which Christ's message was first prepared, then given and sent out into the world—a providentially determined history. It represents about the first significant effort to write general history since Augustine and was a tremendously influential work.

he could not interfere in France against the monarchy or the laws and customs of the realm).

If Bossuet was ponderously orthodox in his vindications of the royal power, the latter years of the Sun King's reign saw the emergence of a more critical spirit. Fénelon (another churchman, Archbishop of Cambrai), a possible precursor of the Enlightenment, wrote his *Télémaque* for the edification of the grandson of Louis XIV, who was expected to assume the throne; it contained some clear thrusts at Louis XIV's policies of "magnificence," which had involved France in costly wars and bankrupted the land. Fénelon's ideal state was a highly regulated one, like Plato's Republic, perhaps a communistic one; but it was one where the rulers avoid luxury and lavish display and do not wage war. The critical, sometimes satirical tone points toward Montesquieu and Voltaire and is unlike the solemn apologetics of Bossuet.[2] Something has gone wrong; and things did go wrong with the Grand Monarchy, which began so brilliantly and raised France to the peak of power and influence in Europe. Louis's pride and ambition caused him to be opposed in war by all the rest of Europe, which in turn brought France almost to her knees. The Sun King went down in anything but a blaze of glory; his death was cheered by all France.

Dominated by the classical idea of unity and symmetry, Louis XIV's state would tolerate no nonconformity. In 1685 took place that action which the historian Jacob Burckhardt described as "the greatest sacrifice ever made to the moloch of unity"—the expulsion of the Protestants (Huguenots) from France. France lost useful citizens, but the Grand Monarchy gained in symmetry. There were many others throughout Europe, inside and outside France, who deplored this act of pride and fanaticism and thought it foretold the downfall of the state. It may have cost James II his throne (revulsion in England against the act rebounded against the Stuart king's attempted policies of absolutizing the country on the French model). After this, the rivulets of criticism began to break through the monolithic unity of the state. Fénelon spoke of a power which had "no foundation in the hearts of the people," which made slaves rather than subjects, an idol with feet of clay.

Another significant figure of the later years of Louis XIV was Fontenelle, secretary of the Academy of Sciences, popularizer of science, proponent of the critical method, Cartesian rationalist, wit, and pamphleteer who was to live ninety-nine years and be the grand old man of the *philosophes* in the age of Voltaire. He harbored an aggressive dislike of "priestcraft," a trait for which the "deists" of the eighteenth century

---

[2]Nevertheless close study of Fénelon considerably modifies the older view of him as a premature *philosophe*. To mention only the most important thing, he was deeply religious, in a less dogmatic but more pietistic way than Bossuet.

were to be notable. In fact, this strain of religious skepticism or "libertinism" sustained a certain existence underground in France all through the century, its leading source being Montaigne along with the left-wing implications of Descartes, of a mechanistic universe, running itself without need of God. It had been too dangerous to say openly; for doing so, in Richelieu's time, men had suffered imprisonment. Fontenelle employed the tactic of disguise: his *History of Oracles*, under pretence of attacking pagan superstitions, contrived to suggest that Christianity, too, contained barbarous relics of the age of superstition. Fontenelle believed that any faith taken on authority was a stupidity, *une sottise*. Like other deists, he considered the existence of God a scientific certainty, but held this scientific or "natural" religion to be the enlightened replacement for an outmoded Christianity based on revelation. He was fiercely anticlerical, depicting priests as imposters and miracle-mongers, another deistic trait. In 1686 he revived the provocative discussion of a plurality of worlds.

To attack the religion was to attack the state, for the power of the monarchy rested on its alleged divine sanction and the Church was an integral part of the political and social order. While England broke ground toward religious toleration few on the Continent yet dared assert that religion and politics, church and state, could be separated. It is here, perhaps, that the versatile Pierre Bayle made his boldest forays. After being driven from France in 1685 during the persecution of the Protestants, Bayle settled in Holland and through his books (*Thoughts on the Comet, Critical and Historical Dictionary*) and his editing of a monthly literary magazine (*News from the Republic of Letters*) became well known throughout Europe. Schooled at the Jesuit College in Toulouse, Bayle had abandoned Catholicism for the Reformed (Calvinist) faith and taught at a Protestant academy in Sedan; but in Rotterdam his colleague Jurieu soon charged him with having abandoned all religion to become an atheist. This was scarcely true, but he had become outspokenly heterodox. His political polemics drew on him the ire not only of France but of King William III of England (William of Orange, of the United Provinces of the Netherlands), who caused him to lose his professorial post. Bayle must have been a gadfly indeed to earn the dislike of *both* Louis XIV and William III who were mortal foes engaged in a great war with each other! His embattled life ended at the age of fifty-nine in 1706. Practically all the next generation of *philosophes*, deists, and critics of society read and were stimulated by his daring speculations, especially the *Dictionary* (1697). (From Holland, books could readily be smuggled into France, eluding the censorship.)

To a lesser degree only than Newton and Locke, Bayle was an authentic pioneer of the eighteenth-century Enlightenment. Speculating boldly on basic questions, his particular interests were the problem of evil, providence in human affairs, free will, the relationship of religious belief to moral conduct, and religious toleration. He indicated sympathy toward the Manichaean or Gnostic heresy, that there is a separate principle of evil in the universe, and was fond of raising the reproach against Calvinism, or against any Christian position, that it made God the author of evil. Perhaps his best-known suggestion—the famous "paradoxe de Bayle"—was that the atheist might be a good citizen, since civic virtues have nothing to do with religion (and, as he was fond of saying, there are very few real Christians anyway). And in all areas, in accordance with his motto that "errors are none the better for being old," he tried to reexamine things, using high standards of factual accuracy and critical intelligence, a theme which the Enlightenment would eagerly follow. Bayle's extraordinary one-man job, the *Critical Dictionary*, is the most important predecessor of that famous Encyclopedia the *philosophes* were to erect as their chief monument some fifty years later.

The historian, Bayle wrote,

> . . . ought to be attentive only to the interests of truth, to which he ought to sacrifice resentment of injuries, memory of favors received, even love of country. He should forget that he belongs to any country, that he has been raised in any particular faith, that he owes his fortune to this or that person, that these are his parents or those his friends. An historian *qua* historian is like Melchizedek, without father, without mother, without genealogy. If one asks him, "Where do you come from?" he must answer, "I am neither French nor German, nor English nor Spanish, etc., I am a resident of the world, I am neither in the service of the Emperor nor of the King of France, but only in the service of the truth. . . ."

Though this rigorous ideal of careful and impartial scholarship might not be new, stress on it was to be a hallmark of the Enlightenment. Meanwhile Bayle's unorthodox speculations exerted as much influence as his high standards of historical accuracy and objectivity. We find the young Montesquieu writing a tract refuting the doctrine of damnation of the pagans, a point popularized by Bayle.

It was against Bayle that Leibniz wrote his *Theodicy*, for Bayle seemed to be skeptic and pessimist. He agreed with John Locke in disliking pretentious theorizing, in rejecting ancient authority and calling for a fresh look at everything, though he lacked Locke's determination to set up a clear, new standard of certainty (see pages 111–17). Bayle restated William of Ockham's belief that religion can have nothing to do with reason; our intellects can know nothing of that; it must be taken on pure faith if at all. Obsessed by the presence of evil in the world—suffering and cruelty fill the pages of history, Bayle well knew—he evidently rebelled at those who spoke of divine providence and benign necessity, whether Bishop Bossuet or Spinoza. His Calvinist training doubtless helped persuade him of the view that the flesh is sinful and this world a place of diabolical temptations. But he wished to rebel against this, not to accept it. Much of the Enlightenment's almost savage pessimism (see Voltaire's classic *Candide*), together with its equally fierce desire to strike out at evil and eliminate it, appears in Bayle.

Because of such as Bayle, Fontenelle, and Fénelon, France was ready to enter another era with the death of the Sun King in 1715. He left a country defeated in war, her bid for world dominion checked, though still the most powerful of European states, a country with exhausted treasury and discontented peasantry. But a long peace lay ahead and prosperity returned. The next king was an amiable weakling who could not inspire the respect that Louis XIV had commanded. The spirit of the age was to be one of criticism, satire, boldness, impiety, combined with a new kind of faith and hope, deriving from Newton and from science, in progress toward an ideal society in this life on earth. In brief, the Enlightenment was about to begin.

Men other than Frenchmen were to contribute to it, even in France. Chief victor in the wars of 1689–1713, England (now, having absorbed Scotland in 1707, better called Great Britain) was the land of Locke and Newton, the Glorious Revolution and parliamentary government, intellectual freedom, civil liberty, and a substantial degree of religious toleration. Its prestige was enormous, and even the great Frenchmen of the Enlightenment, Montesquieu and Voltaire, would borrow plentifully from English sources. Of all these sources, the most important single one was John Locke, whose book on human knowledge must next be considered.

Before temporarily leaving France, however, let us summarize its significance, under the great monarchy, for the intellectual world: it concentrated talents at one bright point, in and around Paris; it subsidized these talents and gave them the boon of the limpid, clear, mellifluous French language, which now became the international tongue of the scientists as well as the diplomatists of Europe. No other place in Europe or the world at this time was so fitted to be the world's intellectual and cultural capital as the French city. It combined the prestige that inevitably accrues to power with style, wit, and ideas. It provided the institutional setting (salons, academies) in an international atmosphere—Paris belonged to the world and not just to France. One could speak of the fading of Rome, associated with a clericalism outmoded during the Enlightenment; of the relative provincialism of London, along with a certain English indifference to ideas; of the still semibarbarous atmosphere of Berlin, not to mention Moscow. These latter places looked to France, their educated classes speaking and writing in French during the eighteenth century. So the stage was set for the Enlightenment, that movement which was so French and yet so cosmopolitan.

Restoration England

" 'Tis a pleasant, well bred, complaisant, free, frolic, good-natured, pretty age," a character in one of Wycherley's plays remarks. Puritanism was definitely *out* in England after 1660, and the most popular literary productions of the day, such as Samuel Butler's *Hudibras*, heaped scorn on it. Though, in 1668, Samuel Pepys confided to his famous diary that "the business of abusing the Puritans begins to grow stale, and of no use, they being the people that, at last, will be found the wisest," the reaction proved enduring against such aspects of Puritanism as republicanism in politics, the ban on the theater and other amusements, and theological Calvinism. It is well to remember that the sober and moral spirit of the Puritan epoch survived the reaction, returning more than a little in the eighteenth century and then triumphing in the nineteenth, and that even during the bawdy gayety of Restoration times the greatest poet was John Milton, a Puritan, while the book destined to perhaps the longest life and greatest number of readers was John Bunyan's *Pilgrim's Progress*. But the current fashion ran all in the other direction. Cromwell's bones had been dug up and scattered to the winds; King Charles II, the Merry Monarch, was back on the throne; his courtiers, fresh from French exile, dominated the scene.

The levity and vulgarity of Restoration England contrasts with the sedate dignity of Louis XIV France. The theme of classical elegance (it was "the Age of Elegance"), and the search for "a politer way of living" is evident in both countries, but in England there was an admixture of coarseness, revealed in the king himself: Charles told dirty stories and pursued common prostitutes in a way that made him something of a buffoon, despite his many virtues, his easy manners, his noble appearance. The Restoration theater needs no comment—that perennially delightful but shockingly immoral stage where

intrigue was plot, obscenity was wit.

There was no English Racine; this was no time for tragedy. And the plays of Vanbrugh, Congreve, and Wycherley are more uproarious and bawdy than those of Molière, less perfectly formed, though quite as witty. English adaptations of Molière, significantly, were made more earthy. In both societies it was the aristocracy and courtiers who set the tone, but the English (we may perhaps think of Squire Western!) lacked the French refinement. The chief English writer of the Restoration era was, however, John Dryden, whose skillful lucidity in classical couplets ushered in the eighteenth century—a versatile professional, a true artist, whose best talent was for satire. Dryden himself came to feel that the age was overrefined, in form not in content, and that it had lost strength and seriousness. He catered to the fashionable lubricity himself, not without some apparent distaste.

The "hardess and smartness" (F. N. Lees) of the Restoration mood is reflected in the cynical misanthropy of the Earl of Rochester, the notorious literary libertine. Rochester belongs with Montaigne, Hobbes, and, just a few years later, Swift, among those who have scarcely found human nature an edifying spectacle. A cowardly, greedy, lustful creature whose apparent virtues are only hypocrisies—thus does man appear to Rochester. This Hobbean view of man was to come under sharp attack in the happier eighteenth century. England during the Restoration (1660–1688) had yet to find her political happiness despite the tableau of court ribaldry. The Merry Monarch sat uneasily on a throne still unsure of its powers and its limitations. The fervent prayer of John Evelyn, that "God of his infinite mercy compose these things, that we may be at last a Nation and a Church under some fixed and sober establishment," was not to be answered until after 1688. England drifted through a period without overt civil war (until 1688) but not without severe disturbance. Bitter controversy became focussed on the exclusion of Charles II's brother from the succession (the former having no legitimate male offspring, though several bastards); Titus Oates raised a national hysteria against Catholics; there were plots, counterplots, executions; there was war, plague, and the great London fire. If the plague drove Newton to his farm and thus forever benefitted mankind, while some saw the fire likewise as a blessing in disguise, England had little success in war and Charles became the subservient ally of mighty France, thus betraying, as many thought, both the Protestant cause and her own national interest. Though courtiers might indulge riotously in sexual license, the nation as a whole had little to celebrate.

But the period was by no means all barren and frivolous. Charles, who spent so many hours worrying about whether he should visit Nell Gwyn, Mrs. Stewart, or the Duchess of Cleveland, had as one of his virtues a genuine interest in science, and thus was not wholly unfit to preside over the age of Newton. The Royal Society, which received its charter in the second year of his reign, brought together the Newtons and Boyles, under the inspiration of the Baconian philosophy. Poets such as Dryden and Cowley, public officials such as Pepys and Evelyn, joined in support of the scientific movement. It was still possible for people to believe in witchcraft—the last trials for this crime lie in the later years of the seventeenth century—but the scientific outlook was growing. Religion in general was not rejected, certainly, except by a few libertines, but it was being detheologized and defanaticized. Anything smacking of religious fanaticism or "enthusiasm" stood in high disfavor because associated with the revolution and civil war: was it not the excessively godly visionaries who had stirred men up to kill their king? The secret Catholicism of Charles, and the open Catholicism of his brother James who stood to inherit the throne, aroused alarm, but it was now common to put the papists and the extreme nonconformist Protestants in the same camp, because they were both foes of moderation and reason in religion. If the former allegedly appealed to blind faith in the Infallible Chair, the latter relied with equal unreason on the fantasies of the inner light. A sensible man knew the dangers of too much religion as well as too little. His major interests would lie elsewhere—if not in pleasure, then perhaps in science, in poetry or drama, in the new study of "political arithmetic" (Sir William Petty), or other useful arts.

With colonial ventures prospering under Charles, England, or at least some Englishmen, gained wealth. After the Glorious Revolution of 1688 she was able under William III to lead the coalition that defeated mighty France in the long war of 1689–1713. By uniting the whole country against him, James II, who succeeded his brother in 1685, inadvertently secured its future power and glory under the Constitution. The political debates accompanying the 1688 revolution have been already noted in the preceding chapter where John Locke's great political treatise is discussed. In fact the foundations of the eighteenth century, in England as well as in France, lay in this seventeenth century *fin de siècle*. It was the age not only of Newton and Locke, but also of the rise of the Whigs and the commercial interests, of religious toleration and rational religion, and of a new style in the arts.

This style was the neoclassical. Englishmen joined with Frenchmen in holding up to admiration the one true way in art, which the Greeks had first found, but which basically is right because "natural." This style was held to be simple, harmonious, lucid, elegant, and agreeable; it abhorred crudeness, gaucherie, pedantry, excessive passion, anything immoderate or lacking in balance. Architecturally, the severely classical style of Palladio, sixteenth-century Italian, was imported into England early in the seventeenth century by Inigo Jones, and then carried on, after some lapse during the confusion of mid-century, by Christopher Wren, who, born in the same year as John Locke (1632), seemed to most Englishmen a not unworthy third in the sacred trinity with Locke and Newton—and who, indeed, a sometime professor of astronomy, shared their scientific interests. Chief architect of the London *redivivus* after the great fire of 1665, builder of St. Paul's Cathedral, Sir Christopher bent the taste of England as few men ever have, and bent it toward the neoclassical. There remained, however, a baroque element in the later seventeenth-century style, manifesting itself in the other great architect (also playwright) of the period, John Vanbrugh, who built gigantic and unliveable mansions (Blenheim, built for the Duke of Marlborough but infuriating to Lady Marlborough, being the best known), had a taste for the Gothic and for medieval castles, and was not admired in the eighteenth-century. With his passing, the restrained, elegant, and sedate style of the eighteenth-century Augustan age came in, the age of Burlington and Kent in architecture.

So it was in literature, along with the other arts. Dryden and others accused the Elizabethans, Shakespeare included, of having lacked refinement, correctness, and order: they were jewels, admittedly, but jewels in the rough, with many impurities that must be removed to make the best literature. Nor could neoclassical taste approve the violent paradoxes and disorderly rhythms of the Metaphysical poets, John Donne and company. So the stage was set for the impeccably wrought, highly intellectual verse of the eighteenth century, when Pope will write rhymed essays and the gentle "pleasures of the imagination" will be celebrated. Gentility set in as the century began, when Jeremy Collier launched his celebrated attack on the immorality of the stage. The search for "a politer way" had suffered from the insolence of Restoration rakes; now the middle classes began to assert themselves. Purged of revolutionary Puritanism, they would make up much of the polite reading public that bought the works of Addison, Defoe, Pope, and others. One of the most significant features of the eighteenth-century literature was to be this emergence of a literary market, freeing the writer from dependence on aristocratic patronage. He might starve in Grub Street, but he might make a fortune like Pope; in any case he was the proud member of a distinct profession, not a fawning courtier or the lap dog of some noble.

And so began what a later historian, looking back across the French Revolution, called "the empire of opinion," chief hallmark, as he thought, of the Enlightenment. There was a public which bought and read books, and writers tried to please this public. The law of supply and demand had taken over in the realm of literature and ideas. To us a commonplace, no doubt, but it had never really been so before. Books had been written and published to meet an educational need, being used in limited quantities by scholars and students; or they were written to please some wealthy patron, usually king or noble. A substantial reading public able and willing to buy serious books scarcely existed before the later seventeenth century; neither did journals and newspapers with a popular circulation. These date from the early eighteenth century.[3]

Pope, remarkably enough as it may seem to us, made his fortune from translations of Homer. A sufficient tribute, this, to the neoclassicism of the day. The English named this "the Augustan age," in imitation of the silver age of classical letters. They aspired to the *juste milieu*, the spirit of moderation. In their polite refinement, English letters probably reflected much more of the Puritan influence than of the Graeco-Roman ethos, but at least they thought they were reproducing the ancient rule of reason in the arts. The progress of England from Restoration to Augustan was a progress toward refinement, gentility, and perhaps attenuation. Our age, Dryden reflected as the century turned,

> . . . was cultivated thus at length,
> But what we gained in skill we lost in strength.

But it was not in literature and the arts that England was to lead the world in the eighteenth century. Her greatest achievement and proudest boast was of the liberty that came to her at last after 1688—an ordered liberty, not a chaotic one, liberty *with* that "fixed and sober establishment" in state and church. It was this liberty that attracted Frenchmen such as Montesquieu and Voltaire, otherwise not much enamoured of British society.

There was another realm of English superiority, of course, one which was suggested by the name of Newton. And to the scientific and constitutional English influences on the Enlightenment was added the prestige of "the great Mr. Locke." Already author of the classic exposition of English liberty, Locke added further to his laurels when in 1690 he produced *The Essay concerning Human Understanding*. It came closer than any other single document to generalizing the basic principles of the new order that all Europe felt to be dawning with the eighteenth century.

Locke's "Essay Concerning Human Understanding"

The name of John Locke was preeminent along with that of Newton during the Enlightenment, and of all writings the former's *Essay concerning Human Understanding* has the best claim to be known as

[3]As is described in Joseph Frank, *The Beginnings of the English Newspaper 1620–1660*, (1961), English journalism put down some tender roots during the period of the Revolution, but these were torn out during Cromwellian and Restoration times; it remained for the post-1688 generation to find the soil in which a free press could grow.

"the manifesto of the Enlightenment." Viewed as an influence on an era, Locke was one of the most important men of ideas who ever existed, worthy to be ranked in that respect with Plato, Aristotle, and Augustine among his predecessors, and Rousseau, Marx, Darwin, and Freud among his successors. Like many great works of popular philosophy, his *Essay* can be subjected to criticism which reveals numerous apparent inconsistencies, but we would be misled by too formalistic an approach. The very inconsistencies of Locke were psychological advantages. Paradoxically, logically consistent systems of thought may be less believable than those which are not so consistent. It was one of Locke's assets that he mediated between philosophy and the common man in a remarkable way. "Had Locke's mind been more profound, it might have been less influential," George Santayana remarked. The same gifts of lucidity and trenchant analysis, combined with a sturdy common sense, that were evident in the political treatises showed up in this other, even more renowned work of the Englishman, in which he tried to make clear just how our minds work and what they should work on.

It was a consciously revolutionary work. The *Essay* wears an air of modesty, but it is false modesty, for Locke expected to sweep aside virtually all previous philosophy. At the beginning he set himself only the humble ambition of "removing some of the rubbish that lies in the way of knowledge." The right way to look at the matter is to first examine our minds before embarking on the road of knowledge, to see what kind of voyage it is they are suited for. If we find that we have only an earthbound vehicle there is no sense in planning a trip to outer space; and of course Locke does find that our minds are limited. If, however, we confine ourselves to what suits them, he thinks, we can build up a body of knowledge on this sound basis that will be certain and real. The solid foundation Locke finds is not Descartes's clear ideas but rather sense experience. Locke early launches an attack on those (presumably the Cartesians) who believe in "innate ideas." (In England, Lord Herbert of Cherbury was the best example.) Perhaps Locke had in mind Aristotelians also. It is hard to find anyone who held that men were born with actual "ideas," but both Aristotle and Descartes assumed an inherent rationality, an ability in the mature mind to assent to certain logical propositions *a priori*. But Locke seems to have assumed this too. The key to the issue may be found in Locke's claim that "there is nothing in the intellect which was not before in the senses"—to which, repeating Aristotle, Leibniz made the classic retort, "except the intellect itself." Locke believed, more or less consistently, that the intellect plays a passive role as a sort of court of registry for sense impressions. There is nothing innate in the mind, Locke thinks; it is a blank page, a *tabula rasa*, on which experience prints everything. "All knowledge is founded on and derives ultimately from sense . . . or sensation." Our most exalted ideas, the most complicated thoughts of genius, all go back to the simple building blocks of sense impressions. Simple ideas become complex ones as the mind adds them together.

The mind does have this not insignificant capacity of forming complex out of simple ideas, by "reflection," according to Locke. Yet one feels that this is a rather mechanical process, and some of Locke's followers were to make it explicitly so via the laws of "association," which determine how ideas are put together—suggested by Locke himself in a later edition of the *Essay*, developed further by David Hartley in England and the French amateur *philosophes*, Condillac and Helvétius, in whose hands it became a rather vulgar ridiculing of all "metaphysics." Locke was rather ambiguous on this point. If the mind does perform a creative task here, his empiricism is impaired. It has long been an obvious criticism of Locke that he smuggled in a good many rationalistic assumptions and thus was not a consistent empiricist, though he started out bravely by raising the banner of pure sense experience. His initial spirit, indeed the entire spirit of the *Essay*, was "in accord with the current distaste for vain speculation" (M. H. Carré). Wishing to expel all pretentious metaphysics and senseless speculations, Locke courted popularity among the hardheaded burghers to which class he himself belonged. It has been said that he represents the philosophical counterpart to Robinson Crusoe, that self-sufficient do-it-yourself man who sprang from the brain of Locke's contemporary countryman, Daniel Defoe. He wished to simplify and he wished to make practical; at the same time he did not want to be a skeptic. So he staked out the rather daring claim that everything was both simple and clear. But, he did not really stick to his empiricism rigorously. Our mind is a *tabula rasa*, he says, and everything comes to it from sensations. And yet, somehow, it has the facility of finding general laws, of attaining to "clear and certain" truth, truth of a mathematical order of certainty and clarity. Between Locke's empiricism and his rational clarity lay in actuality a logical hiatus, which Berkeley and Hume were to expose to view. Locke was sure that "the understanding has a native faculty to perceive the coherence or incoherence of its ideas and can range them right." It can reason. Is it then really a *tabula rasa*, getting everything from experience?

One of the ways in which Locke attempted to solve this problem was by the distinction between primary and secondary qualities of things, a distinction earlier introduced by Galileo, as we know. "Solidity, extension, figure, motion, number" are taken into our minds exactly as they are, Locke held; these qualities are essential attributes of things, really "there," and we perceive them as they are. The secondary qualities of color, sound, odor, taste, feel, are not in the objects but in our minds.

We get all our knowledge through the senses, Locke realized, and this raises difficulties. He sometimes almost realized that if we get knowledge only through our senses we can never have the certainty he claimed for his method. We are in fact left almost in hopeless skepticism. We know sense impressions, or our own "ideas," and these may well be knowable, but how can we know they correspond to what exists in the outer world? They are, on Locke's own analysis, not the *same* as the objects out there, and there is no guarantee that they are anything like them. An image on your eye retina is not the same thing as the thing you are looking at, and if we are to put all our bets on it for what we know, clearly this knowledge must lack certainty in the sense Locke meant when he said that our knowledge of the outer world is both certain and real. Paradoxically, Locke raised the severest of skeptical doubts in the course of his attempt to demonstrate certainty. The "direct copy" theory of perception, which assumes that what is out there is seized by the mind exactly as it is, came to seem naive to many philosophers after Locke. Between us and the object, Locke reminded us, lies the screen of our senses.

Very little thought is required to know that at least some of the perceptions we have are not "out there." A color-blind person makes us realize that color is dependent on our visual apparatus, for example. Borrowing the distinction between primary and secondary qualities from Galileo, Locke conceded this point for the latter but tried to save the former for objective knowledge. Berkeley was to show this distinction untenable: size and shape are just as "subjective" as smell and taste, when one thinks about it. All represent knowledge given us by our special sense apparatus, not known directly and immediately.

Other objections have been lodged against Locke. He is not rigorous in his terminology, something a great philosopher must be: thus, he uses the key word "idea" to mean both a sensory impulse from without and a notion within the mind, two different things. To the careful analyst, then, who reads Locke with the advantage of the acute criticism that came later, the English sage can seem like one of those writers who start out briskly with an air of "I'll clear all this up for you" only to bog down in difficulties and flounder to an inglorious finish. Promising to put all knowledge on a firm foundation, he really ended in a sort of despairing skepticism, or solipsism (that is, all I can know is my own mental world) —which were the positions reached by his two leading British successors, Berkeley and Hume. As Isaiah Berlin observes, Locke "ends by creating two worlds," the subjective one, which we can know and work with but which contains no guarantee of its objective truth, and the external world from which we are separated by the screen of our "ideas." This was far from his original intention.

But it is hardly fair to judge a thinker by what remains of him after several generations of critics have worked him over. In any case, there is no doubt but that countless persons felt in reading Locke that a revelation had dawned, the scales had fallen from their eyes, the empire of knowledge seemed born anew. A little robust common sense had kicked out all the obscure metaphysics, opening the windows and letting in the light. Observation, proof, science were the watchwords. The vain visions of the past were swept away, and philosophy, descending from heaven to earth, from mystery and obfuscation to fact and truth, became both useful and intelligible to every man. "The light of common sense has spread over Europe," the Enlightenment *philosophes* would say, and Locke, as Isaiah Berlin observes, almost invented "common sense." One sees in the inimitable Voltaire's satirical tale, *Micromegas*, how gleefully the *philosophes* accepted Locke as the only sensible, because modest, philosopher, exposing the pretensions of all the other schools. "It was his glory to free the world from the lumber of a thousand vulgar errors," Sterne had his Tristram Shandy exclaim. "He appealed to the experience and conscious knowledge of everyone, and rendered all he advanced intelligible," Bolingbroke wrote admiringly. Much later than that, in 1829, an American disciple paid tribute: "In the *Essay concerning Human Understanding* intellectual science appeared for the first time in a clear and intelligible shape, unmingled with the vain and visionary fancies which had previously disfigured it, and accessible to the plain good sense of every cultivated mind." The feeling of making a fresh start, by chucking overboard the ballast of unnecessary complications and tedious verbiage to get down to simple fundamentals, came from Locke.

Some romanticists who came after the Enlightenment and reacted against its weaknesses were prone to blame its esthetic insensitivity on Locke: He had taught men to ignore beauty, art, everything but the pedestrian facts. "It is the death of every religion, of every exquisite sentiment, of every sublime impulse," complained Joseph de Maistre. Locke did have much of the philistine in him. His biographer, Maurice Cranston, notes that when he visited the cathedrals of Europe, he was interested only in their measurements! In the eighteenth century the "man of Locke," virtually the man of the Enlightenment, was prudent, cautious, practical; he was Benjamin Franklin, a good soul and a useful citizen, perhaps a wit but seldom a poet, content to leave the sublime and misty reaches of experience alone, averse to speculating on ultimate questions because these are a waste of time. The "touch of cold philosophy" blighted poetry for Enlightenment man.

But during the eighteenth century men turned with relief to the Lockean method and found it fruitful in various directions. Liberating them from the old, it suggested new directions. Generally speaking, it meant what Pope wrote, "the proper study of mankind is man," not God. More specifically, the Lockean concept of the *tabula rasa*, the blank mind which experience can shape into anything, suggested the importance of education and raised the exciting vista of changing human nature itself —for the better, presumably—by improving the social environment. When Helvétius, later, announced that "The character of men originate in their external circumstances," he was extending Locke, no doubt, but it was a natural extension. Lockeanism joined hands with Newtonianism, too, in boosting the experimental, empirical method, in raising the stock of the practical sciences. It encouraged the confident expectation that this method could attain knowledge that was both "real and certain."

In all areas Lockeanism encouraged experimentation. In literature, those most struck by the *Essay*, like Sterne, were least likely to remain harnessed to the neoclassical proprieties. An enemy of prejudice and mental laziness, Locke resembles Francis Bacon, and perhaps Montaigne, in some shrewd remarks on human prejudice, error, and irrationality. To Locke, rational thought is of the highest importance:

> Temples have their sacred images, and we see what influences they have always had over a great part of mankind. But in truth the ideas and images in men's minds are the invisible powers that constantly govern them, and to these they all, universally, pay a ready submission. It is therefore of the highest concernment that great care should be taken of the understanding, to conduct it aright in the search of knowledge and in the judgments it makes.

But most men "seldom reason at all, but do and think according to the example of others," while others "put passion in the place of reason." And a third sort, though seeking to follow reason, lack "that which one may call large, sound, roundabout sense" and so go astray rather in the manner of Bacon's idol-worshippers: they ride a thesis or dramatize a theory. Let men get certain principles firmly implanted in their heads, having received them in childhood, and these become "riveted there by long custom and education, beyond all possibility of being pulled out again." Locke set the force of his robust common sense against prejudice of this sort, against emotional thinking and against authority, that is, "the giving up our assent to the common received opinions, either of our friends or party, neighborhood or country," a thing that "keeps in ignorance or error more people than all the others together." Here spoke the authentic voice of the Enlightenment.[4] Emancipated alike from meta-

---

[4]The quotations in this last paragraph are from a work of Locke's called *The Conduct of the Understanding*, which he intended as the last chapter to be added to later editions of the *Essay*, but which he never finished and which was published after his death along with some other fragments.

physics and authority, it would venture forth with the practical reason to extend the frontiers of real knowledge by independent thinking.

The *Essay concerning Human Understanding* spawned numerous controversies, as might be expected of a well-known book with a provocative thesis. To a certain extent Locke basked in the sunlight of his friend the great Newton, and like the scientist carried the day among up-to-date intellectuals with relatively little opposition. Yet there were critics. Bishop Stillingfleet of the Anglican Church found "Hobbism, skepticism, and infidelity" in Locke, believing that his radical empiricism would destroy Christianity by undermining all universals or general concepts. By 1713 Bishop Berkeley (to be considered later) had converted Lockeanism into immaterialism; prior to then, there were one or two others in this vein, for example, Arthur Collier. John Norris, in a work first printed in 1701, approached Locke from the point of view of the Christian Platonism so well established in England through the Cambridge school, with some influence also from Father Malebranche's modified Cartesianism. These were rather abstruse works, but Berkeley, at least, caught the eye of almost all educated people with his startling leap into sheer mentalism (nothing exists *except* ideas) from a Lockean foundation. Subsequently, David Hume showed the skeptical possibilities latent in Locke, and David Hartley developed the mechanistic psychology. The "way of ideas" introduced by Locke led variously to mentalism, to skepticism, and to determinism.

It also led to deism. This is treated in the next chapter. Bishop Stillingfleet had suspected that if one refused to accept any knowledge except that which is founded in sense perception, one would sweep away the grounds of belief in Christianity and perhaps all religion. Locke was charged with materialism: a disguised Spinozist, he ruled out any real knowledge of substantive qualities and in so doing implicitly ruled out God. William Carroll was one such critic, in addition to Stillingfleet, who foresaw the skepticism that was present here in embryo and would appear fully in David Hume. Locke himself was a pious, believing Christian, who thought not only God's existence but the Christian revelation susceptible of clear demonstration. But his method and outlook opened the way to doubts, joining with other influences in this direction, especially those of Bayle and Fontenelle, the French Cartesian rationalists.

Leibniz

Among those who disputed with Locke was the powerful thinker who exerted great influence not only on his German world but throughout Europe: Gottfried Wilhelm Leibniz. A scientist, he had disputed with

Newton the priority of the discovery of the calculus, an unseemly feud in which the fault was at least as much on the English side. The form in which subsequent mathematics embodied the calculus was to follow Leibniz rather than Newton. As to priority, it would appear they arrived at it independently about the same time, a thing by no means unusual in science. Leibniz published first, the secretive Newton having done his work in private. A philosopher, he debated with Locke and Samuel Clarke, and had his admirers even in France against the Lockean-Newtonian outlook. Leibniz was a profound and subtle thinker, and a difficult one; he was influenced deeply by Platonism, by scholasticism, as well as by the Cartesian and Spinozian philosophies which were exciting in his youth (he lived 1646–1716[5]), and he tried to make a synthesis of all of these. He was too metaphysical for most of the eighteenth-century *philosophes*, who on the whole found Locke's simple empiricism much more to their liking. Yet the power and originality of his thought could not be denied. His versatility expressed itself in many other activities and schemes such as organization of the Berlin Academy of Sciences, a plan for the reunion of the churches of Europe on the basis of a scientific theology, and another for the political reunification of Europe. He left behind many unpublished papers in which recent scholars have found evidence of a tremendously powerful mind, anticipating in some ways recent developments in the sciences.

Leibniz did not accept Locke's empiricism, pointing out that there are *a priori* truths, truths of pure reason which do not derive from sense experience and are more certain. That the sun will come up again tomorrow is a truth of a different sort than the proposition $2 + 2 = 4$. He made the rejoinder to Locke's "there is nothing in the intellect that was not before in the senses" by adding, as had Aristotle, "except the intellect itself." The empiricism of Locke contrasts with the rationalism of Leibniz; exactly this dualism and tension characterized eighteenth-century philosophy. Men turned to the observed, sensed, experienced fact, finding freshness and truth in this reality as opposed to the arid abstractions of past metaphysics. But at the same time they expected the facts to yield general laws, of the most exact nature; they took it for granted such generalizations would be forthcoming. Did they get the laws from the facts or did they make the facts fit the laws already derived from pure Reason?

Against Newton, Leibniz criticized absolute space and time, as well as the conception of matter as solid discrete particles; in this respect he

---

[5]Born in Leipzig, he grew up in an academic atmosphere, his father being a professor; attended the great universities at Leipzig and Jena; as diplomatic representative of the Elector of Mainz, visited Paris and London in the 1670s where he met eminent scientists and philosophers, also visiting Spinoza in Holland.

seems to anticipate extremely modern, Einsteinian conceptions. He also anticipated the twentieth-century invention of symbolic or mathematical logic. He was indeed a great mathematician.

Leibniz's own picture of the world was interesting but secured little support then, being regarded as purely speculative; today, it may not seem so fanciful. Leibniz declared the universe to be made up of "monads" which are tiny units of mind each of which mirrors the universe but does not interact with anything outside itself. Perhaps the most striking feature of this *is* that each monad is a "point of view"; each reflects the universe differently in having a different position. The monads were in part an effort to overcome Cartesian dualism; they were also a reaction against Spinoza's monism. Leibniz's is an extremely pluralistic universe, each of its tiniest components being different (which seems surprisingly modern—compare with Pauli's exclusion principle). At the same time each component is interrelated with every other in that no monad could be changed without changing every other. In this system there is a divinely preestablished harmony. Leibniz integrated scholastic arguments for the existence of God into this strikingly original picture of the world, influenced by the Cartesian science and the Spinozian philosophy and today seen as relevant to the amazing revelations of modern subatomic scientific investigation.

Most famous in the eighteenth century because of Voltaire's ridicule of it in *Candide* was Leibniz's "best of all possible worlds" optimism. There must be a sufficient reason for everything, Leibniz held, including even God's will. God selected this world from many possible worlds, not arbitrarily but for a reason. The world has its necessary laws and correlations; once a particular world was chosen, all things in it had to be as they are and have been, since everything is interrelated. God, in effect, willed every action of past history and all future events, as part of a pattern necessary to the whole structure. But God could have chosen to will many other "possible worlds." He chose this one because it contained the least possible evil. In every world, some evil must necessarily exist; in the beginning, God, His perfect brain functioning like some gigantic computing machine (we may conjecture), figured out which world would contain the least evil and created it.

One of Leibniz's last works was his *Theodicy* (1710), an effort to explain how it is that the evil we see is the least possible amount of evil. It had been stimulated by Bayle's pessimism. This substantial work treated a question that fascinated the whole eighteenth century. Rousseau's subsequent answer, that good must include free choice and thus involve the possibility of evil, is one of many considered by Leibniz. Perhaps his most prominent one is this: any *created* world is bound to be imperfect, imperfection being a necessary attribute of created being.

Only God is perfect. If we ask why he created any world outside himself, we can answer that existence, even imperfect existence, is better than nonexistence; or that the perfection of the world demands a hierarchy of being, the imperfect required to set off the perfect. As Leibniz wrestled with such problems, including that of free will (in man and in God), we are likely to feel he has lost himself in imponderable depths, and like Voltaire we may throw up our hands and point only to the real evil we can see about us.[6]

Those who think of Leibniz as propounder of misty German metaphysics and dubious dismissals of evil would do well to remember another side of this incredible genius: his practical technology. The eminent historian of science Giorgio de Santillana lists Leibniz's contributions here as including "aeronautics (he invented the name), acoustics, optical instruments, clockworks and planetariums, navigation, canals, steering devices, carriages, wheels, wheel bearings, and machine tools."[7] With Bacon, Descartes, Pascal, Huygens, and others of the great scientists of the century he shared a burning desire to convert theoretical knowledge into practical power over nature and did not neglect this as a field of labor. Here was the indispensable framework of that "industrial revolution" which was in reality no "revolution" at all but a long process of social, intellectual, and cultural change over several centuries; the decisive step was taken in the seventeenth.

Leibniz's system, including its optimistic rationalism, might excite the laughter of some but it contributed to the Enlightenment. It was not orthodox Christianity and aroused the deepest hostility of the German clergy. It was boldly speculative. Though Leibniz's "metaphysical rationalizations were quite contrary to the spirit of the Enlightenment" (N. L. Torrey) in some respects, disagreeing with its empiricism and materialism (instead of materializing the soul, one *philosophe* complained, Leibniz had spiritualized matter), in other ways it was not contrary to the Enlightenment and influenced it profoundly. Leibniz was at bottom a rationalist who tried to resolve the most profound moral problems by the use of his reason. He was also scientist and mathematician. Rather more conservative by temperament than most of the eighteenth-century *philosophes*, he did not like their destructive spirit when he saw it in Bayle and predicted, accurately enough, that such criticism would eventuate in revolution. Yet clergymen accused him of atheism, and he was undeniably close to Spinozism at times.

---

[6]Leibniz's was but the most famous of a large number of eighteenth-century theodicies; among others, one may mention William King's *Essay on the Origin of Evil*, much discussed in England in the 1730s and a leading source for that celebrated poem, Alexander Pope's "Essay on Man." The original Latin version of King's tract, the work of an Irish bishop, dated from 1702.

[7]*American Historical Review*, April, 1959, p. 625.

All in all, Leibniz like Locke made his contribution to the intellectual ferment of the century at the beginning of which he died. In eighteenth-century Germany the popular rationalist Christian Wolff perpetuated Leibniz's influence in a somewhat simplified and debased form. Germany was less ready for the Enlightenment than England or France. It was more pious and less inclined to free thinking, the most creative movement at this time being the religious Pietism centered on the University of Halle. Philipp Spener, a Lutheran minister, began in 1666 to try to infuse spirituality into a rather decadent Lutheranism; from these German reformers and mystics, including the earlier seventeenth-century figure, Jacob Boehme, John Wesley was to borrow a great deal when he began in the 1730s to try to revive the Church of England.[8] Leibniz suffered considerably at the hands of the conservative German clergy and found it difficult to publish his writings in his native country. It was in France that he attracted the most attention.

The French historian of ideas, Paul Hazard, called this period from about 1680 to 1715 a time of "the crisis of the European conscience." The ideas incubated in these years hatched and took wing in the eighteenth-century Enlightenment; what had been in the shadows emerged into the open; the speculations of a few "rare spirits" became familiar to all literate men. The generation which began with the thought of Hobbes and Spinoza and produced Locke, Newton, Bayle, and Leibniz could well claim to have fathered the Enlightenment. The critical spirit was born, along with scientific empiricism and a new outlook in politics and in the arts. It was the prologue to the eighteenth century.

[8]Boehme was a considerable figure; Hegel later said that he was the only original philosopher between Plato and himself. His mysticism unquestionably affected William Blake, Saint-Martin, and the eighteenth-century German pietists who influenced Goethe. Thus Boehme is an ancestor of romanticism, his influence being postponed until after the Enlightenment had run its course.

5

The Enlightenment:
Deists and "Philosophers"

It was time that a philosophy at once nobler and truer presided over the destinies of the human race . . . [than] that discouraging philosophy which regards error and corruption as the habitual state of societies. . . .

MARQUIS DE CONDORCET

*. . . Truth, by no peculiar taste confined,
Whose universal pattern strikes mankind.*

THOMAS WARTON

Deism

The seventeenth century had been an Age of Reason—impossible to deny that when one thinks of Galileo, Newton, Descartes, Spinoza, Hobbes and Locke and Leibniz. That is to say, more precisely, its major thinkers had striven to perfect a method of scientific analysis that was careful, rigorous, logical, and naturalistic in that it did not refer directly to supernatural causes. God was assumed to exist as an ultimate guarantee of an orderly universe, but one sought the laws of nature in examination and analysis of the phenomena themselves. "We are not to look into the Scriptures for the English constitution," one of Locke's Whig followers observed drily. Neither was it any longer possible to look into them for the truths of science. And, in fact, a few were even beginning to ask whether it was wise to look there for the truths of religion! One should not accept anything on authority, and if the Bible claimed to be the revealed word of God it would have to prove itself. The beginnings of serious Biblical criticism are to be found in the seventeenth century, most notably in Father Richard Simon's *Critical History of the Old Testament* (1678), which doubted the Mosaic origin of the Pentateuch in a way quite modern.[1] Further, if one could prove God's existence and discover the rules of morality by reason alone, of what use were these old Jewish tales? So a small number of bold and perhaps impious spirits were beginning to assert, usually *sub rosa*. And many others, not willing to engage in such shocking speculations, felt that Christianity would at least have to square itself with modern scientific reason. They were confident it could.

This tension between religion and science, theology and rational philosophy, was an old issue in Europe, as witness medieval scholasticism. The eighteenth century was in this respect another scholastic age, with some of the terms changed. It too tried to reconcile reason and Christianity, with a few willing to dismiss the latter altogether, some on the other wing ready to throw out reason to keep religion, but most hopeful of an accommodation.

Charles Leslie, at the turn of the eighteenth century, seized his pen to assuage the anguish of a lady who "had been stagger'd with the arguments of Deism, even to distraction." Was Christianity, she asked in horror, "but a fable," with "no greater ground to believe in Christ than Mahomet"? Leslie comforted the tender doubter with "A Short and Easy Method" of refuting the deists. Most, assured by the examples of Newton and Boyle, thought the deists could easily be confuted. But it was not to be so short and easy. The debate was just beginning in 1700, and hardly died down in England until 1740, by which time, as Bishop Joseph Butler remarked in the preface to another celebrated book against deism, "it is come . . . to be taken for granted by many persons that Christianity . . . is now at length discovered to be fictitious."

The critical spirit predominated. The more conservative complained in vain that nothing was sacred; God himself was put on trial; the Sacred Books were asked to present their credentials before the bar of Reason. The Enlightenment spirit, born between 1690 and 1730, expressed itself above all in this inquisitive skepticism that probed old myths and took nothing on faith. So it is logical that the most exciting debate of the Enlightenment was about religion, ranging those critical spirits who called themselves "deists" against the more orthodox Christians. It must immediately be added that equally typical of the Enlightenment, along with its bold criticism, was a faith of its own in something called Reason. Deists, as their name indicated, believed in a deity. They thought his ex-

---

[1]That this Roman Catholic priest joined the heterodox Spinoza and Hobbes in bold Biblical criticism reflects in part a desire of some Catholics to embarrass Protestantism, for it was the latter who held that "the Bible and the Bible alone" constitutes religion.

istence could be demonstrated rationally. They were not forlorn unbelievers wandering in a wasteland of doubt, as were some later agnostics and atheists, but true believers, in their own way.

The eighteenth century was not entirely an irreligious age. Deists and skeptics themselves were, after all, a minority, and the century produced John Wesley as well as Voltaire. But most of its intellectual leaders were not interested in speculation about ultimate ends and were weary of theological debates. There had been too much of that in the past. The age was one of the *secularization* of thought. "Religion, ceasing to be the master interest of mankind, dwindles into a department of life which it is extravagant to overstep," as R. H. Tawney wrote in *Religion and the Rise of Capitalism*. And R. G. Collingwood (in *The Idea of History*) has defined the Enlightenment as an endeavor to "secularize every department of human life and thought." Arnold Toynbee has reminded us that for most men at most times in history, religion *has* been "the master interest." But the Enlightenment rebelled against this habit. It was a century when many wanted to get rid of religion for all except the utilitarian purposes of underwriting the validity of secular science, and of securing social morality.

John Locke, in addition to his other famous works, was also the author of a book called *The Reasonableness of Christianity*. A pious man, in his way, he seems to have been led to undertake his famous *Essay concerning Human Understanding* by a desire to know how far we may have certainty in matters of religion. At the time he wrote, there was in England a general turning away from the theological squabbles, the sectarian fanaticism and the violence of the Revolutionary period; "enthusiasm" of all sorts fell into disfavor. The keynote of the hour was moderation, and the moderate revolution of 1688 reenforced it. Yet the dominant classes in eighteenth-century England had no desire to encourage atheism or any radical unorthodoxy in religion, if for no other reason than that Christianity was still widely felt to be the buttress of morals and therefore of political society. (The iconoclastic Pierre Bayle, writing from Holland, caused a scandal at this time by arguing that an atheist might be a good citizen; few respectable people agreed with him.) The hour was ripe for a more moderate way in matters of religion, in which a defanaticized Christianity could be shown to be nothing more than good solid reason, or "common sense."

To this end wrote the Anglican Latitudinarians including some of the Cambridge Platonists, a group we have already mentioned in connection with their wish to play a mediating role between religion and science; from about 1700 to 1720 a leading disciple of this school was the Anglican scholar and philosopher Samuel Clarke. Within the Church of England, Latitudinarians prevailed against the High-Church element, suspect as Jacobite-Tory after 1688 (followers of the deposed or abdi-

cated Stuart line). Latitudinarians resembled the early advocate of toleration, Castellion, in urging that the articles of faith ought to be made "few
and plain," with a minimum of dogma, a maximum of Christian morality, less "enthusiasm," and more good works. Theologically, Calvinism
went out of style as too extremist and perhaps revolutionary; Arminianism—the milder, free-will, moralistic position of the Dutch Remonstrant
to whom reference was made earlier—became popular. The nonconformist groups—Presbyterians, Quakers, Independents—both lost in popularity and toned down their own doctrinal zeal.

Locke, therefore, was only one voice among many raised in behalf
of a milder, rational Christianity. Persecution had become obsolete. With
the ending of the Licensing Act in 1693, there began in England an era
of press freedom which was scarcely impaired throughout the eighteenth
century, until at the end of it the storms of the French Revolution did so.
Christianity was to be submitted to the test of free discussion in an age
of reason; its votaries, including Locke, believed that it could pass such
a test triumphantly. The belief that nothing in Christianity is contrary
to reason (though there may be some things *beyond* reason unaided by
revelation) was fairly standard Christian belief; certainly the medieval
scholastics had held it. In the eighteenth century, "reason" was a term
more likely to connote Newtonian science than Aristotelian philosophy,
and the favorite argument in favor of religion was, for a long time, that
the orderliness of nature as revealed in its majestic laws presents overwhelming evidence in favor of an intelligent Creator, and that this Creator provides the constant framework for the operation of those laws.

Much was made at this time of the agreement of Christianity with
natural morality, both Locke and Samuel Clarke claiming that ethics was
or could be an exact science whose precepts corresponded admirably to
those of Christianity; while Lord Shaftesbury, an admired and much-
read essayist, backed the theory of an innate *moral sense* (or what
amounted to this) in men, source of the natural religion. Reason invaded
ethics; men were no longer content to accept the moral creed on Scriptural authority, but must prove that it rested on reason. They might or
might not hold that it rested on reason *alone*. Rational Christians, quite
orthodox, would say that reason confirms revelation; the bolder would
suggest that reason supplants it. It was in the two zones of morality and
Scripture that the debate centered. Holding that reason may know the
truth about God and the moral principles, deists counterattacked Scripture by pointing to its inconsistencies and absurdities. Of all the disputes
to which free discussion of religion gave rise, Biblical ones proved the
most embarrassing to the devout. For the text of Scripture abounds in
difficulties and uncertainties.

In brief, the offer to submit Christianity to the test of reason began
a series of disputes in which a fairly small number of unorthodox Chris-

tians or anti-Christians made grave troubles for the orthodox. Between about 1690 and 1730 a good percentage of the books published in England related to the trinitarian controversy or the "deistic" one, with some other assorted questions concerning the Bible thrown in. In regard to the first, those who argued that the Bible and/or "reason" afford little support to the conventional doctrine of the Trinity were able to make out a strong case; the controversy split both the Nonconformist and Anglican churches. The antitrinitarians thus dealt a severe blow to "orthodox" Christianity, for the trinitarian position had been a pillar of orthodoxy in virtually all Christian churches of the West ever since the famed Council of Nicaea at the very beginning of the Christian era (325 A.D.). Few if any of the antitrinitarians were anti-Christian. But in their wake came the deists, some of whom undoubtedly were.

Deism was the position that reason alone, without revelation, is sufficient to bring us to a right understanding of religion and morality. Deists must be distinguished from those who, like Locke, Clarke, and Shaftesbury, had said that Christianity is consistent with reason, without meaning that we can dispense with the former and use only the latter. It is quite possible to argue that these Christian rationalists opened the door to deism and infidelity, inadvertently. But there is a large distinction, surprisingly overlooked in some accounts of this movement, between believing Christianity is rational and believing it is unnecessary. The latter defines what was called deism in the eighteenth century.

Usually the deists, including John Toland, Matthew Tindal, and Anthony Collins, paid tribute to Christian morality, and to Christian concepts of God, though they sniped at aspects of Christian doctrine; they said that this fine religion is no other than the natural religion available to the unaided reason of all men. No special revelation was necessary to promote it; to believe that is Jewish superstition. Christianity had been corrupted by this irrational Hebraism, and also by Greek metaphysics, so that it contained many impurities accrued through the centuries. But Jesus himself had been an excellent moral teacher who taught substantially the same ethical precepts found in Confucianism, Mohammedanism, Stoicism, or any of the great world creeds. At bottom, in all that matters, these are alike, and this is because all men have the same rational faculties or perhaps innate moral sense. (The deists were not all of the same mind in details.) Christianity, to quote the title of a deistic book, is a "re-publication of the religion of nature"; it is "as old as the creation." Christ appears as a combination of Newtonian scientist and homespun philosopher who derived his moral teachings from reason alone.

Shaftesbury and Francis Hutcheson, a Scottish professor, postulated a moral sense, related to the esthetic sense, which though not "innate" can be developed from basic tendencies in human nature. It leads to disinterested benevolence. Shaftesbury and Hutcheson were concerned to refute Hobbes's view of man as essentially egoistic, though they did not deny a place to self-interest. Shaftesbury was an elegant writer whose essays were much admired and contributed not a little to the eighteenth-century educated Englishman's picture of the well-bred gentleman.

But Bernard de Mandeville shocked the public by arguing, in his *Fable of the Bees*, that selfishness conduces to the welfare of society: "private vices are public virtues." Luxurious living, for example, keeps the economy going, and wise statemen govern by harnessing men's baser instincts. Mandeville ridiculed Shaftesbury's genteel do-gooder with a robust cynicism that annoyed but stimulated. This ethical debate, which had other offshoots, was a ramification of the deists' search for standards of morality independent of religious authority, rooted somehow in "nature" or in "reason." While Locke had been content to leave morality to the authority of the Bible, the eighteenth-century British moralists were not; the "parade of reasoning" about matters hitherto reserved for authority, which so alarmed conservatives, marched freely through the domain of ethics. Could one discover a code of conduct by the use of the unaided reason, one that could not fail because clearly discernible in "nature?"

There were many absurdities in the deist position and it never commanded the allegiance of first-class minds in England. Conyers Middleton and especially David Hume had, by mid-century, shown how wholly unsupported by the facts is the deist position that there is a natural morality or a natural religion, monotheistic and enlightened, which all men, even savages, perceive by the gifts of their reason. Bishop Joseph Butler, in a thoughtful and long-celebrated work called *The Analogy of Religion, Natural and Revealed, to the Constitution and Course of Nature* (1736), made it luminously clear that one does not find clear moral principles in "nature." But in a negative sense the deists and other miscellaneous critics of orthodox religion had done a great deal of damage. The whole dispute, giving rise to hundreds of books (the vast majority by more or less orthodox churchmen), tended to cast doubt on the certainty of Christianity, in the sense of any one accepted, orthodox creed; most people probably decided that so much disagreement among the learned meant that one should simply ignore theology. The deistic writers, who were shrewd propagandists, while they failed to establish their positive creed, perhaps succeeded in what may have been their chief intent, to embarrass and discredit traditional Christianity.

English deism passed beyond the waters, to become more famous when it was put into the epigrams of Voltaire. While the British Enlightenment carried on with the imposing figures of Berkeley, Hume, and Adam Smith, to whom we shall return, it was in France that this movement of the mind won its greatest successes and attained its greatest fame. The extent to which the French *philosophes* learned from the English should not be forgotten: both Montesquieu and Voltaire were Anglophiles, Newtonians, and Lockeans. Voltaire was directly indebted to the English deists. One of them whom he met early in his career was the exiled Jacobite, Lord Bolingbroke, one of the deistical writers. German illuminati, too (see Lessing), looked to England as a source of "enlightenment." But so far as concerns deism, France had a certain tradition of this sort too; freethinking had followed in the wake of both Montaigne and Descartes. Descartes's friend Father Mersenne had felt compelled to write a tract against *The Impiety of Deists, Atheists, and Libertines of This Age*. Father Simon and Spinoza had pioneered in critical studies. Fontenelle's work had been noted. Voltaire as a young man discovered the shockingly Epicurean philosophy of the "libertine" Abbé de Chaulieu, proclaimed and practiced in Paris.

But not much of this had been able to see the light of day and circulate freely. Only in England, at the beginning of the century, were thought and publication free. There one might read increasingly bold attacks on the authenticity, credibility, consistency, and even the morality of Scripture—attacks which scandalized many people, but were not suppressed. The English deists had ushered in a century of unprecedented boldness in questioning every dogma, every received opinion. If God himself could be put on trial (as someone said of the deistic debate in England), what was sacred?

In England, the 1730s brought a partial reaction against the wave of "infidelity" that had damaged Christian orthodoxy in the 1720s, during the unitarian and deistic controversies. Bishop Berkeley, who wrote against the "minute philosophers" or pygmy atheists, was one distinguished member of the reaction. So was Bishop Butler, whose book has been mentioned. Of the others, the most notable were the pietistic mystic, William Law, a religious writer of real power, who had been led by the protracted argumentation to abandon rationalism in religion altogether, and John Wesley, probably the greatest Christian of this century, founder of the evangelical movement in England. The powerful preaching of Wesley, directed at the lower classes and frankly emotional, shocked most respectable Englishmen, whether Whig or Tory, high church or low, as much as deism did. Methodism was disreputable, and few outside the wretched poor would have anything to do with it for a long time. It was of the highest importance for the future, but it outraged every instinct of the Age of Reason. The respectable upper and middle classes in Augustan England did not wish to be atheists or deists, yet they deplored all religious "enthusiasm" and were fond of a devitalized low Anglicanism, or unitarianized Puritanism, which asked little of them except the bourgeois virtues. Unitarianism, Erasmus Darwin remarked at the end of the century, was a featherbed for a dying Christian. Wesley, and later the evangelical Anglicans, believed this to be so, as did Jonathan Edwards in the American colonies of Britain. They feared that Christianity was becoming secularized and reduced merely to a code of morals. Educated people were beginning to disbelieve the Biblical tales. Wesley and Edwards were great men but they had little luck in turning back this tide of laxity, which fed on prosperity and complacency, as well as on new knowledge and ideas.

Deism took a sharper turn in France than it did in complacent Whig England. The clergy, there, was much more a part of the privileged order, with vast economic power, a monopoly of education, and a strong influence on politics. It was also likely to be more reactionary: whereas the compromising Church of England bent before the deistic storm, the great religious orders in France did not. Victorious early in the century their foes the Jansenists,[2] the Jesuits tended to hold the upper hand from 1700 to 1760. Flexible in some ways, the Society was not apt to be on matters of dogma and fought the "libertines" furiously. Religious controversy throughout the noonday of the Enlightenment— 1730–1760—was much more acrimonious in France. In Voltaire and Diderot, deism lived on as an integral part of the great French *philosophe* movement.

In 1764, Voltaire was still repeating the deism he learned in his youth, and his "Profession of Faith of the Theist" of that year in his *Philosophical Dictionary* (he had come to prefer "theist" to "deist" though the idea was the same) may serve as a recapitulation of the deistic credo. God exists. He is a remote deity who probably does not concern himself directly in the affairs of men. But it is good for the people, at least, to believe that he rewards virtue and punishes sin. There is a universal, original, primitive religion, simple and rational. All religions derive from this same source. Socrates, Mahomet, Confucius, Jesus—at bottom they all held the same universal religion of nature. It is graven in every heart; its injunctions might be reduced to these, "Worship God and be just." Priests and obscurantist metaphysicians corrupted the simple message of Jesus so that it became incomprehensible, and then they persecuted people on the basis of their mumbo-

[2]A papal pronouncement condemned Jansenism, for which, it may be recalled, Pascal had fought; the great Jansenist center at the convent of Port-Royal was destroyed. Jansenism did not entirely cease to exist, nevertheless, and may be found playing a strong part in the history of the period; it was important in the French *parlements* and their opposition to the crown.

jumbo. But when these false guides are overthrown, tolerance will prevail. Priests are probably unnecessary; however, a public church is a convenience and under the guidance of the philosophers God should be worshipped in an orderly manner. This reformed deistic church will promote good citizenship and brotherly love. Such, in outline, was the position of many of the eighteenth-century "philosophers," who like the sage of Ferney thought that a new day had dawned for mankind, whose light was "common sense" and simple lucid truth.

One should stress, again, the firmness with which most men of the Enlightenment believed in God, along with the scorn in which they held orthodox Christianity. There were some atheists, later in the century, but these were scarcely typical. More representative was d'Alembert, the French philosopher, scientist, and encyclopedist, who dreamed like Descartes of finding the single Law of Nature, one great ultimate principle which would reduce all phenomena to order. D'Alembert thought that such a law would be the final glorious proof of God's existence, testifying to his wisdom and grandeur. Atheism leads to despair, or is a product of it; the Enlightenment was optimistic. Its God had nothing in common with ancient myths, which were said to be unworthy of him; in being the God of the physicists and mathematicians, he took on the greater magnificence in their eyes.

It seems worth repeating that one of deism's most striking contradictions, on which it perhaps was impaled, was that implicit in its extreme rationalism, which led it to affirm "natural" religion yet deny that most men were capable of it. Spinoza had preceded Voltaire in this: the mass of people are not rational, must be led by their passions, hence need religion. "Il faut une religion au peuple," but not to the "philosopher." Deists alleged that all men have within them the light of reason enabling them to perceive all necessary religious truths without the unworthy crutch of revelation; but, on the other hand, almost all of them added that in fact most men do not have such ability, only the enlightened few do. To reconcile the contradiction they were driven to assert (a typical deistic utterance) that a conspiracy of priests had corrupted mankind and kept them in bondage. But often they conceded that many men would *always* have to be led by their irrational hopes and fears rather than by their reason. And then they might even urge, as did Benjamin Franklin, that it would be wise to conceal from the people the secret that their faith was not literally true. Perhaps Christianity presents in metaphorical form the same truths the philosopher clothes in reason—a proper Christianity would certainly do so—and so is a great instrument of good. Franklin observed that he came to think that Christianity though perhaps not strictly true was certainly useful, while an outspoken deism while true was not useful. It was a path that Voltaire himself may be said to have followed. The deists reasoned their way into silence and ended back in the camp of orthodoxy.

Voltaire and Montesquieu

We must return to describe the great age of ideas that arose in France during the *philosophe* period, the epoch of Voltaire, Montesquieu, Rousseau. The death of Louis XIV in 1715 produced in France a feeling of the end of an era, and liberation from the hand of solemn authority. The *salons* and the brilliant men of letters, accepted into high society where they traded *bon mots* with the aristocracy, were legacies from the seventeenth century; but now a lighter note creeps in, and a more critical one.

One of the first signs of the new spirit was a sprightly book by the Baron de la Brède, better known as Montesquieu. The *Persian Letters* were printed in the Netherlands, a convenient place for publishing books too dangerous to issue in France, thence of course to be smuggled across the border. This work which appeared in 1721 turned out to be one of the great literary successes of history. It capitalized on the new public awareness of the lands of the Middle East. European interest in both China and the Islamic lands was renewed toward the end of the seventeenth century stimulated by travellers' accounts and by translation of some literary works from these countries. (The deistic discovery of an alleged universal natural religion owed something to this smattering of knowledge about Confucianism and about Mohammedanism that had recently reached Europe.) The young Gascon noble appears to have owed a large debt to the Italian Giovanni Marana's *Letters of a Turkish Spy* (*L'Esploratore turco*) which preceded his book by some thirty-seven years. The Enlightenment was to be an age of satire. (Already on the European scene was Jonathan Swift, the Irish wit and critic of society, whose *Gulliver's Travels* followed Montesquieu's work by five years.)

In Montesquieu's book two Persians visit Europe and pass comment on its curious customs, comparing them to their own, in letters to each other. The book's popularity must be put down to its frequent excursions into such captivating subjects as the culture of the harem, but it was also a work of serious social criticism. There were some rather bold criticisms of identifiable European potentates living or recently dead, such as Louis XIV, as well as some general political observations reflecting an interest in Hobbes, Locke, and the social contract; there were also strongly anticlerical notions—which Montesquieu, all his life, entertained and which are typical of the mood of the Enlightenment.

Monks are dervishes, the pope is a wizard, religious rites are superstitions, from which the moral is drawn that only a good life counts and all the various religions of mankind are of value only insofar as they conduct to it; disputation about theology is absurd and toleration is the only sensible rule. The *Persian Letters* contained much deism, along with an interest in the study of comparative civilizations and of political institutions, such as led Montesquieu to write another and greater work more than twenty-five years later.

The book was a morning portent of the scintillating French Enlightenment, that witty and serious, critical and embattled age of which Montesquieu is one of the immortal leaders. He was to be surpassed in fame, literary fecundity, and sparkle by at least one, whose career had already been launched in the early days of the post-Louis XIV regency —the great Voltaire.

The young Voltaire was a wit and man-about-town whose brilliant conversation and charming manners made him the darling of fashionable Paris society. A successful playwright in his twenties, the world seemed this young man's oyster, despite the scrapes he got into either for amatory or political reasons. In 1726 he went to England on the occasion of a row he had gotten into with the Chevalier de Rohan-Chabot over an actress, Voltaire (or Arouet, as his real name was) being then thirty-two. According to many accounts, this visit to England for a period of three years changed Voltaire's life; previously he had been lacking in serious intellectual purpose but now he found it. While he liked neither the English food, climate, nor society, all of which he found to be about equally dismal by comparison with the French, he was deeply impressed with English liberty, as shown especially in the deistic controversy, and above all with the teachings of Newton and of Locke.

Actually the story is not quite so simple. Voltaire had amused himself and the town with his epigrams and his adventures before the English experience; he continued to do so afterwards. He had not entirely lacked seriousness, and he encountered English thought through the exiled statesman, Lord Bolingbroke, as early as 1719. He had received an excellent education from the Jesuits, whom he long admired; he had read Bayle, and hobnobbed with those in France who as "libertines" secretly mocked Christianity. His first known writing (1713) was a treatise on the problem of evil, and his first important play, a tragic drama on the theme of Oedipus, presented a challenging and serious idea—an attack on the stern and vengeful God of Calvinists and Jansenists.

Nevertheless, there is something in the view that the sojourn in Britain was a landmark in Voltaire's life. Upon his return he settled down to work more seriously. He became a missionary to the French on behalf of Locke and Newton. He was of course not the only apostle of this sort. His rival in love and science, Maupertuis, attached himself to the same cause, and if learned Newtonian ladies were soon refuting Cartesian savants the popularity of these two amorous philosophers may be held partly responsible. Voltaire was converted to a serious mission, to the study of mathematics and the writing of philosophy. He settled down at Cirey with his mistress, an intellectually gifted woman, the Marquise du Châtelet, and they worked. Voltaire became very rich; to his other talents he added a shrewd business sense, a "talent for high finance" (Nancy Mitford). (Investing shrewdly and always collecting his interest, Voltaire also gave away large sums to friends or even to people he did not know, of whose misfortune he had learned). He lived in luxury at Cirey and conducted far-flung business operations through his agents; but at Cirey a routine of reading and writing was adhered to.

With this conversion of Voltaire to a life of "philosophy," and with the publication of his *Lettres philosophiques* (*Letters on the English*) in 1733–1734, the Enlightenment may be said to have been officially launched. In 1736, expeditions to Peru and to Lapland, the latter led by Maupertuis, brought proof of the Newtonian theory, the question being whether the earth was flattened at the poles, as it indicated, or not, as the Cartesians claimed. The results, Voltaire quipped, flattened both the earth and the Cartesians. This is not to say that the battle of Newton against Descartes was finished. Voltaire's enemies, who were numerous, ridiculed him for his book *Elements of the Philosophy of Newton, Popularly Presented*, which he had difficulty getting properly published (1738), and he gloomily remarked that "in France one has to believe in the vortices to be a good citizen." Still, this was largely a prejudice, made up of French national pride. Mme. du Châtelet, to whom, one suspects, Voltaire was attached as much for her knowledge of mathematics as for her physical charms, took over this area of thought at Cirey and later published a better exposition of Newton than Voltaire's, though she had a liking for Leibniz of which Voltaire did not approve.

With Prince Frederick of Prussia, soon to be King Frederick and then Frederick the Great, Voltaire, in 1736, began his correspondence and friendship—another great landmark of the Enlightenment years, the era of the *philosophes* and their friends, the would-be philosopher-kings.

While Newtonian science and Lockean philosophy represented a cause close to the hearts of the *philosophes* at all times, Voltaire could not fail to include a vein of social criticism, even more barbed and open than the veiled allusions of Montesquieu's *Persian Letters. The Lettres philosophiques* omitted no opportunity to contrast France unfavorably with England, the land which had produced not only Newton and Locke but also freedom, a land whose useful and virtuous citizens be contrasted with the idle and sybaritic French aristocracy (a commentary which comes somewhat strangely from Voltaire, in view of his own previous existence). Voltaire, who seldom could refrain from letting his pen run away with him, so offended the French in this work that he again had to retire to an outlying district. But the mildness of the punishment is to be noted. So far from enduring merciless persecution, the critics of government and society in the eighteenth-century France usually had at most to fear exile to some provincial country house. While under the ban for his *Lettres*, Voltaire actually made merry for a time at the Duke of Berwick's Army headquarters on the eastern frontier, where a small war was then going on (eighteenth-century wars generally disturbed few of the amenities of life). Even if writers were sent to the Bastille, as Voltaire once had been earlier, they were given sumptuous quarters and treated virtually as guests of the king—a most civilized sort of confinement. "Singular prisons," remarks a French historian, "where one is imprisoned without a trial, but where one could write books which were to shake the foundations of the social order"! While Voltaire chided it for falling short of the freedom enjoyed by Englishmen, the French government through most of the eighteenth century really had no desire to persecute its men of letters and at most subjected them to inconveniences. Nevertheless, the *ancien regime* with its train of stupidities and evil, ill-led by the lazy, weak-minded Louis XV, was to receive many a barb from Voltaire.

By 1750 Voltaire had become middle-aged yet his fabulous career still had many years to run, and some of his greatest works (*Candide*) and crusades (the Calas affair) lay ahead; he would never be tame nor his pen ever still. He was now a member of the Academy, as well as official historian to the king with a residence at court if he chose (of course he did not); he was capable of writing panegyrics to the king. He was an international institution and his plays, mediocre though they might sometimes be, automatically were sell-outs. He received a medal from the pope (Benedict XIV), with whom he was on good terms (Benedict was something of a *philosophe* himself, to be sure). He secured *lettres de cachet* himself to be used to silence his foes—rather an inversion of what is popularly supposed to be the case. He continued to exchange compliments with Frederick the Great, and soon began to do so with the Empress of Russia. The French public itself was amused by but perhaps grew a bit weary of his constant quarrels, intrigues, and love affairs. After the death of his mistress and fellow Newtonian, the extraordinary Mme. du Châtelet, in 1749,[3] Voltaire lived for a while in Potsdam with Frederick, quarreled with that equally volatile genius, finally settled down with his niece (also his mistress) at Ferney just across the border from Geneva, Switzerland, about as far from Paris as one can get in France. There he spent virtually all of the rest of his life. He never stopped writing and remained the very incarnation of the Enlightenment movement, a role certainly not diminished by the famous Calas case, which made him a symbol of opposition to intolerance and religious bigotry. We shall return to him again. But he now shared the stage with younger men.

Montesquieu, too, made his last and greatest contribution in 1748. *The Spirit of Laws* was a book he had worked on for at least a dozen years and which represented his *magnum opus*. It has been called the first really scientific approach to government and politics. It claimed to be a systematic treatise, empirically based, on the laws and customs of all peoples, and thus may be seen as the pioneer work in sociology, too; while Montesquieu made some contributions to the embryonic science of economics. (The social sciences were well mixed up together in their infancy.) Hobbes and Spinoza, and even Locke, had been abstract, theoretical, and general in their approach, whereas Montesquieu was, or at least seemed to be, historical, empirical. There is nothing of the social contract in Montesquieu, because this was a theoretical concept, a model, which one scarcely meets in real history. Regardless of whether Montesquieu meets the test of empiricism—his scholarship is naive by modern standards, and we may still feel that the best of him is not "empirical" but speculative—this book immediately took its place as the greatest work of its kind yet written, and it exerted an influence on all who came after it. In Italy, Beccaria, the Italian penologist, wrote under its inspiration, and in Russia, Catherine the Great tried to formulate a code of laws based on it. It came close to being the political bible for all the Enlightened.

Today it seems a curious if undeniably brilliant work. One part is a classification of governments according to types, reminiscent of Aristotle, except that Montesquieu has a greater sense of history. Of the three forms of government, republics are suitable for small city-states, and their hour has passed. Monarchies are the form for present-day Europe; a despotism, with monarchical power unchecked by the feudal

---

[3]The Marquise died in childbirth, delivering a child acquired from one of her many casual affairs, the father being neither Voltaire nor, needless to say it, her husband. The pregnancy itself appears not to have seriously disturbed Voltaire, but the loss of his beloved Emilie saddened him greatly.

classes, is appropriate to a huge empire such as Rome held. Each form has its "principle" or informing spirit, without which it is lost: virtue for republics, honor for the feudal monarchies, fear for despotisms. This is stimulating though not so original as some of the rest. From this typology we rather abruptly transpose to the celebrated section on the influence of climate and geography on political institutions. Though such writers as Hippocrates among the ancients and Bodin among the moderns had speculated on climatic influence, Montesquieu pursued it with a unique thoroughness. His conclusions were often dubious enough: that northern peoples are more courageous than southern, that Orientals are intellectually indolent. The peoples of hotter climes, Montesquieu claimed, make love more ardently, and as for music, he had heard the opera in Italy and in England, and attributed to the climate the former's superior liveliness. These are certainly naive reflections, yet they exhibit a lively curiosity about the causes of cultural variation and were bound to stir controversy. His views were not very consistently worked out, and he wavered between the physical and the moral causes of the differing natures of civilizations, recognizing the complexity of causation. This section was a beginning essay in the problem of historical causation, a problem which still exercises historians in our age, with little agreement yet. But Montesquieu foreshadowed the historical systems of such later thinkers as Hegel, Comte, Marx, and today Toynbee.

This is not all: a last, slighter section of *L'Esprit des lois* traced the growth of Roman and feudal law through the Middle Ages, a pioneer historical essay of considerable significance. How the three parts fit together has given rise to much discussion, many finding an essential disorder in Montesquieu which some have tried to correct by rearrangement and editorial comment, others insisting that there is really some integration in the work. The truth would seem to be that Montesquieu like so many of the early pioneers of the social sciences had bitten off an impossibly large chunk. A general science of all of society is scarcely possible, we know today. The Newtonian ideal of a single great law, or a few relatively simple laws, for all social phenomena, was a will-o-the-wisp which generations of social scientists were destined to pursue in vain, one of the last of them being Karl Marx. Montesquieu contributed some keen insights into a number of different questions, while in the main showing a bent towards the historical. He was fascinated by the question of why civilizations differ, why they rise and fall, why this government develops at one time and that at another. These are legitimate questions, also extremely difficult ones, and no one "law" can explain them all. Nor in his day was the necessary evidence available. Some of Montesquieu's history is entirely fanciful.

But in true Enlightenment manner Montesquieu searched for laws in the new scientific sense: "necessary relations which derive from the nature of things." He wanted to apply the methods of Newton to the phenomena of human civilization. He sought, in a most stimulating way, to expose relationships between social phenomena. This quest directed attention to the study of society as an autonomous area to be treated with objectivity and rigor, a quest which needless to say proved extremely fruitful. At the same time we must recognize that no one yet has made an exact science out of history and sociology, and it seems unlikely that they ever will, in the sense the eighteenth-century *philosophes* meant. But for that century the notion was an exciting one, fairly close to the central theme of the age: the science of Newton and Locke conquering all, sweeping away ancient error even in the realm of human affairs and ushering in a more enlightened epoch. Montesquieu died in 1755, but his spirit continued on.

Montesquieu too was an Anglophile, regarding the English constitution as the most admirable example of enlightened political reason. It has often been pointed out that his exposition of that constitution was false, since he presented it largely as a balance of forces, between king, Parliament, and judicial bench, whereas in fact the Whig oligarchy ran the country (by fairly corrupt means). There is some truth in this. But England *was* the freest and most tolerant society in Europe in the eighteenth century, and in admiring it the French *philosophes* were true to their values. Liberty and toleration were the virtues they most admired. Though French progress in this direction came more slowly than in Britain, it made its way. By the 1740s publishers were daring to print works that previously could not have openly appeared.

Diderot and the Encyclopedia

The leading publicist of this bolder phase of the Enlightenment was a handsome and versatile young man who emerged from provincial poverty and obscurity. In the early works and career of Denis Diderot one can see at work all the intoxicants of the new freedom. Though his *Pensées philosophiques* (1746) has been called "one of the most important books of the eighteenth century," it seems largely a rehash of English deism; what was original was not the thought itself, but daring to print it in France. (A good many deistic tracts circulated clandestinely in France between 1720 and 1750.) There was an attempt to suppress it, but no longer could one so easily control such matters; it circulated and was read. Diderot and another young man who arrived in Paris in 1742 to become his friend, Jean-Jacques Rousseau, were of humbler origin and at first of less respectability than Voltaire and Montesquieu, who moved naturally in the highest French society. They were also more radical. But the time was ripe for them. Both Diderot and Rousseau were men of authentic genius, original in their thought, well read in the classics. The female-dominated Paris salons, always ready to welcome literary genius, soon eagerly took them up. (Diderot was also extremely handsome, Rousseau glamorous.)

There were other "philosophers": Condillac, D'Alembert, Helvétius, D'Holbach. In the exciting atmosphere of Paris, always an intellectual capital without peer, men could now fully absorb not only Locke and Newton, but Bishop Berkeley, the acute British critic of Locke, as well as Voltaire and Montesquieu and many others. The sciences were being rapidly developed and were fashionable. D'Alembert, an illegitimate son of Mme. Tencin the celebrated salon hostess, became a great mathematical physicist; Condillac built a mechanistic psychology on the foundations of Locke and David Hartley; another Englishman. Buffon, the famous French naturalist, had begun his long *Histoire naturelle*. The versatile Diderot was, among other things, a minor inventor and scientist. He was also moralist, psychologist, philosopher, novelist—and encyclopedist. It was natural that the most brilliant and versatile of the *philosophes* should edit the great enterprise which filled the 1750s and became the most famous intellectual landmark of the times.

Encyclopedias were hardly new, and two at least of a sort to bear comparison with this one had already appeared, Bayle's and one by the Scotsman Ephraim Chambers (1728), to both of which the French *Encyclopédie* owed a heavy debt. Nor were the *philosophes* above plagiarizing from the Jesuit *Dictionnaire de Trévoux*, 1704. But the new encyclopedia was to be much more comprehensive than these older ones. It combined Bayle's flair for stimulating ideas with Chambers's stress on the arts and sciences. Men generally agreed that there was much need for such a publication. After a number of false starts the enterprise ended up in Diderot's hands—not surprising when we consider that he combined a facile pen with a remarkable breadth of knowledge, to which virtues he added an extensive acquaintanceship among the literati of Paris. The one drawback, in the eyes of publishers and authorities, was his Voltairean penchant for writing troublesome manuscripts. These ranged from an indecent novel (*Les Bijoux indiscrets*) to his unorthodox religious views, expressed again in 1749 in *Letter on the Blind*. In the latter work Diderot seized on the case of a man born blind whose sight was to be restored, to draw some typically Lockean conclusions: having different sensory experience, a blind person will have different notions of everything, including God.[4] We are reminded of that well-known poem by Rupert Brooke, in which the fish conceives of God as

> Immense, of fishy form and mind,
> Squamous, omnipotent, and kind.

In the course of these ruminations Diderot discharged a good many of his opinions designed to upset the devout, opinions largely derived from Bayle and earlier English and French deists. Diderot's views were more extreme than Voltaire's, who, though a deist, thought belief in God important for morality and social order; Diderot agreed with Bayle that an atheist could be just as good a citizen as a believer. To believe in God was "not at all important."

Therefore the authorities descended upon Diderot in 1749 and escorted him to the Vincennes prison under cover of a *lettre de cachet*, seriously interrupting the progress of the Encyclopedia, but probably giving it some valuable free publicity. Well-treated in the prison, allowed to read, write, and even apparently to visit his mistress by night, Diderot was released after a few months, having promised not to repeat his "intellectual excesses." It was while en route to visit Diderot at Vincennes that his friend Rousseau decided to write an essay on the arts and sciences which won him his first literary fame. The first volume of the Encyclopedia, edited by Diderot and D'Alembert (the major share of the work was always Diderot's) and duly licensed by the king, appeared in mid–1751. Withstanding quarrels among the editors, troubles with the censors, and the vicissitudes of Diderot's private life, volumes then appeared annually until 1759, when with Volume VIII in press a royal decree suddenly condemned and suppressed the whole Encyclopedia.

Alarmed conservatives believed it to be a vehicle for "deism, materialism, and irreligion," a prejudice which the sensational book of Helvétius, *De L'Esprit*, printed in 1758, helped establish through guilt by association. This book, written by a wealthy financier and amateur philosopher, brought out into the open a tendency of Enlightenment thought to sanction a morality of naked egotism or hedonism. At any rate the Encyclopedia was held up for six years during this tide of reaction. A serious war was then going on, too—more serious than most eighteenth-century wars—between England and France. The *philosophes*

---

[4]The intriguing question of whether a man born blind who had his sight restored would recognize by sight an object he knew by touch had first been raised by William Molyneux in 1692, and variations on it made up a favorite eighteenth-century philosophical pastime. See John W. Davis, "The Molyneux Problem," *Journal of the History of Ideas*, July–September, 1960.

and encyclopedists were considered not only indifferent to patriotism but Anglophile in their intellectual tastes. But with great tenacity and faith Diderot, now virtually alone, continued his work on it and was rewarded by seeing it finished in 1766. To the seventeen volumes were subsequently added eleven volumes of plates and seven more of supplementary material and index.

Anybody who aspired to be anybody in France bought the Encyclopedia, as they bought the volumes of Buffon's *Natural History* or the plays of Voltaire; in the celebrated La Tour painting of Mme. Pompadour, the king's mistress, there is a volume of the Encyclopedia conspicuously displayed in the row of books on her desk. To it is commonly attributed a vast influence in disseminating the ideas of the Enlightenment. Printed under government approval, it was at least nominally subject to censorship; but the chief of the censors, Malesherbes, was a man of genuine tolerance, almost a *philosophe* himself, and for a long time the censorship was lax. It is scarcely possible in a few words to give much of an idea of the contents of so many fat volumes. It might be observed, first, that this Encyclopedia would strike a modern reader as rather unlike his impression of that species—flat, objective, factual, impersonal. This one abounds in graces of style, in purely personal asides, the use of the personal pronoun, little bursts of rhapsodic prose. (Could we find, in a modern encyclopedia, "O sweet illusion of poetry! You are no less charming to me than truth itself. May you touch me and please me until my last moments?") Its selection of topics was somewhat whimsical and arbitrary: whatever interested Diderot he put in. This habit once backfired. Though the Encyclopedia as a rule showed little interest in places and history, having only a few lines for example under the subject "France," it included a long article on "Geneva," perhaps under Voltaire's influence, which discussed Calvinism and other religious deviations in a way that irritated both the Genevans and the French ecclesiastics.

Stress on scientific, mathematical, and technological subjects is marked; typical of the Enlightenment, the Encyclopedia exalted the practical and downgraded the pretentiously metaphysical. It pecked away at orthodox religion in various ways, with ironic asides and with articles on pagan gods that might be construed in a double sense, with attacks on the Jesuits and praise of Mahomet, etc. Politically it did not often appear radical, but Lockean principles found their way into numerous articles. In many ways the Encyclopedia served to make known the new ideas. It was so useful that it became indispensable; but its practical knowledge was served up liberally if subtly sprinkled with propaganda for those causes the *philosophes* held dear.

Despite the crisis in the affairs of the Encyclopedia 1759–1763, the party of the *philosophes* had become a powerful one. Though never without enemies, they were so fashionable that satirists began to hold *them* up to ridicule, because they were so potent and haughty an element in "the establishment." Their friends at court included the imperious Pompadour and the chief minister, Choiseul. Voltaire had joined the Encyclopedists, in part, though he stood a bit aloof from their main group and never was at all intimate with Diderot; he had lent his name to a number of articles. (Even by his ideological allies, it seems, the notorious pen was feared, and the man not loved. Later Voltaire issued his own *Philosophical Dictionary*.) The reign of the *philosophes* was to be interrupted, however, by a quarrel within their own ranks.

The Later Voltaire

A note of pessimism or at least chastened optimism crept into the older Voltaire, in what were his most magnificent years. According to some, this indefatigable writer whose literary career lasted for more than sixty years, exhibits no pattern of philosophical consistency. Though everything he wrote is luminous, when added up it presents a "chaos of clear ideas." A man who wrote with as much facility as most people talk, he can hardly be blamed for an occasional contradiction. In general, Voltaire seems to have changed his mind in the direction of a gloomier outlook as he aged. A natural process, no doubt—enhanced in Voltaire's case by the death of his mistress, the souring of his friendship with Frederick the Great, by the war of 1756–1763, and by the Lisbon earthquake of 1755.

Voltaire endowed the latter disaster with immortality. The earthquake and tidal wave in the beautiful capital city of Portugal was a major catastrophe by any reckoning (other places in Europe, too, were affected in lesser degree by the quake and the great storm). Needless to say, this was hardly the first dreadful calamity in human history. But for the eighteenth century, it was one of peculiar significance. In the words of the eminent Voltaire scholar, Theodore Besterman, it "fell like a thunderbolt on the whole of the Western world, and wrought a permanent transformation in every thinking man's philosophy." Perhaps Besterman exaggerates. But the earlier Enlightenment, including Voltaire, had tended to subscribe to an optimistic creed, in its extreme form reaching to Pope's "Whatever is, is right." A good deist, Voltaire along with other deists as well as rational Christians believed in God and an orderly, harmonious universe; he believed that man was rational and, having been put on the right track by Newton and Locke, would proceed now to march forward with reason to the abolition of absurdity and evil. These rosy hopes were sorely tested by Voltaire's experiences both private and public. The Lisbon earthquake hit him just wrong. He began to speak of "the bloody tragedy and ridiculous comedy of this world." He denied progress in history and wrote of cycles, "a continual alteration of day and night." He showed less respect for human nature.

He scarcely can be said to have given up hope. The poem on the Lisbon earthquake ends with the hope that "one day all will be well," though it is not well now. The conclusion of Voltaire's masterpiece, *Candide*, suggests the means: let us cultivate our own garden. But the sardonic laughter that fills the adventures of the unfortunate Candide is at the expense of those who think that this is a benevolent world. Not merely is the world filled with suffering and cruelty, but this evil is capricious, striking without rhyme or reason, as the Lisbon earthquake struck that city for no apparent reason, sparing others just as wicked, and killing all kinds of people there without discrimination. And no one is the master of his fate. During the Seven Years' War, while he was writing *Candide* and giving vent to other pessimistic utterances, Voltaire wrote of the world as "mad," almost unbearable.

For Voltaire this disillusionment acted, oddly, as an energizing principle. The optimism of Leibniz and Pope—all is for the best in the best of all possible worlds, as he chose to put it[5]—made for complacency. Who can be much stirred to make war against evil if "whatever is is right?" Seeing that all is wrong, Voltaire stirred himself to put some of it right. To cultivate our garden is to do whatever we can against evil in our daily lives. Rejecting cosmic optimism, we dig in and in a tough-minded way tackle reform piecemeal.

Never far from Voltaire's crusading sights was the intolerance of organized Christianity. His youth had been surrounded with the Jansenist controversy, and in the 1720s when he came of age intellectually the deistic movement was at its peak. It was not difficult to glimpse in the French church evils in need of reform; the monasteries and abbeys were mostly in decay, the higher clergy constituted a substantial portion of the privileged aristocracy, often behaving in a most unspiritual manner, and except for the Jesuits the clergy made no great contribution to the intellectual life of France. Voltaire's outbursts against the "infamy" that must be "crushed" perhaps become more understandable in the light of such facts. We know that he was a deist, holding that revealed religion must be replaced by natural, priestcraft by philosophy. On the other hand he believed in the need for religion—"the people need a religion," if not the enlightened few. Students of Voltaire's religious views have

---

[5]It seems clear that Voltaire misunderstood Leibniz, or in his bitterness chose to distort his position. See pages 119–20.

found him quite ambiguous, undecided whether he opposed Christianity root and branch as a legacy of ancient superstition or whether he wanted to reform it. His relationship with the church was evidently ambivalent, involving both love and hate. He continued to engage in wickedly witty exposures of the Bible's contradictions and absurdities, in order to discredit revealed religion; while on the other hand he showed much more interest than did Diderot and other *philosophes* in purifying and using the church. In his old age he attended church and showed a keen interest in local religious orders around Ferney. He admired the Quakers, least theological of all Christian sects.

His running battles with elements of the clergy culminated in 1762 when the case of Jean Calas of Toulouse provided him with a prize specimen of clerical intolerance. There was actually little religious persecution in eighteenth-century France, though not until 1787 was toleration enacted into law. Research has demonstrated that the Calas case, which Voltaire made infamous, was not a typical happening, however deplorable; it came about under unusual circumstances, which owed something to the war France was waging against two Protestant powers, and was a rare instance of anti-Protestant hysteria in eighteenth-century France. (A few years later, during the Gordon Riots of 1780, anti-Catholic hysteria broke out in England, where religious toleration had seemingly been well established.) The Calas case was that of an elderly Protestant shopkeeper accused of murdering his son to prevent him from turning Catholic, and condemned to a barbarous execution against what seemed the plain weight of the evidence. Its ultimate reversal, not in time to save the unfortunate Calas, was a tribute to the zeal and ability of Voltaire.

It is widely believed that toleration was one of the chief virtues and contributions of the eighteenth-century philosophers. This is true insofar as they combatted religious intolerance and clerical bigotry, but it should be pointed out that they were scarcely prepared to tolerate everything. The biographers of both Diderot and Voltaire have commented on the fact that the *philosophes* wanted free speech for themselves only, not for their foes, whom they intrigued to get suppressed just as the anti-*philosophes* wished to suppress them. Arthur M. Wilson suggests that, paradoxically, Malesherbes the censor was the most tolerant since he wished to let both sides have a hearing within the limits of propriety and political safety; neither of the contending factions would have allowed the other a hearing at all if it had had the power to suppress. This was a ruthless war, though conducted mainly with words. The philosophers held strong beliefs; it was their mission to purge the world of error and install Reason. Reason is one thing and not another, and to believe strongly in it is to embrace a form of intolerance, even if one chooses to regard it as enlightened intolerance. Voltaire was not prepared to tolerate the "infamy" of bigoted clericalism! Nor was he typically tolerant of anything he regarded as stupid or wrong—which included a considerable number of things. That he contributed to the exile of Rousseau (discussed further in this chapter) seems possible.

Voltaire like most of the *philosophes* (Rousseau being the chief exception) was not very democratic. Few people were in the eighteenth century. He usually spoke of the people as *"canaille,"* and once he observed that the *canaille* will always remain the *canaille*. Shoemakers and servants could never become philosophers! Peter Gay, author of an excellent book on Voltaire's political views, does the best he can to rescue the hero of rationalism from an attitude somewhat embarrassing to many of his modern admirers, but can find only a few fragmentary prodemocratic utterances (mostly in his old age) to weigh against a great many statements on the other side. Voltaire's position here was logical. The world was to be rescued by philosophical reason, and this had to come from the few who represented the vanguard of enlightenment. Eventually, no doubt, everyone would be enlightened, but at this time and for a long time to come the ignorant multitude would be the ally of the priests. The moral absolutism of Voltaire's group was hostile to democracy, in the sense of letting things be settled by majority vote. Their prime objective was to enthrone reason, and for this they looked on the whole to the "enlightened despot." The dictatorship of Reason was to them much preferable to a democracy of ignorance. Condorcet, Voltaire's disciple, observed that it is easier for a charlatan to mislead the people than for a man of genius to save them. "A prince greedy for acclamation will never receive the admiration of posterity," Mirabeau wrote in praising Frederick the Great. Some of the Physiocrats (discussed later) were such proponents of enlightened despotism that they held to a doctrine of the irresistibility of reason: the prince could not possibly act otherwise than in accordance with it!

These last comments are merely by way of noting some differences between the *philosophes* and modern liberal-democratic ideologies. These were later movements, to which the eighteenth-century philosophers contributed something but which in many ways were essentially different. The eighteenth was an aristocratic century, up until the explosion of 1789, and its intellectuals showed this as much as its politicians and social leaders. We may note that neoclassicism, the reigning spirit in the arts and in life's very style, was aristocratic in that it stressed order, hierarchy, and refinement. To welcome all the generous confusion of individual eccentricity, social upheaval, and exotic experience would have to wait for romanticism, whose full emergence only came after the Enlightenment had had its day. There was only one of the *philosophes* who pointed ahead to, among other things, romanticism and democracy, and it was his fate to be estranged from the rest of his fellows.

Rousseau

Jean-Jacques Rousseau seemed born to be the perfect foil to Voltaire, and in their complete contrast and their clashes lies much of the drama of the French Enlightenment. (The quarrels of these two giants are still carried on, quite as venomously as then, by some of their twentieth-century epigones!) The utter disparity extends to their lives: the sophisticated worldling, Voltaire, successful from the beginning, as opposed to the failure, Rousseau, who was little better than a tramp until sudden success came to him near his fortieth year; the Parisian against the provincial outlander; the man at home in the highest circles of society versus the *gauche* rustic; the conqueror of all women opposed to the man who became tongue-tied at their approach and was a great lover only in his fantasies. Extended to the area of doctrine, Voltaire was the skeptic, wit, and cynic, Rousseau the intense, serious, sentimental believer; Voltaire pessimist, Rousseau optimist; Voltaire aristocrat, Rousseau democrat; Voltaire classicist, Rousseau a founder of romanticism. They shared a rare gift for popularizing ideas, for embodying in their attractive works of literature the key intellectual issues of their time. "He invented nothing but inflamed everything," ran a celebrated comment on Rousseau, one almost equally applicable to Voltaire. That their talents and general position in the intellectual spectrum were so similar made their clash the more intense. Between them they came close to summing up the century.

The youth who ran away from a not too happy life in Geneva at sixteen was all his life a reader, a thinker, a dreamer, but socially inadequate; no man of the world like Voltaire or extroverted genius like Diderot was he. He arrived in Paris in 1742, not a boy prodigy like Voltaire to whom the world was ready to open its arms, but a man of thirty who had spent an aimless, vagabond life, thus far without a single worthy achievement. In his fascinating *Confessions* Rousseau, under the guise of ruthless objectivity, manages to convey the impression that not he but his environment, or perhaps the sins of others, were responsible for his deplorable youth; but his own innate laziness and oversensitivity were involved too. He did have this sensitivity and he could always write; his descriptions of nature and of the interior life were to bring a new dimension to European prose.

He came to Paris fancying himself a musical scientist, having invented a new system of musical notation, which turned out to be something less than the sensation Rousseau thought. Before long this rather rough diamond was shyly making his way into the glittering salons. He gained an appointment as secretary to the French Ambassador at Venice, which turned out to be a fiasco, Rousseau regarding his employer as a half-wit and the ambassador dismissing him for intolerable insolence. Rousseau was to spend his life in quarrels—clearly his was a most difficult, even psychopathic personality. Some further years of discouragement awaited Jean-Jacques after this misadventure, during which he accumulated bitterness against the brittle Parisian world which he was not socially sophisticated enough to cope with and which refused to recognize his talent, so he thought.

He was rescued by the Prize Essay, which gave him a chance to put into acceptable literary form his resentments against society. "Has the revival of the arts and sciences contributed to purify or to corrupt morals?" Rousseau took what is generally assumed to be the unexpected side, though the savants of the Academy of Dijon, a sober provincial capital, probably welcomed an answer in favor of the latter alternative, on old-fashioned Christian principles. What was unusual was that a clever Parisian writer would so argue, as Rousseau did. Rousseau later described his sensations upon reading this topic as akin to a religious conversion, a flash of illumination showing him his whole course hereafter, such as Descartes had experienced in November, 1619. This was in October, 1749, when he visited Diderot then languishing in Vincennes prison. "I saw another universe and I became another man." He wept.

Though Rousseau's thesis that civilization is always corrupted by the arts was logically vulnerable to attack (it received on a careful count sixty-eight replies, and Rousseau later admitted its defects), it is hard to deny that the purpose it really had was a plausible one. Rousseau meant, in effect, that the Paris society of would-be literati kept by amorous ladies posing as patrons of the arts, of courtiers and snobs, of luxurious waste and spectacular immorality, was corrupt and corrupting, and less of an intellectual capital than it thought. There was enough truth in this to strike home. Even Voltaire had to retire from Paris in order to do serious and sustained work. The atmosphere of brilliant conversation mixed with sexual and social intrigue might be fun, but was it philosophy? Rousseau gave expression to a widespread feeling against this Sodom with its fleshpots as well as pseudophilosophers.

Egypt, Greece, and Rome had fallen because of the enervating effects of luxury, Rousseau argued in the Prize Essay. As manners become more refined, sincerity is lost. And is not all our knowledge in the end vanity, vanity? Do we not end in skepticism? Echoing Montaigne's "Que sais-je?" Rousseau condemns the pride of human intellect. At the same time, with some inconsistency, he praises Bacon, Descartes, and Newton, because they have brought useful knowledge. He was not really against all "civilization," then, but only against certain features of the corrupt, supersophisticated upper class civilization of his time. But in general his tone stressed "back to nature" as a remedy for too much of the artificial. He praised the Spartans and the Scythians; honest peasants are better than courtiers; a man innocent of too much "book learning" is better off than the learned. To which Voltaire replied, contemptuously, that Rousseau wished mankind to go back to a four-legged existence.

Paris society was prepared at first to treat the Discourse as a *jeu d'esprit*, not meant seriously. Indeed there was something paradoxical in a man competing for a prize by writing an essay proving that all such intellectual activity is debilitating and corrupting. (The Spartans, whom Rousseau holds up for admiration, presumably did not hold literary competitions.) Rousseau was overwhelmed with invitations, and his boorishness was accepted as delightfully in character with his views. But, whether from shyness or principle, Rousseau refused a presentation to the king and a royal pension (this upon the occasion of his successful operetta, *The Village Soothsayer*). Soon thereafter he began to quarrel with the whole set of Paris *philosophes*, who were now accustomed to assemble at the salon of the atheist, the Baron d'Holbach.

It was not a long step from the primitivism of his first Discourse to the later works in which Rousseau seeks further to show that man in his natural state is good, but that society as it exists corrupts him. Among the shockers emanating from this thesis were (1) that love and marriage are disastrous inventions of civilization, representing a sort of female plot and (2) that private property is another baleful contrivance, the result of bold usurpation, bringing in inequality, greed, and war. This last opinion Voltaire found particularly disagreeable. It drew from him the comment that in assailing private property Rousseau again was striking at civilization itself.

Rousseau went on to suggest that the social contract which created the state was conceived in duplicity and fraud, being a conspiracy of the rich to enslave the poor. Thus the existing state was illegitimate, he implied, and a wholly new start on a democratic basis was needed. Rousseau reasoned his way to positions which stand at the beginning of modern democracy, socialism, and anarchism, though with him these were mere ideas which, we feel, had little more than a rhetorical content. But they were to be quoted in deadly earnest during the French Revolution, a generation later. For Rousseau was read; few could resist the peculiar magic of his prose. It may well be claimed for his *Social Contract* and *Discourse on the Origin of Inequality* that they were the most electrifying social message the European world had ever received since the days of primitive Christianity.

The Discourse on the Origin of Inequality was written (1755) in response to another essay proposed by the Dijon Academy, though this time Rousseau did not get the prize. "What is the origin of inequality among men, and is it authorized by natural law?" Jean-Jacques was inspired to clarify some of the rather muddy ideas he had poured out in the first essay. In the second one he gives us his picture of man in a hypothetical state of nature. Rousseau's natural man is very different from Hobbes's; a happy, healthy being, not knowing the unhappiness that comes from civilization with its stresses and strains, he has few needs and can satisfy these. While defending his legitimate self-interest, he feels pity for the sufferings of others and has a social sense. It is rather a Garden-of-Eden picture—Rousseau's version of the state of primal innocence. Why then did men leave this pleasant state; whence came the Fall? In effect, Rousseau blames it on greed and selfishness. A few, at least, had the fatal itch to seek wealth and power, beyond what they needed, and at the expense of their fellows. Private property made its ominous appearance, and the state arose to protect property. Since then things have on the whole gotten worse.

It might be noted that there is a contradiction here, if Rousseau says that man it naturally good, yet lost his primal virtue because—he is bad! Or at least some men are, and the rest evidently cannot resist them. Elsewhere he dwelt on the two natures in man, a higher and a lower. But if these two natures exist they must always have done so, and one is left wondering why men were happy once and no longer are. Or is it all simply a figure of speech, this primal state of nature? Rousseau is full of "bipolarities," unresolved dualisms; but so, doubtless, is the human heart itself, of which he was so matchless a student.

In *Le Contrat social*, 1762, Rousseau went on to indicate how this fraudulent contract of government, imposed falsely on the people by a few rich schemers and establishing a despotism, could be made legitimate: there must be an entirely new contract, a contract not between rulers and ruled but between all and all. Before writing this celebrated tract, Rousseau published his two "novels," these three works all coming in 1761–1762 in a burst of creative activity marking the climax of his career. His literary success reached a peak with the didactic and sentimental novels, *La Nouvelle Hèloise* and *Émile*. By the time they were published he had detached himself formally from the party of *philosophes*. He had quarreled with Diderot; he had broken with the society lady who had been keeping him as her pet *philosophe*; he had left Paris to go live in the country; he had written a letter to Voltaire full of hatred. ("I do not like you, sir. . . .") "I have absolutely detached myself from the party of the *philosophes*," he wrote in 1761. "I do not like it at all when they preach impiety, and this is a crime they will never

pardon me for." Rousseau added that he was yet a foe of religious bigotry and would never please the party of the devout, either. The most
famous passage from his novels is "the Profession of Faith of the Savoyard Vicar," an impassioned hymn of worship to the deist god of nature
which did, in truth, please neither the pious nor the impious; it was
deeply religious, yet wholly unorthodox. Rousseau's fate is summed up
in the lines of William Blake, later:

> Mock on, mock on, Voltaire, Rousseau.

He was associated with eighteenth-century atheism and infidelity though
opposition to this was exactly the basis of his quarrel with Voltaire. To
be sure Rousseau ferociously assailed the falseness and hypocrisy of
organized Christianity for which he would substitute his own religion
of nature. He was a truer "deist" than most who went by that name,
for to him God and religion were really important. Other eighteenth-
century deists felt, like Diderot, that the matter was of no importance,
or, like Voltaire, that it was useful to maintain belief in God for utilitarian reasons.

Voltaire now thought Rousseau quite mad, and indeed he was
somewhat headed in that direction (a painful ailment adding to the natural imbalance of his temperament). Without many friends among the
rich and powerful, Rousseau was persecuted for *Émile* and for that famous tract, *The Social Contract*, printed in 1762, and had to flee France.
He was not far wrong in charging an unholy alliance of the Christians
and the philosophers against him.

La Nouvelle Héloise is a passionately sentimental parable on the
theme of virtue, the virtuousness of a beautiful woman who overcomes
the temptation of the flesh (though she did fall once) to remain true to
a husband she does not love, and to convince even the man she does
love that there is a higher form of friendship than the physical. It was
one of the most successful novels in all history, all the women and half
the men of Europe, so it seems, being reduced to tears over it. With it
romanticism was born, it is often suggested. Here Jean-Jacques was a
prophet. But he owed something to Samuel Richardson, English author
of *Pamela* and *Clarissa*, for the fashionably sentimental theme of virtuous maiden seduced. This was an age of sentimental novels.

Émile is a treatise on education, enshrining Rousseau's conviction
that "All is well when it leaves the hands of the Creator of things; all
degenerates in the hands of man." This, his central message, was later
explained by a great French critic as follows:

> Strip off the artificial habits of civilized man, his superfluous wants, his
> false prejudices . . . return to your own heart, listen to its intimate

sentiments, permit yourself to be guided by the light of instinct and conscience; and you will rediscover that primitive Adam . . . long buried under a crust of mould and slime, but which rescued from its enclosing filth can again be placed on its pedestal in all the perfection of its form and in all the purity of its whiteness (Taine).

Émile has been called the "basic treatise of modern education" since it shows awareness of the need to treat the child as a developing personality. The child is not a small adult, as Rousseau accused Locke of believing, and cannot be reasoned with. He posits stages of growth; thus from five to twelve is a prerational age, when the senses dominate and when education must appeal to concrete experience. Between twelve and fifteen, one should introduce the subjects which demand intellectual qualities; later comes the instilling of morality, finally initiation into the mysteries of sex. Here again we meet Rousseau's favorite idea, that children are naturally innocent and good, though he recognized a certain tendency toward evil and was not altogether consistent on this point. He was sure that a "natural education," building on nature rather than going against it, is the best. Existing education was based on false principles. "Do exactly the opposite from what is usually done," Rousseau advised, and you will probably be right! His attack on wet nurses resulted in a fad for nursing their own children that affected even women of the nobility. The familiar primitivist theme emerges also in a truly Spartan regimen to be imposed on the poor children (sleeping with open windows in winter, etc.), while Rousseau also takes advantage of the occasion to deliver a lecture on the superiority of a simple, honest craft to less worthy occupations: we should all be carpenters or something of the sort.

It was in *Émile* that Rousseau placed, also, the famous Creed of the Vicar of Savoy, previously mentioned. The Vicar knows largely by intuition that God exists, though there is some use of the argument from design. He tackles the problem of evil, which Bayle and Voltaire found so strong an argument against any religious view of the universe, and urges that evil must exist because it is necessary to free will. If men were not free to choose, if they were only automatons, virtue could have no value. Free will enables men to choose the good and thus endow it with value. If they do not choose it, they rightly suffer because of their choice. The latter proposition will strike many as most dubious, but Rousseau's answer is one of the classic ones and he presents it with eloquence. The point is, essentially, that to have good we must also have evil, its opposite. This is true, but it does not meet the question of why there is, or seems to be, unnecessary, superfluous, and anomalous evil in the world. It may be granted, for example, that in order for us to enjoy food the sensation of hunger must exist; but why should people suffer starvation? Rousseau, however, was a consistent optimist, having written an answer to Voltaire on the Lisbon earthquake.

The Vicar proceeds, after this excursion into a thorny field, to present a most unorthodox version of immortality. There is no mention of the Christian doctrine of Redemption. Virtue is its own reward and vice brings its own punishment, in the hearts of the wicked. Rousseau could not of course accept the Christian doctrine of Original Sin. Human nature at bottom is good. Corruption there had been, but Jean-Jacques's version of the fall, we know, was a very different one: men abandoned the life of simplicity and equality to pursue wealth, set up private property, and thus bring on a train of woes. This can be corrected, for men have not lost their free will nor do they bear any inherent taint of sin.

The Vicar ends by calling for a purer, simple, less dogmatic religion, indeed a religion without dogma, resembling the Pietistic or quietist sort. When he is eighteen and ready for his moral education, Émile listens to the Vicar. He then goes to Paris, but significantly leaves that "city of noise, smoke, and mud, where the women do not believe in honor nor the men in virtue." Émile returned to the country, where he had further adventures, with love and sex, which we need not detail. That the book was banned, even in Holland as well as France, was due to the offense it gave to orthodox religion as well as to the potent *philosophe* party, and to its latent political radicalism. (The germ of *The Social Contract* was here.) To Voltaire and the rest of the *philosophes*, rationalists all, this was the worst sort of nonsense, calculated to wipe out the gains made by Reason and return mankind to primitive barbarism. They ridiculed Rousseau, and helped get him banished, but they could not wipe away the impression Rousseau's writings made on a wider reading public than the Encyclopedia or the plays of Voltaire reached.

The Social Contract

Rousseau the romanticist, the primitivist, and the individualist, the Rousseau who counselled a return to bucolic nature and later wrote the charming *Reveries of a Solitary Walker*, does he stand in puzzling contrast to the Rousseau of *The Social Contract*? For in this famous tract there is seemingly a great deal of statism and socialism. Calling for a completely new organization of society, a new social contract to replace the fraudulent old one, Rousseau spoke up for equality and for a kind of democracy, and yet he almost abolished the individual's rights. For this new society deposits all power in the community and makes of the popular will a General Will that is something collective, not to be confused with the mere sum of individual wills.

We can resolve or explain the contradiction by recalling that Rousseau's central thesis was the natural goodness of the individual, evil being the work of society. From this one may go in either of two directions. One may decide that since the individual is good, society is altogether unnecessary. This anarchist position was adopted by some of Rousseau's followers (see particularly William Godwin, discussed on page 212. Sometimes Rousseau learned this way, but in the main he adopted another line. Society, so far from being unnecessary, is the allimportant determinant of the individual; the task is to reconstitute it, turning it from a corrupting force into an ennobling one. And the good society must not be founded on selfishness, that is, individualism, but on unselfishness, that is, the community. It should be the ideal society, carefully organized, in brief, a utopia. And so Rousseau was led to describe a kind of democratic-socialist utopia in *The Social Contract*.

How did the state originate? Not from the family, as Filmer claimed; nor is it organic and natural, as Aristotle held. Against Hobbes, Rousseau protests that men would never have freely yielded themselves up to the Leviathan state which enslaves them. The state does properly originate in a contract, but thus far there has never been such a true contract; some men, the stronger and less scrupulous, have simply imposed their will by trickery and force. The multitude has been gullible, but it will soon awake. Men are to enter into a social contract on the basis of equality in order to insure their liberty. They will enthrone no king but set themselves up as their own rulers. Their sovereign is—the general will. This is the will of all. It is the People collectively and politically. But, in the view of many of Rousseau's critics, he no sooner delivered the people than he reenslaved them—to this abstraction, the General Will. For it seems that the General Will is not just the sum of individuals, it is an ideal, representing what the people ought to will if they willed rightly. Moreover the individual owes all rights to this state; unlike Locke's social contract (which was popular with most of the *philosophes*), this one reserves no "natural rights" to the individual. Rousseau perceived that there can be no "rights" outside of society; one has no "rights" in a state of nature, one only has the rule of might.

Rousseau certainly did not mean to sanction a totalitarian state; indeed, he could not have known what that meant. He did not foresee even the uses that would be made of his General Will by fanatical dictators during the French Revolution that broke out only a few years after his death. Still, Rousseau's political theory is decidedly statist, and its lineal descendant may be Hegel. There is even to be a civil religion, a kind of official deism, which every citizen is required to accept and for the repudiation of which he may be punished by death! Foes of Rousseau have often made him out to be a proto-Fascist in recent years and their chief argument is this enforced state religion. But it should be pointed out that, at least according to some close students of Rousseau's thought, he is describing an ultimate perfect state, when selfish interests have become completely merged in the General Will and social solidarity has become perfect. It is not clear that Rousseau would have supported policies of persecution. He does think that the ultimate loyalty of the individual in a perfect society must be to that society, and not to some outside power. It is the same conclusion Plato reached, and Rousseau may justly be accused of being illiberal in the technical sense; but the inquisitorial features of his political system have been exaggerated. Rousseau was in fact much influenced by Plato's Republic and the same decided impatience with any individual dissent from the laws, the same organic conception of the state, may be seen in his *Social Contract*. It sets up something of a puzzle: the war between Jean-Jacques and Jean-Jacques, between the romantic individualist and the authoritarian statist.

The same combination of democratic zeal with almost totalitarian dictatorship will be found in the French Revolution. "Jacobin democracy" was an offspring of Rousseau, and modern socialism has sometimes been traced back to him. So has modern Fascism. It is remarkable how much of the modern world burst through in the thought of the man from Geneva. But certain recent writings on Rousseau, popular but erroneous, have grossly exaggerated his totalitarian side. Though this debate is likely never to be resolved in view of the puzzling nature of the individual-society relationship and of Rousseau's contradictory utterances, it is worth noting that some of the most recent and careful examinations hold that Rousseau was basically on the side of the individual, that he intended no leviathan state, and indeed comes out looking almost like John Stuart Mill. (See Alfred Cobban, *Rousseau and the Modern State*, revised edition, 1964.) As Cobban remarks, "To the end a hard and insoluble core of individualism remains in his thought and refuses to be dissolved away by the rising tide of communal values." Some misunderstanding has arisen through a failure to note Rousseau's distinction between state and community. The "General Will" is the will of the community; it may be expressed imperfectly, or not at all, in the existing state, and indeed is, like democracy, an ideal hardly ever realized in the real world, Rousseau says. He did not, like Hegel, deify the state, only "the people."

"Primitivism," the myth of a "golden age" in the past, or of the "noble savage," may be traced far back into history and indeed is one of the archetypal images or myths of mankind.[6] Thus Rousseau may be fitted into a long tradition, or said to have repeated one of the oldest and simplest ideas known to man. But his version of the myth is tailored for modern man by being given a new twist. Most golden age myths simply assume an ideal, blissful, paradisial time "in the beginning," when according to some versions men were immortal, talked to God, had no sins, did not need to work. The Christian rendering of this myth was distinctive in seeing the Fall as paradoxically fortunate, since man could not have stayed in this primal state and must advance through history to a final stage that will be better than the first. Rousseau made this more explicit, and secularized it. Human nature was perhaps once pure, man was once free; there was a taint, the taint of cupidity, and it led to a fall into private property, materialism, irreligion, immorality. Redemption can come if men truly repent of their evil and resolve to build a new society, tearing themselves wholly loose from the corrupt old one. This new society restores the perfect harmony, freedom, and equality of the original state of bliss, but on a higher level. Such was the popular version of the vision of Jean-Jacques. Was it profound or naive, a myth for modern man to live by or the oldest of hallucinations?

Rousseau did not look in the direction of the enlightened despot as much as did Voltaire and the rationalist *philosophes*. The ideal government to him was a pure democracy, and if this is impractical (and he thought it was) there still ought to be as much direct participation in government as possible. It followed that the unit of government should be small. A larger nation might be some kind of federation of these small units; from Rousseau came a strong influence in the direction of federalism, that is, a weak central government. This must always be borne in mind, too, when one hears Rousseau called a cryptototalitarian. His tightly knit political communities were to be more like city-states; the democratic unanimity they were required to have is what does frequently crystallize in small cohesive communities. Rousseau could hardly have approved the extension of this to a large state. He is quite sure that no one can delegate his portion of the general will to anyone else, even

[6]See Lovejoy and Boas, *Documentary History of Primitivism and Related Ideas in Antiquity*, 1935, and Chapter 2 of M. Eliade, *Myths, Dreams, and Mysteries*, 1960. Professor Lovejoy once pointed out, correctly, that Rousseau is not strictly speaking a "primitivist" in that he did not think that man could, or even should, remain in the earliest stage of animal-like existence. The term to Rousseau must be understood only in the sense that he had much to say about the early stages of human life and contrasted modern man with these, often unfavorably.

by election: the representative principle found no friend in Rousseau, who were he alive today would doubtless laugh at our boast that we are democratic because we get to choose someone every few years to represent us in legislature or executive.

So Jean-Jacques is more accurately to be seen as a proponent of small communities, strongly democratic and socialistic, loosely linked together somehow in a federation. It should be remembered that *The Social Contract* was meant to be but part of a larger work on government, which he never completed, though portions of his political theory may be seen in other writings, such as the interesting constitution he wrote for Corsica.

It has been pointed out that Rousseau was really no revolutionary and therefore the men who made use of him to that end in the great French Revolution were inventing a mythical Rousseau.[7] Apart from his sensitive mistrust of crowds and violence, there is this hostility in Jean-Jacques to centralized states, which is exactly what the radical wing of the Revolution wanted and which was one of the most enduring results of the Revolution. But the implicit if not explicit revolutionary content of Rousseau's thought should not be overlooked. Mably and Morelly developed a real Rousseau, if not the only one. He was prophet of the absolute renewal, the total reform of a hopelessly corrupt civilization, as well as the theorist of democracy. It is not wrong to see in him the most profound of all the stimuli to the Revolution, even though the direction taken by the Revolution did not follow in detail his vision of the good society.

This complex "problem of Rousseau" needs to be briefly summarized, in conclusion. Perhaps the best way to look at Rousseau is in terms of his "bipolarities" (Jean Wahl) or paradoxes. Man is born free, but enslaves himself; he is naturally good, yet naturally corrupt; he hates authority, yet needs it; he must have religion, but will submit to no gods; history is a record of horrors, but may end in utopia. And so on. Rousseau, whose magic of words seared each of these insights into the mind of Europe, meant many things to many people. He was the preacher of equality and democracy, of simplicity and socialism; he inspired both a return to nature and an optimistic futurism. Students of his thought still quarrel about his meaning and agree that he was both misunderstood and hard to understand. But quite plain people thought

[7]See especially articles by Gordon H. McNeil, "The Anti-Revolutionary Rousseau," *American Historical Review*, July, 1953, and "The Cult of Rousseau and the French Revolution," *Journal of the History of Ideas*, April, 1945. And see further below, pages 203–6. Called upon once to write a constitution for the existing state of Poland, Rousseau showed himself quite conservative, seeking to build on traditions rather than start all over.

they understood him perfectly, and were inspired to change the world.

Voltaire remained a mighty force until his death in 1778, and took on the stature of a revered immortal in his last years. His final visit to Paris in 1778 was a tremendous triumph. Rousseau spent the years after 1763 in unhappiness and almost madness, though he produced some deathless writings (including the unique *Confessions*). He died in the same year as Voltaire. About to dawn were the style and mood of romanticism, of which Rousseau was a prophet and the political and social democracy of the French Revolution, when his name would be on many lips. So would Voltaire's. No one was in a political sense less revolutionary; yet the Revolution made a cult of him, no less than of Rousseau, seeing him as "the first philosopher who waged a frontal attack against prejudice, superstition, fanaticism, feudal privileges and all kinds of tyrannies." Together, the two great eighteenth century "philosophers" helped induce the Revolution; then, during it, they would at length be pitted against each other.

6

The Enlightenment:
Skeptics and "Scientists"

At certain times the world is overrun with false skepticism. . . . Of the true kind there can never be enough.

JACOB BURCKHARDT

I do not like your men of the eighteenth century. They are too simplistes.

HENRI BERGSON

British Skepticism

If the apostasy of Rousseau did something to end the idyll of the Age of Reason, even more effective in unravelling its confident rationalism was another betrayal from within stemming from the British Isles. Thence had come the decisive influence on eighteenth-century thought, that of Newton and Locke. A few decades later, the same wind bore to the continent the disturbing news that Locke's philosophic successors in the lineage of British empiricism had reached some unsettling conclusions. They had taken Locke's basic assumptions and followed them, not to certainty but to skepticism, not to realism but to "immaterialism." Something of this has already been suggested in the section on Locke.

Bishop George Berkeley was an outstanding scientist as well as philosopher, who directed keen criticisms at Newton and Locke, because, rather like Pascal in the previous century, their outlook seemed to him shallow and materialistic. His *De Motu* (1721) seems remarkable today for its awareness of Newton's error insofar as he assumed an absolute space and time; like Leibniz, this astute Irish clergyman partly anticipated Mach and Einstein. And Berkeley saw, too, that no scientific theory can claim to be describing the nature of things as they really are; all we can say is that it is a set of symbols that works, by means of which we gain predictability within a certain range of phenomena. This is what most modern physicists have had to accept, and it makes Berkeley into a real prophet. At the time, not much note was taken of it.

Author of a study of visual perception that long remained a classic of experimental psychology, the Bishop of Cloyne[1] was a vigorous personality who interested himself in social reform in his native Ireland (*The Querist*), tried to establish a college in Rhode Island, disputed with the deists (*Alciphron*) and with the Whigs. A conservative, he hoped to confute the impious materialists with his idealism. A strange enthusiasm for the virtues of tar-water as a cure for diseases was one of his eccentricities. But Berkeley had a keen intellect, and his idealism, regarded as his greatest eccentricity—this crazy bishop seemed to think he had abolished matter—actually embodied a signal contribution to philosophy. Though he also knew Continental philosophers such as Malebranche and Leibniz, Berkeley always held John Locke in great respect but conducted a systematic criticism of his theory of knowledge. His own "immaterialism" he claimed to be strictly empirical, logical, and even commonsensical. If we examine carefully what happens when we perceive something, and if we are careful in our use of terms, we cannot avoid concluding, Berkeley thought, that Locke had failed to finish his analysis of that process. Locke had pointed out that we have "ideas" of external objects, knowing them only as they appear to our minds as ideas or, as would be said today, sense data. Thus what we know of the table in front of us is a series of sense impressions concerning its size, shape, color, texture, etc., brought in by our various sense organs. We do not know the thing directly, but through our senses. So far so good; where Locke erred, Berkeley believed, was in supposing that some qualities, the "primary" ones, inhere in the object, are really "there" as a substance or substratum. The primary qualities of size, motion, and number, Locke had held, are not *dependent* on our senses as are secondary qualities (color, odor, taste, etc.). But Berkeley believed that in reality there are no primary or substantive qualities, but that all are equally subjective, dependent on our senses. So he argued brilliantly in a series of Dialogues (1713) scarcely matched since Plato. Locke had retained the

---

[1]Berkeley studied philosophy at Trinity College, Dublin, then became a Fellow of that college, after which he was made Dean of Derry and then Bishop of Cloyne, of the Anglican (Irish) Church. Like many eighteenth-century Anglican churchmen, he was basically a man of learning for whom the clerical position served almost as a sinecure.

remnants of medievalism in his substantive view of reality. We find on careful analysis, that the "thing" can be dispensed with. It is only a collection of sense data!

It does not exist, then, unless it is perceived. *Esse est percipi*: to exist is to be perceived. For a nonliving object, the statement that it "exists" can have no meaning except to say that someone perceives it, or could perceive it. Berkeley challenged the reader to find any other meaning for the word than this. In this sense, then, reality becomes mental. Only "spirits" (minds) and "ideas" (sensory data fed into minds) exist. Berkeley constantly insisted that this line of reasoning was empirical and logical; he was in no sense affirming anything mystical. His "idealism" differs from the later type, stemming from the nineteenth-century German philosophers, in that they affirmed a mysterious, ineffable spiritual substance, while Berkeley would have no part of any substances. Modern philosophers would tend to say that Berkeley was right in abolishing substantive qualities of things, though the use he made of this "phenomenalism" in arguing for a world of spirits and of God might go too far. Berkeley roundly asserted that he left the world just as it had been: "Everything is as real as ever. I hope that to call a thing 'Idea' makes it not the less real." And, he added, if you boggle at the thought of eating and wearing "ideas," the word is not important; so long as you agree that "we eat and drink and are clad with the immediate objects of sense which cannot exist unperceived."

The bishop went on, of course, to argue for the existence of God on the grounds that the ideas that appear to our minds must be caused by the "omnipresent eternal Mind." We *cannot* have an "idea" of God, that is, know him directly as a sense perception; but we infer his existence from the existence of sensible objects, which must be caused by something and have a Perceiver. The world that we know is, in effect, God's thoughts—an attractive picture, though doubtless a departure from Berkeley's empirical science. Still, he had been empirical and had reasoned acutely, so acutely that despite a tendency to dismiss him as overly paradoxical, he dealt a serious blow to commonsense Lockean rationalism. The idealist position, Diderot wrote uncomfortably, is the most absurd but is the hardest to refute. Berkeley had partly undermined Enlightenment materialism.

That part of his analysis which proved the most enduring, and has ever since been widely accepted in philosophical circles as incontrovertible, was his attack on the inherent or substantial qualities of things. If such qualities exist, we cannot know them, for they appear to us through our senses only, and all we can say is that we have picked up signals from out there and transposed them into an idea or image of the thing. When we say "the desk is brown," as Berkeley noted, we are not technically right, because brown is a color, and colors can only be known by beings with sense organs. The color, then, is not in the desk but in us. "No sensation can be a senseless thing." The shape, size, or weight of a thing is not really any different; these too are the results of our senses.

David Hume

David Hume then took the ball from Berkeley as the latter had taken it from Locke. Hume, the most acute philosophical mind of his generation, was a Scotsman of rather humble birth who early conceived a passion for "the pursuits of philosophy and general learning" and between the age of twenty-five and twenty-six, while living frugally in Paris, composed *A Treatise of Human Nature*, published in three volumes 1738–1740. In his words it "fell deadborn from the press." Revised and republished in 1752 as *An Enquiry concerning Human Understanding*, a title sufficiently indicative of the Lockean influence, it did rather better, and his other writings on a variety of topics helped him to gain considerable fame. These included a celebrated *History of England* as well as essays on moral, religious, and political topics. His reputation for religious skepticism if not atheism barred him from the professorial chair he coveted at Edinburgh University, but when he visited Paris in 1763 he was lionized by the *philosophes* and was widely recognized throughout Europe as the greatest philosophical mind of his day. His repute since then has not diminished; he remains the outstanding British philosopher.

With his daring speculation, his freedom from prejudice, the breadth and range of his intellect, and his acute reasoning, Hume was very much a man of the Enlightenment, indeed he might almost be called its most typical figure. But the position he reached, that of a thoroughgoing skepticism, made the Enlightenment's optimistic rationalism most uncomfortable. It started it on the road to decline ending with Kant's philosophy, Kant in turn having been inspired by Hume.

Hume's path was that of a consistent empiricism, offspring of Locke and Berkeley; he showed that it leads to skepticism. The *Treatises* sought to apply the scientific method to the study of man. Like Locke, Hume began by examining the mind, in order to determine the nature and scope of human knowledge. He improved considerably on Locke's examination of the knowing process. What Locke called "ideas" Hume broke down into (a) sense impressions and then (b) the images formed in the mind as a result of this sense perception. Hume's analysis is considerably more detailed and careful than Locke's or Berkeley's. Without entering very far into it, we can take note of the fact that it led Hume to his famous skepticism in the following ways:

(1) Accepting Berkeley's criticism of any substance or substratum in material objects, he rejected the bishop's belief in "spirits" or minds, pointing out that the same kind of analysis can be applied to them. There is no substance called "the mind," but only a series of psychic happenings. How can we prove from experience "I exist"? All we really know is that acts of perception are being performed.

(2) More significantly, Hume entered upon a long examination of the nature of causal inference. All reasoning we do about factual, empirical matters, he found, is reasoning of this sort, finding relations of cause and effect. In other words if we do any purposeful thinking about the external world of objects, other than simply to record its presence, we must introduce causal inference—as when I decide the baseball travels *because* I struck it with a bat or the ice melts *because* it has grown warm. But at the end of his analysis Hume was led to conclude that there is no certain proof of the validity of any such inferences. That one object is contiguous to another—the ball to the bat—and that there is a temporal order—the ball travels after being struck by the bat —is experienced and therefore known for sure. But we do not experience cause and effect; we only assume it. The assumption rests on repeated experiences in which the same thing happens; but this cannot prove that it always will happen. It may be said that the "course of nature continues always uniformly the same," but this is not demonstrable, and so it can have only probability, even if high probability. It is really a matter of faith. There is nothing in sense experiences to compel us to believe that one event causes another. We are forced to conclude, or at least Hume was, that not reason but "custom" supports our scientific laws. Habitually, we assume that what happened in the past will happen in the future, a thing that "reason would never, in all eternity" be able to demonstrate. Subsequent philosophers have found it difficult to refute Hume's position here, for what it is worth.

(3) Hume's disabused explorations of the ways of the human mind led him to other skeptical conclusions. "Reason" really plays little part in life. Hume devoted a good deal of attention to moral philosophy and found that in regard to our actions "reason . . . can never pretend to any other office than to serve and obey the passions." "Morality is more properly felt than judged of." Reason can tell us nothing of values. Moral judgments rest on feelings of approval or disapproval, which relate to our pleasure or pain, and cannot ultimately be reasoned about. Those people, and Locke was one of them, who claimed that "morality is susceptible of demonstration" were quite in error. There are, of course, moral feelings fairly common among men, as for instance a

widespread aversion to murder, cruelty, deceit, etc., and these are entitled to great respect, but they are not rational, that is, we do not reach them by logic. They are simply feelings, emotions, which cannot be logically dealt with. Men do of course reason about them but to little avail.

Hume's close and careful definition of "reason" emerges with particular vividness in his analysis of moral decisions. "Reason" is not just a state of being calm and judicious. Men commonly say they are pitting "reason" against "emotion" when they restrain some wilder immoral impulse. But in fact they are arming one of the calmer emotions against the more passionate, Hume argued. "Reason" is one of two operations: either abstract reasoning of the sort performed in mathematics and logic, a comparison of ideas, a discernment of their relations to each other (as, four is more than three and two plus two equals four); or empirical, experimental reasoning such as finds and verifies facts in the external world. And on examination it appears that neither can determine moral choices, though they may assist, playing some such "handmaiden" role as Augustine envisaged for reason. For example, if we have to decide whether to go to church or not we can use our powers of observation to count the churches around us and measure the distance to them; we can calculate the habits of our neighbors, examine the Bible for error, read the history of the church, and conceivably do a thousand other things that involve the reason. But Hume insists that when we make our decision we must pass beyond reason to an affective or emotional disposition: we either do or do not want to go to church, and that is it. Reason could never tell us whether this is right or wrong, for that is not its province. In a celebrated passage Hume observed how often moralists make the shift from "is" to "ought" without noticing it; but one cannnot properly do so, and in this point is contained, he says, the whole problem of ethics. It is wrong to say that Hume banished reason from the realm of ethics; but he does say that "reason is, and ought to be the slave of the passions, and can never pretend to any other office than to serve and obey them." Contemporary philosophers have come to very similar conclusions, that assertions of value are beyond reasoning about, they are simply "emotive."

(4) Hume, it hardly needs saying, did not regard the existence of God as demonstrable by reason. He did not claim to be an atheist and evidently thought it probable that there is some general principle of order in the universe based on intelligence. But this is only a guess and far from a provable certainty. It stands on the same plane as cause-and-effect; not found in experience or reason, though we accept it on faith. We may choose to believe, but this is a sheer act of faith—"fideism." Both the deists and the rational Christians were in error, Hume mani-

festly believed, when they talked about reason supporting religion of any sort.

(5) In his political writings Hume reached equally skeptical conclusions. He seems to have begun confidently in the expectation of finding a "science" of politics but quickly decided that political phenomena can yield no such laws as mathematics, that "all general maxims in politics ought to be established with great caution." He joined Montesquieu in dismissing the social contract as fiction, and added that it was not even a necessary fiction. For instead of inventing this feeble myth as a sanction for government one might as well say that government rests on utility, "on opinion only." He rather agreed with Locke and especially Rousseau, whom he knew and befriended during the latter's ordeal of exile and persecution, that men could live well enough without government; he thought the American Indians showed this. But with the increase of wealth and the growing complexity of society government gradually arose because it was useful; there was no explicit contract, though the idea of one might be a symbol, or historical shorthand, for what happened. Force and violence are the aspects of human political history most in evidence thus far (an agreement here with Rousseau, too.) Hume ridiculed Locke's "tacit consent." Most men are forced to live in the country in which they were born. Insofar as they owe obedience to their government, it is because of the utility of government. Society could not today exist without government, so there is a duty of obedience; but if government ceases to be useful, for example if it should become "intolerably oppressive," its claims on our obedience cease.

A government is good or bad, then, in proportion to its usefulness to the community. Paley and Bentham, following Hume, were soon to define this usefulness as the sum of happiness; Hume was one godfather of the utilitarian school, which will be discussed later. This does not indeed take us all the way, because one must then define what is "useful." But at least it disposes of all sorts of efforts to legitimize authority by political metaphysics—hereditary succession, or the divine right of kings, or the social contract. Hume is skeptical here in undercutting a number of sacred cows and also in rejecting abstract reason as a guide in such matters. Political society is in fact rooted in instinct and habit. Custom is a better guide than reason. It is a short step from Hume to Edmund Burke, who regarded rationalism in politics as positively dangerous.

Hume's interest in history was no aberration: he knew that political beliefs and loyalties are the outcome of long social evolution. No one willed them, they grew; men cannot alter them at will, for the "cake of custom" resists rational manipulation. Only time may, or may not, bring further progress and enlightenment. In the eighteenth century, history, which had stood low in the seventeenth century, began to attract more and more serious interest; Hume and Voltaire are the best examples. History becomes not just an idle amusement or a source of practical knowledge of statecraft, but a depository of wisdom and what truth there is, a guide to life.

It must be pointed out that Hume was far from drawing gloomy or enervating conclusions from his skepticism. On the contrary, he was at pains to emphasize that, after all, our healthy human instincts override these quibbles of the reason, and properly so. We *are* moral, we *do* believe in God, and in scientific laws—not because of reason, but because of instinct, or the will to live. This is quite natural and deserving of respect. Reason not only is the slave of passion, it *ought* to be, in daily living. If we pause to reason, Hume says, we are afflicted with doubts, and life would stop if all men were philosophers, which fortunately they are not. (Pierre Bayle, that other great Enlightenment skeptic, had made the same point.) "Most fortunately it happens that since reason is incapable of dispelling these clouds, nature itself suffices to that purpose." I dine, Hume said, converse with my friends, play a game of cards, and then my philosophical speculations appear "cold and strained and ridiculous"; I realize they are a mere game. A game worth playing, but still only a game. One of the perhaps pernicious features of British empirical and positivistic philosophy, as some have thought, was thus begun by Hume: its divorce from real life, to become a verbal game.

But at least Hume carried his skepticism through to the end, for the skeptic must be skeptical of his own skepticism. "A true skeptic will be diffident of his philosophical doubts, as well as of his philosophical conviction." And to mistrust reason is to fall back on the instincts, on habit, on "custom" as Hume most often calls it. These are sound guides in life, if not in philosophy. In this sense, it must be noted, Hume was not a "skeptic." We can and should trust our instincts.

To refute their countryman, the Scottish "commonsense" philosophers, including Thomas Reid, Thomas Brown, and Dugald Stewart, abandoned empiricism and conceded the existence of some "innate ideas" or intuitive principles, trying, in this patchwork manner, to save the structure of "common sense." One can see in them the Enlightenment philosophy in some disarray, perhaps, and yet one can see the powerful drive to keep its clarity and certainty, and not to be led into a bog of confusion by too much reasoning. It is the central paradox of the Enlightenment that what it meant by "reason" was really a religious belief in clarity, and that reason itself slew this sort of reason. The chief murderers of Enlightenment "clear light of reason" were those archrationalists, Berkeley and Hume.

Certainly with Hume there is not much left of that confident expectation of a wholly new method which would yield certainty. This is true if we consider that Hume thinks, quite like Montaigne, that we can know virtually nothing for sure from "reason"—nothing, at least, that matters. On the other hand, the scientific method of careful observation and exact analysis had no finer practitioner than the Scotsman. And he had certainly greatly advanced human knowledge if he had deflated human reason. The Enlightenment could hardly be the same after Hume, but it might still be a kind of Enlightenment.

As we have seen, Hume himself encouraged a tendency to dismiss his conclusions as possibly fanciful. He is often considered today to be the greatest of all British philosophers, and no one has ever convincingly refuted his skeptical arguments in many particulars. But like Berkeley he encountered a reluctance of his age to take him seriously. Only in quite recent times, perhaps, has he come fully into his own as a philosopher. In the eighteenth century, "the deductions of Berkeley and Hume from the empirical philosophy of ideas did little to deflect the course of that philosophy. The outlook of Locke and Newton continued to rule" for some time. (M. H. Carré).

One or two other comments about Hume: His delightful open-mindedness is illustrated by his once helping one of his critics, who had assailed him in a way Hume thought could be improved upon, so he offered to sharpen up some of the criticisms! He helped his rivals get published. One apparent inconsistency in his rejection of all absolutes was his addiction to neoclassicism in matters of style and taste, on which he wrote some essays: he believed in the moderate, dispassionate, simple and correct style, rejected Shakespeare and Milton, and thought a now-forgotten dramatist named John Home superior to the Bard. Thus he was not immune to at least one of his age's blind spots.

Hume's thought is of a far richer texture than these brief remarks can suggest, of course. His influence has come down to us in innumerable ways and is still operating. We have mentioned the contemporary analytical and positivist philosophers; Hume also influenced Edmund Husserl, who stands as one of the founders of the type of philosophy regnant in France and Germany today. Thus he might be said to be a common denominator in all present-day philosophizing. His ethical and political thought has been equally influential. While Edmund Burke and Jeremy Bentham carried on his lineage in two rather different directions politically, his friend Adam Smith found inspiration in Hume for the foundation of modern economic theory, and nineteenth-century British liberalism owed much to the tolerance and catholicity of the Scotsman. Absolutists and "crusaders" have usually not liked him because of his crusty skepticism, yet some highly unorthodox and influential moderns have shared this spirit. One thinks, for example, of the American jurist Oliver Wendell Holmes, Jr., who held the "humbug" of utopian socialists and reformers in robust contempt, but was himself a deeply probing questioner of all kinds of sacred cows. Wherever the dispassionate critical intelligence operates, free from all prejudices and prepossessions, there is the spirit of David Hume, destructive or bracing, as one may choose to call it. Pretty clearly it is both, and to repeat, it dissolved the more positive faith of the Enlightenment along with other forms of faith.

The Birth of the Social Sciences in the Enlightenment

The eighteenth century, needless to say, held "science" in great repute. "The philosophic spirit is, then, a spirit of observation and exactness," D'Alembert wrote in the Encyclopedia. Observe, experiment, analyze; frame clear, exact general laws on the basis of careful research— here was the infallible method, child of Descartes and Newton, now supposedly brought to perfection. Nothing remained except to extend this method to all those areas still languishing in superstition and disorder. The spirit of the century was that of Bayle: "errors are none the better for being old"; let us by efficient mental work clean up all the sloppiness and credulity of the past. It was also that which Alexander Pope expressed in the famous line, "the proper study of mankind is man."

Through the century, further advances in the natural and physical realms encouraged belief in scientific progress. At mid-century, electricity became the universal toy, as savants and amateurs arranged demonstrations of the mysterious force. In 1746 Van Musschenbroek invented the Leyden jar, and in 1752 Benjamin Franklin came over from America to conduct his famous experiments showing that lightning is electricity. At the end of the century Alessandro Volta found how to store electrical energy in a primitive battery. Men built primitive steam engines and locomotives, ascended into the sky in balloons as great crowds watched (in Paris in 1783)—and began the "industrial revolution." Kay and Crompton and Arkwright and Newcomen and Watt launched Great Britain into the age of machine technology, though the consequences did not clearly show up until the beginning of the next century. The automobile, the railroad, the airplane, the telegraph, and the mechanized factory could be glimpsed in embryo in the eighteenth century—just barely discernible, but sufficiently to suggest the fascinating picture of almost unlimited technological progress. In the realm of theory, such mathematicians as d'Alembert, Lagrange, and at the end of the century Laplace refined and perfected the Newtonian mechanics.

In other areas of science, Buffon described the forms of living things while the Swede, Linnaeus, classified them and Maupertuis and Diderot speculated about their origins in a way that foreshadowed nineteenth-century evolutionary theory. Chemistry began its somewhat belated revolt against Aristotle and proceeded during the course of the century to make itself into a modern science, a path traversed roughly between Stahl (1717) and Lavoisier (1783).

Nevertheless it was the study of Man that held the center of the stage during the Enlightenment.[2] Here was the exciting frontier, where one could combine the humanistic interest so strong in this age with the equally respected scientific method of Newton and Locke. Today, we are inclined to see the imperfections in eighteenth-century social science, its oversimplifications and excessive optimism. Its error would seem to lie in the effort to reduce humanity to physics, to make of man and of society Newtonian machines. But it cannot be denied that it founded the social sciences as they have developed in the modern world—economics, sociology, historical studies, political science, psychology, anthropology. They all emerged from the womb of the Enlightenment, and their parents were such general luminaries of the age as Hume, Voltaire, Montesquieu. The latter's pioneer step in political science has already been noticed, as one of the classics of the French Enlightenment. In the 1760s and 1770s, interest began to focus principally on *les economistes*, or those known in France as Physiocrats (= government or rule by Nature).

Economics

In the background of economic theory lay certain ethical interests and problems of the century. Modern economists, strictly "scientific," might be surprised to learn that their study began life as an offshoot of the study of morals; but in a very significant way it did. Adam Smith, the greatest of all eighteenth-century economic theorists, was a professor of moral philosophy who before he wrote his immortal *Wealth of Nations* (1776) produced a treatise on the moral sentiments (1759). A book that impressed the Physiocrats deeply was Helvétius's *De l'esprit*, the tract that caused such an uproar in 1759 because it stoutly supported a hedonistic ethic—good is what brings pleasure, bad pain. In a milder way Lord Shaftesbury, Francis Hutcheson (a Scottish mentor of Adam Smith) and Hume had argued similarly. For economic science, the sig-

---

[2]It is, indeed, possible for C. E. Raven to write (*Natural Religion and Christian Theology*, 1953) that science suffered a "sudden and complete eclipse" in the eighteenth century. By comparison with the seventeenth, there are certainly few really great names.

nificance of this was that this science assumed as its basic postulate an "economic man" who always seeks to maximize his happiness. "To obtain the greatest amount of pleasure, with the least public expense, is the perfection of economic conduct," Quesnay, first of the Physiocrats, announced at the beginning of his pioneer study, the *Tableau économique* (1758). Without this "economic man," there could hardly be a science of economics. "Economic man" believes that worldly happiness is the end of life and is prepared to strive for this goal in systematic, predictable ways. Apparently one of the presuppositions of economic science in the modern sense was the widespread acceptance of this hedonistic ethic. It may seem obvious to people today; but the Enlightenment's persistent "pursuit of happiness" reflected a somewhat new bent. The Greeks had preferred wisdom to happiness, the Romans power, medieval men sanctity; even Calvin and the Protestants, who allegedly introduced the elements of a "capitalistic ethic" (hard work, frugality, sobriety) had not meant to place worldly success as the ultimate desideratum.

Another prerequisite was economic individualism. The new students and practitioners of "political economy" took for granted that the self-reliant, independent individual, liberated from domination by various groups, is the typical unit of society. Much in social as well as intellectual evolution had been preparing for this. Hobbes, Locke, and Rousseau had helped with their sovereign individuals who came together to create government. An equally familiar ingredient in the new economic thought was the idea of a social harmony that somehow results from the combined actions of individuals. If we have individual economic men —as Adam Smith will say, "Every individual continually exerting himself to find out the most advantageous employment for whatever capital he can command"—what prevents this from being a chaos of conflicting wills, a recipe for social anarchy? Fortunately, as Smith put it, Providence has provided by means of an "invisible hand" that the advantage of society as a whole is served when individuals strive for their own gain. Portions of *The Wealth of Nations* accept the idea made famous by Bernard Mandeville—the proposition that "private vices equal public virtues." Men scrambling for gain and desiring in their greed to live luxuriously supply work for the poor and bring wealth into the nation. This notion of a social harmony clearly owed much to the analogy of Newton's universe, in which particles work together to form a single great system.

Prior to the Physiocrats and Smith, speculation on economic questions had by no means been lacking. Already Montesquieu (1748) had brought forward the idea of a general science of social phenomena. All the French Physiocrats acknowledged a debt to the *Spirit of the Laws*. Ever since Bodin, an undercurrent of serious economic theorizing accompanied a great deal of practical pamphleteering, addressed to particular issues. John Locke himself, and his contemporary Dudley North, had contributed ideas. In France, Cantillon's *Essai sur la nature de commerce* circulated in manuscript early in the century (it was not printed until 1755), and Melon's 1734 *Essai politique sur le commerce* was another attack on "mercantilist" economic thought.

A word on this earlier economics known as mercantilism is in order here. Thinking about economic subjects was not new. After Adam Smith, it became fashionable to dismiss all that had gone before as both random and irrelevant—simpleminded, unsystematic, filled with error. To this earlier body of economic writings, extending from the late sixteenth to the earlier eighteenth century, the term "mercantilism" was rather cavalierly applied—the term being a later invention, designed to classify various phenomena, rather like "feudalism" was applied to the political order of the Middle Ages by modern historians. More recent students are inclined to doubt both that the term will suffice, or that it is fair to dismiss all this literature as at most of historic interest. Mercantilism was said to have been a program for building up economic strength in obvious ways, looked at from a commercial point of view, its judgments usually piecemeal and simple. But, while it may be agreed that much of this thought lacked order and system compared to the "classical" economists (Adam Smith and after), these pioneers paved the way for later syntheses and were the first to postulate that man could, by taking thought, guide his actions to increase wealth. In the seventeenth century, William Petty's "Political Arithmetic" dreamed of applying Cartesian mathematical analysis to economic phenomena. In general, the mercantilists were more optimistic about the possibility of planning for economic improvement than were their more distinguished successors. But they also saw that sometimes there are "laws" that defy the will of statesmen, and so came to suggest that the wise politician tries to go with "nature" rather than against it.

Whatever their merits, the earlier writers on economic subjects came to be superseded in the age of the Physiocrats and Adam Smith. Mercantilism was accused of fostering unnatural interference with "liberty of trade." The old economic order, whether approved by all the "mercantilist" theorists or not, was regulatory and discriminatory. It was protectionist. Imports competing with native manufactures were evidently bad, since they threw native artisans out of work, and so were restricted or prohibited. Losing gold and silver was also felt to be an evil, while gaining the precious metals was a good. "Good" trade was encouraged by subsidies; such was the exporting of native manufactures in return for foreign raw materials. Tariffs, prohibitions, subsidies tried to assure a "favorable balance of trade" and the protection of domestic manufactures. In addition the state sometimes attempted to control wages and prices.

Scattered attacks upon this "system," which was susceptible to corruption, were not entirely absent before 1750, and sometimes took the form of suggesting that "liberty of trade" might be preferable to this cumbersome apparatus of special privileges. David Hume launched a major theoretical assault when he pointed out that the favorable balance of trade is an illusion which economic laws always defeat in the long run. For a favorable balance brings in specie, which causes prices to rise, and thus exports to fall off. Conversely, if a nation has an adverse balance its prices will fall and it will gain markets. Thus an equilibrium is bound to be struck. (Substantially the same point was made by the French pioneer, Cantillon, about the same time.) Hume's economic speculations, though less extensive and systematic than his friend and fellow Scotsman's, Adam Smith, helped prepare for the latter's.

But the Physiocrats, beginning with Quesnay, were the first to build a system on the premise that economic activity should be entirely free. Quesnay, court physician to Louis XV, was soon joined by the Marquis Mirabeau (father of the French Revolutionary statesman) and many others to form a party or school that was easily the most significant such movement in France in the 1770s. Voltaire, with characteristic wit, said that about 1760 France became bored with plays and epigrams and started talking about wheat. The French economy was in trouble from the war of 1756–1763 on until the Revolution broke out in 1789, one symptom of that distress being a chronic inability to balance the national government's budget. So the Physiocrats' attack on the old system, with proposals for sweeping reform, was bound to receive a hearing though it might meet opposition from entrenched interests. The Physiocrats were, perhaps, too dogmatic to be successful reformers. But their dogmas made intellectual history. They insisted upon full liberty of economic activity, based on individual property rights in a freely competitive economy. This meant dismantling the whole structure of governmental regulation, it meant throwing down tariff walls, it meant drastically simplifying the tax system. At bottom, it meant treating individuals as economic equals (equal in rights, by no means necessarily in wealth or station, for men have unequal talents).

The Physiocrats had a pronounced agrarian bias. A startling feature of their creed from the modern viewpoint was its denial of any value to commerce and industry. France was then an overwhelmingly agricultural country, one peculiarly favored for agriculture as compared to her great rival England, so this was less an eccentricity than it may seem. Aristotle had ranked agriculture first, "because of its justice," and Benjamin Franklin, the American sage, declared that farming was the only honest way of making a living. So this bias against commerce and industry was widespread and deep-seated. It had been prominent of course in medieval Christianity. Physiocratic doctrine held that only agriculture produces a surplus. Commerce is only a barren exchange, manufacturing adds no more than the value of the artisan's labor; but the soil is productive. This agrarianism was actually related closely to the Physiocrats' free-trade liberalism. They backed their demand for the elimination of all taxes except one, on land, by the argument that all taxes must in any case come from that source, the only one that creates value. And they proposed to throw trade open to competition because they thought that rich merchants were gaining an illicit profit by monopoly. Free competition would ensure that no merchant or manufacturer got more than his just reward. French physiocracy did not lead so easily into the economics of the industrial era as did Adam Smith in Great Britain. Though the Physiocrats have achieved immortality as founders of the modern science of economics in a general sense, they rather withered on the agricultural vine, dying out with the coming of the industrial century.

But neither must Adam Smith be put down as an apologist for "capitalism." Because the nineteenth-century bourgeois-industrialist economists (Ricardo, Senior, Mill) stemmed from Smith, foes of industrial capitalism in the nineteenth century often believed that Smith was its apologist, but this was hardly so. First, Smith on occasion scolded all who pursued wealth, praising the simple, frugal life. He much admired Rousseau, as well as Voltaire. More notably, he did not like merchants at all. He had considerable sympathy for the agricultural community, and in a most remarkable chapter on "The Laboring Poor" he indicated far more sympathy with the plight of this class than was common in his day. The workers, Smith thought, were oppressed and cheated by their employers, who conspired to keep their wages low. They were victimized by excise taxes, which bear unfairly on the poor, keeping their wages too low to the detriment of the nation. All this, and more in *The Wealth of Nations*, testifies to a radical and anticapitalist strain in Smith. It is ironic that he became known as author of the businessman's bible.

The Wealth of Nations fully endorsed the Physiocrats' program of economic liberty. Let the government cease subsidizing and regulating, and much inequity and iniquity will disappear, Smith believed. Enhance the individual's scope of action, and energies will be unleashed leading to economic progress for the whole community. "Superintending the industry of private people, and directing it towards the employments most suitable to the interest of the society" should be no part of the duty of the state. Let the sovereign power defend the nation's shores and perhaps run its post offices and schools, while administering justice with an even hand; beyond that, let each individual look to his own interests, which he knows best and can best advance. Government is in no way fitted to carry on economic functions. That no one can efficiently operate an enterprise in which he does not have his own interests at stake was a principle which led Smith to reject not only government in business but also the joint-stock companies, ancestors of the modern corporation. Smith would not have been a friend to the huge modern corporation, any more than he was to the monopolists and absentee owners of his day. Essentially he spoke for the small entrepreneur. He apparently believed, or half-believed, that the principle of *laissez-faire* would also benefit the "laboring poor," by striking at their chief oppressors, the rich monopolists.

Smith's first comprehensive textbook of economic science treated the whole range of economic phenomena in a way that determined the pattern of all future writers on the subject. His favorite theory, if one could be singled out, was that of the division of labor (though he was not the first, by any means, to think of this). Increased economic efficiency results from specialization. The tailor does not make his own shoes, but buys them from the shoemaker, who does not make his own clothes but employs a tailor; and thus both profit. It should be the same way in international trade. Mercantilism refused to trade with the foreigner; but if the foreigner can make something cheaper than we can, let us buy it from him and send him in exchange something we make cheaper than he does. Free trade, obviously, linked closely to the doctrine of the division of labor. The fewer obstacles to trade in the world, the more opportunity there is for specialization.

Smith did not go so far as the Physiocrats, whom he regarded as overly dogmatic, in denying productivity to commerce and industry. He made use of the labor theory of value, to be found earlier in primitive form in John Locke (and indeed Locke did not originate it) who had declared that the earth produces nothing until men work it and therefore "It is labour then which puts the greatest part of the value on land. . . ." "The value of any commodity," Smith wrote, "to the person who possesses it, and who means not to use or consume it himself, but to exchange it for other commodities, is equal to the quantity of labour which it enables him to purchase or command." Thus began a theory destined to a long future, adopted by both Ricardo and Karl Marx in varying ways until abandoned a century after *The Wealth of Nations*. Smith, however, did not assign to labor the right to all wealth produced; both "stock" (capital) and land have legitimate claims; profit and rent are part of the cost of production, the former because of the role of interest and the reward for risk. Smith was somewhat cloudy on the exact relationship. Here as elsewhere he began the discussions that others would carry on during the next century. Another example is the theory of wages, and the doctrine that population always drives wages down to the subsistence point, later associated with the name of Thomas Malthus.

His book came close to being the book of the century; one has only to think of compiling a list of the century's most influential books to realize that it would be one of the few obvious and unanimous choices, along with *The Spirit of the Laws* and *The Social Contract*. Before long, political economy was being cited by statesmen, as for example by William Pitt the younger, as authority for the dismantling of mercantilist regulations. The new views made their way slowly but inexorably. In France, Voltaire long remained loyal to the mercantilism of Colbert, against the attacks of the Physiocrats.[3] Frederick the Great passed from mercantilism to free trade, aided by the influence of the brilliant Count Mirabeau, subsequently prominent in the first phase of the French Revolution, whose father the Marquis Mirabeau was a well-known Physiocrat. Baron d'Holbach's *Système social*, an avant garde political tract of 1773, shows strong physiocratic influence. With the enthusiasm of missionaries the Physiocrats sought to disseminate their creed, though they encountered censorship and, even more serious, ridicule: an age that demanded wit in its men of learning found most of these tracts of the *economistes*, unhappily, rather tedious. But Smith among others succeeded in making economic science readable, and as for the ideas of the economists, they seemed to spread as if the times were on their side. A new body of scientific thought had been born, destined to become a permanent fixture in the West. The younger Mirabeau raised a typical voice in praise of "this simple and profound science which is called *economic*, and which in our day has finally demonstrated principles long ignored and unknown. . . . Men will be happy only when it will have become familiar to kings."

In time it did. It may be noted, again, that the Physiocrats were bold reformers in their day. One of their basic principles was that everyone regardless of class should be considered equal for purposes of taxation. This is close to being what the French Revolution was about. The economists postulated as one of their fundamental theses that men should be treated alike, each to count as the same. Their other fundamental thesis was, of course, liberty—men to be left alone, freed from arbitrary and unequal restrictions or favors. These were radical principles at that time, little though some later radicals might like them. The wealthy and privileged were their enemies. The economists were

---

[3]Interested at first, he went into farming near Ferney, draining marshes and planting clover, but failed to make money and turned against the agrarians; see *L'Homme aux quarante sous*, 1768.

faithful to Enlightenment precepts, moreover, in regarding men as much the same everywhere: theirs was a rationalistic internationalism which produced "citizens of the world."

We should take note especially of the ways in which economic science fitted the outlook of the Enlightenment. It sought great general laws, like Newton's; it tried to make of the social organism a machine, comprehensible through being governed by ascertainable principles. Its idea of liberty or laissez-faire was based on the view that society would "go of itself" like any good machine, like the world-machine unveiled by Sir Isaac. The social world should display as much natural order as the physical one. It ought not to be a mere pushing and pulling of wills, but an orderly system. Find the key, and the machine might be wound up thereafter to run itself in obedience to the unchanging laws of economic behavior.

Historical Writing

The Enlightenment spirit, insofar as it searched for the hard, ascertained fact and was impatient of sloppiness in research, and likewise in its rejection of supernatural for natural explanations in human affairs, was favorable to historical research, and there was a good deal of history written in the eighteenth century, some of high quality. Among the greater men of letters who wrote serious history were Voltaire and Hume; more famous than either the former's *Age of Louis XIV* or the latter's *History of England* (both popular books) was Edward Gibbon's classic *Decline and Fall of the Roman Empire*, a subject that had also interested the historically-minded Montesquieu. These works were based on more thorough research than most previous ones (the rationalistic seventeenth century notably disparaged history) and they also showed some capacity for analyzing and interpreting the facts. Some, therefore, have credited the eighteenth century with founding the modern study of history.

On the other hand, the Enlightenment really did not have a highly developed historical sense. It had a prejudice against much of the past, feeling that all it contained was error. D'Alembert expressed a wish that the past might be abolished; Voltaire was only interested in "the age of reason," dawning with Descartes. Many of the *philosophes* were intrigued by the idea of progress, and wrote sketches, as did Condorcet, of the successive eras of the human race as it marched onward and upward, but their views on all but the last one or two eras were rather fanciful. They had little interest in national history or awareness of national differences. History is written for many reasons, but history as a serious and sustained object of investigation probably depends upon a belief that knowledge of the past is vital to our understanding of the present, and of the human situation generally—a belief that to *understand* anything we must study it genetically, by tracing its growth. This in the main the Enlightenment did not have. The *philosophes* did not see what relevance the history of the more remote epochs had to anything (Montesquieu was an exception here) and, feeling that the solution to present problems lay in some sort of social science, they had little desire to use history as a means of attaining knowledge about the present.

The great exception to Enlightenment present-mindedness was Giambattista Vico, often seen today as the greatest theoretical pioneer of modern historical studies. Vico held that human history is the most knowable of subjects—a refutation of Cartesian scientism—since men have made it and can therefore understand it; he felt that understanding of the past enables us to understand the present, offered a good many practical rules of method for historians to steer by, and understood very well that past epochs were not like our own. He speculated about a cyclical pattern in history. Vico was an amazing genius who contributed striking ideas not only about history but about language, myth, and the evolution of the law. But, writing in Naples, he was not well known outside his own region for a long time; he probably influenced Herder and the German historians of the later romantic era, but few others during the eighteenth century. Vico and subsequently the German romantics held that each epoch and people of history has made its unique contribution to the whole, none better or worse than another, each "equidistant from eternity" in the words of Leopold von Ranke. This obviously encouraged the careful study of every part of the past as worthy in its own right. This was not the dominant eighteenth-century view; few past epochs had been worthy at all, most had been sunk in hopeless ignorance, only the modern period represented anything of value. Nor had this modern epoch grown organically out of the past, for on the whole this explanation by tracing origins, the genetic approach, was alien to the Enlightenment mentality.

Yet a series of eighteenth-century tracts speculated about the course of human development and brought to birth the idea of progress. The Greeks, and Renaissance humanists such as Machiavelli had practically no conception of a progress toward social perfection. It has been noted that one needs only a slight logical alteration in the Christian scheme of a progress towards final salvation to give you the secular version of the millennium. Logically slight, the change was nonetheless substantively enormous; it brought heaven down to earth, and seemed to substitute the hopefulness of a real utopia for the gloom of a dubious one after death in some intangible paradise. Near the end of the century, in a famous essay on the progress of the human mind, the Marquis de Condorcet, a Voltaire disciple, divided European history into ten stages of development, of which he thought his own era the ninth, on the verge of reaching a final one marked by indefinite "perfectibility." More speculation than empirical historical investigation, such beliefs in an orderly plan running through all the past provided a framework favorable to the study of the past.

History is perhaps a conservative study; it burgeoned on the outlook of Edmund Burke after 1790, according to which human society is a complex organism slowly growing, not to be rearranged arbitrarily by a social blueprint, perhaps scarcely subject to the will of man at all. Modern historical as well as sociological studies stem from the post-French Revolution schools of conservative thought, more than from the Enlightenment. Though Hume is an evident exception, the eighteenth-century *philosophes* in the main were too rationalistic and optimistic for this sort of view. They believed in an ideal order of society, worked out by reason and put into effect by political engineers. The conception of a slow and endless growth could not have pleased them. More congenial to them was the headlong rush toward Utopia.

The fact remains that they laid the foundations of historical science in their methodology of exactness and criticism. And during this century the great public museums, libraries, and archives came into being to facilitate the historian's work, a matter of the first importance.

Other Social Sciences

Though worthy of more extensive treatment, the other sciences of man must be sparsely summarized. A kind of psychology lay very close to the central themes of the Enlightenment: Locke's *tabula rasa* mind, which built "complex ideas" out of "simple ideas" or sense impressions, formed the basis for an examination of the knowing process, which Hume, as we have seen, carried forward to a most careful and detailed analysis. David Hartley, an Englishman quite famous in his day, worked out a mechanistic psychology based on the "laws of association," which long appeared in the textbooks of psychology. Eighteenth-century Lockean psychology was what we would now call "behavioristic," that is, it tried to reduce mental phenomena to mechanical, predictable reactions to external stimuli. This had overtones of social reform. "If I can demonstrate that man is, in fact, nothing more than the product of his education," wrote Helvétius, "I shall doubtless reveal an important truth to mankind. They will learn that . . . to be happy and powerful nothing more is necessary than to perfect the science of education." The mind, being subject to the exact laws of learning, can be manipulated as one chooses by careful control of the environment. If this today may raise repellent images of totalitarian brainwashing, in the eighteenth century it meant a hopeful means of wiping out evil and securing indefinite progress. The mind is infinitely improvable because infinitely malleable; there are no fixed, innate limitations—no original sin, for example. Thus many construed the Lockean psychology as carried on by such as Hartley and Helvétius.

Implied was an educational revolution, and there were more reformers than Rousseau in this area. Such reformers, like the Frenchman La Chalotais, believed that one learns by doing—"man is made for action" and criticized traditional methods of study for being too bookish and intellectualist. They were the forerunners of what in twentieth-century America would be called "progressive" education.

Enlightenment psychology is the ancestor of much modern experimental psychology, behaviorist or Pavlovian; and one may even claim for it deeper insights. There are speculations in the far-ranging works of Diderot that anticipate Freud, and the shady figure of the Marquis de Sade, author of scabrous and indecent novels, can be seen as beginning the study of sexology. However, this "depth psychology," venturing near the irrational pools of the unconscious, was not typical of the Enlightenment, which was "externalist" rather than internalist, seeking in society the factors that determined the individual mind. One of the most scandalous but significant books of the *philosophes* was *L'Homme machine*, by the physician La Mettrie (1748), in which he boldly asserted that man is only a machine. While the ethical consequences La Mettrie drew from this were alarming (machines are not responsible for their actions, crime does not exist, the only proper goal of life is sensual pleasure), the idea itself rather coincided with the main bent of Enlightenment thinking about the mind.

Of Vico the historian and Montesquieu the political scientist it may be said that they could as well be called sociologists. The term was not coined until the nineteenth century (by August Comte); the thing itself, if we define it as a scientific approach to social phenomena, greatly interested the eighteenth-century savants though they lacked the resources to carry it out. It would be better to say that history, sociology, psychology, and political science were all mixed up together, in this their infancy, as the "science of man." Only later did they get broken down into specialties. Economics was long known as "political economy," indicative of the linkage. Here again, on the organizational side, orderly collection of statistical data and its preservation started. It is, for example, only toward the end of the eighteenth century that accurate data on population becomes available.

Buffon, the naturalist whose *Histoire naturelle* ranked among the most distinguished scholarly works of the century, extended his range (1749) to *The Natural History of Man*. Why and how do the various races of man differ? Information about such matters was as yet extremely sketchy, but the quest was begun. Montesquieu's *Spirit of Laws* speculated on the cultural differences among men, tracing these to climate and geography, as we know. Information about strange people began to flow in: the first real knowledge about Chinese history and culture; the first translations from Hindu literature by Sir William Jones and the Frenchman Anquetil-Duperron.

It was only a beginning; most of the work remained to be done. But the idea was born. Montesquieu expressed it: human laws and customs, in all their bewildering diversity, do not represent merely "fantasies," but are explained by laws ("necessary relations derived from the nature of things"); and particular laws lead to more general laws, in an ascending hierarchy. At the end, the single law of man, Newton's gravitation principle in its social counterpart. This was the will-o'-the-wisp that drew Enlightenment man on. He was destined never to find it, but the quest aroused men of genius to scholarly labors for more than a century thereafter, and still does.

The Diffusion of the Enlightenment

We have thus far dealt mainly with the Enlightenment in France. France in the eighteenth century was by far the most important nation in the Western world; apart from its enormous prestige in the arts and sciences it had (as some people today may fail to realize) a far greater population than any other European country—four or five times as many as Great Britain, more even than Russia at that time. It also had, in Paris, its one great city where all its brilliance came to a single point, and Paris belonged to the world.

We have also mentioned the English Enlightenment in so far as this meant Locke, Berkeley and Hume, and the brilliant "Scottish inquiry" that culminated in Adam Smith. The English eighteenth century deserves a little more than this. It had a rather different flavor than the French, for England was more self-satisfied. No irresolvable political and social crises seemed to disturb her equanimity, as in France, where despite economic progress the problems of administrative reform and social hierarchy plagued the state until, receiving no solution, they erupted in the Revolution of 1789. The British had had their revolution. Having somehow achieved stability and liberty after nearly a century of turmoil, the British after 1715 showed no disposition to rock the boat, but felt, with the long-time "prime minister" Robert Walpole, that it was best to let sleeping dogs lie (*quieta non movere*). There is not much sharp social criticism, and almost no political discontent, in England until we reach the 1760s, and then the protest is mild by the standards of the French 1789. There is no English Voltaire, no English Rousseau, no crusade against the church. If Voltaire meant little to England, that redoubtable Englishman, Dr. Samuel Johnson, could see only madness in Rousseau. Undemocratic and somewhat corrupt the eighteenth-century constitution might be, but it brought England prosperity, peace, and liberty. Even the critical mind of David Hume could find little to complain of in political England: he gave thanks that he could write freely in "a land of toleration and of liberty." By the 1770s this had changed somewhat in that a few were beginning to clamor for a more representative and democratically elected Parliament, others for legal and not merely *de facto* religious liberty and equality. But they still battled complacency, the natural fruit of success.

Complacency, gentility, decorum, and a little too much moderation may mark the English eighteenth century, against which the gloomy rages of the great Dean Swift beat in vain. Yet the "Augustan age" had great charm. Its architecture, Palladian-classical, was stolid and unadventurous, perhaps, but it built pleasant and eye-pleasing homes for middle-class as well as aristocratic Englishmen, and many, many gracious churches. Its literature was a delight, with all its limitations by the later standards of romanticism. A social art, it aimed to instruct through pleasing, to teach good manners, to make gentlemen; it knew nothing of the strident romantic urge to individual self-expression. Augustan England read the amiable essays of Joseph Addison, discussed Robinson Crusoe's bourgeois virtues, laughed with Fielding and Gay (whose satire was essentially gentle and constructive, compared to the Continental style), and shed gentle tears with Richardson and Cowper. A limited literature no doubt, but a charming one. Its greatest poet in the first half of the century was the incredibly skilled craftsman Alexander Pope, who aimed to say

What oft was thought, but ne'er so well expressed

(for, "works may have more wit than does them good"). Its greatest literary figure in the 1760–1780 period was the master conversationalist, poet, critic, and lexicographer Dr. Johnson, who presided over the best talk England ever heard, casting his epigrams into the waiting ears of Boswell. All this is literary history. It is also intellectual history, for a whole set of ideas, about nature and man and God and society, lay beneath this composed stylization. But these ideas, Lockean and Newtonian, neoclassical and rationalist, may be omitted here on the grounds that they were fairly similar to the French Enlightenment or have already been noted.

On the Continent in other places than France, French styles tended to dominate European life as has seldom been the case at any time. Frederick the Great of Prussia chose to speak and write in French; the same was true in Russia. In the eighteenth century, France continued the cultural domination begun in the seventeenth, there being nothing in Europe to compete with her Voltaires, Montesquieus, and Rousseaus, nor with her artists either. It is true that the *philosophes* made a point of preferring Italian opera to French—and importing it. Englishmen who made the "grand tour" for their education, as became the custom at this time, went to Italy as well as France. But French style, the exquisite Louis XV style, reigned supreme in furniture, decoration, and architecture. Some of the German courts took up this "rococo" fashion and did even better with it; today one can hardly surpass the gems of this vintage at Munich, Ansbach, and Würzburg. But the style was originally and basically French; French manners and dress also set the fashions. With imitations of Versailles all over Europe, from Copenhagen to Lisbon, small wonder a French architect wrote in 1765 that "everywhere you will find our architects occupying the first position. Our sculptors are equally diffused everywhere. . . . Paris is to Europe what Athens was to Greece; she furnishes the artists to all the rest of the world." He might have added, the ideas.

It will not do, nevertheless, to neglect the other countries. The Enlightenment was cosmopolitan. Not often were any of the *philosophes* caught being patriotic or nationalistic; they spoke, rather, of ideas knowing no boundaries, of reason being the same everywhere, of a single race of man. Montesquieu, in a much-quoted sentence, said that he did not wish to know anything that was good for France but bad for humanity. Voltaire once quite shamelessly wrote an ode to French military victory, when he wished to get something from the king, but he more typically hated wars and armies, and loved learning and pleasure wherever it might be. He once congratulated Frederick of Prussia on a victory won over the French! Lessing, the German *philosophe*, rejoiced that he had exchanged his fatherland for the human race. So, if the French writers dominated the eighteenth century, they did not do so in any spirit of arrogant nationalism, but offered their intellectual wares generously to anyone in any country who might wish to respond.

In Germany the legacy of Leibniz through Christian Wolff has been mentioned. The generation of Lessing (*c.* 1745–1770) reacted against this rather arid rationalism and reached out to France and England. Gotthold Ephraim Lessing was notably fond of English thought, but devoured everything of worth in both countries. Critic, scholar, dramatist, and philosopher, Lessing reveals the versatility of the eighteenth-century *philosophe*; and, if he reacted against Wolff, he still had the cool rationality, the passion for clarity, which marks off the Enlightenment from the romantic movement ahead. Like Voltaire, Lessing's works are scattered over many fields and are somewhat fragmentary; but no writer ever exerted more influence by applying a lively, critical spirit to all things—contributing, as Lessing said, to the *fermenta cognitionis*, the ferment of the mind. Retaining Leibniz's optimism, Lessing wrote *The Education of the Human Race* to suggest that man's progress towards full reason and truth unfolds gradually through history.[4] This was a harbinger of that notable German interest in history which bloomed subsequently with Herder, Fichte, and Hegel. But such sketches of an outline of history showing some plan of progress were typical of the Enlightenment, Condorcet's being the best known.

Lessing, "the founder of German literature" as he has perhaps too exuberantly been hailed (after all, there was Martin Luther and there was "Simplicissimus"), had a flair for style and an itch for controversy, both *philosophe* traits; he was less impious than most of the French, declaring himself impatient of the shallowness and dogmatism of the "freethinkers." But not without reason, in view of his interests, personality, and tone, has he been called "the typical man of the Enlightenment." And he did much to arouse a rather somnolent Germany to a more vigorous intellectual life, marked by a critical spirit, high literary and scholarly standards, the reception of fresh ideas. He prepared the way for the most brilliant generation in German history, the one that produced Goethe, Schiller, Herder, Kant, and Fichte.

Among other German *illuminati*, mention might be made of J. H. G. Justi (1720–1771), a kind of German Benjamin Franklin full of practical projects such as postal service and transplanting the silk industry from Japan; a wide-ranging writer on political, economic, and educational reforms, the father of "Cameralism"; believer also in enlightened despotism.

Other countries also responded to the lure of the Enlightenment. The Marquis de Beccaria, of Milan, built on Montesquieu in his cele-

---

[4]Providing a possible solution to our friend, the problem of evil: evil lessens with each generation, as God's plan unfolds, everyone contributing his mite to its extinction. It is a higher good to allow mankind to participate in the extermination of evil.

brated treatise on *Crimes and Punishments,* which, in turn, inspired Catherine of Russia in her attempt to reform the legal code of backward Russia. We have mentioned the Neapolitan philosopher, Vico, whose "new science" was historical sociology. A reawakened sense of history seems to have been a mark of the Enlightenment throughout Italy, as was an effort to modernize antiquated structures of law and government. Tuscany, as E. W. Cochrane has pointed out, became deeply interested in French thought in the age of Voltaire, Montesquieu, and company; the conception of Enlightenment (*illuminismo*), though with a certain difference, struck Florence who bestirred herself for the first time since the glorious *cinquecento* and showed a receptivity to many of the new ideas.

"Enlightened despotism," meaning the rationalizing and simplifying of government, more orderly systems of law and penology, and a degree of acceptance of mutual obligations between ruler and ruled, came to Florence as it did to other countries—Spain, Russia, Austria, Prussia. In Spain, the Enlightenment revived another people whose intellectual and political life had seemed to decay with the loss of power after the "Golden Age" of the sixteenth century. The degree of somnolence is indicated by the fact that (so scholars tell us) in the year 1705 only four books were published in all Spain, and these trivial. Descartes, Gassendi, and Newton were condemned as pernicious error, most scientific subjects banned altogether. Spain lay steeped in ignorance and superstition as the inglorious reign of Charles II, "Carlos the Bewitched" came to an end in a great European war fought over the spoils of the helpless Spanish empire. In his reign autos-da-fe were still held, that is, public mass burnings of religious heretics. The eighteenth century brought a certain awakening. There was a scientific stress, expressed in expeditions sent to South America and in new colleges of mathematics and engineering. There were publications of the complete editions of Spanish authors of the past, such as Miguel Cervantes, along with the rise of newspapers and *tertulia,* groups comparable to the French lodges where middle-class people gathered for serious discussion of new ideas. The appeal of French ideas became great enough to alarm pious traditionalists who lamented that "libertinism, immorality, luxury, enervation, all the vices characteristic of the French, have spread enormously among us." Certainly an exaggeration, at least until quite late in the century: the Spanish Enlightenment was limited to a few. The great twentieth-century Spanish writer J. Ortega y Gasset even claimed that Spain—it was its basic difficulty—had missed the Enlightenment altogether. But more careful studies of eighteenth-century Spain considerably modify this sweeping statement on the other extreme. There *were* vigorous spirits aroused to prod the land of The Cid and Cortez out of her long sleep. Padre Feijóo was almost the Spanish equivalent of Locke, Voltaire, or

Lessing: reformer, assailer of ancient error, inquisitive investigator of all kinds of subjects. He was, however, himself a Benedictine monk, and in general the Spanish Enlightenment was much less impious and anti-clerical than the French. It did produce reformers who assailed the slave trade, the subjection of women, mistreatment of American Indians, legal inequality, the special privileges of the nobility. They did not attack the throne, but looked to it for the force to reform a stagnant, backward society. The Spanish Enlightenment spread to the New World as may be seen in the universities there. Charles III brought enlightened despotism to Spain, with a special concern to promote economic development.

The Swiss, Pestalozzi, elaborated an educational method from the hints given in Rousseau's *Emile*, at the end of the century. The catalog of Enlightenment influences is almost endless. Americans know of that influence as it shaped their nation at its birth through the thought and culture of those splendid specimens of the Enlightenment, Thomas Jefferson, John Adams, Benjamin Franklin, Tom Paine, and other "citizens of the world" at home in the intellectual circles of Europe—especially England, but, France too. The papacy, and other churches, were even penetrated by it, repugnant though some of it was to them. The Church of England was "latitudinarianized" to the verge of deism.

The Jesuits, militant right arm of Rome since 1540, were dissolved in 1773, a victory for their enemies the *philosophes*, though in fact there were also reactionary enemies of these learned educators, including sovereigns jealous of their power and resentful of their loyalty to the pope. Frederick and Catherine, the two leading enlightened despots, refused to publish the brief suppressing the order. The banning of the Jesuits in France, which occurred in 1764, took place as the climax of a long campaign, in which the traditional accusations against the Society were renewed: wordliness, an accommodating attitude toward sin, free will and rationalism in their theology, lack of loyalty to the crown (ultramontanism), and even alleged belief in regicide. An attack on the king in 1758 by a young man who had worked for the Jesuits lent credibility to this latter charge. These were hardly the charges of progressives against reactionaries, and they were brought by Jansenists and Gallicans, in a wave of hysteria that owed something to the war. But at the same time Jesuit education came under fire as obsolete, stressing as it did rhetoric and the classics; the call was for more modern languages, science, history. When the Jesuits were closed down, no fewer than eighty-four colleges in France closed too, evidence of the Society's virtual monopoly of higher education. The resulting crisis gave rise to a good deal of educational philosophizing and experimentation (as it did also in Spain). The Society was not restored until 1814, as a part of the reaction against the Enlightenment and the French Revolution.

Pope Benedict XIV was on suspiciously easy terms with Voltaire.

Many an English and French bishop adopted some of the views or attitudes of the *philosophes*. Complaining that the devices of wit and satire alone attracted the public, some clerical defenders of the faith attempted to imitate Voltaire's style while opposing his opinions.

By the 1770s, old Frederick of Prussia had been joined by Catherine of Russia as well as by Joseph II of Austria and Charles III of Spain in the circle of Enlightened Despots, adopting and attempting to put into practice the ideals of the Enlightenment. The mutual admiration between the *philosophes* and these monarchs from far less cultured parts of Europe is a curious and revealing chapter in the history of the Enlightenment. Today, most of Voltaire's manuscripts and the library of Diderot repose in Russia, thanks to the fact that Catherine was more interested than anyone else in obtaining them. The fluctuating love affair between Voltaire and Frederick is well known; the Prussian king invited other French savants to his court. Not only Frederick and Catherine but a number of lesser rulers, in Naples, Tuscany, Denmark as well as Spain, attempted to undertake the role of philosopher-king, new style. As noted, this meant the reform of administration, the promulgating of new legal codes, more humane punishments for crime, in line with Beccaria's dictum that the purpose of penology should be to rehabilitate and not to exact revenge, and sometimes more basic social and economic improvements. Joseph II sought to end serfdom in his backward domains, though Catherine did not. Frederick wrote lucidly on the duties of a sovereign to his people, accepting responsibility for their welfare and upholding the rule of reason and law even though this rule was embodied in the monarch. Enlightened despots promoted religious toleration. Doubtless these verbal tributes to enlightenment were not always honored in practice by the potentates: Catherine seemed pathetically out of touch with reality; Joseph II failed to make many of his reforms stick; Frederick refused to assail a social structure based on inequality. But much was done, and the failures were not always due to a lack of good will. Eighteenth-century enlightened despot reform laid the foundation for nineteenth-century democracy and nationalism, it is increasingly recognized (for example, by recent historians of the Italian *risorgimento*). When all is said, enlightened despotism stands largely vindicated as an extraordinary example of the power of ideas in politics.

It is worth repeating that the political thought of the *philosophes* and especially of the Physiocrats tended toward enlightened despotism. "The happiest government would be that of a just and enlightened despot," as Raynal wrote (*History of the Two Indies*, 1770). Perhaps, indeed, the philosopher-king would not do anything except let "nature" rule: Quesnay, asked by the king what he would do if he were king, answered "nothing"; but he would be wise enough to let the Laws reign. He would himself be the embodiment of sovereign Reason.

If Catherine's despotism was Enlightenment-influenced, so was the ideology of rebellion against despots. A. Radishchev, chief pioneer of the Russian radical tradition, came back from a German university training, where he had been sent by the Empress to learn jurisprudence, with other learning, picked up from Helvétius and the more radical *philosophes*, which led him to assail serfdom and despotism. For this he suffered arrest and exile. (See Radishchev's *Journey from St. Petersburg to Moscow*, 1790, edited 1958 by R. P. Thaler.) It is well to bear in mind that enlightened despotism was not the only fruit of eighteenth century thought, as 1789 was to prove.

It might be added that there were faint stirrings of cultural nationalism here and there which could result in anti-French and anti-Enlightenment feelings in the future. Lessing told the German writers that they should stop imitating the French and begin to create their own style. Nationalism asserted itself; in the long run, Prussia was not going to follow Frederick in rejecting its own tongue and modelling thought on the French pattern. Frederick himself, ironically, became the greatest of German national heroes. The rebellion against the Enlightenment that began as early as Rousseau and was in full swing by 1800 included a strong measure of nationalism, as against the cosmopolitanism of the eighteenth century, which in practice often meant acceptance of French cultural domination.

To another religious or cultural group of Europe, too often overlooked in histories of ideas, the Enlightenment meant a great deal. The story of Jewish thought is one that often paralleled the Christian world. The Jews had their own great medieval Aristotelian scholastics, especially the celebrated Maimonides. In Renaissance times Jewish mysticism, stemming from Hellenistic Gnosticism and embodied in the Kabbala, paralleled Neoplatonism and fascinated some of the humanists. At this time, of course, Hebraic studies grew in importance for all of scholarly Europe, the mastery of this language in order to study the Bible and ancient literature more carefully being one of the humanists' proudest achievements. And, in the eighteenth century, we find rabbis applying Newton to the Jewish religion just as Christians did. Though the rabbis of Amsterdam excommunicated Spinoza, rationalism deeply affected the Hebrew community of Europe. In the seventeenth century, it might be added, the Jews had their equivalent of Reformation fanaticism in the messianic movement of Sabbatai Zevi; when this played out, a rationalist reaction set in, just as in Christian Europe.

The Enlightenment was, for Judaism, a time of "emancipation," since the western European states were beginning to admit them to citizenship and to participation in the common culture—a process aided no little by the rational, tolerant, and cosmopolitan outlook of eighteenth-century thinkers. Jewish thought responded in kind. Most famous of Jewish *Aufklärers* was Moses Mendelssohn, friend of Lessing. Mendelssohn urged his fellow Jews to accept citizenship in the states of Europe and participate in European culture—which did not mean that they should cease being Jews, for, distinguishing between civic practice and communal tradition, one could be both a good German and a good Jew. To Christians, Mendelssohn undertook to explain the nature of Judaism, clearing up misunderstandings and smoothing the way for increased toleration. With Lessing (*Nathan the Wise*), he preached that religion is not a matter of creed, there are diverse ways to God; therefore Jews and Christians are not, in an enlightened age, rivals but colleagues. Mendelssohn's form of deism, if it can be called that, found the basis for new unity between the two great religious traditions, seen as variant routes to the same destination rather than as jealously exclusive special revelations.

The diffusion or spread of the Enlightenment can be discussed in a time as well as a space dimension. When did the Enlightenment end—or did it? The term is usually employed to mean, roughly, the eighteenth century, or the century between Newton and Locke and the French Revolution, 1689–1789. It may, occasionally, be extended back to embrace the seventeenth century's scientific and political revolution—clearly one has trouble excluding Descartes, Hobbes, and Spinoza from its broader purview. Or, confined more narrowly, it might be equated with the era of the *philosophes*, roughly equivalent to the long career of Voltaire and matching the times of Rousseau, the Encyclopedists, and perhaps as an appendage the Physiocrats. That would mean about 1720 to 1778. So there is a tendency to look upon it as ending toward the close of the eighteenth century.

In some sense that is undeniably true. We come to the movement known as romanticism, another and a different "spirit of the age," rebelling against the precepts of the Age of Reason, cursing its gods and deifying its devils, about as sharp a reaction as the voluminous history of the tides of taste ever recorded. We come, too, to the French Revolution, itself perhaps a product and result of the Enlightenment but a convulsion after which everything had to be different. Immanuel Kant is another mighty turning point; we may if we choose count the Königsberg philosopher among the men of the Enlightenment—he accepted that honor proudly—but, again, he altered the world of thought so that quite new directions became inevitable. All in all, the 1789–1815 upheaval constitutes *the* great revolution of modern history, in all spheres of life. The specific atmosphere and mixture of ideas that prevailed throughout much of the eighteenth century could never again be as it was.

Despite this, the Enlightenment continued, of course. That is to say, important traces of its influence survived in the nineteenth and twentieth centuries; like all great adventures of the mind it left its permanent mark on the mentality of subsequent generations; nothing after it could be the same. It would take a large tome to trace all such influences in detail. Only a few examples follow here. Philosophy, in its academic sense, still is bent on the direction David Hume turned it through most of the Anglo-Saxon world. Economic theory, if it has gone much beyond Adam Smith, bore the mark of his particular outlook until quite recent times, and perhaps still does. More generally, the optimistic rationalism characteristic of the Enlightenment has survived even the social tragedies of the twentieth century, especially in the United States. We owe the idea that there is and will be "progress" to the eighteenth century, that science and technology help us most in this advance, that men are creatures destined for worldly happiness. Though an increasing number of intellectuals have come to doubt these things, probably a majority of ordinary people still hold them. Modern liberalism and socialism are outgrowths of the eighteenth century, along with much of social science. The goals of public policy today are those shaped by the Enlightenment: material welfare, happiness. Then one thinks of such things as religious toleration, humanitarianism, legal equality, freedom of discussion—of democracy and social equality—all of which grew mainly out of this century.

At an even deeper level, it is pretty clear that our basic habits of thought and our use of language owe more to the Enlightenment than to anything else. Though we may like to quote Shakespeare and the King James Bible, we no longer normally write baroque prose; and while we may still go to church, relatively few participate in that passionate religiosity so prevalent in the sixteenth and earlier seventeenth centuries.[5]

Limitations of the Enlightenment

Since the Enlightenment brought forth so many laudable things, it is natural to ask why the romantic period rejected it, or portions of it,

---

[5]The scientific movement produced criticism of traditional rhetoric, as too pompous and ornate, and demanded a style that would be clear and plain. This literary revolution would seem to have affected modern language more than any other.

in disgust; why, in brief, we didn't just stay in the Enlightenment rather than move past it. The romantics saw what might be called the philistinism of the Enlightenment, or its disparagement of poetry, original imagination, anything sublime or "enthusiastic." The latter was a bad word to the eighteenth century. The emotions and the unbridled imagination were under deep suspicion, as sources of pernicious error. They might even lead men back to religion! Locke advised parents to stifle the poetic impulse in their children, believing this to be the realm of fantasy and untruth; Newton considered poetry to be "ingenious nonsense." This "touch of cold philosophy" did not of course succeed in destroying all poetry, but it did tend to reduce most of it to a tame and didactic—and artificial—level. Verse was allowed to sprinkle sugar on the truths of science, but not to create its own: "truth shines the brighter, clad in verse."[6] Voltaire and D'Alembert confessed frankly that, as the latter wrote, "Our works of imagination are in general inferior to those of the preceding century," because "the philosophic spirit, which wishes to see everything and suppose nothing, has spread over into belle-lettres."

The question of the eighteenth-century style or styles may detain us for a moment. Voltaire's heroic couplets, so much admired in their day, have now lost their savor, as have the novels of Rousseau, which tried to express emotion but only succeeded in breaking through to a sticky sentimentality. Both the "rules" applied to literature by neoclassical canon, and their timidity in the presence of strong emotion, seem to stand between most eighteenth-century writers and any power of conveying genuine feeling. With its drive to purify, elevate, and clarify, the neoclassicism of the century seems overly genteel, as well as overly intellectualized in its poetry. Its high priests, such as Joseph Addison in England, did not bar all sentiment or even passion ("enthusiasm") but these qualities were under deep suspicion. It was "an age of prose," as Matthew Arnold declared, but not of poetry; an age of science and clarity, which failed to reach the domains of the heart where other and more profound truths dwell. And as the century wore on this refinement becomes overrefinement and we get the rococo style, or something similar which often went (in France) under the name of *bel esprit*. This refers to a prettifying that is delightful but undeniably represents

---

[6]The poet Thomson sang of how Newton
     Untwisted all the shining robe of day;
     And, from the whitening undistinguish'd blaze,
     Collecting every ray into his kind,
     To the charm'd eye educ'd the gorgeous train
     Of *Parent-Colours*. . . . .
Marjorie Nicolson, in *Newton Demands the Muse*, classically treated this type of eighteenth-century verse that drew inspiration from science.

a decline from the high seriousness of the earlier classicism. In music, it was the so-called Italian style for which Rousseau did battle (it is a bit strange to find Jean-Jacques rococo, but such his music was), a lighter, gayer music. In painting, it was the exquisite, artificial, faintly lascivious frivolity of the Fragonard-Greuze-Boucher school. In architecture, the rococo is diminutive, delicate, as is Louis XV furniture. One cannot complain much about the taste that could produce such splendid ornaments, but one is perhaps entitled to wonder whether a society so *raffiné* had much vitality left. Today, significantly, the word *rococo* in the French language carries strong overtones of the weakly decadent. It was, after all, the style of the last years before the deluge.

Taine claimed, in a celebrated work of the nineteenth century, that neoclassicism was to blame for the false clarity that perverted Enlightenment political science. Its delights may not be denied: the ease and wit of Pope's verse, the music of Bach, Handel, and Mozart (a progression here toward the rococo), the beautiful decorative style of buildings, the painting of the French masters or of the Venetian, Tiepolo. The argument between classic and romantic is an endless and fruitless one, for people weary first of one and then of the other—lucidity, order, restraint, versus passion, excitement, adventure. But it is clear that at the end of the eighteenth century one of these cycles had run its course and was showing signs of decay. Nor was it in touch with genuine social reality; an aristocratic and genteel art, it told of the triflings of the boudoir or displayed a highly idealized "nature."

The young Goethe described how he and his friends were no longer shocked by the deism and materialism of the *philosophes*; they were simply bored. It was all external and superficial, ignoring realms of human experience that are deeply laid and perennially attractive. They associated this superficiality with the highly artificial style of the late Enlightenment.

Taking its revenge against neoclassical overrefinement, a certain type of literature appeared in the eighteenth century, far from well-groomed, which itself, however, was unsatisfactory. This was the perverse and immoralist novel, carried to its most notorious extreme in the works of the Marquis de Sade. A scandal not without interest, Sade carried to extremes another side of the Enlightenment, its hedonistic ethic, suggested by Helvétius and La Mettrie: one should make the pursuit of sensual pleasure the aim of life. Many eighteenth-century novels, including the delightful but notorious *Fanny Hill*, celebrate the pleasures of carnal appetites. But this hedonism might seem either simply vulgar or as in Sade quite disgusting. It is possible to criticize the Enlightenment for lacking a higher ethical standard. Even if we regard Sade as a sport, it is clear that having rejected the higher passions of religion and art, major Enlightenment figures offered simply the pursuit of happiness.

That celebrated phrase represented a major interest of the era. Paul Hazard in his history of Enlightenment thought devotes a chapter to "Happiness," noting how many books, pamphlets, stories, and poems addressed themselves to this topic. Along with "Why evil?" "What is happiness?" might be called the century's leading question. It felt strongly that the time had come to make men happy here on earth, not in heaven, and that fanatical ideals such as led men to kill and torture each other must be exposed as frauds. It remained then only to be happy here and now, in solid, commonsensical ways. But when one came down to it, it was not at all clear in just what this happiness consisted. If merely in material things and sensual gratifications, one could accuse the age of lacking nobility and of degrading man to an animal. Or we may be reminded of the story John Stuart Mill told, in criticism of the utilitarian ethic, about the gentleman who always hid the candy around his house because he enjoyed it only when he came upon it unexpectedly! If you doggedly search for "happiness" as such, you may not find it at all; it is a by-product of other quests.

Diderot's *Supplement to the Voyage of Bougainville*, 1772, a latter-day piece of the famous *philosophe* and encyclopedist, presents a picture of the happy Tahitians, whose natural sexuality knows no shame until the white man arrives to spoil the party with his morality. This has been praised as a fine anticipation of Freud and Margaret Mead, but the least that can be said is that Diderot seems much less aware than these moderns of the price at which unrestricted sexual indulgence is bought, and that the tropical-island solution will hardly do as a simple model for Europe and the West.

The libertine Enlightenment, as it might be·called, shows a progression, or regression, through the century. The novels of Richardson, to which Diderot and Rousseau acknowledged a great debt, were disguised as sermons, a feature which Rousseau imitated in *Héloise*. The attempted seduction of Pamela, the abduction and rape of poor Clarissa, are presented as triumphs of virtue over depravity in that the virtuous girls meet their trials with Christian fortitude and in some sense triumph over their persecutors; but the evil details are related with an evidently salacious delight. Sade's *Justine* is Clarissa without sympathy. Her outragers are the wise ones; innocence is superstitious prudery. The constant argument in the Marquis's books is that the most apparently execrable impulses are "natural," and to oppose them is to be an obscurantist. "This odious thread of brotherhood, so praised by unspeakable Christianity," must be overcome; love is a dangerous weakness, since it interferes with pleasure. If it be objected that Sade cannot be taken seriously, the answer is that he does represent the extreme wing of a prominent eighteenth-century group, and perhaps a logical culmination of the hedonistic and materialist philosophy. Laclos's *Liaisons dangereuses* is another immoralist work of art, and a good one.

"Bathed in eroticism," the age found in Casanova, fabulous sexual adventurer, a not untypical figure; the Italian was something of an amateur *philosophe* (like Sade), knew Voltaire and Diderot, moved in and out of high society, and left his *Memoirs* as one of the leading personal documents of the century. He is said to have recruited girls for Louis XV's notorious private harem at Deer Park. Clearly there is nothing wrong with love; but an obsession with erotic pleasure for its own sake is notoriously the enemy of love (Sade frankly admitted it) and leads to a moral dead end. Seduction of the innocent in Laclos, humiliation and torture of the sex object in Sade are the last recourses of jaded appetites. Such practices were of course not invented in the eighteenth century, and indeed the main stream of pornography flowed from ancient and Italian Renaissance sources. (See especially Aretino.) Yet the pleasure-seeking aristocratic society of the eighteenth century, relieved of "superstitious" fears about divine retribution and fed on a seductive diet of amorous novels and paintings, indulged its sensual desires more openly and extensively than at most other times. And to this purpose such of the *philosophes* as Helvétius, Holbach, and La Mettrie clearly contributed something.

The picture of eighteenth-century style is a more complicated one than these remarks would suggest. It experimented in all directions. The polite good breeding and complacent Whiggery of the Steele-Addison school in Britain finds its foil in Swift's savage pessimism, or, in another direction, in the robust realism of Fielding and the lubricity of Richardson. While Rousseau wrote rococo music, he encouraged in other ways (as we know) a severe classicism, denouncing the artificiality and luxury of the court art of *fêtes galantes*. There was a rerevival of classicism after about 1760, associated with the painting of Joshua Reynolds in England and David in France, with Wincklemann's archaeological uncovering of ancient treasures, and with Dr. Samuel Johnson's virile criticism. But there is a little Gothic revival too, expressed in Strawberry Hills and horror novels. The intense artificiality of the rococo school, again, is countered by the almost savage realism of a Hogarth or a Smollett. The main impression is of a restlessness and experimentation. Some students find that dissatisfaction with the tamer sort of classicism *and* the more effete sort of rococo pushed art and expression after mid-century in at least two main directions: a more exactingly realistic classicism, and the cult of feeling or sensibility of which Richardson, and Rousseau the novelist, were such renowned exponents.

This last mood settled rather deeply over literate Europe in the third quarter of the century, partly replacing "rationalism" though sometimes simply paralleling it. (Rousseau could write *Julie* and *The Social Contract* almost simultaneously.) "Men of feeling" wept and gushed in naive sentimentality. A meditative and melancholy mood was fashionable. The "Night Thoughts" of the English poet Edward Young were translated into many languages and enjoyed a huge success: the school of the cemetery, brooding much on sadness and on death. Gothic shadows and the fate of poor Pamela afflicted the same people who were reasoning their way to atheism. In 1784, Albergati's heroine, Laura, has been deranged by four books: *Candide, Julie,* Young's *Night Thoughts,* and Holbach's *System of Nature.* For those little accustomed to unorthodoxy it must have been a dizzying combination. What strikes us is the rationalist, satirical, scientific Enlightenment cheek by jowl with the most arrant sentimentalism. But the latter fashion was very much the "in" thing from about 1760 on.

With all its successes and failures, eighteenth-century art was destined to be overwhelmed by the rushing torrents of romanticism, and for a long time came to be a byword for a literature *manqué.* Twentieth-century critics are more objective than nineteenth about this. It may be agreed that romanticism brought in personal statement, individual insight, penetrating intuition, as these had not been known before. The eighteenth-century style was more formal because more social. One did not strive for originality, but for the familiar; one used (and was "confined by") traditional language and traditional *genres.* A literature of the *salon* or the drawing-room, it reflected the tastes of a society probably more cultivated *in its average* than any that has ever existed, but with no conception of the individual genius, the far-ranging soul thirsty for adventures beyond those of the run of mankind. The estrangement or alienation of the artist from society, the modern theme, had not yet begun, or was just barely beginning. If the eighteenth century had a myth, writes Ricardo Quintana, it was the myth of the normal man, of the shared experience. How different from romanticism! We must remember these things in evaluating the Enlightenment style.

The End of the Enlightenment

It may also be said that the Enlightenment's faith in itself faltered when it began to see through its own "myth." It was, in the shrewd phrase of Whitehead, an "age of reason based on faith." It had begun in the golden confidence that scientific empiricism would lead to certain general laws. But empiricism issued in skepticism, or failed to find those simple all-embracing laws that were expected. The faith of reason was a faith in clarity, that everything would come out neatly; it was a faith in science without metaphysics. There was a concomitant belief that "nature" and science give clear guidance in morals and religion. All this was oversimplification or grave confusion. Science is not normative, value-giving; nor can we endow the "laws" of science with anything more than a tentative, operational validity. The concept Carl L. Becker made famous as "the heavenly city of the eighteenth-century philosophers" is indicated here: these philosophers actually had kept the medieval Christian faith in a providential world order, while switching the terms to make it an earthly rather than an other-worldly paradise, revealed by scientific reason rather than by theology. (Gordon Wright: *The philosophes* scoffed at miracles, yet believed in the miracle of human perfectibility.)

Something pretty basic to the eighteenth century's confusion of thought on these fundamental issues may be discovered in the ambiguities of the word *nature*. We do not need to be told that it was a word very close to the heart of the age. It was to "nature" that the neoclassical writer appealed, also the deist leaving behind revealed religion, the social scientist looking for an exact canon in human affairs, the moralist seeking the right rule of human conduct. Arthur O. Lovejoy in an essay on " 'Nature' as Aesthetic Norm" once set forth some eighteen different meanings of the word and pointed out that the principle of "following nature" was fatal to neoclassicism, since "nearly all forms of the revolt against neoclassical standards evoked the same catchword" (see *Essays in the History of Ideas*). As Joseph Butler had pointed out to the English deists, "nature" is wholly ambiguous. Eighteenth-century man had read into it order, simplicity, regularity; one could as well read, as some Romantics did, irregularity and disregard of the rules, by the free spirit, following "nature" rather than convention. It was, perhaps, the most elemental cause of the Enlightenment's fall that it had appealed to "nature" in the confident expectation that here was a clear, unequivocal standard of authority, but the reverse turned out to be true.[7]

Finally, of course, that great apocalyptic event, the French Revolution, helped bring the Enlightenment to an end. The Revolution looked to the eighteenth-century philosophers for its inspiration and ideas; but, in the first place, it soon swept far beyond their decorous prescriptions to explore political frontiers previously unheard of, and, in the second

---

[7]The Marquis de Sade provides a good example of the utter confusion into which the concept of "nature" had fallen toward the end of the era. To attack nature is to conform to her, since nature is strife; "the only real crime would be to outrage Nature," but this is impossible, since Nature herself contains all crimes, hence there is really no such thing as crime, etc.

place, it was so massive that men could not help thinking of it as ushering in a new epoch—by implication, closing the old one. Then the reaction to its violent excesses entailed opposition to all those ideas that
had presumably inspired it. Intellectual Europe tended to follow Burke
and Maistre in rejecting the Revolution and the intellectual movement
that lay behind it. The titanic struggles of the twenty-five years after
1789 left the entire civilization forever altered, socially, politically, and
intellectually.

The extent to which the ideas of the *philosophes* caused, or helped
cause, or shaped the direction of the great French Revolution has become one of the classic debates in intellectual history. Few deny that
Voltaire, Montesquieu, Rousseau, and Diderot contributed much to it,
by undermining respect for old institutions, encouraging hope of a better social order, and, in Rousseau's case at least, suggesting that on the
ruins of the existing social order a new and more perfect society would
arise. They obviously did not create the various grievances, discontents,
and stupidities which formed the fuel for the Revolution; they did not
cause nobles to be greedy, kings feeble, merchants ambitious. But they
supplied the match that touched off this flame, and conceivably they
guided it to become a great and significant movement rather than the
sort of aimless rioting and protesting that had been going on for centuries.

It is, however, equally accepted that the *philosophes* and Encyclopedists expected neither revolution nor democracy and were distorted by
the revolutionaries, who read into them their own wishes and goals.
During the Revolution the words of Rousseau, Voltaire, and Montesquieu
were to be on everyone's tongues; they were words often wrenched out
of context and given a meaning that would have startled their authors.
We can see that now. We know, for example, that Rousseau's political
ideas were subtle, complex, and perhaps contradictory, but, rightly
understood, support nothing like the case for revolutionary national
democracy that a Saint-Just and a Robespierre thought they did. What
this suggests is that the dynamics of history embraced both thinkers
and actors in a common current which neither fully understood. Ideology was a part, but only a part, of the total process that made up this
titanic historical event.

Friends and foes of the Revolution are likely to agree that the
ideas of the Enlightenment thinkers played largely a negative role, destructive rather than constructive. In general they wished to sweep away
what they called superstitions, or corruptions, or artificialties, or outmoded laws; as for what would take the place of the old society, they
appealed quite vaguely to reason, or nature, or natural law. If Voltaire
thought that men released from monkish religion would be fully ra-

tional, and that would be enough, Rousseau suggested that men with their accretions of unnatural civilization scraped off would be perfectly good, and that would be enough. The Physiocrats and Adam Smith added that society could run itself if left alone, once the clumsy apparatus of state intervention and social inequality was dismantled. These people did not really see any social problem, except to get rid of what existed. The charge of "nihilism" has been levelled at the *philosophes*— destroyers, not builders. They were innocent of any such intention, but it is easy to see why the charge might be made.[8] The first revolutionaries did not think this was nihilism—quite the reverse. They naively believed that all would indeed be well when the Old Regime had been put out of business. But in fact they had to learn the hard lesson that men are not by "nature" sufficiently rational or virtuous, to make the good society automatically come into existence.

Friends of the Revolution think that it was enough glory for the eighteenth-century philosophers to have made possible the destruction of an unjust and unreasonable political and social order, to have raised the banner of reason and humanity, to have pointed out the general direction mankind was to follow without knowing exactly which roads it was to take—enough, and more than enough, for one generation to do. Foes have always alleged that Voltaire, Rousseau, and company falsified man and falsified history, thus causing European man endless anguish. It is possible that even yet we do not have enough experience of the modern world to be able to judge objectively between these clashing ideologies. But no one denies that the French Revolution ushered in the specifically modern epoch of history, or that it partially reflected the grand ideas and emotions of the eighteenth-century philosophers, at the same time as it ended their era.

[8]It was frequently made at the time, by opponents of the *philosophes*. "Ils ont l'art de détruire, mais ils n'élèvent rien," Charles Palissot remarked in his comedy of 1760, *Les Philosophes*.

II

Main Currents
of Thought
in the
Contemporary World:
1789 to the Present

The nineteenth century falls rather naturally into three parts, from the viewpoint of Zeitgeist and history of ideas. The morning is the romantic and revolutionary age, lasting from about 1789 to 1832 or perhaps 1848. It is marked by convulsions both political and moral, another intellectual revolution, and a great deal of creativity, emerging from its storm and stress. Its heroes of thought are Kant and Fichte and Hegel; Chateaubriand, Saint-Simon, Fourier; the romantic poets; the renovators of political philosophy; the creators of new social doctrines. It is an age in which men felt old moorings give way and wondered where the storm would blow them. Then, during the noonday of the century, calm returns and there is time to take soundings. Doubts and tensions remain, but this Victorian period is marked by relative stability, and by the undertaking of extraordinary efforts at synthesis. This is the time of Comte, Marx, Darwin, and Mill.

The evening brings its gloom and uncertainties; unquestionably a darker mood strikes Europe late in the century, from about 1885 down to the stunning collapse of 1914. If the average man remained complacent and hopeful, post-Darwinian and post-Marxist Europe produced a crop of amazingly insightful thinkers who were exploring domains never heretofore much known, zones of fearful nonsymmetry. The unconscious irrational, or the prerational, interested the men who dominate this epoch—Nietzsche, Freud, Bergson, Sorel, Max Weber. In part, this mirrored the experiences of an epoch which brought vast movements of population from farm to city, vast increases in population with the accompanying problem of "mass," almost terrifying technological "advances." In this period the artist and intellectual tends to be estranged or alienated from society, yet becomes creative as never before.

Of all watersheds, 1914 is rivalled only by 1789 in the modern world; nothing after the terrible world war could be the same. Shattered visions of infinite progress littered the postwar landscape, and Western man suddenly found that he had no other values to fall back on. He tried to invent new ones, tried even to recover old ones, but watched his world descend into even lower depths of war and degradation. The response of thought to the challenge of "decline and fall" was at times nothing less than heroic, if likewise nothing less than desperate. If the future does not call it the age of Lenin and Hitler, it may decide to know it as the age of Toynbee and Sartre. Withal, it was the age of Le Corbusier and Picasso, Lawrence and Joyce, and others who have expressed the contemporary idiom. We are midstream of it and can hardly evaluate it, but because its waters are our own, to swim around in them and try to sense which way the current goes is one of our greatest pleasures and needs.

This second portion of the book, then, tries to take European man from the French Revolution through the nineteenth century and into his current fix. It begins with him emerging from the Enlightenment into romanticism, from an aristocratic into a democratic society, from an agrarian and commercial era into the industrial-technological one. It leaves him perhaps a confused and buffeted creature, the victim in part of too much knowledge, too many ideas; but at the same time needing to rethink and put to use his manifold inheritance of thought and expression.

7

Romanticism
and Revolution:
1789-1815

*What is the good of curbing sensuality, shaping the
intellect, securing the supremacy of reason?
Imagination lies in wait as the most powerful enemy.*

GOETHE

I have seen the beginning and the end of a world.

CHATEAUBRIAND

At least three revolutions, the French, the romantic, and the Kantian,
occurred in the 1780s, with their direct impact carrying on through
the next several decades to leave a deep mark on the entire modern
world. To these, general history must perhaps add the Industrial Revolution. Contemporaries were prone to regard them as but different aspects
of a single revolution. Thus the conservative Francis Jeffrey in 1816,
discussing "the revolution in our literature," attributed it to "the agita-
tions of the French revolution . . . the hopes and terrors to which it
gave occasion." (Some recent scholarly students of romanticism have
been inclined to endorse this verdict.) And the German poet Heine,
speaking of Immanuel Kant, remarked that "with this book (*The
Critique of Pure Reason*) an intellectual revolution began in Germany
which offers the strangest analogies with the material revolution in
France . . ."–and, he added, to the reflective mind is of equal importance.
This judgment was endorsed by Karl Marx who observed that the
Kantian revolution in philosophy was the intellectual counterpart of
the French Revolution in politics. It only remains to connect Kant with

romanticism, and of course that is a common juxtaposition—not that the two things were quite the same, but that Kant's successors and disciples, Fichte and Schelling, provided philosophical grounding for the romantic poets.

Clearly these three important developments, in politics, literature, and pure philosophy respectively, did interact and sometimes blend. It is not clear that they were of similar origin. Kant was working on problems bequeathed to philosophy by Locke, Berkeley, Leibniz, and especially Hume; he wrote his chief books before the Revolution, and his basic position does not seem to have been affected by that event, though it stirred him deeply even in his ivory tower at Königsberg. (But Jean-Jacques Rousseau demonstrably influenced both Kant and the French Revolution.) The Revolution, needless to say, owed nothing directly to the German philosopher on the shores of the Baltic, whose abstruse speculations were unknown in 1789 to all but a few. As for romanticism, which also can be traced back to Rousseau, it most clearly announced its arrival in Germany around 1781, with the writings of Schiller and the young Goethe, in a context that seems neither politically revolutionary nor at all interested in technical philosophy. The young Goethe was mostly interested in mystical religion. Schiller's *William Tell* was to inspire many a revolutionary, but it was not written until 1804.

Causation in history is a tricky problem, never simple. Monistic dogmas which assert the invariable priority of one factor, such as technological change or the rise of a social class, do not stand the test of careful criticism. Material, social, and intellectual factors continually interact on each other. It is not clear that they do so within the matrix of a single system, so that one can speak of the unity of an historical epoch. Any historical period contains within itself many processes and themes, not necessarily all knit together in a seamless web; there are always loose ends.

One can say with assurance that there was restlessness and malaise in the 1780s. The American Revolution, an event of the profoundest significance for Europe, not least France, concluded successfully. The French monarchy was in deep trouble before 1789, reeling toward bankruptcy, apparently unable, since the failure of the Turgot reform effort in 1776, wherein new King Louis XVI began bravely, only to fall back, to install necessary reforms. In Great Britain, a political organism weakened by the American defeat faced impending great changes, as reformers demanded a more democratic and representative Parliament. In the realm of literature and thought, there were some equally disturbing signs. The German drama of *Sturm und Drang* (storm and stress) was a strong reaction against Enlightenment classicism, while the turn toward mysticism and religion expressed itself in France in such figures as the popular *philosophe inconnu*, Saint-Martin. (Hamann, Swedenborg, and Blake are other examples in diverse quarters of Europe.)[1] The 1780s was a glorious decade that gave us Mozart and the American constitution as well as Kant, in many ways the climax of the Enlightenment. But the leaders of the great *philosophe* era were falling away. Voltaire died in 1778, Rousseau in the same year, Hume in 1776, Diderot in 1784, d'Alembert in 1783, Condillac in 1780, Frederick the Great in 1786. Buffon and Franklin were octogenarians. These illustrious passings signalled the demise of an age. Many sensed change in the air—even before the French Revolution arrived to confirm it.

Though Enlightenment strains continued on, to be seen in such prominent schools as British utilitarianism and Political Economy, the Revolution ended by discrediting much of it. It was accused, by the important conservative manifesto of Edmund Burke, of having led France to disaster through its simplistic and abstract conception of man, its utopian quest for a perfect social order. It was now said to have been metaphysical, a charge it had once itself levelled at the past. It had invented fantasies and called them Reason. It had thrown out the really important things in life, such as religion and tradition and concrete human ties, in favor of slogans about the rights of man which, in practice, only invited godless men to slaughter each other. Europe, the conservative foes of revolutionary France believed, would have to purge herself of this disease which, erupting in the Terror, had its roots in the sick cynicism of Voltaire, the wild dreams of Rousseau. In Burke and his numerous followers strains of romanticism interacted with the reaction against the Revolution that affected most of Europe's major intellectual figures by 1798, continuing on through the Napoleonic wars and into the post-Napoleonic Restoration.

The French Revolution

Recent historians of the French Revolution tell us that we should not speak of a *French* Revolution. "In fact, the French revolution was only one aspect of a Western, or more exactly an Atlantic revolution, which began in the English colonies in America shortly after 1763, extended through revolutions in Switzerland, the Low Countries, and

---

[1]Robert Darnton, *Mesmerism and the End of the Enlightenment in France* (1968) interestingly recounts another reaction against rationalism that appeared in the 1780s, becoming almost a mania for a time. Darnton points out that mesmerism had a distinct radical component, being adopted as a kind of anti-Establishment gesture by a number of the future leaders of the Revolution.

Ireland, before reaching France between 1787 and 1789" (Jacques Godechot). From France, it bounced over to Germany, Switzerland, Italy, and other parts of Europe. One might object that it is foolish to compare the rumblings in Holland or Ireland with the French Revolution for significance and scope, and that the later revolutions came about precisely because France's had done so. But it is certainly true that the French Revolution from the beginning exerted a worldwide influence, and, if this was because of French prestige and influence throughout Europe, it was also because the Revolution produced ideas for which the whole Western world was ready.

What were the great ideas of the Revolution? Some of them seem self-evident and therefore pedestrian today, but they were not so familiar then, and they were given vibrant new meaning by the marvelous events of 1789: popular sovereignty, self-determination of peoples, equality of rights. And nationalism. Frenchmen joyously toasted "la patrie" of which they were all, equally, the children now: no more Bretons, Angevins or Dauphinards, any more than nobles and commoners. The whole conception of the political society changed. The king could no longer be king of France, he must (if he stayed) be king of the French, for he owed his power to the people. The special privileges and rights of the nobility, renounced by the nobles themselves in an orgy of ideological altruism, were no more; all citizens were equal before the law, with equal access to office, equal liability to taxation. Much of the Revolution's mystique went into that word *citoyen*. The Nation, then, was born—a community of men sharing equally in rights and duties, not a class hierarchy. If people did not like the government they had, they should have a right to change it. And they had a right to speak up freely, according to the Declaration of the Rights of Man and Citizen, that great manifesto of the Revolution.

Those who alleged a certain vagueness and utopian character in the ideology of the Revolution would of course be right. It was an apocalyptic moment, and all kinds of millennial ideals came forth. Universal peace was one of them, ironically enough in view of what the Revolution in fact soon brought to Europe. Numerous orators repudiated the very right to make war, and the Assembly solemnly adopted a resolution of this sort in 1790. Two years later, France was at war with the monarchies of Europe and only that incurable ideologist, Maximilien Robespierre, was still (for the time being) a pacifist. It had been expected that all mankind would be brothers. In fact, "popular sovereignty" or "self-determination" entailed war, because Europe's political order did not correspond to this principle. Nor would it have been possible to decide what this slogan meant exactly, in practice, in many parts of Europe.

Faced with the need to transform the largely negative character of the initial revolution (the first Constitution resounds with "il n'y a plus" —"there no longer exists"), men fell back in good part on eighteenth-century ideas. Rousseau especially was to be quoted incessantly by leaders of the Revolution. Enlightenment political theory tended to be vague and utopian. Nor was it all of a piece. Montesquieu disagreed with Voltaire, Voltaire with Rousseau, and Rousseau, if not with himself, at least with some of his followers. It is easy to identify at least three major strains in the Revolution, perhaps more. The first period of the Revolution was in the hands of moderate men, who did not wish drastic change; the intellectual idol of this phase was Montesquieu, the goal a limited, constitutional monarchy on the English model. Then, in terms of the chief Revolutionary factions, came the Girondin, Jacobin or *Montagnard*, and *sans culotte* or perhaps Babeuvist forces—in broader ideological terms, roughly liberal, democratic, socialist.

The Girondins admired Voltaire, his disciple Condorcet being one of their brain trust. Not lacking in revolutionary zeal, the party of Brissot, Condorcet and Mme. Roland was anticlerical, antiaristocratic, and inclined to a doctrinaire liberalism, based on Montesquieu and Locke along with Voltaire (though Mme. Roland also admired Rousseau, an ambivalent figure, as we know). These were the upper bourgeoisie, insofar as a class label might be roughly pinned on them. They believed in natural rights of the individual and were suspicious of excessive state power. Constitutional government with "checks and balances" but not too much democracy appealed to this group, who perhaps betrayed their bourgeois outlook as much in their deistic anticlericalism as in the law against workers' associations passed in 1791. Anglophile admirers of the British constitutional system, they bequeathed much to nineteenth-century French liberalism, always weaker than in Britain but not without its influence. They lost out in the struggle that developed, were destroyed, and sent to the guillotine by their enemies on the Left. It is significant that under the impact of events they moved toward democracy. Initially hostile to universal suffrage, some of them came around to it. Condorcet's constitution of 1793, which never went into effect, included universal suffrage and a single legislative assembly, ideas approved by the American friend of this group, Benjamin Franklin. But executive and judicial checks on the will of this assembly were to exist. If the Gironde moved close to a type of democracy under the pressure of events during the Revolution, its position should be distinguished from Jacobin democracy.

The left-wing Jacobins developed an unusual conception of democracy based on Rousseau's social contract and general will, or their construal of these concepts. Their goal was equality, and the idea of the general will together with the mass or mob action on which their power often depended caused them to glorify the people *en masse*. Robespierre and Saint-Just accepted a dictatorship of Reason, with themselves representing the "people." This strain of thought had relatively little regard for individual rights or parliamentary institutions, which seemed to it selfish and corrupt. The Jacobin constitution of 1793 provided for no separation of powers, no limit on the power of the state, no guarantees of individual liberties. It sanctioned a plebescitary or democratic dictatorship, based on the popular will but with power delegated to a small number of men. Jacobin democracy with its frank worship of the mob spirit is difficult for Anglo-Saxons to grasp, but it has been a potent tradition in France. Democratic in a deep sense, with a feeling for the common man *en masse*, a desire to bring the people directly into government (Robespierre wished to build a stadium holding twelve thousand people to allow the crowd to watch the legislators), and a passion for equality, its disregard of legal processes and individual rights may have been reflected in the Reign of Terror, though that abnormal episode ought not to be charged to ideology alone. (Later Jacobins showed a keen concern for individual justice: consider the glorious fight of Georges Clemenceau, a century later, on behalf of Captain Dreyfus.)

Robespierre was the great ideologist of the Revolution and leading personality during the hectic bloody days of the Republic of Virtue. It is significant for his love of Jean-Jacques that he believed in the worship of a Supreme Being; atheism, he declared, is aristocratic. He was a believer, but his true God was a kind of abstract embodiment of the People. Effective mass orator, he was coldly unhappy in most of his relationships with concrete, real people. With a sensitivity that caused him to tremble at the sight of blood, he could order the death of thousands in the name of humanity. All that Edmund Burke meant when he accused the Revolution of abstract theorizing and a want of practical judgment is embodied in Robespierre, the man of austere principle who hated the intrigues of practical politics and ended a bloody dictator because he would not compromise.

Robespierre was not the most radical product of the French Revolution. Jacobinism was not socialistic though it accepted the supremacy of community over individual, in the spirit of Rousseau's social contract. Danton, Robespierre, and Saint-Just assumed a right to regulate property in any way necessary, but the social order they believed to be best was one in which every citizen held a little property, as Rousseau had suggested. This might well be designated as a petty-bourgeois or artisan-workman utopia.

Socialism did appear in the French Revolution though it did not get far. Babeuf and Buonarroti, revolutionary socialists, attempted an insurrection in 1795 (the Conspiracy of the Equals) but failed badly. Never-

theless they began a powerful tradition. Their thought was crude, but
their feelings strong; somewhat inarticulately they hated property,
commerce, luxury, while extolling the virtues of poverty, equality,
honest labor. They, too, took their inspiration chiefly from aspects of
the writings of Jean-Jacques, which partially articulated their natural
class feelings. Morelly, an obscure writer, had developed Rousseau's
thought in a more socialistic direction just before the Revolution. Mably
and Holbach also wrote in a similar vein and reached large audiences.
These were mostly poor men and their words are significant as among
the first sounds from the lower depths. Like the Levellers and Diggers
of the English Revolution, the left-wing Jacobins and the Equals spoke
briefly for classes of men hardly yet represented at all in literate
thought; the revolution had stirred the pot sufficiently to bring them momentarily to the top, then they subsided. But this time their voices were
not forgotten. Buonarrotti survived to become a link with the socialism
of the 1840s, and Parisian revolutionary radicalism lived on in other
firebrands such as Blanqui. This *sans culotte* socialism spread over
Europe quickly, making an appeal to doctrinaire representatives of the
poorer classes. It was, after all, close to elemental Christianity. Russo,
the Italian Babeuvist, echoed Savonarola's medieval call to the rich to
throw away their jewels.

These extremes tended to discredit the Revolution. The initial joy
with which it was greeted all over Europe turned to disillusionment as
the 1790s wore on the Revolution led to civil war, persecution, terror,
international war. At first all the intellectuals of Europe were enchanted
by it, including dozens who later became its bitter foes. "Bliss was it in
that dawn to be alive." Not only Wordsworth but Maistre, Chateaubri-
and, Kant, Fichte, Novalis, Goethe, Coleridge, Southey, and many others
felt this. Rousseau had passionate admirers in England, like the father of
Thomas Malthus, who asked only to be known as "the friend of Rousseau." Gilbert Wakefield, a Rousseau disciple, was imprisoned in 1799
for allegedly expressing a wish that the French would invade and
conquer Britain. Everyone at this time, too, was reading Gibbon, whose
Decline and Fall of the Roman Empire, which he had finished in 1787
after more than twenty years of labor, radiated a republican spirit—or
did it only seem so in the atmosphere of 1789? The Roman state had
begun its collapse with the very first emperor, and Christianity had
finished it off, the great historian seemed to be saying.

But the Revolution seemed to lose its way and turn to violence,
rapine, and injustice. It ended with the Reign of Terror and the awesome
spectacle of the revolution devouring its own children. The result was a
reexamination of the premises of the Age of Reason, and a rejection
of them that aided the turn toward romanticism.

The Revolutionaries had seemed to cling to eighteenth-century rationalism. It was not the romantic Rousseau they worshipped, but the utopian rationalist of *The Social Contract*. Before his suicide in a revolutionary prison, Condorcet, the disciple of Voltaire, wrote his hymn to unlimited human progress under reason. The Republic of Virtue and of Terror paraded the Goddess of Reason through the streets. Volney (*The Ruins*, 1791) theorized that empires fall from an insuffciency of natural religion and too many priests. Robespierre, in his meteoric path upward to grand inquisitor and then downward to victim of the Terror he had instituted, carried Rousseau's words with him everywhere. Little wonder that some who watched turned away in disgust from eighteenth-century thought, holding it responsible for the failure of the Revolution.

Critics of the Revolution

Edmund Burke's great indictment of the Revolution stood out above all others. It was eloquently answered by Tom Paine and others; the conservative reaction did not entirely sweep the field. But it tended to dominate. Historians still debate the element of validity in Burke's charges against the Revolution, but it would probably be generally agreed that he was right in holding that *philosophe* thought on politics was both too vague and too doctrinaire, in an area where these qualities are peculiarly dangerous. A recent scholar has observed concerning the thought of Helvétius and Holbach that they "must answer for the fact that they ultimately offered nothing beyond pious wishes" for an enlightened despot, ignoring "institutional structure" altogether.[2] One can readily find fantasies in which it was simply assumed that revolution would somehow install good government and do away with all evils—crime, hatred, deceit, envy, lawsuits, prisons, poverty, etc.—presumably by a sweep of the pen. No more monumentally innocent thought can be imagined. It can still be found in the Revolution of 1848.

The famous Declaration of the Rights of Man and of Citizen, manifesto of the Revolution, is a case in point. Attempting to reduce the formula for political justice to a few axioms, it revealed considerable confusion and subsequently was completely ignored. It might mean everything or nothing. "Men are born and remain free and equal in rights." "The purpose of the state is to secure the citizen in enjoyment of his rights." What exactly were these rights, and how could the state

[2]Everett C. Ladd, Jr., "Helvétius and D'Holbach," *Journal of the History of Ideas*, April-June, 1962.

maintain them? They were said to include "the unrestrained communication of thought and opinions," as well as "a sacred and inviolable right to property"; but in both cases there might be exceptions, "in cases of evident public necessity." Similarly equivocal were statements that "the law ought to prohibit only actions hurtful to society" and "ought to impose no other penalties but such as are absolutely and evidently necessary." Would anyone disagree about the principle, but could any two people agree on the all-important matter of just what these actions and penalties are?

Critics of the "natural rights of man" school (Hobbes, Bentham) have claimed that such rights are either equivocations or tautologies— meaningless slogans. But clearly they have an emotional value. At this time, their concrete referents were real enough. For example, Robespierre in his younger days attacked the law that "inflicted civil infamy upon the innocent family of a convicted criminal" (John Morley) as well as another that denied civil rights to children born out of wedlock. Such remnants of irrational barbarity fell before this wave of political reform. The reforms of the Revolutionary era were real enough, though stated in an abstract way. And had they not been so stated, they might never have been secured. In their attempt to bring about the final perfect state of mankind, the Revolutionary ideologists overstated their case and spoiled it, but en route to its ultimate failure as an apocalyptic movement the Revolution achieved all sorts of useful changes in the lot of mankind. The old order of inequality, with its relics of the seigneurial system in the countryside, its unequal taxation and denial of equal economic opportunity, its unjust and arbitrary laws, disappeared forever. This is what the Revolution meant, and why it has always been celebrated joyously in France.

But it meant something else in England—something suggested by that cartoon in which an ugly assassin armed with faggot and dagger is offering to give "liberty" to Brittannia. Secure (as most Englishmen thought) in their own liberties, the work of history and experience not slogans and theories, Brittannia looked with horror on the bloody and turbulent French scene, and found herself at war with revolutionary imperialism. From this position she produced the leading works of the counterrevolution, most notably that of Burke.

Edmund Burke's renowned book of 1790 is as famous as any tract in the history of politics, and about as controversial as any. *The Reflections on the Revolution in France* has been and probably always will be the subject of violent disagreement. But its distinction is usually admitted even by those whose ideology forces them to be its foe on principle. Burke claimed that the revolution went wrong because its leaders tried to scrap an entire political system and put a new one in its place overnight; he related this mistake to the outlook of the *philosophes*, the political rationalists whose method lacked realism in an era where abstractness is fatal and the nondoctrinaire approach is vitally necessary. On neither of these points has he lacked adversaries, then and later. But he made a strong case on both scores, though it may be hard to see how the mistakes could have been avoided. It is true that the wholesale abolition of an entire order in France in 1789 created immense confusion during the transformation period. "Feudalism" was declared at an end, which meant the dissolution of such institutions as the army, local government, the judicial system, the clergy. As for the *philosophe* political ideology, it did indeed consist in good part of general maxims without careful attention to detail and so was more helpful in tearing down than in building back up.

Whether Burke's analysis of the Revolution was right or wrong, the events in France stimulated him to formulate his political philosophy. A soaring eloquence and dazzling sense of the subtle texture of actual politics lent to Burke's book a memorable quality; as a piece of literature, it is one of the pioneer works of the new school of romanticism. The leading idea emerging from this eloquence and this subtlety was that society is a vast and complicated historical product which may not be tinkered with at will like a machine; it is a repository of collective human wisdom to be regarded with reverence, and if reformed at all it must be with due respect for the continuity of its traditions. There were other related ideas: that a political community is something made by history, an unanalyzable bond between men which makes free government possible; that the social organism has its "natural aristocracy" which the commoner sort of men must and do, in a healthy society, respect; that general rules and abstract principles are no help in politics.

With a disdain for the "abstract rights" proclaimed by the French, he tried to make clear the real rights of man: Burke certainly believed in rights, but he stressed the degree to which men in entering civil society must give up some of their liberties in order to gain the advantages of government. He distrusted the restless innovators who had no patience to search out the wisdom of their ancestors but must draw amateur blueprints for the total reconstruction of society, as if they were the first to think. The science of government is not for these, whose visionary schemes "in proportion as they are metaphysically true, are morally and politically false." These "smugglers of adulterated metaphysics" knew not man—or God. Burke was pious and felt that political society was sound only on Christian foundations. To Burke two human needs were evident above all: history, and religion. Man is a religious animal who, if he did not have Christianity, would turn perforce to some other, and probably less satisfactory faith—not a bad prediction of what has actually happened in recent times. He is a social animal, who would be no more than a beast if he were cut off from the fabric of ancient custom and tradition that sustains him. Reverence toward God and toward the social order are therefore the two great duties, and they are linked, for history is the revelation of God's purpose.

There is irony, and perhaps confusion, in the fact that Burke accused the *philosophes* of being "metaphysicians," they whose banner always bore the motto "Down with metaphysics." He turns their own weapon against themselves. It seems that Burke is right, if we think of some of the cruder post-Rousseau political pamphleteers. They were utopian fantasists without the least practical knowledge of politics. But Burke's own empiricism has roots in the better sort of Enlightenment political thought, Hume and Montesquieu especially.

The Irish politician deeply influenced all subsequent conservative political thought. Edition followed edition of the *Reflections*, all over Europe. Louis XVI personally translated it into French. For this popularity, its timeliness, and what seemed an uncanny prophetic quality (Burke announced the failure of the Revolution before it had failed, it seemed) were partly responsible along with the richness and color of the style. Stripped of its rhetoric, Burke's thought may not appear extraordinary, but its phrases would echo long afterward.

Perhaps it was not necessarily "conservative" in the most obvious sense of this word. In suggesting an empirical approach to the enormous complexity of human affairs, in place of the vague sloganizing of the *philosophes*, Burke may well be viewed as the founder of a real science of social reform, rather than as a hidebound conservative. He was certainly not opposed to change, if properly carried out, and his own career, that of a person of humble birth, consisted of one passionate crusade after another. His biographer, Philip Magnus, identifies many; the more famous were his crusades on behalf of American independence, Ireland, India (the Warren Hastings affair), and against the French Revolution. "The most urgent need of his nature was always some great cause to serve—some monstrous injustice to repair." This tempestuous Irishman was temperamentally as little a conservative as well can be.

But there was of course the conservative Burke, or, since he almost created the school, the Burke traits that came to be thought of as conservative. The feeling of piety for the social order, the mistrust of harebrained reformers with a one-shot plan, the organic conception of social growth, these were the foundations of the conservative faith. A great deal of Burke has been accepted as essential political wisdom for anyone who wants to participate in politics as it always is and must be, rather than merely shout slogans from a distance. A modern socialist, Harold Laski, declared that "The statesman ignorant of Burke is lost upon a stormy sea without a compass." The features of Burke's outlook less palatable to most moderns include his belief in aristocracy, with the accompanying rejection of equality.

The *Reflections on the Revolution in France* was a work of genius, written at white heat, blazing with indignation and charged with eloquence—an eloquence that is a bit too much for some modern readers ("Burke never takes the trumpet from his lips") yet makes a gorgeous effect. It deeply influenced his generation and contributed not only to the anti-Revolutionary cause but to the romantic taste. In his youth, in the 1750s, a struggling young lawyer turned literary man, Burke had written a treatise called *The Sublime and the Beautiful*, which has often been seen as a landmark in the evolution of taste from neoclassical to romantic. He argued that while the realm of the "beautiful" is indeed subject to the familiar classical rules about harmony, proportion, elegance, etc., there is another realm, the "sublime," which inspires fear, awe, which does not civilize and socialize us as the classical does but makes us feel alone, exalts and exhilarates us. Burke was always a little romantic, his career was exceedingly so, and his last great work is, perhaps paradoxically, as romantic in style as it is conservative in content. So in a way the great spokesman of the counterrevolution was a revolutionary, too.

The Bonapartist Era

Insofar as he was trying to defend tradition and "prescription" as the "guardians of authority," Burke was swimming against the tide of the times. Despite its excesses and horrors, the French Revolution happened and, as Lord Acton later remarked, "it taught the people to regard their wishes and wants as the supreme criterion of right"; it accustomed men to change and swept away the old order beyond hope of recovery. Even Burke did not imagine, realist that he was, that it would be possible to restore the *status quo ante* in France. Soon the troops of France spread the Revolution all over Europe. The dictatorship of Napolcon (1800–1814) turned most of thinking Europe, even thinking France, against the Revolution, but the Bonapartist victories continued to overturn the old arrangements of Europe.

Against the rule of Napoleon, a good many of France's leading men of letters protested and went into exile, though some (like Bonald) came back now that the anarchy was over and order had been restored by a vigorous ruler. Benjamin Constant, Mme. de Staël, and Chateaubriand headed the brilliant crowd of refugees, to whom Bonapartism was purely and simply tyranny. There were others, like Goethe, who never lost faith in Napoleon, seeing in him the man of destiny whose mission it was to unite Europe under a single progressive law. In France, beginning in the period just before Napoleon (the Directory), the so-called Ideologues reacted against political failure and disillusion by becoming severely objective, seeking to study the human mind as strict scientists. (They were perhaps the ancestors of those antiseptic moderns, the "behavioral scientists.") This was the time of Laplace, Lamarck, Cuvier, and other great French scientists, indicating that the more detached subjects could flourish under Bonaparte. Laplace crowned the "classical mechanics," perfecting Newton, and was the author of a famous *Système du monde* which undertook to explain the operations and evolution of the universe without recourse to Newton's *deus ex machina*. ("Sire, I have no need of that hypothesis," he responded when Napoleon asked him about God.) Cuvier and Lamarck began the controversy over evolution. The Italians, Galvani and Volta, were installing the age of electricity. Napoleon did admire the sciences and thought it important to encourage them in every way possible.

Within France, however, political controversy could hardly exist and freedom of speculation was limited. Not that Bonaparte was, personally, anything other than the most emancipated of thinkers. Enormously cynical, he delighted in shocking people with his atheism in private conversation; but, believing that "only religion gives the state firm and lasting support," he would not tolerate any public irreligion. "You must form believers, not reasoners," he told the teachers of a state school for girls. Since "the stability of marriages serves the interest of social morality," the Code Napoleon was severe on adultery, but privately Napoleon called it "a mere peccadillo, an incident at a masked ball . . . a most common occurrence." Women he regarded as "mere machines to make children," and intellectuals and artists he affected to despise; therefore Mme. de Staël, an intellectual and artistic woman, was his *bête noire*. But many of Napoleon's outrageous opinions were, as they so often are, a kind of defense mechanism of an ego unsure of itself in this domain, and cannot quite be taken seriously. He claimed, for example, to be "insensitive to what is called style," but he obviously was not. An omnivorous reader, he missed little that went on in the world of art, science, and philosophy and often commented on it shrewdly. Nevertheless we feel he was sincere when he wrote that "the statistics of my army are, as far as I am concerned, the most enjoyable literary works in my library and those which I read with the most pleasure in my moments of relaxation!" But one should not be unjust to this remarkable man; in some ways his insatiable curiosity especially about scientific matters was hardly less than epochal. On his expedition to Egypt in 1798 he took along two hundred scholars to investigate that fascinating but still largely unknown land of antiquity. He shared and advanced the historical and orientalist interests of the times. He did not, however, admire the new literary fashion of romanticism that belonged to his foes, Mme. de Staël and Chateaubriand. Speculative thought and letters did not flourish in France in the years of Napoleon.

Abroad, the leading theme was a rallying of forces against Bonapartism. The *mystique* of the French Revolution gradually lost what force it had had in England. In 1794, Tom Paine's reply to Burke (the *Reflections* did not lack answers), *The Rights of Man*, sold like hot cakes and the London Correspondence Society caused a fear of the French Revolution happening in Great Britain. William Godwin's *Enquiry concerning Social Justice* was very much in the French spirit, a rationalist utopia based on the ideal perfection of individuals. Though repeating Rousseau's indictment of existing property relations as theft, Godwin's utopia differed significantly from most of the French in being antistatist. In Britain, the idea of a natural order of society took the laissez-faire form: society will run itself if left free from interference. The Physiocrats also believed this, but the idea took deeper root in the Whiggish environment of England. Tom Paine claimed that "the common consent of society, without government" can perform all the necessary functions heretofore discharged by government. The rest ought to be dispensed with, and would be as men approached perfection: "government, like dress, is a badge of lost innocence." Laws regulating property and morality are, as Godwin observed, useless if men are not virtuous, and unnecessary if they are.

The combination of Smith, Rousseau, and the spacious fields of America with her sturdy, self-reliant citizens brewed this heady dogma in the mind of Paine. That it was not exclusively American was indicated by Godwin, father-in-law of the poet Shelley and husband of the women's rights author, Mary Wollstonecraft—a group around which much of the political Left in Great Britain revolved. Godwin was so suspicious of the state and indeed of all forms of institutional organization that he attacked public education, among other things. "Did we leave individuals to the progress of their own minds," Godwin believed, "without endeavoring to regulate them by any species of public foundation, mankind would in no very long period convert to the obedience of truth." This was the ultimate laissez-faire. Godwin believed, as H. N. Brailsford once remarked, that all men are as rational and virtuous as Swift's Houyhnhnms.

England was to be the land of liberalism, and Godwin no doubt is significant for the British bent of mind. But after some initial popularity he was regarded as a crank, and was the only man ever known to have caused Coleridge to lose his temper. British opinion turned away from the French Revolution and all radical thoughts during the long wars with France. Coleridge was among those who, earlier enthusiastic for the Revolution, "threw away his squeaking baby-trumpet of sedition" and combatted the revolutionary heresy with all his strength. Coleridge ranks with Burke, to whom he owed much, as a founding father of English conservatism. But the sometime radical journalist, William Cobbett, joined the anti-Jacobin cause too, indicating that this mood was well-nigh universal in Britain. The Evangelical movement within the Church of England, led by William Wilberforce, was a reaction against the deistic laxities of the eighteenth-century church, thus a reproach to the infidel French.

But controversy remained to the end. William Hazlitt, the famous literary critic and essayist, was described by a friend as "prostrated in mind and body" when he learned of Bonaparte's final defeat; "he walked about unwashed, unshaven, hardly sober by day, and always intoxicated by night" for weeks, until one day he awoke as if from a stupor and never touched alcohol again. His friend, Haydon, author of the above description, believed that Napoleon had criminally betrayed the true cause; and yet on the great man's death in 1821 reflected in his diary that "posterity can never estimate the sensations of those living at the time" about Napoleon—how his rise, his glory, and his fall affected men. Shelley found himself warming again to Bonaparte when he saw what followed:

> I hated thee, fallen tyrant! I did groan
> To think that a most unambitious slave
> Like thou, should dance and revel on the grave
> of Liberty. . . .
>
> I know
> Too late, since thou and France are in the dust,
> That Virtue owns a more eternal foe
> Than Force or Fraud. . . .

These were exciting times. It is not surprising that romanticism arose in those twenty-five hectic years from the first dawn of revolution in 1789 to the final defeat of Napoleon in 1815.

Nationalism

Germany gave birth to nationalism, in reaction against humiliation by the French. Herder and Fichte, giants of German thought, preached it along with humbler writers and organizers of youth (Arndt, Jahn, Kleist). The Enlightenment had been cosmopolitan. Fichte became convinced that this was another one of the errors made by that now politically discredited era. If France gave the world the Enlightenment and the Revolution, did not Germany have something to give? Every nation has its day, and the German day might be the greater for being so long postponed. Defeated in war by Napoleon, the Germans were assuming the cultural and intellectual leadership of the world in this time of Goethe, Schiller, Kant, Beethoven. A cultural people should have a great state. Germany must wake up politically as she had done artistically and culturally. (*Addresses to the German Nation, 1807.*)

J. G. Herder's contribution to nationalism stands out in the intellectual career of a many-sided genius. Romanticism blended with nationalism in his thought. It was a humane and liberal nationalism, by comparison with some manifestations of that spirit; it meant, to Herder, the self-fulfillment of peoples who thereby make their contribution to the brotherhood of man. He glorified the people, the *Volk*, exaggerating a strain already met with in Burke (there is wisdom in the collective consciousness of the people, that is, in traditions). Herder went seeking the songs of the people "on the streets, in alleys and fish markets, in the simple roundelay of the peasant folk." He has been compared to the American poet Walt Whitman in this respect, and indeed he deeply influenced Whitman. Mystical adulation of the national genius could lead in dangerous directions, perhaps, but at least Herder did not suggest them. He simply believed that nations exist, that peoples have their national cultures, and that these should be developed as the source of a valuable literature and art. The democratic element in this romantic nationalism is apparent.

Napoleon I met his downfall in 1814–1815, and conservative Europe gathered at Vienna to try as far as possible to restore order based on principles of tradition, prescription, monarchy. But forces had been set in motion which could not be halted though they might be slowed or deflected. Between 1815 and 1830, Restoration France and conservative Europe produced some notable attempts to develop the conserative ideology, but it also saw the elaboration of the liberal, democratic, and socialist political philosophies. These political "isms" will be dealt with in the next chapter. Meanwhile we may note that of all these, the most potent "ism" in the nineteenth century was to be nationalism, affecting even the smaller and lesser peoples of Europe. The English and the French had long suspected they were nations, the Germans were finding it out, the Italians soon would discover it; but also we catch a glimpse of the Danes, who previously had had no inkling of their separate nationhood, seeking to restore the ancient Danish tongue and old Danish customs, while Gothicism in Sweden represents a similar impulse. The Belgians will find that they cannot live under a Dutch

king, no matter how beneficent his rule and how logical and beneficial
the larger political unit is, for they are different. Nietzsche, in a char-
acteristically impatient moment, burst out that Napoleon had tried
to unite Europe but reactionary nationalism had interfered to botch
his plans. It may later have seemed reactionary; but for at least the
first half of the nineteenth century nationalism was regarded as liberal,
progressive, and democratic. It meant the right of peoples to be free
and self-determined, not merely because freedom in any of its guises
is a good thing, but because the idea had been deeply implanted, by
such as Herder, that each people has a sacred mission to make its unique
contribution to the symphony of nations. And it meant, concretely
speaking, the struggle of Germans to escape the dominion of France,
later of Poland to throw off the tyranny of the Tsar, or Italy to free
herself from the Austrian yoke. For better or worse, Europe was to
divide into numerous national cultures in the nineteenth century—a
process accompanied by disruptions and upheavals. This vast and
epochal process was in part a movement of the mind. More will be
said about it later. Certainly that other of our three revolutions, the
romantic, had much to do with it.

Immanuel Kant and the Revolution in Philosophy 1724–

Born in 1724, the man who became the greatest of modern philosophers did his most creative work in the 1780s, against the background
of the crisis in Enlightenment thought. Rousseau made a deep impression
on Immanuel Kant, as he did on so many of this generation. Indeed
little that was discussed during the Enlightenment escaped the attention
of the omniscient little professor of Königsberg. The young Kant,
brought up in the reigning German philosophical school of Leibniz as
systematized by Christian Wolff, showed strong scientific interests and
entered into some of the typical *philosophe* controversies: thus, we find
him contributing his bit to the Lisbon Earthquake argument. But it was
particularly the work done by Berkeley and Hume to undermine the
confident certainties of rationalism that engaged his attention. It was
only in his middle age that Hume awakened him from his "dogmatical
slumber." He found Hume's skepticism most unsatisfactory and, like the
Scottish "commonsense" philosophers (but more effectively than those
simpler souls, whom he ridiculed), determined to rescue men from it,
restoring their confidence and vitality. Kant was an *Aufklärer*, a spokesman of the Enlightenment. But his powerful mind in attempting to
refute Hume penetrated into ground beyond the frontiers of that movement. He made what he called a "Copernican revolution" in philosophy

and was, in later years, compared to the French Revolution in his impact on thought: "With this book (*The Critique of Pure Reason*) an intellectual revolution began in Germany which offers the strangest analogies with the material revolution in France, and, to a more reflective mind, appears to be of equal importance. . . . On both banks of the Rhine we see the same break with the past, all respect for tradition is revoked" (Heinrich Heine).

One of Kant's major objectives, then, was to rescue science from Humean skepticism. Hume, it will be recalled, took his departure from Locke's empiricism, which held that the only real knowledge comes from sense experience, and there is nothing in the mind except what comes to it from the senses. He demonstrated—and Kant accepted his demonstration as "irrefutable"—that through the senses alone the human mind cannot encounter reality at all, nor can it have a science founded on anything but "opinion." We have only an unrelated sequence of sense impressions. The principle of cause-and-effect cannot be derived from experience; we simply assume it arbitrarily; it may only be an accident of our mental processes.

Kant's reply was roughly as follows: the mind or intellect, so far from being passive or negative, contains the organizing principles which *impose order on experience.* The mind contains forms and categories, which are the basic concepts that give meaning to experience. These "fundamental conditions of thought itself" are a priori, that is, not derived from experience. Kant, in what he describes as the hardest metaphysical work ever done, specified these forms and categories: two forms of perception (space and time), twelve categories of the understanding (for example, cause and effect).[3] (These correspond to the types of judgment of Aristotelian logic, that is, the types of quantity, quality, relation, modality.) All minds contain these categories, thus mind is a fundamental unity.

Thus our minds condition and indeed determine knowledge by being as they are. Agreeing with Leibniz, Kant denied that there is nothing in the mind except what the senses bring in: there is the mind itself, which sorts out, classifies, relates this raw material, making it intelligible. We will not here, of course, follow Kant in all his arguments and terminology. From his powerful analysis, it is enough to say, emerged a picture of mind as creative, not passive, and of reason as something a priori, thus rescued from the skepticism of an empiricist

---

[3]Kant's categories are: quantity: unity, plurality, totality; quality: reality, negation, limitation; relation: substance and accident, cause and effect, community; modality: possibility, existence, necessity. It is usually held today that Kant's categories, too dependent on the logic of his day, do not hold up; but this is not to say that basic categories of the understanding do not exist.

approach. Goethe interpreted Kant to mean that "had I not borne the world in myself by anticipation, I would have remained blind even with eyes that see." It is not our senses that enable us to experience reality, but a preformed structure within the mind that prepares us to receive and understand sensory impressions. It is not the "solid" data of sense which provide the basic cement of science, it is something given within the mind, something like those "innate ideas" Locke had sought to banish as too mysterious or occult.

Because of a debate that arose, it must be added that Kant was evidently not an "idealist" in the sense that some of his followers were. He does not say that reality is a creation of the mind. Things are out there, and in striking our senses they provide the indispensable, primary data of knowledge. The point is that we could not "understand" them if we did not have minds equipped with a rational structure. Kant is pointing out that the world outside must appear to us in a certain way because of the kind of mind, as well as the kind of senses, that we have. If we put on red-tinted glasses, things look red, though they really are not all red; and we have also our built-in sensory apparatus, so that colors, odors, etc., appear to us as they do because of the way that apparatus works. Kant adds the important point that things appear rational—classifiable and subject to order, such as cause and effect, identity, comparison—not because of the way *they* are but because of the way our minds are. The mind makes sense out of experience; it would be senseless without mind. But the external world exists; Kant is not denying that, nor that we must have its stimuli for the mind to work on in the knowing process.

This was only part of Kant's examination of the knowing process, and it must be added immediately that the sort of knowledge we have been talking about—scientific knowledge, taken from experience as worked on by the categorizing intellect—was not, to him, knowledge of ultimate reality. This domain of science is perfectly valid; Kant's goal was to rescue science from skepticism, and to represent him as a foe of science (the view is not uncommon) is a gross error. He himself made some contributions to the sciences, in which he was always interested. But it is a particular sort of knowledge, appropriate to the practical or useful realm only; it is knowledge of appearances, not of substance. In the famous Kantian language, it is the *phenomenal*, as opposed to the *noumenal*, world. It relates to the properties of things, not the "thing-in-itself." Kant's other great objective, the inspiration for which he perhaps derived from Rousseau, was to rescue the realm of *value* from the scientists. Thus he sets up two sharply different categories. The realm of science, which is useful knowledge, deals with the phenomenal world, the world of appearances. The realm of value,

of moral and esthetic experience, is intuitive and deals with the noumenal world, the world of substantive reality. Kant thinks that the two
realms must not be confused. One of his achievements was to riddle the
proofs of God's existence derived from the facts of physical nature—
arguments extremely popular during the eighteenth century, especially
the "argument from design." From ontological argument to argument
from design, Kant devastated all these venerable "proofs" with such
effectiveness that few have dared revive them since. The proofs appropriate to science have nothing to do with God, Kant believed. For they
can never give us values.

There is nevertheless the noumenal realm. Kant was not quite sure
whether we can know it at all. He seemed to think that in moments
of moral or esthetic experience we can glimpse it fleetingly, and these
hints were to be built upon by the romantics who followed him. The
human soul, a thing-in-itself, by quite other roads than the analytical
reason may make contact with other things-in-themselves. Kant seems
ambiguously poised between the Enlightenment and romanticism here.
On the one hand he said that he "had to deny knowledge to make room
for faith," which he clearly much wanted to do. His most widely quoted
sentence is that in which he proclaims the equal wonders of the two
realms, the starry heavens and the moral law. On the other hand Kant
seldom departed from his Enlightenment hard-headedness, was certainly
no mystic by temperament, and was not at all sure about our being able
to make contact with the noumena at all. Perhaps we are condemned
to live in the phenomenal world as far as intellectual activity is concerned, while being aware that there is another world, the real world,
which we can never know at least in this life. Each of Kant's realms is
flawed for man. From the scientific, phenomenal one we can get clear
and useful knowledge, but it is knowledge of appearances only. From
the spiritual, noumenal realm we could get ultimate truth if we could
reach it, but ordinarily we cannot do so.

Kant nevertheless at times put great stress on his rescuing of religion
from the clammy grip of science so as to restore faith to its true estate.
The existence of God, freedom of the will, the soul, these things cannot
be proved by scientific argument. But when we move from "pure
reason" to the "practical" or moral reason we are in a realm which is
in its own ways quite valid though different. Pascal's "the heart has its
reasons" was close to Kant's meaning. Man's moral consciousness exists
and is entitled to great respect though its knowledge is not the kind
appropriate to science.

It is interesting to compare the dualism of Kant with the other
great dualisms of Western thought—Plato's, Ockham's, Descartes's. To
Plato, the realm of essences or ideas alone is real and knowable; to Kant,

it is alone real, even more so, but it is scarcely knowable, certainly not knowable by the reasoning intellect as Plato thought. To Descartes, there are two realms, the physical and mental, one the domain of necessity and the other of freedom; there is something of this in Kant but, again, Descartes felt the physical world to be perfectly knowable in a way that Kant could not. Kant is closer to William of Ockham, and to Pascal. Science is one thing, religion another; two wholly different kinds of cognition are appropriate to them; we cannot pass from one to the other.

Kant's successors tended to quarrel about what he meant, and it is plain that with but a slight twist his "critical philosophy" might be made the foundation of several different systems. Some Kantians forgot about the thing-in-itself and became either idealists, arguing that the world is completely a mental construct, or positivists (phenomenalists), urging that we do not and cannot know what ultimate reality is and had better remain content with the orderly arrangement of our observations. Others developed Kantian noumenalism in a Romantic or mystical direction, stressing the role of the poetic or religious intuition in touching the deepest reality by nonscientific methods. Kant himself, as we have said, was hardly a romantic by temperament; but the romantic era was beginning as he wrote and his immediate followers in Germany tended to be either idealists or romantics, sometimes blending the two. There is no doubt a sense in which Kant is the uncle if not the father of romanticism. But we ought not to forget that the bulk of his work was directed towards clarifying scientific philosophy and that his contribution here was enormous. It is part of the wonder of the Königsberg philosopher that he greatly advanced both of those different domains of the mind which he so sharply separated, the scientific and the esthetic-religious.

Kant's dualism nevertheless was unsatisfactory for many who had been accustomed by the Enlightenment to clear and final conclusions. Phenomena and noumena, pure reason and practical reason, seemed completely divorced, a situation not felt to be satisfactory. Fichte and Schelling, his immediate successors in Germany philosophy, sought for a unifying principle that would weld the divided self and divided world of thought together. Impressed by Kant's "transcendent" structure of reason, they wished to broaden it so as to bring pure and practical reason together under one roof. Kant stimulated future philosophy by the problems he left, as every great philosopher does.

But in both of Kant's two realms, the "Copernican revolution" is evident: the human mind is creative, not passive, whether it is working as scientist or as seer. It is an active agent, far from the wax of Condillac; it imposes order on nature, even in the scientific process. Kant reminded scientists that Galileo had understood the necessity of hypothesis, asking questions of nature; pure empiricism is poor scientific method. The creative mind is as much a necessity in science as in poetry. This is well understood today; Kant probably more than any other modern thinker established it firmly.

Kant made significant contributions to political and ethical thought, too. For our purposes it will be sufficient to note the *liberal* implications of these. The Kantian ethical rule or "categorical imperative" (an objective, necessary command) included the principle that persons must be treated "as an end, and never as a means." In making *duty* a linchpin of his system, Kant may have betrayed his Prussianism; but his political thought was generally liberal. It stressed individual freedom, the moral autonomy of the person, human beings as ends. There were even a few Kantian socialists in the nineteenth century, who pointed out that the rule of treating people as ends and not as means, as persons not as things, invalidates the labor system of capitalism, which makes the workingman a commodity.

These liberal features, along with the attack on rational proofs of God's existence, caused Kant's writings to be banned for a time in his native country. But his political thought also stressed the reign of law, obedience to duly constituted authority; it sought to resolve the dilemma of liberty and authority (a dilemma of which Kant was very conscious) through just and general laws. History is the story of the education of mankind toward freedom under law. Thought should be free. Kant was one of those who "wished to be warmed by the fire of the French Revolution but not burnt up by it," he was a moderate liberal with a horror of violent revolution. He believed a republic to be the best form of government and his thought worked in a liberal-democratic direction. It has been argued otherwise; but if Kant stresses authority, he also believes in liberty. His political thought is perhaps a little trite; his well-known essay on universal peace does not take us much farther than the usual utopian exhortations. But Kant's deep respect for the individual was rooted in his great Critical Philosophy: one can readily see that he made the human mind and the inner self more important and sacred than did the Lockeans. They would have it determined, passive, dictated to by external conditions; to Kant it is hub and focus of all, it is self-determining and free insofar as noumenal, and even in its phenomenal aspects it dictates to nature rather than being dictated to. The final purpose of all creation, Kant suggests, is the full realization of man as a moral being.

Kant came soon to be regarded as the greatest of modern philosophers (Hegel disputed the title with him in the nineteenth century, but clearly Kant made Hegel possible) as well as a notable contributor to moral and political ideas. It seemed that he brought an end to the typical Enlightenment philosophy by rejecting both its empiricism and confused skepticism in favor of a new form of rationalism. The peculiar Enlightenment formula of commonsense empiricism was not tenable after his criticisms and reconstructions. He also gave hints to both the romanticists and the liberals, to whose influence the next generations largely belonged. The intellectual revolution of this era was bigger than Kant, but he was somehow an integral part of it.

Post-Kantian Philosophers

The grand lineage of German philosophy in its golden age began with Kant and ended with Hegel, a half century later. In between lay several others, most significantly Johann Gottlieb Fichte and Friedrich Wilhelm Joseph von Schelling. Here a very brief summary will suffice. Fichte, brought up on the writings of the French *philosophes*, praised the French Revolution and subsequently wrote much of significance on political, social, and economic subjects—especially his famous *Addresses to the German Nation* (1807), inspired by the Prussian defeat at the hands of Napoleon, which we have mentioned. He also had a good deal to say about religion, and was in fact dismissed from the University of Jena in 1799 largely because of his excursions into this arena, bringing on him the charge of atheism. (A sort of pantheism would, of course, be closer.) He was not very romantic in temperament; philosophy, he thought, should be a science. But he adopted and preached a philosophy of idealism, believing that anything else leads to determinism and materialism, which destroy human dignity. According to the vision of reality that Fichte developed, the universe consists of an absolute Ego which is like our own consciousness, a unique, free activity which strives to realize itself in perfect self-awareness and is the foundation of all nature. Leaving aside the technical jargon, which probably mystified all but a few, this vision of reality dramatized the human will or consciousness as hub and center of the universe because an expression of the absolute spirit of which the universe consists. Spirit or idea makes up reality, and our spirits, represented by our basic consciousness, an indescribable but intuitively certain thing,[4] are the concrete manifestations of this world spirit. One might say without too much distortion that according to Fichte each of us is God, or a part of God—if we equate the "abso-

---

[4]Consciousness is the foundation of all thought and experience, yet we cannot find it in thought or experience because it cannot be objectified, cannot be made an object of thought or experience, Fichte pointed out. This seems to be true and resembles the point made in recent times by Sartre and the existentialists.

lute" or "world spirit" with God. So, if Fichte was technically not a "romantic," he introduced an intoxicating idea which in the broader sense was very romantic: that the world is spiritual, that we are a part of that spiritual world, and that in moral experience especially we can touch the uttermost sublimities of the universe.

Schelling, a disciple of Fichte and friend and collaborator of Hegel, whom he influenced, produced a stream of writings, especially between 1797 and 1802, which developed the idealist outlook into what he called Transcendental Idealism. He put greater stress than Fichte on physical nature as the objective form of the Absolute and pointed out the road Hegel was to follow in many respects. Perhaps the most striking feature of his thought was its representation of the artistic creation, the act of esthetic intuition, as the supreme achievement. In it the unconscious and the conscious forces, representing the two forms of the Absolute, are fused in synthesis; it is in art that the infinite manifests itself in finite form.[5] Coleridge and all the romantic poets absorbed Schelling eagerly, for understandable reasons; he provided a metaphysical basis for the artist such as had never before been known. Romanticism's glorification of the poet as seer, as "unacknowledged legislator of the human race," as discoverer and purveyor of loftier truths than the merely logical, relates closely to Schelling's thought. Much later in his career, Schelling opposed Hegel's excessively abstract rationalism by offering a kind of foreshadowing of existentialism; he influenced Kierkegaard, who listened to his lectures at Berlin in the 1840s. He came to reject all abstract, conceptual thinking as "negative philosophy," inferior to concrete, existent realities. He showed a keen interest in the history of religious mythologies, like Jung in our time. In this his earlier preference for art may perhaps be seen continuing.

Fichte and Schelling may seem to have travelled a long way from Kant, who so far as he lived to meet their ideas evidently repudiated them. But Kant had started them off. This extraordinary spate of German philosophizing concluded with the titanic figure of Hegel, consideration of whom we shall postpone for a moment. The whole of it cut a wide swath in intellectual Europe in the first half of the nineteenth century. It combined keen and searching thought with daring speculation and a good deal of moral sublimity. Later, especially in the non-German world, it seemed excessively "metaphysical" and might be dismissed as empty bombast. From another point of view, it revealed

[5]To further explain, the unconscious is the real, or objective, physical world, the conscious the realm of the ideal and subjective. Both are parts of the Absolute. Their destiny is to be merged in one, the objective becoming merged in the subjective and vice versa. This happens when the artist shapes nature, or cooperates with it, as Michelangelo carving a statue.

about as radical a perspective as Europe had seen. For it may be noted that Fichte, Schelling, and subsequently Hegel offered a philosophical alternative to religion, substituting their Absolute for the Christian conception of God. A prominent feature of this metaphysical faith was man's place in it as almost the equivalent of God. The Absolute was not quite just the individual human Ego writ large, but it came close to being that, at least in the popular interpretation of these philosophies. The human consciousness reflects and participates in the divine. Man's art and moral experience are in effect cosmic forces working in and through him. German idealism united with romanticism to deify the mysterious forces working in the human soul and so to introduce that theme of "titanism" so marked in the nineteenth century, and according to some so dangerous. "Glory to Man in the highest," as the poet Swinburne sang.

At any rate the lofty and searching inquiries of the great German philosophers of the Kantian age captured mankind's imagination. Near the end of the century the South African, General Jan Smuts, having made his fortune and reputation by the age of thirty, decided to retire. "I prefer to sit still, to water my orange trees, and to study Kant's 'Critical Philosophy,' " he said. It could have been any thinking man's dream. Kant—together with his children—came close to meaning *philosophy* for the nineteenth century .

The Germans soon found their way to England, chiefly by way of Coleridge. They were less well known in France until around 1850; the Enlightenment carried on more strongly there, represented by Condillac's empirical psychology. But eventually the impact on French thought, and on Italian, was to be strong. Meanwhile France was not without idealist and romantic philosophic strains, as for example, Maine de Biran and Victor Cousin.

The Origins of Romanticism

Romanticism is often said to have begun with Rousseau, and particularly with that amazingly successful novel *La Nouvelle Hèloise*, which had all Europe weeping in 1762. Certain romantic affinities can be found in other eighteenth-century writers, notably the English poet James Thomson (d. 1748), while the poets Gray and Cowper are often classified as "preromantics" bridging the gap between Dryden and Pope on the one end and Wordsworth and Coleridge on the other. (And, indeed, it is possible for Geoffrey Clive to separate out a whole "romantic Enlightenment.") It may be questioned, though, whether "preromanticism" is a very useful concept. The criterion is passion or emotion, but this is not really the right one. The sentimentalism of the age of Julie and Pamela made itself at home in the Age of Reason, and had little in common with what later came to be called romanticism. But at any rate Rousseau strongly influenced practically all the romantics of the next generation or two; it is hardly too much to say that in France the figure of Jean-Jacques, shrouded in mists of legend, became deified. Before long the German writers Goethe and Schiller took up the romantic manner, the former's *Sorrows of Werther* rivalling *La Nouvelle Héloise* in its ability to reduce all manner of people to tears, while the *Sturm und Drang* (storm and stress) plays of the early Schiller were to be show pieces of romanticism for many years. (*The Robbers* was written in 1781.) The chief disciples of Rousseau at first seem to have been the Germans; in France the influence of the rationalist Enlightenment continued, with Voltaire getting his tremendous triumph in Paris near the end of his life in 1778. But the restless decade of the 1780s, with its Saint-Martin mood, has been mentioned.

Then came the Revolution, which tended to halt literary and intellectual life, diverting all attention to the political melodrama being enacted at Paris. Some Frenchmen for a time suspected romanticism as too German to be patriotic. But in 1801 to 1805 French romanticism asserted itself with the powerful figure of Chateaubriand, the leading literary personality of his day. With *Atala* and *René* a new mode of literature had arrived, it was widely recognized. Chateaubriand was the father, as Rousseau was the grandfather, of all subsequent French romantic literature.

Meanwhile in England the young poets Coleridge and Wordsworth were experimenting with a new poetry they rightly felt to be nothing less than revolutionary. They along with the poet-seer William Blake began English romanticism in the years just before the turn of the century, but it remained obscure for some time. Blake printed his own books *Songs of Innocence* (1789) and *Songs of Experience* (1794), but they were neither noticed nor understood for a number of years. He was known slightly as designer and engraver, but evidently not at all as poet, until well into the nineteenth century.

The Revolutionary and Napoleonic wars were going on; Chateaubriand became an exile from Bonaparte's dictatorship and even Coleridge and Wordsworth took up political pamphleteering. In Germany, romanticism continued to flourish uniquely: a group that included Frederick Schlegel and his brother August in Berlin, Novalis and Schelling at Dresden and Jena, called themselves Romantic and threw out ideas important to the philosophy of the movement, to which it is necessary to add the theology of Schleiermacher (1799) and the music of Beethoven (1800). All this was in the years 1798–1801—romanticism's moment of creative fruition. But its popular triumphs lay ahead.

Picking up momentum, romanticism reached its maximum of influence in the years 1810–1830. Wordsworth and Coleridge began to achieve fame and were joined by Shelley, Byron, and Keats to make up the most renowned group of poets in England's history, all of whom are customarily labelled "romantic." In 1813 the Swiss-born Mme. de Staël, a glamorous figure who wrote, made love, and fought Napoleon with equal verve, popularized the Germans in France with her celebrated work *D'Allemagne*. France succumbed to romanticism between 1820, when Schiller's *Maria Stuart* (composed in 1801) took Paris by storm, and 1830, when Victor Hugo's *Hernani* caused the wildest tumult in the history of the French theatre but emerged triumphant. Hugo and Lamartine, along with the novelist Alexander Dumas, the avowed leaders of the romantic movement, were the most popular and distinguished writers of their age. At the same time the painter Eugene Delacroix headed a school which called itself romantic.

In the 1830s a "romantic" influence may be seen in many directions, and indeed for the rest of the century that influence never ceased to exist, being so absorbed into the texture of thought and expression that "nothing after it could be the same." But it became diffused. A partial reaction against it set in. We must not think of romanticism as ever quite sweeping away all opposition. In France, where a strong classical tradition existed, Hugo was denied admission to the Academy five times, the last time in 1836, and warfare between romantic and classic never ceased to enliven the theatrical season, at least. (In 1829 the Academy denounced romanticism as that which "puts in disorder all our rules, insults our masterpieces, and perverts mass opinion.")[6] In England, embittered literary reactionaries helped bring on Keats's early death, his friends believed. The greatest German literary figure in history, Goethe, who contributed to romanticism early in his career, eventually declared that classicism is healthy and romanticism diseased. Unconverted "classicists" always existed and indeed there was something of a classical rerevival contemporary with romanticism. If we grant that the romantics had carried away most of the prizes by 1830, they were under attack from the younger generation of the forties and fifties as too pompous and theatrical. Broadly speaking this next generation preferred to absorb its romanticism, if at all, in carefully filtered form.

Yet between 1760 and 1840—to take the widest time span (the

[6] S. O. Simches, *Le Romantisme et le goût esthétique du XVIIIe siècle*, 1964, documents the extensive survival of eighteenth-century taste, classical and rococo, at the high tide of the romantic.

creative zenith coming then in the middle of it)—Europe had been hit by something new, exciting, and controversial. We have yet to define what this was, having only named its landmarks. What was romanticism? The question has puzzled the more literal-minded for a century. A definition is elusive. It is possible to declare that this inability to define romanticism is the scandal of the century. The word took on many meanings. The romanticism of Chateaubriand was Catholic, and reacting against the Revolution, became Royalist; but the romanticism of Victor Hugo was (eventually—Hugo began as a conservative) republican, liberal, even revolutionary. It was romantic to suffer, to pray, to fight (as Byron did for Greece), to venture on far voyages, to commune with nature, to have a sense of history. It was romantic to love passionately and transcend the conventional moral boundaries, but the eighteenth century, now old hat, had done this too, like all other centuries. It was romantic to read about the Middle Ages, and to admire the pseudoprimitive bard Ossian,[7] but also to adore the days of classical antiquity— "fair Greece, sad relic." Fate was romantic; so was soul-baring. What was not, if done with the proper spirit? Romanticism was a mood and a style much more than a doctrine; moods and styles are hard to define.

The ambiguity of the term is carried over into everyday speech, in which today the word "romantic" is widely but quite variously used. It can mean charming, or pretty ("What a romantic place!"); mysterious; old ("romantic old house"); sexy; quaint; young and exciting; impractical, visionary, dreamy; heroic and glorious. To be sure it cannot mean *anything*; one would never use it to mean dull, mediocre, staid, cautious, and this tells us something; yet its range of meanings is quite wide and even includes possible contradictions.

As the early nineteenth-century revolution in ideas, romanticism "has become a label for half a dozen things that have only an accidental connection" (Christopher Dawson). He instanced the following: expressing one's emotions, love of nature, intuition as a source of truth, the quest for new experience, the view of society as organism rather than machine. This is not an exhaustive list. In drama it meant departing from the classical "rules," to the great indignation of the traditionalists; in poetry it meant, to Wordsworth at least, using simple rather than "literary" language and writing about plain people rather than fancy

---

[7]Between 1760 and 1763, the Scotsman James MacPherson published three volumes purporting to be literal translations from the legendary ancient Gallic poet Ossian, a sort of Celtic Homer of the third century A.D. Suspected by a few at the time and confirmed by later scholarship was the fact that little if any of this material really came from such a source, most of it being made up by MacPherson himself. But this "romantic" verse enjoyed wide popularity throughout Europe, much though Johnson inveighed against it ("Sir, a man might write such stuff for ever, if he would abandon his mind to it").

ones.[8] In a clever essay Arthur O. Lovejoy once showed that these various meanings can be made to seem flatly contradictory, and suggested that we must speak of romanticisms—not one thing, but a number, that happened to coincide in roughly a single period and have sometimes gotten badly confused. Romanticism, Lovejoy pointed out, has meant a belief in progress and a spirit of reaction; a return to Christianity and a naturalistic humanism; also various other philosophies arrantly at odds with each other. In concluding that "the word 'romantic' has come to mean so many things that, by itself, it means nothing," Lovejoy came near the truth; and yet of course we must not conclude that therefore it did not exist at all. The mood of an age may be nonetheless real for being illogical. Future historians will find it as difficult to say exactly what existentialism was as present ones do to define Renaissance, Enlightenment, or romanticism. Historical phenomena take on many accretions as they pass through society; they become involved with other phenomena and eventually lose themselves in the common stream. Any major movement of the mind inevitably accumulates a crowd of different associations and meanings as it spreads. It becomes rather like our political parties: too big to stand for any one creed on which all its followers might agree, except the vaguest sort of generalities. But we do not for this reason infer the nonexistence or meaninglessness of Democrats and Republicans. It is, in fact, possible to argue the reverse: that whenever we find a doctrine that everyone knows about but no one can quite define we are in the presence of a major intellectual revolution.[9]

Without question romanticism was such a revolution. We are in danger of losing this truth if we seek too narrow or precise a definition. Behind the *forms* of romanticism, which were various, lay a deep spiritual change, often vague but nonetheless mighty. Critics of romanticism, then and later, charged that it was a fever which rejected all discipline and, by being out of proportion with nature, refusing to accept boundaries, became a dangerous malady, "an assault delivered on the modern soul by all the combined forces of disorganization" (René Doumic). To them it was nothing less than the destruction of the sense of balance on which European civilization had rested ever since the Greeks invented classicism with its message of nothing in excess, everything in proper proportion, each element in its due place. On the other side, friends of the new spirit believed that it had for the first time emancipated Europe

[8]The word *romantic* derives from the medieval "romances" so named because written in the vernacular (French) rather than in classical Latin. Thus in returning to popular speech, and trying to find folk themes, romantics were loyal to the basic meaning of their movement.

[9]It is also possible to point out that "the indefinable word is the essential one" (Chesterton): such terms as love, good, blue cannot be defined, but only illustrated, because irreducible. Perhaps romanticism is such a case.

from a timid orthodoxy and opened minds and hearts to poetry, to real religion, to true philosophy, to sincerity rather than artificiality. It was, said Sismondi, a "Protestantism in letters and the arts," a demand for liberty against authority in style; some have added that it was nothing less than an ultimate Protestantism (without dogma) in all ranges of life —a defiant Promethean rejection of all constraints on the free spirit of the individual man.

Types of Romanticism

Leaving such sweeping claims aside for the moment, we may try more precisely to state the range of romantic attitudes. First, romanticism began in *reaction against* the eighteenth century, that is, against rationalism, mechanistic materialism, classicism, all the dominant ingredients of the Enlightenment. There comes a time when youth tires of the orthodoxy of its elders which, once itself revolutionary and exciting, has come to seem pallid and dull. Youth looked for new ideas and found them in Rousseau, subsequently in Kant, Fichte, Burke. A chief weakness in the Enlightenment was its neglect of the imagination, its externalism and absence of anything inward or deeply esthetic. It denied religious emotion; it ignored the mystery and terror of existence in its effort to make all things clear. All common sense and broad daylight, it became uninspiring and unthrilling. It lacked what the French call *frissons* or thrills, and its literary style was, or came to seem, flat, conventional, unenterprising. Likewise its ethic of selfish hedonism, along with its mechanical and materialistic view of the universe, could appear as ignoble or dull.

Consequently the romantic era is filled with cries of rejection. "I, for my share, declare the world to be no machine!" exclaimed Thomas Carlyle, repeating the German idealists. The eighteenth century had said that it was. Burke speaks of reason being "but a part, and by no means the greatest part," of human nature, while Coleridge says that the "calculating faculty" is inferior to the "creative faculty." This rejection of the analytical reason in favor of an intuitive "eliciting of truth at a flash" was very close to the heart of romanticism and represented, in good part, another reaction against the Enlightenment. In literary form, romanticism rebelled against the "rules" imposed on drama or poetry by the classical formula, and against classicism's preference for the general rather than the concrete. "We are not to number the streaks of the tulip," classicism had pronounced. Romantics wanted to do just that. Romantics sought religion—a source of *frissons*, if nothing more— because rationalists scorned it. Chateaubriand declared that nothing is pleasing except the mysterious; the mysterious had been the great common enemy of all the *philosophes*. So, too, with "enthusiasm."

That which had been sensible moderation now seemed like torpor, or worse. The eighteenth century, "soul extinct but stomach well alive" in Carlyle's phrase, became a byword for crass materialism; Thackeray called it an age of gluttony. "The man of Locke" was to be scorned. "I mistrust Locke," Schelling announced; virtually all the romantics shared this contempt for that earthbound philosophy.[10] "Unable to believe but terrified of skepticism," the peculiar "heavenly city" of the eighteenth-century philosophers with its "faith of reason" was now seen to be uninhabitable. Carlyle spoke for the romantic generations in repudiating its hedonistic ethic or pleasure-seeking spirit as unworthy of man: "the pig philosophy" he called it. (It was still vigorously alive in Carlyle's Britain in the guise of Jeremy Bentham's utilitarianism; the two schools could not abide each other.) This reaction against "the pursuit of happiness" as swinish sensualism pushed the romantics into some very lofty poses: man was once again to be Promethean hero, world-conquering adventurer, sublime sage or saint—anything except that simpering courtier of the eighteenth century whose only goal in life was to satisfy his creature comforts. Keats, who certainly celebrated the sensual pleasures, regarded them as the doorway to transcendental realms of knowledge, not as ends in themselves.

The Age of Reason had been an Age of Prose; and so romanticism meant poetry, or a new kind of poetic prose such as Chateaubriand wrote. Romanticism was after all primarily a literary movement, though it spilled over into all branches of life. Eighteenth-century poetry had become on the whole unsatisfactory. "Crushed by rules, and weakened as refined," this polite literature usually failed to communicate sincere feeling, was overly formalized and abstract; it was Dr. Samuel Johnson, no romantic,[11] who noticed this much:

> From bard to bard the frigid caution crept
> While declamation roar'd and passion slept.

Hazlitt, though not uncritical of the new poets, affirmed that

---

[10]Some romantics made use of Locke (compare the young Hugo), but if so they read him as meaning that the senses, that is, the feelings, and immediate experience, are to be trusted above the abstract reason. Ernest Tuveson, in *The Imagination as a Means of Grace: Locke and the Aesthetics of Romanticism*, 1960, has explored this line of Lockean development in the eighteenth century.

[11]From his famous Dictionary, definition of "Romantick":
    1 Resembling the tales of romance; wild. . . .
    2 Improbable; false.
    3 Fanciful; full of wild scenery. . . .

> Our poetical literature had, towards the close of the last century, de-
> generated into the most trite, insipid, and mechanical of all things, in
> the hands of the followers of Pope and the old French school of poetry.

In revenge, the romantic poets gave full vent to what Locke had disparaged as "the conceits of a warmed or overweening brain." For a later
taste as well as an earlier, they sought too many "grand effects," they
bared their souls overly and gushed too much. Still, few would deny the
mighty debt to literature owed to the poets of the romantic generation.
They revitalized language, and, among other things, brought poetry to
the people. Too vast to be estimated is the force exerted on millions of
people, heretofore hardly reached by the printed word, by romantic literature: think of Musset and Hugo in France, Shelley and Wordsworth
in England, Goethe and Kleist in Germany, Emerson and Longfellow in
the United States, Bobbie Burns in Scotland. These and their imitators
molded the consciousness of the nineteenth century, it is not too much
to say. They made poetry something more than rhymed reason; as image
and symbol, haunting the imagination, it shaped the feeling for life in
its own unique way.

Mounting "an insurrection against the old traditions of classicism,"
the romanticists achieved a virtual revolution in the canons of art and
literature. One measure of that revolution may be found in attitudes
toward the art of the Middle Ages. Ever since the Renaissance, Gothic
architecture had been dismissed as crude and barbarous. Gibbon said
that the Piazzo San Marco in Venice contained "the worst architecture
I ever saw." Ruskin, only a few decades later, pronounced it the most
beautiful of human creations (*The Stones of Venice*). Each of us must
make up his own mind about this, but in general the romantics prevailed, most people today grant the beauty of St. Mark's and of the
Gothic cathedrals in general. The French Revolution started to pull down
those "piles of monkish superstition"; the Gothic Revival of the 1830s
tried to renovate them and imitate them. Similarly, it may surprise us to
learn that the poet Dante had been held in considerable disdain. Whatever their other prejudices against things medieval, most moderns have
become accustomed to think of the *Divine Comedy* as among the immortal masterpieces of world literature, but in the eighteenth century
Thomas Warton had spoken of it as "disgusting" and a follower of Voltaire pronounced it the worst poem in all the world. Dante's reputation
was made by the romantics, by Blake, Byron, Shelley and Coleridge,
enthusiastically seconded by Carlyle, Tennyson, Browning, and Ruskin
a bit later. A popular product of the romantic revolution, much fancied
today by collectors of the unusual, was the Gothic novel, with its eerie
atmosphere and supernatural events, its werewolves and ruined abbeys

and diabolical happenings. Thus the taste for the medieval could go to extreme lengths. The mysterious, the exotic, the irregular, the sublime and even the grotesque now became appealing.

In a similar way the taste for wild nature, for mountains and deep forests, was largely a romantic reaction; pure neo-classical taste considered the Alps hideously unkempt and would have gone some distance out of the way to avoid them.[12] "Nature" was a word much on eighteenth-century lips, but it did not usually mean the woodlands wild. Rousseau's *Reveries of a Solitary Walker* passed down to Chateaubriand and to Lamartine's *Meditations*; and everyone knows how important nature was to Wordsworth and Thoreau. This attachment to the trees and flowers and hills had, or came to have, a metaphysical foundation which, forming a link to philosophical idealism, is one of the leading ideas of the age. Rousseau believed vaguely that nature soothes and calms us, returning us to fundamentals and reminding us of deeper truths than those of human society. Wordsworth, without much philosophy, felt keenly

> . . . a sense sublime
> Of something far more deeply interfused,
> Whose dwelling is the light of setting suns
> And the round ocean and the living air,
> And the blue sky, and in the mind of man;
> A motion and a spirit that impels
> All thinking things, all objects of all thought,
> And rolls through all things.

In Germany, where philosophy had been stimulated by Kant, and where romanticism from the first interacted with it, this pantheistic sense of spirit in nature, "rolling through all things," received explicit formulation. How Kant's critical philosophy created a revolution in philosophy, and how this led on to the other great German philosophers (Fichte, Schelling, Hegel) has already been pointed out. There were philosophers who specifically called themselves "romantic"; and there were idealists, like Fichte, who contributed to the popular conception of romanticism in certain ways. Broadly speaking, the result was to present a vision of reality as basically spiritual, and to suggest in some sense a unity of this world spirit linking man to nature. The post-Kantians in

---

[12]Despite neoclassical preference for neat symmetry, the eighteenth century had permitted a place for much that was not "beautiful" but nevertheless somehow impressive, under the title of "the sublime." Romantics—*cf.* the young Burke's notable essay—developed this concept. Especially was this true in England, never as orthodoxly neoclassical as France. "Mountain gloom and mountain glory" (Marjorie Nicolson) was celebrated by some eighteenth-century sublimists.

various ways postulated a fundamental knowable unity, spiritual in nature—a mind-stuff underlying and giving form to the appearances, corresponding to the mind-stuff we have in us, and which we contact when
we are using our minds creatively. Fichte called it the Ego, adopting an
idealist position in which thought is the basic reality and stressing moral
experience; Schelling spoke of the Absolute, of the union of object and
subject in the human consciousness, and of the paramountcy of esthetic
experience. All this might seem rather Teutonically mystifying to most
people; on any showing it was difficult and academic, for these worthies
of German philosophy were all university professors. But it got outside
the classroom, as the poets Novalis and Hölderlin and Richter transformed its abstract words into concrete poetic symbols. And as esthetic
doctrine it was tremendously influential.

Many people came to hold, more or less loosely, something like
this idealist-romantic position, meaning that we can see God or a higher
reality in Nature, actually commune with it, feel its basic kinship to our
own souls. Nontechnical, semipopular romantic idealism may be found
in Thomas Carlyle's first book, *Sartor Resartus*, wherein this vivid
writer gave expression to the idea that "the external world known to our
senses and explored by our sciences is mere Appearance. Reality is its
divine, unseen counterpart, standing to Appearance as Soul stands to
Body" (D. C. Somervell). "Transcendentalism" became a byword among
both French and American literary men of the period 1820–1840; the
name of Ralph Waldo Emerson is enough to remind Americans of its
potency. This heady doctrine might persuade men that all the appearances, social conventions, for example, are a fraud, and that each of us
can be godlike if only he dares to search his own soul. It was close to
mystical pantheism, a heresy long known to Christianity, whereby the
god-intoxicated man felt that he might communicate directly with deity.
Often it had explicit roots in Neoplatonism; William Blake's mysticism
has been traced to this source, and these writings were also prominent
in the omnivorous reading of Coleridge, who claimed that he had found
mysticism in many of the ancients before he read the Germans. There
was also a discovery of the Indian religiophilosophical tradition at this
time. "The pantheism of the Orient, transformed by Germany," E.
Quinet wrote in 1841, was responsible for what he called a *"renaissance
orientale."* (But the discovery and translation of the Hindu classics owed
most to an Englishman, Sir William Jones, and a Frenchman, M.
Anquetil-Duperron.)

The romantics added the thought that it is above all the Artist, the
Poet, who feels the Infinite Spirit in him when he creates. Working intuitively, he "elicits truth as at a flash" (Coleridge), truth deeper than
the experimental or analytical. His poetic images are symbols of nature,
keys to reality. The visionary-religious element in romanticism is per-

haps to be found in its most remarkable state in the works of William Blake, the English artist-seer-poet. Taking quite seriously the identification of his own thoughts with the soul of the universe,[13] Blake believed it was the mission of the poet and artist to be a religious prophet, endowing the old religious truths with new meaning. A "symbolist" before the French school that was to bear this name later in the nineteenth century, a discoverer of the "archetypes of the unconscious" before Jung, Blake gave new names to the gods and spoke of building a "new Jerusalem" in England. His haunting, childlike songs touch closely on perennial religious and moral experience.

The church called the New Jerusalem was associated not with Blake but with the writings of the eighteenth-century Swedish seer Emanuel Swedenborg (d. 1772), whose visionary writings interpreting the Christian scriptures became popular, especially in England, in the early nineteenth century. There is still a Swedenborgian society in England; there was considerable American interest, too. The German romantic theologian Friedrich Schleiermacher (*Discourses on Religion*, 1799) sought to transpose Christianity from dogma to interior experience—a faith experimentally true, true to the meaning and purpose of life when its doctrines are transformed into concrete human terms. This idea grew familiar in the nineteenth century and merged with the "liberal" Christianity which dismissed Biblical literalism arguing that the "essential" truths of Christianity are deeper and broader, and often absorbed such secular goals as liberty or social justice. Romantic theology stressed inward emotional experience as a criterion of faith, and interacted with a revival of evangelical, pietistic Christianity. Already begun by the Wesleyans in the eighteenth century, this movement was quite popular from about 1780 to 1825. Various fervent if unorthodox sects arose. Alexander of Russia succumbed to one and tried to write it into the Holy Alliance of 1815; the socialist Saint-Simon preached a "new Christianity" to go with his Enlightenment social science. The Evangelical movement within the Church of England, beginning at the end of the eighteenth century, greatly influenced the whole Victorian era. Within Catholicism, the celebrated "Oxford Movement" produced John Newman and others in England in the 1830s; in rebellion against materialism and utilitarianism, these apostate Anglicans shared with the romantics a poetic and spiritual emotionalism, a sense of history, a medievalism. Some Oxonians stayed within Anglicanism but revived the "high church" tradition.

This return to religion was popular: witness the American "great revival" of the earlier nineteenth century on the frontier, or the evangeli-

[13]Compare Gerard de Nerval, the French romantic poet: "The human imagination has invented nothing that is not true, either in this world or the next."

cal movement in Britain which reached the lowest classes. But many of the major writers shared it. Chateaubriand's *Genius of Christianity* was a leading work by one of the most celebrated of romantics; Wordsworth and Coleridge, if not Shelley and Byron, sought Christian piety. Eighteenth-century scoffing at the gods was no longer in vogue. Often unorthodox and verging on pantheist heresy, the feeling for religion was not the less strong for that.

Politically, romanticism was ambiguous. Coinciding with the French Revolution, it could not help but interact with it. At first, the romantics hailed the Revolution with delight, joining figuratively with the young Wordsworth as he danced with the French people. Then they turned against it listening to Burke's great indictment, which is charged with many feelings close to the heart of romanticism. The Revolution stood for eighteenth-century rationalism and failed for that reason; it was, in fact, reactionary. Most Romantics distinguished between the French Revolution as a particular historic event and the broader movement of history it imperfectly embodied. They did not doubt that humanity was on the march, seldom wanted to go back to the eighteenth-century "old regime," but agreed that the French Revolution had degenerated in a cynical and vulgar imperialism, because of its false groundings in Enlightenment materialism. In his famed history of the Revolution, Thomas Carlyle regarded it as having failed because it did not (until Bonaparte) produce any "great man." But the advocate of hero worship condemned the Old Regime also for having failed to provide inspired leadership, a sure sign of decadence. Romantics might, like Wordsworth, retain a rather naive Godwinian faith in human perfectibility, believing however that this utopia would come through man realizing his *inner* powers of consciousness, something not to be attained by changes in forms of government.

Coleridge's political odyssey may be taken as typical: interested in politics and at first enthusiastic for the Revolution, he wrote an ode on the storming of the Bastille; his *Ode to France*, 1798, records his disillusion and despair. "In Mr. Burke's writings the germs of almost all political truths may be found," he thought, but he also thought Burke had gone too far in his hatred of the Revolution. There must be a moral basis of policy; Kant's categorical imperative, that persons are not to be treated as things, is the great foundation. Coleridge was a staunch foe of economic individualism and of the pseudoscience of political economy, which he regarded as "solemn humbug." The mystic bonds that tie men together shape the almost sacred entity of Society, which is a reflection of the divine, as much so as physical nature. This *organic* view of society, opposed to the eighteenth century's alleged atomistic individualism, was a marked romantic trait. Coleridge's political insights are deep, but he failed to communicate any very coherent platform; he had too much awareness of the complexity of things, and felt the great need was not for a program but for human understanding.

The others in the galaxy of great English Romantic poets illustrate the political ambiguity of romanticism. If Wordsworth and Coleridge ended as Tories, Byron, by far the most popular poet of his day, was an aristocratic revolutionary, who defended the Luddites, died fighting for Greek independence, and wrote much about rebels; though, in view of Byron's life, we cannot but feel that he more nearly spoke his mind when he asked for "wine and women, mirth and laughter." Shelley, that "beautiful and ineffectual angel," was also full of revolt at times:

> Men of England, wherefore plough
> For the lords who lay ye low?

but more full of poetry and the love of beautiful women. The greatest of these poets, John Keats, simply had no discernible politics; nightingales interested him far more. "Romanticism," the authors of a book about it assert, "fostered sympathy for the oppressed . . . and looked forward to a new social system, a Utopia." (W. V. Moody and R. M. Lovett) So it did, doubtless. But another writer (C. Grana) tells us, with equal accuracy, that "Romanticism included a revival of political traditionalism, neo-feudal at times, decrying social fragmentation and exalting a sense of unspoiled community, born of spontaneous loyalty to ritualized customs." And we should have to take account of others who, like Keats or Alfred de Musset, were innocent of political convictions altogether.

But the great events of revolution and war wove themselves through the texture of feelings of all the writers. Stendhal, in his essay on "Racine and Shakespeare," remarked that those who had lived through such times, who had experienced the Terror and marched with bloody feet through Russian snows with Napoleon, could no longer be moved by the chaste tragedies of classicism. The blood stirred by these mighty happenings, and warmed by revolutionary slogans, simply could not be aroused by the older proprieties. It demanded stronger meat and drink. The political thought of romanticism was diverse, but whatever it was it demanded and created excitement. The young Hugo, worshipping Chateaubriand and abhorring the Revolution, was royalist, conservative, and even reactionary, but it was out of strong emotions and also a love of liberty. He simply thought that a false liberty and democracy had led to despotism, the enslavement of the people in the name of slogans about equality. Later he became a liberal, radical, or revolutionary (reversing the conventional picture of men growing more conservative with age). The fact is that Hugo was always passionate, always idealistic, always libertarian; the modes in which he expressed this spirit changed with the times, that was all.

Nevertheless the confusion in romanticism is amply evident in its political thought. We have only to observe that an organic view of society is widely regarded as most typical of it, but how are we to adjust this vision of collectivism with the spirit of revolt and individual self-expression, even alienation, also obviously a romantic attitude? Between Coleridge opposing the English reform bill of 1832 and Hugo on the barricades there seems a decided gulf. No doubt German philosophy could provide a shaky bridge between the ego and the cosmos, but there seems little to be gained by trying to cover positions so various with a single term.

The Meaning of Romanticism

A century of scholarship and criticism has sought in vain for a single definition of romanticism. From this, some have drawn the conclusion that the term is useless, that no such thing existed, rather a number of different things that somehow got lumped together owing to sloppy thinking or "label-itis." In any case, was romanticism the same in Germany, France, Great Britain, Spain? Plainly it took on regional variations. Should not one study the concrete—this Spanish poet, that German philosopher, Wordsworth, Keats, Coleridge—and forget about the elusive general? This has almost been the direction of literature studies in recent decades. Still, the term *romanticism* survives despite all efforts to kill it. It survives because it *is* a useful term to cover a number of striking if not identical cultural phenomena of the period around 1780–1830. Large terms are needed, though they are necessarily imprecise. The philosophy, literature, and general *Zeitgeist* of this period had enough in common over large areas to justify the use of some general word to describe it. Possibly we should use several terms; but we can, if we like, choose to subdivide the one term, qualify it, mark the exceptions—but retain it.

All kinds of definitions, divisions, and distinctions have been offered. Of these, it seems useful to distinguish the *negative* romanticism which was a reaction against the Enlightenment, against neoclassicism, materialism, hedonism, etc., from the positive romanticism which was largely a gift of German philosophy—the philosophy of subjective and intuitive truth, spiritual nature, and the poet's role in bringing the two realms together in conscious creative experience. It may be useful, too, to sort out things which got interlocked with romanticism but were not essentially of it such as the political explosions of the times, nationalism, democracy, the reaction against the French Revolution. It is also helpful to sort out things which while characteristic of numerous romantics were not at all new, such as Byron's sexual morals. And the careful student will take note of national differences. Thus the English romantics, despite Byron and Keats, were a much more chaste and prudent lot than the Germans, as a recent scholar has pointed out, reflecting the stability of English life and its strong bourgeois morality. French romanticism wore the badge of anti-Revolution with special prominence. Romanticism was weakest in Spain and Italy, especially in the latter, perhaps because of the pervasive influence of classicism on the Italian landscape. (The Gothic had been weakest there too.)

When all is said, the romantic revolution must be linked to the French Revolution as a vital aspect of what was perhaps the most exciting and creative period of modern times. If one wishes to hazard a definition of the basic factor in this intellectual revolution, it would be *subjectivism* or the participation of mind in shaping reality. It has been said that no one previously had conceived the knowing process except in terms of the object known; now the subject came into the picture. The mind partly creates the external reality it grasps. Coleridge objected that "Newton was a mere materialist. Mind, in his system, is always passive—a lazy looker-on in an external world. . . . *Any system built on the passiveness of mind must be false.*" This was the central insight of the romantics, and it will be seen, then, how important Kant was. And in this sense romanticism, though many aspects of it went out of fashion after a time, has left its stamp on the contemporary Western world.

Subjectivism worked itself out in the unique romantic conception of the free individual, freed from the rules, from moral conventions, from all external restraints because he is the Creative Genius. In the concept of genius, romanticists found their central literary conception. Bound by no rules, he makes his own. By no means everyone is a genius, but conceivably all *might* be. At any rate they do arise—a Homer, a Shakespeare, a Goethe—and they make the pattern for others to follow. In the last analysis we follow and should worship the actions of genius. Carlyle, in his famous *Sartor Resartus*, repeated the message of Goethe as an antidote to skepticism and lethargy: arise, WORK, do what thou canst do. Hero worship, and the gospel of work, affected people in all walks of life in the nineteenth century; they were romantics without knowing it.

It may be suggested then that romanticism was a literary and intellectual counterpart of the new principle of individualism in society—and this despite the fact that romantics often inveighed against individualism. The Old Regime had been corporative and organic, a society of estates and classes; after the French Revolution, one had a society of equal individuals. The literature of the eighteenth century, as we earlier noted, was a social literature which sought essentially not to express the personal soul but to communicate the common ideas. Romanticism was the former. Men had begun their modern fate of loneliness in the crowd, or their modern privilege of individual self-development, as one may choose to put it. It is true that the family remained, and was to be all the more stressed in Victorian times; but classes were dissolving (in France, and to a lesser degree in England), free competition in the market place was becoming the arbiter of success, the church was fading, the stable order of countryside would soon be challenged and overcome by the city's anonymity. A collection of individuals replaced "society," as Jeremy Bentham and the utilitarians divined. One stood or fell by one's own unaided efforts. Romanticism was a literary retreat to the individual ego which, seen or not as part of a larger world soul, remained as the one solid basis of life.

Arthur O. Lovejoy, that great student of ideas, found the fundamental romantic trait to be diversity, as over against Enlightenment standardization and simplification—the search for unique particulars, rather than universals and generals.[14] So stated, the change embraces a great deal of this age of revolution, counterrevolution, and romanticism. The French Revolution, seen as the climax of the eighteenth-century desire to simplify and generalize, encountered Burke's opposition based on the complexity of political life, which must be handled concretely. Kant, faced with the choice between naive materialism and straightforward skepticism, fashioned a philosophical fabric that was far more intricately woven. Nationalist diversity replaced cosmopolitanism. All were interconnected.

Romanticism's stress on diversity relates to some general features of nineteenth-century civilization. That civilization was in many ways more diverse and less unified than the older one. Aristocratic and cosmopolitan, the eighteenth century had *a* style, even though one might note exceptions to it. The nineteenth was to be eclectic in its architecture, pillaging the past for borrowed styles; it was to offer a "generous confusion" of modes in the arts and in ideas; it divided into separate national cultures. It was a much more pluralistic civilization. Man was parcelled out in men, as the poet Rossetti put it—which he, looking backward nostalgically, took to be a sign of the decadence of Europe. Unconsciously perhaps, romanticism reflected the atomization of European society.

---

[14]In *The Great Chain of Being*, 1936 written after the essay "On the Discrimination of Romanticisms" quoted earlier, and suggesting that Lovejoy found his way to more unity in romanticism than he had once seen. See also his paper, in a symposium on "The Romantic Movement," *Journal of the History of Ideas*, June, 1941.

8

The Birth of Ideologies: 1815-1848

From the thunder of Napoleon battles, to the jabbering of Open-vestry in St. Mary Axe, all things announce democracy. Democracy is everywhere the inexorable demand of these ages, swift fulfilling itself.

THOMAS CARLYLE

I alone shall have confounded twenty generations of political imbecility and it is to me alone that present and future generations will owe the beginning of their boundless happiness.

CHARLES FOURIER

The European Situation 1815–1848

The profusion of political and social "isms" in Europe after 1815 was a consequence of the situation men faced in that year. Especially acute in France, the crisis affected all Europe, for none of it had been untouched by the Revolution and Napoleon, and much of it had been as profoundly altered as France herself. Bonaparte had destroyed the old order in Italy and Germany and had brought sweeping innovations wherever his legions marched. Now the Revolution and its great leader were vanquished. But was it possible to go back to the old regime of 1789 as if nothing had happened? Even the most reactionary did not really believe that. If one could not believe in either the old order or the new, what lay ahead? All over Europe, men felt the need to take soundings and mark out some course. Europe seemed to be rushing into a yawning void. Clearly the old Europe was dead—ten centuries of civilization washed out. The new Europe had failed, morally and now physically, from the Reign of Terror to the coup d'état of Bonaparte and so to his military defeat after a terrible war. But Europe was going on, filled with all kinds of half-understood dynamisms such as democracy, industrialization, etc. Did they portend destruction or creation, rebirth or decadence?

In France, the impulse to order showed itself strongly. Laissez-faire liberty did not appeal to the rationalist French mind. Both conservatives and socialists shared a desire to define and shape the reconstruction of a positive social order. But this must be done in a new way, and there was widespread realization that science and fact, not metaphysics and dogma, had to form the foundation. In Great Britain, liberal individualism was much more prominent. In both countries, political and social ideologies constituted the leading intellectual interest. Even in Germany is that true; for while the great Hegel reigned as the last of the classical lineage of German philosophy, and produced a system some found too metaphysical, Hegel's chief interest was in human history and its political order; his disciples included critical historians such as David Strauss and social ideologists such as Karl Marx.

For the greatest need in Europe after 1815 was for political and social reorganization following the destruction of the old order by the French Revolution. The peace settlement at Vienna in 1815 tried to do this in the arena of practical politics; it partly succeeded and partly failed. Popular movements such as nationalism in Germany and Italy, or working-class radicalism in Britain and France, reflected the deep disturbances of a society undergoing rapid economic change along with political uncertainty.

Socially, one marked the decline of the old aristocracy and the rise of a new class, an upper bourgeoisie of commerce, finance, and industry. The period of a few years from 1815 to 1830 witnessed a generally conservative spirit, the product of the reactionary victors of the long war against Bonapartism; in France, it is the time of the attempted Bourbon restoration, in England the Tories continued their power, and in Germany Prince Metternich's Austrian conservatism controlled affairs. But the underlying social realities defeated the attempt to preserve aristocratic domination. The revolution of 1830 sweeps aside the restored monarchy in France; the great Reform Bill of 1832 signals the demise of old-fashioned Toryism in Britain.

The middle classes had begun their long reign. There was at this time considerable class consciousness among spokesmen for this group. Power must be transferred from the landed oligarchy to the "intelligent middle and industrious classes," said Richard Cobden, an oracle of British liberalism. These classes distinguished themselves from the "mob" below as carefully as from the aristocracy, or what was left of it, above —from both of which they differed in possessing the traits of industriousness, sobriety, and morality, they thought. They were serious, frugal, upright, hardworking and, according to some critics, hardhearted. Certainly they were builders of wealth in this vigorous morning of the Industrial Revolution, very proud of their achievements, inclined to be scornful of those who contributed less, as they believed. Distinctions must be noted within the "bourgeoisie"; the term is too broad to be meaningful. In France, at least, the "grande bourgeoisie," who dominated the 1830–1848 Orleanist Monarchy, was a haughty coterie of rich bankers and industrialists who were "political liberals but social conservatives," having little regard for their social inferiors and absolutely no taste for democracy. In France, the 1830 revolution brought a "liberalization" of the suffrage to the degree that perhaps one in forty adult male Frenchmen voted as compared to one in seventy-five before. In Great Britain, after the great Reform Bill of 1832, one in five had the vote. In the Continental revolutions of 1848 a lower bourgeoisie joined with workers in demanding universal suffrage. Britain escaped that revolution because to a much greater extent her lower as well as upper bourgeoisie were enfranchised.

The word *bourgeois* became an epithet in two circles: the socialists and the literary men. It was alleged that the middle classes were indifferent to the arts as well as to the sufferings of the poor. The stereotype of the bourgeois (as he appears in a Daumier caricature, for example) had some basis in reality. It is true, for example, that the Benthamite *Westminster Review* regarded literature as inappropriate to civilization, while the liberal *Economist* along with Herbert Spencer coolly considered it better to starve the poor than to administer public charity. But we must remember the strength of this "industrious and intelligent" bourgeoisie. By and large, they *were* in possession of a large share of those not altogether contemptible characteristics, industry and intelligence. They were creating wealth as it had never been created before. If their natural habitat was the bourse or the factory rather than university or parliament, they did produce powerful spokesmen in this age: not merely Samuel Smiles with his propaganda of self-help, but such as Cobden, Bright, Thiers, Guizot.

It is necessary also to keep in mind the point once made by Balzac, the astute French novelist and observer of the "human comedy": if the bourgeoisie destroyed the nobility, a combat would immediately ensue between the bourgeoisie and the people beneath them. The weapons with which the bourgeoisie had brought down the aristocracy—charges of special privilege and unearned income, demands for more democracy and equality—could obviously be turned on them by the others. Coleridge, opposing the extension of the suffrage in 1832, warned the middle class that they would be unable to stop by giving the vote just to themselves, but would eventually have to give it to all. Carlyle warned them that by refusing to look after their workers they would drive them to social revolution; for the feudal landlords had at least given protection to their serfs, whereas the new factory owners gave them no human sympathy, only an inadequate wage. So the "social question" arose early and socialism became a factor, though unable to overturn the rule of the bourgeoisie. Few serious thinkers were ever quite happy with the new organization of society, or lack of it, under middle-class industrialism.

Results of the French Revolution

The most basic change wrought by the French Revolution (in principle, for most of Europe) was that which Henry Maine capsulized in the phrase "from status to contract." The Old Regime had been hierarchical, organic, inequalitarian, and corporative. Treating people neither as individuals nor as equals, it had yet contained a place for all within the society. Within fifty years of the French Revolution Thomas Carlyle could develop a considerable nostalgia for it, on the grounds that the serf at least had had a protector, humble though his role was. The Revolution proclaimed equality and freedom. Men were free to make their own way; they were also free to starve. The medieval peasant had held his land and his duties by custom (status); the nineteenth century worker had lost this security, he could rise, but if he fell there was in principle no one to rescue him.

From this enormous change issues a whole series of nineteenth century ideological statements. The socialists were indignant that human labor had been turned into a commodity, and claimed that "bourgeois freedom" was only a disguise for the greater exploitation of labor. More objectively, historians pointed out that the opposition of classes had been increased, not diminished, by the abolition of the old feudal ranks of society; for now all were theoretically equal but marked off from one another by just the possession of wealth, a thing more likely to breed jealousy and bitterness. The gap between rich and poor became greater, not less, and the poor had less protection. In *Past and Present*, Carlyle asked his contemporaries to consider "Gurth, born thrall of Cedric the Saxon," who, though not exactly "an exemplar of human felicity . . . to me seems happy, in comparison with many a Lancashire and Buckinghamshire man, of these days, not born thrall of anybody!" "The Revolution ended one inequality and gave birth to another," as a later French writer summed it up. The new inequality was both more obvious and less tolerable. Plutocracy had replaced Aristocracy. Legal, juridical equality meant a rat race in which the weaker or unluckier were ground into the dirt by the more energetic and less scrupulous.

If the new "bourgeois" leaders could sometimes express feelings of disdain for the lower classes, they did not entirely neglect their welfare. Rejecting most plans of state assistance in accordance with their approval of the "night watchman" state which only "prevented crime and preserved contracts," bourgeois liberals could not deny that their maxim of "a fair field and no favors" required some social services. Education was perhaps the leading case of this sort. "The schoolmaster was abroad" in these years, in Europe as well as in the United States, where the name of Horace Mann became a household word. Guizot, who scorned the multitude, nevertheless put through the educational reform of 1833, called the charter of French primary education. It was far from installing free and universal elementary education, but by requiring every commune to maintain a public primary school it began the movement that led in this direction. Probably the nineteenth-century bourgeoisie have been overly blamed for their alleged callousness toward the poor and the workers. Still, their creed did not allow for much social welfare legislation by modern standards. The political economists wrote their basic textbooks. The great nineteenth-century economists were engaged in developing a highly specialized, formidably exacting branch of knowledge, with rare success; they were arbiters of public policy and beacons of light to the powerful industrial bourgeoisie.

Writing in 1831 on "The Spirit of the Age," young John Stuart Mill remarked that "a change has taken place in the human mind. . . . The conviction is already not far from being universal that the times are pregnant with change, and that the nineteenth century will be known to posterity as the era of one of the greatest revolutions of which history has preserved the remembrance, in the human mind, and in the whole constitution of human society." In 1830 France had a revolution, sweeping aside the restored Bourbons and establishing a constitutional monarchy; in 1832 Great Britain, too, entered into the Liberal era with the passing of the great Reform Bill after a severe political struggle. But with the progress of the so-called industrial revolution, the rise of what Carlyle named the "social question," and a steady trend towards popular democracy, there was to be no stability on the basis of the 1830–1832 settlements, which provided for neither a democratic suffrage nor a welfare state. They were in fact political and social orders dominated by the upper classes and offered little to either the workers or the lower middle class, who were to join in making the revolutions of 1848, proving, however, incompatible allies. The 1830s witnessed a rise of interest in socialism and related ideas, brought violent insurrection to some districts (for example Lyons in 1831) and then gave way to the "hungry forties," at the end of which major revolutions swept Europe from one end to the other.

An unprecedented ferment of social and political thought prepared the way for the revolutions of the year 1848, a secondary tremor hardly less earth-shaking than the first quake of 1789. Various sorts of socialism, democracy, social democracy, liberalism, mingled in another apocalyptic moment, when many expected the deferred social millennium. Again came apparent failure and disillusion. But in fact 1848 marked the permanent arrival, if not the absolute victory, of both democracy and socialism; after that they dominated the European scene for a century. The ideas that grew up in this 1815–1848 period are the political and social ideas or ideologies on which the Western world has been living ever since. They are, then, of the utmost importance.

Conservatism

The rise of a conservative ideology began with Edmund Burke, and all subsequent members of this school were basically indebted to his *Reflections on the Revolution* (see above, pages 206–10). Coleridge, as we have noted, built on Burke's foundations in England, though his political thought was somewhat scattered. Writing under the impact of his own later (1798) disillusionment with the French cause, he did not go as far as Burke in rejecting all rationalism in politics; he joined him in the respect for tradition, the organic sense of society, and the feeling for a moral order in history. His influence flowed down through the nineteenth century as a strong philosophic source of British enlightened Toryism; John Stuart Mill declared that Coleridge and Jeremy Bentham, the utilitarian, were the two opposing seminal figures in nineteenth-century British thought. The contrast must be noted, for American students: British and European conservatism has been an enemy of laissez-faire. Coleridge believed in government regulation of manufacturers, government aid to education, the duty of the state to enhance the moral and intellectual capabilities of its citizens in all sorts of positive ways. Conservatism abhorred, and was set over against, the individualism of the "liberals," who preached free competition and no state intervention in the economic order. It can be related to the rural squirearchy, was certainly not equalitarian or levelling (Coleridge opposed the Reform Bill of 1832), but was deeply humanistic and more likely than liberalism to support governmental welfare measures for the poor. The leading hero of factory reform and other humanitarian measures in early industrial England was the Tory, Lord Shaftesbury. The Coleridge tradition passed to such writers as John Ruskin, who described himself as "a violent Tory of the old school" and violently denounced the materialistic and unprincipled society of industrial England. It also passed to Benjamin Disraeli with his conception of a democratized Conservative party leading the way to social reform on behalf of the workers.

It was in France, though, that the conservative ideology developed most prominently, in the Restoration period after 1815. There were a few liberals in post-Napoleonic France (1815–1830), for example Benjamin Constant and Mme. de Staël, those old foes of Bonaparte, who stressed constitutionalism, civil liberties, a limited monarchy, parliamentarianism. In this camp too one might put Chateaubriand, his career now turned to statesmanship as he struggled to make the system of parliamentary monarchy work. But even these French "liberals" do not seem to have had much of the spirit of Benthamite individualism, then becoming dominant in Britain. Nor were they the dominant voices, distinguished though the thought of Constant was. France in the 1820s produced two brilliant streams of thought from opposite directions: Right and Left. These were the conservatives and the socialists. The conservative camp included Joseph de Maistre and the Vicomte de Bonald as its chief ornaments.

Born in 1753, of aristocratic Savoyard family, the first of these was early a follower of Rousseau. In the 1780s he became interested in the occult Christianity pursued in the circle of the Marquess de Saint-Martin, "the unknown philosopher" as he signed himself, but dropped the attachment when the Church pronounced against it. A provincial senator, happily married, Maistre would never have made himself a famous figure in the history of thought had it not been for the French Revolution. Initially, he was known as a liberal or even a Jacobin. But he fell afoul of the Revolution in 1793 and went into exile. At Lausanne in Switzerland, he frequented the society of M. Necker and his celebrated daughter, Mme. de Staël, and met Gibbon the historian. At that time he began to put together his thoughts on the origins of the Revolution, the reasons for its failure, and the means of reconstructing France. These were themes to which the thoughts of many men turned in these dramatic years.

Bonald was in exile in Heidelberg at the same time, and Maistre wrote to him in 1796 that "your spirit and mine are in perfect accord." They had to wait out the Napoleonic years; Bonaparte, though he read and admired a book of Maistre's in 1797, could not secure the loyalty of the man who had made himself the spokesman of French royalism. Maistre worked as a diplomatist for the King of Sardinia, going to St. Petersburg as ambassador in 1803. The rugged integrity of this Savoyard (a people noted for this trait), who separated himself from his family whom he deeply loved, whose faith in France did not waver through the darkest days, added to the eloquence of his prose and the charm of his personality. He was a writer of genius and a scholar of great learning, as even his foes conceded. In St. Petersburg he wrote his chief works: *On the Pope, On the Gallican Church, Evenings in St. Petersburg.* After the fall of Napoleon and the restoration of Louis XVIII,

Maistre returned to France to receive considerable acclaim, and his books, now published in France, earned him the reputation of chief theoretician of the Bourbon restoration; he died in 1821 just as he was gaining this long-deferred but well-earned recognition. Bonald, whose ideas were quite similar (he lacked Maistre's grace of style but was rather more systematic), lived on to reign as the high priest of the monarchists, joined among others by the youthful and fiery La Mennais, who would later take up a different crusade. But of these Maistre's writings are the best known.

Negatively, Maistre's thought was marked by a cold fury against the whole *philosophe* school. He wished to "absolutely kill the spirit of the eighteenth century." In this sense these "Ultraists," as they were known, were reactionaries. The lucid intellect of Maistre concluded that the *philosophes* had introduced the poison that had induced the sickness of the Revolution; the poison must be purged from France's body before she could be restored to health. Maistre would not even allow Voltaire and company the virtue of common honesty. They were great criminals; to like Voltaire is the sign of a corrupt soul; the very visage of the great satirist bespoke his service of the Devil. Locke, Hume, Voltaire, Rousseau were all evil or at the very least horribly misguided men. Here Maistre was simply a polemicist, a vigorous and eloquent one, turning Voltaire's weapons against himself and assailing the mockers as they had once assailed the church.

However, once the poison had been cast out, these "reactionaries" saw the additional task of reconstructing society and tried to show how it might be done. Here they proved immensely stimulating and influenced many who did not at all share their ideological preconceptions; they even, and most notably, influenced the socialists, Saint-Simon being the best example.[1] Counterrevolutionaries, royalists, Catholics, conservatives, these men cannot be written off as sterile reactionaries. They combined keen intelligence with penetrating insights into the weaknesses of the liberal or democratic order, while also contributing some fruitful ideas about methodology in the social sciences. They were aware that one could not go back to 1789, much though they may have regretted the Revolution, which Maistre could only explain as having been sent by God to punish France for her sins! Maistre was not the "prophet of the past" as a wit dubbed him. It was necessary to establish a new political

---

[1]John Morley in his essay on Maistre commented at length on the fact that pretty obviously the great reactionary valued religion and the church less for their inherent truth than for their social utility. The stress of analysis is on the part that such institutions must play in stabilizing society. In this sense, Maistre himself is almost a "utilitarian."

philosophy; this was the age of ideology, with mere habit no longer sufficing; "the intellectual principle has taken priority over the moral principle in the direction of society," as Maistre put it. Living in a France which had seen the failure of the Republic and then (defeated in frightful war) the collapse of the dictatorship that succeeded it, and which now found itself trying the uncertain experiment of a restored Bourbon monarchy, Maistre and Bonald hoped to explain clearly why republics always failed and only monarchies could provide political security. The task stimulated them to a wide-ranging investigation of political and sociological phenomena.

Their argument made extensive use of the idea that the natural order of society is historical and traditional, while individualism and democracy are diseases resulting in social anarchy. Take away the discipline imposed by church, monarchy, nobility, each in its proper place in the orbit that is natural to France (nations have character; each has a form of government suitable to it; you must not tamper with this truth by an arid rationalistic universalism), take this away, and the result will be disorder, corruption, decay. Written constitutions are crude and artificial; the true constitution of a people is written in the hearts of its people and expressed in its ancestral customs. The school of Maistre, Savigny, and Haller[2] was historical; they held that wisdom in politics comes from experience only, that is, from a discriminating study of the past, and from the understanding of national character as revealed in history. Abstract theory had caused much damage, they believed, ignorance of and contempt for history being the prime source of political error.

Their arguments in favor of absolute monarchy may now make tedious reading, but the conservative school had a considerable influence on nineteenth-century thought. Bonald has been called the founder of sociology; he certainly influenced Comte, who is more frequently granted that title. Alexis de Tocqueville's famous *Democracy in America*, which might be called the pioneer work of sociological analysis, was much influenced by these writers. (See La Mennais's comments on democracy in his 1825 book, *De la religion considerée dans ses rapports avec l'ordre politique et civil*, volume I. It looks as if Tocqueville were testing the hypotheses of La Mennais: that democracy leads to despotism, enshrines mediocrity, causes people to be restless, rootless, and godless, and makes money the only idol.) Whereas their recommendations for the good

[2]Savigny was spokesman for the historical school of jurisprudence in Germany, Burkean in its stress on the organic evolution of the law rooted in tradition. Haller, a German Swiss, held similar views. The latter's nostalgia for the Old Regime in its corporate, organic, and inequalitarian aspects was especially strong.

society came to little, their critical analysis of the social changes over-taking France, their investigations of such matters as what effect the loss of religious faith or of social hierarchy will have on politics and society, were truly stimulating. Their appeal from the abstract theories of the rationalists to positive historical facts and careful sociological investigation bore fruit in many students after them, who admired their methods while not necessarily sharing their political prejudices.

A deep awareness of the tragic aspects of the human situation marks Maistre's thought, and is deserving of respect. It will hardly do to banish Maistre because he points out that the plight of humanity is not a consoling one. In politics he was a conservative, yet not illiberal; he wished to see the monarch checked by tradition and by local institutions in a "pluralistic" society, as in the Old Regime. His recent editor, Jack Lively, has pointed out how close he was after all to Rousseau, whom he thought he hated. Like Bossuet, Maistre distinguished an "absolute" monarchy from an unlimited or despotic one. In a notable argument set forth in *Du Pape*, he argued that the papacy might mediate between the sovereignty of the state and the liberty of the individual. The argument impressed few, least of all the pope; but it indicates Maistre's desire to mitigate the authority of the state (which he felt necessary) in some way lest it become tyranny. He did not think democracy the answer, not at least for France (he conceded that England had it in her national character to live as a republic). It would only lead to a new Bonapartism. How accurate that prophecy was the events of 1848–1851 would reveal. Too much the polemicist, and marred by corroding hatreds, Maistre remains a major figure because of his flashes of rare insight.

A recent writer (Benjamin N. Nelson) has observed that "a society founded on sheer egoism . . . will undergo atomization, anomic loss of a sense of belonging." It then leads to totalitarianism by reaction, modern totalitarianism being an effort to substitute for "subtle and satisfying forms of organic solidarity" by "imposing the yoke of mechanism." In other words, a natural community being absent there is flight from the intolerable rootlessness and anonymity of modern urban life, towards some kind of statism. The case for the conservatives of nineteenth-century France must rest on some such point as this, and it would seem to be one of enduring pertinence.

British utilitarianism and Political Economy postulated the free, self-reliant individual, the "mainspring of social progress" because his energies were released by the knowledge that what he gained would be his own, capable of enriching himself, and thereby also enriching the nation, capable also of enlightening and educating himself. But an accompaniment of this far from unworthy idea was the loss of a social sense. The market was an impersonal force, though it regulated the relationships of society—impersonal and selfish. Society became only a collection of individuals, and thus something necessary to man was lost; for though he likes to assert his individuality he cannot do without membership in a community. The conservatives whatever their sins in other respects surely performed a valuable service to modern Europe in defending the community against atomization.

Moreover the conservatives typically disliked industrialism as well as mass democracy, and they had a deep sense of human dignity. Their values tended to be rooted in the stable society of the countryside where everybody knows everybody else and the impersonality of the city is abhorrent. In both England and France there were "Tory radicals" throughout the century who sided with the working class against the capitalists on matters of social reform. They produced a strong vein of social criticism. Coleridge, Carlyle, Disraeli, and perhaps Ruskin might be put into this category in England—a distinguished heritage of social thought, by no means reactionary, holding up the ideal of a society that was aristocratic, but not plutocratic, socially responsible rather than irresponsible, opposing the social neglect of laissez-faire with a paternalism of the upper class.

Saint-Simon, the socialist, acknowledged his debt to Bonald who taught him that society is "an organic machine whose every part contributes to the movement of the whole," it is not a mere collection of separate and unconnected individuals. The conservatives and the socialists had something in common, and that, an important idea: the social principle. But the conservatives saw society as the will of God, favored obedience to political authority, believed religion to be a necessity, abhorred revolution, and could scarcely accept either equality or democracy. Agreeing in the conviction that society must be ordered and organized, wherein they both differed from the nineteenth-century liberals, conservatives and socialists disagreed about the nature of that organization, and its source. For the socialists held to an Enlightenment faith that human reason might contrive an ideal organization and establish it all at once. Conservatives, with a wisdom they thought they had learned from the melancholy experiment of the Revolution, held this to be impossible, and disastrous. For no opinion lay closer to the heart of conservative doctrine than a mistrust of what Burke called "the fallible and feeble contrivances of our reason." It mistrusted political theories, and believed that we must fall back on existing rooted institutions, which represent a kind of collective wisdom of the ages and which have at least worked. The liberals and radicals believed man could do better; the conservatives feared he might well do worse. They would rely on the allegedly natural social order, which seemed to mean just the *status quo*. Their defect was that the age was seething with change, and there was no stable order of things.

Liberalism

Though conservatives tried to put down an anchor against the currents of change, no task was less promising in this first half of the nineteenth century. It was, as a recent historian has observed, the most revolutionary half-century in history up to that time. Everyone felt whirled away by the pace of change; "We have been living the life of 300 years in 30," Matthew Arnold's father, the famous schoolmaster, remarked. "Can we never drop anchor for a single day, On the ocean of the ages?" Lamartine poetically wondered. By and large, it was a hopeful half-century, with all its perplexities and turbulence, much more hopeful than the latter half. There is an exuberance about its writing that reflects this basic optimism; one sees it in the titanic creative energies of a Dickens or a Balzac, as well as in the explosion of hopeful solutions for all the problems of humanity. "The period was full of evil things, but it was full of hope," Chesterton wrote in his book about Charles Dickens. Its typical giants, like Victor Hugo, dreamed vast dreams of progress and threw themselves furiously into their tasks. So it was not, on the whole, a good time for conservatives, and after a few years of success attendant upon the fall of Napoleon they gave way to more hopeful people, who presided over an era culminating in the great liberal-democratic-socialist revolutions of 1848.

Liberalism was a term rather like Romanticism, broad and vague, and still is. By general agreement it was strongest in Great Britain, which had an ancestral sort of liberalism (though the word was not used in any systematic way until the 1830s) embracing civil liberty and parliamentary government. The English had not known absolute monarchy and had been living under the mildest of European governments since 1688. Fondly recalling such landmarks as the Magna Carta and the Bill of Rights, Englishmen considered themselves freer than any other people and typically looked with amused contempt on the political broils of the French and other continental lesser breeds. The storms of the French Revolution caused some curtailments of this liberty between 1795 and 1820, producing toward the latter date, at the time of "Peterloo" and the repressive Six Acts, what has been called the ugliest estrangement between English government and people since 1688. But this did not last, and under Whig auspices a series of parliamentary measures between 1825 and 1840 could be called "liberal" in that they extended the range of freedoms, both commercial (removal of tariffs, monopolies, restrictions on trade), personal (freedom of press, religion), and political (more representative elections to parliament, extension of the suffrage in 1832).

There were other aspects to this "liberalism," for example opposition to factory legislation and to trade unions, which may seem illiberal by modern standards but were in accordance with maximum freedom of individual entrepreneurs from government regulation. Free speech was restored: in 1819 the Habeas Corpus act had been suspended, journals and pamphlets taxed, publishers imprisoned for criticizing the king, but by 1832 these restrictions had been substantially removed. (On the Continent, Metternich more successfully repressed freedom of the press—a "modern scourge," the great conservative said, inconsistent with organized society—and seven German professors at Goettingen became martyrs to the censorship of ideas which was a part of the "Metternich system.") In 1828–29 the Catholic Emancipation Act and repeal of the Test Acts removed political disabilities from non-Anglican Christians, though the Established Church remained and Jews were not similarly relieved for thirty more years.

It cannot be said that the Whigs who supported these last actions were moved by flaming slogans about the rights of man; they were practical measures. The Reform Bill of 1832, bitterly opposed as it was, left four out of five Englishmen without the vote. At the same time, in the name of "liberal" principles the most "liberal" Englishmen supported the harsh Poor Law of 1834 and fought the Ten Hour bill. Even the most radical of them, like Francis Place, felt that granting any great amount of welfare relief to the laboring poor would "encourage idleness and extinguish enterprise." A courageous band of Englishmen fought to abolish slavery within the British Empire, but a considerable number of these were not "liberals" but Churchmen and Tories. All in all, early nineteenth century liberalism was a somewhat curious thing as we view it today, and it requires some explanation.

It was associated with two notable intellectual systems of the period: the utilitarians, and the Political Economists. Utilitarianism was the offspring of that strange genius, Jeremy Bentham. Bentham had been writing as early as the 1770s and was an old man in 1810 when his school began to become prominent; he belonged to the later Enlightenment and never departed from it in essential spirit. Decidedly no Romantic, Bentham was a thoroughgoing rationalist, a scoffer at religion, a man without poetic instincts and almost, it seems, without emotions. John Stuart Mill, son of Bentham's leading disciple, described in his famous autobiography the inhuman regimen under which he was raised, and which finally caused him to have something like a breakdown, his relief coming only when he found consolation in poetry and philosophy. After this dramatic and symbolic experience, Mill wrote a series of essays in which he presented Bentham and Coleridge as the two seminal influences of the century. The romantic conservative and the utilitarian liberal, rivals and opposites, sent forth two different strains of thought and feeling which even Mill's wise and catholic mind could not quite reconcile though he strove to do so.

The lineage of utilitarianism can be traced back to various earlier sources. Helvétius, the French *philosophe*, had announced as a momentous discovery the apparently trite idea that good government is that which secures the greatest happiness of the people. He also shared, if somewhat confusedly, the Physiocratic idea that about the best thing government could do to this end was to leave men alone—certainly, to leave trade alone. The recipe for maximum happiness was left somewhat vague in the pages of Helvétius's *Treatise on Man*. In Britain Francis Hutcheson had used the phrase "greatest happiness of the greatest numbers," and David Hume had arrived at a form of "utilitarianism" when in his criticism of the social contract he had concluded that it was a fiction that might be dispensed with: "It is therefore an opinion only that government is founded." That is to say, there is no sort of sanction for government, on rational analysis, except the usefulness of that government in the eyes of its citizens. (Hume could scarcely have supported Bentham's view that an objective, rational standard of utility is possible, however.) William Paley, in his influential textbook *Principles of Moral and Political Philosophy* (1785), accepts this and defines utility as the sum of happiness. A law is good or bad accordingly as it increases or lessens this total of well-being.

Based on Enlightenment hedonism, utilitarianism was severely rationalistic, sweeping aside claims of sentiment or habit in government (the charismatic, customary, and bureaucratic forms of authority, as we might say today, following Max Weber) and requiring laws and institutions to justify themselves on the practical grounds of welfare achieved. Utilitarians were the direct opposites, and of course the violent adversaries, of Burkean conservatives in wishing total and immediate reform on theoretical or *a priori* principles. Sweep away the whole of a decrepit, illogical system, they urged, and replace it with a bright new model built on scientific foundations. They proposed breathtaking changes: instead of two houses of parliament there should be just one, aristocracy along with monarchy should go, the common law should be replaced by a codified law; prisons should be reformed, schools should be reformed, everything should be reformed. Most radical of all was the suggestion of democratic, i.e. universal manhood suffrage, which the utilitarians reached in typical fashion by reasoning that each man is the best judge of his own interest and "each should count as one." In behalf of these proposals the followers of Bentham, including James Mill and many others, wrote pamphlets, edited magazines, tried to elect members of Parliament, and in general crusaded eagerly, inspired by their belief that they had at last found the exact science of government.

An interesting and powerful group, they reached their peak in the 1820s as an organized movement but radiated influences down through the whole century. If they were in many ways exceedingly "radical" (a name they proudly adopted), they were in other ways not so much so, according to some standards. They stoutly defended private property, basing their case on the self-interest of free individuals. There was always some tension between the reforming and the individualistic tenets of Utilitarianism. In the 1820s they worked closely with other "radicals," including workingclass groups, and helped push through the Reform Bill of 1832. After that they tended to lose their crusading zeal (perhaps the inevitable fate of a movement) and to become more conservative, or more pragmatic, working piecemeal for specific small changes and dropping their demands for total reconstruction of all society. They did not cease to do useful things; to take but one example, though an illustrious one, Edwin Chadwick undertook the sanitary reform of London in the 1840s as a utilitarian disciple. From the total reconstruction of society to sewage systems was a considerable decline though not necessarily a discreditable one. But later utilitarians tended even more strongly toward *laissez-faire* or the limited state, which respected individual property rights and did not regulate private business. In this respect they adopted the views of the Political Economists and parted company with socialists. The utilitarian position had always based itself squarely on the enlightened self-interest of individuals.

Bentham and his followers believed they had formulated an exact science of government. Hardheaded, they rejected the Natural Rights school, which was one form of liberalism reaching back to John Locke and the Whig revolution. Such alleged rights, apart from and above positive law, are either meaningless or false, they held. "Liberty" is not an absolute right, concrete liberties must be embodied in legislation to be meaningful and the nature of such legislation should be determined by exact investigation into real circumstances. Bentham shared with Burke this one trait, at least, that he wished to get rid of metaphysical rubbish in politics and law and bring everything back to the touchstone of measurable human happiness. He believed that he could measure human happiness. The sum of individual happiness is the social goal, at which legislation should aim. Bentham thought that he could perform the herculean task of providing an objective measuring-stick for happiness on which all might agree. He invented a "felicific calculus."

The Benthamite principle of social welfare as the sum total of units of individual happiness, a total which could in principle be measured rather exactly thus providing the basis for a science of welfare, lasted a long time; as late as 1920 A. C. Pigou, British economics professor, claimed to have solved the problem of finding this exact science (*The Economics of Welfare*). The effort to make an exact science of welfare economics must nevertheless be regarded as a failure and illusion. Bentham's notion of it certainly was inadequate and received many criticisms and subsequent restatements. But for all his extravagances Bentham had a genius for practical reform. From his tireless pen flowed a series of projects for the practical reform of everything: schools, prisons, courts, laws. Some of them were fanciful, some ingenious. By sheer energy and perseverance, Bentham and his followers (James Mill being the first and chief) forced upon the public constant consideration of the questions, "What good is it? Can it be improved?"

Utilitarianism spread beyond its native shores to exert an influence in other countries, as far afield as Russia, Spain, and Latin America. It offered a simple and rational rule for reform and had the merit of avoiding nebulous sloganizing as well as revolutionary radicalism; it was hardheaded and practical. But its individualistic foundations rendered it less acceptable in France. There the key social theorists of this period, whether conservatives like Maistre, socialists like Saint-Simon, or bourgeois thinkers like August Comte, stressed the social principle and were more statist.

It was this school of utility that Carlyle attacked as piggish and which sent the amiable Coleridge into a rage. Bentham and James Mill cared nothing for the arts, dismissing poetry as nonsense in the best or worst tradition of the Enlightenment; they cared nothing for "society," seeing in it nothing more than a group of individuals. Selfishness and hedonism seemed enshrined in their utterly unheroic ethics. The romantic-conservative, Coleridge-Carlyle temperament could not understand them. Nor, indeed, were they anywhere popular at first; they were radicals, as Lord Brougham remarked in 1827, "in their religion intolerable atheists, in their politics bloody-minded republicans. . . ." Bentham's immense body of writing (of which the best known was *Principles of Morals and Legislation*, 1789) is marked by few if any graces of style. It is rather more prolix and formless than the works of his forerunners in the English tradition, Hobbes and Locke; but it does swarm with ideas for practical reform. Bentham's creed of self-interest has doubtless gone out of style in the twentieth century, but it appealed mightily to the nineteenth-century bourgeoisie and was conceivably a suitable polity for that day—witness the enormous growth of wealth in Great Britain. His method of attacking social reform piecemeal, assailing it with factual research and avoiding large nebulous slogans, continued on in the Fabian Socialists later, the goal being rather different but the method similar. It seemed to suit the English genius—individualistic, empirical, mistrustful of general ideas and metaphysics. And it can be interpreted as a creed for the English bourgeoisie in particular.

Political Economy

Closely related to and allied with Utilitarians in the camp of British liberalism were the Political Economists. In the early nineteenth century the brilliant beginnings in economic thought made by the French Physiocrats and Adam Smith reached maturity in the writings of such men as Thomas Malthus, David Ricardo, J. B. Say, and Nassau Senior. Say along with Sismondi kept up the French contribution, but in the main the British took over this subject. Perhaps this was because its determined individualism suited the British temperament, tradition, and experience. It is significant that Sismondi defected to socialism, while in Germany there were "romantic" economists such as List and Mueller who rejected the individualistic premises of the British "classical" economists. In Britain, too, the great Scottish writer Thomas Carlyle joined Coleridge and other poets and moralists, dismissed as mere amateurs and sentimentalists by the economists,[3] in deploring the "dismal science." But it flourished and developed influence uniquely in the British Isles. The prestige of the Political Economists reached a high point with the publication in 1817 of Ricardo's *Principles of Political Economy* followed by Say's *Treatise* in 1821. Popularizations such as those of Mrs. Marcet (1816) and Harriet Martineau's stories in the later 1820s carried the message from on high to the common man in somewhat simplified and adulterated form. It was the message of the hour, almost bedside reading for modish literates; it became "high fashion with the blue ladies to talk political economy." This ascendancy continued, on the whole, the assumption being that an exact science had been perfected. In 1856 a distinguished member of Parliament remarked that "Political Economy is not exactly the law of the land but it is the ground of that law." Leaders of government sought the advice of the economists and parliamentary committees turned to them for guidance.

What was the message? The Economists were in fact not a completely homogeneous group by any means. They had their heated de-

---

[3]John Stuart Mill in his discriminating and appreciative essay on Coleridge said that "in political economy he writes like an arrant driveler, and it would have been well for his reputation had he never meddled with the subject." In turn Coleridge regarded Political Economy as "solemn humbug."

bates. It is possible to identify a left wing and a right wing, led respectively by James Mill and J. R. McCulloch. Malthus and Ricardo engaged in a memorable debate about effective demand, to which John Maynard Keynes returned a century later in search of new truth and found Malthus righter than Ricardo though for a century it had been thought otherwise. As for the greatest of them, David Ricardo, it is hard to know where to put him. Though often associated with the most brutally pessimistic of those who spoke of an "iron law" keeping wages down to the sustenance level ("the natural price of labour is that price which is necessary to enable the labourers, one with another, to subsist and perpetuate their race, without either increase or diminution"), he led to a kind of socialism, and was best known for denouncing the landlord as virtually the enemy of society, thus precipitating class war in England. Ricardo evidently believed much less than Adam Smith that there is a natural order of harmony in economic affairs. He saw the landlord and the factory owner as natural foes. Rents raise the price of food, which raises wages, which causes profits in manufacturing to fall. And it was difficult to avoid the conclusion, on Ricardo's premises, that the wage worker is at war with the employer, since the latter must force his wages down in order to keep his profits up. The long struggle in British politics over repeal of the Corn Laws, or protective tariffs on grain, during which liberal manufacturers like John Bright attacked Tory landlords as parasites, sprang in good part from Ricardo's theory about rents; while Owenite socialists took their inspiration from his Labour Theory of Value and Karl Marx built a system on it.

Yet of course the main message, especially in the popularized version of Political Economy, was that of individualism and laissez-faire. Smith and the Physiocrats had claimed that in accordance with a law of nature the "invisible hand" causes individual and social objectives to coincide, the rule of laissez-faire generally sufficing, via competition and the profit incentive, to secure the most efficient production and distribution of wealth. "The whole art of government," Smith had thought, "lies in the liberty of men and things." His successors may have moralized less, but they continued to assume that the free competitive system is the best and that state intervention seldom serves a useful purpose. It now became a mark of ignorance not to recognize as much; Ricardo was more cocksure and dogmatic on this than Smith. "Mercantilism" was well on its way to becoming a synonym for the dark ages of economic thought. Merchants and statesmen began to accept free trade, which had by about 1820 (witness Baring's petition from the London merchants to Parliament in that year) become business orthodoxy. Say's law of the market posited automatic adjustment between production and consumption. The wage fund theory indicated the futility of any "artificial" attempts, such as by trade unions. to alter the sum available for wages. In one of Miss Martineau's little tales, a strike takes place, and some wage increases are granted as a result, but the owner then informs the men that he will have to fire some of them. If some workers get more than their share, others will get less.

In another of her stories, it is explained how public expenditure on the poor raises tax rates, which discourages capital and thus intensifies the problem of unemployment. And the Reverend Thomas Malthus had by this time profoundly affected many with his famed tract on population, revealing that population always tends to increase up to the limit of sustenance, thus ensuring perpetual poverty unless something really heroic is done to break the gloomy cycle. The "hard line" Poor Law of 1834, based on an attempt to deter rather than relieve poverty, by making welfare relief both hard to get and unpleasant, was actually far from a new medicine. In the eighteenth century Bernard Mandeville, Daniel Defoe, Arthur Young, and a host of others took it for granted that "the poor have nothing to stir them to labour but their wants, which it is wisdom to relieve but folly to cure," that in brief the poor must be kept poor or they will not work, and charity only encourages idleness. "It cannot fail to happen," Turgot had written before Adam Smith, "that the wages of the workman are limited to what is necessary to procure him his subsistence." But the prestigious teachings of Political Economy were thought to have lent credence to this venerable belief.

James Mill observed that capital tends to increase less rapidly than population, nor can the growth of capital be forced; it must make its own pace. The classical economists would certainly have listened with bewilderment or perhaps amusement to the recent debate about just how you go about "creating economic growth" by the activities of various governmental agencies. Their world was strictly bounded by the limitations of nature, they saw the laws of diminishing returns and increasing population as probable barriers to any great improvement in the overall lot of the human race. They permitted themselves only an occasional hint of a brighter future.

Yet they became the respected arbiters of policy. This was a triumph not only for their obvious intelligence but also for the readiness of the middle classes to receive the message of hard work and austerity. Classical Political Economy appealed to the Puritan spirit of the industrious small manufacturers and businessmen who were climbing from poverty to riches in the favorable economic climate of England during and soon after the Napoleonic War. The slogan of the industrial middle class was self-help. The creed which Carlyle thought a monstrous, inhuman "gospel of mammon" seemed to them the law of life and of progress. As Great Britain assumed the leadership in industrialization, it was the presence and the power of this class, more perhaps than any other single factor, that was responsible for her success. They had energy, and the system of laissez-faire capitalism provided them with incentive.

The British economists were both much admired and cordially disliked, and excited a vigorous countermovement. Socialism took its point of departure from the economic inequalitarianism as well as the economic individualism or selfishness of their teachings. Bentham, who had supported political and legal equality, accepted economic inequality. There must be, he wrote, equality in the sense that each man is entitled to the just fruits of his own labor. But since men have unequal talents and energies this will mean unequal rewards. Compelling people to share the fruits of their labors with others, the only practical way of securing economic equality, not only violates justice but will prove disastrous. Coleridge reached exactly the same conclusion—a rare example of agreement between the two leaders of rival schools. It is difficult to overstate the importance for the nineteenth century of this apparent truth that you must choose between civil and economic equality, you cannot have both; as students of ethics would put it, the problem of personal versus distributive justice.

The great utilitarian admitted that on other grounds equal distribution of wealth was desirable as contributing to the greatest happiness of the greatest number. (The principle of diminishing utility, he pointed out, means that the addition of a unit of wealth to one who already has a good deal of it brings less pleasure than it does to one with less of it.) Thus was posed the dilemma: in the name of social justice and economic efficiency one sanctioned inequality and hence unhappiness.

Into the making of British middle-class liberalism, expressed in the famed "Manchester School" headed by John Bright and Richard Cobden, went some other ingredients than the intellectual doctrines of Utility and Political Economy. Bright was a Quaker; Manchester was a provincial center. The rising capitalists of the Industrial Revolution were heavily nonconformist in religion, outside the old aristocratic establishment; they were new men. As dissenters they had had to fight discrimination; Bright said he had to be a liberal because of the persecutions his people had endured. Scripture played as much part in the Manchester creed as Political Economy. The Bright-Cobden school went into their great crusade against the Corn Laws, symbol of a hated landlord aristocracy, with Bible phrases on their lips and the spirit of a moral crusade in their hearts. Tennyson ridiculed Bright as "This broad-brimmed hawker of holy things," a selfish moneybags hypocritically pretending to be religious. But the close student of Bright knows there was more to it than that. Self-interest was there, Political Economy contributed its share, but so did a kind of Puritan conscience, which was something

more than a mask for self-interest though it is easy to see why its enemies made this charge. A part of the Liberal creed was that passionate
hatred of militarism and war which led Bright to stand out courageously
against the Crimean War. If his Quaker faith dictated pacifism, so did
the tenets of economic liberalism: free trade would do away with war,
which was an avocation of the idle aristocracy; nonintervention should
be the rule for nations as for individuals. Thus did religion, economics,
and interest blend together to make up the faith of liberal England.

Thus, clearly, there were several strains in early modern liberalism,
not always in exact agreement with each other; yet they all tended to
agree broadly on a negative conception of the state, on something approaching laissez-faire as an ideal. The Natural Rights school of Locke
stressed resistance to arbitrary and tyrannical government while enshrining private property as one of the basic, inalienable rights of man.
The utilitarians built their system on the rational self-interest of free
individuals. The Political Economists never forgot their Adam Smith
origins, holding to a conception of the automatic economic order which
goes of itself if kept free of bungling statist tinkerers. To this must be
added the religious nonconformists whose whole history disposed them
to be suspicious of establishments and rules imposed by the state.

Of course, the achievements of the French Revolution in general,
meaning the liquidation of the old class society (which came more slowly
in England but did come), left a kind of automatic liberalism in effect.
The Old Regime having been destroyed, men became equal. Equal under
the law, that is; of equal rights, opportunities, status. That such an
equality might mean, practically, a larger amount of real, economic
equality did not occur to men until they saw what happened. Socialism,
Harold Laski has written, was based on "the realization that the liberal
ideal secured to the middle class its full share of privilege, while it left
the proletariat in its chains." With allowance for rhetorical embellish-
ment, the statement comes close to expressing the essence of the matter.
Liberty—the liberty of everyone to prosper or fail in accordance with
his energies, abilities, and luck, the law maintaining a scrupulous im-
partiality and the state refusing in any way to intervene to protect the
weaker or less fortunate—meant inequality, and even injustice. It meant
that those who succeeded had both the protection of the law and the
accolades of society, while those who failed, for whatever reason, might
expect to hear only that most ancient of cries, *vae victis*.

Socialism

At about the same time as conservatism and liberalism, socialism
entered vigorously upon the scene. In 1822 Charles Fourier, son of a

Besançon merchant, published his *Traité de l'association*, a work not exactly greeted with wild acclaim when it appeared, one among multitudes of strange schemes for the total reconstruction of society, but destined in time to a greater fame than any of these. Between 1814 and 1822 the eccentric Count Saint-Simon, who modestly called himself a combination of Bacon, Newton, and Locke, sent forth a spate of books on the basis of which his claim to be the first important socialist has usually been approved. Meanwhile in Britain, Robert Owen, the Scottish factory owner, was popularizing by example his plan for a more social organization of industry; thousands came to New Lanark to inspect it. Sismondi had broken with the laissez-faire economists, repelled by their selfish atomism and apparently callous disregard of human beings. The word *socialism* does not seem to have come into use until the 1830s, but the idea itself was forming, clearly, in the 1820s. "Associationalism" was a term then in use.

Naturally, it had earlier roots. Leaving aside the strong tradition of communalism in both Platonism, the Church, and medieval feudalism, and that of Christian millenarianism present from medieval times, we can find strands of socialism in the Enlightenment, along with the stronger element of laissez-faire individualism. By no means consistently a socialist (indeed, he sometimes called private property "sacred"), Rousseau in one memorable passage, which shocked Voltaire, regretted the origins of private property in an initial act of usurpation. Someone said, "This is mine!" and got away with it, ending the idyll of primitive communism and ushering in greed, civilization, and all their accompaniments. From Rousseau's concept of the General Will—the will of society as a whole, something more than the sum of individual wills—many of his disciples derived a strong statism. Rousseau's *Social Contract* taught that all rights are derived from society, without which they could not exist; the state therefore is justified in regulating property; there is no absolute right of property; if property exists it is at the sufferance of society. Rousseau believed that private property should be permitted to exist but should be approximately equal and represent only what one earned with one's labor. Moreover he considered the pursuit of wealth an evil, a source of modern society's ills. Though to describe Rousseau as a socialist would be to commit an anachronism, some of his attitudes fed into the nineteenth-century stream of this school. His influence did not encourage the kind of socialism that stressed greater productivity and wealth, for he thought the good life was one of Spartan simplicity.

Morelly, called "the only consistent communist among the eighteenth-century thinkers," combined Rousseau's General Will with his attack on private property to arrive at a crude socialist theory. Equally crude, yet fervently sincere, was the thought of those who backed

"Gracchus" Babeuf in his rather pathetic Conspiracy of the Equals in the latter days of the French Revolution (1795). Robespierre, that "child of the ideas of Rousseau," had been willing to use the power of the state ruthlessly in accordance with the General Will concept, but had basically been a Jacobin democrat who did not wish to abolish private property. Babeuf, however, advocated a "distributive socialism," a common pool of property, to which everyone brings what he earns and which is then carved up equally. "Nature has given to every man an equal right to the enjoyment of all goods." The same nature that provided the basis for bourgeois property rights might be turned in another direction. A passion for equality and a belief that private property creates inequality moved these simple, poor people.

Like romanticism, socialism is a large word covering a multitude of rather different things. There have been various sorts of socialism, though one may link them all by certain common denominators. The first half of the century brought forth a profusion of schemes and plans, some of them seemingly weird and most impractical, yet supplying the basic ideas for all subsequent socialist thought. The eagerness with which men produced and imbibed socialist ideas in this period relates to the general feeling that some new plan of social reorganization was desperately needed; to a discontent with the liberalism of legal equality *cum* free competition; and to the continuing ferment of ideas stemming from the Enlightenment, romanticism, the French Revolution.

The pioneer socialists were a colorful and interesting lot. Robert Owen, though born a poor boy (one of 13 children, he went to work at the age of nine), rose to become a wealthy and successful factory owner in a rags-to-riches story. A man of boundless energy, he went into business for himself at the age of 18 in Manchester, getting in on the burgeoning cotton textile industry, and later bought the mills at New Lanark in Scotland destined to become internationally celebrated. But he also found time to read and was clearly influenced by the "philosophic" ideas of Rousseau, Godwin, and other Enlightenment thinkers. At New Lanark he set to work reforming the ignorant, degraded mill hands (largely children) who worked long hours in unsanitary and dismal surroundings. He reduced working hours, improved housing, established schools, banned alcohol, set up communal stores where goods were sold at fair prices, organized pension and sick funds—and found that it paid, for the workers worked better. He was the benevolent dictator of a model community to which visitors began to come from all over the world. Owen's fame as an enlightened employer was such that when he visited the United States in 1825 he was invited to address a special joint session of Congress. He was at this time a respectable example of philanthropy and "benevolence," widely approved qualities, but he soon lost his respectability as he embarked on a variety of schemes for the total reformation of society. He attempted to found a highly unorthodox Rational Religion, a kind of secular social morality which may be compared with Saint-Simon's New Christianity (see below). But most of Owen's enormous energy went towards attempts to duplicate the New Lanark idea of planting other model socialist communities, sinking the whole of his substantial fortune into such schemes. Though the community at New Harmony, Indiana (which Owen bought from the Rappites[4]) is the best known, there were numerous others of varying sizes in the United States and the British Isles. They invariably failed, but attracted thousands of eager experimenters, enchanted by the thought of helping to found what Owen called a New Moral World, to be marked by the spirit of community rather than selfishness.

The Owenite communities, like the later Fourierist ones, seemed, alas, to prove the validity of the liberal-utilitarian claim that men are moved only by their self-interest. The Owenites adopted a simple form of Ricardian socialism in which they attempted to devise a medium of exchange based on labor power, to escape capitalistic exploitation of the worker. This proved unworkable. Owenite communities tried to abolish the family, seen as a bastion of private property and egoism, in favor of some form of communal living arrangements—a feature which, along with the religious unorthodoxy, shocked and alienated the neighboring populace. The communities were ill-managed, since Owen could not be everywhere and few of his disciples possessed his organizing genius. They attracted a gorgeous miscellany of unscreened free spirits, cranks, idealists, misfits, and parasites. Often in America the abler members caught the spirit of frontier individualism and went off to become proprietors for themselves. An endless number of such reasons might be given for the almost invariable collapse of these enterprises. Owen was not discouraged; he later, in the 1830s, threw himself into the Grand National Trade Union cause, which also collapsed after a spectacular beginning. Owen never tried to found a political party, regarding himself as missionary and educator. In its day the Owenite movement made a tremendous stir. "In the peak years 1839–1841," writes J. F. C. Harrison, author of the best recent book on Owenism, "two and a half-million tracts were distributed; 1450 lectures delivered in a year, Sunday lectures attended by up to 50,000 weekly." More than 100 Owenite journals existed at various times. In the 1820s, when evangelical religion

---

[4]The early historian of socialism, J. H. Noyes, called the Shakers and Rappites "the real pioneers of modern socialism." These were religious communitarian sects, the former being an offshoot of Quakerism, while Father Rapp stemmed from the German Pietistic tradition (cf. the earlier Moravians and Mennonites). Essentially this was just a version of Christian monasticism.

was popular, Owenism took on the qualities of a sectarian religion; later, there were Owenite Halls of Science.

After all this stir, the Owenite movement died away upon the death of its remarkable founder in 1857, leaving little behind except a memory. (The cooperative movement, largely fathered by the Owenites, is an exception.) The same was true of other British socialist tentatives of this period, associated with the so-called Chartist movement among the working classes. They seemed to lack adequate intellectual foundations. Was it the incurable individualism of the English that caused the failure of socialism there?

The French Socialists

France gave birth to more doctrines of *mouvement social* than any other country. Sismondi, in 1819, attacked laissez-faire economics, urging that the state intervene to regulate the use of property for the well-being of the community. Political Economy based itself on an assumption of human selfishness and took human nature as it is. Adam Smith had posited the "economic man," seeking his own advantage, and made this self-seeking individual the key to his system; so did Ricardo, perhaps even more. That every man wishes to obtain additional wealth, as efficiently as possible, Senior made his starting point. It should be noted that the supremacy of individual desires was a keystone of the whole structure of liberal economics. Suppose the state directs men to produce something they are not producing. The view of the classical economists was that this must mean a diversion from what is desired to what is not; and this was a sufficient refutation in their eyes. Some romantic economists protested that the nation might wish to elevate itself by choosing a standard of production other than just what people want; it might wish, for example, to create more musical instruments and fewer evening dresses for wealthy women. This cannot be refuted by the classical economists, except that they would simply dismiss it as "uneconomic," that is, going beyond their system. They would add that a directed economy must burden itself with an expensive bureaucratic system whereas the undirected one is largely self-running. But in large measure they identified efficiency with meeting the desires of individuals.

It was this individualist and egoist principle that critics of liberal economics, including Sismondi and, in Germany, Fichte, resented and assailed. Their moving impulse was an ethical desire to create something nobler than a selfish scramble, a "mere congeries of possessors and pursuers," as Lord Keynes once called it; or, again, a rational impulse to *plan* rather than leave matters to a chaos of contending individual wills.

The difficulty was that this drove you to highly authoritarian structures in which an intellectual elite planned for and governed the entire community.

Whereas it was the poor man's simple passion for equalizing himself with the rich that inspired Babeuf, an intellectual passion to impose order, to *plan* the whole economy, was especially marked in the case of socialists such as Sismondi and, especially, the extremely important Frenchman Saint-Simon.[5] Saint-Simon did not suggest equality, but rather a hierarchy. He looked upon society as one great workshop whose efficient organization was the main task of modern times. Science could surely answer this need, Saint-Simon thought, and he proposed an elite of social engineers planning and running society on scientific principles. He rejected democracy; the crowd cannot govern. He added, later, the need for a new public religion, a "new (rationalized) Christianity," also presided over by a priestly elite. One can see why this eccentric nobleman has appealed to the present Communists of the Soviet Union, who grant him a place with Marx and Lenin among the makers of modern communism. On the other hand, Saint-Simon did not suggest class war or the dominance of the "proletariat." The new elite should seemingly be drawn from the industrialists and engineers. "Technocracy," a later scheme which enjoyed a brief vogue in the 1920s and 1930s, expressed more nearly what was in Saint-Simon's mind than Marxism. Perhaps, indeed, this is the way the world is going, whether in the West or in the Communist world today.

Rather like Jeremy Bentham in England, Saint-Simon was an eccentric who succeeded in planting an idea that percolated down through the nineteenth century in his native France. The Emperor Louis Napoleon (1851–1870) was one of his influential disciples, even writing a book on *The Extinction of Poverty*. Certain aspects of his thought were carried on by August Comte (see below, pages 296–302). Saint-Simonianism was not necessarily "radical," as noted; its "captains of industry" might be industrialists, and Saint-Simon was quite willing to accept even the Bourbon monarchy if this regime would back his plan. Like the Physiocrats of the preceding century, Saint-Simon preferred enlightened despotism to democracy. He announced a new epoch marked by industrialism and the power of scientific and technological knowledge, and he

[5]Claude Henri de Rouvroy, Comte de Saint-Simon (1760–1825) was a French aristocrat who traced his ancestry back to Charlemagne. He fought in the American Revolution, was wounded at Yorktown. During the French Revolution he made a fortune in financial speculations, narrowly escaped the guillotine, and then like Owen poured all his fortune into his schemes for a new moral and social world, dying in dire poverty. Between 1802 and 1825 he exuded a stream of writings and journals and left behind a cult.

called for a new aristocracy, to replace the defunct orders of church and nobility. He stressed increased productivity, to satisfy material wants, agreeing with Bentham that the social goal is "happiness," which he defined largely as the satisfaction of physical wants. All this could be as attractive to a businessman as to a proletarian, perhaps, though the element of state compulsion might repel him. As a matter of fact, Saint-Simon inspired most notably a number of public-spirited administrators who wanted to impose a rational plan on the disorderly economy of laissez-faire. (One of the leading Disciples, Pierre Enfantin, later was prominently associated with the building of the Suez Canal; a passion for huge enterprises of this sort marked the Saint-Simonians.) The French down to the present have shown less enthusiasm for the free, unregulated economy and society than have the English. It is possible to see at work here the urge toward order and lucidity of the French mind, always influenced by classicism and rationalism. It might be added in regard to Saint-Simon that he was not a nationalist, but advocated and predicted a European society and economy.

Saint-Simon and Thomas Carlyle who owed much to him, reiterated their message that Europe had entered the industrial age, the "mechanical age," a new epoch calling for wholly new methods of government and thought; they called attention to the fact that the "social question" (Carlyle) was the burning issue of modern times and would not be solved by laissez-faire negativism. They did not have any exact blueprint for this new order but were sure that the "captains of industry" would have to assert leadership rather than content themselves with profits; they were sure that society needed a plan ("That Chaos should sit empire in it, that is the Worst," Carlyle exclaimed.) These ideas, vigorously expressed, exerted an incalculable influence in Europe. It is impossible to imagine Marx and the other later socialists without this background. Saint-Simon, who lived in direst poverty and was laughed at as a crank, takes on great stature as one of the seminal minds of modern times, as we view the nineteenth century in perspective. Perhaps modern society has turned out to look more like his vision than any one else's, including Bentham or Marx.

Charles Fourier, a sweet and saintly sort of person, thought in terms of social harmony, cooperation, "association." He may be regarded as the prototype of that variety of socialist to whom these things are values in themselves. In him it is easy, though, to detect the continued influence of the eighteenth century. Like the Physiocrats, he presumes a preordained harmony and a perfect plan for society; only, unlike them, he does not believe in the separateness of the individual atoms but thinks they must be placed in association according to an exact formula. Everybody has his precise niche in Fourier's carefully constructed plans. Science, speaking through Fourier, has determined the organization of the community down to the last detail. The ideal community must contain between sixteen hundred and eighteen hundred people, with a certain proportion of each occupation and age group and psychological types; they are to be housed in certain types of buildings; they rise at specified hours, etc. There are communal dininghalls; no one is to be left—or let —alone. It is rather monastic (Fourier was a religious man) and rather depressing. It had the attraction of being a precise plan, where others had been vague. It suggested the perhaps enduringly important idea of a balanced society. And Fourier promised the elimination of all vice, crime, unhappiness. The state will become unnecessary. Fourier declared that his scheme was completely voluntary. He hoped by setting up model communities to demonstrate by example the superiority of his cooperative system to the competitive anarchy of the economists, against whom he launched violent diatribes. He wished to make labor enjoyable instead of unpleasant. Many experimental communities did indeed come into being inspired by the pages of the *Treatise on Association*; most of them were not very successful, as we might guess. There were some rather unusual features of the Fourierist community, such as polygamy.

We can smile at Fourier, but we may be surprised at the number of people who took him seriously enough to try out his scheme. Harriet Martineau, the liberal Englishwoman who may be supposed to have had no special love for socialists (Coleridge regarded her as an incorrigible social atomist), wrote that the principle of cooperation "will now never rest till it has been made a matter of experiment." It was. Numbers of the sturdy individualists of New England founded Brook Farm on Fourierist lines, with predictable results. The fad for socialist communities, to which Robert Owen and his son had contributed, took on fresh life under Fourier's influence. Though it was (and still is) common to laugh at Fourier's dreams, this retired merchant who fed his cats and waited each day for the millionaire who would finance his schemes to save the world was an interesting and important figure. In his theories of the "passional attractions" have been seen anticipations of Freud. More than Owen or Saint-Simon, Fourier was a keen psychologist who tried to base his social system on an examination of human nature. He did not, like the Owenites, wish to abolish private property, because he thought it too deep a human instinct to eradicate. The trick is to harness this force and make it serve the public interest. The proper collaboration of interests, as well as passions, leads to a happy community. (On the other hand Fourier, a bachelor, went even farther than Owen in desiring to dissolve the family; instant divorce by agreement would be the rule.) A gentle and nonrevolutionary socialism, hating strife, seeking concord, bucolic and joyful, Fourier's utopia was perhaps not a thing of this world. Yet it was the most appealing of all visions of men living together in happy communion, and in certain ways it was the most shrewdly realistic.

Etienne Cabet, author of the utopian romance *Voyage to Icaria* in 1839, was a slightly later specimen of French socialism. He was a "communist" in the sense of vesting total ownership and absolute power in the community—a veritable police state, suppressing all freedom of thought, in the name of an ideal society where economic efficiency was joined to perfect social harmony. The "Icarians" joined the Owenites and the Fourierists in establishing social communities in the New World (Illinois, Iowa, Texas), one of which survived until 1898 though in general the utopian ideal was not realized in practice.

Thus there were various kinds of socialism. Agreeing in their desire for some sort of social control over private property and individual rights, the socialists differed in the degree of control they would exercise, in its manner, and in its institutionalization. In the thought of Saint-Simon, Fourier, and Cabet, socialism is sometimes vague and often foolish; but it was an exciting beginning.

Modern socialism and communism have lain so heavily under the influence of Karl Marx that his predecessors in this field sometimes are forgotten. A recent and quite good book on Marxism does not even mention Saint-Simon, Fourier, and their numerous offshoots; it says that Marx is the "heir of Jan Hus, Thomas Moore (*sic*), Thomas Paine, and Jean-Jacques Rousseau." Doubtless he was, but in a much more meaningful sense he was the heir of the numerous socialists who had filled the press of Europe with their schemes and debates all through the years when Marx and Engels were growing up. Marx had more theoretical and philosophical talent than most of them; he syncretized a great many of their systems, marrying revolutionary Babeuvist communism to Saint-Simonian and Owenite conceptions in a Hegelian ceremony. But he really created few if any of the various ideas he strung together so ingeniously. To a large extent this creativity belonged to the half-mad Saint-Simon and the eccentric Fourier, along with their whole generation of (mostly French) messiahs of "social science."

More of them appeared than there is space for: the names of Jones and Harney in Great Britain, of Rodbertus and Weitling in Germany (before Marx), and of the numerous disciples and offspring of Saint-Simon and Fourier in France are among them. (Victor Considerant carried on Fourier's work. A remarkable group of Saint-Simonian "Apostles" formed a community in Paris where they attempted to live the famous formula of "to each according to his need, from each according to his ability" before dispersing to carry the message into the world.) Here was a veritable chaos of socialistic ideas. Socialism before Marx reminds one of Protestantism before Calvin—in danger of perishing from its very profusion and popularity, in need of discipline and unity to save it. A rigorous logician of iron will would come in both cases to impose that discipline, at the cost of variety. Karl Marx would have recourse to the resources of German philosophy in this task, so that it is logical at this point to turn to the thought of the last and perhaps greatest of the German classical philosophers, flourishing during these years.

Hegel

French political and social thought, British economic theory, and German philosophy, these were the three outstanding areas of new ideas in the period 1815–1830, it was frequently said. In 1831 died G. W. F. Hegel, Kant's successor as the leading German philosopher and much more a system-builder than the essentially critical Kant. Hegelianism so far triumphed in academic circles that by the end of the century even in Great Britain and the United States (where there was a certain resistance to this kind of thought), the leading philosophers were largely of this school, while in very unacademic circles it had also spread widely, especially through the theories of Karl Marx and other socialists who owed much to Hegel.

Hegel's was a vast, labyrinthine and, according to some, impenetrable system which despite its difficulties exercised this enormous influence. It may be well first to ask what message, stripped of all the technicalities, ordinary cultivated men got from Hegel. One of them, the Russian socialist Belinsky, who wrote that when he read Hegel he was overcome with emotion and the world took on a new meaning, got the message from Hegel's famous formula "What is real is reasonable and what is reasonable real." This meant that all of history is the unfolding of reality itself, the idea or mind of the universe; what happens in history is in effect the writing of a book of which God is the author. For those who believed Hegel, history and human affairs no longer were chaotic, jumbled, or meaningless; every great event had its place in an unfolding plot which when the book was finished would be seen to have no loose ends, nothing put in without purpose. As Belinsky wrote, "For me there was no longer anything arbitrary or accidental in the course of history."

Undoubtedly Hegel's approach to human history *was* a revelation. He did not invent it; to go no farther back, an interest in history as rational process was taken up by Herder, pupil of Kant, who wrote an essay on the "Idea for a Universal History from the Cosmopolitan Point of View" in 1784, on which Kant commented, following which Fichte,

Schelling, and others made it a leading topic in German philosophical circles. The famous formula of thesis-antithesis-synthesis, the dialectic of history, which Marx took from Hegel, was evidently first suggested by Fichte, not Hegel. (Nor did Hegel consider it the only kind of process.) The original impulse to the new historicism probably came from Vico, writing in the earlier eighteenth century (*The New Science*, 1725, 1744); but we have already noted how little that Neapolitan philosopher was in step with his times. Voltaire was much more typical of the Enlightenment in seeing the past as without any continuity or regular path of development; a record largely of "crimes, follies, and misfortunes" illuminated by occasional and rather inexplicable epochs of reason; most of it without any interest to the philosophical mind. (What point in studying the superstitious Middle Ages or the ghastly wars of religion?) Yet at the end of the eighteenth century one of the great paths of discovery for the European mind was that of continuous secular progress, and others besides Hegel saw it. Saint-Simon incorporated into his socialism, before Hegel and Marx, the notion that history has a will of its own: "The supreme law of progress of the human spirit carries along and dominates everything; men are but its instruments. . . ." He was at pains to correct those eighteenth-century philosophers who saw only darkness in the Medieval period; not only had it played its necessary part in its own day, but from its womb came the next age: "If historians had analyzed and examined the Middle Ages more deeply . . . they would have recorded the gradual preparation of all the great events which developed later and would not have presented the explosions of the 16th and following centuries as sudden and unforeseen." From Rousseau had come what F. C. Lea has called "the romantic myth": progression from alienation to reunion, through civilization to a higher perfection at the end of historic time, when a perfect art, fully realized personality, and an ideal society would exist. Such popular elements of historicism lay about in every direction when Hegel applied his philosophical skills to the task of shaping from them a huge intellectual synthesis.

German philosophy had been searching for the underlying ideal unity of things. Hegel would show that this was a process working itself out in history. Behind the apparently fortuitous jumble of events, the philosopher-historian can discern a great process at work, which is nothing else than thought, the Idea, working itself out in reality. History is a logical, rational process.

We have begun with the historicism[6] of Hegel, which undoubtedly

---

[6]*Historicism:* defined here as the idea of history as a process above and beyond individual human actions; a will or destiny embodied in history which imposes itself on individuals.

(Belinsky was right) constituted his greatest attraction. It was an exciting idea; we may ask what its implications were. For one thing, it stimulated great interest in history. Later historians, more positivistic by temperament and disillusioned with Hegel's overly rational history, have disparaged him, but all historians probably owe their basic professional debt to Hegel. (The conservative political theorists, too, encouraged the study of history.) It was in Germany that the great historical profession of the nineteenth century began, with such contemporaries of Hegel as Leopold von Ranke and B. G. Niebuhr developing the "scientific" historical method (use of archival source materials, careful criticism of the documents). We cannot seriously become interested in history so long as it has only an antiquarian or story-telling value, however amusing it may be; to be elevated to the dignity of a leading professional study history must be thought of as revealing significant truths about man and the universe. Bonald and Maistre saw in it the training school of politics; Hegel saw much more: nothing less than God's Will immanent in the world, the unrolling of a great purpose.

Hegel should be defended against certain criticisms of his history that are frequently encountered. He did not say that all events are logical, or that the pattern of history can be determined without reference to the events. The actions of history are the outward expression of thoughts, and these thoughts form a logical, necessary chain of reasoning. We should study the actions, the empirical events, but we should not stop there; we should "think them through" to discover their inner logic. This still seems sound enough method, whatever mistakes Hegel made in his actual historical reconstructions. The mind of the historian, it is clear, must supply *some* sort of structure for the facts, which by themselves are without meaning. Hegel of course felt that there was a single objective pattern into which all would fit, a faith few historians find relevant to their tasks today.

The three main phases of history, according to Hegel, have been the Asiatic, characterized by absolute monarchy, followed by the classical Graeco-Roman, marked by individual freedom, and finally by the Germanic-European which fused the two earlier civilizations in a synthesis of freedom in the context of the strong state. Hegel's disciple F. C. Baur applied the dialectic to New Testament studies by finding the thesis in Jewish nationalism, antithesis in Pauline universalism, and synthesis in the mature Church which emerged in the second century. An eagerness to make the facts fit this framework led Baur into some serious mistakes. One may judge from him both how stimulating and how dangerous the Hegelian formula might be. Few historians outside the Marxist camp any longer regard it as more than occasionally useful. There is clearly *something* to the thought that a reaction often occurs: romanticism was a reaction against the Enlightenment, for example, while some of the postromantics tried to combine both in a synthesis. But the Hegelian formula is much too pat and would have to be used with care; in any case, one must see if the phenomena fit it (and often they do not) rather than insist that they must.

It is interesting and typical that Hegel defined his historical epochs in political terms. To Comte, as we shall see, the key lay in modes of thought, while Marx found it in the technological-economic sphere. Hegel's preoccupation with the political probably reflected the urgency of that problem in the Germany of his day, disunited and seeking to find its political unity. Hegel has been accused of an excessive nationalism, especially German nationalism, but in his time this was considered liberal and progressive. The key institution of the present age, Hegel felt with some justification, is the nation-state. He bequeathed to most German historians, and indeed to most nineteenth-century historians in all countries, a belief that the proper subject matter of history is politics; "history is past politics," in the definition of E. A. Freeman, the British master. While there was a subsequent rebellion against the narrowness of this definition, it might be defended on the grounds that the political order has usually given the distinctive stamp to epochs and peoples, from the oriental despotisms of earliest times through the Greek city-states, the Roman Empire, feudalism, and down to the age of the territorial state. If tomorrow should bring a world-state or even a federated Europe, this development would surely be so striking and significant that an epoch would be named for it. The "primacy of politics" is often a sound position.

History was actually only a part of Hegel's system, though the most celebrated part. He started with that idea of a single transcendental spiritual reality, so attractive to the post-Kantian romantic philosophers. Hegel had a rather unromantic temperament and made fun of his friend Schelling's "Absolute" as a sort of vague nothingness, or everythingness. He wished to clarify it. Hegel had a logical mind; was not this ideal reality nothing but logic, the logic of the universe, dialectical reason itself? Reality is at bottom thought in motion. What Hegel in common with the other German idealist philosophers called the Idea, or the Absolute, underlies all other phenomena, nature and mind; it exists objectively. When we speak of Hegel as an idealist, we should remember that his was not a subjective idealism but an objective idealism: the Absolute Idea is out there, independently existing—God, if one likes— not a creation of my mind and yours. Most romantics, we recall, shared this belief that there is an unseen spiritual world of essences, of which the world known to our senses is only the external manifestation. Hegel simply defined it as logic. It is in motion, *a dialectical process*, like a conversation in which the first statement is made, then answered, a new statement made, and so on. Progress is made; things proceed towards fuller freedom and eventually to the Absolute's complete self-realization. In all things, the dialectic works. Hegel made some effort to show that it may be found in physical nature and the plant and animal world as well as in human affairs. Nature and History are the two great realms of the knowable, the two modes of the Absolute. But the former is static; only in the latter does the creative process go on.

Process and organism are Hegelian keynotes. As opposed to the static formulations of Enlightenment thought, he has everything in motion, to be grasped only when its growth and development is understood; no one better reveals the nineteenth century's genetic, evolutionary outlook, or contributed more to implanting it. And, though somewhat obscurely, Hegel believed that the universe was not like a machine but like an organism, a view closer to both the older and the newer conceptions than to eighteenth-century mechanism. His logical methodology was based on the organic approach: nothing can be understood except by reference to the whole of which it is a part. With specific reference to the Kantian categories, Hegel held them to be bound together in a unity; not isolated and separate, but aspects of a single entity, the mind, which itself is a part of all the rest of reality. (That is why the real is rational and the rational real: our minds and the universe are parts of a single whole, hence obey the same laws.) We are almost back where we were before Descartes taught men to dissect, to break things down into simple components for purpose of analysis. Hegel was the philosopher of process, and of organism.

All this may seem rather difficult. Many found Hegel hopelessly difficult. But the spirit of his philosophy, when one gets hold of it, hangs together and communicates a special vision, an excitingly new one in its day. We asked what some of its implications were and may resume that discussion. Belinsky, our Russian friend, drew from Hegelianism some highly conservative inferences: it seems to teach that whatever is is right, like all systems declaring the universe to be perfectly rational. With particular reference to history, it apparently requires us to believe that whatever has happened is for the best: in the Lisbon Earthquake controversy, Hegel would assuredly have been on the side of Rousseau and the churchmen against Voltaire's pessimistic protest. He has been accused of teaching that might makes right, and there is a certain truth in this, for "the hour strikes once for every nation" and whoever has the power at a particular moment of history is presumably in the right. Some nations are "world-historical" ones destined to contribute more than others to the pattern of history. And everything, including war, is a necessary part of the pattern. When Napoleon and Hitler were winning they were right, presumably, though when they were losing they were wrong; like all deterministic systems, Hegel's does not really tell us much, for we never know what the pattern is until after it has happened. Hegel in any case believed that individuals are the unconscious tools of the world-force, they have no wills of their own.

Yet this view of the past greatly encouraged historical research by inculcating a deep respect for each epoch of the past, which made its unique contribution and is therefore worth studying for its own sake. One did not demand that it conform to current prejudices and thus commit the sin of an excessive "present-mindedness," distorting the past by forcing it into a mold of recent construction. One studied each era of the past as if, in Leopold von Ranke's words, it was "equidistant from eternity"—just as much a part of God's plans as our own age. German historians like Ranke, who led a great nineteenth-century renaissance of historical studies, were not Hegelian metaphysicians but they did broadly share this outlook which saw order and purpose in the events of history and hoped to lay bare the whole mighty plan by their industrious researches.

Politically, Hegel might best be described as a conservative liberal. An ardent Bonapartist in his day, Hegel's chief political work was a product of the reaction (*Philosophy of Right and Law, 1821*). He believed in constitutional government but preferred monarchy to democracy and opposed individualism. He shared some of the presuppositions of the upper bourgeoisie who greatly mistrusted the mob though in a certain sense they were liberal. Certainly Hegel claimed to believe in progress through orderly government—progress toward freedom. But his version of freedom was the so-called positive one. Freedom, that is, was not to him the negative practice of just letting people alone. The proper definition of freedom is realization of possibilities, Hegel believed. This may be made clearer by the example of the child, whom we compel to go to school, though if we gave him his will he would doubtless prefer the freedom of play. We are preparing him to be truly free by expanding his possibilities of growth. (Rousseau's "forced to be free" will be recalled.) Ignorance is slavery; the savage who is "free" is really far less free than the modern man who is bound by the rules of a state. No creature is absolutely free, but free only to realize its natural possibilities. A bird is free to fly, but not to swim. Man, as a creature of reason, realizes his freedom by developing his rational potential, and to do this requires making many sacrifices of his liberty of action. He must live in an organized state, obey its laws, and serve the interests of the community.

Hegel's stress on the state as the highest unit led on to social-welfare protests against extreme individualism (see particularly T. H.

Green in England, discussed later). When Hegel glorifies the State we should understand that he uses the term in a rather special way. In his system it is the dialectical synthesis of family and civil society, or in his jargon the union of universal and particular in the "concrete universal." In more commonplace terminology, this means that the State (as an ideal) is the highest development of the community, the place where a perfect society would find its completest expression. Hegel, in brief, does not conceive of the state as a leviathan standing over against its subjects, ordering them about and intimidating them; it is more like Rousseau's General Will—the common rational spirit of the whole community—made manifest. This view appealed to moderate, liberal men because it claimed not to sacrifice the individual completely to the state, nor was it socialistic. According to Hegel, it is only as a citizen that the individual becomes wholly free and possessed of rights. This feeling for association against individualism, though with a conservative cast, made Hegel a significant founder of the more moderate movements of social reform. And if Hegel was a conservative, his disciples do not show it. While some went to the Right, and some to the moderate center, the "young Hegelians" including Karl Marx and Ludwig Feuerbach became materialists and atheists. Belinsky, too, was a socialist or anarchist.

Hegel was apparently a Christian, but Kierkegaard, the Danish pastor who is now considered the chief founder of modern Christian existentialism, accused him of devitalizing Christianity, by rationalizing it and making it abstract. There is some truth in this. Hegel's new version of scholasticism made reason and religion coincide, but the highest synthesis is philosophy; Christianity is the symbolic or mythical mode of expression presumably meant for minds incapable of philosophy. Christianity is done the honor of having its representations agree with Hegel's philosophy though in a slightly inferior manner. If many Christians had their faith confirmed by finding that it agreed with the most advanced philosophy, others like Kierkegaard resented the relegation. One could easily, with Feuerbach and Marx, forget about religion and take the philosophy alone. It could then readily be converted into a materialistic determinism. Hegel was closer to the atheism of Marx than he may have realized. One finds, for example, that in Italy Hegelianism was adopted by the anticlericals and laicists. The state represents the highest ethical ideal, and is above the church, they held. The Roman Catholic Church, when in 1864 it produced its great Syllabus of Errors or list of modern heresies, included Hegelianism as a form of anticlerical liberalism. Actually, Hegel excluded religion from the historic sphere, regarding progress as social and political, not religious; in sharply separating private religion from public, political matters he was in a traditional Lutheran scheme.

Hegelianism exerted so strong an appeal in good part because it was a complete system, an organic whole, an exceptionally unified, "total" philosophy. It was the first of several such in the nineteenth century—Comte's was another, then Marx's and Spencer's. Of these at least one, Karl Marx's, owed its basic traits to Hegel. It was an evolutionary system, thus incorporating the nineteenth century's most characteristic point of view. By comparison with Kant, the evolutionary or historical element stands out; Kant had failed to see, Hegel thought, that reason is not static. What is true today was not true yesterday, and Hegel believed he had found here the answer to Kant's alleged proof (through the "antinomies") of the logical contradictions in any speculative metaphysics that goes beyond our experience, such as the nature of God or the origin of being.

Hegel's remarkable system of rational metaphysics based on historicism and dialectical evolution was hard to overlook; some have hated it, regarding it more as the scandal than the glory of the century, but like Marxism, its lineal descendant, it demanded attention and commanded allegiance because of the boldness of its stance as a complete reconstruction of human knowledge.

At the end of the century there was a decided reaction against the rigorous monism of Hegel's system. William James thought it a stuffy house with not enough air in it. In our time the "historicism" of Hegel, insofar as it meant a closed and deterministic system, has been assailed and convincingly refuted.[7] The enormous influence of Hegel is evident as much in his opponents as in his disciples. In protesting against Hegel, two giants of unorthodoxy in his time created movements of future significance: Schopenhauer and Kierkegaard, both of whom reacted against Hegel's cosmic rationalism and optimism to produce ideas of the irrational (Schopenhauer's "Will," a blind striving cosmic force) and of completely undetermined freedom (Kierkegaard's individual existent person). Today Kierkegaard's "existential" religion is more popular than Hegel's rationalized religion.[8] But Hegel's vision of an organic rather than a mechanistic universe was prophetic, and his stress on process, evolution, development, has been basic to the modern mind. His influ-

[7]Karl Popper, in the important but argumentative book *The Open Society and its Enemies*, Vol. 2, 4th ed., 1962—the work of a modern philosophical analyst with a bias toward liberalism—attributes practically all the sins of the modern world to Hegel's baleful influence (pages 25–80). L. T. Hobhouse blamed the First World War on him. This seems a little extreme!

[8]In an early work which was long considered his least impressive, *The Phenomenology of the Spirit*, Hegel threw out suggestions which have found their way into present-day existential and phenomenological thought. Thus, rather startlingly, his genius contributed something to the modern school that is often thought of as based on criticism of his main system. For further remarks on this, see pp. 461–470.

ence can hardly be overestimated. Moreover, there has recently been a significant revival of interest in Hegel.

Another novel and attractive implication of the many-sided Hegelian structure may be mentioned. In effect, very nearly, God is man, according to this philosophy—not the individual man, but humanity collectively in its historical evolution. The historic process is "the march of God through the world." The world spirit grows and develops through human history. From this one may derive a new explanation of the riddle of the human situation, with its lofty aspirations and its frustrations. Each of us has in him something of the universal man, whose nature is nothing less than potential perfection, the self-realization of the world. But each of us also is a particular person, bound to one time and place, destined to make only a tiny contribution to the splendid temple of reason that will someday be finished. Hence our soaring aspirations and our limited achievements. We can nevertheless do what our talents permit us to do in the confident knowledge that it does fit somewhere into the great plan. Nineteenth-century optimists who believed in progress found that Hegelianism fitted comfortably into their scheme of things.

Hegel inspired or reenforced a large amount of nineteenth century nationalism of the messianic sort; perhaps a less appetizing outgrowth than some of the others—we can see what Hobhouse meant when he accused Hegel of encouraging war—yet in some parts of Europe a liberal or revolutionary ideology. As an example, Count August Cieszkowski (1814–1894), Polish nationalist and Hegel disciple, used the Germans (Herder as well as Hegel) to support his vision of a great Slavic state which would adorn the next and perhaps last stage in the evolution of mankind. Hegel's influence in Russia and other parts of eastern Europe was strong for a generation—about 1835 to 1860—and contributed no little to the great nationalist myth known as Pan-Slavism. Historicist messianism throve on a simplified version of Hegel, who taught that history has a goal toward which all is tending; and nationalism did too since the philosopher had seen "historic peoples" and their states as the vehicles of historical destiny. This sort of Hegelian historicism is obviously deeply laid within the popular modern mind. In his study of a twentieth-century American politician, Henry A. Wallace, Dwight MacDonald noted the theme of an "American hour" in world history, prepared for by all previous happenings. God has brought forth the United States in due time to do His bidding in the cosmic drama of historic man. Each nation might, gratifyingly, find the god of history on its side.

To a generation confused by many new ideas and by drastic political and social change, Hegel offered an apparently satisfying unity, which found a place for everything and discerned the order behind the baffling facade of events. Faced with the question whether liberals, conservatives, or socialists were right, the Hegelian could answer, all are—each in its place and time, each a part of the final synthesis. Confronted by revolutions and counterrevolutions, wars and political turmoil, he could hold that all these occurrences are part of a necessary pattern. Hegel also found a place for both reason and Christianity, which many had seen as locked in mortal conflict: just different ways of stating the same truth. Hegel's synthesis which seemed to harmonize all things was almost as impressive as that which Thomas Aquinas had offered at the peak of medieval civilization in the thirteenth century. It proved equally fragile. Some found it distressingly abstract, a mere house of words. Others converted it into materialism and atheism by discovering that there was no need to posit Hegel's spirit underlying the natural world. Still others used the idea of historical destiny to justify all kinds of revolutionary and nationalistic causes. While Hegel's vast influence on modern thought is not in question, it radiated in all directions and lost its unity.

Hegel's Disciples

More may briefly be said concerning the offspring of Hegel, a progeny of some importance to the modern world. Hegel influenced practically all schools of thought in Germany, also British idealist philosophers of the later nineteenth century such as F. H. Bradley and Bernard Bosanquet, dominant in the British universities for some time, in Italy the philosophers Benedetto Croce and Giovanni Gentile, and many others. Socialists made use of him, historians knelt at his shrine, both the religious and the antireligious seized on pertinent aspects of his thought for their purposes. He lent authority to conservatives and radicals, reformers and foes of reform. His ability to be all things to all men is perhaps an indictment of Hegel as well as tribute to him.

A few notable descendants need to be pinpointed. Karl Marx, the most remarkable of these, will be dealt with subsequently. Marx in his youth belonged to a group known as the Young Hegelians, who were all left-wing exponents of a modified Hegelianism. Among these, Bruno Bauer and David Strauss showed a decided interest in Biblical and religious studies, Strauss's critical biography of Jesus being one of the century's most sensational books, while Ludwig Feuerbach treated the theme of religions in a more general way. All the Young Hegelians believed that Hegel's thought represented the most advanced creation of the human mind thus far. But they thought it needed restatement, a very sweeping sort of restatement, in a sense really the abandonment of

Hegelianism. For Hegel had been wrong in his idealism. He should be turned over, "set right side up." Reality is actually material, and ideas are only a projection of physical being. The idea of God had been invented by men as a symbol for all their ideals and goals; as such it served a useful purpose, but may now, at a higher stage of self-awareness, be abandoned. Theology becomes anthropology, in Feuerbach's words. We realize that only man exists, and "politics must become our religion": the goal of man's perfection through his own social action is to be explicitly recognized.

Feuerbach was far from a great philosopher, but this somewhat vulgar materialism, atheism, and (in the specifically modern sense) humanism was extremely significant. Large numbers of moderns have accepted it as their "philosophy." August Comte was even then pointing out that the nineteenth century had witnessed the birth of the Positive Age, replacing the ages of Theology and then Metaphysics. The new God was materialistic science, the only goals practical, mundane ones. The Absolute as well as God would have to be relegated to the realm of fairy tales. It is remarkable that Hegel led in this direction, but in fact it *was* possible to stand him on his feet in this way. (Hegel himself pointed out that science was relegating art as well as religion to the sidelines in the modern age.) Marx was the most celebrated of those who did so, after Feuerbach.

The young Marx's intellectual life was immersed in the debates of the Young Hegelians. He tended to define his position in criticism of them, as for example *The Holy Family* (1844) versus Bauer, and the *Theses on Feuerbach* (1845). In his early manuscripts, which remained unpublished until recently, he also does incessant and rather obscure battle with Hegel's *Phenomenology*. Marx remained strongly under the influence of Hegelian concepts even as he struggled to go beyond the master. Hegel, it should be noticed, instilled in his followers a desire to surpass him just because they were his disciples. For had not Hegel taught that the dialectic goes on, and each age has its own statement to make? Hegel had made the ultimate statement for his generation; the next generation must say something else, something beyond this. The Hegelians of the years after the master's death in 1831 tended to think that he had brought pure philosophy, speculative thought, as far as it could go. What remained? To translate this thought into action, to change the world and not just understand it. The age of metaphysics had ended with Hegel, the age of humanism had begun.

The element of political ideology, then, in the seemingly metaphysical system of Hegel, becomes evident. The great object of knowledge is history, and especially political history; and at the end, by a slight alteration in Hegel, we decide with Feuerbach that "politics must become our religion." The sole aim and interest of man is to discover and create the good society on earth, with the aid of his scientific intelligence.

Social Romanticism and the Revolution of 1848

The ideas of Fourier, Saint-Simon, and Owen, formulated during the 1820s, enjoyed considerable popularity in the 1830s and 1840s and were joined by others. The disciples of Saint-Simon tended to split up, but the movement nevertheless went on. As their 1830 manifesto stated, they rejected the equal division of property and accepted the "natural *in*equality of man," thus favoring a hierarchical society; but "each is placed according to his abilities and rewarded according to his works" by planning and coordination, property being held by the state and not individuals. (The one-time secretary of Saint-Simon, August Comte, who will be dealt with separately, can probably not be classed as a socialist, though the influence of Saint-Simon remained on his thought in the form of a stress on authority and the subordination of individuals to the state.)

The most popular French political tract of the 1830s was probably the *Paroles d'un croyant* by La Mennais, or as he now called himself (the change is significant of a democratic shift) Lamennais. We may recall him as an enthusiastic disciple of the "reactionaries," a decade earlier. He now became an equally enthusiastic social democrat. The change is not so great as we might imagine, for most French socialists acknowledged some debt to Maistre and Bonald. The "words of a believer" came from one who was a Catholic priest, but was not long to be, for the Church would not tolerate his left-wing views. His romantic eloquence made him the man of the hour and enthusiastic followers proclaimed Lamennais the new messiah, while Metternich, the statesman in charge of keeping down revolutionary discontent in Europe, grumbled about "this anarchist . . . fool . . . abject being." No work had more to do with the Revolution of 1848. In this and ensuing books, the Breton priest expressed a lyrical if vague awareness of a "tremendous revolution going on at the heart of human society," a revolution which was the march of "the peoples" and would produce a "new world." He denounced "wage slavery" and castigated the rulers of society for neglecting their responsibilities to society. "If you reject peaceful reform you will have reform by violence." The obvious British counterpart to Lamennais is Thomas Carlyle, whose electrifying prose called attention to the "social question" in an enduring classic, *Past and Present* (1843).

Lamennais and Carlyle represented a blending of romanticism with social reform in what has been called "social romanticism" (D. O. Evans) or "political Messianism" (J. L. Talmon). The late romantic writers Victor Hugo, Lamartine, and George Sand were caught up in it. As David O. Evans observes in his little book on *Social Romanticism in France 1830–1848*, "*Les Misérables* was the culmination of a massive literature of social novels and dramas which flourished between 1830 and 1848," including those of Sand and Balzac, from whom Friedrich Engels said he had learned more than from all historical and economical treatises put together. The ground was thus prepared for that remarkable revolution of 1848 of which the leaders were a poet, Lamartine, and a social theorist, Blanc. As one might expect from romantic poets and novelists, the spirit was rather more emotional than logical. The mood was messianic or apocalyptic; the "people" were on the march, tyrants trembled on their thrones or in their counting houses. A splendid new world would dawn after brave deeds by popular heroes had overthrown them. The French Revolution, heretofore unpopular, was rehabilitated by historians like Michelet and Quinet, not to speak of Louis Blanc. Had there not been something splendid, if terribly splendid, about that volcanic upsurge of the People? They had announced their arrival with an explosion which signalled the great revolution of modern times, the democratic revolution.

Lamartine and Hugo were not really socialists, 1848 was to make clear. Under the impact of that event, a split developed between the republicans or democrats and the working-class socialists which helped doom the revolution. Prior to 1848, these two strains mingled in a chorus of slogans about social justice, popular rights, and the march of the masses.

In England there was something similar, if more restrained befitting the national temper. There was nothing restrained about the Scotsman Carlyle, or such working-class spokesmen as the Irishman Feargus O'Connor. The novels of Dickens and Mrs. Gaskell contain their share of social protest. The Chartist movement was a more impressive organization of the actual working-class people than anything in France. But Britain already had her liberal reforms and she had a national Parliament with deep roots in the national tradition. The great debate of the 1840s turned on the relatively concrete issue of free trade versus protection. During this struggle to repeal the tariffs on grains, Richard Cobden and John Bright organized the Anti-Corn Law League and carried political debate down to the grassroots level. Great Britain avoided revolution in 1848 and proceeded toward social democracy at a more moderate pace.

Democracy might now be observed in relatively successful operation in the United States of America. In the mid-1830s Alexis de

Tocqueville returned from his visit there to write *Democracy in America*, one of the political classics of the century. Countless others went to America and wrote travel books, but Tocqueville's was a uniquely philosophical mind. He wrote against the background of a considerable discussion of democracy in France at this time. And he brought to the task the new ideas of a social-scientific methodology as proposed by Bonald, Saint-Simon, Comte. Consequently *Democracy in America* is a good deal more than a travel book; it is a work of systematic sociology. Highly praised at the time, it has kept a considerable repute ever since. It is a truly objective work, not a partisan one: Tocqueville was amused to find that some thought he had written against democracy and others that he had written for it. A liberal noble, Tocqueville reminds us a great deal of Montesquieu; he had learned from Burke, too, as well as many others. The integrity, moderation, and wisdom of a book that nevertheless sparkles with ideas has earned it its high standing in the literature of politics and society.

The question Tocqueville was really interested in was whether this new thing, democracy, which his historical sense told him was inevitably on the way, could be reconciled with liberty and with traditional European civilization. Was it a triumph of barbarism from within, a revolt of the blind masses certain to destroy culture? Would it lead to a new despotism? These things had been said. The social scientist in Tocqueville wished to test them by a method more fruitful than mere theorizing. So he went to the United States and observed.

Social scientist that he was, Tocqueville was not free from ideological influences. A moderate, a liberal, he wished, he said, both to "allay the terrors" of the reactionaries and "calm the ardor" of the radicals. Perhaps Tocqueville found in America what he wanted to find—as it has been alleged. The charge is only partly true. He did find a mixture of good and bad. For example, Tocqueville allayed the fears that democracy meant wild instability, dictatorship, destruction of property, and irreligion. Here in the democratic United States property was safe, religion flourished, and there was no fear of violent revolution. Give power to the people and they will become responsible, Tocqueville implied; democracy has its own safety valves. On the other hand, he found science and literature mediocre in the United States, the uncommon man intimidated by the mass, and he feared that this was a law of democracies; he was among the first to complain of democratic conformism and the "tyranny of the majority." To some of his contemporaries in Europe he apparently taught that democratic society destroys liberty. But in the main his temperate and sympathetic appraisal helped the republican cause in France. Tocqueville himself, though by no means an egalitarian, served in the shortlived Second Republic born of the Revolution in

1848 and never learned to love the despot who ended its life, Louis Napoleon. Liberty was his passion. He loved England, as Montesquieu had, and John Stuart Mill was one of his friends; thus he seems close to British liberalism.

His moderate note was unusual in France in the 1830s and 1840s. Among the new socialist voices of the 1840s there was Pierre-Joseph Proudhon, a man of the people himself, whose chief message was to abolish unearned increment and unproductive property: "What is the producer? Nothing. What should he be? Everything." An enemy of statism, Proudhon suggested "mutualism" or farmers' and workers' co-operatives as the answer to economic injustice; he was an ancestor of the anarchist-syndicalists, and perhaps also of the populists and Henry George agrarians. But his revolutionary spirit appeared in his advocacy of class war, his call to the working classes to rise up and throw off their chains, as the Communist Manifesto of 1848 put it. Marx later ridiculed Proudhon for the crudeness of his thought, but he influenced Marx, being in the 1840s and 1850s the best known of the radical socialist theoreticians. Proudhon had no faith in democratic processes as such; "social reform will never come out of political reform, political reform must emerge from social reform." "Universal suffrage is the materialism of the Republic." But Proudhon seldom stayed long in one position; he seemed "determined that none should share his views." Marx was right about the shoddiness of much of Proudhon's thought. But he possessed a style, an aptitude for phrase-making, along with a burning sense of social injustice.

Paris was discontented and bored with the prosaic "bourgeois monarchy" of Louis-Philippe, which had come into existence in 1830. Though liberal enough to permit free speech and encourage education, its constitution denied representation to all but a few and its social philosophy was largely laissez-faire liberalism—its motto, "enrich yourself." The dominant class was the "grande bourgeoisie." In the cafes of Paris lesser men listened to Proudhon's call to revolution. When the revolution came he disagreed with it; "they have made a revolution without ideas," he declared. He laughed at the panacea of the influential socialist Louis Blanc: state-owned factories. To Proudhon the root of the matter was demand, not production. Leave the working class without adequate purchasing power and the state factories would stagnate quite as much as privately owned ones, for want of a market. Proudhon's was the classical statement of the underconsumption theory of economic depression.

Proudhon's *What is Property?* (1841) had been preceded by Louis Blanc's *The Organization of Labor* (1840). At this time also, it may be recalled, Etienne Cabet's *Voyage to Icaria* appeared, with its message of utopian communism. Blanc, an indefatigable writer, produced a stream of works in these years including a laudatory history of the French

Revolution and a *History of Ten Years*, in which he cataloged the sins of the capitalistic Orleanist regime. Blanc stood for a blend of Jacobin democracy and socialism that perhaps lacked logical consistency but was proclaimed with great eloquence; it rejected Saint-Simonian authoritarianism in favor of a more democratic political order, yet was socialist in its attacks on private property in the means of production. Blanc did not, like Proudhon, call for violent revolution, or like the intrepid Blanqui, socialist working-class leader, seek to practice it. He evidently believed that the people would freely vote for socialism if given a chance. The results of the elections of 1848 severely disillusioned him, and he appears then to have discovered for the first time that France was a country of peasants and not of Parisian left-wing journalists. At that time he retreated somewhat from democracy. Later, however (he lived well into the Third Republic), he continued to support a moderate, democratic, and "gradualist" socialism against Marxists and Anarchists.

Among other rebels and prophets who led the way to 1848, there was the Italian Giuseppe Mazzini, a passionate Genoese who as a youth joined the *Carbonari* and vowed his life to the cause of national liberation for Italy under a popular government. He spent most of his life as an exile in London but returned during the revolutions of 1848 to take part in those tumultuous events, presiding over the short-lived Roman Republic of 1848–1849. His prolific and eloquent pen gained him a place as one of the chief writers of this time and a great leader of the Italian *risorgimento*, which in 1860–1861 became the most exciting movement in Europe. If the gallant soldier of liberty, Garibaldi, was the most popular figure of the Italian national political revival, Mazzini was its spiritual leader. Belonging as it does to the generation of "social romanticism," the eloquence that so bedazzled his contemporaries may seem bombastic and hollow today, though on the whole it wears better than most of that sort of thing. Mazzini, with Louis Blanc, belonged among the democratic socialists. Hostile to liberalism because it was too negative and selfish, he affirmed the value of both democracy and "association." He was equally against class war and individualism; all men should be brothers, there should be solidarity, and there should be religion, a religion of humanity. Mazzini quickly quarreled with Marx and Bakunin in the First International; he was too radical for Italian liberals, who fought him for control of the *risorgimento*, but too conservative for the left-wing proletarian rebels. Like Blanc, he called himself a republican and obviously derived from Rousseau and the French Revolutionary tradition; he was an Italian Jacobin. (Northern Italy had been as eager for the French Revolution as France; Mazzini's father had lived under the Ligurian Republic.) But his stress on national liberation and a social-democratic *mystique* put him in the center of nineteenth-century ideology.

Lamennais, Blanc, Proudhon, and Mazzini supplied a good part of the fuel for the engine of revolution that roared down the track only to crash in 1848. Broadly speaking they formed a brotherhood of social protest with generous ideals, but they failed to agree and their thought was often vague. These limitations must probably be held responsible in good part for the failures of 1848. Nevertheless the ferment of social thought in this generation must be recognized as a powerful force in modern Europe. It produced most of the ideas, in embryo, on which social reformers of all sorts have been living ever since.

But the experiences of 1848, a year which began with democratic revolutions all over Europe and ended with the confusion and discomfiture of these revolutions, caused a temporary reaction against all forms of "social romanticism." In general, the sad failure of the Revolutions of 1848 was like a large bucket of very cold water poured on the slogan-intoxicated men who had begun them so hopefully. All over continental Europe the sobering up was much in evidence; people felt that there had been too many daydreams and vague formulae, too little precise thinking. The reaction was toward realistic means and limited objectives. Like all reactions, it went far in the opposite direction. The feeling spread that power alone counts, and practical methods of politics. It was a German (evidently Ludwig von Rochau) who coined the word *Realpolitik;* but the same idea could be found from one end of Europe to the other. Thus 1848 was almost a repetition of 1789, in that the ideals and ideas which inspired it turned out to be too vague and were held to have caused more harm than good because of this flaw: zeal without knowledge. The counterparts of Rousseau and Voltaire were Proudhon and Mazzini; with more of romantic fire, they had as little of concrete social engineering. If Bonald and Maistre had suggested a more realistic approach, this was swept aside because they were conservatives; if Saint-Simon demanded science, he had in reality supplied only ideology. Evidently much yet remained to do before that ideal human society could become more than a vision or dream. Again there was a reaction away from utopias.

Not until the 1880s did the socialist movement really revive; only in the 1860s did it show any spark of renewed life. "Social romanticism" and indeed romanticism of all sorts went out of fashion among men of letters. The success of the Italian national liberation movement in 1861 might seem to be an exception to this; but in actuality this miracle was the work of realists and moderates, not of Garibaldi and Mazzini. During the French Second Empire, when another Bonaparte arose on the grave of the Republic, the reigning intellectual system was the austerely scientific credo of positivism.

But it is also true that bourgeois liberalism of the "classical" type became less harshly dogmatic. It too had had its heyday between 1830 and 1848; the uncompromising features of the *grande bourgeoisie's* political and social outlook had had not a little to do with bringing on that outburst of resentment, the revolutions of 1848. After 1848 the suffrage was less restricted, despite the apparent failure of that revolution. Even Napoleon III was careful to have his mandate affirmed and reaffirmed from time to time by universal suffrage, which has never ceased to exist in France, whatever the regime, since its installation in 1848. Dogmatic laissez-faire, too, received less emphasis. Napoleon ran something of a welfare state, the realistic conservative Bismarck installed sweeping welfare measures in Germany, and Great Britain began to move in that direction soon. *Realpolitik* turned away from romantic visions of utopia, but it also turned away in some measure from the absolute dogma of laissez-faire, equally visionary.

Whatever the final verdict, this generation of 1815–1848 must be granted primacy in the modern Western world, perhaps repaying close study more than any other one by those who wish to understand presentday problems, dreams, and outlooks. These ideologies—liberal, socialist, nationalist, conservative—are still the basic value structures for most people in Europe and its offshoots.

9

Classical Ideologies
of the Mid-Nineteenth Century:
Mill, Comte, Darwin

The history of the human race is the history of growth.

FREDERIC HARRISON

*If there is the mob, there is the people also. I speak
now of the middle classes—of those hundreds of
thousands of respectable persons—the most numerous
and by far the most wealthy order in the community.*

LORD BROUGHAM

The Mid-Victorian Era

After revolution and romanticism receded in 1849, Europe entered upon a period which could well be described as the classical age of the nineteenth century. It was the mid-Victorian era, with all the phrase conveys: middle-class domination, comfortable bourgeois virtues, industrialism and free trade, political stability with an undercurrent of working-class distress. Victoria, the personification of the bourgeois virtues, reigned only in Great Britain, but Great Britain led the way into the industrial age, and in other places, notably Germany and the Low Countries, "Victorian" phenomena could be observed.

In Great Britain at mid-century, the classical school of economics reigned, its laissez-faire injunctions slightly modified by the post-Ricardian economists, but only slightly; by 1846 it had converted most statesmen. Along with it flourished the popular ideology of self-help, making perennial best sellers of such books as Samuel Smiles's *Lives of the Engineers*, the stories of poor boys who made their way to wealth and glory: Faraday was a blacksmith's son, Stephenson a collier's, Telford a shepherd's. George Orwell, the modern essayist and novelist, remarked that his father had read only two books in his life, the Bible and Smiles's *Self-Help*—probably a typical Victorian intellectual history. The powerful London *Economist* assumed dogmatically and without any question that the sum of private interests "is always the same as the public interest." Free trade conquered in the struggle concerning repeal of the corn laws (grain tariffs) in the 1840s. While the factory laws removed the worst abuses of child and woman labor, the country having been stirred by Parliamentary investigations into this cruel scandal, there still remained no protection for adult male workers against the law of the market in wages; the trades unions had barely begun their long march to respectability and power in 1850. (They did not receive legal recognition until 1870 and were not a strong factor before the 1880s.) With government as well as wages cheap, in this incredible paradise of private enterprise by modern standards (no taxes, no labor unions!), industry and invention flourished, the nation seemed to grow rich, and British power, influence, and prestige were never greater. Victoria came to excel even Queen Bess as a long-lived symbol of greatness.

This was the heyday of the middle classes, whose peculiar ethos permeated the era. Recently arrived through hard work and frugality, the middle classes radiated respectability. This was the "age of improvement," as historian Asa Briggs has named it. Some have spoken of a "mid-Victorian combination of Puritanism and Enlightenment." French morals were frowned upon (witness the reaction to Swinburne), also those practiced by English romantics and lords in the Regency era just prior to Victoria's accession. Such magisterial organs as the *Edinburgh Review* dispensed the dogmas of "free trade and tight morals," high intellectual seriousness, and a robust common sense ("masculine sanity," G. M. Young calls it) along with a deplorable lack of taste and imagination in the arts. Indeed, the arts were often declared to be a waste of time. The middle class doubtless shared some traits all over Europe, but Puritanism and individualism were not so prominent elsewhere. In regard to Puritanism, it may suffice to recall that over in Vienna, on the banks of the beautiful blue Danube, the bourgeoisie at this time built a culture marked by its music, gayety, and charm. Nor could the French bourgeoisie ever have displayed that egregious prudery found among the British middle classes, who (so we are told) segregated the male and female authors on library shelves.[1] Nevertheless, the high

---

[1]Victorian prudery must not be misunderstood as an anemic rejection of the sexual impulse, however. As Walter E. Houghton points out, "The major reason why sex was so frightening to the Victorians was the glaring fact that . . . sexual license in England not only existed on a large scale but seemed to be increasing." The romantic cult of free love (Shelley, Byron) survived, and French socialism and bohemianism threatened from across the channel. The Obscene Publications Bill of 1857 reacted to a large popular literature of pornography. The Victorians knew

seriousness and earnest moralism of the Victorians was a bond that
stretched broadly from Samuel Smiles to Matthew Arnold, whatever
other differences the merchant and the poet-intellectual had. The wish to
edify and to improve, to overcome evil and spread enlightenment, was
at the bottom of it—no unworthy spirit, despite the prudery into which
it might stray. For all their blind spots, the British middle classes, strong
and energetic, led the way to prosperity and success, and wished to build
a vigorous society in their own image.

On the other side of the picture, callousness, poverty, ugliness, and
degradation caused Carlyle, Ruskin, and others to protest against the
very foundations of this civilization, alleging it to lie in selfishness and
materialism. Hazlitt had written that "the carriage that glitters like a
meteor along the streets of the metropolis often deprives the wretched
inmate of the distant cottage of the chair he sits on, the table he eats
on, the bed he lies on." Shelley had burned with indignation at the factories of England and the suffering they imposed on the hapless creatures who labored incredibly long hours at work that was both body-
and soul-destroying. Coleridge had declared that if society disclaimed all
responsibility to the poor, as the economists and liberals preached, then
the poor would feel no sense of belonging and would eventually rebel
in a class war. Disraeli in 1844 wrote in his celebrated novel *Sybil* that
there were indeed two nations in England, the rich and the poor, utter
strangers to each other.

John Ruskin claimed that the ugliness of the factory towns, and
the appalling lack of artistic sensitivity in the country generally, were a
part of the social order, knit deeply into the outlook of the middle
classes whose ideology was a blend of Puritanism and utilitarianism,
both absolutely hostile to all the arts. Certainly, until near the end of the
century, the slums of London and other cities showed a subhuman
degradation seldom if ever equalled in Europe, and until the 1880s very
little concern about this was displayed by anyone; it was not society's
business, but the individual's. In *Unto This Last*, Ruskin voiced an eloquent protest against the economics of irresponsibility and the social
creed of selfish neglect.

Dickens in *Hard Times* (1854) flagellated a society that had just
finished congratulating itself, upon the occasion of the great Crystal
Palace Exhibition, for its infinite progressiveness. It is a world made up
of Bounderbys, greedy capitalists unscrupulously pursuing success, and
Gradgrinds, who, aided by utilitarianism and Political Economy, have
reduced life to statistics and forgotten its beauty. The city has become a

---

that sex was a potent force—so potent that, as Matthew Arnold observed, it needed
restraining rather than encouraging.

place of loss of identity in the lonely crowd; the factory is a scene of ugliness and inhumanity; the bourse and market-place erase human connections. And this society does not even deliver its one specialty, more and more material goods, for hundreds of thousands are in want and "hard times" may throw the whole economic system into confusion.

The protest voice, thundering indignantly like Carlyle's and Ruskin's and Dickens's, exposing the structure of exploitation as did, for example, Charles Kingsley's famous tract *Cheap Clothes and Nasty*, indicated a considerable Victorian social conscience. Not until after 1880 did it have much effect, but it undoubtedly prepared the way for the breakthrough against laissez-faire that then occurred. Carlyle became unbalanced in his hatred of the liberal orthodoxy and discredited himself by some of his later pronouncements, which have a fascist ring to modern ears. (Such were the abjurations against parliamentary "talking shops" and in favor of strong, silent dictators; the contempt for democracy; the worship of heroes; the scorn for humanitarianism, seen as shabby sentimentalism. The Tory socialist became more and more the Tory.) An incomparably vivid prose stylist, Carlyle was read by the Victorians but they discounted his views as chronically wrong-headed. (See John Morley's characteristic essay on Carlyle.)

Eminent Victorian Thinkers

His leading disciple in Victorian times was John Ruskin, already mentioned. Ruskin began as a student of architecture, making himself the Victorian oracle on this subject and prophet of the Gothic Revival, with *The Seven Lamps of Architecture* and *The Stones of Venice* (1849–1853). He believed that all great art comes from a sound society; the Gothic, he thought, stemmed from the free medieval craftsman, not yet become a degraded appendage of the machine. Ruskin carried on Carlyle's fierce hatred of modern industrialism and unregulated capitalism. Shaw said that Ruskin's jeremiads made Karl Marx sound like a Sunday School teacher. He increasingly thundered at modern soullessness and destruction of beauty; "we manufacture everything but men." In his later years he tried to create medieval orders dedicated to social service. With a prose that had the power to move men, he stimulated and influenced an incredible number of successors: William Morris and British socialism, Tolstoy, Proust, Gandhi, Frank Lloyd Wright. The historian of the Manchester School (W. D. Grampp) credits Ruskin with doing more than any one else to discredit and destroy the old laissez-faire creed. A little mad in his old age, he launched his diatribes like an Old Testament prophet and was increasingly ignored, but seared the souls of a dedicated few. His stature today is recognized and his reputation as a great Victorian secure. Few have so influenced certain aspects of the modern mind.

The other great eminent Victorian critic of society, Matthew Arnold, was a poet and critic who also branched off into political and social thought. Hardly a popular writer, he tremendously affected literate England and no one better carried on the grand traditions of European culture in an era of bourgeois philistinism. He preached no panacea, but like John Stuart Mill aimed at a "certain temper of mind"—a civilized mind, broad, intelligent, critical, refined. Civilization, he reminded his progress-enchanted Victorian readers, does not consist of material things and of mere numbers; it is a development of intellect and taste. In *Culture and Anarchy* (1867), Arnold rejected anarchy in cultural matters and asked for use of the state to promote the arts and letters. Like the French esthetes by whom he was much influenced, Arnold looked largely to literature for salvation: "the best poetry will be found to have a power of forming, sustaining, and delighting us, as nothing else can." The Barbarians and Philistines of industrial Britain might, he sometimes thought, be converted to sweetness and light. Though savagely critical of their taste and manners, Arnold admired the energy and curiosity of the middle classes and did not entirely despair of their conversion. Arnold essentially upheld an ideal of high culture—the best of the great Western tradition from Homer to Baudelaire—as best he could in a time of cultural decay, as he saw it. No one felt more keenly the decadence of the modern, with its "sick hurry and divided aims," or longed more for some kind of healing faith to cure the disease of modern skepticism. He also besieged the parochialism of the English from his position as connoisseur of world literature, aware of the value of the modern European greats (German as well as French—Goethe and Heine were among his favorites) as well as of the ancient classics.

If Matthew Arnold, perhaps the most civilized of all the Victorians, was a critic of the narrowness of the bourgeoisie, the "philistinism" of the middle classes as well as the crudities of the landed gentry, the fact is that almost all the greater Victorian writers were critics of their society. The charge of complacency will not stick against Tennyson and Browning, the great Victorian poets, though they have been accused of it.

The most celebrated and symbolic thinker of mid-Victorian England was John Stuart Mill. His early career may be familiar to many from the well-known account of it in his *Autobiography*. Brought up in the strictest Benthamite discipline, he rebelled and turned to Wordsworth and Coleridge for relief. His searching essays on Bentham and Coleridge reveal the patient catholicity of his fine mind, looking for the value in each figure while peeling off the dross. He became interested in Comte, finding in his discipline and social sense a corrective to British individualism though there was much in the Frenchman he could not stomach. Indeed Mill, who lies buried with his wife at Avignon, always owed much to Frenchmen, something to be remembered when one sees comments on his "typically British" philosophy. He read the novels of Dickens; he formed a firm friendship with Carlyle for a time. Tocqueville's great work on democracy attracted him; Kant and Hegel mostly repelled him, being too metaphysical for Mill's essentially positivist mind. In the long run the mark of Bentham prevailed: Mill was essentially the rationalist and liberal. But his thought has been summed up as a series of compromises, and no nineteenth-century thinker read more widely and sympathetically than Mill.

What compromises did Mill suggest? Empiricist and positivist in his philosophy, he refused to say with the Kantians (as he construed them) that the laws of thought are merely mental categories; he held them to exist objectively, and he prepared a systematic treatise of inductive logic. Classic defender of the liberty of the individual, he showed some sympathy to Comte and French socialism, up to a point; fearing the element of compulsion that lurks in every socialist scheme, he approved voluntary cooperation. In his famous textbook on the *Principles of Political Economy*, his foundation was individualistic capitalism yet he was prepared to entertain exceptions to the rule wherever a sound case could be made—and the exceptions, it has been noted, grew with every edition of the *Principles*, so that Mill has been claimed as an ancestor of English socialism (Fabian). Skeptic in religion, near the end of his life he felt the bankruptcy of "scientism" and edged cautiously toward belief in a finite God; at any rate he recognized the human need for religious experience. He had always been willing to temper the narrower individualism of the Benthamites with some of Coleridge's feeling for the community. Doubting sometimes about democracy because of his love for liberty, he believed the strongest argument for it to be that it is a process of education; and Mill always remained the optimist, feeling perhaps that all men were potentially as rational as himself. British empiricism was deeply engrained in him, and a part of that tradition was an openness, including Locke's doctrine of a malleable human nature (Mill believed this strongly) and Hume's dislike of dogmas. Resolutely open-minded he remained all his life, and thus has seemed the classic "liberal."

His strongest hatreds were of censorship, intolerance, conformity— anything that interfered with individual liberty. His best-known work, the essay *On Liberty* (1859), to which his wife, Harriet, a remarkable woman, contributed much, is the classic argument for the maximum of individual liberty. "The only purpose for which power can be rightfully exercised over any member of a civilized community against his will is to prevent harm to others. His own good, either physical or moral, is not a sufficient warrant. He cannot rightfully be compelled to do or forbear . . . because in the opinion of others to do so would be wise or even right." (Mill stressed that this was in a *civilized* community; "barbarians" would do best with an enlightened despot.) The goal and purpose of mankind, the only end worth striving for, was to Mill the complete development of the individual's powers to the highest possible point; he quoted Humboldt and remarked that "few persons, out of Germany" comprehend this, suggesting a Kantian or romantic source of his doctrine of freedom.

The argument of *On Liberty* then majestically unfolds for liberty of thought and discussion. The doctrine we suppress may be true, unless we assert infallibility for received opinion; or, if not true, it may contain *some* truth; or, even if it contains little or no truth, dissent is necessary to prevent intellectual stagnation; if we do not have to defend our creed, we will forget why we hold it.[2] Mill next makes it clear that under certain circumstances speech cannot be free, as when it is "a positive instigation to some mischievous act." Justice Oliver Wendell Holmes later observed that there can be no freedom to cry "fire!" in a crowded theater, and this is about what Mill meant. One always wonders when reading Mill how far agreement could ever be reached on the exact or even approximate boundaries of the limits he mentions. Holmes used the above principle to ban free speech in war time by those who allegedly did not support the war, a ruling which others thought to be an outrageous violation of civil liberties. But Mill seemed to think that these boundaries can be made clear.

He believed at any rate that the liberty necessary to human dignity and growth was all too lacking in the modern world. He stressed the danger from the "tyranny of the majority," which had replaced regal despotism as a threat to liberty. "That so few now dare to be eccentric marks the chief danger of the time." Everything was becoming standardized, from shoes to ideas, and Mill complained, as so many have done since, of the mass culture that was stamping conformity and mediocrity on everyone. Reverting to his effort to defend the individual, Mill sought to meet the objection against his own criteria that, after all, everything we do *does* concern others. About all that Mill succeeded in doing was to reassert his position. When we have finished reading this extraordinary essay we are likely to feel that while Mill has presented an incom-

---

[2]Mill's fellow Victorian, the great Roman Catholic John Henry Newman, adjusted his religion to liberalism by arguing, similarly, that heresy is necessary to faith. Unless error forces us to clear thinking, we do not perfectly know our creed.

parable discussion of the issues and made an eloquent appeal for the free individual, he has not resolved the ancient dilemma of liberty versus authority, the individual against society. He has expressed a preference for the individual; but anyone who prefers to stress society's claims can easily turn most of Mill's formal arguments against him. (One such Victorian answer to Mill was written by James Fitzjames Stephen, *Liberty, Equality, Fraternity*.) But this tract with its magisterial style and high seriousness remains one of the great Victorian period pieces.

Mill's social-economic views, while also fundamentally "liberal," were not complacent. He questioned in a well-known passage whether all the machinery thus far invented had yet lightened the toil of a single person, and said that "the restraints of communism would be freedom in comparison with the present condition of a majority of the human race." In the *Political Economy* he defined property as what one has "produced by one's own exertions" (or received by legitimate gifts from one who did so earn it). But he held that the worker in the factory is not entitled to the whole of his produce, because machinery and materials are also involved. He often expressed sympathy for the ideals of socialism while doubting that it could work without compulsion in the present state of human nature. As noted, he was willing to make exceptions to the rule of economic individualism and the list of these steadily increased.

But as the classic mid-Victorian liberal, Mill fought for such causes as votes for women (his essay "On the Subjection of Women" is almost as famous as "On Liberty"), Jewish admission to Parliament, freedom of the press, and freedom for the orators on soapboxes in Hyde Park, which he once saved by a filibuster when he sat as an independent member of Parliament. Mill may be credited with almost single-handedly giving liberalism the larger meaning it has since conveyed to the minds of Anglo-Americans, of "an attitude rather than a set of dogmas" (Theodore M. Greene)—the attitude of open-mindedness, dispassionate and skeptical consideration of all views, faith in a process, a method, a climate of opinion rather than in any particular creed. Liberalism had previously meant, much more nearly, the doctrines of atomistic individualism, hedonism, and also laissez-faire: the "economic man" of Adam Smith, the calculating pleasure-seeker of Jeremy Bentham. As such, it had been a somewhat narrow and barren ideology, if a potent one. Generous-minded men, filled with large visions of hope in human brotherhood, men such as Mazzini, for example, who despised what he knew as "liberalism," were repelled by it, declaring it to be selfish and materialistic. But Mill imparted to English liberalism his own catholicity and libertarianism, his steadfast faith in the free individual as something spiritually noble. "The saint of rationalism" has recently been seen (by Maurice Cowling) as really at heart a kind of narrow-minded fighter for his own particular set of preconceptions; but this view is unusual and the interpretation strained: Mill's typical spirit is quite the reverse. Under his influence even liberalism's deep-seated fear of the state could melt; for no dogma is sacred, only the individual is, and perhaps he may be defended and strengthened by some forms of state aid.

Mid-century liberalism was represented in France, where it was weaker than in Great Britain but far from nonexistent, by Prévost-Paradol, whose *France Nouvelle* (1868) is a kind of Gallic *On Liberty*. (Both Mill and Prévost-Paradol, as a matter of fact, were influenced by Alexis de Tocqueville, perhaps the greatest liberal of them all and another Frenchman.) Prévost-Paradol regards democracy perhaps a bit more favorably than Mill, seeing in the people a check on Parliament, though he would have the popular will checked by an upper legislative chamber not popularly elected, an independent judiciary, and strong institutions of local government. This decentralization and pluralism carried echoes of the Ancien Regime in a France strongly centralized since Napoleon; antistatist and antisocialist, but libertarian and to a degree democratic (universal suffrage), Paradol's "New France" would indeed have been a new blend of ingredients in the French tradition, and was not so far from what soon came into existence in the Third Republic. He wrote it in the last days of the Second Empire, when even Napoleon III was making his way toward the "liberal Empire." After his defeat in war and the subsequent shock to French pride, against all expectations a liberal-democratic republic arose from the ashes and gradually put down roots in France.

This tribute to the spirit of the age was matched by Great Britain's step in liberalizing the suffrage in 1867, after intensive debate and much lamentation from those who feared the death of liberty as well as stability at the hands of a mobocracy.[3] A new era of politics came in the wake of the Second Reform Bill, with new leaders and new issues. It was, for Britain, the decisive turning point of the century politically, the First Reform Bill of 1832 having really not brought any marked change in the aristocratic tone and tenor of British political life. Whether the delicately balanced British political mechanism could really survive democracy, commentators as wise as Walter Bagehot honestly doubted; it was as much a gamble here as in France. But in both countries the feeling was that there could be no turning back, and for the rest of the century the task was adjustment to this potent force, mass democracy. Nothing influenced thought nearly as much.

Many dynamic processes were at work transforming Europe and the world in this epoch. Italy and Germany attained their national uni-

---

[3]These "Adullamites," as John Bright derisively christened them, led by Robert Lowe, contributed the most brilliant and enthusiastic speeches to the great debate. Mill, though he supported the bill, shared some of these doubts about it.

fication (1860–1871) in the most exciting developments on the Continent. Russia freed her serfs (1861) and began slowly to advance toward a modern industrial civilization. Europe achieved her greatest power ascendancy of all time in the world, expanding after 1870 all over the globe in the era of "imperialism." Wealth, power, and success in the realm of politics and social structure, (relatively, at least) brought a mighty surge of confidence; belief in progress approached the status of a religion. Technology inspired daily gasps of wonder and practical science almost monopolized public attention, for this was the age of Faraday and Edison, Gauss and Siemens, Pasteur and Hertz. The national cultures of each European state came of age as popular education and patriotic history held up to admiration the success story of each people: England from Alfred to Victoria, France from Capets to the Republic, accounts of slow but inevitable growth.

Spiritually, Europe was far from at peace; the surge of material power and wealth carried in its wake grimmer phenomena, such as industrialism's bleak landscapes and exploited workers, or a bourgeois vulgarization of culture. It also brought the celebrated Victorian crisis of religious faith. But the classic age of the nineteenth century produced some classic ideologies. Among the most important figures were August Comte, Karl Marx, and Herbert Spencer, as well as Mill, all of whom might be described as synthesizers of social doctrine, creators of systems of secular ideology. Charles Darwin fathered a scientific ideology for the age of science. Socialism, liberalism, and democratic nationalism assumed the stature of popular creeds by which men lived, with traditional Christianity's hold generally declining. Romanticism received a check, or at least a dilution: literary realism and naturalism became prominent, bearing strong social themes—we are more likely to meet novels about working people or ordinary burghers than about exquisite souls or North American savages.

Europe was becoming more populous and more complex; far more people were being drawn into the charmed circle of literacy and intellectual culture each year. National education systems grew up in these years, transforming the populace of western Europe from largely unlettered to almost completely literate—elementary education, not secondary, as yet, but still an advance of incalculable importance. For the intellectual historian, this increase in the percentage of people to be considered as part of "the European mind" is as significant as the absolute increase in population, so notable a feature of this era which was dramatically diminishing the death rate through epochal advances in medicine, public health, and food production and distribution. Together, they accomplished a numerical revolution of staggering dimensions. The age of the masses was beginning.

But there were large differences between the nations of Europe in this respect: while England, on one extreme, gave an elementary education to just about every child in the kingdom by 1895, Russia advanced much more slowly and Italy had only about half defeated illiteracy. The industrialized countries of western Europe opened a large gap between themselves and the more "backward" peoples of eastern Europe, not only in education but in wealth, social mobility, degree of popular participation in civil liberties, and in government.

No single theme exhausts the richness of the generations lying between the revolutions of 1848 and the end of the century; indeed, eclecticism was a notable feature of the epoch, a drawing on all past styles in architecture, for example. But on the whole, intellectually speaking the dominant motif continued to be that of social ideologies, now extended into massive synthetic systems. Pure philosophy and religious speculation went on, but do not stand out for us as characteristic. Comte, Marx, and Darwin will always hold their rank as the classic statements of the century, whatever ravages time may make on their once proud systems. Comte and Marx offered what we see today as systems of secular religion based on science (though Marx would have vehemently denied that he created a religion). Darwin, strictly a scientist, revolutionized many areas of thought and infused strength into ideologies stressing evolution. These are the three giants of the nineteenth century's noontime, as Nietzsche, Freud, and Bergson were the masters of its twilight period.

Comte and Positivism

Comte's first writings go back to the early 1820s, when he was working under Saint-Simon; the crux of his positive philosophy appeared in six volumes between 1830 and 1842. Partly overlooked during the romantic revolutionary excitement of the 1830s and 1840s, Positivism emerged, somewhat transformed, to become the reigning intellectual orthodoxy of the Second Empire, 1851–1870. Through John Stuart Mill principally, Comte's influence spread into England. It is recognized now as one of the leading systematic philosophies of the century, though, in common with the similar great "social syntheses" made by Marx and Spencer, its rating may not be high. These vast edifices of thought which tried to subsume everything in one system seem incongruous today; they were the work of amateurs who assumed omniscience. But the intellectual energy that went into them cannot be denied, and for the nineteenth century they were the nearest thing there was to a new synthesis of knowledge. Basil Willey has commented that Comte was a nineteenth-century schoolman, basing his *Summa* "not on dogmatic theology, but on dogmatic science."

He did feel acutely the need for a complete reconstruction of ideas to replace the "intellectual anarchy" that was an aftermath of the French Revolution, a feeling he shared with Maistre, Saint-Simon, Hegel. As Saint-Simon's secretary, he came to feel that the socialist count was too much in a hurry. He was right in seeking to found a new science of society based on the positive facts and scientific method, wrong in leaping to his conclusion about the shape of the new society. But when Comte branched out on his own he showed himself quite as doctrinaire as Saint-Simon. Certainly the note of authority was strong in his plan for social reconstruction. Order must be reestablished in Europe, and having found the right foundation Comte proposed to make everybody accept it, by means of a suggested authoritarian social structure of which the high priests of positivism were to be the directors. Comte was as anti-individualist as any socialist, though he preferred to keep private property and the family. He was, if anything, more so. John Stuart Mill, who was attracted to some features of positivism, pronounced Comte's social plan "the completest system of spiritual and temporal despotism which ever yet emanated from a human brain, unless possibly that of Ignatius Loyola." Its hostility to representative government and approval of the Napoleonic dictatorship gave it its standing under the Second Empire.

Comte thought he had laid the foundations for social reorganization in his philosophy. The method appropriate to modern times is the scientific or "positive." Comte put forward his famous "three stages" theory of human development, according to which society passes from the theological to the metaphysical to the positive stage, based on the dominant mode of thought typical of each period. His history, like Hegel's, was highly speculative; it seems impossible to fit the actual facts into this scheme. For example, anthropologists no longer accept the progression within religion as postulated by Comte, from fetishism to polytheism to monotheism. Historians would have to point out among other things that science appeared as early as the ancient Greeks and metaphysics as late as Comte's contemporary Hegel. If we reduce the Comtean formula to the statement that primitive peoples are not capable of modern thought, it becomes little more than a tautology.

In brief, the same objections to so staggeringly oversimplified a scheme may be raised against Comte's as against other examples of this sort of thing: Marx's five stages, Hegel's three political epochs, etc.[4]

---

[4]In Italy the "new science" of G. Vico, dating from the eighteenth century, came into its own at this time. Vico's phases of all civilizations were the religious (theocratic), heroic (aristocratic), and humane (democratic).

Nevertheless, these "philosophies of history" though now outmoded were exciting at this time and the nature of their appeal may readily be seen. We have already discussed this in connection with Hegel. Comte had at least this advantage over the German, that his historical system purported to rest on the facts and not on a speculative theory, thus was attuned to the scientific age. So discriminating a critic as John Stuart Mill thought the three stages an illuminating and reasonably accurate key to the natural evolution of civilization.

Europe was now in the positive stage, and needed to reconstruct its civilization on that basis. To Comte this meant, to repeat, a highly organized social order. The existing stage of liberty and laissez-faire he regarded as the interlude of anarchy between two eras, an anarchy he proposed to bring to an end as speedily as possible. The new scientific order would not be less organic and hierarchical than the older orders dominated by priests and metaphysicians.

Positivism means the method of observed facts, handled with the use of hypothesis but refraining from any conclusions about the substantive nature of reality. Comte agreed with Kant that science studies only the phenomena. In his own words: "The human spirit, recognizing the impossibility of obtaining absolute ideas, renounces the search for origins and goals of the universe and the effort to know the innermost causes of things, in order to concentrate on discovery, by experiment combined with reason and observation, of the effective laws, i.e. their unchanging relations of succession and similarity." This was not exactly new, and Ernest Renan later reproached Comte with having said, "in bad French," what all scientific minds had known for two hundred years. This was not quite fair; it had really only been known widely and clearly since Kant, and Comte undoubtedly revealed some of its practical implications. He was perhaps philosophically more astute than Marx, though the latter held a Ph.D., for Marx assumed a dogmatic materialism which Comte knew was untenable: we are not justified in saying what the essence of reality is. (Marx held a low opinion of Comte, perhaps in part because he was a rival; "this is miserable compared to Hegel," he thought. Lenin would follow Marx in discarding positivism or phenomenalism for a direct-copy theory of sense perception which seems naive but permits a full-blooded materialism. The Marxists have seemingly felt there is something wishy-washy about positivism, inappropriate to revolutionaries.) Comte felt that we are not justified, either, in atheism, only in accepting the impossibility of having certain knowledge about God. Science is descriptive only; we should not even speak of "causes," only of "observable sequences."

In his Course of Positive Philosophy Comte undertook to arrange the sciences in a logical order; his, obviously, was a mind delighting in tidiness. From the most abstract, mathematics, we proceed through astronomy, physics, chemistry, biology, and finally to the most concrete, sociology, a word of Comte's invention which has stuck in our vocabulary. Sociology, at last possible in the positive stage, steps forward to become queen and capstone of all the sciences. Of this last and greatest science Comte, of course, regarded himself as the discoverer.[5] It included what we should now call social psychology, economics, politics, history, and originally ethics. Later, Comte put ethics and religion at the top, above even sociology, and gave the world the Religion of Humanity.

Comte seems hopelessly to have confused his multiple roles as social scientist, social reformer, and inventor of a new religion, though he believed he had unified them. As one of his British disciples, Frederic Harrison, observed, "Positivism is at once a scheme of Education, a form of Religion, a school of Philosophy, and a phase of Socialism." Could it be all these things at once, effectively? As a school of philosophy it has survived, though Englishmen would be more apt to think of Hume as its founder. Sociology has survived as a discipline, but many others than Comte have contributed to it, and its scope is much narrower than Comte conceived. The Religion of Humanity for a time showed a surprising vitality. Positivist societies were formed in England and France for the worship of great men; there were Comtean churches as far afield as Brazil. (Positivism had a considerable popularity in Latin America.) This was in George Eliot's mind when she expressed her poetic wish,

> O may I join the choir invisible
> Of those immortal dead who live again
> In minds made better by their presence.

Hero-worship had a considerable Victorian vogue, in wider circles than Comte's disciples; quite evidently it "inherited the functions once fulfilled by a living Church" (Walter E. Houghton)—it was a substitute for religion. From Sam Smiles to Ruskin, many a Victorian author held up to admiration, for inspiration, the lives of great men. But as such, the Religion of Humanity fell far short of its author's expectations. Positivism served chiefly as a rallying point for the militantly antireligious.

In regard to positivism as "a phase of socialism," if we may so define it, it never had much appeal. Comte's social utopia most closely

---

[5]It is to Comte's credit that he recognized that each of the sciences has to have its own methods; you cannot "reduce" social science to biological, or biological to mathematical. Certain sociologists who seem to wish to convert social phenomena into statistics are ignoring the warning of the founder of their science, that this sort of procedure often "disguises, under an imposing verbiage, an inanity of conceptions."

resembled an iron dictatorship of social scientists, which is perhaps a fate to be avoided. In practice, he sanctioned the ill-fated "democratic despotism" of Napoleon III. But it may be conceded that Comte did something to advance the cause of socialism by his criticisms of laissez-faire and by his belief that the social instincts evolve with humanity. The path of development is from selfishness to altruism, he taught.

Louis Napoleon's regime, established in 1851 on the ruins of the Second Republic, was much influenced by Saint-Simon and Comtist ideas and undertook some interesting if inconclusive experiments in state socialism. Its economic and social policies were not failures, the collapse coming from an ill-advised foreign policy and defeat in war at the hands of Prussia. But its denial of representative government and full liberty caused its demise to be unlamented. Comte and most of his followers rejected individualism and democracy as the equivalent of anarchy.

If many of the details of Comte seem absurd, his central conception may be a valid intuition of modern man's problem. It is easy to agree with Comte that modern European civilization is "positivist." Is it possible to have a civilization on this basis, that is, without faith in God, without a metaphysic, with only science and technology, which supply our wants very well but give us no values, except to go on supplying more and more wants? Is modern society condemned to be "fissiparous," with no unity—soulless, with no values?

Many of Comte's successors were absorbed in just such problems. Positivism became extremely fashionable in France between 1850 and 1870. Its disciples included Emil Littré the lexicographer, Claude Bernard the psychologist, Hippolyte Taine, critic and historian, and Ernest Renan, one of the most brilliant and versatile French men of letters of the century. This group tended to reject Comte's dabblings in religion as an eccentricity, and accepted only his scientific method. They distinguished themselves from atheists and materialists in the manner indicated: we cannot know ultimate things or essential qualities, only the observed phenomena. They evidently thought, however, that science does give certain knowledge, which a thoroughgoing phenomenalist (*vide* Hume) could hardly believe. They searched for a religion of science. Most of them finally became aware that science itself cannot give us values, ideals, goals. Insofar as we have these, they must come from outside science.

Renan, a passionate seeker, deeply troubled by his skepticism, looked long for a religion he could square with his scientific outlook. He rejected Christianity on the grounds of evidence (his *Life of Jesus*, his best-known work, shocked the orthodox all over Europe by its critical handling of the supernatural claims), and he rejected Hegelianism as too metaphysical. He occasionally came close to doing what some disreputable young poets were about to do, make a religion of art. Like Matthew Arnold, his British contemporary and perhaps kindred spirit, Renan felt the need for religious experience and suggested an esthetic equivalent. But a "religion of science" remained his lifelong quest and he failed to find it, ending in skepticism. He came closest to finding it in a positivistic version of Hegelianism, a theme of progress running through history which gives evidence of God.

In France after 1870 positivism suffered a decline. True, there were some eccentric survivals, especially the leader of the reactionary, nationalistic *Action Française* movement of the twentieth century, Charles Maurras, and also so vigorous a literary personality as Julien Benda. But strong forces in French thought rejected "scientism" and returned to metaphysics and religion in flat defiance of the positivists. (Compare Henri Bergson, or the Catholic revival, or more recently existentialism; in literature, symbolism and surrealism.) Intellectual France has never since felt much attraction for positivism, apparently having received a thorough immunization in the 1850–1870 period.

In Italy, positivism reigned as the leading philosophical school in the later part of the century, its chief systematizer being Roberto Ardigo. Comte's influence in nineteenth-century England (and the United States) was far from negligible: in the former, to the well-known names of John S. Mill and George Eliot one must add a number of others. A British disciple was Richard Congreve, Oxford don in the 1850s, whose pupils included the leading publicist of English positivism, Frederick Harrison, and also E. S. Beesly. But Comte's influence extended to men who were not in any sense "disciples" but whose own independent thought received definite impulses from positivism: powerful voices such as Herbert Spencer, H. G. Wells. In Germany, Comte's direct influence was not great, but there was a parallel movement in the form of "back to Kant"—the positivist or phenomenalist Kant, in reaction against the romantic and Hegelian metaphysics; one might also include the materialism of the Young Hegelians (see pages 277–79). By and large, the 1850–1880 period was uniquely "positivist."[6] Anglo-Saxon philosophy since World War I has been invaded by other forms of positivism (logical positivism) which owe less to Comte than to other sources, though there are affinities. This more recent chapter in intellectual history will be handled later.

[6]James H. Billington, "The Intelligentsia and the Religion of Humanity," *American Historical Review*, July, 1960, discusses the vogue for Comte among Russian intellectuals in the 1870s; the French positivist tended to supplant Hegel and to precede Marx as the leading influence from the West on Russian sociopolitical thought.

In the broadest sense, it might be said that modern Western civilization is positivistic, in that metaphysical or religious modes are not congenial to it. This would be true of the average mind, the common man's, more so than of the intellectual's or artist's. Everyday life is so surrounded with the technological and the scientific, so extensively "rationalized," so conditioned to mechanical models and explanations, that conscious mental life runs naturally and normally in grooves that can be called "positivist," that is, scientific, rational, nonmetaphysical, averse to mysticism or any truths not immediately verifiable by experiment or demonstration. For better or worse, that is the kind of culture most people live in. "What grows upon the world is a certain matter-of-factness," Walter Bagehot wrote. He blamed it on business as well as science. So Comte, though far from inventing this feature or being the only thinker to express it, identified himself with a basic trait of modern civilization. And his belief in a tightly organized, hierarchcal society ruled by the scientists may not miss by much the modern forms of totalitarianism.

Literary Realism

The specific post-1848 atmosphere was, of course, highly conducive to a positivist reaction against the romanticism, idealism, and sentimentality of the previous generation. All over Europe, men in all walks of life felt what Napoleon III's minister, Emile Ollivier, expressed when he said "We have collected in our hearts enough images, sentiments, aspirations, too many. . . . We must, to make these things useful, fill ourselves with practical facts." This was the generation of Cavour and Bismarck, as well as of Pasteur and Darwin: the realistic, fact-minded generation. The reaction extended into literature, which reacted strongly against romanticism, by retreating to a realistic, even humdrum description of the ordinary. Romanticism had begun to fade by the 1840s and was almost fully out after 1850, despite lingering vestiges. In France, the "art for art's sake" movement accused the romantics of sentimentality and sloppiness, demanded a greater sense of form and discipline, and also rejected romantic subject matter ("Deliver us from the Middle Ages!" cried Theophile Gautier, the leading spirit of this school.) "Art pour l'art" insisted upon more careful craftsmanship as well as less moralizing and philosophizing in literature. These French writers were disgusted with bourgeois society, retreated to a private world, became rebels and "bohemians" and thus began a literary attitude destined to carry on into the later period. Flaubert, the leading novelist of the 1850s and 1860s, practiced a severely objective, "scientific" approach to literature, and dealt realistically with far from heroic people.

The book of the hour was *Madame Bovary* (1857), which is among other things a savage satire on romanticism. Poor Emma, a lady of some spirit and intelligence, trapped in marriage with a clod in the provinces, dreams of Prince Charmings and a grand world but is led to destruction by her inability to grasp reality. Yet Flaubert includes a hatred of this stupid society in which Mrs. Bovary, a person of potential creativity, is trapped. She is Jude the Obscure and Tonio Kroeger and all the American "rebels against the village" of a half-century and more later. Flaubert, like the poet Baudelaire, was a bitterly alienated personality. For them Art was a retreat from a most unsatisfactory world, an ivory tower: "Give me the highest one possible," cried Flaubert. A fierce hatred of the existing bourgeois society accompanied an extreme disillusionment with politics, associated with visionary romantic schemes and dreams. The thing about *Bovary* that most startled and upset Flaubert's readers was its amoralism. No edifying moral was drawn; it was a sad piece of life ending in tragedy and left at that. Even Sainte-Beuve complained that "The good is too much absent; not a single character represents it," while Ruskin contrasted such "foul" fiction, utterly demoralizing, with "fair."

The same lean, spare, detached style, using irony, "dry," shaped with fastidious craftsmanship, could be found in the poems of Baudelaire and in the writings of other great "realists" of this era such as Flaubert's friend, the Russian emigré Turgenev. Its detachment went with a mood of pessimism. The philosopher for this disenchanted post-1848 antiromanticism was, in its gloomier moods, the brilliant misanthrope, Arthur Schopenhauer. In his younger years Schopenhauer had challenged the great Hegel but failed to win adherents; in his old age, after 1848, he became fashionable. Philosophically, Schopenhauer asserted that the universe is not Hegel's Reason but is Will, a blind amoral striving expressed in us as wanting, desire, appetite. In seeing the world as an arena of power, without meaning or purpose, and in seeing reason as a tool of instinct, Schopenhauer's vision came close to Darwin's though expressed in quite different terms. He recommended art as the only antidote to an intolerable existence—other than that extinction of the will which Oriental philosophy aspired to as the ultimate wisdom. In esthetic contemplation we can achieve a degree of disinterestedness and thus escape from the tyranny of the will. An interesting and highly readable philosopher, Schopenhauer appealed to this generation both in his elegant pessimism and in his estheticism.

The French writers shocked the English; but in Britain too there was an antiromantic reaction. The great Victorian novelists—Thackeray, Trollope, George Eliot—followed what might be called the cult of the commonplace; "the setting of tragedy moves to the abodes of the humble," observes Mario Praz, whose book on the Victorian novel is titled *The Hero in Eclipse*. A democratic art, celebrating the simple virtues of ordinary people, may be found here. The great poet Robert Browning examined man as he is. This Victorian literature differed as far as possible from the French in that it observed the Victorian reticences about sex and was highly edifying and morally earnest, as well as basically optimistic (though George Eliot was as aware of a crisis of faith as was Matthew Arnold). The exceptions, like the Francophile Swinburne, were scandals. But the same theme of realism may be seen in both, and it is in good part a reaction to the excesses of romanticism.

The Darwinian Revolution

The progress of science had continued, at the end of the eighteenth century and into the nineteenth. More precise calculations on the moon, planets, and comets perfected the Newtonian system. The discovery of the planet Uranus and the satellites of Saturn owed most to the German-born English astronomer, Herschel. Having measured accurately the distance to sun and moon, and arrived at a notion of the fantastic distances of the stars, astronomers by the end of the century came upon the stunning fact of the existence of other *galaxies*. Herschel and Laplace formulated hypotheses concerning the origin of the stars and planets. The latter in 1796 summed up the *System of the World*, presenting it almost rhapsodically as a triumph of scientific method and a proof of the orderliness of nature.

There was also the breakthrough in chemistry. It is interesting that Coleridge, speculating about the influence of scientific ideas on other branches of knowledge, thought that the discoveries of Scheele, Priestley, and Lavoisier, "reducing the infinite variety of chemical phenomena to the actions, reactions, and interchanges of a few elementary substances," would affect philosophy and other fields of thought no less than Newtonianism had done in the eighteenth century. It did not quite prove so, but the influence was hardly negligible. It may be significant that Fredrich Engels, when illustrating the laws of dialectical materialism in the physical sciences, tended to use examples from chemistry.

The path of progress in electrical phenomena, from Volta and Galvani at the end of the eighteenth century to Michael Faraday's discovery of the generator in the 1830s, prepared for that mighty invasion of the life of man by electricity later in the century (electric lights, trolley cars, etc.). But with all due regard for these celebrated achievements, destined to alter the lives of millions and contribute to their welfare, the most significant developments in the sciences in the nineteenth century, at least from the standpoint of thought in general, lay in the realm of biology, of life, especially its evolution. The Frenchman Pasteur has been called "the Galileo of Biology" (Karl Popper) because of his contributions to bacteriology and medicine; but in the history of ideas by far the largest figure is Charles Darwin.

The road to Darwin's theory of biological evolution actually led through another science. The science of geology came into its own in the closing years of the eighteenth century. The Geneva geologist, de Saussure, seems to have been the first to use the term, in 1779. It may be said to have attained full status in 1788 when the Scotsman, James Hutton, presented his "uniformitarian" theory. All during the eighteenth century there had been speculation about the meaning of fossils and about the earth, but it was often fanciful. The German mineralogist, A. G. Werner, proposed a hypothesis in 1780 that the earth was originally engulfed in ocean, which subsided leaving behind the various formations, minerals, and fossils. This was the "catastrophist" or "neptunist" school, which had many followers, in part because it squared well with Biblical stories. Hutton then caused a sensation by proposing to account for the phenomena by the steady operation of the same natural forces over what then seemed immensely long periods of time. This was "uniformitarianism," and it stirred the wrath of some religious critics because it could hardly be adjusted to a literal reading of the Old Testament. Between the Catastrophists and the Uniformitarians a lively competition ensued—which is always good for the progress of a science. We would say today that both were partly right; but concerning the matter of the time element Hutton was right, and this revolution in time constitutes on any reckoning one of the great changes in man's conception of his world. Coming between 1788 and 1830, this revolution is comparable in some ways to the seventeenth- and eighteenth-century revolution in astronomy: to the immensity of space, it has been well said, was added the immensity of time. "Oh, how great is the antiquity of the terrestrial globe," Lamarck, the French paleontologist, exclaimed. "And how little the ideas of those who attribute to the globe an existence of six thousand and a few hundred years duration from its origin to the present!"

There were those, during the period of conservative domination in England from 1794 to 1820, who attacked Hutton and his followers as dangerous subversives; so also Lamarck in France. But as data were collected, especially in the area of paleontology, rigid conservatism had to give way. The Reverend William Buckland, an Anglican clergyman, became a leading geologist and fathered a sort of compromise between scriptural and geological views; he seemed to uphold the Deluge, yet the Bishop of Chichester noted his ambivalence in a witty paraphrase of Pope on Newton:

> Some doubts were once expressed about the Flood:
> Buckland arose, and all was clear as mud.

At this time geology, it has been said, became something like the favorite outdoor sport of the English upper classes; certainly it flourished there preeminently, though French scientists such as Cuvier and Lamarck made signal contributions.

It remained for Charles Lyell, in 1830–1833, to write the definitive geological synthesis. Lyell was a thoroughgoing uniformitarian, and he brushed aside religious objections as irrelevant. His geology formed an important part of the background for the biological discoveries of Darwin; "I feel as if my books came half out of Sir Charles Lyell's brain," Darwin once wrote. The time-revolution disposed of one obvious objection to an evolutionary theory, while increasing knowledge about fossils suggested its possibility. But Lyell was not an evolutionist. He could not find in the fossils sufficient evidence for the transformation or progression of species, that is, one actually growing out of another. Indeed for many centuries this had been the invincible obstacle; it was a stumbling-block to evolution comparable to that which the problem of motion had presented to the Copernican theory. As in the case of the slow acceptance of the Copernican hypothesis, one finds here that Biblical prejudices played a smaller part in delaying the evolutionary theory than is often suggested. The real difficulty lay in overcoming the dogma of constancy of species, which the biological evidence seemed to support. No examples of such change of species seemed to be found in nature; the evidence, notably the sterility of animal hybrids, showed the opposite.

Since time immemorial, reaching back to Aristotle, European thought had speculated about a "great chain of being," a logically complete range of life forms arranged in a hierarchy from lowest to highest. The chain ascending upward may suggest evolutionism to us, but it was always then conceived as a *static* hierarchy, a plan emanating from God's mind which was pleasing in its order and which was given for all time. Forms stayed as they were and did not change. The chain of being might be conceived as organically related, like a single great body or like an electrical circuit, and it could evolve into an evolutionary theory. But the traditional doctrine did not entertain any notion of evolution through time, of the transformation of species by gradual and natural means. Aristotle held that the world was created from all eternity and had no beginning—a most profoundly unevolutionary outlook. This is not to say that no one had ever proposed the idea of evolution. Among the ancient Greeks, who canvassed all ideas, Anaximander and Empedocles suggested it. As in the case of astronomy, Aristotle prevailed over their view.

The eighteenth century had shown an enormous interest in biology. Buffon was one of the most popular writers of the age, and other distinguished *philosophes*, including Maupertuis and Diderot, speculated on the origins of life and the nature of species, speculations quite natural in any curious age released from conventional explanations. Biology was somewhat of a factor in romanticism and German philosophy, suggesting organic to replace mechanistic images. Diderot and Maupertuis may readily be seen as anticipating Darwinism, but again, there seemed no convincing evidence for transformation of species, and the great authority of Buffon was, on the whole, it would seem, thrown against it. These stimulating writings did serve to arouse great interest in the question. It can be said that this period between about 1750 and 1850 was like that century that elapsed between Copernicus and Newton: the question had been raised, there was much interest in it, and growing knowledge; eventually a master jigsaw-puzzle worker would fit all the pieces together.

The pieces to be fitted together came, in a fascinating manner, from many different areas of thought. Darwinism constitutes one of the most interesting of all studies in intellectual history because it shows how much science is a part of the "climate of opinion" of its day. The idea of "survival of the fittest" which Darwin was to turn to such good account as an explanation of biological evolution was suggested to him by Thomas Malthus and Herbert Spencer. Reading Malthus's *Essay on Population*, which expounded the tendency of population to increase faster than food supply, Darwin saw that this must lead to a struggle for survival in which the less durable organisms would die and fail to reproduce themselves.[7] As for Herbert Spencer, this Victorian oracle preceded Darwin in setting forth a ruthlessly competitive natural order. The idea of natural selection through competition in a world where some must go under because there is not enough sustenance for all, came first from the economists. It was "in the air" by the 1830s and Darwin, a naturalist, picked up and applied it to his field of study. He had his hypothesis many years before he presented his proofs in 1858.

From 1800, Europe seemed to be grasping for the concept of evolution, though not until 1858 did Darwin (and, almost simultaneously, Alfred Wallace) cage the elusive idea. The romantic approach to science known as *Naturphilosophie*, an interest of some German philosophers, thought in evolutionary terms, and sometimes believed in transmutation, but, not strictly scientific, its explanation was closer to what later became known as vitalism, that is, a life force immanent in nature which

[7]"It at once struck me that under these circumstances favorable variations would tend to be preserved, and unfavorable variations would be destroyed. The result of this would be the formation of new species."

strives to fulfill itself. Schopenhauer, the interesting German philosophical pessimist, strongly believed that this life force appears in us as an instinct to live which nature uses to trick us into striving, so that the species may be reproduced, an outlook some of which may have worked its way into Darwinism. We need hardly remind the reader how historical-evolutionary the popular systems of Hegel and Comte were; this undoubtedly conditioned men to think in terms of the genetic, developmental explanation of things.[8] So it seems that the century conspired to bring about the theory of evolution.

Already, before Darwin, the French paleontologist Lamarck had proposed a theory to account for the evolution of species. He believed that developed characteristics could be inherited. There are (to choose an example) Polynesian swimmers who have developed in the course of generations an unusual lung capacity, enabling them to stay under water (so we are told) as long as six to eight minutes. Lamarck would have explained this as, perhaps, many people today might do unthinkingly: each generation stretched its lungs by long practice and then handed on this lung power to the offspring. This is wrong, according to modern biologists, who follow Darwin; what happened was that people with unusually large lungs became divers, and the others did not, or perhaps drowned. Darwin usually disparaged and ridiculed Lamarck, whom he accused of intruding desire or purpose into the picture, as if the bird's *wish* to fly gradually succeeded in stretching an organ into a wing. Evolution is simply the mechanical result of survival value, on Darwin's more "scientific" explanation. Some birds happened to have more nearly wing-like organs and these survived, the process being repeated for many generations. Lamarck's theory, of course, rested on the vulnerable hypothesis of the inheritability of acquired traits, though to be sure Darwin did not entirely avoid this, either.

In 1844, the Scottish encyclopedist Robert Chambers published, anonymously, *The Vestiges of the Natural History of Creation*, a work which substantially set forth the Darwinian hypothesis though without Darwin's careful accumulation of scientific evidence. It caused a considerable stir of controversy. Thus the state of the question when Darwin arrived was about as follows. The hypothesis of evolution, in the sense of the transformation of one species into another, all descending from one original form of life, was already familiar, but the evidence for it did not seem sufficient to overcome long-standing and apparently

[8]But Hegel, an evolutionist in his philosophy of history, was not so in his philosophy of nature. There is no temporal, only a logical relationship between man and the lower organisms. "Nature and history are different things," and "Nature has no history" were Hegelian axioms. The cycle of nature is endless repetition from which nothing new evolves, contrary to the situation in human history.

strong objections to it—chiefly, the seeming fixity of species, as attested by the sterility of hybrids, but also certain moral and theological prejudices. Geology and paleontology, however, had strongly suggested its possibility. The "climate of opinion" was favorable to the evolutionary outlook, and some economic writers had called attention to the struggle for existence. It was urgent, it seemed, to either prove or disprove the assertions of Chambers, which had aroused controversy. The Lamarckian theory was not convincing.

Rapidly developing scientific knowledge in a number of fields, and far-ranging scientific expeditions over the whole face of the globe had produced much new data about life on earth. Darwin himself had sailed on the famous *Beagle* voyage, 1831–1836, studying and collecting zoological evidence. As he observed the unusual forms of life on isolated islands, such as the giant turtles on Galapagos, he became convinced that species are not immutable; if so, why should different environmental conditions give rise to different plants and animals? Darwin had his hypothesis by 1835, and his theory, from Malthus, by 1838; he spent the next twenty years patiently assembling every possible strand of evidence with which to tie it all together. (As early as Chambers, i.e., 1844, Darwin had a manuscript, but he would not publish it until he had made it entirely convincing.)

At length, Darwin assembled all the pieces and gave an answer which convinced most independent minds of his day. In so doing he wrote the most important book of the century, by rather general agreement, and took his place along with Galileo and Newton among the greatest of scientists, those who have altered the entire mentality of man. A poll of distinguished people taken at the end of the century to determine the ten most influential books of the century showed that *The Origin of Species* was the only book on every list. Today, the story would hardly be different, though one or two others might also gain unanimous support. A.D.—after Darwin—all was changed utterly.

Darwin's achievement has occasionally been disparaged, because so many other people *almost* hit upon his idea, but the soundest judgment remains in his favor. While scientific discovery like technological invention is always a social product, no credit may justly be taken away from the man who has the genius to make that discovery. Darwin was a very plain and straightforward professional scientist, without philosophical pretensions. His last work was on *The Formation of Vegetable Mould through the Action of Worms*! Subsequently he was drawn into some philosophical issues which were perhaps beyond him. But the combination of scientific research and clear thinking found in *The Origin of Species* is very nearly up to Newtonian standards.

Darwin, then, did *not* originate the theory of evolution. What he did do was (1) provide a wealth of evidence for it, that is, for the mutability of species and (2) propose the theory of natural selection to account for it. Darwin convinced most people that evolution had occurred, and today scarcely anybody doubts it. Assembling data from paleontology, anatomy, experimental breeding, and other fields, the new view represented a triumph for thoroughness and collation of scientific research, a victory which rightly enhanced the prestige of science as a social institution. That is to say, it became clear with Darwin that scientific discovery is less the fitful inspiration of genius than the certain result of steady accumulation of data and the patient collation of it. Darwin had genius, but his warmest admirers confessed it was the genius of infinite pains rather than superhuman intelligence.

Darwin was persuasive not only because of the empirical evidence he drew together but because of the striking hypothesis he put forth to explain how evolution takes place. It is noteworthy that the two things were intimately connected: Darwin began his great twenty-year campaign of fact-collecting *after* he hit upon the theory of natural selection, from which we may infer that a good theory both stimulates and directs research. But it could be that the hypothesis was wrong as explanation, that evolution indeed has occurred but not in the way that Darwin imagined. The theory of natural selection has been modified since Darwin, principally by an understanding of the mechanism of heredity, which was not generally known until 1900.[9] Today few if any biologists deny natural selection's importance but the function of mutation, including macromutation or the accidental production of extreme variants, has brought in an additional factor. The majority of scientists think that variations in heredity *plus* natural selection account for evolution. There are a few who question whether natural selection is really a *major* cause of evolution. (No one can deny that it occurs, and plays *some* part.) It should be noted that Darwin was wrong insofar as he proposed slow and gradual evolutionary change, declaring that "nature makes no leaps." Modern mutation theory stresses the sudden leaps. The giraffe did not get his long neck inch by inch, as Darwin thought, but by monsters of long-neckedness that sporadically appeared and proved to have survival value so runs the current view, roughly, as against original Darwinism. Darwin's view that offspring blend the characteristics of their parents rested on ignorance of the mechanism of heredity (as he knew) and entailed difficulties he could not solve.[10]

[9]The Austrian monk Gregor Mendel published his pioneer findings in 1866 but they were ignored by the men of science until 1900.
[10]If a slightly longer-necked giraffe did appear, by mating with an ordinary one the effect of the mutation would be partly lost, on Darwin's supposition. Modern genetics has established that heredity does not work by simply blending the parental traits; in the genes all traits are preserved and may appear unimpaired in some later individual.

All this may be studied in textbooks of biology or zoology. Clearly Darwin was the founding father of large and important areas of modern biological science, whatever modifications of his original theory new knowledge has made necessary. Our interest is in his impact on wider areas of thought, and in the sharp moral and religious controversies that ensued.

Reactions to Darwin

"With the one exception of Newton's *Principia*, no single book of empirical science has ever been of more importance to philosophy," Josiah Royce wrote. Equally important to social and religious thought, and soon brought into the hustings of popular debate, Darwinism eventually affected just about everything in the modern world. It was immediately controversial, as Darwin had foreseen. Most epoch-making books have been greeted in total silence and had to wait years to be accepted as important: Marx, Freud, and Nietzsche, for example, all took around twenty years to gain recognition. *The Origin of Species* sold out on its first day of publication and made its author immediately famous. Many were dismayed, a feeling not confined to clergymen and little old ladies, shocked at the refutation of Genesis. Some of the keenest minds of the age, and some of the least orthodox, joined in the dismay. George Bernard Shaw wrote that "If it could be proved that the whole universe had been produced by such selection (Darwin's "survival of the fittest"), only fools and rascals could bear to live." Von Baer, the distinguished German scientist, refused to believe in a theory that made men "a product of matter" and debased them to the level of animals, while the Professor of Geology at Cambridge, Adam Sedgwick, declared that acceptance of Darwinism would "sink the human race into a lower grade of degradation than any into which it has fallen since its written records tell of its history." Was not Darwin another Schopenhauer, his science teaching that only accident and blind will rule the universe, or, if gods, "gods careless of our doom," as Matthew Arnold put it? Apart from the fate that might overtake orthodox Christianity, were *any* moral values possible in a Darwinian world? The implication that man is no unique child of God endowed with a soul, but rather an offspring of the amoeba by way of other animals, was disturbing; so was the view of all life as an amoral struggle, "nature red in tooth and claw," filled with pain and death, the sacrifice of countless individuals to the species. Still more so was the indication that the universe is nothing but chance and luck.

Though Darwin made some gesture of appeasement to the religious in his book, he was not a religious man, and steadily grew less so. In his

Autobiography—the undeleted version—he explains how he first re-jected Christianity about 1840 and later also dropped the "theism" that appears in the last two pages of the *Origin*. He undoubtedly shared the position popularized by his vigorous proponent Thomas Huxley as "agnosticism." The acrimony with which the war between science and religion soon began to be waged owed much to the belligerence and even arrogance of Huxley, as well as to the blindness of his most famous adversary, "Soapy Sam" Wilberforce. Huxley and Bishop Wilberforce met in a debate in 1860 on which occasion a famous exchange of insults took place, the clergyman observing that he would rather not claim a monkey for an ancestor and Huxley retorting that he would rather be descended from an honest ape than from one who though endowed with brains refused to use them! These two were hardly typical specimens. Huxley was driven by a rage against the clergy which led him to write privately of an urge to "get my heel into their mouths and sc-r-unch it around"; he made the wholly inaccurate statement that "Extinguished theologians lie about the cradle of every science as the strangled snakes beside that of Hercules"! By no means all clergymen rejected Darwinism —some soon began to find it agreeable to theism—while its foes in-cluded many nonclergymen, scientists among them. Roman Catholics were more inclined to accept, or at least to tolerate, Darwinism because they were freer from Biblical literalism.

But Darwin undeniably moved away from religion. His life story reveals one who early was quite pious but whom Lyell's geology led away from Biblical Christianity; then the hypothesis of natural selection destroyed in his mind the classical arguments for natural religion, drawn from the evidences of design and purpose in organisms. His concluding paragraphs in the *Origin* point to a theism which was in fact quite widely adopted: it is not less wonderful, but *more* so, that God chose to plant the seeds of all life in a few simple forms rather than create each species separately. But Darwin abandoned this position, as a study of his letters and subsequent published writings reveals. There was too much chance and too much evil in the biological world he saw to permit him to believe in a benevolent plan. "I cannot persuade myself that a beneficent and omnipotent God would have designedly created the Ich-neumonidae with the express intention of their feeding within the living bodies of caterpillars, or that cats should play with mice." It was the old Problem of Evil that destroyed Darwin's faith, along with the mud-dle and untidiness in the evolutionary picture which went far to dis-credit the notion of an orderly plan. Darwin was certainly not, like Huxley, a naturally irreligious man. He simply was driven by the evi-dent facts to lose his faith in a "beneficent and omnipotent God." If reproached for destroying religion, he could only answer that he did not invent these harsh facts; they existed.

The thought also struck him, later, that the mind of man itself is a product of the evolutionary order, thus merely a tool of survival. This same idea was to jolt others. The result was evidently to dethrone intelligence or soul as a separate principle, making it merely a factor in evolutionary adaptation. Oddly enough, this would seem to destroy science along with theology, as having any higher validity; everything would have to become just a weapon in the struggle for survival. At any rate Darwin's somewhat confused speculations mirror those of many others; all had been thrown into disorder by this amazing new knowledge. Unwilling to be dogmatic, Darwin called himself an "agnostic," though a recent careful study of his religious views concludes that it would not be too unjust to equate them with atheism. Darwin found absolutely no evidence for a divine creation and providence; that he was not an atheist was owing only to his reluctance to be dogmatic about anything. Perhaps —who knows?—such evidence might appear in the future. Darwin did not find it.[11]

The Aftermath of Darwin: Evolutionary Controversies and Philosophies

I find no hint throughout the Universe
Of good or ill, of blessing or of curse;
I find alone Necessity Supreme;
With infinite Mystery, abysmal, dark,
Unlighted by the faintest spark
For us the flitting shadows of a dream.

So wrote James Thomson in "The City of Dreadful Night." Thomson was by nature a pessimist, but he was not alone in drawing gloomy conclusions from Darwin and science. At a time when belief in the divine inspiration of every line of Scripture was still regarded as the sole foundation of Christianity (Gladstone, the great Oxford-educated Liberal statesman, so argued in 1865), and Christianity was regarded as the foundation of the social order, the discrediting of Genesis was no small matter, and the blows that came from Lyell and Darwin fell on a body already bruised by those of the positivist historians and the schools of Biblical criticism. The theological-Biblical debate has today lost in im-

[11]The disciples of Darwin have continued to be militantly antitheist. Thus Julian Huxley, grandson of Thomas Huxley and distinguished twentieth-century biologist: "Newton's great generalization of gravitational attraction made it possible and indeed necessary to dispense with the idea of God guiding the stars in their courses; Darwin's equally great generalization of natural selection made it possible and necessary to dispense with the idea of God guiding the evolutionary courses of life" (*On Living in a Revolution*, 1944). Huxley's comment on Newton is inaccurate, in that eighteenth-century men did not so construe Newtonianism.

portance, for most Christians no longer construe the Scriptures so literally, but as late as 1925 in the United States (the Scopes trial) it retained considerable power to arouse emotions. Wider than this was the moral debate, concerned with the question of whether Darwinism did not destroy all values by eliminating purpose and design from the universe; many who were not at all orthodox Christians joined in disapproving a creed apparently consistent with no sort of belief in rational order in the world. In one of his books the Victorian author Winwood Reade told of a young man's suicide, under the impact of Malthus and Darwin, whose books he placed, bound in somber colors, on the table in his room, the *Essay on Population* labelled "the Book of Doubt" and *The Origin of Species* labelled "The Book of Despair." Yet others were able to accept Darwinism as meaning progress.

The great debate went on with endless ramifications. A classic story is that of P. H. Gosse, lay minister and naturalist (father of Edmund Gosse, whose *Father and Son* is a Victorian classic), who, struggling to reconcile his Christian faith with his science, hit upon what he regarded as a brilliant answer: God had created the world "prochronically," at a particular and arbitrary moment in its life, *as if* its past history had existed (*Omphalos: An Attempt to Untie the Geologic Knot*). He was laughed out of court. By 1872 Darwin could write that "almost every scientist admits the principle of evolution," and also the theory of natural selection as its means of operation. Yet Louis Agassiz, the famous American (Harvard) naturalist, would not accept Darwin and spent the rest of his life laboring to prove this "monstrous" theory false. Samuel Butler, Victorian freethinker and critic of religious orthodoxy, began by admiring Darwin but came to think that the Cambridge scientist was a deceiver who supplied the wrong explanation; Butler accepted evolution but not natural selection, and was led back to Lamarck via St. George Mivart, the Roman Catholic biologist, author of *The Genesis of Species* (1871). In *Evolution Old and New*, 1879, Butler attacked the scientific establishment as more bigoted than the religious. Bernard Shaw also became a neo-Lamarckian, but moralists found this more appealing than scientists.

There were harmonizers and accommodaters who sought to show that even Darwinian evolution is consistent with divine purpose. Was there not something sublime in the ascent of man through the eons from primeval slime to intelligent and spiritual being (Henry Drummond)? Admit the cruelty and suffering, one still had as an undeniable fact the grand result. Asa Gray, the American naturalist, complimented Darwin for having *restored* teleology to nature! There was design, if "on the installment plan": Darwin himself had once been reduced to awe at the greater wonder of God contriving to draw all life from a single simple beginning. In any event, as Mr. and Mrs. Carlyle had pointed out, whether we are or are not derived from the amoeba is irrelevant to our spiritual life. Josiah Royce, the distinguished American philosopher, held to an evolutionary idealism and pointed out that the human mind does seek values, is not animal-like: these are facts as incontrovertible as Darwin's, if puzzlingly different from them. Darwin had not and could not make man a brute. He had given him new and puzzling knowledge, but so long as human consciousness exists it will rise above matter to seek understanding and the good.

There were also vitalist approaches to evolution which pointed out that Darwin had not addressed himself at all to the important question of what really (in a final sense) causes the evolutionary process. Granted that natural selection does take place, and with an apparent blindness and cruelty (millions of individuals, whole species even, may perish because of some accidental change in their environment), it would seem that other factors are present, too, including an intelligence that runs through all life. The behavior of organisms is often so remarkably purposive that one has difficulty in attributing everything to a mechanistic process. At any rate can natural selection account for the emergence of life itself? There is also running through life a will to live, as Schopenhauer and Bergson noted. Can this inextinguishable vitality be the result of a mechanical process? It must have been there to begin with, though strengthened by natural selection. Perhaps this life force is really the "cause" of evolution, natural selection only the means it uses. If we see a large group of men running a long race, and notice that some of them fall or drop out, while a few run strongly and forge to the front, it would seem odd to say that the cause of the winning of the race (evolution) is the fact that some drop out from unfitness (natural selection), without raising the really interesting question, why are they running? Why do they bother with this rigorous competition at all? Why do they not all sit under a tree and rest? Darwin pointed out that there is competition in nature, and refrained from speculating about the reason. Good; but was he justified in implying that the question has no importance and need not be raised? If natural selection is made into a dogma, it may divert our eyes from other questions of great moment and distort our outlook on nature. So, at least, Henri Bergson was to argue.[12]

The outcome of all these efforts at accommodation with evolution was perhaps uncertain, but in general men learned to live with it, sometimes by making a separation between animal world and human world, nature and value. On this view a great change had taken place in "na-

---

[12]There were other French vitalists—Vandel, Mercier, Varagnac, and more recently the celebrated Jesuit father, Teilhard de Chardin.

ture." "Nature" to the eighteenth century had suggested order, harmony, benevolence, indeed something to be imitated, an agreeable model for man. After Darwin nature might be thought of as fascinating but it was in part terrible and it was not a proper model for human beings. But on the other hand, there were those who embraced the new "naturalism" which placed man in the setting of the natural order and did not separate him so sharply from it as had, for example, the Cartesian or Kantian dualism. Darwinians were "monists" (their foes said materialists) who could not accept any mind-body dualism, any separation between the physical world and the mental. The human animal is an organism like any other, responding to his environment and in part shaping it as he responds. Man became a part of the biological natural order as he had not been before.

If some of the more thoughtful drew pessimistic or tragic conclusions from evolution, most people probably integrated it casually with the reigning belief in progress. Constant and inevitable progress does take place on Darwinian terms, progress of the species or race if often at the expense of individuals. Organisms adapt to their environment and grow steadily more efficient; if the unfit perish the fit live, and life evolves from lower organisms to higher. It was one version of the "idea of progress" for which Victorian stability and economic prosperity provided a favorable atmosphere. Is not the mighty spectacle of nature surging forward over the corpses of countless individuals an inspiring one, if awful?

Philosophically, Darwinism helped discredit idealism or intellectualism. Young philosophers like John Dewey abandoned Hegel for some more naturalistic outlook. Mind, it seemed, must be a product of evolution, ideas of natural selection. Mind could hardly be detached from the organism and erected into a separate principle. If we even believed that the universe makes sense, as Nietzsche was fond of saying, is this not just because those of our ancestors who could not make sense of it failed to survive, and natural selection bred those who did? An instinct, will, or life force may throb through the universe, but intellect is its tool; reason is a survival trait. A character in a Shaw play remarked that the modern view is not "I think therefore I am," but "I am therefore I think." A new reason for distrusting reason had appeared: reason is a product of the nature it purports to understand. If I believe in God, or say that the universe is orderly, I may be doing so because of traits bred into the intellect by the struggle for survival, and if I am tempted to assume the absolute truth of these beliefs I am caught up by remembering that my mind itself is an evolutionary product, hence essentially a survival tool, like the monkey's tail or the giraffe's neck! This "irrationalism" might take various forms: pessimistically, it could be presented as grounds for despair with blind will and instinct ruling the universe; optimistically, it might be said that human intelligence is no less a creative tool for being a part of the natural order. But there remained a fundamental difference between all the new thought and the old, in that for many it was no longer possible to set the human mind *outside* nature. Being a part of nature, the mind had to give up its proud claim to be able to understand it as one understands something from which one is detached. The mind is just that part of our organism that participates in a certain way in the great game of life. Man was no longer Pascal's "thinking reed," his intelligence set against the world.

The implications of Darwinism are too numerous to be recorded. "Evolutionary views have deeply penetrated our present thinking in almost every conceivable field. . . . It has become regular procedure to study phenomena in terms of their development. . . . Interest in evolution has moved out of academic circles even into the field of commerce and industry."[13] Perhaps this judgment attributes too much to Darwinism as such, for the bent of the nineteenth century toward historical explanations and the idea of progress was rather more general; Darwinism may be seen as only a part of this larger pattern, which included such independent forces as Hegelian philosophy, Burkean political thought, aspects of Comteanism, and the maturing profession of historiography. But it is interesting to note that John Dewey, in his famous assessment of Darwin's impact on philosophy (*The Influence of Darwin on Philosophy*, 1909), attributed to him the enthronement of "the principle of transition" or seeing things as involved in processes of change, rather than as Platonic "eternals." Clearly Darwin did exert the greatest force in this direction. For unlike Hegel and Comte he seemed truly scientific. Dewey added that Darwin had shattered the closed metaphysical system of Hegel in favor of a pluralism and experimentalism. One did not simply postulate movement here, one *studied* it, looking closely at every natural object with the eye of the scientist, but looking at it in motion, in process. Thus to many living in the later nineteenth century a whole new vision of things opened up, and evolutionism seemed a refreshing breeze blowing over the somewhat desiccated landscape of idealism.

The rise of science as the prevailing mode of thought, predicted by Comte, owed more to Darwin than to any other one figure. Many noted this change at mid-century. Mark Pattison dated it between 1845 and 1850. Oliver Wendell Holmes, Jr., the great American jurist, reminiscing many years later, thought that of all the intellectual gaps between generations, that between his own and his father's (about 1865) was the greatest: "It was the influence of the scientific way of looking at the

13Walter J. Ong, in *Darwin's Vision and Christian Perspectives*, 1960, pp. 1–2.

world." He mentioned, in addition to *The Origin of Species*, Herbert Spencer and Henry T. Buckle.[14] Buckle was an amateur historian, author of a multivolume *History of Civilization in England* (1857–1861), the Toynbee of his day, whose volumes lined the shelves of many a Victorian library, and who sought to reduce history to an exact science. More famous yet was the apparently omniscient Herbert Spencer, who did not confine himself merely to human history but claimed to have reduced the whole of the cosmos to an exact and evolutionary, science.

Spencer, the most celebrated of mid-Victorian philosophers, was a sort of combination of Comte and Darwin. Like the former, he was a tremendous synthesizer of every field of knowledge, under the general rubric of a scientific or positivistic method—a synthesis which greatly impressed his contemporaries, eager for an integration of thought, but which has since considerably depreciated in value. Someone has called him "the Marx of the middle class"; he could equally well be called the British Comte. A distinctive feature of his philosophy was its stress on evolution, a stress indeed not lacking in Comte, Hegel, and Marx, but which in Spencer is even more pronounced. Influenced by Lyell and von Baer, he popularized "survival of the fittest" before Darwin. Unlike the Cambridge scientist, Spencer proceeded to set about creating a full-scale philosophy of evolution. While Darwin was largely content to nail down the lid on evolution with a large supply of experimental facts, Spencer assumed the case closed and set off on cosmic speculative adventures with it.

The entire universe obeys the same laws of evolution, Spencer affirmed. He wished to show that the evolution not only of life but of the physical cosmos and human society could be reduced to the same laws—an exciting idea, indeed. The laws Spencer found were as follows: things invariably evolve from (1) the homogeneous to the heterogeneous, (2) the undifferentiated to the differentiated, and (3) the unintegrated to the integrated. "From a relatively diffused, uniform, and indeterminate arrangement to a relatively concentrated, multiform, and determinate arrangement." The cosmos began with separate, simple atoms uniformly dispersed through space, and will end, presumably, with highly organized structures working together in a single complex system (rather the reverse of the "primeval atom" theory now popular). Human society began with isolated individuals performing simple tasks without specialization and proceeded towards an order at once more diverse, specialized, and interdependent. Writing voluminously with an encyclopedic knowledge few could match, Spencer tended to bowl over opposition by

[14]Leonora C. Rosenfield, *Portrait of a Philosopher: Morris R. Cohen*, 1962, p. 321.

the sheer weight of this formidable erudition. Darwin called him "about a dozen times my superior" and said Spencer would go down as the greatest thinker of the century. He was certainly the most popular of all serious thinkers, to judge by the sale of his books. "Probably no philosopher ever had such a vogue as Spencer had from about 1870 to 1890," wrote the American publisher, Henry Holt, who had the enviable privilege of selling Spencer's books in the United States. (Between 1860 and 1903, some 368,000 copies of Spencer's various works were sold in authorized editions in the U.S.A., countless others in unauthorized ones.)

Spencer combined with his evolutionary outlook a Comtean positivism (it came to him from more native sources) which insisted that scientific laws are descriptive statements only, telling us nothing about essential natures or origins. The latter doubtless exist but are "unknowable." Like Kant, Spencer invites us to a certain sense of awe before this realm, but we can have no real knowledge about it. Positivists have generally been divided between those who say that there is no point in even talking or thinking about what we cannot know, and those who would not rule out our speculations and intuitive insights into it provided we do not confuse these with knowledge of a scientific order. Spencer belonged to the latter group; he does not forbid us from speculating about the Unknowable. Still, faithful Christians classed him among the "agnostics" who did so much to undermine religious faith. At the same time, it is obvious that (like Marx) he really offered a sort of religion, in the trappings of science.

But in time many of his generalizations came to seem rash, founded on inadequate evidence, made by one who was determined that the facts prove his theory. A Victorian giant, Spencer's reputation has fallen perhaps faster than he deserved, for he seems at least the equal of Comte, Hegel, and Marx. But like those other ambitious "scholastics" he was certainly guilty of letting his speculations outrun the facts on which they were supposedly based. Little if anything now remains standing of his vast intellectual edifice.

Social Darwinism

By far the most notable feature of Spencer's exuberant thought was its application of evolutionary ideas to human society; and of all the spokesmen for what was termed "social Darwinism" he was the most renowned. There is some irony in Spencer being known as *the* "social Darwinist" since his conception of biological evolution (which he formulated before Darwin's was published) was more Lamarckian than Darwinian (he believed in the inheritability of acquired characteristics). On the other hand, he fully accepted the Darwinian notion of a struggle for existence as the key to evolution. "Survival of the fittest" was his term. An editor of the *Economist* at one time, Spencer knew the tradition of laissez-faire liberalism before he turned to evolution and shows us the intimate connection between the two. John Maynard Keynes, the modern economist, wrote that "the principle of the Survival of the Fittest could be regarded as a vast generalization of the Ricardian economics." Typically British, the principle of individualism remained powerful in his evolutionary synthesis. While society grows more complex with progress, it also grows freer and more diverse. The evolution of the individual is toward greater freedom and less constraint. Competition is the key to progress. Spencer's complacent identification of the poor with the unfit who may safely be left to die out is in good part responsible for the later dislike of his whole philosophy. The oft-quoted passage in *Social Statics* (first published in 1851, revised in later editions but not changed in any significant way) argued that "to prevent present misery would entail a greater misery on future generations"; "when regarded not separately but in connection with the interests of universal humanity" individual suffering is seen to be for the best. Spencer was sure that "As civilization advances, government decays"; in this opinion, he was as far as possible at odds with Comte, whom in some other ways he resembles. He takes us back to the Godwinian anarchists at the beginning of the century. He was the principal source of a revival of radical antistatism in Victorian England, against which however there was to be a strong reaction after 1880.

"Social Darwinism" has been a loosely used term. There are in fact several different ways of applying the formula of evolution via natural selection or "survival of the fittest" to human social development. Spencer sometimes mixed them up. One could postulate a competition, first, between whole *societies*, perhaps between nations or states, which compete against each other peacefully and sometimes go to war against each other. Applied here, a social Darwinist might hold that such competition is healthy, even that war tests the character of a people (Hegel as well as Spencer occasionally said this), that out of this struggle for survival between social units we get increasingly efficient societies. Spencer presented this sort of social Darwinism at times, declaring that societies are organisms akin to individual bodies, being functionally organized and experiencing growth; they are tested by their environment and evolve from small and simple to large and complex types.

Or, again, evolution via competition might be said to occur among specific social *institutions* such as the family. As E. B. Tylor, another social evolutionist, put it, "the institutions which can best hold their own in the world gradually supersede the less fit ones, and . . . this incessant conflict determines the general resultant course of culture." Finally, competition with resultant progress could be applied to *individuals*—the form of social Darwinism most often associated with Spencer. Here, there is perhaps a logical distinction to be made (Spencer sometimes confused them) between *biological* competition—the sickly dying off, the healthy surviving—and *economic* competition. In any case, the competition between individuals *within* a society is clearly a different thing from the competition *between* societies and some have thought Spencer guilty of inconsistency in holding both ideas. But he thought, more or less consistently, that free competition made for the best society and the best humanity as well as the best individuals ("best" meaning most efficient, best adapted to the challenge of the environment).

Beyond any doubt Spencer freely mixed ideological elements into his alleged science of society. He owed much to the tradition of liberalism reaching back through the Manchester School to Locke and Hobbes, and he perhaps owed something too to the school of Burke, which had tended to see society as an organism too complicated safely to tamper with. Spencer's world view betrayed his own time and place, just as Comte smuggled his Saint-Simonian predilections into a system supposedly scientific. Yet Spencer gave a great boost to the supposed sciences of sociology and anthropology. The latter rather clearly dates from Darwin and Spencer; it was born under evolutionary auspices. It was assumed that "primitive" peoples represent the first stage in a ladder of development, comparable to the biological ladder; they are our ancestors, in the same way that simple forms of life are the ancestors of the human race. There are universal stages, and laws of development. For example, in religion animism always comes first, monotheism last, in a single straightline path of evolution. Today these views have been discarded or enormously qualified, but the study of different societies gained its initial impetus from an expectation that research would uncover simple laws of development. Thus E. B. Tylor, less dogmatic and more empirical than Spencer, nevertheless expected that in time the laws of development would be revealed; "human institutions like stratified rocks succeed each other in series substantially uniform over the globe." Skepticism about such grand laws of evolutionary succession appeared by the end of the century, when anthropologists tended to find that each primitive society is unique and can be fitted into no schematic pattern. But for the English-speaking peoples Spencer was the fountainhead of both anthropological and sociological science. And the fact that sociology failed to become an important academic discipline in England until quite recently, suffering a severe setback in the first half of the twentieth century, is due in part to the discrediting of Spencer about 1900.

Spencer's brand of "social Darwinism," with its sanctioning of a ruthlessly competitive social order ("root, hog, or die" is the law of life, the American social Darwinist William Graham Sumner bluntly put it), created something of a dilemma for other Darwinians, less inclined to grant indulgent smiles to a capitalistic society. In 1893 Thomas Huxley, the aggressive champion of Darwinism, argued in a well-known series of lectures that in human affairs natural selection is *not* the rule to follow. Progress, he said, consists in working *against* nature and evolution, "checking the cosmic process at every step." He could agree with Matthew Arnold that

> Man must begin, know this, where Nature ends;
> Nature and man can never be fast friends.

"It is an error to imagine that evolution signifies a constant tendency to increased perfection," Huxley wrote. What survives, because it is the best adapted, is not necessarily or usually the best in an ethical sense. Unguided evolution may well lead to moral regression and social failure. Thus did Huxley in part withdraw his faith in evolution.

Clearly this must be so. Victorian social Darwinists usually wished to approve a fairly civilized process of competitive economics, against any sort of state socialism. But if one applied Darwinism to human society literally and thoroughly, one would evidently revert to the prehistoric jungle. The biographer of Adolf Hitler (Alan Bullock) tells us that the only idea the infamous Nazi dictator held to was "a crude Darwinism." To Hitler this meant that only power counts, individuals may be ruthlessly sacrificed, the ill and injured put to death, whole races wiped out because allegedly less biologically fit. Anyone stupid or evil enough to take this sort of social Darwinism at its full value would seem to find in it sanctions for the law of the jungle applied *à outrance*. Though nature might be "red in tooth and claw" in the animal world, no sane person could wish to reduce the society of man to such a condition.

There were those who pointed out that even in the subhuman biological realm conflict is not the only rule. Cooperation also exists as a means of biological survival, as numerous examples of symbiosis and social organization in the animal world testify. Moreover the will-to-power, the life force, the instinct to survive that pulses through all living things, can be "sublimated" so that it works for good rather than evil. Mankind, in particular, evolves by inventing new modes of social cooperation; it has passed to a higher phase of evolution, *rational* evolution, involving the use of brain power rather than brawn. Animals do this to some extent; man has made it supreme. Why should "natural selection" mean physical strife and bloodshed? There is more survival value in the intelligence that organizes peace and social welfare. It was possible in this way to turn the argument against Spencer's cult of dog-eat-dog competition. And, in fact, after 1880 western Europe turned rapidly toward social-welfare modifications of the competitive economic order.

In "Why Darwin Pleased the Socialists," G. B. Shaw made the point, half-seriously as usual, that it took the capitalists down a peg to be told that they were rich not because of their virtue or the design of providence, but simply by accident. Darwinism's hostility to religion, along with its reinforcement of a naturalism that looked squarely at harsh social facts, rendered it pleasing to the Left. The most notable literary offshoot, the Naturalist school of Emile Zola, Jack London, and others of the sort, was daring, brutally frank, and much interested in the lives of the lower classes. Zola was not really a socialist, since he thought, consistently enough with a Naturalist outlook, that no one was to blame and everyone was a victim of circumstances, the capitalists no less than the workers. But no one is likely to read *Germinal* without acquiring a good deal of sympathy for the coal miners. So "social Darwinism" did not always mean rugged individualism of the sort most pleasing to expectant capitalists (John D. Rockefeller and Andrew Carnegie greatly admired Darwin). Socialists sometimes tried to appropriate Darwinism. In his preface to an 1894 book on socialism and science, the British socialist Ramsay MacDonald asserted that "Darwinism is not only not in intellectual opposition to socialism, but is its scientific foundation." That struggle is the law of life, that conditions change and institutions must change too, were principles easily bent to radical usages. It may be relevant to add that Darwin, Huxley, and Spencer were all compassionate men shocked at human suffering and hopeful of alleviating it, and that they all believed progress possible. Spencer was a vigorous anti-imperialist, who believed also that war was obsolete in the modern world. He deeply influenced radicals as well as conservatives, and, in fact, was by nature much more a rebel and an outsider than a member of the British intellectual establishment. So we would be wrong to think of "social Darwinism" only as a creed congenial to the successful. It revealed what Nietzsche called "that Janus-face possessed by all great ideas."

The Idea of Progress

At least one substantial common denominator in all these nineteenth-century ideologies was Progress, that idea the nineteenth century so generally bowed to. "The history of the human race is the history of growth," the English Comtean historian Frederic Harrison proclaimed, as "the meaning of history." The Hegelian, holding that the spirit of God dwells within the historical process and guides it to ultimate completion, and the positivist, refusing to acknowledge such a metaphysical hypothesis as God or Absolute, were equally sharers of the optimistic world view that found in history a steady advance from one beginning to one end, and that a glorious one. One thought that Progress worked through the Absolute without man even being aware of it; the other believed that only in rejecting the Absolute and becoming conscious of his human powers did man learn to advance; neither doubted the existence of Progress. Marx, next to be considered, inherited the Hegelian spirit; Comte's lived on in many bourgeois versions, liberal or conservative, of the idea of progress. (J. B. Bury, in his classic study of this idea, wrote that Comte did more than any other thinker to establish it as a permanent fixture on the mental landscape.) Mill agreed with Comte on this, and Darwin taught most men that incessant advance is the law of life, though doubtless they mistook him if they thought he believed in a purposeful progress. Spencer's incredibly popular evolutionary ideology proclaimed a steady advance, onward *and* upward. A disillusioned post-1919 critic, Emil Brunner, called the idea of progress "an axiomatic belief which needed no proof nor could be disproved . . . a pseudo-religious creed, which to negate was a kind of blasphemy." One can round up some doubters, but there were not many at the high tide of Victorian optimism, and as late as 1908 the distinguished statesman-philosopher of Great Britain, Lord Balfour, proclaimed that "there are no symptoms either of pause or regression in the onward movement which for more than a millennium has been characteristic of Western civilization." What seems remarkable to us is that these beliefs in progress assumed not only a steady onward and upward movement, but a movement of the entire society. We would be inclined to say today that some things doubtless "progress," if we define the term in certain ways—technology becomes more efficient, scientific knowledge accumulates—but other phases of life remain much the same and some deteriorate. It would be a rash man who would claim that art, morality, even political wisdom have advanced. The nineteenth century optimists supposed that the society is a unit which progresses as a whole, so that every part of it is engaged in constant improvement.

This optimism, fed by a steady procession of technological gains, survived the Darwin-induced crisis of faith. And it is a tribute to it that even the greatest critic of Victorian society, Karl Marx, embraced it too, in his way.

10

Nineteenth-Century Ideologies: Marxism

If previously the gods dwelt above the earth, now they have become the center of it.

KARL MARX

The fundamental problem of social science is to find the law of motion according to which any state of society produces the state which succeeds it and takes its place.

KARL MARX

Foundations of Marxism

A native of the city of Trier on the French border, Karl Marx first became acquainted with Friedrich Engels in Paris whither he had gone in 1843. Prior to this, attendance at the University of Berlin had exposed him to the school of Hegel, though the great philosopher had died a few years before, in 1831, and this was a lasting and significant influence, much though Marx might disparage certain aspects of Hegelianism. Marx obtained his Ph.D. at Jena with a dissertation on the ancient materialists, Democritus and Epicurus—an appropriate topic for him in view of his long commitment to philosophical materialism. A career in the German universities might have been in the offing for the brilliant young man, as it had been for Hegel and would be for Nietzsche; but Marx was always uncompromisingly radical. He had adopted the atheistic and naturalistic views of the young (left-wing) Hegelians of whom the foremost was Ludwig Feuerbach. Outspoken impiety doomed his chances for a professorial post.

In his early years Marx produced a body of writings of a quite romantic nature, reflecting a deep concern at the plight of the individual in society. These remained unpublished until quite recent times, when they have attracted much interest. Marx turned to journalism, then went to Paris to breathe the intoxicating air of that intellectual capital in the giddy forties, when the socialist ideas of Fourier, Saint-Simon, and especially Proudhon were being discussed. Here also came colorful Russian revolutionaries such as Michael Bakunin. The meeting with Engels resulted in a friendship for life, bringing to Marx support both financial and intellectual on which he was often to lean. The two men seldom disagreed, an unusual partnership, and one of considerable moment, for without Engels, a man of some means, Marx could surely never have spent his life writing books which few bought. For Marxists, it would seem to be an awkward fact that the proletarian theory owes its existence to the money of Engels, a capitalistic factory-owner. (Engels was the son of a German textile manufacturer, manager and part owner of a branch his father set up in Manchester, England, ultimately inheriting the business on his father's death. Marx himself was of bourgeois lineage, son of a moderately well-to-do lawyer.)

Marx eagerly imbibed socialist ideas in Paris. Soon came the revolutions of 1848, and the *Communist Manifesto*, a brief work written by Marx and Engels for a left-wing organization, which had little influence on the events of 1848 but was destined to lasting fame as the most concise and eloquent statement of the Marx-Engels position. (The first draft of the *Manifesto* had been made in 1847, before the Revolution.) For by this time the main contours of Marx's thought were pretty well set. Like Darwin, he had his thesis and would spend the rest of his life supplying the documentation. The excitement of 1848 probably never left Marx; he spent the rest of his life preparing for other revolutions, which never came. Marx returned to Germany to edit a newspaper in Cologne for a time, but to his disgust the revolution failed and he was forced to leave the country. He came to London in 1849, home of all refugees, and lived there the rest of his life, happily married[1] but perennially poverty-stricken until the last twelve years of his life (he died in 1883 at 65). He would not adopt the suggestion of his mother-in-law that he write less about capital and make more of it! He burrowed in the British Museum library, wrote, and organized communist associations. As an organizer he left something to be desired, the famous First International of 1864 amounting to little at the time. His chief opus was *Das Kapital*, the first and only completed volume of which appeared in 1867, written in

---

[1]The picture of Marx's happy marriage must now be somewhat tempered by the account of his fathering an illegitimate child, a family scandal suppressed in good Victorian manner. In their later years the Marxes were far from congenial.

Marx's native tongue. A second and third volume were edited after Marx's death by Engels from his fragments, a fourth later by Karl Kautsky. Marx's failure to finish his *magnum opus* probably indicated problems in his theory he could not solve. There were other tracts, polemical, journalistic, or theoretical. He died and was buried in relative obscurity in London, though his fame was beginning to spread on the Continent in the last years of his life. He was surrounded by a faithful corps of German socialists.

His intellectual background was an unusually rich one. He had experienced the best of German, French, and British thought. Having gotten philosophy virtually from the mouth of the great Hegel, he then drank up socialism in the cafes of Paris at a vital moment, and went on to study economic theory and economic history in London, where he laid the great library of the British Museum under heavy contribution. He kept abreast of current thought in this age of ideas and proved to be one of the ablest of all synthesizers. He blended German philosophy, French social doctrine, and British political economy in a system that could well claim to have drawn on all the best minds of the nineteenth century and forged them into a harmonious unity. With considerable confidence, to say the least,[2] he believed that he had superseded all previous thinkers and ushered in a new age of man of which he was the pioneer theorist. On his death he left a movement, organized as the Social Democratic party, which soon was the most vigorous and successful socialist party in Europe and went on to play a vital role in modern history. Of this movement the Communist party was an offshoot. The success of these parties could be traced directly to the vigor and apparent clarity and profundity of Marx's thought.

At the same time, critics thought they detected major flaws in Marx's system early, and it never received much acceptance in the academic or professional worlds. Some of his own followers conceded by 1900 that since his main prophecies had turned out wrong, his theory would have to undergo fundamental revision. Accepted today in one part of the world at full value as the greatest thinker of modern times, he is widely regarded in the other as an intellectual mountebank who really founded a peculiarly narrow and intolerant religion. There are yet others who think that Marx was truly one of the seminal thinkers of

[2]He was in fact intolerably arrogant according to some accounts. Carl Schurz's comment is classic: "I have never seen a man whose bearing was so provoking and intolerable. To no opinion which differed from his own did he accord the honor of even a condescending contradiction. Everyone who contradicted him he treated with abject contempt. . . . I remember most distinctly the cutting disdain with which he pronounced the word 'bourgeois,' and as a bourgeois, that is as a detestable example of the deepest mental and moral degeneracy, he denounced everyone that dared to 'oppose his opinion."

the modern era but that he suffered at the hands of his own excessively enthusiastic disciples, who made him into a messiah and built a church around him in a way that he would not have approved. So there is a Marxist puzzle. What no one doubts is the enormous influence of the ideas produced by Marx and, lest we forget, Engels, who accepted the intellectual superiority of Marx but was himself a prolific writer.

Dialectical Materialism

Most people probably associate Marxism with either (1) the economic analysis of capitalism, purporting to show its inevitable destruction from its own "contradictions" and replacement by socialism or communism or (2) the broader materialist interpretation of history, which alleges that the fundamental causal factor in social change at any time is the technological or economic. But it is necessary to begin, as Marx did, with the philosophical framework of *dialectical materialism.* "Materialist in substance and dialectical in manner," this philosophy sought to combine the Hegelian dialectic with a materialist view of reality. It is important to grasp Marx's position here, to realize the curious way he attempted to combine a scientific with a metaphysical outlook. In many respects, Marx was hard-headedly empirical or positivistic, that is, he would not accept knowledge that was not evident to the senses. In his mature years he shared the outlook of Comte and Darwin and ridiculed "speculative idealism." Nevertheless he insisted on retaining Hegel's dialectical *method,* the formula of dialectical movement. This, Marx claimed, is how things actually do behave. When we look at nature or history we find that everything exhibits in its activity and development a dialectical pattern of action and reaction. The dialectic is a characteristic of matter. It is important, but difficult, to know whether Marxists assert this as an empirical observation, which in that case might not always be true, or as a dogma beyond criticism.

Marx and Engels were quite insistent that dialectical materialism *is* Marxism. "Dialectics," Engels wrote, "is nothing more than the science of the general laws of motion and development of nature, human society, and thought." It unifies the sciences, which are found to be one, everything obeying the same dialectical laws. This element of Hegel lingered on in Marx; and indeed for the philosopher who was his master Marx had a high regard. Hegel had only got the terms reversed; reality is not mind and idea, as he thought, but brute matter; yet he had correctly divined the way reality *behaves.* Dogmatic Marxists have always equated the dialectical method with the scientific method, and assume dialectical behavior to be an inherent property of all things.

As stated by Marx and Engels the three laws of the dialectic are (1) the transformation of quantity into quality, (2) the interpenetration of opposites, and (3) the negation of the negation. These rather mystifying formulae may perhaps be clarified by the following examples. (1): Water suddenly becomes ice at a certain point of coldness, thus a qualitative change takes place as a result of a series of quantitative changes. Or, a revolution finally takes place after years of cumulative pressures. Pile one thing on another and at a certain point you cease to have just a pile of the same things, you have something entirely different. A humbler and possibly facetious example might be the inflating of a tire: keep putting in air, and finally at a critical juncture you get not a tire but an explosion. (2) and (3): Change is the rule of nature because everything contains within it its own opposite, which negates it and in turn will be negated. The seed contains within itself the plant that it will turn into; the plant will decay, giving rise however to new plants. A social order, such as capitalism, creates out of its own body the socialism destined to destroy it. Socialism thus interpenetrates capitalism, and negates it. Struggle and conflict punctuate this process: the old organism produces its violent destroyers.

As applied to the sciences, it has seemed to critics of Marx that the dialectical method does not mean much, or if insisted upon as a dogma, is harmful to science. Soviet Russian scientists work like western ones. Whenever (as happened on one or two occasions, notably in the Lysenko case) there has been an effort to force on them a Marxist scientific orthodoxy, the results have been unfortunate for science. Either dialectical materialism is so commonplace that even "bourgeois" scientists follow it without knowing that they are doing so (like Molière's M. Jourdain talking prose!) or else it is a failure. The attempt to distinguish a Marxist science from a bourgeois one, with the former being superior, clearly has failed. Nevertheless from Marx and Engels on down to such unlikely philosophers as Stalin, Marxists have insisted that dialectical materialism is the distinctive foundation of their science, and the famous analysis of capitalism is meant to be but a special application of it. In our time scientists in the Soviet Union have suffered pains and penalties because they appeared to stray from the dialectical path. Not only human affairs, but the natural sciences are expected to conform to dialectical principles. To be a Marxist, one must be able to enter into the spirit of the dialectical universe and visualize things in motion and in contradiction, giving birth to their own opposites, negating and renegating, occasionally bursting through the barriers of quantity to create a new form. A vision not unlike this is to be found in the more recent school of Emergent Evolutionists, who in other ways do not resemble Marxists, however. They stress the freedom and unpredicability of life, ever proliferating in unexpected ways, whereas Marxism is deterministic, though to be sure there is a Marxian problem in this regard.

Many of the examples given by Marx and especially by Engels are from the natural sciences (the freezing of ice and the sprouting of the seed are theirs). But no one associates these German worthies with a revolution in chemistry or biology.[3] Many do associate them with a revolutionary new conception of the historical process, as well as with the first effective socialist economic analysis. They applied the dialectical method to these areas more consistently and successfully. It is well, though, to remember that this method was the tool of thought they always used, and that they held it to be of universal validity, *the* scientific method.

The dialectical method was after all Marx's distinctive contribution. Today because he is the most famous socialist or communist he is often thought of as the man who invented socialism, but this, as we know, is not so. The protest against the suffering of workers under capitalism antedated Marx, as did the idea of social ownership of industry as a remedy for the evils of "capitalism." The Chartists, Robert Owen, Saint-Simon and Fourier, Proudhon, Blanc, etc., all came before him. We have previously discussed these pioneer socialists. In Rousseau's vision of an original state of primitive communism, when there was no wickedness and exploitation, followed by the Fall due to eating the apple of private property, there is much of the basic vision of Marx, too, the latter more sophisticated, spelled out in greater detail, but in its archetypal essence quite similar.

Likewise, other concepts associated with Marxism such as the class struggle and the class conditioning of morality and thought were hardly original. "Of all maxims none is more uncontested than that power follows property," Joseph Addison remarked early in the eighteenth century, an idea which may have come to him from James Harrington. John Stuart Mill, in *On Liberty*, a contemporary work (1859) but one not influenced by Marx, whom Mill at that time had probably never heard of, observed (parenthetically) that "Wherever there is an ascendant class, a large portion of the morality of the country emanates from its class interests and its feelings of class superiority." Mill could have found this in the ancient historian Thucydides, among others. As any sociologist must, Herbert Spencer had also confronted the problem of the role of ideas in social change and had concluded that ideas are *largely* a

---

[3]Marx and Engels knew about Darwin, of course, and regarded him as possibly congenial to their system. Engels claimed in his funeral address on Marx that Marx had done for the social sciences what Darwin did for the biological. But the attitude of Marx is indicated in his request to Engels to "study Darwin and see if there is anything there we can use"!

product of "surrounding conditions" including "the social state." Spencer was concerned to stress the emotional determinants of rational processes: "Ideas do not govern and overthrow the world; the world is governed by feelings, to which ideas serve only as guides. . . . Though advanced ideas, when once established, act upon society and aid its further advance, yet the establishment of such ideas depends on the fitness of society for receiving them." Though a reasonably crude and confused statement, Spencer's is at least as adequate as Marx's thoughts on the subject.

Also, the labor theory of value, on which Marx based his famous analysis of capitalism, came to him from Adam Smith and David Ricardo, while socialists such as Thomas Bray had already, before Marx, claimed that "by a fraudulent system of unequal exchange" the workman's just wage is taken away from him by the capitalist.

Of all these ideas Marx made a unique and powerful synthesis. The dialectic enabled him to tie them all together in a seamless system, much like Hegel's in that respect. There is a plan and a purpose to history, Marx claimed; and moreover there is a method, the understanding of which enables us to decipher the meaning of history and thus collaborate with it in its purposes. He claimed to have provided this key that unlocks the golden gates of social science and shows us how every event fits into its place. The key was dialectical materialism.

We might think that a dialectical philosophy would stress freedom and not determinism, for it is expressly opposed to a mechanistic outlook on nature, holding rather that the world is not static but like a developing and proliferating organism, or like a conversation. We can scarcely predict the results of a dialogue in which a statement is made, is contradicted, restated, again objected to, and so on. This may be a good way to knowledge, but it is hard to see how we could know the outcome in advance.[4] We could argue that God does; but Marx, of course, did not believe in any God. He held that only matter exists— matter in motion, in evolution. Marx was a determinist, believing that the laws of matter's motion can be precisely determined and used to predict the future. This world made up only of dynamic matter knows where it is going, and sharpwitted men can know it too. Some critics of Marxism have wondered how Marx could exclude God or the Absolute

---

[4]Neither inventions nor scientific theories can be entirely predicted, and these are what Marx regards as the basic factors; much less can future political and economic developments. Prediction in general is possible only for a very short time ahead, and for very general things. These points have been most fully established by present-day philosophers, especially Sir Isaiah Berlin (*Historical Inevitability*, 1954) and Karl Popper (*The Open Society and Its Enemies*, 4th ed., 1962 and *The Poverty of Historicism*, 1957).

yet insist on a rational, purposeful world, obeying regular laws. Or is Marx a pantheist, like his fellow apostate Jew, Spinoza?

All we can say is that Marx shared to the full the positivist bias, that is, he wished to be scientific, to believe only in "facts," to dismiss such nebulous abstractions as God or the Absolute. He got this from the materialists of the eighteenth century as well as from the scientific atmosphere of his own time. But he married it to the very different system of Hegel. The marriage may have been incongruous, but it produced some lusty children.

Historical Materialism

Marx's theory or philosophy of history occupies the central place in his thought. He was strongly impressed by the "historicism" of Hegel, and often spoke of the processes of history as operating independently of men's will. The historical process is an "it" that sweeps men along without regard to their wishes; one thinks of Thomas Hardy's phrase, the "immanent unrecking." This conception of a world-historical force was strong in Marx as it has been in all its disciples; that is why Soviet leaders are so sure capitalism is doomed and communism will triumph —this is not just a matter of probability or possibility but a certainty, decreed by the iron laws of history. Marx did not wish to think of the "laws" of society and history as merely descriptive of trends or tendencies, in the positivist sense, but rather as decrees imposed for all time, existing objectively and requiring men to conform to them. Nor did he wish to think of many small areas for social investigation, but of one great pattern sweeping through all history—a romantic and apocalyptic vision.

On the other hand he also had a considerable feeling for the active participation by men in shaping the historical process. This activism appeared in Marx in his famous statement that philosophers must not merely describe the world but must help change it, in his own career as organizer of the First International and participant in other political movements, and in his statement that with the arrival of his philosophy men passed from the "kingdom of necessity" to the "kingdom of freedom." Marxists have of course made their great place in the modern world by this sort of dynamic revolutionary activism. Is this inconsistent with a deterministic outlook?

Whatever the possible discrepancies in logic, such a combination of activism with determinism produces a potent psychological stimulus; a similar combination was found in Calvinism. Adherents of Marxism feel that history is on their side and so they are bound to win, as well as serve nature's purposes; yet they can collaborate with nature, helping to make history by understanding its laws. Marx probably meant that (1) history is only determined within broad limits, leaving scope for variation in the particulars and in the pace; like a very large boulder bouncing around in a large and uneven chute, it will eventually reach the bottom but may pursue an uneven course and may be temporarily delayed. Present-day communists assume that capitalism will eventually be destroyed but do not specify time or place; it might be now or in two hundred years; the process might move next in Vietnam or in England. In this way a general determinism can be reconciled with a practical voluntarism. (2) As in all social determinism, one must concede that men are a part of the social order and in acting and willing they play their part; fatalism is not the same thing as necessitarianism.

Here as elsewhere, Marx was somewhat impatient of fine-spun theoretical discussions, though theory was important to him. It has been pointed out that Marx uses terms like "condition" and "determine" (*bedingen* and *bestimmen*) much too loosely and indiscriminately. They do not mean the same thing, obviously. There is a significant difference between saying that human intelligence is conditioned (influenced) by society and saying that it is determined. No one would deny the former, almost everyone the latter. There is a characteristic flavor of rhetorical exaggeration about much of Marx's thought. In his materialistic explanation of history, that is, the theory that "material" factors (technological, economic) are "basic" in history while other factors may be relegated to a secondary role, such confusions of terminology and thought appear in profusion. Yet nowhere did Marx prove to be so stimulating and provocative as here.

Marx differed from Hegel, of course, in finding the motive forces of history in material factors, in the "productive forces," by which he evidently meant tools and the economic relations derived from them. Strictly speaking, the motive force of history is the class struggle ("All history is the history of class struggle"), but the techniques and modes of production of any given period determine the class structure. The windmill, said Marx, gives us feudalism (he would have been nearer the mark, according to modern economic historians, had he said the plough and the stirrup). He went on to claim that all the rest of civilization and culture depends on this economic foundation. In his speech at Marx's funeral, Engels put it this way: "The production of the immediate material means of subsistence and consequently the degree of economic development attained by a given people or during a given epoch form the foundation upon which the state institutions, the legal conceptions, the ideas on art and even on religion . . . have been evolved, and in the light of which they must, therefore, be explained. . . ." Marx, he claimed, had been the first to notice this "simple fact." This is the "materialist interpretation of history."

Here we encounter difficulties. If Marx and Engels are saying that men can not think, write, worship, etc., without first finding some means of sustenance, then they are asserting an obvious truth, surely not original, to which no one would object. If they mean that the mode of production and the economic relationships of society influence or condition modes of thought in significant ways, it is also difficult to disagree with them, and once again the idea is hardly original, though Marx surely gave it more striking expression than any other writer one can think of. If however it is claimed that (1) all ideas and institutions are determined by the economic "substructure" and (2) play no real part or independent part in life or history, the claim appears almost self-evidently false. The saints may have been deluded, but they gave up their possessions to follow a religious ideal; others, including philosophers, adventurers, soldiers, political reformers, scientists, have followed their gleam without significant reference to capitalism or any other economic order. Marx himself is a classic example of a man possessed by ideas to the exclusion of pecuniary motives, and the system he created is a prize instance of the power of an ideology. In this respect he is not a unique case, as he may have implied, for history is filled with the prophets crying in the wilderness, philosophers teaching in the marketplace, angry young men (and some old ones) denouncing the existing "establishment." There are manifestly human drives of a very fundamental nature, other than the desire to rule and the desire for gain: drives sexual, esthetic, intellectual, spiritual. It strains our credulity to believe that Beethoven and Brahms wrote their music to serve the bourgeoisie and cover up their shameful exploitation of the workers, yet this is what Marxism requires us to believe. Engels and Marx conceded that this might be done unconsciously, without the individual being aware of it; but that is *really* what is motivating him, nonetheless.

What did Marx mean? He and Engels are not very clear. The "superstructure" consisting of all that is not economic is said to be only a "reflection" of the economic "substructure." Social change can only take place in the latter, the former following along in its wake. Also, "the ruling ideas are those of the ruling class." It is clear, though, that Marx was no crude economic determinist (such as would, for example, explain Milton's poetry by his occupation) and also that he granted at least some ideas a powerful place in history. He undoubtedly knew too little of the history of human thought and action to support his bold generalizations and he tended to conceal by vague language some difficult problems. At the same time he was onto something in proposing an investigation of the origin and social relations of religions and philosophical systems. Nor can it well be denied that there are such things as ideological systems designed to support political regimes—that, indeed, institutions excrete ideologies as a normal function. The situation was much more complicated than Marx imagined when with typical dogmatism he proposed some outrageously exaggerated formulae, but he opened up fruitful fields of inquiry.

Marx's singular allegation, then, is approximately as follows: Ideas and ideologies of all sorts, legal and political institutions and processes, artistic and literary expression, all of religion, culture, and politics, all except the technological or economic comprise the "superstructure" and are ultimately dependent on the latter. Changes in the superstructure do not take place without prior changes in the economic foundation, to which they respond; or, if such changes take place, they are not significant. Marx evidently asks us to believe not only that Christianity is a tool of the ruling classes to divert and pacify the masses (not necessarily a deliberate tool, for remember that Marx holds that this process may be and indeed normally is unconscious), but that all other phenomena in some sense are the same. The class structure cannot be escaped. The bourgeois judge who thinks he is administering perfect justice is really doing so within the boundaries of the capitalist order and so engaged in defending it. Presumably Stravinsky wrote capitalistic music and Cézanne painted bourgeois pictures, much though these artists themselves despised "bourgeois" culture. Marxist literary criticism has applied much ingenuity to exactly this sort of demonstration. Freud was a capitalistic psychologist, according to present Soviet orthodoxy—a view which certainly would have surprised him. Though this is the evident import of Marxist theory, it should be pointed out that Marx himself did not conform to it: he was a great lover of classical Greek drama, which evidently had for him a value independent of its function in the class struggle.

Most people today are inclined to listen sympathetically to claims for the primacy of technological or economic change because they know what a dynamic agent it has been. The most common sort of "cultural lag" is perhaps the sort caused by a rapid advance in technology to which ideas and institutions have not adapted though such adaptation is required. One might instance national states in an age of nuclear weapons. But this is not the only possible kind of "lag," and the reverse might be true. We might come up with a new idea or theory that forced changes in our physical equipment. Freudian psychology has modified our teaching practices and resulted in a new profession with at least some physical equipment (couches!), for example. A new theory of military strategy causes our government to build different types of weapons, abandoning others. It is important to note that Marxists are committed to the proposition that the economic factor is the *only* independent variable, not just that it is one possible variable. Nobody doubts that technological and economic forces are important; the Marxists hold that nothing else is important.

Karl Popper presents an interesting example: Suppose, he says, that all the existing physical plant and scientific apparatus were destroyed, but the knowledge behind it, in books and human brains, were left in existence—the physical apparatus could be rebuilt, though no doubt with great expense and difficulty. But suppose the plant were to remain and the knowledge be lost—as might happen if primitive savages suddenly replaced modern man, and had no knowledge of modern technology. Then the machinery would fall into disuse and perish. In this sense, Popper concludes, knowledge, ideas, seem more "basic" than physical equipment, tools. What his example really indicates, however, is the impossibility of ever separating tools and brains; what he postulates could not happen. Since the beginning of mankind, tools and knowledge have evolved together in intimate association as aspects of the same process. We could not have brains without tools nor tools without brains. The skillful hand and the contriving brain (to borrow a phrase of James C. Malin's) go together. The experimental laboratory and the theorizing intellect must collaborate to make science and technology possible. Marx erred in attempting to separate the two things and make one of a different order than the other. As a matter of fact, he wavered in his view of scientific knowledge, sometimes putting it in the superstructure and sometimes in the foundation—a significant ambiguity.

It seems especially important to recognize the sense in which the strictly *political* element may be primary. The story of some of the new nations today underscores the fact that economic development can scarcely take place until stable government has been secured. Until a political unit is secure both internally and externally, investment, trade, and labor can hardly function in any successful way. Unwise political decisions may cause deterioration of the entire economy, as has apparently happened in some South American countries with great economic potential but a poor political foundation. The political process is often, it would seem, more "primary" than the economic. If man has to eat before he can live, he also has to cooperate in social units before he can eat, or at any rate live much above the level of the beast. Anyone with much experience of the world knows that political processes exist in their own right, independently of economic ones. The fact that we often divide history into epochs based on politics is an indication of this political primacy. The age of the Roman Empire, the age of feudalism, the age of the national state—and, if such evolution took place, the age of the world state—unquestionably suggest politics as the decisive factor. These political classifications have at least as much claim to primacy as the age of slavery, of manorialism, and of capitalism. Political processes are acted upon by economic ones, but then the reverse is also true.

One of Marxism's most startling failures is its inability to mark off any significant difference between the various *national* cultures. France, Germany, Great Britain, and the United States must all be substantially alike, except insofar as they are in slightly different stages of capitalist development, because they are all "bourgeois capitalist" states; but everyone except the Marxists knows that in important respects these nations differ because of the role of tradition, that is, because of their different historic experiences. The Marxists expected revolution to come first in Britain because capitalist development had proceeded farthest here. They overlooked the potent reasons why revolution was *least* likely in the land where due to a complex variety of historical factors the political constitution was the most stable in Europe. With their eyes fixed on only one set of forces, they were blind to the central facts of British history. Marxists were disgusted with the failure of socialism to take root in the United States and could only declare that somehow, for unknown reasons, the American workers were hopelessly "petty bourgeois" in their outlook. Again, Marxists least expected revolution in Russia—a country for which, ironically, Marx entertained the deepest disdain—because it was economically backward.[5] This is not to say that some investigators did not creatively pursue answers to the interesting question why these various peoples utterly failed to conform to the Marxian theory. Again, Marx may be given credit for stimulating much fruitful inquiry, but it was necessary to go beyond his system to find the answers.

Such argumentation can go on indefinitely. Clearly Marx started an interesting debate, but just as clearly he failed to finish it. More sophisticated modern discussions of this problem make Marx seem crude and dogmatic. But he did present the first approximation of a theory that subsequent historians and sociologists such as Max Weber, Karl Mannheim, Karl Popper, and others were to work on.

Like Comte and Hegel, Marx divided history up in a rather arbitrary manner into a few great epochs, his division based of course on economics: primitive communism, ancient slave society, feudalism, capi-

[5]This at times reached extreme proportions. In 1848, at the time of the Slavic conference in Prague which confused the German and Austro-Hungarian revolutions, Marx and Engels wrote in their newspaper that the Slavs should be exterminated, "wiped from the face of the earth," since whole peoples may be "reactionary" and the Slavs are such a race.

talism, and communism.[6] In a rough way one might say that these
describe the history of Western civilization in certain of its aspects, but
they scarcely exhaust the subject and seem inherently no more valid
than Hegel's political classification or Comte's intellectual one. (For
non-Western civilizations, they are less accurate.) The fact is that we
can look at history in various ways, each equally valid. We can arrive at
different periodizations, depending on our criteria; each one will be
useful for its purpose, but not objectively truer than the others.

According to Marx the dynamics of history spring from the inner
contradictions of the first four of these epochs, issuing in class conflict
and revolution. The dialectical principle expresses itself in this process
of clash and conflict, with one order emerging from the womb of another. The oppressed class or classes represent a negation or counter-
statement destined in time to destroy the old society. Feudalism brought
forth bourgeois capitalism from its own contradictions; capitalism in the
same necessary way gives rise to the proletariat and to socialism. "The
material powers of production, at a certain stage in their development,
come into conflict with the existing relations of production. . . . Then
comes the period of social revolution." To repeat, men are the unwitting
instruments of historical destiny. The bourgeois does not want to create
socialism, but he cannot help it, it arises from the very things he must
do.

Marx's vision of the historical process made a powerful appeal to
the imagination. History not only has a plan and a meaning, but it is
tremendously dramatic. Something of his Jewishness surely emerges in
this essentially apocalyptic account of man's journey through time to
reach a mighty climax at the end. For at the end, we are given to understand, with the triumph of the proletariat over the capitalists, we reach
the end of history.[7] There are now no more classes to create another
negation and another turn in the great cycle of history; this last victory
of the submerged ushers in the classless society, and we have come full

[6]A "socialist" stage which follows the overthrow of capitalism and precedes
the establishment of communism was suggested by Marx, presumably a short-
lived transitional period. In the Soviet Union it has turned out to be quite protracted. Pure communism, the final stage, is marked by the withering away of the
state and by all manner of perfection.

[7]Condorcet had placed human history near the end of its days, and so
apparently had Hegel; in 1841 so judicious an intellect as Matthew Arnold declared, in his Oxford inaugural address, that the modern age bears all the marks
of being "the last step" in the story of man. This somewhat curious finalism
can perhaps be traced to several sources, but chiefly would seem to have rested
on observation of the tremendous growth of modern Europe, in political units,
population, extension of power, increased popular participation, etc. Could one
imagine anything larger than the nation-state, except the world state, an obvious
finality? Or any further extension of democracy except to the lowest class, the
proletariat?

circle from primitive communism to communism as the highest stage of human society. In the last phase human nature is cured of all those defects which were the result of its being "alienated" from itself, and is whole again, a harmony rather than a discord.

Marx's Analysis of Capitalism

In his *magnum opus, Capital,* Marx sought to apply his method in detail to the existing social situation. Here he drew on Ricardo and the classical economists as well as on socialism and the dialectic. Marx stumbled upon difficulties, and failed to complete his book, but he left a deep impression upon the budding socialist movement with this major effort of economic theory.

Prior to Marx many less weighty socialist theoreticians had charged that the factory owners exploited, in other words, cheated, their employees. Indeed, this had emerged for all to see in the famous Parliamentary investigations into conditions in the textile factories and mines in England—on which Marx and Engels drew heavily for their ammunition, though their philosophy would seem to deny that these bourgeois bodies could be capable of such exposures.[8] The revelation of brutally long hours and pitifully low wages, frequently using child labor, while the owners drew large profits, had projected the "social question" (in Carlyle's phrase) onto the conscience of Europe when Marx was still a juvenile. In France, there had been the great insurrection of silk weavers at Lyons in 1831. The notion quickly grew that the wage system was a method of exploitation. A workers' jingle current before the *Communist Manifesto* was written (1847) made the point:

> Wages should form the price of goods
> Yes, wages should be all,
> Then we who work to make the goods,
> Should justly have them all.

This was a crude statement of the labor theory of value on which Marx erected his economic analysis.

The labor theory of value may be traced a long way back; it was forcefully stated by Adam Smith and adopted by Ricardo, where Marx found it. Later economic theory was to discard it as unscientific, but Marx seized upon it and attempted to work out all its implications. It was still partly economic orthodoxy in Marx's time though the "bour-

---

[8]Engel's *Condition of the Working Class,* 1844, made extensive use of the testimony before the Parliamentary committees.

geois" economists did not put it to the uses Marx did, needless to say. Value was "cost of production" which included materials and the natural reward of capital (the result of "abstinence" from present consumption) as well as labor. Senior had pointed out that some things have much value without any human labor at all: the pearl I chance to find in my oyster, for example! Yet remnants of the Ricardian labor theory of value existed in classical economics as represented most popularly by J. S. Mill at this time. The clean break with it was not to be made until Alfred Marshall and W. S. Jevons about 1870.

The labor theory of value, plus the subsistence theory of wages, suggested to socialists that labor does not get its full and just price because wages are determined in the market, by the principle of supply and demand, whereas the products are sold for their "true" price, based on the amount of labor put into them. The difference was said to represent a surplus of value appropriated by the capitalist. Robert Owen had tried to change this pernicious system by using a currency reflecting units of labor, so that the price of a product would be exactly the amount of labor put into it. This naive idea proved entirely unworkable. Agreement could never be reached on just how many labor units commodities are worth, a major objection to the labor theory of value being that labor values submit to no accurate quantitative measurement. One carpenter might make a table in half the time another took; and how could you compare highly skilled labor to unskilled—how many hours of carpenter labor is one hour of an expert surgeon's time worth?[9] In practice, the market price based on supply and demand would prevail anyway. The only alternative would be an elaborate system of administrative pricing based on the arbitrary decrees of a state bureaucracy, a system with many disadvantages and few advantages.

Marx ridiculed the labor-exchange idea. He believed that only the abolition of capitalism—of private property in the means of production—would solve the problem, and he used the labor theory of value not to support labor-exchange or social-credit schemes, but rather to demonstrate, as he thought, the dynamics of capitalism as it worked towards its self-destruction.

Among the features of capitalism which seemed alarming in Marx's time were the periodic panics or depressions that afflicted it, tendencies toward monopoly, and of course the low wages and deplorable working conditions that frequently were the lot of the factory hands, to which one might add the demoralizing separation of workers from their tools and products, as they worked with machinery owned by others to produce goods that were not theirs to sell. For all these observable features

---

[9]Marx attempted to meet this objection by postulating a "socially necessary" amount of labor for every commodity, but this hardly removed the problem.

of the nineteenth-century economic order in western Europe, Marx tried to supply explanations based on "laws." The whole of his argument was designed to show that capitalism is a doomed system because it is unavoidably digging its own grave. The labor theory of value is the foundation stone for Marx's concept of the *falling rate of profit*, which is chiefly how he explained crises, consolidation, and the increasing misery of the working class.

Profits must come out of labor. Therefore the increasing use of machinery forces the capitalists to exploit their workers ever more mercilessly. They are forced to adopt machinery because of technological advances and competition; but as they increase the proportion of this "constant capital," as Marx called it, they have less and less of labor power or "variable capital" from which to make profits. Today it seems odd that Marx should have supposed that mechanization destroys profits by displacing human labor. We should assume that it would be more likely to *increase* profits, by cutting down the wage bill or stepping up efficiency of production. But he had his eye fixed on the labor theory of value, from which his conclusion seems logically to follow. This is the chief of the "contradictions" of capitalism according to Marx: that as it progresses, measured by the use of advanced machinery, it must intensify the misery of the working class, for profits must be squeezed out of human labor power. The more machinery used, the lower the wage of the worker has to be.

Strive as they will, the capitalists cannot however prevent their profits from declining. Of this unhappy fact another result is that some manufacturers are driven to the wall and fewer and fewer capitalists exist, holding bigger and bigger enterprises. This, too, unwittingly prepares for socialism; the huge industrial concern is already socialized, and at the last there are scarcely more than a handful of capitalists left to be taken over by society.

Having demonstrated to his own satisfaction that the workers were getting steadily more miserable and capitalists fewer, Marx went on to suggest an explanation for the depressions that periodically afflicted capitalism. His most original and characteristic explanation was that these depressions are a periodic annihilation of fixed capital which delays the collapse of the system by temporarily increasing the proportion of variable capital, in other words, labor. Depressions are the result of a need to destroy the machinery that capitalism feeds on yet cannot digest, a sort of periodic regurgitation. It is sometimes inaccurately said that Marx explained depressions by underconsumption, that is, by the failure of the consuming classes to be given enough purchasing power; but this was the theory of Marx's scorned rival, Proudhon, and he does not assign it the main role as economic villain.

Criticisms of Marx

The labor theory of value on which Marx leaned so heavily was soon to be abandoned by economists, and today most of them think that it will bear little or none of the weight he put on it. His explanation of depressions, then, along with his theory of profits and wages, seem invalid. As for his predictions that small business would succumb entirely to big, and that with the advance of machinery people under capitalism would be worse off and not better—the doctrine of the declining rate of profit and the increasing misery of the working class—these things have not come about, though at times they may have looked plausible. By the end of the century many of Marx's own followers came to feel that a wholesale revision of his economic theories was needed. The main stream of economic analysis travelled away from Marx, and in recent times John Maynard Keynes unquestionably spoke for professional economists of virtually all schools in calling *Das Kapital* "an obsolete economic textbook." But Marx's doctrines have of course exerted an enormous influence on the Soviet Union since its revolutionary birth in 1917. Still, economic practice even in the USSR does not owe much directly to Marx, who failed to describe in detail the economics of socialism. He thought he had charted with scientific accuracy the last fatal illness of capitalism, and all Marxists continue to believe that "capitalism is doomed."

Perhaps it is, but apparently not for the reasons Marx gave. Sometimes it is suggested that Marx was a good prophet in a general sort of way though he missed many details; for has not our economic order, even in the West, travelled a long way from the unregulated individualism of the nineteenth century toward a "welfare state" system which is in the broadest sense socialistic? It has indeed, but we should note that Marx has not really proved a good prophet here. The welfare state or "interventionist" economy (the French have a word *dirigiste*—directed —which is useful) was not really what he had in mind. Marx believed the state would die; his vision of the future was essentially anarchist, or perhaps utopian. Social ownership of the means of production did not mean to him statism. About this he had little to say, to be sure. One cannot really give him much credit for anticipating the course of the future. Bear in mind that he expected the middle class to be ground to bits, the class struggle to become more acute, the factory workers to grow ever poorer until they rebelled, and the capitalist order to end in revolution, with private property in the sector of production disappearing. In all these respects he proved a poor prophet. It took a disastrous war to bring socialist revolution to Europe, and then it came to a backward, almost precapitalist society, quite contrary to the expectations of most Marxists.

Even as Marx was writing *Das Kapital* economists such as Stanley Jevons were criticizing the labor theory with devastating effect, doing away with the mystical idea of a true or inherent "value" of a commodity that is not the same as its market price. They substituted a sophisticated version of supply-and-demand, the marginal utility theory.[10] Others pointed out that Marx's surplus value would not do; why should not competition cause it to disappear? It was argued that capital is certainly productive, which Marx denied. But if in the eyes of experts not much was left of Marx's elaborate theorizing in his *magnum opus*, which he left unfinished, it remained a compelling document. In many portions of the book Marx abandoned the pretence of scientific objectivity to emit thunderous indictments of working conditions in the factories and the iniquity of capitalism. And the whole seemed an impressive vindication of the larger dialectical philosophy. Apparently Marx had shown in detail how capitalism destroys itself and in the process creates socialism, its "negation" which had always been included in itself. Socialism emerges out of the very womb of capitalism, as the dialectic predicts. Capitalism brought into existence the working class, forced it into the factories, and reduced the number of capitalists thus inadvertently "socializing" the economic order and the technological system; it created advanced machinery, broke down parochial social units to create the national and even international economy and also accustomed men to a rational, materialistic outlook. According to Marxists capitalism had an indispensable historical role to play, and until Lenin they practically all felt that every society must work its way through capitalism before it is ready for socialism. There was an ambiguity here, to be sure, revealed in the later history of the Marxist movement. One might choose to dwell on the horrors of capitalism, the misery it caused the workers, the need to destroy it; or one might point to its inevitability and the things it achieved to prepare the way for socialism. But it is the latter that is most characteristic of Marx as op-

[10]Developed almost simultaneously by Carl Menger in Austria and M. E. L. Walras in Switzerland along with Jevons in England, marginal utility analysis represented on charts the curve of diminishing utility as an individual—or, by extension, a nation—acquires successive units of a commodity. To a hungry man the first loaf of bread is extremely valuable, but each successive additional one decreases in its value to him. The final increment, the marginal one, determines exchange value. "Commodities exchange at ratios such that their marginal utilities are equal" (Edmund Whittaker). The student may consult textbooks of economics for full understanding of the principle. Employed by the influential economists Alfred Marshall in Britain and J. B. Clark in the United States, marginal theory tended to dominate academic economics in this "neoclassical" phase. Marshall's *Principles of Economics* supplanted Mill as the standard textbook.

posed to the mere moralists whose outlook he despised because it was not "scientific."

Perhaps the leading source of confusion in evaluating Marxism has been its enthusiastic believers' insistence upon the scientific, rational character of their creed, whereas they seem really to have committed themselves as an act of faith to a kind of religion. However fine and courageous a thinker Marx was, his overly ambitious system contains so many contradictions that, as Karl Popper (a sympathetic critic) observes, and as we know all too well today, those who remain dogmatic Marxists, like the communists, "must become mystics—hostile to reasonable argument." They repeat the formula by rote and refuse to listen to objections; they ignore the real world and live in a dream world. It has become increasingly clear that theirs is a form of faith which has taken on the outer trappings of scientific positivism while preserving the inner structure of an emotional ideology. Many have pointed out the startling resemblance of Marxism to the psychological structure of religion, especially the Judaic-Christian framework transposed into secular terms. We have the original innocence of primitive communism, followed by the Fall (private property), the coming of the doctrine of salvation, the nature of evil and the struggle against it, finally the apocalypse and last state of blessedness. It is clear that this secular religion was in the making before Marx, for Rousseau and the Romantics contributed much to it; he gave it final form and further equipped it with enough intellectual content to satisfy a rational age. In a fine phrase of Professor J. Herman Randall, Jr., "Marxism is the last of the great Romantic faiths, lingering on in a scientific world."

Anglo-Saxon empiricism has typically accused Marxism of being, as Bertrand Russell put it, an "irrational dogma," which Marx took *a priori* from the speculations of Hegel and then found facts to fit, rather than proceeding in true scientific manner. Scientists, to be sure, may use hypotheses, but these are held tentatively and modified where experiment indicates. Most Marxists have held their beliefs as a sacred dogma beyond fundamental alteration, any "revisionism" being treated as dreadful heresy. Marx once said he was not a Marxist, and we perhaps cannot fairly blame the sins of his disciples on him.[11] The Communist Party of the Soviet Union in Stalin's era colors our view of Marxism; but for all we know Marx would heartily have disapproved of Stalinism—

---

[11]There is a sense in which it is logically impossible to be a "Marxist." Marx held that thought changes with the conditions of life, which are in perpetual change; thus no thinker is valid beyond his own time, and Marx if he were alive today would think quite differently than he did. Acceptance of Marx's central thesis rules out the permanent validity of any body of thought—including Marx's!

many of his disciples among, for example, the Trotskyites have said as much. (Marx never liked Russians very much, as we know.) In recent years Marxism has become much more flexible and varied, with all kinds of "revisionists" participating in a renaissance of Marxist studies, much of it out of Eastern Europe. Marxism has interacted with existentialism and with Christianity in a series of dialogues. It does seem to be much more a religion than a science, something admitted today by all but the most old-fashioned, hidebound Marxists. As such, it has displayed a remarkable vitality, indicating that it possesses much relevance to the modern situation. There remain many awkward questions about the status of a body of thought claiming to be exact and objective truth, and final truth at that, when as a matter of fact it appears to be a religious myth if not a metaphysical dogma. These same questions, one recalls, were raised about Christianity in former times.

The characteristic of such "ideologies" is that they are held with a quivering emotionality that erupts into antagonism when any article of the dogma is criticized, and that the holder of the ideology is dominated by it, constantly engaging in efforts to make other phenomena, and other people, conform to his vision. The person possessed by a religion or an ideology can doubtless be described as neurotic, yet this possession may be a source of great energy and dedication. History has been shaped mainly by the "true believers," from the prophets of Israel and the Christian martyrs down to the leaders of the French and Russian Revolutions. And it seems plain that Marxism has proved a potent faith.

Marx represents a blend of simple, emotional faith with a critical and rational intellect. Often he furiously condemned and ridiculed the simpler variety of socialist as "utopian" or soft-headed, wooly-minded. Yet he himself appears in some respects simplistic and utopian. Despite his protests he was essentially not scientist but prophet. Judged in this light, he has received praise from some in our time who have rejected his philosophy as meaningless and his economics as outdated. As a moral critic of capitalism, voicing a protest against its alienation of the worker from his work, its destruction of esthetic values and human dignity, Marx adds his powerful bass to a whole chorus of such nineteenth-century indictments. He would have indignantly rejected the classification of his thought as ethical, but his moral criticism seems to have survived his pseudoscientific theorizing, through most of the Western world. He was the founder not, as he thought, of the social sciences but of the greatest religious movement of modern times.

Marxism is for millions in some parts of the world today a faith to live by, and we may well ask why—wherein lay its peculiar potency as a religion? The answer would seem to be in its strong combination of emotional-ideological with rational-scientific factors, a combination, if you like, of the Enlightenment and romanticism; or a new *Summa*, like St. Thomas's, blending faith with reason. If today we are inclined to "see through" the allegedly rational and scientific portions of Marx, this is not to deny that they were there and could carry great conviction for all but the most searchingly critical intellects. One way in which Marxism seems curiously old-fashioned today is in its absence of any sense of the irrational or nonrational factors in man. Marx scarcely has a psychology, and modern Marxists have usually strongly resisted Freud, Jung, and the existentialists, calling them bourgeois and decadent. Likewise Marxism contributed little to the study of politics as such, a rather strange neglect for a political creed. Politics is the mirror of economic-class interests, which are clear and calculable, without separate identity of its own, according to Marxism. All this testifies to an old-fashioned, Enlightenment rationalism in Marx.

The religious features gave expression to a powerful ethical imperative: one's duty was to advance the course of history by assailing the evil of capitalism and thus to prepare the way for the final kingdom of righteousness. Like Calvinism, socialist historicism made you feel that the fates were fighting on your side, and thus was a great energizing factor. So in many ways this was the "religion of science," or the scientific religion, for which Comte and Renan had searched. He who adopts Marxism may well feel that he understands the world, and from this he sees what he must do to serve the good cause.

It may be unnecessary to add that this Marxist religion, an intolerant one, could lead to ruthless behavior. Lenin's pronouncement is well known: "morality is what serves to destroy the old exploiting society." Hegelian historicism encourages the morality of being on the winning side, we know; to this, Marxism added a ferocious hatred for the old "exploiting society" and a keen desire to hasten the coming of the revolution. The Communist followers of Marx and Lenin were prepared to employ cruelty, force, treachery, and deceit so long as these weapons were used against the bourgeoisie in behalf of the socialist revolution. These features were more evident in the Russian followers of Marx than among the milder Social Democrats of the western countries, but they are easily drawn from his doctrines.

In many ways the social ideologies we have been considering, though they were tremendously influential, were out of touch with realities in their age. Of Comte, Marx, and Spencer alike, A. D. Ritchie has observed that "All three smell of the midnight oil and the ivory tower. They none of them have the proper smell of places where collective or public human action occurs, where discussions go on and decisions are made." It is difficult to object to this characterization. Few more pronounced "outsiders" ever existed than Comte and Marx, impoverished obscurities in their lifetimes, writing books nobody read until some years later. But not so unusual (Bentham is a good example, Rousseau another) is the phenomenon of the eccentric recluse-philosopher who proves to be a fountain of ideas destined to the utmost importance when taken up by others. These ideologies we have found emerging from the nineteenth century answered some great need. They all thought they were sciences; but clearly today we must see them as more nearly "miscellaneous prejudices dressed up to look like science." They did not serve any useful purpose in meeting practical problems of the day, such as statesmen and businessmen faced in their daily affairs.

Yet they were, or became, very popular. Nobody now reads the works of Comte or Spencer, yet a century ago "Spencer's books were read all over the world in many languages by thousands of devoted disciples." Marx's still are. The reason for this is that these imposing systems of thought offered to restore to European man his lost vision of an integrated universe, the source of values. In brief, they substituted for religion, and for the metaphysical systems of the past. Comte was right in divining that modern man had lost his capacity for traditional Christianity and metaphysics. He had not and could not lose his need for religion in the broader sense—as a fairly simple, comprehensible, satisfying picture of the world revealing its structure and purpose. Walter Marshall Horton has defined the human needs which faiths satisfy as three: "the need for an ultimate object of trust and devotion; the need for a final goal of hope and endeavor; the need for a concrete connection between trust and hope . . . ," in other words, a way of salvation. The increasingly numerous and somewhat disoriented masses of modern life, often uprooted by industrialism from traditional societies and cast into the maelstrom of an anomic civilization, have urgent needs of this sort. They may cling to traditional religion but increasingly they have adopted substitutes. No doubt this explains the significance of the nineteenth century's classical ideologies.

Other Forms of Socialism

Not well known in Europe until the 1880s, Karl Marx's formidable system thereafter tended to mold and dominate Continental socialism but never had that kind of success in Britain and never monopolized the field anywhere. Socialism was far broader than Marxism. It ranged, taking the term in its largest dimensions, from a fairly conservative bourgeois right wing, including Christian Socialism and moderate welfare-state reformism, to a revolutionary far left which by the 1880s had come to be designated "anarchism." In between lay many species in rich variety. Marx's contemporaries included Michael Bakunin, the Russian revolutionary, with whom he did many a battle; Louis Blanc, in exile in England after 1848 but tough enough to outlive the Bonapartist regime and return to France in 1871; Mazzini and Garibaldi, the Italians who became internationally famous in 1861; and the American, Henry George, whose book *Progress and Poverty* exerted a remarkable influence in Britain and parts of the Continent. Then there was William Morris, Ruskin's disciple, poet and craftsman, who popularized "guild socialism," a return to the spirit of medieval artisans. Proudhon, the French "mutualist," long retained a strong following in France, and the First International of 1864 produced quarrels between the Marxists and Proudhonists. In Germany, Ferdinand Lassalle, a romantic figure who disagreed with Marx on some matters, was a more important leader in the 1870s than the latter.

Then, within a few years after the major reception of Marxism and its success in the 1890s in capturing the strongest socialist groups on the Continent, came a major effort to "revise" Marx in the light of new developments; while in Great Britain the important Fabian movement rejected Marxian theory to build a more eclectic but extremely effective brand of reformist socialism. All this and more is part of the rich history of socialism and social reform in these latter decades of the nineteenth century, when Europe moved rapidly toward an order both more urban, industrial, and democratic. A brief review of this long story follows.

Revolutionary socialism, or working-class socialism of any sort, sank almost out of sight after 1848 for some time, suffering from repression and disunity. The Second Empire in France jailed Proudhon, exiled Blanc, and stifled press freedom while "buying off" the workers with its great public works projects. With the softening of Louis Napoleon's regime in 1860, socialism revived somewhat, only to be crushed again in the gripping episode of the Commune of Paris, 1871. Working-class socialists were accused of fomenting class war in Paris and the reaction again brought severe repression. This phase of French socialism was Proudhonist. Under the banner of "mutualism" these followers of the Besançon-born working man, who died in Paris in 1865, manifested a hatred of the state and centralized power that marked them off sharply from other socialists. They thought proletarian revolution should lead to a decentralized, "federal" political structure, for Proudhon could see no purpose to the existing state except militarism and the repressive defense of property, both of which would vanish with the bourgeoisie. The economic order would be one of cooperatives, the workers in each factory, farm, or store jointly managing it. Somewhat fuzzy and inane, Proudhon's utopia had the merit of upholding liberty; he accused Marx of fomenting a new tyranny while Marx sneered at the simplicity of the Frenchman's economic ideas. In this respect Proudhon repeated the charge brought by the celebrated Russian revolutionary, Michael Bakunin, against Marx: he was both too dogmatic and too authoritarian, and would lead to a new state tyranny. (The prophecy proved uncannily accurate.)

In 1871 when the Parisians decided to secede from the rest of France after the abdication of the Emperor Louis Napoleon (defeated by the Germans in war), they were acting in large part on Proudhon's ideas. (Communes were proclaimed in several other French cities.) There were to be sure other kinds of socialists, including the extremely romantic revolutionary followers of Blanqui, legendary insurrectionist. Blanquists, Proudhonians, and other socialists and radicals formed a decidedly inharmonious group among the Communards, whose defeat might be blamed in part on this dissension. The defeat of this revolt, and the brutal reprisals, caused the death or banishment of some 20,000 "Communards" and crushed French working-class radicalism to earth for another generation. One of the casualties was the First International, organized in 1864; always a scene of contention, it split, with the "Federalists" or "Anarchists" (Proudhonists) taking over what was left of it for a while only to see it die in 1877.

From the shattering defeat and civil strife of 1870–1871, France headed slowly toward the Third Republic, under which freedom would revive and a new socialist movement gradually reappear. In Germany, laws against the socialists were enforced in the seventies and eighties while at the same time Bismarck tried to alleviate the lot of the workers with Europe's first state-administered social welfare system, including old-age pensions and insurance against sickness. But the German Social Democratic Party, now firmly Marxist, survived the persecution, developed able leaders and a magnificent organization, and after being legalized in 1890 following Bismarck's removal from power, went on to become one of Germany's largest political parties (*the* largest by 1912) and the dominant force in the Second International. The latter world organization dates from 1889–1890 and enjoyed considerable success until 1914, its international congresses and its annual May Day demonstrations being impressive. It counted 12 million members by 1914; the war destroyed it.

Reformist Socialism

The 1880s and particularly the 1890s saw a widespread interest in social legislation on all fronts; it is the watershed for the change of direction from laissez-faire economic liberalism to a more socially conscious, state-interventionist order. There were many signs of this change and many versions of it.

In Britain, the prosperity and stability of the 1850–1870 period washed away Chartism and Owenism, marking the high tide of liberalism in its individualist, antistate phase. But the '80s bring a significant change. In 1881 the philosopher T. H. Green began at Oxford University a school of social thought influenced by Hegel and stressing the social origin of rights, the social responsibilities of property. The rapidity of change in outlook may be judged from a comment of Lord Milner: "When I went up to Oxford (in the early 1870s) the laissez-faire theory still held the field. . . . But within ten years the few men who held the old doctrines in their extreme rigidity had come to be regarded as curiosities." This was a respectable revolution. Green borrowed from Hegel a feeling for the claims of society and the positive role of the state, without any admixture or revolution or violence. At University College, London, economist Stanley Jevons undermined dogmatic laissez-faire by simply asking for scientific, empirical investigation in particular areas to determine "where we want greater freedom and where less," a solution of problems piecemeal, rather than in accordance with some general formula. This was the path taken by the Fabian socialists. It was a reaction against the dogmatic individualism often proclaimed by Victorian liberals (for example, Auberon Herbert and the Non-Interference Union) as much as against dogmatic socialism.

In 1887 the young Irish critic, essayist, orator, novelist, and playwright George Bernard Shaw introduced Marx (as he was soon to introduce Nietzsche) to the British public. But the sharp-witted young men with whom Shaw joined to form the Fabian Society at about this time soon rejected Marx's labor theory of value and with it the rest of his economics: they retained only his moral indignation at the alleged stupidities and wrongs of a capitalistic, acquisitive society, and this they got from others besides Marx—from Carlyle, Ruskin, Mill, Morris, Nietzsche. The Fabians emerged from the chrysalis of something called the Fellowship of the New Life, founded by a remarkable Scotsman, Thomas Davidson, in 1882. The Fabian Society broke away from Davidson's group in 1884. Shaw joined it in 1885. He had turned socialist after listening to Henry George. Fabianism was eclectic in its origins, not imprisoned by a dogma, and permeated with the spirit of British empiricism. Initially, after Jevons and Alfred Marshall had discredited the Marxian labor theory of value in favor of a marginal utility theory, the Fabians tried to elaborate a general theory of exploitation on this basis, using the Ricardian theory of rent. But before long they decided that "abstract economics" was not of much value.

A mentor of Fabian founder Beatrice Webb was Charles Booth, author of an exhaustive pioneer social study of *Life and Labour of the People of London* (9 volumes, 1892–1897). "The *a priori* reasoning of political economy, orthodox and unorthodox alike, fails from want of reality," Booth wrote. Booth had been influenced by Comte and by the German historical school of economics (Schmoller). The result was an economics mainly historical and descriptive; the chief works of the Webbs were massive historical studies of local government, trade unions, and poor relief. Problems should be tackled piecemeal with the aid of thorough factual documentation, they believed. Fabian pamphleteering was often hard-hitting, and bitterly critical of bourgeois society. But the movement's enduring importance lay in the patient accumulation of facts and ideas directed at particular abuses, under the guidance of the industrious Sidney Webb and his wife, Beatrice.

Clearly a faith was at work here: the Fabians did not doubt that socialism was a higher form of human society, the next rung on the ladder of social evolution, and they worked for it with a missionary spirit. The following statement, by C. E. M. Joad, may suggest something of the mood, as he recalled it in later years:

> England before 1914 was a land of gross social and economic inequality, in which the poverty and misery of the many were outraged by the luxury and the ostentation of the few. Under Socialism we believed the poverty and misery would disappear and the inequality be rectified. This was the first, fresh springtime of the Fabian Socialism, and we saw ourselves marching in irresistible procession with Shaw, Webb and Wells—slightly out of step—in the vanguard, to the promised land of State ownership of the means of production, distribution and exchange which we believed lay just around the corner.[12]

In their early days at least, the Fabians were not too scholarly to take part in demonstrations and harangue working-class audiences. On November 13, 1887, Shaw, William Morris, Annie Besant, and other intellectual socialists were roughed up by the police at a demonstration in Trafalgar Square. After this they chose the path of gradual change by parliamentary means, their duty being to furnish the politicians with the facts of industrial life, so fully and plainly that even a politican could not do otherwise than recognize the necessity of social legislation. In this they were remarkably successful. If, prior to World War I, there was in Britain no very large Labour or Socialist Party (there was a small one, with less than 10 percent of the seats in the House of Com-

[12]"What I Still Believe," *The New Statesman and Nation*, May 19, 1951.

mons),[13] this was largely because the older parties, especially the Liberal Party, had been quietly infiltrated by a good deal of social-welfare doctrine.

If they rejected Marx's economic theory, the Fabians agreed with his faith in the future of socialism. It was, they thought, evident that socialism was the wave of the future. But it would come gradually, was coming everyday, rather than all at once in one great revolution. Parliamentary democracy and other institutions of self-government would ensure its peaceful adoption. The Fabians placed great stress on local government; contrary to a common opinion, they did not propose the nationalization of all industry, but at this time (pre-1914) hoped that the county and borough councils, recently established in Great Britain, would own and operate a great deal of it. They did believe in public ownership as a panacea that, by driving the landlord and capitalists out of business, would increase the workers' share and lead to an era of plenty for all. In this they were often quite naive.

But Fabian tactics helped ease the way to acceptance of social welfare principles by moderate men in Great Britain. Under conservative auspices, paternalistic perhaps and including such things as municipal ownership of utilities ("gas and water socialism") and state-run health insurance or old-age pension plans, it could attract broad support; in 1889 a British peer remarked that "we are all socialists now." The sheer facts of life in a complex, interdependent industrial society forced men to modify laissez-faire capitalism. Bismarck declared in his great speech to the German Reichstag on social insurance legislation that the modern state could not disclaim all responsibility for the welfare of its working-class citizens; if it did, it would invite revolution. More modestly, Birmingham industrialist Joseph Chamberlain found that the upper classes could not ignore sanitary conditions among the lower classes in a modern city, because cholera germs were no respecters of class lines.

Also, trade unions became accepted and respectable and gave the workers a modest voice in the affairs of industry and the state. They were at least a force to be reckoned with, backed by the weapon of the strike. In the 1900s British trade unions overcame the Taff Vale decision, making them responsible for damages in a strike. Bitter strikes swept France and Italy as well as Britain, in this decade. While in France "syndicalists" dreamed of accomplishing the revolution by a great general strike, trade union leaders were apt to scorn the socialist intellectuals who preferred theoretical argument to "practical work inside the labor movement." Orthodox Marxism deplored the "opportunism" of trade

---

[13]The parliamentary Labour Party was born in 1900. On its doctrinal side it owed something to the rather eccentric Marxism of H. M. Hyndman, and rather more to William Morris's Socialist League, as well as a little to the Fabians, but it was much more motivated by practical trade-union goals prior to World War I.

unionism which aimed at nothing more than getting some workers a bigger slice of the rewards without "changing the system." But in Germany the unions and the Marxist social democrats struck a close alliance. (The French unionists, by contrast, rejected such a relationship.) By 1906, it was the unionists who had the stronger position, but they accepted the SDs as their political arm. In all the countries of western Europe, the unions, growing rapidly in the 1890s, were strong in the 1900s.

"Socialism" in this sense, as a pragmatic modification of laissez-faire capitalism in trade-unionist and state-welfare directions, became an accepted part of the late Victorian political landscape, though not without its bitter controversies: as late as 1910 in Britain the Lloyd George budget, including an income tax for social insurance financing, inspired an opposition which ended only in the "swamping" of the House of Lords and the passing of a Parliament Act sharply reducing the power of the peers to block legislation. There followed what an English newspaper called "the greatest scheme of social reconstruction ever attempted"—the National Insurance Bill of 1911.

Marxist Revisionism

Quite different was the situation in Germany, where a strong Marxist party developed, by far the strongest and best-organized one in Europe. The German Social Democrats won great prestige by their success against Bismarck's efforts to destroy them. After 1891 save for one brief period the SDP thrived on legality, having shown it could survive illegality. It was a well-disciplined mass organization, publishing its own newspapers and led by educated Germans of the caliber of August Bebel, Wilhelm Liebknecht, Eduard Bernstein, and Karl Kautsky. Entering into close association with the trade unions, in 1912 it was the largest single political party with one-third of the electorate. The Social Democratic leaders accepted the possibility of overthrowing capitalism by peaceful, democratic means. In the meetings of the Second International they opposed the radicalism of the anarchists and preached the inevitability of socialism on the basis of Marx's theory of the self-destruction of capitalism, the dialectically necessary triumph of socialism. Unlike the Fabians they did not view socialism as a piecemeal program but awaited the day when the entire capitalistic system would crumble, meanwhile generally refusing to collaborate in government with the "bourgeoisie."

Bernstein went further in the direction of reformism. His efforts to "revise" Marx touched off a battle of words within the GSDP in which revisionism was finally rejected. Bernstein believed that Marx's prophecies about the decline of capitalism and the increasing misery of the working class had proved false. Small and medium property had not disappeared, but were even increasing; the working class was getting better off, not worse off; the class struggle had become less acute, not more so. Drawing conclusions from this, he suggested a reformism not far in spirit from British Fabianism. He held that political democracy, having arrived in western Europe, made it possible to establish socialism by parliamentary means. "In all advanced countries," he urged, "we see the privileges of the capitalist bourgeoisie yielding step by step to democratic organizations." The party refused to accept this gradualism in theory, remaining officially committed to the winning of the proletarian revolution by means of the class struggle. It would not participate in governments in collaboration with the "bourgeois" parties. It almost read Bernstein out of the party, though he was an old and dedicated servant. But while rejecting gradualism the large majority of the party accepted legalism. Engels himself, living on into the 1890s, announced that "The time of revolution carried though by small minorities at the head of unconscious masses is past." The path to the revolution would be a democratic and parliamentary one.

Similar issues agitated the French Socialist party which, rent by schism, managed to achieve unity in the 1900s but not unanimity. In 1899, after the socialist Millerand had accepted a post in the government headed by the left republican Waldeck-Rousseau, the French socialists earnestly debated this policy, and it was the occasion for exchanges between their two outstanding leaders, Jules Guesde and Jean Jaurès. Jaurès argued that it was good to penetrate bourgeois positions in this way, for would not the capitalist regime fall little by little, and how could it fall if its outposts were never occupied? But Guesde carried the day, by a narrow margin, with an eloquent exposition of socialist orthodoxy: the doctrine of the class struggle, of the solidarity of the working classes, of the utter incompatibility of socialism and capitalism: there could be no "mixture" or in-betweens, it was a matter of either-or. In the 1914 elections the party won about a sixth of the seats; like its German counterpart it refused to take ministerial posts in any government in which it would share power. Right wing-left wing tension still existed, with unity maintained only at the cost of a rather imprecise program. French socialism was complicated by the presence of strong traditions other than Marxism. If Guesde, "Torquemada in lorgnettes," was a rigid Marxian dialectician, Jaurès, the greatest man in the party and one of the great Frenchmen of his generation, was a deeply civilized humanist who drew on many other sources than Marx. For Jaurès, Leon Blum later wrote, socialism was "the summation, the point of convergence, the heritage of all that humanity had created since the dawn of civilization. . . ." Proudhonist and other elements still lingered on in France despite a strong Marxian incursion.

Similarly in Italy there were reformist, revisionist spokesmen (for example, Filippo Turati) arguing that democracy had rendered revolution obsolete, but finding bitter opponents on the left to whom this was dangerous illusion. In Russia, the Marxist debate took a not dissimilar turn. Marxism entered Russia via the remarkable intellect of G. V. Plekhanov, a self-educated but exceedingly well-educated man who, exiled like so many other politically conscious Russians, lived and wrote for many years in Switzerland. In the 1870s the political faith of revolutionary Russians was populism, a courageous, self-sacrificing but intellectually not very clear movement, based on a belief in the uniqueness of Russia and especially of her communal peasant population. The "big three" of earlier Russian socialism had been Belinsky, already mentioned as a Hegelian; Bakunin, the fabulous revolutionary who, influenced in Paris by Proudhon, became an anarchist and attacked Marx for his statism; and Alexander Herzen, the powerful publicist who came to Paris in 1848 to receive a shattering blow from the "June Days" when the workers' insurrection against the Republic was savagely repressed. With the aid of a German historian they discovered in the *mir* or Russian peasant village an allegedly natural foundation for Proudhonian mutualism. Subsequently somewhat discredited, Bakunin and Herzen nevertheless deeply influenced the populist movement of which the Social Revolutionary Party was the political offshoot. In the 1860s the *mir* socialists, though not a violent group, were repressed by the Tsar's government; Chernyshevsky and Pisarev were imprisoned, Moscow University closed in 1868. The result was the famous "To the People" pilgrimage of young idealists in the 1870s, which suffered rude disenchantment and brought about the arrest of hundreds; and then, in desperation, a wave of revolutionary terrorism. This too led nowhere; and in opposition to the romantic excesses of populism, which resorted to assassination, climaxed in the killing of Tsar Alexander II in 1881, the cool, analytical approach of Marxism was welcome. Marxism in Russia in the 1890s had the effect of turning minds from illegal revolutionary pamphlets to the systematic study of economics, sociology, and history; the stress was on a well-grounded intellectual outlook, careful planning, no childish adventurism. Marxism even allowed some to accept the progressiveness of capitalism. It was a weapon against agrarian populism with its revolutionary terrorism.

A civilized, even fastidiously esthetic intellectual, Plekhanov believed in the Marxist laws of historical evolution and counselled waiting for a democratic revolution which would come about spontaneously after Russia went through a capitalist phase. Instilling Marxist precepts into a generation of Russian revolutionaries, Plekhanov found some of these disinclined to wait. In 1903, Lenin proposed the creation of an elite of professional revolutionaries, trained to seize power. To Plekhanov's orthodox Marxism this was little less than Bonapartism or Blanquism. The majority of the Russian Social Democratic Party followed him and a split occurred. Lenin's "bolshevik" group was in fact in a small minority most of the time, the "mensheviks" a more numerous and prestigious group. 1917 was to bring victory and fame to the stubbornly independent Lenin; prior to that, he was thought to have departed widely from Marxian orthodoxy, and was isolated at the far left of the socialist spectrum.

To sum up the Marxist debate: on the Continent, though not in England, Marxism prevailed as the reigning orthodoxy in the socialist or social democratic parties which were well organized and gaining adherents, on the eve of 1914. But within the parties sharp debate took place centering on the issue of whether class struggle, revolution, and the complete destruction of capitalism at one stroke had not become an obsolete program in the era of democratic politics, trade unionism, and welfare capitalism. The usual answer was to refuse to abandon Marxism for Fabian gradualism (Bernstein) but also to reject stress on violent revolution through illegal or conspiratorial means (Lenin). The majority of socialists held to their faith in an apocalyptic revolution that would change the entire system, but thought this could come peacefully as soon as their political party won a majority of the electorate, and they refused meanwhile to take any share of power. Their rate of growth between 1890 and 1914 held out some hope that this might happen. But this compromise was an uneasy one, and gave rise to a degree of internal tension. Between Albert Thomas and Jules Guesde in France, Eduard Bernstein and Rosa Luxemburg in Germany, or Plekhanov and Lenin in Russia, one found a considerable ideological and psychological distance. This ambivalence can be directly related to unresolved dilemmas at the heart of Marxian doctrine; particularly between voluntarism and determinism, elitism and democracy, revolution and evolution. On one side there was the call to action, to an uprising of the downtrodden led by revolutionary heroes; and on the other there was the belief that the objective laws of historical development were fast preparing the way for the inevitable triumph of democratic socialism.

Anarchism

Viewed more broadly, Marxism itself was a kind of center between a right and left wing of the entire "social" movement. To its left lay the anarchists, who seldom could be contained in the same party with the socialists though the congresses of the International provided a place for a less than friendly exchange of views. (The socialists passed resolutions against the anarchists at the International and told them they were not welcome, but, as trade union delegates, some anarchists always got in.) Anarchism was weak in Germany (though sometimes spectacular), stronger (as "anarcho-syndicalism" or direct action through the trade unions) in France, still stronger in Italy and Spain where the condition of the lower classes was more desperate and industrialism was less advanced. An "anarchist" might be a peace-loving enemy of centralization, a Proudhonian friend of liberty and cooperation; but in the 1880s and 1890s a much more familiar type resorted to assassination and other violent actions. They all disbelieved in the value of political action through elections and parliaments. Some of them were Marxists, or partial Marxists: what they had learned from the master was that economics determines all, that representative legislatures are a sham to cover the dictatorship of the bourgeoisie (this from Proudhon, too), and that capitalism owns the state and always will until smashed in the proletarian social revolution. After the revolution, there would be no more parliaments or states anyway, anarchists held; there would be the pure freedom of the classless society—no government at all. Most anarchists were inclined to be far out on the voluntarist wing of Marxism, so far as to be beyond the pale of party orthodoxy. They stressed the freedom of men to change their situation by acting; nothing is predetermined. They might go as far as Georges Sorel (treated later, under the irrationalists) in deciding that socialism is simply a myth, a religion, not a science at all. Sorel found Marx most unimaginative and the social Democrats exceedingly dull—even bourgeois! A good example of such trends within socialism is Labriola, the Italian anarchist; a little later, Henri de Man, the Belgian.

The rapid growth of trade unions as an indigenous, spontaneous process encouraged some social thinkers to believe—as the Russians had believed about the *mir*—that here were "the units upon which the future society will be built" and others to theorize that the revolution would come about not through parliaments but by means of the general strike, when all the workers simultaneously would put down their tools and bring the economy to a halt. Sorel was identified with this position for a time, until he became disillusioned with the trade unions as agents of revolution.

Many varieties of anarchism existed and indeed by their very nature these individualistic radicals could not be regimented into any one creed. But significant numbers of them tried to foment revolution, preparing the workers for it by preaching or, better, by action. Ultraanarchists engaged in a wave of assassinations in the 1890s that shocked not only the bourgeoisie but also the social democrats, who denounced them furiously. Others dreamed of the general strike as a revolutionary weapon, and meanwhile tried to stir up all the strikes they could to give the workers practice.

It is depressing to record so much hate, but the anarchists were idealists who had many of them known the suffering of the most deprived classes in the community. Their intellectual antecedents were vague but plentiful: all the denouncers of injustice and leaders of revolt from Spartacus to Marx, all the haters of ruling-class sham from Lucretius to Baudelaire. If they were educated they knew these; most were not, except for scraps of second-hand learning. They were the extremists of a revolution, the Black Panthers of the nineteenth-century proletariat. Much of their spirit got into the Russian Revolution which, nominally Marxist, was led by men who shared a good deal of the anarchist *ésprit*. Lenin was, really, a borderline case. But during the Revolution the anarchists were to be ruthlessly destroyed by the victorious Bolsheviks.

If the anarchists stood to the left of the Socialists or Social Democrats, there were many on the Right, among whom we have named Fabians, simple trade unionists, and bourgeois upholders of the welfare state. British "Lib-Labs" or trade unionists often seemed highly out of place at International meetings taken up with debates between German Marxists and Italian anarchists. Lord Harcourt, needless to say, who had said "we are all socialists," would hardly have been welcome there at all! Conservative upholders of the status quo, pillars of society, might show an interest in mild socialism. Bismarck, as well as England's Disraeli and Joseph Chamberlain, and Italy's Giolitti,[14] held that some concessions to the workers would keep them from following madmen into violent revolution; if to conserve is to preserve, preservation demanded an end to the irresponsibility of laissez-faire. In 1890, the Emperor of Germany, Kaiser Wilhelm II, having just fired Bismarck and repealed the antisocialist laws, called an international conference to consider "international labor legislation." In France, following the turmoil of the famous Dreyfus Case, the bourgeois left wing (Radicals, and soon Radical Socialists) flirted with socialism: basically Jacobin-democratic, men like Aristide Briand and Georges Clemenceau were prepared to tax big property for the benefit of small, and the government budget of expenditures on welfare rose sharply. The *Solidarisme* of politician-intellectual Leon Bourgeois found nature as well as society filled with cooperation and interdependence, rather than dog-eat-dog competition. At the same time these Radicals showed no sympathy toward anarchist violence, and used troops to break strikes.

Of these varieties of socialism, one more at least needs to be mentioned: Christian socialism. The great papal encyclical *Rerum Novarum*, 1891, was the most famous pronouncement here, though there were

[14]Who according to Denis Mack Smith "had studied *Das Kapital* with application and profit." Giolitti was the almost perennial Italian prime minister between 1900 and 1914.

Protestant versions also. It was not difficult for the Church to approve a kind of socialism. Christian dislike of materialism and selfishness, the doctrine of stewardship by which the rich should aid the poor, the deeply implanted Christian concern for the meek and disinherited, all might be turned in this direction. Catholic social doctrine gained prominence earlier in the century from the writings of Lamennais, but the Breton firebrand had run afoul of orthodoxy. Albert de Mun and La Tour du Pin subsequently brought to Catholic social doctrine an interest in the corporate economics of the Middle Ages; politically, they were conservatives. Pope Leo XIII was deeply interested in the cause of regaining the working class for Christianity. *Rerum Novarum* opposed modern capitalism and while rejecting "materialistic socialism" called for a fundamental reorganization of economic life to correspond with Christian principles. In France and Italy Catholic trade unions were organized, many priests devotedly dedicated service to working-class education, and there were individual examples of capitalists (like Leon Hormel) moved to experiment with "the Christian factory," but it is doubtful if the Catholic Social movement achieved very much. In England, an unusual group of Christian Socialists had emerged in the 1850s, including notably Charles Kingsley, F. D. Maurice, and John Ludlow; this died out for a time but there was a revival toward the end of the century, which tended to merge into the broader movement of social reform (T. H. Green, the Fabians, etc.) without achieving much identity. Christianity had lost most of the proletariat to the secular religion of socialism. Karl Marx was its new prophet.

By the 1900s, there were those who thought this secular socialism was dying of dogmatism and an obsolete, simplistic set of *idées fixés.* (See the remarks of Benedetto Croce, in *Cultura e vita morale*, 1911; or the view of Charles Péguy, leading French writer of the 1900s who broke with the Marxists to become a kind of Christian socialist.) In western Europe, considering the subsequent history of social democracy of all sorts, this was probably true. We need not be reminded that there were other parts of the world where it had quite a role to play. For western Europe, the later nineteenth century was the great age of this secular religion or ideology: the Age of Marx.

The Rise of Historical Studies

As a footnote to Marx's exciting if controversial historical scheme, we might add that history was becoming of serious interest to many in the nineteenth century. Despised in the seventeenth and developed only in rudimentary ways in the eighteenth, it received its philosophical certificate of legitimacy from Burke, Herder, and Hegel and became a respectable academic citizen in the mid-nineteenth century. For example, a chair of modern history was first established at Cambridge University only in the eighteenth century and for long after that amounted to little, but leaped to the front in the era of Lord Acton. The great historians— Voltaire, Gibbon, and on to Macaulay and Michelet in the earlier nineteenth century—had been amateur *literati*, more noted for their literary gifts than any professional competence, though often they did do capable research; now, beginning in Germany (especially at the University of Göttingen), history came of age as a specialized profession marked by the "scientific" use of materials, careful research in the primary sources, with thorough criticism and collation of knowledge. Making possible this advance was the collection and organization of historical materials in the great libraries, archives, and museums of Europe, something that was accomplished only toward the end of the eighteenth century.

The romantics stimulated imaginative interest in the past; German philosophers saw it as the unfolding of Truth, Burkeans as the school of political wisdom. It became possible to widen the range of historical studies to include social and economic history; this was partly a matter of having access to the sources of such knowledge, such as the records of medieval manors, but also partly the perspective of an age acutely aware of economic and social issues. In general, with the retreat of confidence in religion or metaphysics to answer the big questions about the meaning and conduct of life, people turned to history. There one found a repository of wisdom and experience, a treasure-house of knowledge throwing light on the present human situation. Darwin and other evolutionary thinkers popularized explanation of a genetic sort. With the arrival of professional methods and the organization of materials, history seemed to be passing from the realm of conjecture and opinion to the status of a genuine science. Quite a few others in addition to Karl Marx had the idea that a real science of history was now possible. Henry Buckle was dogmatic about it in England, Mill thought so more cautiously; the German scholars, doing their arduous detailed research, felt that some day, somehow, the fruits of painstakingly accurate spade work would be gathered in the form of a universal synthesis. French positivists agreed.

The belief in a science of history in this sense—the sense indicated by historian J. B. Bury when he declared in his inaugural lecture as Regius Professor at Cambridge in 1902 (succeeding Acton) that "there will no longer be divers schools of history," only one, true history, since history is "simply a science, no less and no more—has almost died since then. But the nineteenth was, beyond question, an historical century;

Bury was not wrong in asserting that "In the story of the nineteenth century, which has witnessed such far-reaching changes in the geography of thought and in the apparatus of research, no small or isolated place belongs to the transformation and expansion of history." The leading ideologies, as we have noted, were historical—Hegel's, Comte's, and Spencer's as well as Marx's. Among the great intellectual figures of the century whose interest in history was much more than incidental one could list in addition Tocqueville, Renan, Mill, Arnold, Newman, and many others.[15]

And the reason for this "historical revolution" was that investigation of the past had become not just the indulgence of idle curiosity or trivial antiquarianism, but something charged with the deepest meaning because it could explain the fate and future of mankind. It could reveal the great laws of development, the cycles of growth of the human race from earliest times to today—and tomorrow. All the great nineteenth-century theories of history posited an ascent from lower to higher, in one way or another. Bitter critic of capitalist society that he was, Marx was as optimistic as any Victorian in the long run: one more turn of the wheel of history and the millennium would be reached.

[15]Acton, together with his German friend the Munich professor I. Döllinger, dedicated historians as they were, formulated an historical theology of Catholicism according to which the Christian truth gradually revealed itself in history through the medium of the Church. Unfortunately the Vatican could not accept this because of its implications that individual popes might have erred (did not have the full truth in the past), etc. It remains an interesting example of the impact of history on the age. "Metaphysics could not be relied upon to promote religion— that could be done only by history," as Acton reported the view of Döllinger.

11

The Crisis
of European Thought:
1880-1914

> [With] the development of intellectualism and the
> rationalization of life. . . . Art takes over the function
> of a this-worldly salvation. . . . It provides a
> salvation from the routines of everyday life, and
> especially from the increasing pressures of theoretical
> and practical rationalism.
>
> MAX WEBER

> It will no longer be a despot that oppresses the
> individual, but the masses. . . . I shall return to the
> Bedouins, who are free.
>
> GUSTAVE FLAUBERT

It is common to mark off a new period of European history beginning
in 1870 or 1871. One obvious landmark was the Franco-Prussian War,
which brought to an end the Second Empire in France, led to the Third
Republic there, and introduced Germany's Imperial Reich as the greatest
state in Europe. The unification of Italy was also completed at this time
with the annexation of Rome and the ending of the pope's temporal
power. There were other landmarks: In 1867, Great Britain made a further extension of the suffrage and followed it within a few years with
other reforms, in education, the army, the civil service, which constituted a significant turn toward political democracy. After the victory of
the unionists in her great Civil War in 1865, which had some influence
on the turn toward democracy in England, the United States experienced
a vast economic boom that contributed not a little to Europe's, while

Germany also waxed prosperous on her new unity, beginning a classic period of international trade and development. Also, one can trace the beginnings of the "new imperialism" to the 1870s.

But periodization is often arbitrary, and it is just as easy to make the break a little later. Neither imperialism nor democracy really got into high gear until the 1880s: witness the Third Republic which was not firmly established until this decade, or British politics where Gladstone's Midlothian campaign of 1881 stands as the first really popular election. It is from the 1880s that we date the rise of trade unions and socialist movements, as the last chapter indicated; there is general agreement that this was the critical decade for the turn away from laissez-faire liberalism. Moreover it was the 1880s which introduced electricity, the automobile, and other miracles of technology, though no decade in the nineteenth century was without its contribution to this process.

For the intellectual historian, some time in the 1880s is preferable as a turning point. This decade produced not only Nietzsche, Freud, and Bergson, in addition to the important social thought just referred to, but also such things as the beginning of a new trend in science, dateable from the Michelson-Morley experiment of 1887, and a revolution in the arts—a revolution best placed here, it would seem, though it straddled the whole period 1870–1914. Involved are such writers and artists as Ibsen, Zola, Dostoyevsky, Tolstoy, the symbolists, and the impressionists. From the other end, one can hardly avoid seeing the 1870s as the evening of the mid-Victorian day, not yet quite done, its great figures still alive. One thinks of Mill, Marx, and Darwin in ideology, of the writers Tennyson, Browning, Carlyle, Ruskin, Arnold, and other "eminent Victorians."

One cannot be precise in such matters. The 1870s, the 1880s, the 1890s, the 1900s, each brought forth its novelties and its men of genius. What no one doubts is that 1914 was an epochal date, the huge war that settled its gloomy cloud over Europe in that year marking the end of an era in everyone's chronology. It is beyond doubt also that the years just before 1914 bore unmistakeable signs of being critically disturbed ones. An unusual number of old truths became uncertain, an unusual number of strange creeds and novel doctrines appeared. This was true in the sciences, where verities not challenged since Newton were overturned in a new scientific revolution. It was true in philosophy, in the arts, and in social studies. It was no less true in religion. It is possible that these years were the critical ones for the future destiny of Western man. Intellectually, they are the most exciting years of all, to one living in the twentieth century, for the ideas born here have largely shaped the mind of that century—something rather comparable to the way the 1688–1720 period set the directions of Enlightenment thought.

Nationalism

This was the time of Western civilization's spectacular conquest of the outer world, when the continents of Asia and Africa were forced to submit to the domination of the aggressive Europeans. This vast process was in the widest sense a tribute to the amazing success of Europe, its higher technical skills, and also its organizing genius. But it brought evil with it and to many thoughtful Europeans it was a dismaying moral lapse, perhaps a symbol of decline and fall. The man in the street certainly found it gratifying; but eventually it would produce revolutions against Western domination on the part of Asiatic and African peoples. For the time being what it most notably produced was an inordinate pride and boastfulness, the jingoism that helped fan the flames of war in 1914.

The outbreak of the worst war in history lay ahead, constituting a terrific moral setback for a civilization that had believed itself on the high road to man's greatest success. In some ways the war reflected the conquest of nineteenth-century Europe by the sentiment of nationalism. Nationalism appeared in the wake of Napoleon's attempt to impose French domination on Europe; Fichte's "Addresses to the German Nation," written when Bonaparte invaded Prussia, might be called its manifesto. It went on after the Peace of Vienna, which tried to ignore it; and it played a prominent part in the revolutions of 1848. Thereafter it was to emerge truly into its own in the era of Italian and German unification, when Mazzini was Europe's leading prophet. It was still potent in the years before 1914 and was a basic cause of the war explosion of that fateful year.

Nationalism was not absolutely new, but its intensity and dominance in the nineteenth century made it a force as never before. "The outstanding feature of European history in the nineteenth century is the growth of nationalities," it has been aptly claimed. Nation-making in Europe goes back a long way, ultimately to the earlier Middle Ages. National consciousness, a different and later thing, may be found at least as early as Elizabethan England and Lutheran Germany. But other loyalties competed with that paid to the state or national group. Throughout the Middle Ages, a man was a Christian first, then a native of his home district, and only after that (if at all) a Frenchman, or German. The Church was universal; so, in theory, was the state, for a long time. Actually strongest were dynastic and feudal loyalties, based on a personal and not a territorial loyalty. Only gradually did the future nation-states become clearly defined; but for an accident or two, indeed, we might have Burgundians today instead of Frenchmen. And in Germany the territorial duchies (Bavaria, Saxony, Swabia, Franconia) remained the focus of patriotic sentiment until fairly recent times.

The decline of competing ideals and the consolidation in their permanent form of the nation-states paved the way for nationalism. But the Enlightenment was quite cosmopolitan. Though the work of knitting together the larger states of Europe administratively and economically went steadily on, the fashion in ideas did not then encourage the growth of nationalistic sentiments. The French Revolution and romanticism did contribute to nationalism, as we know it, and yet there remained a substantial element of international feeling among men of letters and learning in the first half of the century. Writing to Thomas Carlyle in 1826, Goethe in his old age rejoiced that "for some time past the best poets and writers of all nations have aimed at what is common to all men," and hoped that this might aid the cause of international peace.[1] There were many transnational European phenomena at this time. Not only were such secular creeds as liberalism and socialism much the same everywhere, but the arts, as well as the sciences, recognized no national boundaries. For example, in music Berlioz was an idol in Germany, Wagner in France—more so than either was in his own country!

But powerful forces were making for nationalism, and writers, poets, philosophers were to get involved. So were historians. The march of nationalism in the nineteenth century accompanied the advance of democracy. The German nationalist movement produced such popular figures as "Father" Jahn, who preached the fellowship and equality of all in the *Volk*—"Freies Reich! Alles gleich!" sang the *Turnerschaften*. The *Volksstaat* or people's state knew no privileged orders, only citizens under the nation, all equal.

Dangerous though it might be, nationalism in the nineteenth century offered a wider sense of community, along with material advantages, to the masses of people. In the exhortations of such prophets as Mazzini, nationalism took on the attributes of a religion, in the same way socialism did, equipped with regeneration, rebirth, and salvation symbols. Born of a spiritual revolution, the national people achieve a sacred brotherhood, which is their destiny and their salvation, and then they go forth to redeem the world. "Nationality is the role assigned by God to each people in the work of humanity; the mission and task which it ought to fulfill on earth so that the divine purpose may be attained in the world." Nationalists talked of universal brotherhood ("He who wants humanity wants a fatherland"); but typically they saw their

---

[1]*Letters from Goethe*, translated by M. Herzfeld and C. M. Sym, introduction by W. H. Bruford, 1957.

own country as just a bit more privileged. Jahn pointed out that the Germans were the central people, the keystone of the West. In different accents but with a similar message, Mazzini reminded his countrymen of their ancient Roman heritage of ruling and civilizing Europe. So did the Pan-Slav Mystagogues.

The rise of popular nationalism in the nineteenth century can be illustrated by the creation of the Joan of Arc cult in France. The "virgin, heroine, and martyr to the State, chosen by Providence to re-establish the French monarchy" (to quote the subtitle of a 1753 book) had of course lived in the early fifteenth century; but her deeds excited little interest at that time and for several hundred years after. Bishop Bossuet's history of France granted her but a few lines, and Voltaire, singularly enough from a later point of view, treated her as rather a ridiculous figure in his play *La Pucelle*. (The *philosophes*, we know, were remarkably immune to the sentiment of nationalism.) A few always kept alive the story of the Maid's bravery and devotion, but until the nineteenth century she remained fairly obscure. Napoleon, in 1803, referred to Joan as a symbol of French unity against English invaders. The Romantics of course were interested in the Middle Ages, unlike the Enlightenment, and we find the British poet Robert Southey as well as the German dramatist Schiller using Joan as a literary theme. Schiller's *Maid of Orleans* (also 1803) was indeed a key document: a German helped give the French their national heroine.

But it remained for the great nationalist historians of the nineteenth century to project the Maid as an image of French patriotism. Of these Jules Michelet was the foremost, and Michelet depicted Joan in eloquent prose as the mother of the French nation. The legend of Joan grew. Finally she was canonized in 1920 as a saint of the Church. Her canonization in French nationalist hagiography had occurred earlier. A notable worshipper at her shrine was the distinguished writer Charles Péguy (who died in 1914 at the Marne). Charles Maurras and the conservative *Action Française* made much of her; but so did socialists and liberals, anticlericals as well as clericals: Joan was the symbol of national unity. Conceivably it was because the French lacked a monarch that they settled their common loyalty on an almost mythical figure from the past. For the British public, of course, the figure of Queen Victoria functioned as a living mother-image and symbol of unity through much of her long reign (1837–1901).

The poet and the historian both participated in this shaping of national consciousness. "A nation," wrote Ernest Renan in a famous definition, "is the common memory of great things done jointly by our ancestors, along with the desire to remain united in order to do yet more of them." The nation, in brief, is a literary creation. The Italian nationalist movement began with Alfieri (1749–1803), who reminded Italians in romantic writings of their past glories. Koraïs performed a similar service to Greece, and an American named Smith is credited with beginning the "Arab Awakening"—so says the distinguished scholar George Antonius—when he revived the study of the Arabic language and literature midway in the nineteenth century. The Irish, who had almost lost their ancestral tongue, tried to revive it, or at least some literary men and Irish nationalists did; the Gaelic revival accompanied the Irish nationalist movement. A revival of Catalonian nationalism in Spain dates from the 1880s; so does Ukrainian separatism in Russia, while in southeastern Europe, an upthrust of nationalism threatened to blow up ancient multinational empires and destroy Europe's shaky balance of power.

In 1896 Theodor Herzl's book, *Der Judenstaat*, laid the foundations of the Jewish revival, focussed on the establishment of a modern Jewish state in the ancestral land of Palestine; the Zionist congresses began in 1897. The Dreyfus case in France and the ferocious persecution of the Jews in Russia, as well as anti-Semitic stirrings in Germany, had brought home to the Jews the fact that Europe was again in the grip of intolerance. Medieval anti-Semitism, the result in good part of religious emotions, had all but disappeared in the tolerant eighteenth century. Now toward the end of the nineteenth intolerance reappeared in the guise of nationalism. (It also had economic, anticapitalist overtones; the myth of the Jew as the sinister International Banker made its appearance. But the main charge against the Jews in the Dreyfus affair was that they lacked loyalty to France.)

Nationalism reached its apogee, or nadir, in the fateful epidemic of jingoism that accompanied the imperialist movement of the 1890s and preceded the great war of 1914–1918. A powerful social process involving all aspects of history, it cannot be left out of intellectual history, for many writers contributed to it. Of these, historians and novelists, thrusting into consciousness the past traditions of the people, were the most prominent. In addition to Michelet, the German historian Heinrich Treitschke, the American George Bancroft, the Englishman Thomas Macaulay come to mind, by modern critical standards rather lacking in strict accuracy, but eloquent and inspired in their evocation of the national story of their respective lands, in whatever guise they saw it. Never was history so popular as in this period when it dwelt on the rise of the nation and the destiny of its people.

Social Darwinism contributed its bit to the nationalist mixture. It is interesting that Herbert Spencer was a staunch anti-imperialist, a relic perhaps of his Cobdenite days; but the view that peoples and cultures are in competition, with the strongest or more efficient rightly surviving, was hard to dissociate from popular social Darwinism. H. G. Wells provides an example of a highly intelligent man and influential writer, moreover, a socialist and rationalist, a man of the Left, who nevertheless believed that Darwinian science had "destroyed, quietly but entirely, the belief in human equality," which meant that some peoples, and some races, are inferior to others; the inferior peoples, "these swarms of black, and brown, and dirty-white, and yellow people, who do not come into the new needs of efficiency," will have to go; "it is their portion to die out and disappear." That international life is a struggle, that those nations not prepared to compete in the arena of power will go down to extinction and will deserve to do so was a widely shared article of faith around the turn of the century; it swept even the United States in the Teddy Roosevelt era and was entertained by quite sophisticated minds. For example, John Davidson, the British poet, influenced by Nietzsche toward the view that "the universe is immoral," enthusiastically supported British imperialism, which he regarded, a la Rudyard Kipling, as having a sanction to rule and rule vigorously over the lesser breeds. The British scientist and mathematician, Karl Pearson, was taught by social Darwinism that races and nations, as well as individuals, are in a ruthless competition for survival from which progress results.

Nationalism rose to an almost frenzied peak in the years just before 1914. Gabriele D'Annunzio, famed flamboyant Italian writer, a weathervane who had adopted almost all possible positions just for the fun of it, became a fierce nationalist about 1909, calling on Italians to sharpen their sword on Africa and then advance on the world, phrases which found an all too frenzied response. The *Alldeutscher Verband*, or Pan-German League, entertained fantasies of German domination of all Europe. In France, Charles Maurras's significant *Action Française* was anti-Semitic and anti-German, militantly patriotic and militaristic (see further page 412). In Russia, and throughout the east of Europe, there was pan-Slavism, various versions of it. In the 1870s, Danilevski had argued that the next turn of the wheel of history would put the Slavs on top, the Latins and Germans having had their turn. Russia, the pan-Slavist Fadeyev declared, must either advance to the Adriatic or retire behind the Urals; it was her destiny to unify all the Slavic peoples of Europe. The personification of nations as having "destinies" was common; no doubt this was what the British philosopher Hobhouse had in mind when he blamed the war on Hegel, this sort of thinking being obviously related to a vulgarized Hegelian historicism. Seeley told the British about their imperial destiny, and according to Esmé Wingfield-Stratford, "The Press reeked with blood and reverberated with thunder" (*The Victorian Tragedy*). "Every important nation had become acutely and aggressively race-conscious," the English historian adds. It was one of the most apparent causes of the first world war.

Democracy

The accompaniment of nationalism was democracy. Here again the preliminaries reach far back, but no previous European age had felt the impact of the ideology and the practice of democracy as the one of 1880–1914. Most liberals of the earlier nineteenth century stoutly opposed universal suffrage. "Because I am a Liberal," wrote a member of Parliament and editorialist of the London Times in 1867, "I regard as one of the greatest dangers with which the country can be threatened a proposal to . . . transfer power from the hands of property and intelligence, and to place it in the hands of men whose whole life is necessarily occupied in daily struggles for existence." Tocqueville and Mill mistrusted democracy because they feared the degradation of intelligence and quality by the imposition of vulgar standards. Comte, as well as Bonald, equated democracy with anarchy, the absence of social order. Spencer wrote that the divine right of popularly elected parliaments would have to be resisted as firmly as the divine right of kings if it should threaten liberty. Many of the socialists scorned political democracy as a fraud, designed to deceive the working classes, who could only win their freedom by a social revolution.

Yet throughout the century there was a democratic thrust, which the generation of Tocqueville and Chateaubriand had felt and which became irresistible after mid-century. It was associated with the economic revolution; it followed necessarily from the bourgeois revolution. Political rights could not be withheld from the masses once political authority became a matter of convenience, not sanctity, and when wealth became more widely diffused. Throughout the century illiteracy declined —thus, in France, from 39 percent to 18 percent by 1878 as measured by conscript soldiers—while the press became increasingly free, and increasingly cheap. In 1870 the Education Act established free primary schools in Great Britain, compulsory within a few years after that. The "penny daily" made its debut about the same time. These are landmarks without equal in popular intellectual history.

In 1867 and 1884, Great Britain took steps towards full manhood suffrage, and by 1910 the women were agitating for it. France never actually lost universal suffrage after 1848, but under the Second Empire it was managed and manipulated in a way that deprived it of much meaning; after 1874, however, the Republic came back. Imperial Germany had a Reichstag elected by universal suffrage though it lacked responsible powers. "An assembly of 350 members cannot in the last instance direct the policy of a great power today," Bismarck held. Perhaps it could not, but in Britain, at least, the system of government by a cabinet drawn from and responsible to the House of Commons found success in these years. All governments had to pay more attention to public opinion—which might or might not be a good thing, critics noted, depending on how enlightened public opinion was. In the realm of foreign affairs, it was all too likely to be xenophobic, shrilly nationalistic, disdainful of the rights of foreigners. At home, those unconverted to democracy complained of unseemly and undignified electioneering methods, of political machines and bosses, of cheaper politicians driving out finer in a kind of political Gresham's Law. But very few discerning people thought that the rule of the few in politics and society was any longer possible. For better or for worse the rule of the many had come to stay.

Intellectuals were inclined to worry about this, perhaps, more than to hail it. In his essay on "Democracy," first published in 1861, and reissued in 1879, Matthew Arnold wrote, "Our society is probably destined to become much more democratic; who or what will give a high tone to the nation then? That is the grave question." A society is of real value not because large numbers of people are free and active, nor because of the creation of wealth; it is valuable insofar as it produces things that are noble and of good repute. When Arnold lectured in the United States or America on the need to "elevate" society, he seems utterly to have failed to make contact with the minds of Chicagoans. But America's sage, Walt Whitman, addressed similar warnings to his countrymen in his old age.

Democracy in itself, considered simply as the principle of mass or numbers, is no ideal, can easily become moral anarchy or mammonism; the old criticism made by Plato was repeated often in the later nineteenth century. Nineteenth-century European thought is filled with outcries against certain aspects or consequences of "democracy." "The crowd is the lie," wrote Kierkegaard. Democracy is "a form of decadence," declared the well-known French writer Emile Faguet, who had been influenced by Nietzsche. "If I am a democrat, it is without enthusiasm," observed the great French political leader Clemenceau, who had once led the popular party, in 1908. A notably hostile Victorian witness was Henry Maine (*Popular Government*, 1886). Nietzsche, treated later in this chapter, expressed hostility to democracy in aspects of his thought. The rule of inferiors, the herd spirit, the debasement of culture to the mass level, were to him among the chief diseases of modern man, to be cured only by the most drastic elevation of supermen-heroes to the helm of state, men strong and ruthless enough to whip and drive the masses toward some worthy goals. Like Dr. Stockmann in Ibsen's play "An Enemy of the People," Nietzsche believed that "the minority is always right." The levelling of the human personality into the conforming mass-man appalled him, and he thought democracy was responsible for this.

The Irrationalism of Nietzsche

"Almost without exception, philosophers have placed the essence of mind in thought and consciousness; this ancient and universal radical error must be set aside. Consciousness is the mere surface of our minds, which, as of the surface of the earth, we do not know the inside but only the crust. Under the conscious intellect is the conscious or unconscious will, a striving, persistent, vital force, a spontaneous activity, a will of imperious desire." Thus wrote the eccentric essayist and philosopher Arthur Schopenhauer, an offshoot of the romantic and idealist German philosophers (see above, pp. 221–23). Schopenhauer's distinction between Will and Reason, the former being fundamental, could be seen also in Darwin's scheme of nature in which the intellect is only a tool of survival, a part of the whole organism which struggles to adapt to its environment. Schopenhauer, the pessimist, thought the world spirit tricks us into making the struggle; the enlightened philosopher outwits the world spirit by suppressing desire, renouncing the game of life. He had been influenced not a little by the Hindu Upanishads, which became known to the West near the end of the eighteenth century and attracted some of the romantic and idealist philosophers.

The Oriental pessimism of Schopenhauer did not make much of an impression but the belief that the will is a deeper force than the conceptualizing reason left its stamp on the European mind. One whose mind was awakened on reading Schopenhauer was the brilliant German, Friedrich Nietzsche. Confronted with what seemed to him a decadent civilization, Nietzsche thought that he had found one cause of its enfeeblement in an excessive development of the rational faculty, at the cost of a creativeness that comes only with the spontaneity of instinct or will. The brilliant young philologist and classicist, whose first book was a study of Greek drama (*The Birth of Tragedy*), traced this disease far back into Western civilization. It had begun with Socrates and Plato, the triumph of logic over literature, reason over will. Another antirationalist of this era, the Frenchman Georges Sorel, independently made this same discovery that Socrates had been the root of all evil rather than of all good as conventionally taught. Excessive development of the rational faculty enfeebles; the habit of conceptual thought paralyzes the will. Europe had intellectualized too long; the result was the weary mediocrity Nietzsche thought he saw about him in this age of bourgeois materialism. In perhaps his greatest work Nietzsche has Zarathustra say, "I saw a great sadness come over men. The best were weary of their work. . . . All is empty, all is indifferent, all was." Western man had lost the capacity for believing in anything, his intellectualizing had led him to skepticism. The only solution lay in a new primitivism that would lead back to heroism.

The Birth of Tragedy (1871) revealed both his deep insights into Greek civilization and his almost frightening originality. Among other things it saw the genius of Hellas as stemming not primarily from joyous optimism (as so often suggested by the romantics) but from tragic suffering, and consisting not in scientific and philosophical rationalism so much as in primitive emotionalism tempered by reason. Dionysus, whose cult engaged in ecstatic and orgiastic ritual dances, became for Nietzsche a symbol of this primitive force, without which men cannot be truly creative. The Greeks had been great because they had Dionysus, as well as Apollo. They had not been rationalists, but men infused with the will to live. Their greatest age was the time of the early philosophers and dramatists, of Heraclitus and Aeschylus. Plato and Euripides already mark their decadence, which Western civilization unfortunately inherited more than their grandeur.

This electrifying reversal of previous perspectives was typical of Nietzsche's sharply iconoclastic thought, his "transvaluation" of values. A lyrical poet as well as a philosopher and deeply learned man, Nietzsche's challenging, radical books were to wake up intellectual Europe in the 1890s. He wrote most of these books in a frenzy of creativity in the 1880s, against the threat of oncoming madness which was evidently the result of syphilis contracted in youth. Widely rejected as a brilliant madman in the complacent atmosphere of pre-1914, a destructive and perverse genius who could not be taken seriously, he stands today as the major prophet of the tortured twentieth century, with its wars and its Caesarism which he predicted

Among his rejections were Christianity (a religion for slaves, denying life), and traditional morality ("morality is the most pernicious species of ignorance"). The supermen needed to rescue a decadent civilization must be beyond morality, for they must be "without pity for the degenerate." Democracy and nationalism, the vulgar superstitions of modern dwarf-men, also were targets for his sneers. More remarkable, and celebrated, was his atheism: "God is dead"; European man had killed him; one could no longer believe in any principle of cosmic order. Nietzsche did find something to believe in, escaping from his terrible skepticism to a "joyful wisdom" which to most others must seem scarcely less pessimistic: the love of life, as it is, in all its disorder, ugliness, cruelty, just because it is life (amor fati: love of fate). We are part of the cosmos, which is a blind incessant striving (it goes around in huge circles, coming back eventually to repeat itself), and we can affirm our own life force by living and striving. We can accept Dionysus, and reject Christ. "You have understood me? Dionysus versus the Crucified" —these were the last words.

The universe is irrational, it simply is. We can reject it, choosing with Schopenhauer to renounce life by suppressing all desire like the Indian *fakir*; or we can accept it, fully realizing its irrationality, pain, and horror. Not easy to understand, and perhaps tending in his later works toward the madness that approached him, Nietzsche at his worst suggests a shocking hatred of civilization and a desire for barbarism; at his best, he reminds us that man can create values by his own nobility though the universe be hostile. The supermen he called for to reshape the human race should not be thought of as brutalized Hitlers, rather as enlightened poet-philosopher statesmen. It must be said in his defense, and has been said by recent students concerned to rescue him from wild misinterpretation, that he despised all nationalism and militarism, including German, and also was no racist or anti-Semite, though the Nazis later made use of him. His wilder ejaculations of rage against the human race can charitably be excused as products of the sufferings of a morbidly sensitive and physically sick man; of enduring value in Nietzsche is the hatred of falsehood and sham, of mediocrity and vulgarity, along with deep insights into human creativity, and a fierce sincerity: one should live one's philosophy. His fantastic sensitivity to ideas makes Nietzsche a barometer registering virtually every variation of the modern mind.

Chief among these insights was an awareness of the role of the darker, submerged, unconscious, "Dionysian" elements in human nature, which by being "sublimated" enter into creativity. For Nietzsche anticipated Freud in many respects. This force is partly sexual, and Nietzsche suggests that Christianity and conventional morality have grievously damaged Western mankind by surrounding sex with taboos. It is, more basically, just the joyous spontaneity of the animal. It is the dithyrambic dance of primitive man. Civilize it, smother it with morality and reason, and you destroy something necessary to man and to culture. The highest culture requires something of the intellectual element but too much of it means decadence.

Nietzsche combined and held in suspension an amazing number of modern attitudes. There is something in him of the alienated artist, saying with Baudelaire, "The world has taken on a thickness of vulgarity that raises a spiritual man's contempt to a violent passion." He is an important precursor of twentieth-century existentialism, in question here being his call for man to create his own values by sheer will-power, as well as his rejection of all merely theoretical philosophy. "I have written my works with my whole body and life," Nietzsche could say proudly. He is the gloomy prophet of the totalitarian state and modern mass-man. But most of all he is the philosopher of the will-to-power or life force—the irrationalist, prober of drives deeper than reason, anticipator of Freud and Jung, psychologist of the unconscious.

In all his moods and guises, Nietzsche is clearly something quite new and different, compared to Victorian orthodoxy. He has the flavor of the *fin de siècle*, over which indeed his influence was spread widely. André Gide, the French novelist, remarked that "the influence of Nietzsche preceded with us the appearance of his work; it fell on soil already prepared . . .; it did not surprise but confirm."[2] As so often happens, an idea's hour seemed to have arrived and a number of people felt it independently at about the same time. One of the ideas this period seemed destined to discover and probe was the unconscious irrational within the human psyche. Almost contemporary with the great writings of Nietzsche in the 1880s came the first work of the Viennese physician, Sigmund Freud.

It would be difficult to overstate the influence of Nietzsche. It is an influence that has been felt much more on the Continent than in England, and may indeed be the most important single cause of that divergence between Continental and Anglo-Saxon modes so often noted today in philosophical circles. Whereas until recent times most British and American reactions to Nietzsche were hostile or uncomprehending, finding no sort of sense in this mad German (see the studies by Halèvy and Brinton), one must grasp Nietzsche, unquestionably, before one can understand the great European moderns, such as Thomas Mann, André Gide, D. H. Lawrence, the German and French existentialists and many others. As a recent writer (Werner Pelz) has commented, "It is not a matter of agreeing or disagreeing with his philosophical conclusions, but of having passed through his corrosives of metaphysical, moral, and psychological doubts. They leave a man scarred or purified; certainly changed." Through this fire the mind of modern Europe has passed.

Nietzsche's political impact was in more than one direction, like Darwin's. Atheist, radical critic of conventional religion and morality, destroyer of all manner or orthodoxies, this most dramatic of thinkers held a natural appeal to the Left, and we find many socialists and anarchists responding to his message, associating it with revolutionary

---

[2] In his article on "Nietzsche and John Davidson," *Journal of the History of Ideas*, June, 1957, John A. Lester, Jr., notes another case of one who "may have been a Nietzschean before he ever heard the name of Nietzsche," but whose native inclinations were stimulated by contact with the German. There were many such instances.

activism. It seemed to suggest an apocalyptic ending to the whole Western past and the inauguration of a completely new age. He was the darling of the *avant-garde*, the bible of the defiantly alienated artist-intellectual. In his name one could throw off traditional religion, defy the conventional moral rules, scorn the bourgeoisie, and predict a day of doom. None more revolutionary; and yet Nietzsche also scorned democracy and socialism, which he linked to the slave-morality of the Judeo-Christian world view. He preached the inequality of man and could be used to sanction imperialism, despotism, and war. Benito Mussolini was deflected from left-wing socialism toward the new cult of fascism in good part by Nietzsche; Hitler and the Nazis subsequently glorified him, even if, as his defenders insist, they distorted him. During the war of 1914–1918, people in the Allied countries fighting Germany quite commonly linked Nietzsche to the ruthless war-making of the Hohenzollern legions, who were depicted advancing on their barbarous mission armed with Nietzschean admonitions to be brutal. If this was an hysterical caricature, the fact remains that German youth just before the war were strongly affected by the cult of adventure and heroism, derived in no small part from the aphorisms of *The Will to Power* (rather tendentiously edited by Nietzsche's reactionary sister) and other Nietzschean writings. "I am dynamite," the sage of Sils St. Maria had said; there was indeed an explosive quality in the rhetoric of this great writer. He could act as an energizing agent on all kinds of different people.

Freud

Sigmund Freud, in contrast to Nietzsche, was not a poet, prophet, and sage, but (apparently) a hardheaded empirical scientist. The Austrian doctor brought strange knowledge from the underworld of the human psyche but summed it up in perfectly rational concepts and offered a systematic clinical approach to it.

Freud is one of the seminal minds of the modern age, by almost universal consent; he ranks with Newton and Darwin as one of those scientists who altered the fundamental conditions of thought and changed Western man's view of himself in basic ways. He ranks also with Marx and Darwin, it is frequently said, among the big three of the nineteenth century. This despite the fact that, like those other two giants, his theories may prove to have been wrong in many details. Freud himself was convinced he had made epochal discoveries: "I have the distinct feeling that I have touched on one of the great secrets of nature," he wrote, and on occasion compared himself to Copernicus and Darwin. Freud was hardly an arrogant man, though inclined to be somewhat dogmatic, and in pointing to the importance of his ideas he was stating only a generally acknowledged truth. The greatest impact of Freudianism came in the 1920s and 1930s; today his place in modern thought seems secure though there is increasingly a tendency to doubt that Freud founded an exact science, or that his imposing structure of thought will prove any more lasting than other speculative ideas. The verdict on Freud may come to resemble that on Marx, in that he will be viewed less as a scientist than as a pioneer who opened up new horizons for others to explore. His name has become a household word, and his influence extends to education, literature, the arts, religion and philosophy, morals, popular culture.

It may be that like other household words Freud is really not accurately understood by most people. But the story of the path to his theory of the role of repression in neurosis is fairly familiar. A physician engaged in treating mental illness, Freud found that patients under hypnosis related events in their lives and that this narration had a therapeutic effect. It was not hypnosis but the narration, it seemed, that was effective. Freud developed the free-association technique and confirmed beyond much doubt the often startling relief from various neurotic disorders that comes from talking things out. (It was a truth, perhaps, that confessors in the priesthood had always known in less precise ways, possibly bartenders too!) On this rather slender underpinning Freud erected some ingenious, exciting, controversial theories.

Freud, who took his M.D. degree in 1881 at the age of 25 and explored these areas of psychiatry during the next decade in Vienna and Paris, presented his views about the cathartic effect of recall of a painful memory in 1893. The next year he added the assertion that these painful, repressed incidents were invariably associated with sexual matters. Thus began his celebrated exploration of sex, including childhood sex experience, with a new frankness. Freud soon presented the concept of the unconscious, as the place into which shameful material gets pushed. The unconscious was already a familiar idea, having been suggested by Schopenhauer and the philosopher Eduard von Hartmann, among others; Freud did not invent this term or discover the existence of the unconscious mind. But he thrust it into great prominence by making it a central part of his theory. Some things, particularly shameful things, get pushed down into the unconscious part of the mind, and festering there cause mental trouble; bringing them up into the light of consciousness cures the illness. Later, Freud drew a picture of the conflict in the mind between the *id*, the primitive unconscious where dwell all kinds of lustful drives and desires, and the *superego* at the other extreme, representing the inhibitions which society and conscience impose. The ego, in between, is a battle ground between these conflicting forces, a place of uneasy compromise between the id and the superego, the antisocial and the social.

Some of the implications of Freud were even more shocking than Darwin. The natural impulses of sex are suppressed because society brands them as shameful; the sexual drive, or *libido*, Freud thought to be the strongest human impulse and the key to life. Man has learned to be civilized at the cost of making neurotics and perhaps emotional cripples. Freud saw a tragic conflict between the demands of the individual and of society (especially in a later work, *Civilization and Its Discontents*, 1930). Sexual drives may be "sublimated" into great achievements. But suppression of antisocial wishes usually leads to varying degrees of unhappiness and neurosis. Freud more than anyone else has been responsible for a tendency in recent times to remove from sex some of the inhibitions and taboos. But it may be worth noting that on his own mature view, this will hardly solve the problem. The id, he believed, holds violent and antisocial impulses which society, and ultimately the ego itself, cannot tolerate. Freud appeared to think that rape, murder, sadism, all kinds of foul and nasty desires, lurk in the unconscious mind; and so any ordered society must in part sit on the lid of this disorderly basement of the human psyche. The superego is also a part of the mind, and its function is to discipline its uncouth relative downstairs.[3]

Nevertheless, the most sensational consequence of Freud was the new frankness about sex. He was not the only one working in this direction; the pioneer Australian sexologist, Havelock Ellis, may be mentioned. In the 1900s (Edwardian England) and especially in the 1920s, a glorious goodbye was said to Victorian "prudery." A typical piece of Edwardian fiction, Elinor Glyn's *Three Weeks*, delights in sophisticated adultery in a manner that most Victorians could simply not have understood. Freud was a serious thinker and a great scientist, not a salacious publicity seeker, and much of what has been done in his name cannot be blamed on him. Yet he did dare, above all others, to bring out into the open what had long lain under a severe restraint.

Additionally, Freud stressed the importance of the child's earliest experiences, of infant impulses of love and hate and erotic play. To some, he had gone Darwin one better, removing from man his last scrap of dignity by exposing him as a creature driven by animal desires, even his finest ideals and creations really a product of secret lusts.

The reply, as usual, was that new knowledge of this sort cannot be

---

[3]Like Darwinism, Freudianism has its long prehistory in which elements of it were hinted at. Thus in the eighteenth century Diderot and Rousseau spoke of the war which rages in the human breast between the natural man and the artificial man. See especially Diderot's *Rameau's Nephew*.

swept aside, however dismaying it may seem at first. To increase our knowledge of man is to make it possible to enrich his life and civilization. To understand the darker side of human nature, which exists and must be dealt with, is a step toward controlling and directing it. Freud himself was no mystic. Hard-bitten and a little cynical, he was a scientist through and through, like Darwin, though in his later years he permitted himself some philosophical speculations. His task was to make it possible for men to live happier lives by removing their mental ills. Freud did not invent the irrational and libidinous side of human nature, but only dared to point to its importance.

In the 1900s Freud was only just getting to be known. *The Interpretation of Dreams*, 1900, took eight years to sell its initial printing of six hundred copies. But the movement was well on its way to maturity, though Freud continued to work and grow, reshaping his thought in the 1920s. After the World War—which he was inclined to regard as an inevitable discharge of the aggressive impulses repressed by civilization —he grew famous, and was awarded the Goethe Prize in 1930. But from 1923 on he suffered from a painful cancer of the jaw, and when the Nazis seized Austria in 1938, the Jewish scientist, whose books they burnt, was forced to flee, dying in England the next year at the age of 83. *Beyond the Pleasure Principle, The Ego and the Id*, and *Civilization and Its Discontents* were the leading books of the 1920s, more speculative and less scientific than the earlier ones. Always a prolific writer, Freud was also always more than a technician; he was a man of wide interests and broad culture, "deeply versed in classical literature as well as the noblest examples of European literature," as his biographer Ernest Jones tells us, and the close friend of such writers as Thomas Mann, Stefan Zweig, Romain Rolland—a man of genius who belonged to the great European intellectual tradition. Yet there was a certain acrid dogmatism about Freud, as about Marx, and this helped lead to the schisms which beset his "movement."

Carl Jung

About 1912 Freud came to a rather painful break with the greatest of those who had followed, or accompanied, him in the pioneer explorations of the unconscious, the Swiss psychologist C. G. Jung. Jung, who lived until 1961, broke with Freud partly because of his belief that psychic energy is not exclusively sexual; Freud would tolerate no questioning of his gospel of the primacy of sex.

There were more basic reasons. Jung was less a scientific rationalist than Freud. Some have wished to deny to Freudianism the title of "science," on the grounds that it makes use of metaphorical and perhaps unverifiable concepts (repression, sublimation, dream analysis, id, not to speak of Oedipus complex and death-wish); but there can be no doubt that Freud approached his task of analyzing the human mind in a brisk, rationalistic spirit. Freud had no use for religion which he believed to be a neurotic manifestation derived from the Oedipus complex. His tendency to "explain away" religious and other ideologies, or modes of expression, as the product of a more "basic" and quite naturalistic condition, links Freud with Marx, Feuerbach, Durkheim, and others of this sort. If to Marx religion is a means of enslaving the proletariat, to Freud it is a means of compensating for a neurotic mind—to the former an excrescence of an unsound social order, to the latter an excrescence of an unsound psyche. This puts Freud in the camp of those who are "rationalists" in the sense of being foes of "religion," who believe that the healthy intellect should rest content with a wholly naturalistic view of the universe. This position is itself, however, an ideology or unprovable assertion of certain values—evidence of a type of mind or temperament, perhaps the type that William James called "tough-minded." (It is also an argument *ad hominem* which can be turned upon its user. If Freud tells me I am religious because of my mental history, I can retort that he is irreligious because of his.)

Jung, on the other hand, incurred the contempt of the scientific psychologists but the admiration of others by wandering into the fields of religion, art, literature, and history. Shocked by what he termed Freud's "materialistic prejudice" and "shallow positivism," Jung might have agreed with D. H. Lawrence who scolded Freud for creating a "technology of the heart." Those American disciples who took Freudian psychoanalysis to be a useful mechanical means of keeping one's psyche in good order represent what Jung and Lawrence were forced to reject. Jung moved toward a theory of the "collective unconscious," which he thought he observed to exist in remarkable ways, and he sought clues to the "archetypes," or patterns of imagery, which are basic to it. These appear in mythological motifs, in fairy tales, in art and poetry, as well as in dreams and in conscious behavior. They are found in all the great religions of mankind and in its literature. A fabulous scholar and polyhistor himself, Jung cast his net widely over civilizations past and present in his search for the archetypes of the collective unconscious. His disciples have tended more toward comparative mythology and toward the analysis of art and poetry than perhaps anything else. He manifested some deeply mystical and religious tendencies.

To Jung, religion and art were essential to the healthy human psyche. The great "myths," expressing as they do the language of the mind at its deepest level, with roots in the collective life of humanity, satisfy our fundamental instincts. Without them, human nature shrivels. Here Jung touches Nietzsche's conviction that modern man is overly rationalized and needs to regain contact with some healthy primitivisms. While Jung, too, always claimed to be an empirical investigator, his critics think that he often lost himself in fanciful speculations. But no other pioneer of what Jung called "the undiscovered self" except Freud himself has so drawn our attention to this strange, fascinating realm that lies within each of us, or so contributed to its elucidation.

Probably Jung's best-known contribution to psychology was his classification of personality types, into "extraverts" and "introverts" with subdivisions. He invented other striking concepts, such as "persona" and "shadow," which roughly correspond to Freud's superego and id. The *shadow* is a figure of the unconscious containing evil, antisocial impulses but also other nonconscious elements. The *persona* is our social role, the part society expects us to play, a mask of artificial personality. This seems to bear some relationship to what the existentialists later called the "unauthentic" or "other-directed" self. The fully mature or integrated personality must dissolve the persona and integrate the unconscious into the self. This is close to Freud's "sublimation" or to Nietzsche's fusion of "Dionysian" and "Apollonian" elements. This basic idea is that elements of the unconscious emotion must be used in the interest of a higher creativity.

"The dynamism and imagery of the instincts together form an *a priori* which no man can overlook without the gravest risk to himself," Jung wrote in *The Undiscovered Self*. Overlooking them, he believed, could be held responsible not only for individual mental illness but also for such social horrors as German Nazism; for the forces latent in the unconscious will break forth in wildly irrational ways if they are not understood and administered to properly. Modern man still lives, he thought, in a make-believe world made up of rational concepts, ignoring the underlying emotional determinants. "The psychiatrist is one of those who know most about the conditions of the soul's welfare, upon which so infinitely much depends in the social sum." The popularity of psychiatry today, growing from nothing to the status of a great profession in this century, offers some evidence that what Jung wrote is true, though we still stand at the mere threshold of real understanding of the self.

Henri Bergson

Better known in the 1890s and 1900s than Freud and Jung and more respectable than Nietzsche, was the French philosopher Henri Bergson, who may also be classed among the irrationalists or arationalists in this "Age of Unreason." Bergson, whose first notable work appeared in 1889 when he was thirty, exerted so strong an influence that by the 1900s he was easily the most important force in French thought, being frequently compared to Descartes, Rousseau, and Comte among earlier masters of an epoch. His lectures at the University of Paris were likened to those of Abelard in the Middle Ages for the sensation they created, and his repute spread widely abroad too. His considerable role in twentieth-century thought is generally conceded. Bergson's gift of style assured him an audience. Like Nietzsche, he used metaphor and poetic imagery because he believed that conceptual thought does not best communicate the nature of reality. Also like the German, he appeared to his contemporaries as a liberator, opening up fresh horizons, calling for creativity and expressing it in his richly gifted prose.

In a romantic manner, Bergson sharply distinguished between the rational, conceptualizing intellect and the intuitive understanding. The former, the scientific, analyzing function, is a practical tool, concerned with useful knowledge, but not truth-giving because reality may not be so divided up and conceptualized. (The student may here be reminded of Kant.) Reality is a continuum, to be grasped by the intuition. It flows through immediate experience, as the "life force" that is in all things. Intuition (meaning instinct become self-conscious and reflective) takes us to "the very inwardness of life," while the intellect is not in this sense in touch with reality. Bergson said that he began his philosophical speculations by considering what is meant by *time*, and found himself led to conclude that the clock-time of everyday life or of the physicist is a convention very different from the real time of experience. The intelligence which analyzes and divides things has given us the former conception which is useful, but not true to experience. When we grasp immediate experience by intuitive means, what we find there is an indivisible continuum, a "duration" that we can scarcely describe save in poetic imagery; this represents a fundamental reality. So it is in other things. Science tells us that the sound of a bell is a series of vibrations, but we experience it as a whole. A melody is not a series of notes; it cannot be described; we intuit it. Science, as Wordsworth had written, "murders to dissect." Reality is indivisible and hence unanalyzable; insofar as we do analyze it, as for convenience's sake we must do, we falsify it.

This is no attack on science within its limits, but it *is* a rather sharp deflation of the pretensions of science to provide complete knowledge, pretensions which at that time existed. "Science consists only of conventions, and to this circumstance solely does it owe its apparent certitude; the facts of science and, *a fortiori*, its laws are the artificial work of the scientist; science therefore can teach us nothing of the truth; it can serve only as a rule of action."[4] Critics of pragmatist and Bergsonian indictments of the "conceptualizing" process as conventional only were not lacking, as might be expected, and often pointed out that these philosophers themselves could not escape the use of conceptual or intellectual language. To do without it would be to abolish thought. To follow Bergson all the way in his intuitionism would be to destroy all analysis and lapse into chaos. It was generally agreed that concepts and reality are not the same thing, also that conceptual knowledge does not exhaust reality or constitute the only mode of dealing with it; but the implication that the two realms are completely divorced, that science tells us nothing at all about reality but only about its own arbitrary signs and symbols, was frequently rejected. Still, the persuasively conducted Bergsonian offensive against science made its impact felt; the chief result was to vindicate and rehabilitate forms of "immediate experience" such as literature, religion, and various mystic or nonrational experiences.

Bergson proposed a vitalistic evolutionary theory, arguing against Darwinian mechanism that life has within it some purposive forces, without which evolution cannot be explained (*Creative Evolution*, 1908). Doctrines of "emergent evolution" received the support of a number of philosophers at this time, the most prominent advocate after Bergson being the British philosopher Samuel Alexander. Reality creates itself gradually, rather than existing from all eternity; life evolves ever new and unpredictable forms. We participate in a universe that is not finished and help in the making of it. A striking idea, and as Bergson noted, a radically new one in the Western tradition, "creative evolution" turned the rather somber mechanistic atheism of the Darwinists into a feeling for the wondrous freedom of a world in growth.

In general, Bergson's persuasively presented philosophy urged the importance of spontaneity, of intuition, and of immediate experience, as over against those "tentacles of cold, prying thought" (Nietzsche) which gives us useful knowledge at the cost of cutting us off from reality. Getting away from cold science and bathing in the refreshing waters of intuition clearly seems to have value, for Bergson. To him as to the American pragmatists, the world properly seen is rich, inexhaustible, vital. Though his stress on spontaneity and immediate experience influenced the existentialists, Bergson was on the whole not a tragic philosopher but a joyous one. The anti-intellectualism or antirationalism of which he may be accused was rather gentle, and to tie this deeply religious man to the subsequent movements of fascism or Nazism appears perverse. Few philosophers have attached such basic importance to liberty. Among his leading disciples in prewar France was the editor and

[4]R. B. Perry, *Present Philosophical Tendencies*, 1912, pp. 230–231.

writer Charles Péguy, who so far as he can be classified might best be
described as a Christian democrat and socialist. He was, in fact, quite
an individualist. Bergson, like the pragmatists, encouraged freedom un-
bounded by dogma and tended not to set up any "school."

The pragmatists[5] and Bergson broadly agreed in their attack on
intellectual or conceptual knowledge. Immediate experience is deeper
and forms the matrix within which intellectual knowledge takes place.
As John Dewey put it, there is an "experience in which knowledge-and-
its-object is sustained, and whose schematized, or structural, portion it
is." We encounter "reality" only in immediate, intuitive experience, as
distinct from intellectual ratiocination. We must reject, as Nietzsche
cleverly put it, the dogma of immaculate *perception*. If we want to know
the music, we do not analyze it into notes or vibrations, we simply hear
it. We can perform, and usefully perform, the latter function, but we
should recognize it for what it is, a secondary and derivative one. In this
respect Bergson and the pragmatists coincided with the aims of Edmund
Husserl, today considered the founder of phenomenology, who was also
philosophizing around the turn of the century though at that time much
more obscure than Bergson. Husserl first used the term "phenomenology" in 1900 to mean the systematic study of how things and concepts
are given to the mind directly, at the deeper, more "real" level, exactly
as it happens and not as it is formalized in conceptual thought.

And in other ways, too, Bergsonism reflected broader currents of
the day which may be seen mirrored in other minds. The stress on the
value of religious experience, *qua* experience, found in William James's
famous lectures on *Varieties of Religious Experience*, could be found
also in the serious interest in supernormal psychical phenomena (to
which C. D. Broad, Cambridge philosophy professor, among others, lent
his name); in George Santayana's interest in the "splendid error" of the
Catholic faith, a great myth: while religions are not of course literally
true, it is a shallow person who thinks he has disposed of them when
he has pointed this out. It could be found in the Catholic Revival among
men of letters, not only in France but in England and in many other

[5]The Englishman F. C. S. Schiller and the Italians Papini and Prezzolini
represented pragmatism in Europe, where it was much less important than in the
United States. The vigorous American William James was a man of international
reputation who knew Bergson as well as Schiller and Papini. Pragmatism had
affinities with the message of revolt and liberation; it denied the existence of final,
abstract truth, asserting that man makes the truth as he acts. Life is an open experiment in which we constantly test our hypotheses against reality and use our
intellects as tools. Pragmatism was popular for a time in Italy around 1900 but
dissolved because of a certain vagueness; it stood for "freedom, creativeness, and
originality" and appealed mostly to poetic writers. Papini subsequently became a
fascist, indicative perhaps of pragmatism's tendency to take on the color of its
surroundings and embrace any active creed that seemed to have vitality.

places. There was unquestionably some weakness in treating religion as not true but useful, or nice to believe. Simone Weil later complained that Bergson presented religious faith "like a pink pill of a superior kind, which imparts a prodigious amount of vitality." But the turning to religion in a self-conscious way, treating it as poetry or a pleasing myth, was very typical of the *fin de siècle* vanguard. Carl Jung, we recall, regarded religion as good psychotherapy.

In Germany, men spoke of the revival of metaphysics, citing Hartmann, Lotze, Eucken; Max Scheler is a good counterpart of Bergson or Santayana—a sensitive, esthetic, introspective, nondogmatic philosopher. In Britain Hegelian idealism was modified in the direction of a greater personalism, and an awareness of the multistructured nature of reality (Bradley, McTaggart). If Bergson contributed to the revival of both religion and metaphysics, and to a nondoctrinaire subjectivism which stressed experience for its own sake—participating in the great stream of life—his most notable influence was on literature. He was very much a philosopher for poets and novelists. He directly inspired the imagist poets and the "stream of consciousness" novel, and had a good deal to do with others of the many literary movements that proliferated—symbolism, expressionism, etc. For Bergson encouraged the artistic imagination to plumb its deepest levels, cutting loose from rational thought in search of spontaneous experience—finding there, he supposed, the utmost reality.

The Bergsonian message, like that of Nietzsche and William James, must be set against the background of science's virtual monopoly of knowledge; he broke through the ban on religious or metaphysical speculations decreed by the positivist regimen. "For the first time since Comte and Kant metaphysics had waged war against scientific determinism on its own ground and won it," Etienne Gilson has written in his recollections of what Bergson meant to his generation. Charles de Gaulle has spoken of Bergson as one who "renewed French spirituality." Later events revealed some of the limitations of this cheerfully affirmative philosophy; it could lead to approval of almost anything that was active and dynamic, like war and fascism.

But Bergson lived on to add to his reputation with the book some think is his greatest, *The Two Sources of Morality and Religion*, published in 1932, a work of rich texture, interwoven with insights, whose general theme conforms to his guiding vision of man as needing to surmount his practical scientific reason with the creative insights of religion and poetry. Standing somewhere between Freud and Nietzsche, Bergson like them was essentially a gifted student of the human interior mind, the subjective dimension, the undiscovered self.

The Crisis in Science

The popular prestige of science stood of course very high, in this period when almost every year brought some fresh technical miracle, whether electric light, phonograph, or automobile. For the more thoughtful, science offered its exciting theories, of which Darwin's natural selection was but the most sensational. The periodic table of the elements, worked out by the Russian Mendeleyeff; the atomic structure of matter, developed by Dalton and others; the law of the conservation of energy, associated with Helmholtz and Kelvin, a striking tribute to the regularity and constancy of natural phenomena; and other great discoveries aroused awe, but not dismay, since they testified to the orderliness of nature and the ability of science to disclose cosmic principles. "The men of science had become the prophets of progressive minds," to an extent that may be measured by a statement in the British *Annual Register* for 1884 that few other subjects except scientific ones received any attention from the intellectual world. Lonely prophets and off-beat poets, despite the attention we have properly given them, did not at this time seriously compete with the scientists either in the popular or the intellectual world.

The widespread confidence in science rested on the belief that it was unfolding an accurate picture of reality, that it was solidly based and could not err, that other modes of knowledge such as metaphysics and religion were obsolete. This popular and slightly vulgar scientific materialism was purveyed in the works of such pundits as T. H. Huxley, John Tyndall, the Germans Emil Du Bois-Reymond and Ernst Haeckel (*The Riddle of the Universe*). But at the turn of the century science was about to lose its confident commonsense air and to confront shattering paradoxes at the frontiers of physics.

The popular, commonsense view of science included such opinions as that reality consists of material bodies, the atoms being thought of as little billiard-balls; that these material objects act in a spatial field and temporal world of the sort familiar to human experience, with an objectively existing space and time; that all bodies obey the same scientific "laws," like Newton's laws of motion and the law of the conservation of energy. The universe was pictured as a large machine, consisting of physical bodies in dynamic relationships. Before long, an astounded public was forced to hear from the mouths of the scientists themselves the refutation of all this. Matter, it seemed, consisted of invisible and perhaps merely hypothetical units called "electrons," which within the atom refused to obey Newton's laws, an example of insubordination without precedent.

Even more surprisingly, time and space as they appear to human experience had to be abandoned, since these are relative to some arbitrary standard and no objective standard exists for the universe as a whole. Newton's law of gravitation, foundation of physical science for 200 years, was evidently not accurate. It became impossible to picture the behavior of "matter" as corresponding to anything within the realm of human sensory experience, either at the subatomic or the cosmic level. The universe was not like a machine, nor was there anything in it that one could readily call "matter"; it was even possible for scientists to hold that reality fades into an idea when we trace it as far as we can. "Matter," remarked Bertrand Russell, became a formula for describing what happens where it is not! Space, time, and matter all turned out to be fictions of the human mind, perhaps not so far from the convenient but unreal abstractions of scientific knowledge according to Bergson.

A starting point for these complex developments was the Michelson-Morley experiment, performed in 1887 by two Americans wholly unaware that they were about to stumble onto a new era in science. They were trying to measure the speed of the earth by measuring the time it takes light to travel with, as compared to against, the direction of the earth's motion. The extraordinary result, after repeated experiments, was to disclose the remarkable fact that no "ether" or other substance exists, for earth and other bodies to move through. There is, in effect, no surrounding atmosphere. All through the nineteenth century, scientists had posited such an "ether" substance because of the discovery that light and electricity acted like waves, hence needed a medium through which to pass; this in addition to its uses as a measuring rod for space and time. The ether had become something of a scandal; necessary as a postulate if the behavior of all sorts of "waves" was to be visualized, it was something no one had ever seen or otherwise established directly as existent. The Michelson-Morley results brought matters to a head. It forced abandonment of the ether, or any conception of a "something" space.

If there is no space, as a backdrop to the universe, there is no absolute standard of motion. All speed is relative to something else. We measure speed on the earth by reference to the earth itself, postulating that it is stable; but of course the earth is in motion around the sun, the planetary system is in motion, too, relative to other systems and galaxies, and so on until we reach the limits of the universe. Then what can we find to measure by? The speed of light, as the Michelson experiment revealed, being the ultimate speed of things in the universe, is a constant that does not vary relative to other motion and cannot be used to measure them by. If there is nothing in the universe that constitutes an ultimate yardstick of measurement, there can be no absolute speed. The same thing is true for distance as for speed. Space and time viewed from a universal and not an earth-bound angle must disappear as absolutes. From this many odd conclusions emerged, for instance, that at the same moment it is a different time to observers in motion in different parts of the cosmos. If right now you are on one star and I on another, it is not the same time for us. If I journeyed to visit you on your planet and then returned to mine in a space-ship, I would find that a different interval of time had elapsed than that shown by my perfectly accurate clock. And so on.

Euclid's solid axioms of geometry were seen to be true only so long as we keep to the boundaries of the earth; for outer space, there are other geometries, based on different physical postulates, which turn out to be equally rigorous logical systems. Thus, it seemed, the quality of objective certainty that had always attached to pure mathematics vanished in relativity, too.

In regard to Newtonian gravity, the difficulty of conceiving a "force" of some sort acting at a distance had bothered Newton himself a little, and had bothered others since. We may recall that Berkeley and Leibniz had explored this weakness in a speculative manner. According to the great scientist Albert Einstein, whose first or special theory of relativity was presented in 1905, gravity is not a "force." We should not think of a pull exerted by objects on each other. Space having vanished in the sense of anything positive like "ether," this adjustment became necessary. Einstein's first theory asked a stunned public to believe that bodies move through the curvatures of space-time which, not being independent of each other, become merged in a single continuum. Others held that the physical principles of the universe cannot be visualized in terms of human imagery at all, they can only be indicated in mathematical formulae.

Whatever else this was, it was not common sense; the scientists were becoming more wildly paradoxical than the artists and poets. At the subatomic level, where in 1897 J. J. Thomson arrived at the concept of the electron or unit of negative electricity as the least unit of "matter," the belief that the atoms could be thought of as miniature planetary systems, with the nucleus as the sun and the electrons circling around it, soon had to be abandoned. Niels Bohr, the Danish physicist who lived until 1962 and became one of the leading theoretical pioneers of the age of nuclear energy, explained that the laws of motion holding for the solar systems do not apply at all within atoms. Thus the laws of Newton, always heretofore assumed to be universal, broke down on both the smallest and largest fields and remained valid only within a zone of fairly gross sense experience. They were crude approximations which worked well enough only when the demand for precision was not too great.

The world within the atom soon became most puzzling, the behavior of electrons breaking all sorts of laws heretofore regarded as sacrosanct. At the turn of the century, Max Planck's quantum theory asserted that energy is emitted discretely and not continuously, in little packages, as it were, and not in a continuous stream. Heat causes electrons to make sudden jumps from one energy level to another. Planck found a "constant," a number which represents the relationship between energy and frequency of radiation, a number which turned up again in Wave Mechanics in connection with the behavior of electrons. Like Kepler's laws, it is a discoverable regularity the meaning of which lay hidden for the time being.

The electrons did not, then, behave as particles of matter would be expected to behave; they did not act at all the way "ordinary" objects do in the everyday world. Further research by Einstein, Heisenberg, and Broglie disclosed that electrons have properties of *both* particles and waves, being sometimes one and sometimes the other, or being something capable of behaving on occasion like both.

Since electrons must be used to observe electrons, and exert a disturbing influence, we can never directly observe electrons, but can only infer their nature. This, to some, was a disturbing reminder that science has limits beyond which human knowledge can never penetrate. Likewise, the behavior of the subatomic particles can be predicted only within limits of probability, thus striking at that certainty and complete determinancy heretofore claimed and thought necessary for physical science. For example, we cannot know both the position and the velocity of a subatomic particle, in the way that we can know them of larger objects. If an airplane is bound for Boston from Chicago, naturally we can find both its exact position and its speed at any given moment. This cannot be done for an electron bound from one place to another. We *can* get general statistical trends, adequate for most predictive purposes, but the individual electron eludes determinacy and predictability. Heisenberg's "indeterminancy" principle, subsequently announced, indicated the unsatisfactory situation at the frontiers of physics. In his book *Physics and Philosophy* (1942), Sir James Jeans summed up the consequences of quanta theory in six propositions: (a) the uniformity of nature disappears, (b) precise knowledge of the outer world becomes impossible, (c) the processes of nature cannot be adequately represented within a framework of space and time, (d) sharp division between subject and object has ceased to be possible, (e) causality has lost its meaning, (f) if there is a fundamental causal law, this lies beyond the phenomenal world, and so beyond our access.

All this represented brilliant advances in the field of physics. Having for two centuries surveyed the land that Newton discovered, scientists now pressed on to a new world, and if at first this world seemed strange that was only to be expected. Nevertheless, this experience forced basic changes in thinking almost as sweepingly as had the seventeenth-century scientific revolution, though the exact directions of change were not clear. Possibly Einstein was playing the role of Copernicus, with the Newton of the new age yet to appear. Breakdown seemed evident in the lack of any one set of rules or laws that applied to all matter, and in the "uncertainty" invading such scientific bulwarks as continuity and causality, not to speak of time and space. The ultimate limits of investigation seemed to have been reached in the effort to track down reality to its smallest ultimate unit, and some philosopher-scientists were prepared to say that this vindicated the idealist position, overthrowing materialism. In the last analysis not even the scientist can get rid of the subjective factor, because as investigator he in part creates the truth; and such concepts, moreover, as atom and electron, space and time, turn out to be mental constructs not necessarily corresponding to objective reality. The interference factor, which makes it impossible to observe the tiniest units directly, cannot presumably be overcome; indeterminacy of electronic behavior also apparently is an ultimate fact, not a deficiency in knowledge that further investigation may remedy.

So far from making science useless, the new ideas yielded knowledge that led to such things as television, nuclear energy, radioactivity, X-rays, space satellites. The Einsteinian formula was brilliantly vindicated by a spectacular observation in May, 1919, the most famous of all those that offered support to Einstein's gravitational theory, correcting Newton's. Of course, the most startling revelation that the strange world of Dr. Einstein was really true came in August, 1945; the mushroom cloud was the final upshot of that innocent experiment in Cleveland in 1887. That $E = Mc^2$ was a deduction from all this theoretical physics which proved out in an awesome way. The absorbing quest of modern physics went on in the 1920s, which was in many ways its "heroic age," and into the 1930s. But the foundations were laid in the pre-1914 period, as were so many other foundations of the modern mind.

What were the implications? Of the theory of relativity, the Spanish philosopher Ortega y Gasset said that it is "the most important intellectual fact that the present time can show." There is general agreement on this, but less agreement, perhaps, on just why. The destruction of the long-familiar Newtonian picture of the world ("very little of the nineteenth-century picture of the world remains today," the editor of a recent survey of twentieth-century scientific thought observes) could hardly be otherwise than a gigantic intellectual revolution, affecting all of culture. It induced a degree of humility and allowed for that revival of metaphysics and that interest in the irrational which were other hall-marks of the times. Science ceased to be simple, perhaps ceased to lean on materialism and mechanism, revealed a "mysterious universe" destined always to remain, in part, mysterious and bumped up against puzzles it could not solve at the very heart of reality. Scientists themselves became a little more humble and talked of the mysterious universe rather than the march toward perfect knowledge. Laymen might still bow before the might of science but they lost their ability to comprehend it. The "world view" of European man since Newton had been dominated by a certain picture of the cosmos as a mechanical model, familiar to human experience. It now became difficult to use any such model.

No one with a knowledge of Western philosophy, from Hume and Kant to Nietzsche and Bergson, could be much surprised by the conclusion that scientific knowledge must be in part subjective, and also incomplete because phenomenal only. The limitation lies within the human sensory apparatus, which can hardly be adequate to full comprehension of the whole of cosmic reality. Why should we suppose that our senses or even our brains, fitted for living in a particular environment, should be capable of grasping and visualizing all this? Reason, employing mathematical abstractions and other tools, can take soundings of nature sufficient for practical advantages; but if by "understanding" we mean an adequate model or picture of everything, this must probably always elude us. In Kantian terms the "thing in itself" is not accessible to the categories of the understanding, while the intuition or imagination can only contact it fleetingly and imperfectly. This is the fate of man, who though marvelously endowed is not God. Ultimately, perhaps, this conclusion was the greatest consequence of the new science. It left man even at the peak of his grandeur, amid the greatest of his triumphs, shorn of his overconfident "titanism" and aware that after the best that science can do, vast mystery must always remain and there is abundant place for a religious attitude toward the universe.

The Crisis in Religion

Religion too was in crisis. Nietzsche had announced that "God is dead"; Freud was an atheist; Darwinism had dealt blows to orthodoxy. The most severe blow to traditional Christianity probably came, however, not from any of these but from the "higher criticism." (In his careful study of *The Victorian Church*, Owen Chadwick finds the higher criticism and comparative religious perspectives far more a cause of Christian crisis than Darwinism.) J. Wellhausen's *History of Israel*, first published in 1878, was a landmark of scholarship. For a number of years before this there had been uneasiness. In 1860 a turmoil in the Anglican Church over the book *Essays and Reviews*, in which some liberal churchmen expressed the view that the Scriptures should be examined like any other book, led to a trial for heresy. Ernest Renan's *Life of Jesus*, and David Strauss's somewhat similar book in Germany, raised eyebrows all over Europe in the 1860s. They were followed by J. R. Seeley's *Ecce Homo* in 1865, not an irreverent book but one which did seek the human, historical Christ. The trend of Romantic and Hegelian theology had been to play down literal Biblicalism.

Wellhausen offered persuasive support to a theory already advanced, that a substantial portion of the earlier books of the Bible (the Pentateuch) was not written until much later than the events they describe, and indeed not put in its final form until about 400 B.C. (the time of Ezra), nearly a millennium after Moses. Wellhausen carried the day among the scholars, especially the younger ones. The second edition of his *History* appeared in 1883 and was translated into English in 1885, giving rise to a considerable controversy. A French scholar wrote in 1894 that "whoever is not totally prejudiced, whoever has not decided in advance that any kind of criticism is false, must accept the idea that the Priestly Code was not formed until after the Babylonian exile."

To some of the pious, this was a shocking conclusion, for it seemed to cast doubt on the Bible as revealed truth, infallible because divinely inspired. The arguments of liberal theologians, that the history of Israel and Judea in the broader sense justified the claim of a unique religious mission vouchsafed to the Jewish nation, carried little conviction to men brought up to believe (as did, for example, William E. Gladstone, the famous British statesman) that the literal truth of every line of Scripture was the impregnable rock upon which Christianity stood.

In 1872, George Smith called attention to a Babylonian version of the story of the Flood—a significant and shattering discovery. The leading feature of the "higher" as distinct from the "lower" criticism was its awareness of an immense literary tradition among the other peoples of the Ancient World, which bore on the Bible at many points. No longer was the Bible seen in isolation, as a totally unique and marvelous book. The Old Testament fitted into an historical context that began to be recovered and understood; thus seen, it perhaps lost none of its wonder nor even its veracity, but it did inevitably become different—a part of human history, not simply the record of a continuous divine miracle. A good deal of the Old Testament has close parallels in the sacred and wisdom literature of the Babylonians and other ancient peoples with whom the Jewish people were in close contact. The uniqueness of the Hebraic outlook—monotheistic, ethical, messianic—remained, but in innumerable details the Biblical story lost its ability to pass as something quite outside the experience of the rest of the ancient world. The Jews could never again be quite the "peculiar people" in the old sense. (This was not displeasing to Hegelian philosophers, who declared the entire "world spirit" of an age to be more significant than single nations or individuals.)

Into this same pattern fitted that immense growth in knowledge about other peoples which was the fruit of anthropological research. Popularized in such books as James Frazer's widely read end-of-the-century success, *The Golden Bough*, this data compelled the conclusion that even primitive religions make use of archetypal beliefs similar to those of Christianity or Judaism. Awareness of Indic thought—a whole world of higher religions—advanced steadily in the nineteenth century. All this worked further toward eroding the uniqueness of Christianity.

By the end of the nineteenth century, also, critical research into the New Testament had arrived at conclusions concerning the Gospels, which included the view that the authors of Matthew and Luke leaned chiefly on the Gospel of Mark as a source, and even the latter contains theological interpolations not taken from Jesus himself. Again, the net result of intensive historical analysis was, roughly, to cast some doubt on the accuracy of the Gospels as accounts of the life of Jesus, and on certain sayings and ideas attributed by them to Jesus. Opening up the problem of the historical Jesus by no means meant destroying Christianity, but simple folk among the pious might understandably think so. A quarrel between "modernists" and "fundamentalists" soon divided most Christian churches. Popularizers of the higher criticism, with an antitheological axe to grind, sometimes exaggerated it and declared that, for example, Jesus never existed and the Bible was a tissue of fables.[6] Scandalized Christians reacted by denouncing the whole critical movement, and it took some time before balanced judgment was restored. In the Roman Catholic Church, "modernism" received a cautious green light from Pope Leo XIII but Pius X, his successor in 1903, checked this move toward liberalism as he did others, as for example, the Catholic democratic movement.

In 1864 Pius IX, embittered by the Italian liberal-nationalist movement which assailed the papacy's temporal power, had issued his cele-

---

[6]Bertrand Russell, the eminent philosopher, held that "historically, it is quite doubtful whether Christ ever existed at all, or, if he did, we do not know anything about him." Russell's *A Free Man's Worship*, 1910, was a skeptic's manifesto.

brated Syllabus of Errors and in so doing placed the Roman Church in a state of war with much of the nineteenth century. Liberalism and democracy, as well as modern science, were declared to be irreconcilable with Christianity and the Church. In 1870, Pius IX had summoned the great Ecumenical Council, first since the Council of Trent in 1563, chiefly to solemnize the doctrine of papal infallibility. The goal was not achieved without a severe struggle, in which many of the German, French, and English bishops opposed the papal party, and after the decrees some liberal Catholics left the Church. Leo XIII, the great Pope who succeeded Pius IX, did not really retreat much from Pio Nono's position. Though anxious to encourage learning, and a friend of the Catholic social movement (see page 359) he continued to assert that the modern state, based on secular individualism, is fundamentally anti-Christian. In Italy Catholics continued to boycott national politics on papal orders, though in France there was finally an adjustment to the Republic. In the 1900s, Catholics who embraced liberal and democratic principles were rebuked. They were reminded that political society must be based on Christian principles, not on liberal skepticism and indifference; in regard to democracy, they were told that the Church cannot attach primary importance to the form of government; it can get along with democracy, but also with other forms, and what matters is that society be Christian, not that it adopt any particular political ideology. Marc Sangnier and the great Charles Péguy were perhaps the leading French Catholic Democrats who finally (1910) received this rebuke.

By that time, the Dreyfus affair had caused a sharp conflict between conservative and liberal France with the clergy ranged for the most part on the former side. The victorious partisans of Captain Dreyfus took their revenge by passing legislation to separate church from state in 1901, the occasion of further bitter exchanges between anticlericals and churchmen. All in all, the Church found itself at war with basic trends in the modern world at this time, and subject to some divisive conflicts. We have discussed the Roman Catholic Church, but the same thing might be said in lesser degree of major Protestant denominations. There were liberals who sought to turn the church's major interest to social reform, abandoning traditional theology and accepting the higher criticism; there were conservatives who feared the extinction of Christianity if it thus merged itself into secular liberalism.

New Spiritual Currents

Strong winds blew in the direction of religion in this era. The trouble was that they tended to be diverted to nonorthodox, even non-Christian varieties of faith. The reaction against scientism, especially powerful in France, led to that interest in moral and interior experience we have already seen in the philosophies of Nietzsche, Bergson, and William James. There was indeed something of a Catholic revival, aided by the conversion of important men of literature. But this religion-seeking spirit more often ignored dogmatic orthodoxy. William James developed the viewpoint in his famous Gifford lectures on "The Varieties of Religious Experience" that the various myths or conceptualizations in which religions are objectively embodied are not fundamental; they are the mere husks of religion. What is basic is the instinct to believe, the need for the human spirit to express itself. One could, presumably, just as well believe in any myth. One might, like the great Irish poet W. B. Yeats, invent a private mythology; one might, like Annie Besant or Mme. Blavatsky, embrace esoteric Oriental religions. The former's "theosophy" became a fashionable creed. The "truth" of a religion became somewhat irrelevant; one could never know that anyway. What mattered was the fact of belief itself.

The point was driven home by a later remark of Emmanuel Mounier, who declared that a century ago almost everyone was either a Christian or else a rationalist opposed to all religion, whereas today there are not too many of either sort. One had faith, but not necessarily a Christian faith, or if so only very loosely.

The greatest prophet of the pre-World War I era was doubtless Leo Tolstoy. The Russian novelist was a personality of such gigantic proportions that he captured the world's imagination, and became a living legend to whose estate at Yassnaya Polyana men came from all over the Western world to do homage. The brilliant novels *War and Peace* and *Anna Karenina* made him famous; but more striking was the spiritual odyssey of the later Tolstoy. Experiencing a deep crisis in which he saw life as absurd and meaningless, this man of passionate "commitment" (to use a modern phrase) was driven to reconsider the most fundamental questions of existence, and after finding neither the abstractions of the philosophers nor the facts and theories of the scientists to be of any help, he ended in a sort of primitive Christianity. There is much in the Russian's agony and redemption to suggest the later movements of existentialism and Crisis Theology. He found that Christ's true meaning had been falsified by formal religion and by rationalistic concep tualizing. Tolstoy found in the simple message of Christ deep truths which no mere formula could express. His religious writings (for example, *The Kingdom of God Is within You*) have tremendous force. He felt, also, the influence of the Oriental religions and tried to find the elemental truths that underlie all the great religions.

Tolstoy advocated and in some measure practiced a return to primitive Christian communism. Powerful denunciations of war and of all forms of coercion made him a hero of the pacifist movement, and in political principles an anarchist. The principle of nonresistance to evil, which Tolstoy could not always obey himself, was the cornerstone of his religious belief. In suggesting a return to a simple life pared of all artificialities he was reminiscent of Rousseau, or of the American sage Henry Thoreau. Tolstoy, a member of the Russian upper class, ferociously denounced the corruption of this class and its European counterpart. Believing passionately in art and literature, he condemned the decadence of European literature and insisted that only the peasant masses were culturally sound, however ignorant of books. In later years he wrote the simplest of parables for the people, though it is unfortunately doubtful that the Russian peasant responded. But a variety of others all over the world did respond, and Tolstoy became a figure almost unique in Western intellectual history. The Russian government, most despotic in the world, dared not touch him though he advocated anarchism, pacifism, and noncooperation with government. The affair of the Dukhobors was perhaps the most astonishing example of Tolstoy's power. He set out to save this sect of Christian communalists from brutal persecution by the Tsarist government, and succeeded in gaining his end and in raising a worldwide fund for the transportation of the Dukhobors *en masse* to Canada.

Tolstoy gave away the money from his literary works and eventually before his death renounced all his wealth. A modern saint, he was formally excommunicated from the Orthodox Church in 1891, which only added to his popularity within and without Russia. The influence of Tolstoy was enormous, though difficult to evaluate. It would be impossible to say how much he contributed to that undermining of the Russian political system which prepared the way for the Revolution of 1917—certainly something, though this process was far bigger than even his outsized figure. He was a hero of the vigorous antiwar movement of this period; for example, we see William Jennings Bryan from the American prairies making his pilgrimage to Yassnaya Polyana. His most prominent disciple in the realm of practical affairs was to be the great Mahatma Gandhi, leader of the Indian independence movement, legendary saint and father of the modern Indian nation. Tolstoy cried out against materialism, capitalism, the corruptions of bourgeois society, and demanded a spiritual rebirth. He did not explicitly become an anti-rationalist, was certainly no mystic, yet his whole-hearted feeling of a need to find positive meaning in life through religious commitment was a more potent blast against merely cerebral philosophy or religion than anything else in his era, probably.

How unorthodox Tolstoy was may be judged from his reply to the edict of excommunication. He denied the trinity, original sin, the divinity of Christ, and all the church sacraments, which he called "coarse, degrading sorcery." He accused the clergy of ignorance and deceptiveness.

Tolstoy's equally great countryman, Fyodor Dostoyevsky, shared with Nietzsche a preoccupation with the idea of God's extinction and what follows from this. In his striking parable of the Grand Inquisitor (in *The Brothers Karamazov*), Christ returns to earth to be arrested and condemned by the wise old Inquisitor, who sees that Christian freedom is impossible for man, enslaved as he is and must be by superstitions. Existing organized religion is a fraud, but perhaps a necessary fraud. Men could not endure pure spiritual Christianity; it is possible for only a few, now. Into this parable, so often reprinted, is packed much of modern religious man's agony and tension. Modern man is depraved, he needs God but cannot find him, orthodox old-fashioned Christianity is bankrupt, the truly religious man today may be the atheist or anti-Christ. Dostoyevsky adopted a belief in the potential mission of the Slavic peoples to redeem decadent Europe because still capable of religion—a kind of spiritual pan-Slavism. Nietzsche himself learned from this Russian genius, who spent some terrible years in Siberian prison camps for the crime of talking against the Tsar's government, then came to reject the revolutionary movement as spiritually shallow. No more significant figure exists for contemporary civilization.

Nicolas Berdyaev has mentioned Tolstoy and Dostoyevsky among those he called the "forerunners of the era of the spirit," the predecessors of the post-1914 Christian revival. Others in this generation referred to by the Russian existentialist were Solovyëv and Cieszkowski (a Pole) from the Slavic world and two Frenchmen, Leon Bloy and Charles Péguy. The latter, initially a Dreyfusard and a democrat, a moderate socialist, and a fine literary craftsman, edited prewar France's most important intellectual journal, the *Cahiers de la Quinzaine*, opening its pages to all kinds of expression. Though a Catholic, Péguy was essentially a free spirit, on whom the influence of Bergson could be seen prominently. Like Tolstoy, Péguy was in revolt against all that was false in a timid and shoddy civilization, and sought to affirm the value of the human soul by preaching integrity, devotion to the spiritual and intellectual life, social justice, dedication to art.

So religion was abroad, but the winds of doctrine were various and confusing. The British scholar J. N. Figgis, writing just before 1914 of *Civilization at the Crossroads*, expressed his dismay at the babel of voices: Nietzsche, Bergson, James, Tolstoy, and Bertrand Russell—atheism, skepticism, intuitionism, the life force, the will to believe, the will to power, etc. Had the European tradition dissolved into a thousand fragments? Did civilization evolve from unity to multiplicity, from the

Virgin to the Dynamo, as the American writer Henry Adams suggested? Some of the manifestations of diversity in the 1900s were wild indeed. In Russia, where the composer Scriabin upheld the artist's role as messiah and announced himself the chosen one, while the poet Ivanov preached the mystical union of Christ and Dionysius in "ecstasy for ecstasy's sake," there was a mood in which "every kind of new religion and superstition proliferated" (Martin Cooper). At the other end of Europe, James Joyce in Dublin encountered the Hermetic Society and the Theosophical Society, where Madame Blavatsky, Annie Besant (who had passed through Fabianism en route to Theosophy) and other modern mystics and would-be prophets were read. Another magician was the Greek Gurdiyev, who offered occult spiritual forces taken from pre-rational cultures and associated with artistic creation. In Italy, D'Annunzio preached the religion of art and of sexual love before settling, deplorably, on the religion of imperialism; spiritually perhaps a fraud, like the dictator Mussolini who so much resembled him, D'Annunzio was a fabulous personality, tremendously popular, expressing much of the *malaise* of the times.

The serious interest in abnormal psychical phenomena (spirit messages, telepathy, clairvoyance, poltergeists, etc.) might be added. As during the fourteenth century when papal control weakened and Europe was swept by witchcraft and magic, so now in the aftermath of Christianity's decline something similar happened. The comparison, at least, may be suggested.

Esthetes and Literary Rebels

One of the great adventures of the last half of the nineteenth century lay in the realm of pure literature. It is impossible to avoid the conclusion that, with the decline of the traditional Church and of any agreed-upon orthodoxy in either religion or philosophy, the great imaginative writers have supplied many of the values of the modern world. Further, it is equally true that art became something of a religion for many in this generation. While criticism from Voltaire and Darwin had eroded Christianity's power to compel unquestioned adherence, there was also disillusionment in this period with scientific rationalism, as we have seen. The philosophers of the era, among whom Nietzsche, Bergson, and William James stand out, tended toward intuitionism or naturalism, rather than rationalism in the sense of formal, conceptual thought, and expressed their views more in poetic metaphor than logical analysis. Perhaps the greatest single advance in knowledge of the era was being made by Freud, who charted the mysterious, nonrational side of the human psyche. Nietzsche's insights, too, haunted all the writers of this era. Thus most of the major currents of the age combined to focus attention on the poetic, myth-making capacities of man.

This was a time when Europe discovered, for better or worse, the depths of the mind that lie beneath rational thought, where myth and symbol reign and strange, formidable powers lurk in hiding. Neither philosopher nor scientist can guide us here, but the poet or novelist perhaps can. In addition to probing the unconscious, these writers gave voice to much of the social criticism that filled the age, criticism of one or another feature of a bourgeois, industrial, democratic society repellent to sensitive souls. But their alienation pushed them toward pure art and toward purely subjective "private worlds" of imagination, for they were disgusted with the public world. Estheticism, art for art's sake, the poet's elevation to preeminence, these attitudes naturally accompanied rejection of the social and moral order by which a hated civilization lived.

The beginnings of this literature of revolt may be found at mid-century or even earlier, when reaction against the older romanticism and disillusionment with a commercial and bourgeois civilization appeared together, a rock flung at Victorian orthodoxy, the esthetic counterpart of revolutionary socialism. The art for art's sake writers, offspring of Gautier and Baudelaire, were from the beginning a rebellious, less respectable lot, whose works sometimes had a *succès de scandale* as well as a genuine success of art. In 1857 both Baudelaire and Flaubert faced criminal prosecution, the former for his *Flowers of Evil* and the latter for the celebrated novel *Madame Bovary*. In England, the Pre-Raphaelites were criticized as immoral, but this was nothing compared to the storm stirred up by the deliberately provocative poet Algernon Swinburne in the 1860s. These writers, as their slogan implied, tended to make of art and beauty a religion, often with results that shocked the moralists. They were aggressively hostile to Christianity and conventional morality. In Swinburne's unpublished novel *Lesbia Brandon* we have the theme of homosexual love (handled also by Gautier in his seminal novel *Mademoiselle de Maupin*) accompanying an estheticism in which people cultivate their senses and live saturated in beauty. Baudelaire's "satanism," which seemed to ask the poet to seek out morbid and abnormal themes, was as famous as his theory that poetry should strive for a purity corresponding to color and music. Swinburne, John Morley wrote indignantly in 1866, was "the libidinous laureate of a pack of satyrs." It is at this time that we begin to hear of Bohemia, where impoverished young painters and writers, the hippies of their day, lived highly unconventional lives.

Whatever the case with Mimi and Rodolphe, Baudelaire, Flaubert, and Swinburne were great writers, and a shocked orthodoxy could not so easily cast them aside. The movement they began swept on, but took somewhat different forms: decadence, symbolism, realism, or naturalism. In all cases the desire to *épater le bourgeoisie*—shock the conventional—went along with an often exaggerated cult of beauty and artistic integrity. Novelists like Flaubert and the Goncourt brothers, in England George Moore, and later the celebrated Emile Zola, dealt realistically with the sordid. Flaubert's famous portrait of the bored and adulterous wife of a provincial doctor in *Madame Bovary* led on to the low-life characters of the Goncourts and Zola: servant-girls, prostitutes, drunkards, criminals. Zola's "naturalism" reflected the impact of Darwinism and was marked both by its claim to be "scientific" and by its rawer sort of realism. The French master produced a huge multivolumed chronicle generously peopled with the vicious and depraved, designed both as a giant tapestry of life in contemporary France and as a demonstration that men are the determinate products of their heredity and their environment. Grim pessimism, man the helpless victim of blind chance, may be found also in Zola's English contemporary and fellow novelist, Thomas Hardy.

The 1880s brought symbolism and the decadents. The latter attained notoriety chiefly through the famous novel by J. K. Huysmans, *A Rebours* (*Against the Grain*), whose hero, Des Esseintes, was the prototype of all dandies, those "super-esthetical young men" whom Oscar Wilde and the *Yellow Book* were soon to introduce to an amazed Victorian public. Emaciated, depraved, and sophisticated, the decadent or dandy felt himself to be the last pale but exquisite flower of a fading civilization, and amused himself with art, vice, and crime. A carefully cultivated exoticism, an extreme artificiality marked this mode of writing. Picking up a copy of the notorious *A Rebours*, Oscar Wilde's hero in *The Portrait of Dorian Gray* felt that "the heavy odor of incense seemed to cling about its pages and to trouble the brain." "The first duty of life is to be as artificial as possible," Wilde wrote, adding that "what the second duty is no one has yet discovered." Cold, cruel, green-eyed *femmes fatales* filled decadent poetry and novels. Homosexual perhaps like Wilde, the dandy might shade into more sinister types representing what Mario Praz has written about as "the romantic agony." An exciting suspicion of nameless sins hung over this literary assault on respectability, around which grouped those who were weary of Victorian primness.

Less obviously designed to shock the bourgeoisie, symbolism, born about 1886, represented the ultimate in Baudelairean estheticism, and produced some great poetry; its goal was to express the inexpressible by an experimental verse which followed the logic of the interior mind, revealing the reality behind the appearances of things by the use of archetypal images of symbols. Much of modern poetry lies under its influence. Verlaine and Mallarmé, later the brilliant young poets La Forgue and Valéry, were its prophets.

This sounds like a more sophisticated version of romanticism, and this is not far from the truth, insofar as the idealist and poet-as-seer elements are concerned. For the poet was indeed a seer, a *voyant*, to the symbolists. But the mood of symbolism was deeply tinged with the related currents of estheticism and decadence. Turning their backs on a disgusting social and material world, many of the symbolists were distinctly other-worldly. Their most celebrated literary character, the hero of Villiers de l'Isle Adam's *Axel's Castle* (which is the title Edmund Wilson gave to his now classical study of this movement), lived alone in a Wagnerian castle studying occult philosophy; when he and a girl who had come to murder him fell immediately and sublimely in love, they decided on suicide because reality could not possibly measure up to the perfection of their love as they felt and experienced it at that moment. Living, Count Axel and Sara thought, is too vulgar; "our servants can do that for us"! In the same spirit, Oscar Wilde once said that "any fool can make history, but it takes a genius to write it"! Art is superior to life. The earlier, "classic" romanticists had not so distinguished and separated art from life.

Around the turn of the century, the more alert young writers of Europe were all smitten with the symbolist message. The young James Joyce, his brother tells us, liked poems that "sought to capture moods and impressions, often tenuous moods and elusive impressions, by means of a verbal witchery that magnetizes the mind like a spell, and imparts a wonder and grace. . . ." Poetry must not be rhymed prose; if it is, there is little point in writing it as verse. Poetry is *sui generis*, its purpose being to convey, not ideas, not conceptual knowledge, but "moods and impressions," the subtle inner world of the mind with its emotional states. This is an appeal to immediate experience—the *données* of consciousness, as the philosopher Bergson called it—which lay very close to the heart of the matter in this period. The French poet Rimbaud, who believed that the poet's vision has power to penetrate a deeper reality and show men how to live (a romantic idea), also believed that the poet can bypass conceptual thought to express reality, somehow, in an immediate, symbolic sense—a conception that may bear comparison to traditional religious mysticism, but was here presented by a man whose life was that of an alienated rebel. This strange and degraded genius has been made the object of a veritable religious cult by some moderns.

The French symbolists' antisocial extremisms may perhaps be excused on the grounds of their intense indignation against a social order that was destructive of all beauty and integrity—the rule of plutocracy, of capitalism, of the bourgeoisie, "a hideous society," as Des Esseintes exclaims. The achievements of the symbolist school are beyond question; they set the tone for modern poetry, especially in France but with a heavy influence abroad, too. T. S. Eliot brought symbolism's manner and mood into English poetry a few years later. Just prior to 1914 the American Ezra Pound, along with T. E. Hulme and others, founded the "imagist" movement in England, influenced by Bergson and related to French symbolism, with some debts also to Japanese poetry.[7] The object was to get at reality in a moment of flashing insight embodied in a single image:

> The apparition of these faces in the crowd;
> Petals on a wet, black bough.

The impulse to create a "pure" poetry, purged of the traditional narrative or argument, was found earlier in Baudelaire and Verlaine and the French school known as "Parnassian" in the 1860s; it is one important ingredient in the modern movement. Its goal was to distinguish poetry from prose by its content as well as its form, a revolt against all previous literary doctrine and against the highly popular Victorian narrative or descriptive poem, such as Tennyson and Browning wrote. Poetry should not be an alternate mode of discourse. In the making of modern poetry the Parnassian strain joins the irrationalist (the mysticism of the Word, Rimbaud's "reasoned disordering of the senses") and the symbolist (allusion, indirect statement, subtle symbolisms) as the leading operative features.

Nietzsche, as well as Richard Wagner, exerted great influence on French thought toward the end of the century. In 1861, when Wagner's music first caused furious controversy in Paris, Baudelaire brilliantly defended it; it had bowled him over much as had the writings of Edgar Allen Poe earlier (the latter a rare example of a decisive American influence on Europe at this time). "The *Revue Wagnérienne* was founded in 1885, not merely to study his music but also his esthetic doctrine— his theory of total art. Wagnerism came to be considered as a complete philosophy of life . . ." (Enid Starkie). As for Nietzsche, his message found some eager ears in *fin de siècle* France. That the great German had so much admired the giants of French literature did not impede

---

[7]A minor chapter in intellectual history in this period relates to the discovery of Japan, so recently and dramatically drawn into communication with the West, by European writers and American ones (Lafcadio Hearn) too—discovery especially of the estheticism that runs through Japanese life. Impressionist painting also owed something to Japanese art.

this reception, of course. Emile Faguet, in his book *On Reading Nie-tzsche* (1st edition, 1904), wrote that "the gist of Nietzsche is that there is no good truth but that which we have discovered ourselves, nor any good rule of life but that which honestly and with effort we have created for ourselves." Wagner and Nietzsche represented the esthetic view of life stressing absolute integrity, loyalty to one's personal vision. To the French tradition that ran from Baudelaire and Gautier to Verlaine and Mallarmé, this was a congenial note.

Also influenced by Nietzsche were the Scandinavians Ibsen and Strindberg, the former possibly the most stimulating and controversial writer of the epoch. Upon the performance of Ibsen's "Ghosts" in London in 1891, a shocked respectability called it filthy, disgusting, and immoral, demanding its prohibition. George Bernard Shaw was impelled to write a book, *The Quintessence of Ibsenism*, in defence of the Norwegian, a book which stands as one of the major critical works of the era as well as a tribute to the vitality of Shaw and of his age. For once, England vibrated to a theatrical controversy as France had often done; *Ghosts* was the modern *Hernani*. In his book on Ibsen, Shaw asked how it was that some hailed the Norwegian as the greatest living dramatist, the modern Shakespeare, a genius beyond compare, while others requested his suppression in the name of common decency and public order. (This occurred all over Europe, not just in England, the alleged home of Victorian prudery.) The answer to the latter question lay in Ibsen's shattering attacks on conventional morality. By later standards Ibsen was hardly daring, but in the 1880s and 1890s his brilliant, successful, interesting plays (as they certainly were then, and on the whole Ibsen's reputation has stood up) were a brand of defiance hurled in the face of the dominant European bourgeoisie. In *Ghosts* (written 1881), an apparently model wife and mother is shown to be living amid lies, unfaithfulness, and corruption, much as Nora Helmer is in the famous *Doll's House* (1879). In *The Enemy of the People* (1882), respectable society persecutes the honest man who would interfere with its material prosperity by telling the truth about the evil source of that prosperity. Hating "Pillars of Society" (the name of one of his plays), Ibsen had no use either for romantic, idealistic reformers. His *Peer Gynt* is a modern Don Quixote who makes himself ridiculous by blindly living as if dreams were reality. With all his symbols, Ibsen was a naturalist too, exploring with Zola the seamier sides of modern life, if a little more subtle in his definitions of the sordid.

Shaw's own plays reflect a considerable Ibsenian influence, with a special flair for the drama of ideas and a flashing, Voltairean wit lacking in the Norwegian. A peculiar sensitivity to ideas marked this versatile Irishman, along with the ability to present these ideas in dramatic form.

Some of his plays expose social evil or hypocrisy in the Fabian spirit; others reflect his fascination with Nietzschean and vitalist ideas then so much in the air. Most of them slightly shocked the public, but amused them so much that they tolerated the unconventional element. Shaw like Voltaire became a licensed iconoclast, privileged to criticize the idols of respectability because he did it in such a scintillating manner. The positive message was socialist but more often after 1900 Nietzschean. Bold, free spirits stride through Shaw's plays, knocking down the proprieties and teaching people to assert their individuality. Following a suggestion of Nietzsche's, Shaw had his Don Juan find that the really best people are in Hell, not Heaven. The common rules are always reversed: girls drink brandy and smoke cigars, while men are cringing and cowardly; honorable professions are dishonorable, and *vice versa,* Mrs. Warren's Profession (the oldest) is really no worse than any other. Shaw's Caesar is a Nietzschean superman, action controlled by reason, beyond good and evil. *Back to Methuselah* popularized the theory of creative or emergent evolution, and indeed the "life force" became a persistent Shavian theme. Shaw lived on to a ripe and creative old age in the postwar years, another trait he shared with Voltaire being an amazingly long literary career. His noonday was between 1900 and 1917, his mission to force novel ideas on bourgeois England.

The new writers, who often themselves thumbed their noses at the crowd, were not always popular. One of the more notable denunciations of the new literature appeared in Max Nordau's book *Degeneration* (1895). Nordau, a rationalistic socialist, saw nothing but "degeneration" in the new literature and philosophy. Nietzsche, Walt Whitman, Wagner, Tolstoy, Ibsen, as well as the French decadents, symbolists, and realists, all he declared to be so many morbid diseases. They were mad, they were antisocial, they were sex-obsessed (sexual overstimulation ruins civilization, Nordau believed). Nordau, one suspects, was almost prepared with Plato to banish the artist from society altogether in the interest of social stability, though he did declare his respect for the "healthy art" of Dante, Shakespeare, and Goethe. Few of the moderns— Hauptmann's *Weavers* was an exception—passed his critical inspection. He rejoiced that the average man remained immune to these siren calls, continuing to prefer music-hall melodies to Wagner, farces to Ibsen.

Nordau's outburst was characteristic more of popular reaction than of avant-garde thought, though he himself was a highly literate person. Nevertheless quite a few scholars and critics reared in the older literature bridled at the new mode of expression, and the mob persecuted it. Oscar Wilde, the chief prophet of the new literature in England in the 1890s, brilliant playwright and epigrammist, ended a broken man after being arrested and jailed for homosexuality. His illness neglected by the prison authorities, Wilde died at forty-six a martyr to the popular dislike of the estheticism he flaunted. The concurrent revolution in the arts and music excited even greater hostility. The riot that greeted Stravinsky's "Rites of Spring" in Paris in 1913, and the similar reception given to Postimpressionist, abstract art in 1911 in England, are famous examples.

The Russian writers, Tolstoy and Gorki, rejected modernist literature and art as unwholesome; see especially the former's *What Is Art?*, which assigned to literature a moral function of communicating values to the masses and indignantly accused the European esthetes of having lost faith in man and civilization. (The latter would scarcely have denied this.) In Italy, on the other hand, the new literature gained some enthusiastic converts. Clearly symbolism and decadence were extremely sophisticated forms, possibly most at home in the older cultures. But Andreyev was one great Russian writer who was influenced by the symbolists.

What seems clear is that there had been a literary revolution. Touched off by Baudelaire and Gautier, it gathered momentum as the century wore on and as the bourgeoisie tightened its grip on Western Europe. The writers flung a challenge in the respectable face of late nineteenth-century society, while at the same time they created fresh styles and announced a new religion, the religion of Art. The alienated artist, or the writer as rebel, the frustrated intellectual as he appears, for example, in Thomas Mann's novel *Tonio Kröger*, is a modern phenomenon. No such gulf between the artist and thinker on the one hand and organized society on the other had been *typical* of any previous age, and in mid-Victorian times Tennyson and Browning, for example, had a socially accepted status not accorded to the defiant decadents or naturalists or symbolists. There is something significant in the fact that upon the death of Lord Alfred in 1892, vacating the Poet Laureateship which he had held since 1850, a long and fruitless quest to fill that honorable office ensued. The best poets were politically unacceptable: the socialist William Morris, the scandalous Swinburne, not to mention those young men like Ernest Dowson who were going off to die in poverty in France. Gladstone, an earnest and literate Victorian, worried about the question but was unable to resolve it. Lord Salisbury, the succeeding Conservative prime minister, contemptuously appointed a third-rate jingler to the post Tennyson had exalted. Thus was the widening gulf between artist and society symbolized. It has been one of the scandals of our century.

A comparable revolution took place in the fine arts. The "modernist" revolution in painting spawned a whole series of new schools, which in general reacted against naturalism and realism. Henri Matisse announced an expressionist credo: "there is an inherent truth which must

be disengaged from the outward appearance of the object to be represented. . . . Exactitude is not truth." Cubism, usually dated from a
Picasso painting of 1907, used formalized geometrical patterns to try to
get at the "inherent reality" of objects. "Futurism," organized by the
Italian poet, Marinetti, announced the end of the old art and the birth of
the new in a manifesto of 1909; the futurist pronouncement included
references to the new physics (space no longer exists, flux and change is
the only reality) as well as to the pace of modern life ("steel, fever,
pride, and headlong speed"). "A clean sweep should be made of all stale
and threadbare subject-matter in order to express the vortex of modern
life."

The impulse behind these movements obviously resembled that of
the new writers. Imbued with a generally revolutionary mood, hostile
to the dull bourgeois society into which they were born, these artists
were further moved by the idea that symbols are the language of the
unconscious mind and reveal new dimensions of the human spirit, or
that by abstract figures one can get at the inmost reality of things. So
they experimented in all sorts of ways, and came up with startlingly
novel pictures.

A new architecture was being born in the 1900s, daring in its
break with tradition. Music, too, underwent revolutionary changes, with
violent experimentation, which defied the conventional and tried to do
something different from any previous composition. In 1913, a riot in
Paris marked the performance of Igor Stravinsky's "Rite of Spring,"
music no less revolutionary than the paintings of Picasso.

If all these new art forms represented anything more than a protest
and a probing for novelty, that something was the intuition of Bergson
or the unconscious mind of Freud. Beneath and beyond merely conceptual or intellectual thought, art as pure expression might get in touch
with a reality denied to logic. Its symbols might be the language of the
human soul at a level deeper than formal thought. These exciting and
disturbing paintings, poems, and musical compositions did certainly be-
speak an atmosphere of revolt and novelty. (Stravinsky's "Rite of
Spring" describes a pagan bacchanalian orgy climaxed by a ritual murder.) They were created largely by "bohemian" artists, Picasso and his
friends being denizens of the Paris slums.

Irrationalism in Political and Social Thought

"Most of the political opinions of most men are the result, not of
reasoning tested by experience, but of unconscious or half-conscious inference tested by habit." This now not-so startling judgment is quoted

406 MAIN CURRENTS OF THOUGHT IN THE CONTEMPORARY WORLD

from Graham Wallas's *Human Nature in Politics*, commonly considered a landmark in the history of British political thought. In this little book, first published in 1908, Wallas, one of the original Fabians, noted that since 1867 "representative democracy" had largely triumphed all over Europe; even the Austrian and Russian empires as of that year seemed to have followed the others in taking steps towards constitutional democracy. But amid these triumphs, students of democracy in the western nations seemed "puzzled and disappointed by their experience of it." It was far from the ideal system its advocates had expected. There were political "machines" (a keen student of them was M. Ostrogorski), and other political phenomena unknown to and unstudied by traditional political theory.

Wallas felt that political science had not learned to study real men in the real world, but dealt with abstractions often irrelevant to it. The largest fallacy was the assumption of rational man, whether in economics or politics, knowing his own interest and serving it. To some extent, Wallas suggested, there had been a decline of rationalism owing to the "de-localizing" of people, who, uprooted from the village where they had a secure place in society, were thrust into the mass anonymity of the city. Also, the intrusions of vast numbers into politics made for the use of symbols and stereotypes—"ballyhoo," the Americans were soon to name it. But above all, the science of psychology had now begun the study of the semirational and nonrational mental processes which most men exhibit most of the time. Wallas opened up a subject other Anglo-Saxon students were to pursue before long. (See, for example, Trotter's *Instinct of the Herd* published during the war, or Walter Lippmann's *Public Opinion* published soon after it.)

Wallas obviously was one who hoped to extend the sway of reason by recognizing, studying, and thus controlling the irrational elements in human behavior. In this he joined not only Freud and Jung but also a group of distinguished sociologists. The years from about 1890 to 1914 marked the brilliant coming-of-age of sociology. It was the generation that followed the trail-blazing during which Comte, Marx, and Spencer had hewed a rough trail. Now came men such as Emile Durkheim, Max Weber and a host of only slightly lesser lights to refine the crude generalizations of the pioneers, while retaining much of their scope and dramatic power. Durkheim carried on Comte, Weber largely began where Marx left off; though British sociology failed to keep up with French and German, the evolutionary hypotheses of Spencer and the social Darwinists formed a significant backdrop to all social theory. Of the stature of Durkheim and Weber there is at any rate no doubt. And the leading social stimulus to the development of sociology was that rapid alteration of environment from rural to urban, traditional to modern society, of which Graham Wallas had spoken. It should be observed that in the hands of a Weber or Durkheim or Robert Michels (who indeed referred to "political sociology") the boundary between socio- logical and political studies was not sharp. "Sociology," as the "scien- tific" study of social phenomena, can be applied to all manner of things; the sociologists of this period were much inclined to apply it to politics. Weber studied the forms of political authority and the origins of the Western economic order; Michels examined the structure of political parties. And the interest Durkheim showed in the relationship between individuals and the community had behind it an urgent feeling about the problems of contemporary European society as it proceeded rapidly into an urban industrial setting.

If we wonder why something called sociology rose to importance at this time, having not existed (at least under this name) before in his- tory, the best answer is that it was precipitated by the disintegration of traditional society, with the emergence of urbanism and what Maurice Barrès, the French novelist, called *uprootedness*. When society is stable the questions which lead one to study it do not arise, it is simply taken for granted. The prominence of sociology in Germany was due to the unusually sudden industrialization of that country in the later nineteenth century, passing from traditional society, marked by the village com- munity, quite rapidly into advanced modern technology with large cities, factories, and the alienation of the individual from society. The leading pioneer of German sociology in the 1880s, Friedrich Tönnies, was preoccupied with the distinction between what he called community and society (*Gemeinschaft* and *Gesellschaft*)—the tightly integrated community, small and cohesive, such as men had generally lived in since primitive times, and the "great society" of the modern state, vast and complex, in which the individual might feel himself freer yet lost. George Simmel, too, one of the early German sociologists, tried to examine the impact of the City, this new environment, on human lives: "The deepest problems of modern life derive from the claim of the individual to pre- serve the autonomy and individuality of his existence in the face of overwhelming social forces. . . ." The urban situation was one of more freedom, greater stimulation, more opportunity for expansion of the mind, but also one of rootlessness, loss of social ties, and consequent disorientation.

The great French sociologist, Emile Durkheim, also made this his theme. He was preoccupied with the loss of social solidarity, as he called it, and thought of sociology as a study that could help modern man find his way to some higher form of it, having lost its primitive type. The term associated with Durkheim, and surely one of the most significant terms of modern times, is *anomie*, which was his name for the uneasiness which afflicts the individual when he has no accepted social authority to guide him. The individual, Durkheim argued, needs such an authority; without it he cannot impose limits on his ego and is not really happy. The individual who feels bewildered and alone in a huge, impersonal world, who has lost the guidance of tradition and religion (which Durkheim felt were very closely connected) and can find no source of values outside himself, who has lost contact with the community—such a person is surely all too typical of modern urbanized and industrialized society, and the pioneer sociologists directed their attention to this problem. Their own personal lives often pointed directly to this interest. They came from the village to the city and experienced cultural shock. The Jewishness of Durkheim and Simmel added to the sense of being outsiders, perhaps. (The brilliant Durkheim felt isolated as a student at the Sorbonne, to which he later returned as professor.) These men would seem to have experienced the crisis of the individual thrown into the vastness and confusion of modern urban life.

Max Weber

The greatest in this golden age of sociology was undoubtedly Max Weber. A scholar whose tremendous range and productivity reminds us somewhat of Carl Jung, Weber, a professor at Heidelberg, suffered intermittently from illness and died in 1920 at the age of fifty-six. A good part of Weber's inspiration stemmed from Marx, whose crudities he wished to refine but whose central conception of a scientific approach to social, economic, and political phenomena he shared. Perhaps best described as a liberal, Weber longed to play an active part in public affairs but in Imperial Germany, of which he was a keen critic, found this path largely blocked. (He did perform some public functions in World War I, which he supported as a patriotic German at least at the beginning but later sharply criticized German policies.) He was a friend of the Social Democrat, Robert Michels, and when the latter was refused a university post because of his left-wing politics Weber bitterly denounced the vaunted German academic freedom as a fraud. All in all, Weber's combination of brilliance, erudition, and courageous political activism stamped him as an intellectual and moral leader of his generation in Germany; and his fame has endured through such of his writings as the stimulating *The Protestant Ethic and the Spirit of Capitalism*, or his lectures in *General Economic History*.

As a social scientist, Weber was aware of the irrational side of politics and made this one of his chief fields. He was fascinated by the forms of political leadership and by the path of historical development in society and state. One of Weber's leading interests was the principle of rationalization. He meant by this in general the tendency of things to get organized and subjected to rules and orderly processes. What Michels saw happening to the German Social Democrats, in their path towards bureaucracy, Weber saw as a universal principle in human history. Beginning in romance or magic, institutions or forms settle down into a stable routine. Music, for example, becomes a science. Government becomes bureaucracy. In this process spontaneity is lost, there is "disenchantment," the pedantic expert takes over from the free spirit; Weber sometimes with Nietzsche accuses the modern world of having lost its greatness of soul, producing petty time-servers rather than heroes. At the same time efficiency gains. There is, however, Weber adds, a limitation to the institutionalized or bureaucratic form of authority; it cannot cope with emergencies, being attuned only to times of stability. In times of crisis we still get a reversion to the type of leadership Weber called "charismatic." The great man arises, commanding allegiance by the peculiar force of his personality or genius. Napoleon in the nineteenth century revealed the charisma as much as Caesar two thousand years earlier, while on a lesser scale religious leaders and leaders of other sorts, continued to appear. (Certainly there was no lack of prophetic figures in the late nineteenth century, from Tolstoy and Stefan George to Mary Baker Eddy and Mme. Blavatsky, exercising leadership in mysterious ways.) Charismatic creations are then institutionalized and reduced to routine, in tradition or bureaucracy. What we do or believe today from custom or because it is enshrined in the routine of law was yesterday the inspiration of some charismatic personality.

Weber shared with his friend Robert Michels, and with Pareto and also Georges Sorel, this interest in the forms and modes of authority— legal, traditional, charismatic, and combinations of these. A historical sociologist, his chief interest was in understanding just how this Western society, with its capitalism, its economic rationality, its powerful political state came to be. Unlike Marx, he saw it not as one inevitable phase of all societies but as a unique thing, created through the centuries, owing something to ancient Judaism. What we may call the sociology of religion fascinated Weber as much as it did Marx and Nietzsche. In *The Protestant Ethic and the Spirit of Capitalism* he presented the famous thesis (often misunderstood) that religious ideas interact with worldly activities to produce a characteristic "style of life," and that Protestantism and Capitalism had something to do with each other. The analysis of modern capitalism also interested Werner Sombart, who more clearly exposed his dislike of its bureaucratic and depersonalizing features.

Weber produced no "system," he is of value because of his stimulating insights into particular areas, illuminating them and adding terms to our vocabulary. In general, Weber like Pareto was pessimistic. Fritz Ringer has recently seen sociology as based on an attitude of pessimistic resignation in the face of modernization—"a heroic ideal of rational clarification in the face of tragedy." In the hands of Weber and Pareto understanding proved oddly sterile. We learn of the world's inevitable imperfections, we reject utopias, and our knowledge is likely to incapacitate us for action. The Italian Vilfredo Pareto, brilliant and versatile thinker, said of his *Trattato di Sociologica Generale* (1915) that if he thought it would have many readers he would not have written it! In criticism of Marx, whom he accused of utopianism, Pareto saw a constant struggle for power between groups and classes, but one that never ends. If Marx's "proletariat" did win, it would become a new ruling class against which others would soon rebel—a quite accurate prediction of what did happen in Communist Russia and other Communist states. In his disabused or cynical reduction of all ideals to selfish power struggles Pareto reminds us of Hobbes, or his famous Italian forbear Machiavelli. Liberty, he would say, is best served when we are aware of the delusions lurking in ideals, aware of the realities of power and thus able to establish realistic checks on it as far as possible. We should aim at a circulating elite, one which draws the potential revolutionaries into the circle of power. But in general Pareto did not prescribe, he only described, and he was not optimistic about the chances of the existing European ruling class. An interesting feature of his sociology was the attempt to classify the basic emotional determinants of ideas, the "residues," in his terminology, which underlie intellectual systems. Thus Pareto was convinced that ideologies may be reduced to certain kinds of power-drives. Few more ruthless exposers of ideals and ideologies have ever written.

This was the essential irrationalism of this brilliant generation of psychologists and sociologists: they were in revolt against formalism, they discovered the deeper, more obscure processes of the mind in which rational thought is embedded and of which it is sometimes a kind of protective screen. The paradox is that in making these discoveries they were using their powers of rational thought; reason undercut reason.

Though enormously learned and often possessed by a disinterested quest for knowledge, these sociologists were far from uninvolved or value-free. They all tended to see a crisis. Raymond Aron says that Durkheim "spoke of sociology with the moral fervor of a prophet," and thought it could save modern man by telling him how to achieve solidarity and avoid anomie. Weber, at times hauntingly eloquent, is a kind of ancestor of existentialism: Karl Jaspers was his student. Pareto, apparently the most objective, was the most embittered, and it is plain that what forced him into detachment was his disenchantment. If you have really given up all belief in fairies, to endure life you must stand off and laugh at it all, adopting an Olympian stance. To many sociologists, their science is patently a strategy for rejecting or satirizing their society. The device of pretending to be a stranger, in order to say "See what odd customs these queer people have! And what absurd things they do!" was an old stratagem of satire, used by Swift and Montesquieu. Certain sociologists do something similar. Someone defined sociology as the village atheist studying the village idiot; we recognize the genre. The point is that sociology itself may be subject to sociological interpretation; it too was a philosophy, a set if ideas arising at a certain time and related to the social conditions of its time as well as to its intellectual antecedents. The main incentive, to repeat, was the dissolving of ancestral customs and institutions during the "modernization" of Western civilization from about 1800 on, the effects of which were keenly felt after about 1870.[8]

New Social Theories: Sorel and Lenin

Perhaps the intrusion of the "irrational" was only a consequence of such rapid, disorienting change. Millions were being uprooted from a stable, centuries-old environment and thrown into a new one. The political theorists responded to this fact in one way or another. Just ahead of them, making most pertinent their comments on political irrationalism, the use of myth, and charismatic leadership, lay Lenin, Mussolini, and Hitler.

In connection with these themes of irrationalism, of literary alienation, of mass society in crisis, we can return to the theme of democracy and of nationalism, so pervasive in this era. Quite often the alienated expressed scorn for the democratic-nationalist culture of deracinated mass men. "I teach that there are higher and lower men." Nietzsche's friend, the Swiss historian Jacob Burckhardt (famed for his study of the Italian Renaissance), thought that Europe would not be healthy until its "natural order of inequality" was restored. Many succumbed to "cultural despair" in contemplating the invasion from below by the new

---

[8]According to Raymond Williams, in 1800 only 3 percent of the people of the world lived in towns of more than 5,000 inhabitants. Today the total is nearly a third. For western Europe, the nineteenth-century trend is suggested by the fact that in 1801 England and Wales, the most urbanized part of Europe, "had less than 10 percent of their population in cities of 100,000 or more" whereas by 1901 this had risen to 35 percent, with 58 percent living in cities of 20,000 or more (Kingsley Davis). For the rest of Europe, the surge toward urbanization came after 1850.

barbarism of mass. Maurice Barrès, one of France's leading writers, associated democracy with the "uprootedness" of modern man who has been torn loose from the soil and deposited in the impersonal neighborhoods of great cities, there to become a faceless cipher. Barrès's program included socialism under a strong authoritarian leader, agrarianism, and anti-Semitism.

A more formidable French political theorist and leader was Barrès's friend, the intrepid monarchist Charles Maurras, founder of the *Action Française*. Maurras was in the tradition of French classicism and rationalism, of Voltaire and Comte. He admired order and stressed the French national tradition, which he saw as classical and rational. He inherited Comte's dislike of modern society as too anarchic and scorned democracy as lacking a principle of order. A prominent theme of Maurras's thought was the need for leadership by an intelligent minority. "The mob always follows determined minorities." The *Action Française* organized the *Camelots du Roi* to engage in agitation and street fighting, an idea subsequently adopted by Fascists and Nazis. Among other ideas it bequeathed to the postwar Fascist movement was that of the "corporate state," a favorite idea of Maurras's that came to him from the Catholic Social Movement in France, especially La Tour du Pin. Though hardly any threat to the state, the *Action* exercised a considerable influence on French university students just before the war. Violently hostile to the Republic in the 1900s, it tended to rally to its support after 1912 with war clouds on the horizon, for it was militantly patriotic and fiercely anti-German. It put out a well-known newspaper, and from Maurras's tireless pen flowed a stream of books and pamphlets. Nationalist, traditionalist, antidemocratic and anti-Semite, Maurras carried on a war against the liberal, parliamentary state and he looms ominously as perhaps the chief forerunner of the "revolutionary conservatism" of the postwar period.

Georges Sorel ranks with Charles Maurras among the outstanding French political theorists in the years before 1914. A Marxian socialist originally, Sorel adopted the irrationalism of the hour and married a Nietzschean and Bergsonian spirit to his revolutionary radicalism. He charged the orthodox socialists with having become bureaucratized and respectable. Their rationalism and materialism, Sorel felt, were quite inappropriate for revolutionaries. Doubtless he was right in recognizing that Marxism is really an apocalyptical religion. He was quite willing to accept it frankly as such. Do not all men live by "myths"? Socialism he compared to the church, the modern strikers being the equivalent of Christian saints and martyrs. He spoke of the social "myth of the revolution," or of the general strike. Sorel, a brilliant political theorist, had lost faith in reason and in society; in combining the twin spirits of Nietzsche and Marx, he suggested something like what later appeared in Mussolini's Fascism or Lenin's bolshevism, for both of whom he expressed admiration. Essentially an anarchist, a hater of the state and coercion, Sorel disapproved of the element of statism and nationalism in Italian Fascism, as he would have rejected Lenin's ruthless state dictatorship. But he did father the idea of a revolutionary elite violently sweeping aside bourgeois civilization in the name of a new myth or religion, that of proletarian socialism. In this "myth" the working class appears as clean, unspoiled, heroic, but brutal enough to dash to pieces the old corrupt order. Without difficulty we can recognize Nietzsche's "blond beasts" clothed in overalls. A civilization must believe in something; modern European civilization under bourgeois leadership had lost the life-giving capacity for such belief. Only the unspoiled proletarians had it: they at least believed in revolution.

At first placing his faith in the trade unions (*syndicats*) to become the agencies of proletarian revolution, Sorel by about 1910 grew disillusioned with them—they were much too materialistic and bourgeois— and turned to a flirtation with nationalism as the revitalizing myth, drawing close to Maurras. This was an ominous precursor of the postwar fascist mixture of revolutionary *élan* and nationalist solidarity; and in fact Benito Mussolini owed a great deal to *Sorelismo*. Thus Sorel drifted even farther away from democracy, in which course he unquestionably went with a significant stream of thought in France from about 1905 to 1914.

On the far left as well as the far right the theory of leadership by an elite appeared. Lenin, destined during the war of 1914–1918 to become a successful revolutionary leader, married a Nietzschean elitism to Marxian social determinism. "Lenin conceived of proletarian revolution as the product of great minds, who, conscious of inexorable trends, would create order and progress out of chaotic elements by organizing the raw material of history in a rational fashion" (Adolf G. Meyer). In this he differed from Marx, who had favored widening the franchise and other democratic political reforms believing that these would facilitate the triumph of the proletariat. Engels, living on into the 1890s, definitely stated that the time of "revolutions carried through by small conscious minorities at the head of unconscious masses" had passed. The socialists of western Europe placed their faith in democratic processes which made it possible to gain power by legal means. If Marx was right, the laws of social development were working relentlessly to destroy capitalism; the number of proletarians along with their class consciousness was supposedly growing so that soon they would be in the great majority. Revolutionary conspiracies were out of date in western Europe, precisely because Marx had revealed the inevitability of the transformation to socialism. But in Russia, where revolutionary conspiracy seemed the only possible recourse against a reactionary absolutism, Lenin sought to reconcile it with Marxism.

To Lenin the proletariat represented the will of history, but only potentially so; it must be organized and shaped by the "vanguard" of trained Marxians. The laws of social development exist, but they must be understood and exploited by this alert leadership. History does not make itself; it is made by men. When the decisive moment has arrived one must strike in a sudden act of revolution. The organized vanguard of the proletariat, disciplined, ruthless, and intelligent, must lead this revolution and install the socialist epoch. A Marxist, Lenin dissociated himself from mere revolutionary adventurism or terrorism, but was equally scornful of the passive, legalistic social democrats of western Europe. They had been corrupted by bourgeois democracy, in his view. Not by parliamentary means but by well-planned and prepared-for revolution would the proletariat succeed in its great mission, and this task called for the leadership of the vanguard elite.

At the Second Congress of the Russian Socialists in 1903 the party split on the issue of democracy; Lenin boldly opted for a tightly organized, highly disciplined elite party prepared to seize power and hold it by violent means. Almost constantly in exile (in Switzerland mostly) during the years from 1900 to 1917, and taking little part in the Revolution of 1905, Lenin read, wrote pamphlets, and edited newspapers; he had scarcely any following and was regarded as a crank. The 1914 war and the subsequent collapse of Russia in the holocaust gave him his chance to become a great revolutionary.

Democracy and the Intellectuals

A German Social Democrat, Robert Michels, a friend of Max Weber and of Pareto, discovered what he called the iron law of oligarchy. Drawing much of his evidence from the German Social Democratic Party, Michels thought the life history of political parties, as well as of other institutions, ran a course from democratic spontaneity to bureaucracy and oligarchy. By 1910 the socialists and the trade unions had grown mature and respectable. They were governed by an elite which made all the decisions and managed the party congresses, the rank and file being content to follow their leadership. The tendency toward oligarchy had afflicted even these groups which might be expected to be the most democratic. The apathy of the masses, the need for leadership, and also the tendency in modern times toward bureaucratic organization—Weber's "rationalization"—are themes that appear in Michels's celebrated study of *Political Parties*, which by 1915 had been translated and published in Italian, French, and English as well as German editions. Political parties are a part of the democratic political order, but they themselves are subject to nondemocratic forces. The right to vote may mean little if the machinery of politics is in the hands of a tightly controlled organization which names the candidates and introduces the issues.

There were, nevertheless, many efforts to come to terms with democracy, which in fact was in successful operation in Great Britain, France, and to some extent Germany and Italy by the end of the century. Until finally rebuked by the pope in 1910, a group of French Catholics, led by Marc Sangnier and the journal *Le Sillon*, undertook the notable experiment of reconciling Christianity with democracy. The neo-Kantian Charles Renouvier presented a philosophical defense of moderate democracy during the period 1872–1890; his disciple, the famous political sociologist Robert Michels, declared that "we are proud to live in a democracy." Perhaps the most notable conversion was that of the socialists. As we have seen, the Marxist social democrats as well as the Fabians accepted the possibility of achieving the social revolution by democratic means. It is also true that conservative and bourgeois circles previously skeptical about democracy grew to accept it, at least in a negative way, in these years.

So an undercurrent of controversy about this silent revolution that was occurring in society and politics runs through all thought in the *fin de siècle* period. Most of the serious thinkers and writers did not travel with the crowd. Indeed, their hallmark is very nearly a rejection of the crowd, of mass civilization, of the breakdown of values, the enthronement of mediocrity. They will use the word *bourgeois* as an epithet; likewise, often, the word *mass* or *popular*. By no means true of all, this is true of those who are the most striking and original: of Nietzsche, the symbolists and decadents, and the major political theorists. They did not find the nationalistic and democratic society of their time satisfactory, and they reacted against it as rebels, "outsiders," deniers and defiers of its conventions.

This is a remarkable feature of modern European thought, whatever we may think about it. The "alienation" of the artist and intellectual from society, these men retreating to a private world, inventing esoteric symbols, or even joining some nihilistic revolutionary movement in their hatred of the everyday world, mechanized, philistine, and commercial as it is, is a peculiarly modern theme. This is not to say that giants of thought were ever particularly popular with the majority. It is rather to say that the majority previously did not enter into intellectual society to any marked degree, while now they did. That which constituted the cultural community had been a restricted circle of the upper class, whether clergy, universities, or *salons*. Now this community was immeasurably broadened, and inevitably at first coarsened. At the same time the texture of thought and expression available to the educated or unusual person became more complex; individual sensitivity was sharpened and refined. So—we may hope temporarily—the gulf between writer and general public widened to a chasm, across which each looked at the other balefully and with bewilderment.

It should be repeated that this estrangement was a new phenomenon. Of the early Victorian writers Walter Allen remarks in his *The English Novel* that they "were at one with their public. . . . They accepted the society in which they lived. . . . The assumptions of their age they fully shared." They might and did criticize, but they did so as those who operate within the family, not as alienated outsiders; they strove to improve the common culture, not throw bricks at it from a distance. Granted that the romantics in some measure began the myth of the alienated, lonely, superior artist, the Victorian age resembled the eighteenth-century society more than it differed from it in its integration, and the Victorian Sage was no bohemian.[9] But when we get to Thomas Hardy near the end of the century, we enter another world; a threshold is crossed about the 1880s, whether we look at poetry, painting, drama, philosophy, or the novel. There is a real bitterness at the world's blind amorality, its utter lack of plan and purpose, its cruelty and its essential barbarity: Hardy's *Tess* does not live in the same moral world as the heroines of Trollope, Thackeray, Dickens, or even George Eliot. Something has happened. In part it was Darwinism, in part capitalism, in part mass culture, in part no doubt other things; the result is clear.

[9]It does not appear to be correct, however, to regard the divorce between popular and good literature as peculiarly modern. In her *Fiction and the Reading Public* (reprinted 1966), Mrs. Q. D. Leavis suggested that in the earlier period—until the mid or later nineteenth century—nearly everyone who could read read the same literature, which was good literature—Smollett, Fielding, Dickens, Thackeray, etc. But others have since established beyond doubt that as long as there was a literate public there was a trash literature. In other words, the average person in the eighteenth century was not reading Fielding and Smollett any more than the average nineteenth century reader was absorbed in Eliot and Hardy; they were reading very much the equivalent of James Bond and Zane Grey. See such studies as Robert Mayo, *The Novel in the Magazines 1740–1815*, Louis James, *Fiction for the Working Man, 1830–1850*, and Margaret Dalziel, *Popular Fiction 100 Years Ago* (1957).

12

The West in Trouble: World War I and Its Aftermath

The best lack all conviction, while the worst
Are full of passionate intensity.

WILLIAM BUTLER YEATS

Men will wish Nothing rather than not wish at all.

FRIEDRICH NIETZSCHE

Intellectual Origins of the War

In 1914 Europe entered upon a catastrophe from which by mid-century she had not recovered. A good part of the twentieth century was to be dominated by the breakdown of international order in that year, leading to four horrible years of mass slaughter, out of which came red revolution in Russia, black revolution in Italy, and subsequently Nazism in Germany—the forms of modern "totalitarian" dictatorship. The war proved scarcely less demoralizing to the victor states than to the defeated. It hurled much of Europe toward bankruptcy and internal collapse. During the war, propaganda took over and truth suffered as never before, and out of the war there emerged a new kind of cynicism, a loss of faith in men and values, such as Europe had perhaps never before experienced in modern history.

It is tempting to find some parallels between this crisis of the political order and the crisis of thought and culture that seemed to exist as of 1914. Historians customarily describe the origins of the World War in terms of diplomatic and political history, and quite properly so: the clash of national interests, the alliances, the military plans, the conferences and confrontations. The rise of nationalism was an obvious cause of the war. Now and again statesmen could be heard observing, in a Darwinian spirit, that struggle, competition, and force are the laws of life. Democracy forced statesmen to take account of a public opinion that was often belligerent and narrow-minded, as well as fiercely nationalist. Diplomacy does not function in a vacuum; politicians are men of their age sharing its prevalent ideas. Historians need to "reconstruct the unspoken assumptions of the men they are studying" and "recreate the climate of opinion in which political leaders operated," James Joll has argued in a thoughtful lecture on *1914: The Unspoken Assumptions.*

These unspoken assumptions of 1914 included a distinct eagerness for war, which the writers and intellectuals shared—something a later generation finds hard to understand, but very much a part of the spirit of the "August Days" at the beginning of the war. The war was extremely popular in all countries at the start. Resisting the war spirit in Britain, Ramsay MacDonald was aware that he was pitted against "the most popular war in British history," a fact to which the incredible rush of voluntary enlistments bears witness. And in the van of these volunteers were the young poets, artists, university students, intellectuals. The story was not different in France, in Germany, in Russia (Hans Rogger has noted the spontaneous enthusiasm for war which swept through Russia in 1914), and soon in Italy. It is difficult to find important leaders of the intellectual community who held out against this martial spirit, and most of them were serving as its cheerleaders. Romain Rolland, one of the few who did try to fight it, cried that "There is not one among the leaders of thought in each country who does not proclaim with conviction that the cause of his people is the cause of God, the cause of liberty and of human progress," and felt himself wholly isolated. The list of "leaders of thought" who did indeed bless the war almost as a holy cause is a lengthy one, and includes most of the great men discussed in the last chapter, those who were alive in 1914. Bergson, Charles Péguy, Freud (who "gave all his libido to Austria-Hungary"), poets and novelists such as Stefan George, Thomas Mann, were as prominent as historians, sociologists (Durkheim, Max Weber on different sides) and even socialists, who forgot their theoretical antiwar principles and rallied to the cause of their country. This was true of such revolutionaries as Kropotkin, Plekhanov, even some of the Russian bolsheviks, Lenin being a rare exception; and of the German Social Democrats, the French Socialists, the British Labourites, with only a few exceptions. In England the idol of the hour was the young poet Rupert Brooke who marched off proudly to die in the war along with so many others who gave their lives as a willing sacrifice to the Moloch of war. To be sure, Rolland exaggerated when he said "not one," for a small minority tried to resist the contagion. Shaw and Bertrand Russell in Britain, Rolland and Georges Sorel in France, Stefan Zweig and Professor Foerster in the German world, Lenin in Russia spring to mind; but they were all but swamped in 1914 by the rush to jump on the war wagon. As the war wore on and lost its glamor, the situation changed. But it is impossible to escape the conclusion that in the beginning the overwhelming majority of the spiritual leaders of Europe heartily approved of the war.

The reasons for this extraordinary belligerence lead us back into some pre-1914 themes. Among the more obvious ingredients in it were (a) a desire for excitement, adventure, and romance, which was associated with the protest against a drab, materialistic, bourgeois civilization. (b) A feeling that the war provided the opportunity for a spiritual renewal through its break with the past and its outpouring of unselfish idealism. (c) An exultation at the healing of a divided society, bridging the gap between classes and between individuals in an organic kind of national unity. (d) A sort of apocalyptic, Nietzschean mood which saw in this catastrophe both an awful judgment on a doomed civilization and the necessary prelude to a complete rebirth.

Clearly all these attitudes involved prewar intellectual themes. In regard to the protest against bourgeois dullness, the connection is obvious. More interesting is the thrill that men of thought secured from what Karl Vossler (writing to Benedetto Croce) called "the magnificent drama of the exaltation of a nation of 70 million people, all without exception one . . . each one living for all, for the Fatherland. . . ." Sophisticated minds such as Max Scheler had come to have as their chief concern "a quest for unity and community in a pluralistic society" and saw in the war a return to the "organic roots of human existence." Barrès's concern about "deracination," the "integral nationalism" of Maurras, and the sociological quest for social solidarity may all be recalled in this connection. A surprising number saw the war as a remedy for modern anomie. It is an outstanding fact that people at the beginning of the war felt an almost mystical exaltation in the surge of national unity that swept through every nation creating the "union sacrée." The men in the trenches also developed feelings of close solidarity in this war, an experience which many soldiers held in high value and hoped to carry into the national life after the war.

Anyone who has studied the mood of 1914 with much care knows that a *mystique* was decidedly present, above all in the young people, and those of poetic temperament, the idealists and the restless ones. War, still seen romantically as an arena of adventure, heroism, and brotherhood, came as a welcome relief from years of pettiness and greed, triviality and bickering. Men turned to it, as Brooke wrote, "as swimmers into cleanness leaping, glad from a world grown old and cold and weary." This mood had been growing in the years just before the war. In France, the period from 1905 on witnessed a sharp revival of what Eugene Weber, who has studied it carefully, sums up as "Discipline, Heroism, Renaissance, *Génie National.*" The conversion of Charles Péguy from socialism to nationalism in 1905 was a landmark; thereafter the former Dreyfusard wrote as a militant patriot, an antipacifist, a fervent prophet of the coming war against Germany. A well-known inquiry into the mood of French university youth in 1913 found that Péguy was the leading influence, along with Barrès and others of the same breed. One of them was Paul Claudel, whose plays and poems radiated heroism and religion and French tradition. In Germany, the years just before the war gave birth to a youth movement whose fierce idealism subsequently was channeled into the war. The *Wandervoegel* of the *Jugendbewegung* were in revolt against their elders, filled with lofty visions of reforming the world, and inclined to a Nietzschean spirit of drastic spiritual renewal accompanied by apocalyptical violence. Poets like Stefan George (and in Russia Alexander Blok) indulged in visions of a purifying war. That the war would bring "the moral regeneration of Europe" was to be held by so relatively mild a philosopher as Henri Bergson.

This frenetic preparation for conflict in the mind of the pre-1914 decade, and the eager way war was welcomed when it came, seemed incongruous later and was therefore somewhat forgotten; it is not well understood today. People soon grew bitterly disillusioned with the war; by 1917 a new mood had set in, which carried through into the despairing postwar years. Yet the spirit of 1914 had existed, and had something to do with the coming of the war. Not that the poets and intellectuals deliberately contrived the war, which seemed to come out of the blue, totally unexpected by the vast majority. But when it came they welcomed it almost as a divine omen and gladly marched off to fight in it, thinking that they were redeeming their own lives and rescuing civilization. "Happy are they who die in a just war," Péguy sang before he marched off to be killed on the Marne in the early days of the war.

The young Bosnians who killed the Archduke Franz Ferdinand and thus provided the spark that set off the flames were themselves aflame with the restless ideas of pre-1914 Europe. Their idols included Gorki, Andreyev, Whitman, Wilde, and Ibsen. They had learned tyrannicide from 1848 romanticism (Mazzini, "William Tell") and revolution from Ibsen; they lived in an atmosphere of youthful literary romanticism, fed by the exciting writers of the hour, with considerable symbolist and decadent influences. They were in touch with the international anarchist movement.[1]

That the war was a just one was, of course, the almost universal assumption, each side firmly believing itself to have been attacked by the other. The socialists rationalized their support of the war by arguing that if they did not fight, their country would be destroyed and with it their movement. The Germans further held that a victory for Russia would be a victory for the most reactionary of European powers. The French similarly believed that a German conquest would be reactionary, wiping out many social gains already made in France. The working class everywhere tended to be strongly patriotic, and the intellectual socialists were not in fact prepared for the kind of situation that occurred. The Second International had often rhetorically declared that the workers of the world would never fight against each other in a war forced on the people by their wicked rulers; but this war did not happen like that. The great majority knew only that their country was being attacked and must be defended. A small minority of the Socialists in Great Britain, Germany and Russia thought otherwise but abided by party discipline. Within a fairly short time Karl Liebknecht in Germany, and Lenin, among the exiled Russian Bolsheviks, went into opposition to the war, while Ramsay MacDonald resigned the Labour Party leadership in England; but these were voices crying in the wilderness for several years. It was dangerous to oppose the war: in England Bertrand Russell was imprisoned, Shaw was snubbed and boycotted, D. H. Lawrence suffered from a feeling of isolation because he could not participate in the *mystique* of the war.

Intellectuals participated in the war to a striking degree. They went off and fought in it, of course, eagerly volunteering in the first rush of battle rapture. They wrote poems to it, hailed it as a regenerating process, celebrated its *mystique*. Many of those who did not serve in the trenches lent their talents to the propaganda side of the war. Arnold Bennett, one of England's leading literary figures, became a director of British propaganda; distinguished historians fashioned handbooks proving the eternal wickedness of the foe (this happened in the United States, too, after the U.S.A. joined the war in 1917), and authenticating stories of barbarous atrocities.

Disenchantment soon set in. The reality of war was anything but romantic. "One week in the trenches was sufficient to strip war of its

---

[1]See among other sources Vladimir Dedijer's article, "Sarajevo Fifty Years After," *Foreign Affairs*, July, 1964, and his book, *The Road to Sarajevo* (1966).

lingering traces of romance," Herbert Read recalled. As the war dragged on and the sickening slaughter mounted, protest against it inevitably arose. In the end, most of those who survived were likely to be ashamed of having been taken in by a romantic view of war. Yet it is well to remember that this was not so in 1914, when a generation of rebels found their great crusade in the war. "We were all flame and fire," Isadora Duncan remembered. Young men lived in fear that the war would be over before they could get into it (it was widely believed that it would be a short one), and of these the educated, university, thinking youth were the foremost. It was the hour of Rupert Brooke ("Come and die, it will be such fun.") In the strange story of 1914 the story of the intellectuals is one of the strangest. The student of intellectual history will find much to connect this state of mind with the ferment of ideas in the preceding generation; for the revolutionary message of Nietzsche, Bergson, Jung, Sorel, Baudelaire, Wagner, and all the rest was just making its major impact on the mind of Europe as the war broke out.

The comradeship of the trenches, alas, is apt to remind us of Adolf Hitler, who carried back into peacetime favorable memories of the war's *Gemeinschaft*. The Storm Troopers were a carryover from the war. Still, others than the Nazis entertained a nostalgia for this aspect of the war and hoped that after it was over a more democratic, less class-ridden society might emerge from it. Yet the most obvious results of the war were fascism, followed by Nazism; and the communism which had gained control of Russia during the almost total breakdown of the Russian state that occurred in 1917 as a result of the war's intolerable demands. Benito Mussolini, brilliant left-wing Italian socialist, broke away from the majority of the party on the issue of Italy's entrance into the war in 1915, which he supported. Free to launch on ideological ventures of his own after this, he fell increasingly under the influence of Nietzschean and Sorelian ideas and emerged in the troubled days after the war as *duce* of the new movement known as Fascism. As for Lenin, few are unaware that he came back to Russia from exile in 1917 following the February Revolution to take charge of Bolshevik strategy and seize power in October, to begin the long dictatorship of the Communist Party in Russia.

The prewar socialists were badly split by the war. Though initially the party supported it, a fraction of the German Social Democrats voted against the war in the party caucus, later brought their opposition into the open, and by 1917 created a major split in the party by voting against the war credits. Though Social Democrats took the lead in establishing the new republic which emerged from defeat in 1919, they had to employ armed force against left-wing socialist uprisings and thus threw themselves into the arms of the Right.

Results of the War

If the war was initially popular, and blessed by the writers, it eventually gave rise to bitter disillusionment. "War is hell, and those who institute it are criminals," Siegfried Sassoon wrote from the trenches. This was the final verdict. The progress of disillusion may be followed in the war poetry—of which this war produced a great deal of high quality. (It remained a writers' war all the way and even in its disappointment produced splendid literature; no other war can compare.) The initial "visions of glory" faded to sorrow and pity and ended in bitterness. The wretchedness, the terror, the nerves tortured by waiting for death, the gassed soldiers, the obscene wounds, even the lice were what the men in the trenches wrote about:

> In winter trenches, cowed and glum,
> With crumps and lice and lack of rum.

Soon they began to scorn the people at home who could have no notion of what the war was really like, and whose knitting of socks or singing of songs seemed a mockery and a sacrilege. A comradeship of suffering and death drew the soldiers close together and sometimes drew them closer to their fellow victims of war in the opposite trenches than to the smug ones at home—or to their own officers. As bitterness developed against the top leadership in this frustrating war which no one could win, soldier-poets wrote of the scarlet majors at the base who "speed glum heroes up the line to death" and would themselves toddle safely home to die in bed. Those who did not die in the first battles but, like Wilfred Owen, lived through almost the whole war (he was killed within hours of the Armistice), could feel nothing but the horror, the pity, and the futility of war. This attitude endured; the romance had gone from war forever and abhorrence of the very thought of war colored the entire postwar era; aiding, ironically, the coming of the next one since a pacifist-minded opinion in the victor countries permitted a revenge-bent Germany to overturn the peace settlement and the balance of power.

The collapse of prewar socialism was not the least of the many interrupted and shattered traditions; discredited by their acceptance of the war, the great majority of its leadership lost control of their own movement in 1917–1919. Lenin's bolshevik faction seized power in Russia and proscribed the menshevik's along with all other political parties as enemies of the Revolution. In Italy, the ambivalence of social democracy helped pave the way for Mussolini's Fascist dictatorship. The Italian

Socialists could not decide whether to be revolutionaries or to defend the democratic constitutional order, and ended by doing neither. When the smoke had cleared, Communists looking to Lenin's Russia had greatly increased their following at the expense of the moderate socialists almost everywhere in Europe, though nowhere except in Russia had they been able to seize the state. Their embittered violence frightened the conservative classes into backing extremist regimes in Italy and, within a few years, Germany. In Great Britain, the war wrecked the old Liberal Party forever and caused a great increase in the Labour Party, which though not communist had a hyperradical wing and pacifist leadership.

The war years produced a large crop of plans for peace in order to prevent a recurrence of 1914. This was true in all countries. There were League of Nations Societies and Associations, Committees for a Durable Peace, Unions for Democratic Control of foreign policy. These plans were not only at variance with each other but wore an odd air of unreality in most cases; intellectuals struggled in an element alien to them and tended toward utopianism. Most of them were disillusioned with the real League of Nations that struggled to an imperfect birth in the atmosphere of power and hate at the Paris Peace Conference of 1919. The hundreds of tracts and pamphlets written during the war ended as less a contribution to human progress than a curiosity for the historian, a fact which contributed no little to the postwar despair. These plans contemplated either a full-blown world state, or, more commonly, the relinquishing of basic control of national policy by states to a League or Association of Nations, along with national disarmament. But the war had if anything enhanced nationalism, and no great power could or would place its security at the disposal of a questionable world organization. The League had little power, and even that little was enough to frighten off the United States, wary of being made the policeman for a hate-filled Europe. Most of the liberals who had so earnestly drawn up blueprints for the postwar world felt that the treaties negotiated at Paris in 1919, along with the League of Nations as adopted, was a betrayal of their ideals and perpetuated oldfashioned "power politics." The postwar years brought a complete revision in ideas about the war's origins. In France, Great Britain, and the United States, nearly everyone assumed it was the Germans who were the criminal unleashers of war; a few combatted this notion even during the war, and immediately afterward a momentous investigation into the causes of the war began—with results that were likely to be "revisionist." If scholars did not seek to show that Russia and France were more guilty of the war than Austria and Germany, they at least concluded, typically, that all had been trapped in a circle of fear where one could not well speak of "war guilt." No nation had been entirely innocent, none criminally guilty; the guilt might be said to lie with a system, or a civilization, or in the nature of humanity itself. This historical controversy gave rise to a vast and interesting literature, which proved only that no historical event is simple enough to grasp scientifically, but which suggested to millions that their leaders had deceived them in charging all blame on the enemy. At the same time the atrocity stories were radically "de-bunked," as propaganda ministers ruefully confessed they had manufactured most of these.

The war violently interrupted everything, and turned all channels of life into new directions. Old intellectual leaders lost prestige, and old circles were broken up; many writers died in the war along with the millions of others. The world after the war was another world, and a new breed of men arose to lead its thought.

Postwar Pessimism

Sickened by not only the physical slaughter of millions of Europe's youth but by the moral carnage of a world convulsed by hatred and lies, the postwar generation was the "lost generation." Lost were faith and hope, belief in progress, confidence in the civilization of the West. By way of introducing what was after all a marvelously creative generation too, we may catalog some of these cries of despair that filled the years destined to follow one Armageddon and precede another. Some of these will be discussed more fully later.

It is difficult to think of any of the great writers of this era—D. H. Lawrence, André Gide, Ernest Hemingway, James Joyce, T. S. Eliot— who did not reject the civilization in which they lived, though it is no less true that this rejection usually antedated the war. They were marked wanderers; the American "expatriates," who joined Gertrude Stein in Paris or Spain, had a counterpart in such as Lawrence, who hated his native England and lived at various times in New Mexico, Mexico, and Italy; or Joyce, a refugee from Ireland who lived in Trieste, Paris, and Zurich. There were, of course, Russian refugees from Communism, Italian from Fascism, and subsequently German from Nazism. Physical flight from the homeland went along with imaginative flight from Western civilization, expressed in Lawrence's admiration for the Etruscans or the Aztecs, in Ezra Pound's importing of Chinese, or what he imagined to be Chinese, literature. "An old bitch, gone in the teeth"—such was Pound's verdict on European civilization, while the usually optimistic, still liberal-socialist H. G. Wells (who coined the phrase "war to end wars" during the war) thought that "This civilization in which we are living is tumbling down, and I think tumbling down very fast." It would be a work of supererogation to reproduce all such comments.

This straying "after strange gods" included a desertion of intellectuals to communism or, less commonly, to fascism. Pound and Wynd-ham Lewis might be placed in the latter camp, but the major movement was toward faith in Soviet Russia as a place where a brand-new and hopeful civilization was being shaped, however roughly. This attitude on the part of Western writers and intellectuals was quite obviously a pro-jection of their own cultural despair onto Russia as wishful thinking, and after a few years as communists or fellow-travellers the harsh realities of Soviet tyranny freshly disillusioned all but the blindest. This was "the God that failed" for a significant segment of serious people, especially in the 1930s, and this "pink decade" will need to be discussed again. Those who briefly believed in the charisma of Mussolini or Hitler as creative forces were also speedily disillusioned, of course. In the 1920s one mostly believed in art or in sex, if one believed in anything; in the 1930s, poets tried to be proletarians and novelists went off to fight in the Spanish Civil War. But the latter gesture turned out to be almost as despairing and futile for most as the former.

If there was whoring after strange gods, there was also an effort to return to ancestral ones. The neo-Anglicanism of T. S. Eliot, Ameri-can-born mogul of English letters (another odd case of literary expatria-tion), had counterparts in the neo-Thomism of a significant group led by Jacques Maritain in France, and the neo-Calvinism and neo-Lutheran-ism of Karl Barth and Emil Brunner. The return to religion resulted from the collapse of liberal beliefs in secular progress. These theologies in some ways were not orthodox, for they usually "de-mythologized" the Bible, perhaps drew on Jungian conceptions, and regarded Christi-anity as existentially rather than literally true. But they found in original sin and Christian humility an antidote to the shallow complacency of those prewar liberals and socialists who had believed in rationality and progress. Perhaps old-fashioned Christianity could be a cure for the dis-eases of a civilization whose sin had been denying its own birthright, succumbing to pride, forgetting the meaning of Christ. Christ was seen less as a preacher of humane ethical precepts than as the apocalyptic or "eschatological" prophet who announced the end of the world and asked men to choose between God and the world. This was especially the bent of Continental neo-orthodoxy, which in the form of the "crisis" theology of Barth came near to Christian existentialism. "It is essential not to have faith in human nature," historian Herbert Butterfield has written. "Such faith is a recent heresy and a very disastrous one." At bottom, the tragic view of life is the true one, asserted many a chastened opti-mist of the postwar years.

Karl Barth's 1919 *Epistle to the Romans* commentary marked a sharp break with the prevailing liberal and idealist German theology, which had seen the course of history as in large part a fulfillment of

God's plan, hence good, a view which could almost blend with the secular idea of progress. The Hegelian influence may readily be seen: God's Reason is immanent in the record of human development, his purposes are realized through Man. Regarded quite widely as the greatest theologian of his times, Barth denied as fiercely as possible (in his initial manifestoes) that God's kingdom is of this world. There is no synthesis uniting God and Man; the two are almost utterly estranged, man is an incomplete creature needing God for fulfillment but unable to find him except in the one tenuous revelation contained in Scripture—the Word. The apparently quite reactionary features of the new theology (variously called "Crisis," "Dialectical," "Kerygmatic,")—back to original sin and Luther's hapless human creatures in need of rescuing by divine Grace—actually made it seem revolutionary. One rejected a corrupt world and refused to accept a flat, vapid, institutionalized Christianity, demanding life-meaning and relevance in one's faith.

The same general features could be found in Martin Buber's Jewish theology, and in N. Berdyaev's voice from the world of Russian Orthodox religion (Berdyaev, initially a Communist, fled from Lenin's police state to Berlin and then Paris in the 1920s). These were exciting voices, some of them far less "orthodox" than Barth. Barth's close associate, Rudolf Bultmann, mediated the message for more modernist minds by his "de-mythologizing" idea, which meant that the language with which the Word is expressed in the Bible is a mere husk containing the kernel of essential, true-to-life statements. The neo-orthodox were normally not "fundamentalist" but "modernist" in their view of the Biblical text, but they rendered this old debate irrelevant by their insistence that the real message is embedded in the myth.

Whatever the variations in their contours, these postwar theologies were alike in rejecting the old belief in Progress. In a book on the subject in 1920 Dean William Inge, the "gloomy dean," saw the idea of progress as "the working faith of the West for about a hundred and fifty years" and found it a fraud. With hope in social progress shattered, the dream of perpetual onward-and-upward laid in ruins by the hideous facts of the mass slaughter just ended and the moral and political confusion that followed it, the world broken and lost, a personal religion became a tower of retreat in the 1920s. Pessimism was not confined to the religious. Oswald Spengler's *Decline of the West* came out of a Germany shattered by defeat, but its message of Western civilization's senility went all over the world and was repeated in varying accents by many others. It was at this time that Arnold J. Toynbee began his even vaster historical study of the rise and fall of civilizations, the first three volumes of which came from the press in 1934. Toynbee has told how, spared from military service by an illness, and watching so many of his classmates mowed down in the war, he felt a special duty to devote his life to an inquiry on the causes of such cataclysmic collapses of civilizations. In the same way, the tragedy energized others who had been spared that fate. (Harold Laski, for example, tells a similar story.) Toynbee was led to nothing less than a gigantic comparative analysis of the life cycles of all the civilizations he could find in world history, and finished his monumental opus only after another world war made the topic even more timely. But his initial inspiration came during World War I.

The book of the hour right after the war was Spengler's, more hastily written than Toynbee's—though in fact Spengler had begun it before the war—but based on the same premise that civilizations, like people, have life-cycles. Needless to say Spengler found many signs of decay in the contemporary West, whose zenith he thought had come in the later Middle Ages.

The Spaniard Ortega y Gasset's brilliant essay, *The Revolt of the Masses*, conveyed a somewhat similar theme of European decadence from lack of creative leadership. Paul Valéry's famous essay on the European crisis and T. S. Eliot's even more famous poem, *The Waste Land*, might be mentioned in this context. Proust's mammoth novel chronicled the decay of French society. Of course, Communists, Fascists, and Nazis all proclaimed the decadence and imminent death of the old society; that they did so helped eventually to rally some support for traditional European civilization, since these rebels against it so obviously purveyed something far worse. But the 1920s echoed with dirges for the passing of the European age.

With Mussolini proclaiming the "lie of universal suffrage" and Lenin the decadence of bourgeois democracy, democracy was under attack and found few defenders in the 1920s. Cabinets shuffled back and forth in France while parties degenerated into factions and only the Communists seemed to stand for principle. M. Tardieu, French premier, retired from politics to write a treatise expressing disillusionment with the parliamentary system. The German Republic established in 1919 had to humiliate itself before the arrogant victor powers as its first act and thereafter lived a precarious life, though it had a few hopeful years between 1924 and 1930 before collapsing under the weight of the great economic depression that struck in the latter year.

During the 1920s the "people" seemed more interested in channel swims, airplane flights, murder trials, mah-jong, crossword puzzles, movie stars, and Mickey Mouse. The Common Man seemed a sad joke, cultural democracy the last absurdity of an expiring civilization—ending, as Eliot put it, not with a bang but a whimper. To Ortega, the Revolt of the Masses meant the end of historic Europe; to Spengler, the Decline of the West began with liberalism and democracy. The war had indeed hastened a trend in Europe to raise up the common man and democratize culture. In the long run this was surely a gain, but in the short run democratization meant cheapening and standardizing. The mass newspaper and journal with their low intellectual content pervaded society, it seemed. The "shop-girl mentality" and the common man as "boob" (H. L. Mencken) were familiar sneers.

Contributing to the gray mood of the 1920s were other things than the war and the mess it had left behind, though doubtless the latter contributed the most. What Walter Lippmann once called "the acids of modernity" had corroded belief leaving behind a cloud of skepticism. These years felt the full force of those deeply subversive ideas developed just before 1914. Freud, for example, now became widely known. Doubtless one can interpret Freudianism optimistically, as many did, particularly in America, regarding it as a new technology supplying medicine for all that ails the mind. But Freud himself was a deeply pessimistic person, especially in his later years, and his books of the '20s, such as *Civilization and Its Discontents*, express a conviction that the battle between the individual and society can never be ended. Ordered society demands that the Id suppress its impulses; "the price of civilization is neurosis." Of course, it was hard not to see Freud as chipping away at the boundaries of the rational mind, pointing to "the cobra-filled jungle of the unconscious" (Chad Walsh) which is the real determinant of human conduct. Freudianism contributed to the iconoclastic mood of the 1920s, to the sexual revolution and the hatred of bourgeois prudery. At times the Freudian message coincided with the return to religion. In an essay on Freud, Reinhold Niebuhr related him to the pessimism of the Barthians; for though Freud was an atheist he agreed with them in seeing man as a tragic figure, torn apart by his conflicts. Certainly the great psychologist, turned social philosopher increasingly in this latter period of his life, believed that men are naturally aggressive creatures who will exploit, rob, even torture and kill their fellows if not forcibly restrained. "Who has the courage to dispute it in the face of all the evidence in his own life and in history?" he wrote to Einstein.

The latter scientist's revolution also worked as a dissolvent of certainties in the 1920s, when the new physics became front-page news. A chapter in Joseph Wood Krutch's *The Modern Temper* (1929), the theme of which was that "Skepticism has entered too deeply into our souls ever to be replaced by faith," deals with the downfall of "the last certitude," science. Einstein, Planck, and Heisenberg might be brilliantly uncovering new truths, but popularly they appeared as destroyers of what had seemed the one solid body of unassailable truth. The circle of skepticism seemed complete when even Science, god of the late Victorians, found the universe mysterious and incomprehensible. The Uncertainty Principle was the discovery of the decade. The day of the signing of the Treaty of Versailles in 1919 brought news of an observation confirming Einstein's law of relativity, and throughout the 1920s the doings of the scientists made big if somewhat mystifying news. Einstein became a household word though the "man in the street" professed to find him as incomprehensible as Gertrude Stein or the surrealists. In the 1920s through the work of Heisenberg and Broglie the startling implications of quantum theory became evident in the dual manifestations of the electrons: they behave sometimes as particles and sometimes as waves, breaking through barriers heretofore assumed to be absolute. It became necessary to resort to something like the "as if" philosophy of Vaihinger (1911) and say that all scientific terminology represents "useful fictions." Observations are real, but these observations can be extended to form such generalizations as electricity, energy, atoms, matter, etc., only as hypothetical mental constructs. It became known, also, that the subatomic particles are subject only to probability and that the observer inevitably interferes with them preventing perfect observation; the limits of science had been reached because no one can step outside the universe, man being a part of it. One might make what one chose of all this, but clearly many old certainties were gone, and the new Einsteinian universe was less tidy: Bertrand Russell said it was more individualist, even anarchist, with no central government! Among the popular expounders of the new physics, Arthur Eddington adopted an idealist position, pointing out that the scientist creates truth, the answers depending on what questions he asks. James Jeans spoke of the mysterious universe and found more room for God than Laplace or Darwin had left. Science was the new mysticism. Alfred North Whitehead explored the implications of the new science for Western metaphysics, showing that the mechanistic framework dominant since Newton no longer sufficed; he and others proposed a "pan-psychism" which saw the universe as composed of organisms; thus electrons and atoms became in a sense endowed with spirit, a return full circle to the Greek-medieval outlook on nature.

The disillusionment of the 1920s appeared fashionably and brilliantly in the novels of Aldous Huxley, which were really fictionalized tracts or sermons. We see, in *Antic Hay* (1923), a succession of object lessons in the failure of values. Gumbril, the hero, listens to the clergyman, and then the schoolmaster, and finds both of them useless; the artist fails him, and so does the scientist. Romantic love is a sham, but the amoralist who tries to find satisfaction in perverse or diabolical behavior is equally absurd. The mordant criticism of all attitudes that try to give life meaning continued in *Those Barren Leaves* (1925) and *Point*

Counter Point (1928); these clever, sophisticated studies in pale melancholy hit the decade just right and made Huxley a household word. That he was the grandson of the famous Victorian scientist and believer in progress made his gloom about the human race the more piquant. A search for values always goes on in the astringent Huxleyan way, and in *Point Counter Point* the memorable character-gallery of failures—scientists, artists, politicians—turned up one slightly hopeful face in a somewhat Lorenzian philosopher (Huxley was a good friend of D. H. Lawrence). Perhaps by a return to healthy instincts one might make one's way out of the desert. *Brave New World* (1932) carried on Huxley's war with modern civilization. In the 1930s he began to find consolation in withdrawal and mysticism. Not a great novelist, Huxley was a subtle prober of values and a sensitive barometer of the moods of his day among sophisticated Europeans who felt themselves in a dying culture and searched almost in vain for a firm intellectual anchorage for their lives. The same spirit may be found in many another novel, poem, or play of the twenties and thirties.

It might be noted that the mood was not, really, tragic in the deepest sense. There is a sunset charm about the dying culture; talk is brilliant, personality and ideas both richly abundant, there are always marvelous books to read. What literate man could really be unhappy in a decade that produced Joyce, Lawrence, Proust, Kafka, and a whole parade of other stunning commentators on the sickness of civilization? A funeral that attracted so many notable pall-bearers had at least its compensations. It remained for World War II to confront Europe with stark tragedy; for the time being, ruminating among the ruins was far from unpleasant. The civilized upper class to which Huxley belonged still existed if it had gone slightly to seed. If this was not "la belle époque" of pre-1914, neither was it yet the nightmare world of Nazism, Communism, depression, and war. The thirties and forties brought these things.

Nevertheless the disgust which their civilization inspired in many European writers was both real and ominous. It could lead them to disaster. One example from many: Louis-Ferdinand Céline, in 1932, wrote *Le Voyage au Bout de la Nuit*, a shocking book, both in style and content, misanthropic much beyond Huxley, scatological beyond Lawrence, a terrible satire on the human race—a book which had a considerable vogue. This talented writer ended an anti-Semite, a pro-Nazi, a collaborator with the German conquerors of France during the war—out of sheer hatred of his native culture, we surmise. He was truly one of those of whom Lawrence wrote in *Kangaroo*, a person driven to defiant estrangement from his fellows.

The Literary Renaissance of the '20s

Tinged as it was by despair, the writing and art of the postwar years had a brilliance seldom matched, for it marked the stylistic maturity of the whole Modernist movement—shocking, perhaps, but dazzingly creative. The literary revolution, whose roots lay in the prewar period, burst upon the general public in the 1920s. Graham Hough has placed "between 1910 and the Second World War" a "revolution in the literature of the English language as momentous as the Romantic one of a century before." Perhaps it came earlier in France. But so far as concerned the English-speaking world such names as Joyce, Pound, Eliot, and Lawrence came to the fore after the war though they had begun their careers just before it. Wyndham Lewis called Ezra Pound, T. S. Eliot, James Joyce and himself "the men of 1914": this quartet who led the revolution in English literature emerged exactly as the war began. D. H. Lawrence's first major novel, *Sons and Lovers*, was completed in 1913; he wrote *The Rainbow* and *Women in Love* during the war. Joyce had *Ulysses* ready to launch on the world at the end of the war years. Elsewhere, too, buds of the prewar years burst into bloom. Paul Valéry and Marcel Proust in France may be instanced. The latter's great symphony of novels, *Remembrance of Things Past*, appeared between 1913 and 1927 though Proust died in 1922 at the age of fifty-one. The German master Thomas Mann reached the peak of his reputation in the 1920s as did the Frenchman André Gide and the Irish poet W. B. Yeats.

Moreover the new art and music, associated with the names of Picasso and Stravinsky, predated the war in its origins but moved into the limelight once the guns were silenced. The year 1913 had seen those famous riots in Paris that accompanied the first performance of Stravinsky's *Rites of Spring*, and also the public tumult aroused by an exhibition of the new nonrepresentational art in the United States. A young American emigré named Gertrude Stein was already buying the paintings of her friend Picasso in Paris—for a song. Picasso was at that time living in poverty among a gloriously bohemian set in the attics of Montmartre. Cubism was born 1908–1910, but the paintings produced by this and other avant garde movements were as yet little more than the obscure eccentricities of certain social outcasts. But after the war, conditions became favorable for the reception of anything new, startling, revolutionary. An embittered "lost generation" of rebels against the purposeless slaughter of 1914–1918 had no interest in defending the values of their fathers, whether artistic, moral, or philosophical.

In Paris in 1919 writers and artists launched their protest against everything; they named it dada (a nonsense word). Everything seemed nonsense—literature, morality, civilization. Action is vain; art is vain; life is vain. All is absurd. Dada was a combination of literary and intellectual sophistication—all has been said, all ways have been used—with the despair of the years 1917–1919, years of slaughter and stupidity. Dada's activities were expression of its bitter derision; it held public meetings, well advertised by post-futurist posters, at which people made nonsensical speeches. Tzara, a Hungarian-Swiss who was one of its chief founders, wrote poems by clipping words from a newspaper article, putting them in a sack, shaking them up, and then taking them out one by one. If most dadaist poems did not go quite so far, they specialized in incongruity:

> The aeroplane weaves telegraph wires
> and the fountain sings the same song.
> At the rendez-vous of the coachmen the apertif is orange
> but the locomotive mechanics have blue eyes.
> The lady has lost her smile in the woods.

Which is not without charm though definitely without meaning.

Needless to say dadaism was a thing of the moment, but its young literary leaders were to be found in the vanguard of other movements of the 1920s. Of these the most important was surrealism. Something of dada's wish to deliberately derange meaning appeared in Surrealism, and also some of its violently disruptive political protest, both however made a bit more constructive and coherent. Surrealism borrowed from Freud and Jung the idea that in dreams and semiconscious states the mind is freed from the tyranny of the rational and can produce fresh, authentic symbols. "Psychic automatism" was its method of writing poetry (suspend thought and let the words come). It may indeed be regarded as a continuation of prewar symbolism with Freudian additions.

Underneath such extravagances there was a romantic faith in the autonomy of the realm of art, which the poetic vision might contact beyond the realm of merely rational concepts. It was a kind of mysticism of art, philosophically an idealism. Surrealism has continued to be the dominant force in French poetry. In addition, the surrealists proclaimed themselves political activists and enemies of "bourgeois" society, which they held responsible for the unhappy divorce of art from life. At first they tended to join the communists, who were the most vigorous foes of the "bourgeoisie," but later they grew disillusioned, along with others, with communist tyranny and intolerance. Their sociology, like their politics, tended to be slapdash in the extreme, though occasionally inspired. It was in painting that surrealism, cubism, and related modernist modes had their greatest success. Gertrude Stein's attempt to duplicate in surrealist prose the success in painting of her friend Pablo Picasso did not really come off, though her personality made her one of the most celebrated women of the 1920s. Her mystifying style ("A rose is a rose is a rose"; "How do you do I forgive you everything and there is nothing to forgive") was perhaps not intended to be understood. ("Nobody knows what I am trying to do but I do and I know when I succeed," Gertrude declared.)

The greater writers of a great age of literature were not always incomprehensible. Of the trinity of major novelists, Joyce, Lawrence, and Proust, only the first departed from reasonably straightforward statement, and he only to any marked degree in his last work, *Finnegans Wake*. The novels nevertheless included daring, experimental, and controversial elements. Joyce's *Ulysses* was banned before publication and stirred up one of the chief literary rows of the decade, matched only by Lawrence's *Lady Chatterley's Lover*. The difficulty lay in the frank approach to sex and the use of words heretofore not permitted in polite discourse. To Lawrence, return to a healthy primitive sexuality was important, not in itself but because he thought people who know how to live know how to love. Sex to him was the key to creativity: taproot of all energies, it is the source of beauty, religion, everything wonderful and vital. So far from being a mere hedonism, this resembled romanticism's doorway of the senses to a transcendent realm of truth and beauty; a great deal bolder and buttressed by modern psychology, to be sure. Lawrence castigated the effete intellectualism as well as the timid bourgeois conventionality of the modern world, feeling acutely the need for something more sincere, more intense, more real. This neoprimitivism sent him back to the Etruscans and the Indians, or, if he had to live in the modern world, to Mediterranean peasants. It sent Arthur Koestler and other Communist converts to the strong, silent workers.

The integrity and "committedness" of Lawrence, as well as his tremendous creative vitality, made him one of the chief of the modern age's seers. Joyce's *Ulysses*, which then so shocked people, has since received wide recognition as one of the greatest literary achievements of modern times. Its "message," if any, was less clear. A vast allegory on the condition of man, a commentary on the futility of human existence, a great symphony in words, an affirmation like Nietzsche and Lawrence of the chaotic abundance of life? Like Eliot's poetry, it made use of startlingly modern techniques to recall modern man to his civilized heritage. Whatever else it meant, it was a triumph of art and meant that the artist shapes and gives reality to the world—a message similar to Proust's. These works were testimonies to the autonomy of art and pointed to a withdrawal of the artist—a withdrawal Joyce and Proust made quite explicit—from society, to go it alone.

The excitement of the new literature owed much to its ability to probe the inner world in all its irrational complexities, its occasional nastiness, its vibrant realities. A Lawrence novel takes us immediately into its characters and makes us *be* them as they struggle with their lives and problems; we are engaged with them. In a famous essay Virginia Woolf accused the older novelists, such as Arnold Bennett, of depicting only the external aspects of people; in wanting to see them from within, as their minds actually work almost minute to minute, Mrs. Woolf was squarely in the center of the new novel.

So there was excitement and creativity in literature, yet also a great sadness, for there is an explicit rejection of the public life. Virginia Woolf's Mrs. Dalloway cannot endure her life as the wife of a leading politician, the whole thing bores her and kills the life of the spirit, found in the cultivation of sensibilities in purely private ways. When Sir Charles Snow, more recently, charged all the literary set with an irresponsible attitude toward politics he had in mind this profound revulsion from the public life that one found in virtually all the great writers of the modernist phase. In the last analysis these artists echoed the decadent view, that in the dying days of a civilization the only consolation lies in art.

The interwar years also brought a new architecture and a new music. Le Corbusier (Charles Edouard Jeanneret) led a whole school of architecture that denounced nineteenth-century eclecticism and demanded buildings for the machine age—"functional" and not traditional. Proclaiming that "the past must be destroyed," this architecture had affinities with futurist art and literature. Walter Gropius headed a similar movement in Germany, where the ill-fated Weimar Republic, destined to succumb to Adolf Hitler's Nazis in 1933, experienced a brief renaissance in the mid-twenties. Munich rivalled Paris as a center of modern art and the Bauhaus architectural and art school, located at Weimar and then Dessau, brought together artists of the caliber of Walter Gropius, Mies van der Rohe, Paul Klee, Vassily Kandinsky. There was perhaps more hope in this new style of building for modern man than there was in the novel.

Both Le Corbusier and Gropius, as well as the American genius, Frank Lloyd Wright, had started their work just before 1914 but reached their creative period after the war. These dates correspond closely with those of the pioneer modernists in painting, music, and literature, and indeed Le Corbusier, who was also a painter, was deeply influenced by cubism and futurism. But almost no one had heard of Le Corbusier, Gropius, the Bauhaus, and "functionalism" before the 1920s, and then they were forced to do battle against outraged traditionalists. One of the larger engagements in this war took place in connection with the League of Nations building at Geneva, supposedly a great symbol of the post-war era, and it is significant that Le Corbusier's modernistic design lost out, even in his native Switzerland, to the sedate neoclassical edifice that still stands there in Geneva. Still, the new style was much discussed and won some triumphs. Dubbed "functionalist," it was in actuality never considered simply as utilitarian by its founders, but was intended to be a modern esthetic. Under cubist influence it tended to be severely abstract-geometrical at first but came to include considerable poetic feeling.

In music, abandonment of tonality was the counterpart of abandonment of perspective in painting and the daring innovations of functionalist architecture; there were such superlative geniuses as Schoenberg and Bartok. There were infinite riches for the eye and ear in these immensely creative years, the years of Picasso, Kandinsky, Gropius, Le Corbusier, and all the others. Though traditionalists might suspect sheer anarchy in their art forms, actually the authentically modern mode in the arts was at work, transforming the way we look at things and hear them, just as it was at work in Einsteinian physics. It is small wonder that this was a revolutionary epoch in other ways too.

Intellectual Origins of Fascism

In the 1920s and 1930s political themes became quite as exciting as literary and philosophical ones even for the intelligentsia. To an overwhelming extent these revolved around the revolutionary regimes that came out of the war in Russia and in Italy: Communism and Fascism.

A result of the demoralization following the war and a disappointing peace, as well as of frustrated national pride, Italian Fascism was hardly a consistent doctrine, but rather a fusion of discontents, successful because of the near collapse of society. It owed something to the fierce strife between socialist trade unions and the industrial capitalists, and to the Socialist's paralysis of will in a divided mind, as well as to the continued failure of parliamentary democracy to function well. A mass movement, it appealed to various inchoate emotions. In part it was the nightmare of Ortega, of Spengler, of Lawrence, and of Huxley come true: a revolt of the dehumanized masses, who were then to be enslaved by the totalitarian state. But Fascism had its intellectual aspects, and made use of some interesting ideas. Its leader, Benito Mussolini, a man of humble birth, had been a left-wing socialist, and was a journalist with an inquisitive and somewhat intellectual turn of mind. He had absorbed at least superficially the advanced political ideas of the pre-1914 generation—from Nietzsche, Sorel,[2] Bergson, and Pareto. He got from them the need for a complete revolution of values, to replace the decadent ones of bourgeois civilization, but also a contempt for materialistic socialism; a belief in elites rather than democracy; in the superiority of intuition over intellect.

Of the Fascist and Communist revolutions, much the same thing may be said as was said of the French Revolution earlier: ideas did not cause them, but they did guide and shape them. Discontents and the breakdown of order existed, the result of war and postwar problems (economic troubles, demobilization of soldiers). There was a host of other accumulated grievances. Italy had suffered from frustration ever since the rebirth of the nation in 1861, an event which was supposed to lead on to the glory befitting descendants of the Romans but instead brought only a series of humiliations. All this would in any case have brought on trouble, perhaps violence; but ideology helped shape this into a coherent, or more or less coherent, pattern of revolution.

The swashbuckling novelist and adventurer, Gabriel D'Annunzio, actually played a more creative part than Mussolini in setting the pattern. A man of ideas as well as of action was D'Annunzio, who put himself at the head of some exsoldiers and marched into the disputed city of Fiume in 1919, accompanying his seizure of it with flamboyant gestures of the sort soon copied by Mussolini—the uniformed private army, parades and mass meetings, the Leader addressing crowds from the balcony as they roared slogans back at him. Admirer of Wagner and Baudelaire, author of decadent novels, D'Annunzio had been a literary prodigy in the 1890s, after which he turned to the preaching of political adventures. "For Italy's younger generation," writes Ernst Nolte, "he was Nietzsche and Barrès rolled into one." He was a poet who became a national hero. He urged the Italians to make war against Turkey for Libya in 1909. Then he plunged into the world war, became an aviator, lost an eye, was decorated for bravery. No one better symbolized the "Leonardist" and "futurist" spirit which was Italy's version of the Nietzschean will-to-power, the Bergsonian *élan vital*. A Dionysian man and a powerful leader of the masses on his own view, he impressed others as an egotist and a charlatan. He was certainly a fertile source of slogans, one of them being the idea that Italy was a proletarian nation which should wage class war—as a united people—against the rich, plutocratic states. The spirit of Fascism was very much this spirit of the

[2]Sorel's influence was especially strong in Italy; see Jack J. Roth, "The Roots of Italian Fascism: Sorel and Sorelismo," *Journal of Modern History*, March, 1967.

romantic gesture, action for action's sake, and the mobilization of mass psychology. One may read here the whole mystique of the avant-garde movement of the day: the Nietzschean incitement to embrace life and "live dangerously," the rebellion against bourgeois legality, the alienated artist's hatred of respectable society, the socialist and anarchist call to revolt. Despite the somewhat disreputable character of Mussolini, there were some ways in which Fascism was smartly up-to-date—more up-to-date than Lenin's Marxism, for it had absorbed the lessons of irrationalism and psychology. It stressed "charismatic" leadership and "superman" activism. The Fascists managed to project an image of dynamic leadership aimed at reviving the Italian nation, sorely distressed and apparently unable to do anything about its troubles. Their weakness was the weakness of the new irrationalism: no system or program, just action for the sake of action, belief in belief itself, creation of "myths" whatever they might be.

To supply the element of nationalism lacking in Nietzsche and Sorel, Mussolini invoked Hegelian strains, popular in Italy for some time. He confided the construction of Fascist philosophy to the distinguished neo-Hegelian philosopher, Giovanni Gentile. The state represents the ethical ideal, and is superior to the individual, Gentile held. Both the individualism of bourgeois liberalism and the divisive class struggle of Marxian socialism are antisocial. Materialism was rejected as ignoble, and an organic conception of society approved. Claiming at first to stand for the individual against the state, Mussolini moved steadily toward more and more statism, a movement of the mind obviously not unaffected by the fact that Fascism had seized the state, and increasingly subordinated the individual to the community.

In addition to the above idea, Fascism seemed to revert to Jacobin conceptions of the general will, of which Il Duce, with his Grand Council of Fascism, was said to be the embodiment. Fascism represented itself as an answer to the degenerate liberalism of the parliamentary system. Also, the idea of the corporate state, developed in Catholic social thought and carried forward by Charles Maurras, became a part of Mussolini's system. Fascism thus appears, on its ideological side, as a pastiche of a number of ideas, with a heavy stress on statism, elitism, and irrationalism. Perhaps its marriage of statism (from Rousseau and Hegel) to the dynamic revolutionary romanticism of Nietzsche and Sorel may be regarded as its most striking achievement. (But the antiromantic conservative thought of Maurras was also somewhat in evidence.) One may argue with some plausibility that Fascism simply grabbed at various bits and pieces of ideas to justify its seizure of power. But it does not seem possible to dismiss its ideological aspects, for these were potent factors. It may be that this was why Fascism and Nazism had such startling success: their leaders were aware of the power of ideas, whereas the anemic liberalism of the time was not. Debased as it was, they offered a religion or faith to live by to modern man, who had need of it. For a few years Italy's most distinguished philosopher, Benedetto Croce, approved of Fascism because it had overcome traditional Italian indifference to politics and the state, revived national morale, and seemingly justified itself by its results. An impressive number of notable Italian writers, artists, musicians, including Papini, Pareto, Pirandello, Puccini, Toscanini, praised the new Italian regime at first. Almost all became severely disillusioned within a few years after 1922.

Mussolini strove to destroy the "lie of universal suffrage" and parliamentary democracy by substituting a strong, heroic elite; he only succeeded in putting Italy under the heel of a corrupt oligarchy. He broke the power of the trade unions but his "corporate state" scarcely provided any creative principle of economic cooperation. Fascism as a new religion was stamped on the mind of youth through control of the educational system and the organization of youth movements, but it soon ceased to interest anyone of intellectual quality. Mosca, the old proponent of elites, publicly regretted that he had ever criticized democracy, for the rule of the Fascists was worse yet. In brief, whatever promise there had been of a genuine new creed or spirit in Fascism soon vanished with only the old face of state tyranny in evidence, this time backed by the resources of modern technology. It is true that Mussolini for a while put on a reasonably convincing performance of the hero-leader, with some "charismatic" appeal. In many ways he was a genuinely talented man. But he wilted under the demands of the superman role and became rather ridiculous. Quite a few of Italy's better minds fled into exile. Others, like the great writer Ignazio Silone, were turned into communists who fought the Fascist tyranny as best they could underground.

German National Socialism owed much to Fascism—Adolf Hitler idolized the Italian dictator—but included some distinctive elements. Like Mussolini, Hitler and his group hated democracy, preached a "national" socialism in place of the Marxist sort which they regarded as poisonous, and were fanatically nationalistic and statist. Nazism, too, thrived on defeat, national humiliation, and the disorders of the postwar era, which were very severe in Germany for several years after 1919. It owed a special debt to Richard Wagner and featured anti-Semitism, not conspicuous in Italian Fascism. It also opportunistically made appeal to all sorts of emotions. It denounced capitalism, communism, the Jews, the traitors who had allegedly caused the defeat of Germany, the pacifists and liberals who continued to weaken her; it demanded a strongly led government capable of voicing the entire national will and leading Germany back to her place in the sun. Its brown-shirted gangs specialized in brutal violence. The Party, with its leadership-principle, borrowed heavily from Lenin's Russian Communist Party in its organization. There were echoes of pre-1914 pan-Germanism in Hitler's program of German expansion; there was also the "crude Darwinism" which caused the relatively ignorant Hitler to act consistently on the principle that life is a ruthless struggle in which the weak, the wounded, and the allegedly "biologically inferior" have to perish. Racism came from Wagner and a few other nineteenth-century writers, such as the Frenchman Gobineau, owing something, too, to the fashion for genetics, which sometimes took the form of belief in racial improvement by selective breeding.[3] From Nietzsche (selectively) the Nazis took slogans about supermen, heroic leadership, and the need to purge the old order ruthlessly.

In the crude thought of the demagogue Hitler, the Jew appears as a scapegoat, blamed for everything: among other things, for capitalism, democracy, socialism, decadent estheticism, modern art and literature, modern skepticism and unbelief. Hitler's taste was severely classical; he shared with Stalin's Communists at least this one trait, a hatred of all modernistic art. In the slightly more sophisticated theorizing of the Nazi "philosopher" A. Rosenberg, the Jew is identified with intellectualism, which is related to internationalism, both to be set off against the sound instincts of a cultural people. Christianity has been corrupted by both Judaic and Mediterranean elements, but there is a sound "Aryan Christianity" which should be encouraged. The decadent phenomena, blamed primarily on Jewish influence, are the internationalist, intellectualist, uprooted, atomistic ones; the sound things are rooted in the soil, national tradition, close group integration, intuition, and custom rather than abstract reason. It is easy to see in this sort of thinking many echoes of German and European thought, from early nineteenth-century conservatism and romanticism, from Wagner and Nietzsche and German sociologists like Frederick Tönnies. They were not all disreputable ideas; perhaps they ought not to be blamed because they fell into the hands of the Nazis. The specifically Nazi contribution was the mysticism of race, which is generally considered to have been complete nonsense. This went so far as to assert that there was an Aryan science and to reject Einstein's theories as Jewish-decadent!

Talk about the "Nordic race" and its superiority was quite common and respectable in the later nineteenth and twentieth century, as may be

[3]Count Joseph Arthur de Gobineau, a friend of Tocqueville and a speculative sociologist in the tradition of Montesquieu, wrote his *Essay on the Inequality of the Races* (1853–1855), purporting to show that the white races and particularly the "Aryan" race alone created civilization. The work influenced Wagner. Flattering to the Germans because it found the highest concentration of pure "Aryanism" to exist in Germany, the theory was the work of a Frenchman anxious to show that the French aristocracy, originally Germanic, deserved its ascendancy.

seen, for example, in England's Cecil Rhodes, whose Anglo-American scholarships, still awarded annually and considered a high honor in the United States, were established for the purpose of knitting together "the Nordic race"; or in such Americans as Josiah Strong and John W. Burgess, a popular clergyman and a leading professor of political science. The United States rang with laments about the "mongrelization" of the native stock through immigration from "inferior" Slavs and Latins as well as Jews. Anti-Semitism was familiar in Great Britain: a recent writer has observed that "fifty years ago anti-Semitism was a political force in England that respectable people supported and with which honourable people sympathized." (Henry D'Avigdor-Goldsmid, *History Today*, April 1964.) The Dreyfus case in France in the 1890s brought forth the first major appearance of modern anti-Semitism. Hitler learned his in Austria. There, the Germans as a minority in a sea of Slavs, Hungarians, and Jews developed an often hysterical pan-Germanism as well as "master race" ideologies. Rosenberg was a Baltic German, again revealing the psychology of the colonist or resident alien. All this is to record the unhappy fact that radical prejudice and belief in racial or cultural superiority was hardly confined to Germany, or typical of it. German National Socialism was destined to write the most odious and detestable chapters of this disease in all history; the ideas were far from exclusively German. Anti-Semitism had been far more virulent in Russia and eastern Europe, where vicious mistreatment of the Jew was common practice; in Germany he had apparently become assimilated and there was no "Jewish problem" until the Nazis invented one.

The Nazi mysticism of race contained an echo of Jung's unconscious archetypes, alleged however to be a phenomena of *race*: each race has its soul, its symbols, its myths, which are carried in the blood. Jung like many Germans was evidently partly attracted to Nazism at first but later emphatically rejected it.

Hitler appropriated some of the ideas of the German conservative writers, a group that included Oswald Spengler, Ernst Jünger, and Moeller van den Bruck, though they did not much approve of him and after seizing power he persecuted this group as relentlessly as others. These thinkers responded to the defeat and humiliation of Germany in World War I by proposing a Spartan recovery program. Spengler and Moeller wrote of the need for strength of will, national resurgence, and a leader capable of embodying in himself the people's will. All weakening forces, such as democracy (alien to the "Prussian style"), liberalism, and class conflict must be eliminated. These ideologies stemming from the French Revolution were the virus poisoning Germany, which must return to conservative principles to regain unity and strength. Moeller and Spengler were the "conservative revolutionaries" who would use revolutionary means to bring about a conservative, that is, nationalistic, goal. But they were not racists and Hitler to them was a disreputable rabble-rouser. There are some striking affinities between these writers and Nazism, but not complete identity.

Ernst Jünger was a spokesman of Germany's restless youth, who just before the war had created a youth movement expressing the urge to get back to nature and renew contact with elemental forces, a protest against the urbanized rationalism of modern life. Something similar existed in France and other countries. After the war, the "fatherless generation" or the embittered exsoldiers were revolutionary in spirit. This youth movement was intensely idealistic, yearning for something much better, earnestly if fuzzily convinced that the existing order—capitalist, mechanical, bourgeois, soulless—was bankrupt. The youth movement with its *Bünde* was separate from the National Socialists but often merged into it. Hitler took advantage of it; in the long run he did not represent its idealism, and it is clear that many young Germans who initially hailed Hitler soon became severely disillusioned with the new slavery his regime introduced. (By that time it was too late.) Radical, revolutionary as it was, young Germany was searching for something to believe in, something exalted and pure. The tragedy was that the figure it thought represented such revolutionary idealism turned out to believe in nothing.

The Nazi and Fascist movements were profoundly anti-intellectual. "When I hear the word 'culture' I reach for my gun," said Joseph Goebbels, Hitler's lieutenant. These movements came to be led by the brutal, the ignorant, and the criminal. They were extremely clever at exploiting the irrationality of the masses, for whom they often expressed great contempt. Keen students of propaganda, the Fascists and Nazis borrowed liberally from all the great mass movements of the past. They employed the language of religious conversion, freely using such words as faith, deliverance, miracle, rebirth, sacrifice. Nineteenth-century nationalism did so too, as we may recall. They took much from the Communists, as well as from ritualistic orders such as Jesuits or Freemasons, and from the army; it has been suggested that they also learned a good deal from American advertising. They played on symbols from the national past. Hitler and the Nazis "looked back into the stream of earlier German thinking and selected that which they found of value to them" (Otto Klineberg). All this was done cynically, in the sense that there was a deliberate use of "myth," a disparagement of objective truth, a frank acceptance of the need to lead the masses by techniques directed at the irrational mind. But all these ideas had been brought forth by such important prewar thinkers as Nietzsche, Sorel, Wallas. The war itself had exhibited the possibilities of nationalistic propaganda and helped undermine respect for truth, as governments resorted to what amounted to systematic lying. Thus in many ways the Fascist and Nazi movements dredged up all the worst in prewar and war culture. They were the evil spirits of Western civilization, but they did not create the evil so much as exploit it. They were intellectual parasites, borrowing the ideas of others to use as tools of power.

The list of distinguished German writers and thinkers who saw something in Hitler, at least for a time, resembles that of Italy in regard to Mussolini; it is a considerable one and included such names as the great philosopher Martin Heidegger, the expressionist poet Gottfried Benn, and a considerable part of the university faculties. At great personal sacrifice a large number of people left Germany in protest against Nazism, or courageously fought it at the risk of their lives. But most of this opposition came after Hitler had come to power in 1933. The fact is that on its purely ideological side the Nazis could make a certain appeal to significant strains in the mind of twentieth-century man. One may see a milder but cognate version of the belief in blood and instinct, in heroism and elite leadership, in such outstanding sages of the period as D. H. Lawrence and William B. Yeats. They too despised democracy and liberalism and yearned for some great purifying movement violently sweeping away the decadent past to bring true leadership.

Hermann Rauschning, himself a participant in the German neo-conservative movement, called Hitlerism "the revolution of nihilism" by which he meant to indicate that it had no doctrinal center at all, no belief in anything. It was an inherently destructive force, committed to eternal dynamism for the sake of dynamism. It was organized neuroticism, the sickness of a nation never quite soundly built and driven mad by the sufferings of war, defeat, and then economic collapse. This analysis itself may suffer from rhetorical exaggeration, but it does convey something of the deep corruption and moral bankruptcy of the Nazi state. Some intelligent Germans hailed it at first because they thought it might bring able leadership. If it had produced a true elite able to govern well, one might have forgiven it its lack of democracy and even some ruthlessness. But it ended in war, the sickening slaughter of the Jews, defeat, and destruction. Thereby all that it had stood for or even suggested became repugnant to mankind.

The Fascist and Nazi creeds glorified war. "War alone brings all human energies to their highest state of tension," proclaimed Mussolini, "and stamps with the seal of nobility the nations which have to face it." The idea that war is a test of a people's moral fibre was an Hegelian as well as a Darwinian one. Hitler believed that the decadent democracies would be incapable of waging war, because their people had been corrupted, softened, debauched. Under National Socialist discipline the German people must prove themselves worthy of history by facing war. Hitler plunged recklessly down a collision course that eventuated in war, a course obviously marked out by ideological elements in National Socialism, both in a negative and a positive way. Negatively, Hitler's ideology convinced him that the democracies with their materialism and un-*Völkisch* cultures were incapable of determined resistance; they would neither fight nor develop a firm national policy, because they believed in nothing, were led by internationalist Jews (apparently the Nazis even thought that Franklin D. Roosevelt was Jewish!), and were inefficiently democratic. Positively, Nazism implied the cult of virility, the test of war. Hitler expected Great Britain to ally with Germany and was prepared to allow the British to govern the seas and their colonial world. He had fallen under the sway of the "geopolitical" ideas of MacKinder and Haushofer, which combined with his belief in Slavic inferiority to direct his ambitions toward a great Eurasian land empire, to be ruled over by Aryan supermen.

It should be stressed that fascism was a Europe-wide phenomenon. In particular, search for the peculiarly "German" roots of Nazism has been outrageously overdone. If it emerged first in Italy, with strongly French intellectual antecedents (Sorel, Maurras) under the leadership of an ex-Marxist who held no brief for Italian national traditions, it sooner or later appeared in all parts of Europe (and America). There were Belgian Rexists, and an Austrian Fascist movement, the *Heimwehr* led by Prince Stahremberg (which predated the Nazis and was destroyed by them after Hitler took over Austria). In Rumania the Iron Guard, preaching return to ancestral customs, rejection of modernism, hatred of the Jew as symbol of capitalism and modernism, combined this sort of deep conservatism with a radical, populist program of land redistribution. There were such manifestations everywhere. In Britain, the man regarded as the most brilliant young Labour Party leader, Oswald Moseley, imitated Mussolini and tried to create a British Fascist party. If fascism failed to capture power in other countries as it did in Italy and Germany, the reasons were chiefly accidental ones of time and circumstance.

Certainly in France the fascist movement could not be described as insignificant. In February, 1934, 200,000 demonstrators attempted to storm the Chamber of Deputies in Paris and fought police in an all-night battle during which thousands of both police and demonstrators were wounded and a number killed—a melee hard to match even in the long and bloody annals of Parisian street uprisings. These protestors were right-wing followers of the fascist leagues, seeking to bring down a left-of-center government. The largest of the French fascist leagues, the *Croix de Feu*, claimed 750,000 members and may have been the largest of all voluntarily recruited fascist groups. Fascism never won in France, partly because there were too many different fascist groups—the old *Action Française* now being joined by several other similar factions.

One of France's leading fascists was a renegade communist, Jacques Doriot. What, in the last analysis, *was* this post-world war phenomeon that so oddly combined extremes of Right and Left? That it *did* so combine things formerly thought to be unmixable opposites is indisputable. It appealed to the young and the outcast, demanded drastic change, practiced violent methods. It sought an image of dynamism as well as youth: Mussolini and Hitler made a point of dashing about on motorcycles or in fast cars and otherwise displaying qualities of energy and *élan*. Fascism's specific programs were normally anticapitalist, appealing to the "little people" against the monopolists; and it called itself socialist, though rejecting the materialistic and class-struggle socialism of the Marxists. Its leaders tended to be one-time Marxists—true at least of Mussolini, Doriot, Oswald Moseley, and others. In all these respects it was radical. But in other ways it was deeply conservative. The demand for national unity, cultural integration, what the Germans called *völkisch* qualities was close to the heart of fascism/Nazism. Their hatred of Jews and Marxists came to the fascists from their dislike of things that disrupted organic culture unity and divided the national community. Their extreme intolerance, their contemptuous rejection of democracy and liberalism, their almost insane attempts to create a national ideology—*German* religion, *German* science—along with their racialist fantasies, all this flowed from the impulse to beat back the tides of pluralistic modernism and recreate a truly organic community. The fascist ideology glorified the country against the city, tried to inculcate blindly obedient patriotism, stressed the family, traditional values, old customs.

This radicalism of the Right was, of course, deeply infused with the irrationalism of the prewar thinkers. An old-fashioned rationalist like Bertrand Russell stood aghast at all this sound and fury, and could only say "The world between the wars was attracted to madness. Of this attraction Nazism was the most emphatic expression." Watching Hitler's parades and mass meetings, listening to his hysterical speeches to roaring, chanting crowds, many others too could only assume that a kind of madness had seized hold of Germany. (In actuality, it would appear, not many Germans paid much attention to the ideology, privately laughing at it; they approved of Hitler because he got things done, restoring Germany to economic health and international success.) But still others pointed out that man, not being a rational animal, has need of ritual and romance, a need neglected in modern times, rationalized, bureaucratized, and mechanized as its life had become. Fascism reminded them that modern Western man is in search of a religion, to replace a lost Christianity, and found here a substitute. It turned out to be a disastrous one.

13

The Pink Decade

Marxism is an all-inclusive whole reflecting our age.
JEAN-PAUL SARTRE

Marxism is . . . an opiate for the people.
SIMONE WEIL

Communism and the Intellectuals

In the 1930s, reaction against Nazism provided a rallying point for the shattered morale of European intellectuals. At this time, they were precipitated in large numbers into the camp of communism. The "red decade," or at least the "pink" one, had begun.

Quite early, the new Communist government of the Soviet Union received significant support from Western intellectuals. "In this muddy age its ten years shine," wrote the American liberal magazine *The Nation* on the tenth birthday of the Russian Revolution in 1927, voicing orthodox liberal-left doctrine. Historians this side of the USSR are likely to find today that it shone mostly with blood. In 1932 the venerable Fabian socialists, Mr. and Mrs. Webb, who had always stood for political democracy and personal liberty, heaped praise on "Soviet Civilization" in a substantial study; they praised it among other things for "liquidating the landlord and the capitalist." At just that time Stalin's ruthless war on the kulaks was driving peasants to starvation in a way one can hardly imagine the Webbs approving. What became almost a stampede of writers and intellectuals to the communist bandwagon later appeared inexplicable, even to the people who joined it. There were, however, some reasons for it.

Bolsheviks and left socialists profited, first of all, by having none of the blood of the world war on their hands. Lenin and a few others, for example, Ramsay MacDonald in Great Britain, had rejected the conflict from the beginning. As soon as the bolsheviks fell heir to collapsing Russia in November, 1917, they issued an appeal to the workers of the world to lay down their arms. They continued to denounce the whole European state system as an iniquitous capitalist scheme and to cloak themselves in the garb of pacifism. Lenin provided a Marxist explanation of the great war—caused by imperialistic capitalism—and socialists alleged that universal peace would follow the extinction of the capitalist system. The unpopularity of the war, and the hatred of all war, that pervaded these years redounded to the credit of the Communists. A good deal of sympathy for the Russian bolshevist government, also, was aroused by the shocked horror with which respectable circles regarded it; by their efforts to destroy it through military intervention in 1919–1920 (though these were feeble and half-hearted), and by their treatment of it as a pariah for some time after 1920.

Perhaps it is not quite possible to explain the pro-Soviet mood in a rational way. It became a symbol for all those who hated the "establishment." The disillusioned and the naturally rebellious, the unhappy young men and women of the "lost generation," saw here a successful revolution, led by a leader of genius and vision, which had overthrown a vicious and reactionary government in Russia. But whatever sympathy the Soviet "experiment" aroused before 1930, it was the impact of the great depression that caused the rush to Marxism. The Webbs, in the study mentioned above, praised especially the Russian "abandonment of the incentive of profit-making, its extinction of unemployment, its planned production for community consumption."[1] The Western democracies struggled almost hopelessly in the mire of economic depression in the 1930s, while in Russia things seemed to go forward with vigor and drive. The first of the great "five-year plans" for the industrialization of Russia was launched in 1928. "There is no unemployment in

---

[1]Fabian socialism was in considerable confusion because its solutions had seemingly not worked. In her diary, Mrs. Webb observed that "we went seriously wrong . . . in suggesting that we knew how to prevent unemployment. We did not." By 1931 there had been two Labour governments in Britain, yet the expected miracles had not come about. "I am beginning to doubt the inevitability of gradualness," Beatrice sighed.

Russia": the explanation might be that there was economic slavery there, but in the grim atmosphere of the jobless thirties even that seemed better than unemployment. As a matter of fact, uncritical books by friends of the Soviet Union poured from the press, indicating that something like a paradise for the working man was being created, with all the old vices missing—vices such as greed, selfishness, prostitution, crime, ignorance. "Planned production for community consumption" had replaced the anarchy of capitalism.

The existence of Fascism and then Nazism polarized political attitudes and diminished the middle position. Mussolini and Hitler excoriated bolshevism, as did all right-wing, conservative people; therefore if you attacked it you could be accused of being a fascist, or as good as one. (Marxist logic featured a method of reasoning by which "objectively" one could be a fascist without even knowing it.) Some very intelligent people admitted that they backed Soviet Russia because it was attacked by those they disliked; they loved it for the enemies it made (*vide* André Gide). Communists did fight fascism and Nazism; they led the way in the famous Spanish Civil War which pitted the two elements against each other. They showed outstanding courage in fighting as best they could the Fascist and Nazi dictatorships in Italy and Germany.

Much aiding this detente with the Communists was the popular front strategy adopted by the latter after 1934. Prior to that the Communist line had been to denounce the moderate Socialists and Social Democrats as "social fascists" and refuse cooperation with them. Some of the fiercest polemics of the '20s were exchanged between the old Socialists and the new Communists, who had split off from the Second International to establish the Moscow-directed Third International. Recognizing after Hitler's triumph that they had gravely underestimated fascism (in their blindness the German Communists actually helped Hitler bring down the Weimar Republic, believing, as their dogma taught, that the collapse of "capitalism" must inevitably lead to socialism and communism), the party line shifted and from Moscow came orders to make friends with all shades of left and liberal opinion and form a united front against fascism. It was one of a number of abrupt and sometimes bewildering shifts which earned the Communists the mistrust of others; but at least it meant, in 1935, that the Communists welcomed the friendship of other left-wing elements, no longer denouncing these as "traitors to the working class" because they refused to join the Communist Party. Soon there was a Popular Front government in France, headed by the venerable and prestigious Socialist Leon Blum, a Jaurès disciple. It had its troubles keeping so various an amalgamation of doctrinaires together, but for a short time about 1936–37 the Popular Front seemed a success.

An additional attraction that may be suggested in explanation (if not extenuation) of the intellectuals' defection to communism was Soviet literature and art. The arts in Russia had not yet been placed in an official strait jacket, destroying their creativity and interest. They were still reasonably free, progressive, and graced by such names as Maxim Gorki, one of the greatest of living novelists in the 1930s (a holdover from the prewar era, but an enthusiastic convert to the Soviet regime); Eisenstein, the genius of the silent cinema; Prokofiev and Shostakovich, the composers. Culturally, today, the world of communism has virtually nothing to attract the educated Westerner; this was not so true in the 1920s and early 1930s. Stalinization of all artistic and intellectual activity did not really get under way seriously until about 1935. After World War II it reached fantastic extremes during the reign of Zhdanov as Cultural Minister, when even music could be denounced as "ideologically incorrect" and scientists were persecuted for not paying sufficient heed to dialectical materialism. It was not yet so in 1930.

So about 1930 writers grew interested in communism. They had grown weary of the weary skepticism of the 1920s. Their mood changed sharply with the coming of the great economic depression and the rise of fascism. They wrote off the esthetes of the 1920s as irresponsibles. "But quite suddenly, in the years of 1930–1935, something happens. The literary climate changes. A new group of writers . . . has made its appearance, and though technically these writers owe something to their predecessors, their 'tendency' is entirely different. Suddenly we have got out of the twilight of the gods into a sort of Boy Scout atmosphere of bare knees and community singing" (George Orwell). Writers became serious, political, almost social-messianic in the spirit of 1848. Conversion from gloom and alienation to hope and social purpose seemed a miracle at the time; only later did Orwell, who went through it, see it as he so wryly describes it above. Writers turned to social realism in the 1930s and pinned their hopes on red revolution. "Drop those priggish ways forever, stop behaving like a stone," the poet W. H. Auden admonished his fellow writers. "Start at once to try to live." Come down from the ivory tower and join a picket line.

Arthur Koestler noted that actual entrance into the Communist party on an active basis, which was his experience, choked off literary expression, but that mild contact with Marxism as "fellow travellers" stimulated any number of writers in the 1930s. John Dos Passos and John Steinbeck wrote memorable works of "social realism" in the United States; Barbusse, Romains, and Malraux in France; Brecht and Seghers in Germany. Some of this mock-proletarianism later seemed ridiculous. The esthetes of the 1920s tried to become democratic "hearties" if not communist revolutionaries; from the Kremlin, the real thing undoubtedly laughed at them, while making use of them as best it could. There was an Oxford Collective Poem made by Mass Observation, so far had the cycle swung from the intensely private art of the previous decade. But the intellectuals' hatred of the Nazi and Fascist dictatorships was real and worthy of respect. This effort to regain a democratic and social content for literature was unquestionably significant and productive of much good literature. It tried to repair the relationship between writer and society sundered since the 1880s.

> Singing I was at peace,
> Above the clouds, outside the ring. . . .
>
> None such shall be left alive:
> The innocent wing is soon shot down,
> And private stars fade in the blue-red dawn
> Where two worlds strive.
>
> The red advance of life
> Contracts pride, calls out the common blood,
> Beats song into a single blade,
> Makes a depth-charge of grief.
>
> _C. Day Lewis_

The flight of the intellectuals to communism reflected in substantial measure their own spiritual predicament. Edward Upward wrote that "I came to it [communism] not so much through consciousness of the political and economic situation as through despair." Koestler commented on "the intellectual comfort and relief found in escaping from a tragic predicament into a 'closed system' of beliefs that left no room for hesitation and doubt." Though not proclaimed as such, but rather as an exact science, the Communist ideology clearly functioned as a substitute religion, too, especially appealing to intellectuals. ("The strongest appeal of the Communist party was that it demanded sacrifice," Louis MacNeice recalled. "You had to sink your ego.") Yet, as such, it proved to be—in the words of a famous symposium on the subject—the god that failed.

The artists and intellectuals who rushed into the arms of communism expected to find there greater freedom, greater creativity, a liberating force. Picasso said that he went to communism as to a spring of fresh water. The great irony is that by 1931 Communism had become a system of slavery and an intellectual straitjacket, so that the intellectuals who entered it were condemned to frustration. The Communist party was being so organized as to destroy all intraparty democracy in the USSR and also so as to put the various other party units firmly under the control of Moscow. Communists in other countries were required to serve the Stalin-dictated party line blindly. In the name of socialist unity they had to agree that the homeland of socialism, the USSR, must be defended at all cost. They were led into the role of apologists for whatever might be done by Stalin, and in the middle thirties this included the astonishing reign of terror that "purged" almost all the old bolsheviks along with hundreds of thousands of others as Stalin systematically destroyed all resistance to his dictatorship. In 1939 it included suddenly becoming the ally of Hitler. While a few agreed to submit their individuality entirely to the party and suspend all ethical considerations for the duration of the battle against capitalism, most found the conditions of intellectual servitude imposed on them intolerable and became disillusioned with the USSR. They might not abandon their revolutionary or Marxist views in leaving the party; they might claim (plausibly) that Stalin had betrayed the revolution and perverted Marx, as well as Lenin. But the exodus from the party that began about 1937 led most of the converts eventually away from the whole Marxist framework. They were led to reexamine Marxism and to see some of its defects, which could be regarded as having led to Stalinism.

Whatever their future destinations, the Left writers departed for them from their Red rendezvous at the end of the 1930s and later treated it for the most part as a mistake. A great deal was written by the one-time Communists about their odyssey in and out of the Party. In his great novel *Darkness at Noon*, Arthur Koestler tried to depict the self-destroying psychology of the Communist who had given over his mind and soul to the Party. Koestler has described his own rather horrifying experience within the Party as a "spiritual discipline" that he would not wish to see expunged from his past, though he came to regard it as an intellectual error. (See *The Invisible Writing*.) A few, like Picasso and Bertolt Brecht, remained; the latter faced and accepted with unusual clarity the decision to lose one's individuality in the Party, to cease thinking and become nameless and faceless, "blank sheets on which the Revolution will write its orders," prepared to "sink into the mud" and "commit any vileness" in order that the cause might prosper. It was a decision any Communist had to make if he stayed in the Stalinist party. But it was a singular position for writers or artists to accept, and Brecht was one of the few great ones able to do so.[2]

Leon Trotsky, Lenin's chief lieutenant in the Revolution, who was driven into exile and ultimately assassinated by Stalinists, provided a

[2]Even Brecht's experience suggests the difficulties of the creative writer under Communism; for his plays, written in a "modern," avant-garde manner, have not been performed in Communist countries though he has been their most distinguished literary property in recent years. In actuality Brecht was never comfortable in the Soviet Union, from which at one time he had fled.

rallying point for some who wished to remain revolutionary Marxists while repudiating Soviet Communism under Stalin. Trotskyites regarded Stalinism as having perverted socialism by the errors of bureaucratization and the cult of personality. They were prone to criticize the lack of intraparty democracy and even the lack of personal freedom in the USSR, yet they remained attached to revolutionary Leninism including the rule of the party as "vanguard" or proletarian elite. On the whole, this group faded out too, after playing some part for a time as the resting place for those disillusioned with events in Russia but not prepared to abandon revolutionary socialism.

An examination of the multitudinous self-analyses of ex-Communists of the '30s and '40s leads one to conclude that the chief reasons for disenchantment were the following: the discovery that Marxian ideology is an illusion blinding one to reality; concern about destruction of moral integrity from having to subordinate truth and standards of decency to the Party cause; the Party's ruthless subordination of the individual to its demands; failure to find artistic fulfillment in Communism, indeed the opposite, a stultifying effect; and eye-opening discoveries about conditions in Russia, especially the tyrannical treatment of people. Inherently undisciplined, freedom-loving artists were usually quite miserable if they actually entered the Party and were required to submit to its iron discipline. Harold Laski, distinguished left-wing theoretician of the British Labour party who was pro-Communist in the 1930s, reacted at length against "deception, ruthlessness, contempt for fair play, willingness to use lying and treachery . . . dishonesty in the presentation of facts." Changes in the party line required embarrassing shifts: A. MacIntyre cites the case of a British party faithful who first lauded Yugoslavia's Tito, then slandered him, then suppressed the latter book when Tito was restored to favor again. What one believed depended on the latest word from Moscow. Stalinism gradually destroyed whatever artistic creativity and freedom of thought there had been in Russia and erected a monstrous tyranny which killed and imprisoned millions. This became increasingly obvious to even the most ideology-blinded partisan.

During World War II, wartime friendship between the Soviet Union and the Western democracies brought a temporary resurgence of Communism within the latter, but the strained relations between Russia and the West after 1945 had the opposite result. Dogmatic Marxism suffered a precipitate decline in Great Britain and the United States. It declined to a lesser degree in Italy and France, perhaps because of a curious affinity between its dogmatic and apocalyptic mood and that of Roman Catholic Christianity. Some of the French existentialists, especially Sartre, were prepared to welcome a version of Marxism—not the obsolete dogmas, the absurd intellectual edifice, but the ethical protest against capitalism, the denunciation of the workers' alienation from his work and from society, which they regarded as the essence of Marx. Of this, more later.

Other Social Movements

There were other "progressive" social movements in the decade of depression which were not Marxist but which assailed the existing order of capitalism. The great economic depression caused a searching re-appraisal of existing, "classical" economic theory. Among the revisers of economic orthodoxy the Englishman John Maynard Keynes stood out as an acute, penetrating, and incisive mind with a gift of literary expression. Keynes, who had challenged conventional public finance methods in the 1920s, came in the 1930s to put his views in the form of a general theory (1936). Pared down to its essentials, the Keynesian view was that contrary to the old theory there is no automatic tendency toward full employment in the free economy (Say's law); rather, there can be stagnation with unused human resources. This is because, among other things, the community's total savings are not necessarily invested in capital equipment. The interest rate, which is supposed to provide the automatic mechanism for insuring the investment of savings (the rate falling as savings rise), may not function effectively because liquidity preference (desire to keep funds in cash form easily obtainable) causes savers to accept a lower return on their money than they could get. Keynes stressed the propensity to over-save and under-invest in a mature capitalist economy; the result can be economic stagnation. The economy cannot be counted upon to right itself, as the older economics taught. It may have to be righted by the intervention of the government. Formerly the approved policy for dealing with depression was for the government to pare its expenditures and balance its budget, and governments did this during the early stage of the 1930s depression, with apparently ineffective results. The new economics called for an un-balanced budget, the government throwing its overspending into the economic stream to break the logjam.

Thus the new economics, as advocated by Keynes and his follow-ers along with some others (the Swedish school was prominent), en-couraged statism though not socialism (public ownership). The private economy can work effectively but it requires regulating with the great fiscal resources of the government used as a balance wheel. Interest rates can be manipulated by government action, the expenditures of the gov-ernment can be varied, taxes raised or lowered according to the needs of the economy at any given time. The Keynesian view, roughly, prevailed, in that orthodox economic theory soon accepted a modicum of the new economics while governments, even conservative ones, accepted their responsibility to "maintain full employment" by use of a variety of powers such as those mentioned. This was an economic revolution and perhaps by implication a political and social one, if a mild one. It cast the "public sector" of the economy in a new and much more active role. It provided, as some saw it, a democratic alternative to communist totalitarianism in the area of national economic planning. To others, the "Keynesian revolution" and the "welfare state" were steps on the "road to serfdom" (F. A. Hayek) only slightly less alarming than red bolshevism; they too reflected the coloration of the Pink Decade.

On any showing, the 1930s was a colorful time, with ideas or ideologies most prominently featured. It suffered subsequently from a severe reaction. That so many earnest writers and intellectuals had eaten of the bitter husks of communism and thought, at least for a while, that it was good bread seemed an astonishing index of their gullibility and has been one of the things responsible for a dismaying amount of anti-intellectualism in the post-1945 world. To be the victim of a merely political "ideology" marked one, later, as an innocent. The thrust of the Western mind toward basic social reform had not ended, but it was perhaps blunted and then diverted by the peculiar experiences of the 1930s.

The infatuation of creative writers with social issues in the 1930s left behind remarkable literary deposits, now somewhat out of style but bound to remain as landmarks for the historian to contemplate, some of them awe-inspiring in their sheer magnitude. For example, Jules Romains, the French novelist, wrote ten thousand pages in his mammoth multivolume novel of social realism, *Men of Good Will*, outdoing Marcel Proust in length if not in quality, and intended to rival Balzac's great "Human Comedy" of a century earlier as a picture of the social world. Politicians, capitalists, industrialists, as well as intellectuals seeking to set the world right, fill these pages. The criticism made of Romains and other novels of this sort (the Englishman Robert Briffault and the American Upton Sinclair were among others addicted to it) is, for one thing, that they really had no first-hand knowledge of capitalists and politicians (or workers!), but invented stereotypes of what Marxist or left-liberal theory required them to believe of such men.[3] Social realism was often wildly unrealistic. And it was frequently unutterably dreary: sermons flavored with melodrama. It was often enough the fruit of a

---

[3]Romains was a Jaurès socialist, which is to say in American terms, roughly, a Norman Thomas socialist, or a Fabian: he had learned his socialism before 1914, in his youth. But the 1930s spawned the "popular front" idea, to bring all hues of the Left together.

blind ideological faith. Romains's huge opus is nevertheless a tribute to the moral earnestness of the writers of the thirties and their desire to bring life back into the scope of art and intellect.

While simple and drastic positions such as Stalinist Communism tended to prevail in the anxious '30s, during which the western world suffered the ravages of economic depression and watched the drift toward another war, there were subtler variations on the theme of Marxism. A recent book by Martin Jay has told in great detail of the Frankfurt Institute for Social Research to which belonged such German intellectuals as Erich Fromm, Herbert Marcuse, and Theodor Adorno, and which specialized in a nondogmatic, more humanistic Marxism. Thrown out of Germany by Hitler in the early thirties, the Institute ended in New York City as part of that great cultural migration of German scholars, scientists and intellectuals which so altered American intellectual life. The moment for this critical Marxism, more concerned with the quality of culture than with revolutionary violence, came much later: Marcuse as an old man was to become the sage of the youth movement of the 1960s, in one of the many odd twists of intellectual history. In the interwar period these sophisticated social theorists discovered Marx's unknown early writings, rejected both Stalinism and Social Democracy as simplistic perversions of Marx, experimented in Freudian existential or phenomenological graftings onto Marxism. They were an esoteric elite at this time but were later to be seen as pioneers. There were other such left-wing groups in Germany during the Weimar years, all of course destroyed by the Nazi revolution, which did not pause to distinguish between shadings of Marxism, the more so since these circles tended to be heavily Jewish (this was true of the Frankfurt school).

Throughout everything, whatever their other disagreements, writers, intellectuals, political leftists, clergymen, and almost everybody else joined in one fervent sentiment: *nie wieder Krieg*, no more war. The war dominated literature. Romains's epic, just mentioned, paused for a whole volume at the battle of Verdun; Ernest Hemingway immortalized Caporetto; the most famous and poignant of all, Erich Maria Remarque's *All Quiet on the Western Front* (*Im Westen Nichts Neues*) cemented the postwar reconciliation of Germans and Frenchmen and Englishmen on the common sentiment of shuddering abhorrence of the whole grisly event. But a few outstanding examples cannot begin to suggest the extent to which the war provided themes for the novel, memoirs, and likewise serious thought. The huge historical *post mortem* into the causes of the war has been mentioned; it extended to the popular level. The fashionable Marxism attributed war to the dynamics of the capitalist system or, more naively, to the conspiracies of munitions makers. Such analyses obviously partook of fantasy more than fact: the widely read book of a

British aristocrat turned Communist, John Strachey,[4] *The Coming Struggle for Power* (1932) predicted a war between the United States and Great Britain as the climax of world capitalism's imminent collapse (and also predicted Communist rather than Nazi victory in Germany). But they suited the spirit of the times. Young men took the Oxford Oath, in England, vowing never again to fight for king and country. A typical extremism of the intellectuals led them to disavow *all* war, without exceptions, without distinction. They repudiated this vow, under the threat of Nazism, in the later 1930s. This feeling was in good part responsible for the weakness of the Western democracies in the face of Hitler's post-1935 Nazi challenge; a generation fed on antiwar literature could not admit the thought of war even against the worst of evils. The final tragic irony of this generation was that it had to go back to war, which it hated, in order to destroy Fascism and Nazism, themselves products of the first war's brutalization of man.

Revolutions in Philosophy: Logical Positivism

A. J. Ayer, the British philosopher identified with "logical positivism" in the 1930s, in some reminiscences recalled that "there was a moment when Philip Toynbee almost, but not quite, persuaded me to join the Communist Party. I have to confess that my reason for refusing was not so much that I disbelieved in dialectical materialism as that I recoiled from the idea of party discipline." There was undoubtedly some connection between the mood of this "revolution in philosophy" (self-styled) and the decade of political radicalism.[5] Logical positivism began life as an iconoclastic doctrine, whatever it may later have become; "the old men were outraged," as Ayer recalls with glee. But its origins went back some years, and led, curiously, to Vienna as well as to the British universities, especially Cambridge.

Logical positivism originated with a group of philosophers and mathematicians active at the University of Vienna from about 1920 until Nazism and war dispersed them in the 1930s, whereupon many of them went to Great Britain and the United States and exerted a considerable influence while blending with certain native traditions in these

---

[4]By no means unusual in England in the 1930s where the Left Book Club, which published such books as Strachey's, the Webbs' *Soviet Civilization*, and the adulatory books on Russia of the "red dean" of Canterbury, Hewlett Johnson, appealed to an upper-class, professional, and intellectual audience.

[5]The Vienna Circle tended to be leftish: Otto Neurath had been a member of the brief Spartacist revolutionary regime in Munich in 1919. The Circle was broken up when the Nazis seized Austria in 1938, its surviving members fleeing to England or the United States.

countries. These men included Schlick, Carnap, Neurath, and Wittgenstein, the latter going to Cambridge University early. They owed something to the prewar teaching at Vienna of Ernst Mach's "empirio-criticism," a careful analysis of the immediate data of experience based on the neo-Kantian view that only sense data exist and we cannot know the thing-in-itself. In Britain, the influence of Ludwig Wittgenstein (*Tractatus-Logico-Philosophicus*, 1921) blended with a somewhat related movement stemming from G. E. Moore and Bertrand Russell, Cambridge philosophers who broke with the dominant school of idealism beginning about 1900. Their roots were plainly in British empiricism; this was the spirit of Bacon, Locke, and Hume, marked by a tendency to avoid all metaphysical flights, concentrate on careful analysis of actual experience, break problems down into their smallest components, watch out for the loose use of terms, and construct no "systems." The early Wittgenstein joined forces with Russell's "logical atomism"; the later Wittgenstein's keen interest in the logical structure of language reenforced Moore's influence to open up marvelous horizons of subtle inquiry to a generation of "linguistic analysts" and "semanticists."

The basic postulate was that philosophical method must be "scientific." Science is not only clear, logical, rational, analytical, but also "verifiable by sense experience." The application of these criteria suggested that for philosophy there is no specific end or content; its function must be to help the sciences—which alone can provide knowledge, since empirical investigation is the only sort of knowledge. "The business of philosophy is not to establish a set of philosophical propositions but to make other propositions clear." To clarify the meaning of words and statements might seem a modest goal but it can be most useful. If science experiments and verifies, philosophy defines and clarifies. Many meaningless problems and much nonsense may be removed by the rigorous analysis of words. Indeed the method might be extended to other fields, such as politics or ethics, to clear up confusions by defining terms, thus locating the problems. The early Wittgenstein held that we may by analysis reduce reality to simple, atomic facts (the Viennese had learned from Russell's "logical atomism") and then frame statements which correspond to these facts.

Perhaps this revolution in philosophy may be best characterized by saying that philosophy ceased to be a "search for wisdom" or a quest for absolute answers, and became instead just the logic of science or the clarifier of scientific methods and concepts. To those who protested that philosophy was abdicating its chief function and leaving modern man, who never so needed help with his values, high and dry, the answer given by philosophers of the new dispensation was that unfortunately this cannot be the philosopher's function. These philosophers were "positivists," that is, they carried on the tradition, with a greater rigor and clarity, of regarding metaphysics (absolute being and value, transcendental reality) as not a true object of knowledge. We cannot really say anything rational about that. If someone, the poet or the seer, wants to speak to this question, let him; this is not the realm of clear logical thought which is the philosopher's. (Reproducing an argument among the nineteenth-century positivists, some of the new positivists said that statements beyond the realm of verifiable sense experience are merely beyond the competence of the philosopher, while others denied the right to talk about them at all.)

The most extreme statement of the new school came from the English philosopher A. J. Ayer in the 1930s. No problems exist, Ayer suggested, except the factual ones of science. All the others can be shown by linguistic analysis to be nonexistent, pseudo-problems. Most of the things philosophers and theologians and moralists had been worrying about through the centuries—God, freedom, spirit, purpose, morals, etc. —were complete wastes of time. They can be shown to be either wrong statements of the problem, or else purely personal or "emotive" projections of the feelings of the individual concerned, about which there can be no fruitful argument. Some of them we can reduce to empirical, testable statements, and these in principle can be solved by the scientist (empirical investigator). The rest must be dismissed as so much empty wind.

The shock effect of this position is evident. As someone has remarked, theologians who were accustomed to being told they were wrong found themselves speechless at being told they were not saying anything at all! Applied to morality, logical positivism might be extremely subversive. Statements of value not being empirically verifiable, they become mere expressions of preference. "I think adultery is wrong" is the same sort of statement as "I hate spinach" or "I dislike abstract art." (Though Hume had said something similar in the eighteenth century, he had been willing to fall back on custom and the consensus of mankind; twentieth-century skeptics had scant respect for either.) It will be recalled that some of the bolder Enlightenment writers had equated right with pleasure and wrong with pain, the only categorical moral imperative being to satisfy one's urges. Sober academic philosophers now indirectly endorsed their hedonism. Strictly speaking, they only pointed out that logical thought can supply no sanctions for behavior; we must look elsewhere for values of this sort. It is open to us to find them in religion or in social utility. At the same time, the frank equation of moral tastes with other kinds of personal taste might be construed as issuing an invitation to moral libertinism. Presumably I should choose my conduct in the same sort of way I choose my neckties—all a matter of personal taste. And if I try to defend one sort of conduct against another by any sort of rational argument, I am talking nonsense.

What was one to make of this breathtaking dismissal of entire realms of intellectual experience? It is now generally agreed that Ayer was much too dogmatic; indeed he has admitted it himself. Logical positivism or something similar has nevertheless remained, in a somewhat chastened form (and, recently, under increasing criticism), particularly in the British universities, as the only respectable kind of philosophy. It has scarcely prevailed at all in the Latin countries. Clearly it represents a severe retrenchment or cutting back, intellectually and culturally, in order to get the advantages of clarity and certainty.[6] Like Locke, these modern *philosophes* advise us to consider only what the mind is fitted for and forget all the rest. The method would seem to have great strengths and also the defects of its merits. It has clarified many questions but has resigned entirely in substantial areas of human experience where certainty is impossible but which nonetheless are urgently important to mankind. Human culture would never have arisen at all, we may well believe, if people had always been as fastidious as these philosopohers. An arid verbalism and a cloistered timidity mark their thought, some have felt. Moreover, it has been urged against them that their verification principle itself, their one test of truth, is an arbitrary, metaphysical assertion; how does one verify the verification principle?[7]

But "the absence of any dogma or jargon, any universal method, any claim to finality" together with the keenness and closeness of its thought has impressed other observers of English philosophy. In the 1920s and 1930s, logical positivism's astringency, skepticism, and almost nihilistic tendencies recommended it. It was in part a kind of nose-thumbing at all the old pomposities; it was a paring back, a getting down to brass tacks preparatory to rebuilding the world of knowledge from the ground up. And in this respect it bore some resemblance to such other phenomena as the prose of Ernest Hemingway. We have only to read the first sentence of Ayer's "manifesto," *Language, Truth and Logic* (1935) to sense this mood: "The traditional disputes of philosophers are, for the most part, as unwarranted as they are unfruitful."

The astringent and analytical spirit appeared also in English literary criticism. The magazine *Scrutiny*, edited by Oxford professor F. R.

---

[6]Its popularity in the universities (not least American ones) seems to relate closely to a principle of rationalization in large professional institutions. This sort of philosophy is not vague, can be precisely graded, is even tinged with the prestige of science.

[7]Wittgenstein's later philosophy, well known only after his death in the 1950s, was in some ways dramatically different from his earlier; it is much more skeptical since we do not know whether our language fits "reality" or not. See further below, p. 483.

Leavis, founded in the 1930s and published until 1953, encouraged what its title suggested, a meticulous line-by-line examination of poetry, in reaction against both the chatty sort of armchair talk about literature which had passed for criticism in Victorian times and against lack of clear literary standards. For somehow it was expected that close scrutiny would clarify standards. The scrutinizers thought of themselves as cutting away large husks of sentimentality with a keen razor of critical analysis, in order to get down to the solid core of real literary value. Like the analytic philosophers, they were to be accused of aridity and pedantry; a fairly strong reaction against them set in 1945. But they succeeded in introducing what seemed like a scientific expertness in the examination of the arts. Somehow this was bracing.

For science commanded great respect. Progress went on in numerous areas of science, though sometimes it seemed rather gloomy progress. It was at this time that genetics became a fashionable study. Psychology, in the universities, lay more under the influence of J. B. Watson, the behaviorist, and the Russian, Pavlov, than of the more speculative theories of Freud and Jung. Eschewing any attempt to analyze interior states of mind, as unsuitable for the scientific method, the behaviorists stuck to measurable observations of external behavior. This was an American school but for a time found considerable international favor. In its more dogmatic moods it was inclined to insist that human nature is determined by its environment in a mechanical sort of way, that life is made up of a series of conditioned reflexes, and that mind, as such, does not exist, there being only a pattern of electric reactions in brain tissue. Very positivist, even eighteenth-century.

"Scientific humanism" was a term much in use; what it meant, roughly, was the possibility of raising mankind to new heights by the use of science alone, with heavy overtones of hostility to traditional religion. But to many the march of science threatened dehumanization. In his *Brave New World Revisited* (1959), written 27 years after his famous depiction of what might be the fate of man in a few centuries when he had been totally organized in accordance with scientific techniques, Aldous Huxley noted the use of Pavlovian theories in the brainwashing techniques practiced by the Chinese Communists. His *Brave New World*, he felt, had all but come true in a mere quarter of a century. Freedom and individuality would be sacrificed to the demands of the machine, large-scale organization, and technological progress. In the years since 1920 there has always gone on a lively controversy between those who hail science and technology as the liberator and savior of man, and those who fear he is being enslaved and spiritually destroyed by these terrible servants. With the spectacular advances in science and technology of these years, the issue became an urgent one. To raise it at the most urgent of all levels, nuclear fission was achieved in 1938 (following the work of Mme. Curie and M. Joliot in 1934 in inducing radioactivity by bombarding certain atoms with neutrons) and would be developed into the atomic bomb during the war that lay just ahead.

Existentialism

The triumph of severely analytical, rational, scientific modes of philosophizing in England, Austria, the Scandinavian countries, soon in the United States (carried there directly by Rudolf Carnap and other Austrian refugees after 1938 as well as by British influences and offshoots of native pragmatism) was, strangely enough, completely reversed in much of the rest of continental Europe, where a highly nonrational sort of philosophy came into prominence in the 1930s.

In the epoch of the world wars European intellectual man lived in a state of shock, in a nightmare world, such as one finds metaphorically projected in the fantasies of Franz Kafka (*The Trial, The Castle*). An unlucky enough man might have watched the mass slaughter at Verdun, seen the bolshevik terror in Russia, observed the black-shirted and brown-shirted hysteria in Italy and Germany, the riots of starving workers during the great depression, fought in the Spanish Civil War, noted the appalling drift to world war again in the 1930s, and perhaps ended in a Nazi concentration camp, after having destroyed whole German or Japanese cities from the air. It was seemingly a world of terror and inhumanity, marked by the almost total breakdown of civilized processes and political rationality. On the other hand, he could have observed extraordinary wonders, too, not only scientific and technological but literary, philosophical, scholarly, suggesting a fund of creative energy in Western civilization that might yet save it. Evidently the chief problem was one of values: something to believe in that sophisticated modern man *could* believe in, something to serve as a directing principle for the aimless power of scientific technology, something to teach to the hundreds of millions of democratic citizens who, now "free," were slaves in their freedom for want of such values.

The serious concern for man as a being who must find values, amid the general wreckage of traditional ones, and act upon them in a nightmare world, is a theme that leads us to the group known roughly as existentialists. Born between the wars chiefly in the writings of the German or German-Swiss academic philosophers Martin Heidegger and Karl Jaspers, "existentialism" (Heidegger talked of his *Existenzphilosophie* while Jaspers used the term *Existentialismus*) did not become well known until just after World War II, when it leaped into international prominence largely owing to the brilliance of one of the outstanding writers and thinkers of modern times, Jean-Paul Sartre. Sartre, once a student of Heidegger's, has been novelist, playwright, editor, essayist, and political activist as well as philosopher (author of the long and difficult *Being and Nothingness*)—a combination of talents which, given the quantity and range of his writings and his role as moral and intellectual leader of a generation, makes him something of a modern Voltaire. Sartre fought in the French Resistance movement of World War II; postwar existentialism received the flavor of the bitter and lonely experiences men went through in this war, whether in the *maquis* or the concentration camps. His fellow Frenchman, the Algerian-born essayist and novelist Albert Camus, killed in an accident in 1960, joined Sartre in leadership of the "second lost generation" after 1945. With all gods really dead now, nothing to believe in, the existentialists quite remarkably turned to man himself to find new values.

Though the experiences of the war are often regarded as decisive in the shaping of existentialism, the fact is that Sartre's mind was formed in the '20s and '30s, and his bitter alienation as well as his ambivalent attachment to Marxism came out of that epoch. He studied philosophy under Heidegger and mastered a good deal of the formal existence philosophy, learning also from the pioneer phenomenologist, Edmund Husserl. But his was no merely academic personality, and he participated in the cultural atmosphere of the between-the-wars epoch. His first novel, published in 1938, set the tone for everything that followed: *Nausea*. It was Sartre's special contribution to take Heidegger and Husserl off the academic shelf and give them sharp relevance to contemporary life: a metaphysics that bore directly on the most immediate life situations of living people. In Sartre's hands it became bitterly pessimistic yet tinged with just a dash of desperate, disabused hope.

Existentialism drew on earlier ideas and indeed one of its attractive features was its absorption of much of the gropings of European thought and expression since 1800, or perhaps even earlier, into one structure; there is something here of a *philosophia perennia*. In one sense it is the ultimate Nietzscheanism. Sartre has written that "Existentialism is . . . an attempt to draw all the consequences from a consistent atheist position." "Dostoyevsky has written that if God did not exist, all would be permitted. That is Existentialism's starting point." If we really grasp the meaning of modern godless man's plight, we are at first reduced to nausea and despair. We must pass through the awful sense of depression that accompanies a real insight into man's condition. He is alone, for he cannot really communicate with others. He finds himself in a world to which he is utterly alien and which has no purpose or meaning. Society, too, is at work trying to depersonalize him, make him into a cog in the machine, make him play a role that crushes his individuality. But on the far side of this abyss (Existentialism is a "philosophy of the abyss," Emmanuel Mounier has said) there is one message of salvation, one ground of hope: man, the human consciousness, is after all left. He is somehow here, able to react; even in feeling despair, he shows the possibility of bestowing value on the meaningless world. As Camus noted, the world is absurd; but then it could not be absurd unless men judged it to be so; this feeling of the absurd itself is the start of philosophy. We are reminded of Pascal's "thinking reed."

Man is unique in the world; his own peculiar kind of being is radically different from all others. Heidegger, who called himself an ontologist, was preoccupied with the nature of Being—of what it means, in general, for anything to exist, and in particular what human existence is. For man, "Existence is prior to essence" Kierkegaard had already asserted. This striking idea found reenforcement in the naturalistic outlook of Darwin, as well as in the psychology of Freud. Reason does not precede and determine man, but vice versa; man exists, and his will to exist leads him to invent "rational" systems, which are thus not ultimate but are a product of his drives, instincts, fears, hopes. It is of the nature of the human being to be unique, a concrete particular not to be understood by membership in a class or group, like other objects. True, insofar as a man is flesh he is the usual kind of being; moreover society is always at work trying to make him into a stereotyped object. But the human personality *ought* to be unique and free, not directed from outside or resembling an object. Heidegger's distinction between "authentic" personal existence and "being-in-the-world" became in Sartre's hands a distinction between being *en-soi* and *pour-soi*—in-itself and for-itself.

Being-in-itself is the mode of being for all things except man—for physical objects, anything that has objective identity. My own past, insofar as I look at it as something vanished and dead, is being of this sort, which is the normal kind of being. It is subject to essences, to generalizing; it is, we might say, the data of science; it is like Bergson's realm of the scientific intellect; it can be conceptualized. But human consciousness, as it exists in our minds every moment, *now*, is a radically different kind of thing—*pour-soi*, in Sartre's terminology. It is actually not being at all, but a kind of "hole in being"—a nothingness, in a sense. This striking analysis of human consciousness owed a great deal to the Viennese philosopher Edmund Husserl, a teacher of Heidegger's, who in turn got much of it from one of Hegel's lesser known writings, *The Phenomenology of Mind*. Thus there is an undercurrent of thought here reaching back to the earlier nineteenth century.

Critics of Sartre (by no means lacking) have reproached him among other things for calling "nothing" what is patently something;

but Sartre's general meaning seems reasonably clear. Our consciousness requires objects to respond to, we cannot have consciousness of consciousness. And our immediate conscious experience is not like anything we can think of; it is just conscious experience. If Sartre's analysis of this elusive substance is sometimes a bit fuzzy, it is a remarkably stimulating effort to examine what seldom has been examined. It provided him with the basis for both his pessimism and his optimism. There can be no God, for our consciousness-being submits to no generalization, there can be no being-in-general. And there cannot really be any happy relationships between people. The other person is an object to me, and I to him. We try to reject the other person's reducing us to an object. The realm of interpersonal relationships is to Sartre condemned to frustration, at best. "Hell is other people," as one of the most famous of his plays points out. The individual could only be happy if he could structure the entire universe to fit his ego, and this of course is impossible.

Yet the nature of this protean nothingness, the *pour-soi* or human consciousness, is to be free, and to create itself. Defined only by his acts, man is free to assign values, to give his life meaning. Sartre and the existentialists do not undertake to tell men what to believe in, how to act, for each of us must decide that himself; to be other-directed is to be unauthentic, to be guilty of "bad faith." Like the positivists, so different from them in many ways, the existentialists refuse to provide us with creeds and dogmas. Their function is to point out the importance of making choices, and the need to make them with utter integrity. One must win his way to authentic personal existence by refusing to be absorbed "in the world" or made an object. Man is an ambiguous creature; condemned to freedom, he has to act, but there is really no creed to tell him how to act (if he believes so, he is guilty of bad faith), and so he is anxious and forlorn. When he surmounts the crisis of feeling the absurdity of his situation, he acts in full understanding of his autonomy as free creator of his own values.

Perhaps the elaborate and, to some people, somewhat mystifying Sartrean ontology is not so important as the ethical message, though it does provide an impressive foundation. The essential existentialism is the message to be authentic, to avoid bad faith, to refuse to be depersonalized. "Existentialism is the struggle to discover the human person in a depersonalized age," William Barrett has written. How can we be authentic individuals? Existentialists give us a few hints. We should reject intellectualism, or merely speculative knowledge; this does not speak to the human condition. We must presumably pass through the crisis wherein we see that there is no God, no meaning in the universe as such, nothing or no one to help us. Then we realize the uniqueness and wonder of man the creator of values. "This world is without importance, and whoever recognizes this fact wins his freedom," one of Camus's characters observes. When we realize that with each choice and act we not only make ourselves but give the whole universe what value it has, we have discovered the dignity of being human. Then we must be "committed," we must believe nothing that is merely idle opinion—what we believe must be for life. Like Nietzsche we must grasp it with our whole heart and soul not merely with the "cold prying tentacles" of conceptual thought.

Perhaps existentialism may be understood by comparing its subjectivism to that of Kant. The Kantian revolution placed the focus of attention on the subject, the mind, rather than the object of knowledge, thus beginning something basic to modern philosophy. But Kant's subjectivism confined itself to the realm of logic, supposedly built into the human mind; it remained rational, merely transferring rationalism from outside to inside, as it were. Existentialism and phenomenology go still further, behind rational thought, which is seen as the product of deeper experience, to a strange world of myth and symbol hardly yet explored. Kant's was a rational subjectivism, theirs an irrational, better infrarational. The rational is *not* the real, as Hegel taught. Existence is not rational, but even absurd; it simply is, and we cannot possibly reason about it—being it ourselves. Only some superhuman being could do that. Existence is a brute fact. We come to realize that men have invented reason to hide their fears or rationalize their desires. Baffled by this knowledge, we must nevertheless choose and act. As Yeats wrote, "We cannot know the truth but we can live it."

Religious Existentialism

We shall return to existentialism, for it persisted and indeed came into its own after 1945 as a major theme of contemporary thought. But at this point we should introduce the companion and variant forms of Sartre's atheistic existentialism, whose parents were Nietzsche and Heidegger. This religious form went back chiefly to the obscure nineteenth-century Danish Lutheran, Kierkegaard, a major rediscovery of the twentieth century (translated into German, 1909, Italian 1910, French 1929, English 1938). "The Kierkegaard renaissance is one of the strangest phenomena of our times," F. Heinemann remarks. But the time had at last become ripe for the "lonely thinker" of 1813–1855, dead at 42, a poor unknown.

Soren Kierkegaard left little mark on his own time (outside his native Copenhagen) and was to remain largely unknown until he became a discovery of the existentialists. He was a savage critic of Hegel's deterministic system, which makes man an automaton. (In this he owed something to the views of F. W. Schelling in his last years.) Such objective thinking—reasoning—destroys the individual, making him a part of the collective. Kierkegaard resisted this with all his being. In proclaiming that "existence is prior to essence," he asserted the primacy of the individual person over any abstraction. He complained that Hegel's system was not "for life" and demanded a faith that was. (Careful students of Hegel complain quite properly that this is unfair, for at times Hegel himself could be quite "existential." Still, the contours of his main system as widely understood doubtless conform to Kierkegaard's indictment.) This was the same thirst for absolute commitment, for a creed related to one's life situation, that we find in Nietzsche, who never read or heard of the obscure Danish parson. But Kierkegaard, unlike Nietzsche, was deeply religious, though his intense personalism caused him to attack the Church as a menace to real faith. Through anxiety and despair the individual must make his own way to God. The Dane's intense suspicion of conformism, the crowd, institutions, phony external substitutes for inward experience, remind us somewhat of certain of the esthetes, and it may be significant that he was a contemporary of Baudelaire (who in the end turned to religion himself).[8] But Kierkegaard, a pastor of the Lutheran Church, also pointed back to the great founder of his church, who demanded a faith based on personal experience and denounced sacramentalism along with the moralism of salvation via good works.

This intense stress on the inner life of the spirit, with its fierce assault on both intellectualized, philosophical Christianity *and* on liberal, moralistic Christianity, was scarcely suitable to nineteenth-century religion, which was going in exactly these latter directions. The "return to orthodoxy" in Continental theology after World War I, previously discussed, owed something to Kierkegaard. Nicholas Berdyaev, a Russian of the Orthodox Church; Martin Buber, a Jew; Jacques Maritain, French Catholic; and the Protestants, Lutheran and Calvinist respectively, Karl Barth and Emil Brunner were influenced by Kierkegaard though they might disagree with him in particulars (see Martin Buber's well-known essay on Kierkegaard in which, from the viewpoint of Jewish Hasidic communalism, he reproached the Dane for being too antisocial, while testifying to the importance of *Fear and Trembling* in his own development).

Buber's *I and Thou* appeared in 1923; Berdyaev, who had known

---

[8]According to Kierkegaard, spiritual development leads one through the aesthetic stage to the moral and finally to the religious. Only in immaturity is one content with mere literary form. But one infers that Kierkegaard had passed through such a phase.

exile under the Tsar and had drifted close to Marxism before the war, hailed the Revolution of 1917 but found himself arrested and exiled by Lenin's dictatorship in 1920, after which he taught, lectured, and wrote in Berlin and Paris. Buber was born in 1878, Berdyaev in 1874, Maritain in 1882; all these men grew to intellectual maturity before World War I but then had their lives sharply altered by that event. They became the greatest of modern theologians.

Christian existentialism touches closely on these imposing figures who have attempted to revive a somnolent religion in refutation of Nietzsche's and Sartre's claim that "God is dead." Maritain has tried to reconcile his neo-Thomism with existentialism. The "crisis theology" of Barth comes close to it, as does the I-Thou experience described by Buber (a distinction between a person's relation to other persons and to things, with God as the "eternal Thou" to be encountered in a dialogue). Paul Tillich and Gabriel Marcel, from the Protestant and Catholic camps respectively, are more explicitly existentialists.[9] The trend was decidedly away from a rationalized religion, a polite and moral one, an easy and conventional one. In dread and anxiety the soul realizes its dire predicament and then makes the "leap" to faith. The individual chooses and wins his existence by reaching out to a transcendent Being who is not "understood" but is encountered, addressed.

Certainly not all modern theologians have accepted existential ideas, but it is interesting and significant that there has been an earnest revival of theology, centering on such doctrines as Original Sin, the nature of Christ, and atonement. Relegated at one time virtually to the scrapheap of vanished dogmas, these issues have once again become important in an era when human pride leading to self-destruction appeared as historic fact. Christian or Judaic thinkers pointed out that we do not need to desert our basic Western traditions and embrace an anarchy of strange beliefs; it is possible to come to terms with the modern experience through the medium of an enlarged but basically traditional religious outlook. The Bible in the words of Rudolf Bultmann has been "de-mythologized"; the assaults of the Higher Criticism have become irrelevant, for it is not the literal truth but the existential truth of this spiritual record that matters. Without God, or some transcendent source of value, man is condemned to destroy himself. He can sit in the wasteland and wait for the end or he can go forth to seek through the mists the God he has lost.

Modern Christian thinkers have tended to see in the totalitarian regimes and world wars of the unhappy twentieth century a conse-

---

[9]Practically all those who use the existentialist approach wish to deny that they are "existential*ists*." Tillich has said that while "the existential element has a definite place" in his thought, "I would not call myself an existentialist."

quence of the despiritualization of man through de-Christianization. Liberalism, capitalism, and materialistic socialism, reducing men to mere factors of production and atomizing them, prepared the way for the terrible explosions of Nazism and Communism, which these thinkers see not as products of the peculiar evil or misfortune of individual nations but as general cultural phenomena of modern Western civilization. ("Germany is not the sin of Europe, but of the entire modern world, the sin of a world so profoundly corrupted that peoples corrupt each other; and the last service rendered by the German people to the old civilization it formerly honored is to show to each nation, as in a monstrous mirror, the image of that which it perhaps is today without knowing it, and which it will surely be tomorrow." So wrote Georges Bernanos shortly after World War II.) Liberty and civilization depend on religious belief. The heroism of members of the Christian churches, Protestant and Catholic alike, in suffering martyrdom at the hands of Hitler's pagan totalitarianism advanced the prestige of religion in Europe; and subsequently the confrontation between the West and Soviet Russian Communism encouraged a definition of the former's position as historically Christian.

Existentialism has been introduced at this point because it was definitely born between the wars, when Martin Heidegger and Karl Jaspers were at work, and Heidegger's student Sartre began his literary career; when the revival of religion with overtones of an existentialist nature took place, through Buber, Maritain, Barth, Niebuhr, Berdyaev. But during that feverish decade of political alarums and excursions, the 1930s, which began with the economic hammer blows of the Great Depression, moved on to Hitler's Nazi conquest of Germany, then to the war brought on by Nazi hatreds and aggressiveness, with Stalin's Five Year Plans and purge trials a part of the picture, little else gained much attention except these economic and political questions. Then came a war more dreadful than the last one, and more inhumane: the terror bombing of European cities by the Allies, the murder of the Jews by the Nazis, incredible and untold suffering, great and sometimes unrecorded heroism. This traumatic experience helped make relevant the insights of the existentialists, and after the war this "philosophy" achieved large popularity.

Politically, existentialism was somewhat ambiguous. It stressed action and commitment, and was defiantly hostile to the kind of society that existed in the West. In its Sartrean form it was bitter, alienated, filled with scorn for the whole quality of contemporary life, inclined to consort with only a small minority of outcasts and rebels. Thus it could blend easily with revolutions of the Left—or with revolutions of the

Right. Its founder, the celebrated philosopher Martin Heidegger, hailed Hitler. Sartre, though, was for many years a Communist sympathizer. Even the religious existentials were, as Reinhold Niebuhr has written of Paul Tillich, "affected by Marxist catastrophism" and in World War II some of them fought cheek by jowl with Communists in the anti-Nazi underground, giving rise to a certain sympathy that endured in the post-war years. On the other hand, existentialism in its very nature was hostile to the dogmatic scientific materialism of the Marxists, to their determinism, and their system-making. To adopt such a dogma is a form of bad faith to existentialists, whose extreme individualism rendered them utterly unfit in any case for the discipline of the Party. Sartre's struggles with communism, which he alternately defended and assailed, constitute a large chapter in the story of his intellectual career. After 1945 Albert Camus and Maurice Merleau-Ponty emphatically rejected communism, quarreling with Sartre, and existentialism became connected with the political quietism and personalism of that decade. The answer does not lie in political nostrums, but in personal development. Existentialism has a conservative side. Believing as it does only in integrity, in behaving according to one's real nature, it is necessarily protean, supporting no one creed or position. All that the existentialist ethic really tells us— perhaps not so new an admonition—is to be sincere, true to our own selves, and not afraid to act on our convictions.

By its own standards there cannot really be an "existential*ism*," the whole idea is to escape *isms*. Each man's truth will presumably be different. In fact, the major figures of the school have disagreed with each other on various questions. Christian existentialists are of course in basic disagreement with the atheistic ones. To Gabriel Marcel, Sartre is "a degenerate disciple of Heidegger," and he disapproved of Heidegger! Sartre has expressed much of himself in plays, Camus in novels; perhaps existentialists have made their most striking contribution in the examination of various concrete life problems. Sartre on the nature of love, and why man is condemned to frustrate himself, a "useless passion"; Simone de Beauvoir on what it means to be a woman; Camus on man as rebel. These and other products of French existentialism are classics of our time. Such plays as Sartre's *No Exit* seem clearly destined to be classed among the serious literary statements of our age. And possibly the most fruitful application of existentialism appeared in the realm of psychiatry, where such men as Binswanger, Boss, and Laing brilliantly developed its possibilities and threatened, in more recent years, to supersede Freudian and Jungian techniques.[10]

Seen in this light, existentialism is an aspect of the modern move-

[10]Further on existentialism and Phenomenology, see pp. 479–83.

ment in literature and psychology, going back to Baudelaire and to James and Freud, with their keen interest in the inner world of man. Existentialism has been defined as "an attempt at philosophizing from the standpoint of the actor instead of, as has been customary, from that of the spectator" (E. L. Allen). It is a dimension of what Jung called "the undiscovered self." Subjectivism is the theme of the contemporary West. And this is why the intellectuals of the 1930s, who tried to be communists, could not do so.

14

Contemporary Ideas in the West: Trends in Thought Since 1945

There are many reasons for thinking that European man is raising his tents from off that modern soil where he has camped for three hundred years and is beginning a new exodus toward another historical ambit, another way of life.

JOSE ORTEGA Y GASSET

Man's existence is now nearing an absolute decision.

ROMANO GUARDINI

Europe After the War

As Europeans awoke from the nightmare of World War II to stand amid the ruins which assured them that the horrors had really happened, they were understandably tempted to reject all the old and start anew. If World War I damaged the respect felt for ancestral tradition, the second such cataclysm twenty years later seemed likely to destroy it. Gabriel Marcel, to quote but one example, has written of "the more than physical horror and anxiety I experienced in walking among the ruins of inner Vienna in 1946, or more recently in Caen, Rouen or Würzburg." Almost any European city between the Channel and Dnieper could have qualified, though German cities suffered most, as a result of the incessant allied aerial bombings. He went on to note that for many the corollary was a total rejection of the European heritage (*The Decline of Wisdom*, 1954). These physical ruins were manifestations of the moral ruins displayed in Hitler's ghastly extermination of the Jews; the gas chambers of Auschwitz and Dachau brooded over a European atmosphere heavy with the smell of death.

Apart from the sheer physical and moral damages of the war, there had occurred what one historian phrased in the title of a book, *The Passing of the European Age*, or as the distinguished German, Alfred Weber, brother of Max, titled a little book of 1946, *Abschied von der Bisherigen Geschichte*, translated as *Farewell to European History*. In 1946 H. G. Wells, who had preached progress toward utopia for half a century, wrote *Mind at the End of Its Tether*, in which he decided that the end of civilization, of man, and perhaps of life on earth was rapidly approaching. A shattered and exhausted Europe was occupied by American and Russian soldiers, both of whom most Europeans looked upon as barbarians from outside. Before long it became evident that the Russians, at least, intended no liberation but a new enslavement to Communism. The Americans were to be looked upon as allies against the menace of Soviet power, and many Europeans were glad to clasp hands with the democratic land of the New World. The fact remains that quite a few bearers of the European culture continued to regard "Russia and America as the same," basically; as Martin Heidegger put it, "the same dreary technological frenzy, the same unrestricted organization of the average man" (*An Introduction to Metaphysics*, 1959).

For those who had expected brighter days with the Allied victory over Hitlerism, the coming of peace and the establishment of the United Nations, the years just after 1945 were deeply disappointing. As economic ruin engulfed Europe, a quarrel between the Soviet Union and the Western powers threatened a renewal of war—another war in the apparently self-perpetuating cycle of "wars in chain reaction," as a French writer (Raymond Aron) titled a book. The war had ended with the ghastly explosion of the atomic bomb over Hiroshima, wiping out an entire city; by 1954 far more destructive nuclear weapons carried by intercontinental missiles were available to guarantee that the seemingly inevitable next war would put a finish to much of the world. Pending this last apocalypse, the world was far from at peace, for there was war in Korea (1950–1953), in Indochina, in Palestine, and elsewhere.

Whoever controlled Europe, Europe and the West no longer held the same monopoly of world power, prestige, and influence as formerly. The world had shrunk, and yet enlarged, as Weber noted: smaller because of modern transportation and communications, it was filled with all kinds of peoples formerly almost beyond the fringes of Europe's consciousness. For the peoples of Asia and Africa, too, in addition to the powerful United States of America, had arrived on the scene. They had gained or were about to gain their independence, they were "out of control" and demanding a place in the sun, and though as yet not powerful states they could no longer be ignored. Loosely united in attitudes shaped by their former vassalage to the West, they were a "third force" in world politics, of vast significance. Suddenly Europe became aware that she was after all a fairly diminutive peninsula on the huge land mass of Eurasia, and that what happened in Iran or the Indies, or even in the Congo and Algeria, was of some consequence. This was a revolution in geopolitical perspectives that announced a new epoch of world history, perhaps the first one since the fall of the ancient Oriental empires.

The other radically new perspective was a technological-scientific one, signalled by the explosion over Hiroshima. What the Atomic Age meant no one could foresee—whether the passing of the human race or its ascent to incomparably higher levels of material civilization. For the time being, it meant assuredly that military power rested overwhelmingly with those who held the capacity to make and deliver nuclear weapons, which included only the Americans and, soon, the Russians. Apart from this confirmation of weakness and dependency, atomic energy drastically transformed basic thought processes about the material world, driving home to all some of the implications of the new physics heretofore appreciated by only a few, such as the disappearance of matter in a sea of waves and electrical energy, the different laws of motion inside the atom, etc. After Hiroshima, no one could regard these things as just interesting theories.

On the other hand, there were countervailing tendencies working against the picture of bleak despair. The terrible war had at least purged Europe of much: of Nazism, anti-Semitism, and even, to a degree, of nationalism. The need to rehabilitate a culture drew men together. Survivors of the terrible experiences of the war, whether living under the nightly threat of terror and death from the skies, or in the hell of a Nazi concentration camp, or as fighters in the "underground," often testified to the strange kind of value in such experiences. Life was given more value by being precarious; simple objects acquired value. Such situations were at least a cure for empty complacency, a reminder of the tragic and serious nature of life, a precipitant of elemental human values. To come up against and face the absolute worst is a kind of purgative; this is the message that emerges from much of the postwar European writing.

Standing together against the Soviet threat, and then building a new Europe from the ashes, a Europe that might at last have learned to unify itself in a federation—these were goals that gave the common life some meaning. Europe began to make a spectacular economic recovery which swept on through much of the 1950s and brought to birth a unified European economy, the Common Market that resulted from the Rome Treaty of 1957 and was expected to lead on by stages to full political federation. Hope returned with the development of the NATO alliance between North America and the states of Western Europe, and with the avoidance of major war. Though life as always was filled with problems, many Europeans saw the light breaking through in the second decade after the war, with prospects even of Europe again assuming its place in world affairs—no "passing of the European age," despite the power of Russia and of America, and the arrival of the non-European peoples. The change between 1945 and 1963 was summed up by Raymond Aron: "In 1945, western Europe was a mass of ruins; today it is one of the most prosperous regions of the world."

Assessment of the very recent past is always a risky business, and what follows in this chapter must be offered with less confidence that what is selected for emphasis represents the enduringly significant themes of this period as posterity will see them. Nevertheless, it is most interesting and important to try to take stock of man's condition today as reflected in his philosophy, literature, his religious, social, and political thought—his world of ideas.

The End of Ideology

Unquestionably the postwar climate of opinion was overshadowed by the sense of catastrophe and disaster, because of war, power, and the bomb. J. M. Cohen, in the concluding statements to his book *Poetry of This Age*, remarked that "events have dwarfed all possible comment" on public affairs and driven the poet to purely personal statement. "All that he can hope to rescue from an ever-imminent disaster will be a moment of love or insight or a clear conception of truth, which, having once been, can never be destroyed." It is possible to wonder whether this contingency of life is really so new. Every man's life is contingent every moment and always has been. Apart from that, earlier generations lived under the threat of starvation, disease, and other afflictions from which many moderns are by comparison almost free. In terms of the totality of human life, the modern world with its massive and longer-lived populations would be far ahead of any previous age even if it experienced a thermonuclear war. (The greatest world problem, according to many, is today *over*population.) Nevertheless, the reminder of man's contingent being, his constant confrontation with death, the possibility of centuries of progress being extinguished in a few moments (which might even be the result of an accident)—all this undoubtedly further undermined nineteenth-century beliefs in a secular utopia or the progress of humanity toward perfection. The "boundary situations" about which existentialists talk seem all too real in the world as it exists today.

Thus the turn to "personal statement," to an insight of the moment and away from the ideologies or total faiths. The retreat from ideologies was a prominent theme after World War II. The political activism characteristic of the 1930s fell to low ebb in the 1950s. "Outside the Communists," a French writer observed in 1952, "French youth is almost totally disinterested in politics today." The same could be said for British youth, German youth, Italian youth. Heroic attitudes struck during the war, in the Resistance for example, had in the main turned sour. The Communist movement continued to attract a few, but not many; the behavior of Stalin and his cohorts had destroyed it. There was a profound reaction against Soviet Russia under the Stalinist dictatorship, a regime which sent millions of people to prison and labor camps without fair trial, showed itself willing to employ every sort of iniquity in the crudest "means justified by the end" credo, and threw international relations into chaos, while also destroying creative Russian thought and literature by a straitjacket of political control. In the sight of Western intellectuals, who had once seen it through a veil of illusions, the last of these was torn from the ugly face of Soviet Communism by the enslavement through military force of the peoples of eastern Europe. And it was seen that this moral bankruptcy was implicit in revolutionary Marxism, because of its deification of the historical process, its fanatical faith in a future utopia held to justify any amount of death and crime now.

To some extent, too, the "end of ideology" has been facilitated by the failure of ideology in the Soviet Union itself. In Stalin's era the high priests of the Communist Party, charged with the zeal and dogmatism of the Marxist faith, made decisions. In the Khrushchev era (1953–1964) and afterward this power tended to gravitate toward bureaucracy, a process summed up by one authority as a "transition from charismatics to mathematics." In general, the element of breathless, apocalyptic exaltation in Russia that was a legacy of the great Revolution and was perpetuated in the Party, tended steadily to wane as rationalization and normality took over. Not even the charisma of Lenin is safe from the corrosions of time and life. If Stalinization debased it, the post-Stalin era completely destroyed it; the New Jerusalem of Marx and Lenin became just another managerial and bureaucratic society.

For some, the moment of final disenchantment was 1948, when the suicide of Jan Masaryk marked the end of Czechoslovak independence; for others, it was 1956, when, even after the death of Stalin and the disclosure of some of the enormities committed during his reign by the new bolshevik leaders themselves, Russian tanks poured into Budapest to put down a Hungarian uprising against Russian rule. The blood shed in the streets of Prague in 1968 was only a dismal postscript to the story of Soviet oppression in all the countries of eastern Europe, most especially in those countries for whose liberation from Nazi power the war had originally been fought—Poland and Czechoslovakia. Meanwhile in Russia itself those who had predicted a humanizing and liberalizing trend following the demise of the terrible Georgian were proved wrong by the subsequent treatment of critics of the Soviet regime. A brilliant and courageous group of young writers who claimed a right to do something else than parrot the official government line was imprisoned or sent to mental institutions. The story of the trial of Daniel and Sinyavsky, and the proscribed writings of Solzhenitsyn and others, became known in the West. At the same time exhaustive research by Western scholars, exemplified in Robert Conquest's *The Great Terror*, stripped the last veils of illusion from the picture of a benevolent Soviet Union, revealing an inhumanity that surpassed even Hitler's. The fiftieth anniversary of the Revolution in 1967 provided an opportunity for reappraisal, and it is significant that even those from the Left were overwhelmingly unfavorable. A bureaucratic society with a bourgeois culture and a reactionary foreign policy, not altogether converted from its nasty habit of killing off anyone who dissented in the slightest from a mindless orthodoxy—Russia was Orwell's nightmare of *1984* come true.

When in the 1960s a more radical political mood returned, it found world Communism divided as never before; one might choose to follow the Chinese brand, more righly emotional and aggressively ideological, or the Cuban brand, none of them in agreement with the others. Communist parties in the West were released from rigidity and freer to develop in different directions. But this meant an end to the one-time god, now fragmented in a host of minor deities, and in fact the new leftists of the '60s were gloriously anarchic, quite undisciplined, wholly unlike the old Communists, though some of them might pay passing respects to Castro or Mao or Ho Chi Minh simply because they were enemies of the West. It was a highly existentialized, extremely unorthodox Marxism that inspired these younger rebels, grown up since the '30s and no longer knowing its idols. We will postpone that story for a moment. The '50s was by and large a conservative decade, and even its despair was quiet. If Marxism was generally rejected, any other fervent sort of political mystique was equally suspect. There was little enthusiasm for democracy—two cheers for it, as E. M. Forster wrote, but not three; it is the worst of all forms of government except for all the others, as Winston Churchill had put it; one accepted it as the elimination of ideologies, not as an ideology. In France, the Fourth Republic set up immediately after the liberation of 1944–1945 was more democràtic than the Third had been, but gave way in 1958 to the considerably less democratic (or at least less parliamentary) Fifth, headed by national leader Charles de Gaulle, hero of the war. The Gaullist state was in some ways progressive, for it aimed at modernizing France technologically. But it proposed to do this chiefly by a Saint-Simonian expertise of government administrators, bypassing the old game of party politics and operating beyond the old ideologies.

Something similar happened in Britain, in that the Labour party, elected to office in 1945 on a tide of socialist idealism, was voted out in 1951 in an atmosphere of considerable disenchantment with its policies. It tended thereafter to become much less ideological. The Conservative party held office from 1951 to 1964. In place of total solutions, political theorists suggested piecemeal solutions (Karl Popper). "Rationalism in politics" is a snare (M. Oakeshott); the art of politics is an adjustment of differences in pragmatic ways. After experiencing all those "cruel or fierce political ideologies [which] have played havoc with human welfare," wrote famed British historian L. B. Namier, the mature political community learns to do without them altogether. Namier gave his approval to the condition described with some degree of alarm by philosopher Stuart Hampshire: "There is a tired lull in English politics, and argument on general principles has largely died. . . . Both political parties are now in this sense conservative, tied to day-to-day expedients." Political writing took the form of close analysis of actual political behavior (such as voting), which often left few romantic illusions about the rationality and responsibility of "the people," or ordinary citizens. Analyses in any wider sense were apt to bypass ideology, too. Bertrand de Jouvenel, writing *On Power* (*Du Pouvoir*), found the most significant aspect of political evolution to lie not in the forms of government, aristocratic or democratic, but in the steady growth of the apparatus of coercion, regardless of forms—the growth of Power.

Similarly in economic thought, argument and analysis were likely to transcend the old issues between capitalism and socialism. For example the discussion of economic growth, carried on in such books as those of W. Arthur Lewis, Colin Clark (*The Conditions of Economic Progress*), and W. W. Rostow, who subtitled his *Stages of Economic Growth* "a non-communist manifesto," noted among other things that ownership of property is not as such a vital factor. Neither David Ricardo nor Karl Marx is very relevant to twentieth-century economic problems, whether they are those of the "affluent societies" of the Western democracies or the youthful near-primitive economics of new African and Asian nations trying to find a short cut to affluence. Even in the Soviet Union, realism began to prevail over Marxian dogma: in the future it seemed likely to do so more and more.[1]

The socialist parties that survived changed their outlook consider-

---

[1] In order to make the Soviet system of state-planned socialism work, an illegal "shadow economy" of private enterprise grew up, comprising perhaps as much as 25 percent of the economy, and winked at most of the time by the authorities. And Soviet policy seemed to be turning in the direction of more decentralization and scope for managerial initiative.

ably; while the German Social Democrats had almost ceased to be recognizably socialist at all, British Labourites quietly abandoned nationalization of industry and a planned economy, in their earlier dogmatic forms, as panaceas for the evils of capitalism. Their experience in the 1945–1951 period of power helped move the British socialists away from these dogmas: for (as Labour leader Hugh Gaitskell himself pointed out) state ownership did not seem to make any significant difference in the condition of the workers, nor did it solve the economic problems with which Britain was faced. Thinking hard, the intellectuals of Labour struggled to find a new rationale for the party, with not much agreement and often some strange conclusions. Labour theorist W. Arthur Lewis, for example, appeared to opt for a more vigorous kind of entrepreneur capitalism—a program that would have appealed more to Nassau Senior than to Karl Marx, one imagines. Increasingly, the Socialist party became as flexible and opportunistic as its rival, the Conservatives; less ideological and more "practical," it simply found *ad hoc* answers to particular problems. It was a participant in the game of democratic politics, the stakes of which were political power; the means to power, wooing a diverse and changeable electorate.

The study of power was an outstanding feature of recent political and social thought. "We have all become intensely aware of power as the major phenomenon in all societies," Raymond Aron wrote. In addition to Jouvenel's brilliant book, the works of the Heidelberg sociologist A. Rüstow, writing in the shadow of Max Weber, may be instanced among the general theoretical studies. The theme comes through in any number of more specific studies of foreign policy and international relations.[2] George Orwell's *1984* gave expression to the frightening possibilities of power in the modern state to enslave its citizenry. This popular fantasy-satire described a condition in which the government disseminates all knowledge. Technology enables the state to control everything, even to read thoughts; "Big Brother" is everywhere. Thought control has become accomplished so thoroughly that men have ceased to think, they have been brainwashed into automatons by their government. This fear for liberty under the conditions of modern life has been a pervasive theme. Here it may be noted that it runs counter to prewar progressivism in that the latter whether Marxist or Keynesian tended to be statist. The new political thought whether of Left or Right has shown a greater mistrust of the power of the state, whoever may be in charge of the state. It has returned to Lord Acton's motto that all power tends to corrupt and absolute power corrupts absolutely.

[2]See also the studies of "power elites" within nations by such sociologists as Theodore Geiger and C. Wright Mills, or such historians as Sir Lewis Namier and his disciples (a very important school in England) or, in France, Jean Lhomme (*La grande bourgeoisie au pouvoir*).

"The mighty invasion of government into economic life," it has been often noted, constitutes "one of the most fundamental contrasts between the twentieth century and the nineteenth." The depression of the 1930s frightened men into accepting large measures of government regulation, a trend aided by the new economic theories of Keynes, while World War II brought total war and with it, of necessity, total organization under government control. It is obvious that modern industrial society is too complex and specialized to be run by the laissez-faire rules of the nineteenth century. Since 1945, a continuing vast military defense program and a "space" program of gigantic dimensions have meant an expanding role of government in most countries. This increasing statism, while ardently defended by a variety of collectivists, including neoliberals as well as socialists, aroused protests against it in the name of the sovereign individual, of spiritual autonomy, and of esthetic and moral values opposed to the reign of bureaucracy and the rule of the machine. Orwell's *1984* may be regarded as representative of such protests. (See also Huxley's *Brave New World Revisited*.[3] And, indeed, students of "dystopias" such as Chad Walsh and Judith Shklar noted the appearance in recent times of a whole category of such literature, contrasting with the utopias of the nineteenth century. (One of the first, which influenced Orwell, came from a disillusioned Russian Communist as early as 1920 —see Yevgeny Zamyatin's *We*.) Utopia has turned into nightmare.

The Popularity of Existentialism

Utopianism, based on optimistic views of human nature, became most unfashionable. A quotation from the distinguished American theologian Reinhold Niebuhr may suffice: "No cumulation of contradictory evidence seems to disturb modern man's good opinion of himself. He considers himself the victim of corrupting institutions, which he is about to destroy or reconstruct, or of the confusion and ignorance which an adequate education is about to overcome. Yet he continues to regard himself as essentially harmless and virtuous." Against this Enlightenment outlook Niebuhr and other contemporaries reacted with ferocity. "It is necessary not to believe in human nature." Carried on by such internationally famous men as Paul Tillich and Rudolf Bultmann, the German neo-Protestant message that originated with Barth and Brunner continued to attract attention. Existentialists of all varieties told the in-

---

[3]In his acute book *The Liberal Mind* (1963), Kenneth Minogue pointed out that liberalism suffers from, among other things, the contradiction of wishing both to enlarge the individual's freedom by diminishing state action and to promote his welfare by increasing state action. Basically individualist, the liberal seeks to harness the state to serve individual purposes, yet finds himself sanctioning an ever-growing network of statist restrictions on personal liberty.

dividual that he is responsible for his own being, cannot put off blame for his actions on society or anyone else, and cannot find salvation in social utopias.

Many in the modern world continue to fear more than anything else the eclipse of liberty and of the free personality under the exorbitant encroachment of statism and mass society. They may differ in their terms, or in the exact identification of the enemy: is it the state, or the democratic mass-man, or machine technology, or all of these? But there is broad agreement about the nature of the problem. "Personality is losing all along the line against power," J. B. Priestley wrote in 1955 ("The Gentle Anarchists"); the popular British author added that the younger generation "takes regimentation for granted" having become accustomed to the loss of liberties which everyone enjoyed until a few decades ago.

This deep concern about the authentic individual in an age that seems to conspire to destroy him has been a leading cause of the existentialist vogue, which continued strongly in the postwar years. The formidable Sartre, philosopher, Resistance fighter, and popular playwright and novelist, edited the most influential journal of ideas, *Les Temps Modernes*, and, flanked by his lady Simone de Beauvoir, presided over a circle that included the glamorous Algerian, Albert Camus. Paris was still the leading center of world ideas. A popular existentialism emanated from its cafés. To a rather bewildered American newspaper observing it in 1947, it was something invented by a Nazi (Heidegger) and was like Nazism a philosophy of "nihilism." But Sartre and Camus had fought the Nazis, and Sartre supported the Communists at least until 1956. And what of the others, like Gabriel Marcel and Paul Tillich, who were deeply religious? The Kierkegaard renaissance continued. There was also a Nietzsche renaissance: previously viewed in England and America as somehow connected with German militarism and with Nazism, the German poet-philosopher now appeared as a mighty prophet of the modern predicament and a perceptive diagnostician of man's fate when all gods are dead. To realize fully that the world has no meaning; to know loneliness and dread; to reject conventional morality and religion; and then, "on the far side of despair," to affirm one's freedom to act and thus to create values—this existentialist recipe soon became known to every undergraduate.

The popularity of existentialism is to be explained less by the talents of its promulgators than by the appeal it made to post-1945 man. He hardly needed to be convinced of tragedy and absurdity in the world, not after Auschwitz and Hiroshima. He was disabused of ideals and wary of ideologies. He had seen the apocalypse happen, not once but twice—and life went on. There was nothing left to believe in—except, as the existentialists declared, life itself, in its concrete particulars. Nazi nihilism and Communist cynicism disgusted him, he wanted to affirm the dignity and value of the human person. But the old religion was dead, for any thoroughly "modern" mind; nor did science and rational philosophy (analytical) offer him anything more than the dry bread of skepticism. Belief in belief itself, the recipe of James and Sorel, entered somewhat into the existentialist recipe for nihilism; it added an imposing body of speculative thought about the individual consciousness, more up-to-date than Freud.

Writers of the hour, such as the attractive George Orwell, who was hardly philosophical enough to have embraced anything so pretentious as existentialist ontology, reflected its basic mood: down with systems, down with generalities, stick to the individual existent person. Orwell told how a Belgian who had called for the death of all Germans saw one real German corpse and changed his whole outlook. The false imagination, as someone said, can hate whole races, nations, and classes; the true imagination cannot hate a real human being. Orwell used his touchstone of human values to reject and assail the Communist pattern of dogma, lies, and hatred, but he also maintained a stance somewhere on the Left as a searching critic of false values in a materialistic and dehumanizing capitalist society.

Though it had its bitter side, and Sartre might be accused of seeing man as a "useless passion" condemned to eternal frustration, existentialism is not, as some have claimed, a wholly gloomy philosophy. Faced with absurdity, we do at first feel dread and anxiety, but then we rise above them to create values by squarely facing our situation and responsibilities. We choose, act, and win through to authentic existence thus endowing the universe with value. Existentialism is an optimistic and activist creed, leading us back to life and not leaving us in a Buddhist rejection of it. It is an expression of the defiant energy of the West in the teeth of all adversity. It is easy to accuse it of intellectual confusion or even charlatanry, but not of passivity. It is not its fault that "God is dead"; that was the fault of modern science and rationalism. It tells us what we may do about this cruel death.

Christian socialism or Christian democracy emerged temporarily after the war as a promising substitute for the older political ideologies. It has the advantage of being nondogmatic and dedicated to the spiritual individual. Under strong leadership (in Italy, De Gasperi was the leading statesmen of the postwar decades), Christian Democrats showed concern for the welfare of worker and peasant and emerged as the strongest political party in France, Italy, and Germany soon after the war. They tended, however, to dissipate from vagueness of doctrine. While political parties bearing their name might continue to exist, these lacked any very specific ideological content. This was natural, for the Christian position is not positively political and may be turned in any number of different directions. Under existential influence, Christianity in the postwar world undeniably carried on its post-1919 revival; but often it meant only the imperative of commitment and involvement, a personalism that cared deeply for the individual and his inner life but did not stand for any very clear dogmatic position.

Like Christianity, existentialism could be turned in almost any political direction; it only demanded sincerity, authenticity, integrity. In a letter to a German friend who had embraced Nazism, Camus wrote

> I continue to believe that this world has no higher meaning. But I know that something within it has meaning, and this is man, because he is the only being who demands it. This world has at least the truth of man, and our job is to prove his case even against destiny itself.

A fair statement of the existentialist case; but why, on these terms, should Camus object to his German friend choosing National Socialism? Camus went on in this letter to appeal to "justice." On existential terms, can there be any such abstraction? Justice must be what I affirm. Issuing a timely call for integrity and individuality, existentialism actually left the rest fearfully vague, and could be accused of an anarchic irrationalism which makes the criteria of truth just one's own fantasies, thus dangerously undermining all critical and realistic social thought.

In the 1950s, a largely conservative decade, existential thought on the whole supported an apolitical, anti-ideological, personalist mood. In the 1960s it blended violently with radical political ideologies. Sartre always claimed that Marxism was the only possible philosophy for modern man, though his Marxism was of a highly unorthodox kind by Kremlin standards. A new wave of radicalism would arrive in the 1960s, featuring an existentialized neo-Marxism (it is treated further below). In the 1950s, despite some absorption of Marxist elements into an existentialist ethic with the approval of Sartre, the leftism of the 1930s was no more, arousing only occasional echoes among the immature and the provincial intellectuals. "Vegetating in the utopias of the last century" as a French writer (Jean Duvignaud) put it, seemed futile; "new dreams must be invented for a new world." Raymond Aron wrote of "the end of the socialist myth."

Other Philosophical Schools

In academic philosophical circles, existentialism's more respectable cousin, phenomenology, made steady gains, especially on the Continent. What Sartre called "a great emptiness, a wind blowing toward objects" the phenomenologists thought they might get at: raw consciousness, prior to all ideas or concepts. These attempts constitute a considerable chapter in the story of recent philosophy. There is no space here to attempt to detail them. It may only be noted that system-making in the older philosophic way has no place in phenomenology. Its practitioners are engaged in a kind of super-Kantian exercise in discovering the nonrational categories of the mind, and these turn out to be numerous, ambiguous, not reducible to any order. Phenomenology bears some relationship to the recent school in literature which describes itself as *chosiste*, or thing-ist: dedicated to the full exploration of objects *qua* objects, the thing for its own sake, not seen as a symbol of anything or as part of any logical scheme. We remain content, in both *chosisme* and phenomenology, with concrete existents, experienced and described as they are, just because they are.

Even those philosophers who belonged to the very different tradition of logical positivism, which we have described as dominant in England and Scandinavia, tended toward some of the same conclusions the existentialists reached, even if they arrived by a different route. The formidable Ludwig Wittgenstein, it will be recalled, was by general agreement the high priest of the positivist school. His earlier work was thought to be rationalist, scientific, and antimetaphysical. Yet even the earlier Wittgenstein had been fascinated by language and aware of the problems it presents. The later Wittgenstein (chiefly in the posthumously published *Philosophical Investigations*, 1953) concluded that language is a screen almost completely cutting us off from reality. The world of facts outside this screen is one we cannot know except as our language permits it. The point would seem to be quite similar to Hume's, that other scientific rationalist who reasoned his way to the most irrationalist conclusions back in the age of the philosophes. The inferences from this skepticism were similar: one falls back on the language of everyday life, for one. Many of the Oxford philosophizers of the analytical school did just that. At any rate they continued to feel that philosophy has no great messages to deliver, being a method and not a creed—its job, to help us clarify our thoughts. Under the influence of Wittgenstein II it tended in the '50s to become ever more absorbed in linguistic word-games. It drew back in horror from any suggestion that philosophers might construct systems, or assert truths, or discover values. Like the phenomenologists, the analysts took things as they found them, preferring concrete particular problems, tending to deflate all abstractions and generalizations.

The New Radicalism

While the 1950s were politically quiet, they were hardly complacent. As the Cold War between the rival power blocs of Russia and the

West threatened to erupt at any moment, in a decade punctuated by international crises (Korean War, Berlin crises, Suez/Hungarian joint crisis in 1956, Cuban missile crisis in 1962, etc.), the development of the nuclear hydrogen bomb and intercontinental missiles kept mankind cringing under the threat of annihilation. Among the most widely read serious books of the decade were Orwell's *1984* nightmare of total war between totalitarian slave states, and Neville Shute's picture of the horrors of atomic war, *On the Beach*, to which one might add William Golding's parable of boys reduced to savagery, *Lord of the Flies*. Such highly esteemed novelists as François Mauriac, Graham Greene, Angus Wilson, Evelyn Waugh presented a gloomy view of human nature derived from traditional Christianity, as did the older T. S. Eliot, whose brilliant modernist delineation of "The Waste Land" now gave place to the Christian humility of *Four Quartets*. The decade was not revolutionary, since it had ceased to believe in Marx's romantic epic of history and had seen his disciples end by establishing a new tyranny. In literature, the decade had turned away rather strongly from socialist realism, whose tracts seemed unutterably dreary.

Signs of discontent began to appear toward the end of the decade. Curiously, the discrediting and then the splitting up of world Communism opened the way to a freer development of the Left. After 1956 some of the communist parties, for example the British, cut loose from Moscow's moorings altogether and sailed off on their own toward some kind of neo-communism. The Italian Communist party moved far away from the rigid dogmatism of Stalin's day to become almost an open-minded party of the Left, willing to discard old shibboleths and seek fresh formulations. In Italy and France a "dialogue between Catholicism and Communism" began, receiving encouragement from new currents in the Catholic Church, expressed in Pope John XXIII's extraordinary 1963 encyclical "Pacem in Terris" which issued a call to liberal thought and social action in the Church. With the fragmentation of the world Communist movement, which began in the late '50s and carried on into the '60s, Chinese Maoist and Cuban Castroist versions of the revolutionary faith became live options for leftists; there was a good deal more charisma and mystique in these than in the old, tired Moscow version, which still hopefully presented its lives of Lenin but was now run by bureaucrats in gray flannel suits. New revolutionary heroes such as Che Guevara appeared. Or, if one preferred milder brew, some of the east European satellites of Russia produced revisionist Marxism which tried to soften the harsh Leninist variety by administering doses of Kantian ethics or other humanizing ingredients. In France a *Union de la Gauche Socialiste*, created in 1957, experimented in a more eclectic socialism drawing on Proudhon, Jaurès, and the Christian socialism of

Lamennais and Sangnier. It dreamed of defanaticizing the Communists and undogmatizing Marx, in order to fit them into this "Popular Front." In brief, the demise of historic Soviet Communism as a world revolutionary faith allowed fresh breezes to blow through the dried-up landscape of the Left and inaugurated a period of confusion but considerably greater vitality there.[4]

But the deeper cause of the new radicalism was unquestionably a new generation, as usual rebelling against the attitudes of its fathers. The 1950s were still dominated intellectually by the generation that had matured between the wars, had known Hitler and Stalin and the Red Decade, experienced the gigantic trauma of World War II, and had ended disillusioned with all ideologies, unable to believe in any utopias. A younger generation, to whom these events were but faint memories, began to find a voice, at first hesitantly, in the later '50s. In Britain, John Osborne's play *Look Back in Anger*, 1956, has come to seem a curiously significant landmark. Other writers and critics asked for more commitment and social relevance; a debate about this, initially between critic Kenneth Tynan and veteran dramatist Eugene Ionesco, enlivened the later '50s. Few mature writers in the '50s dared to say a word for social realism, which raised memories of the dreary propagandist tracts of the '30s; Ionesco was existentialist and personalist and was almost as famous as Samuel Beckett whose *Waiting for Godot* was the classic existentialist stage statement of the forlorn human condition. The Angry Young Men now demanded action. It was not altogether clear what they were angry at—at Britain's declining power, at the "caste system" of a still somewhat snobbish society, or just angry, with the natural rebelliousness of youth. By comparison with the rock-throwing militants of a decade later they were quite mild, and many of them, like Kingsley Amis and John Braine, later became conservative. But their somewhat incoherent protests together with their demand for a less quietly resigned voice in literature marked a certain turning point.

With France somnolent under De Gaulle and Communism in disarray, the British writers commanded the center of the world stage for a time. Activism coalesced momentarily in a strong pacifist campaign, influenced among others by the nonagenarian philosopher Bertrand Russell (always a maverick), which culminated in the Campaign for Nuclear Disarmament along with attacks on American foreign policy and demands to take Great Britain out of the North Atlantic alliance. The dec-

---

[4]Relaxation of pressure from a supposedly monolithic world Communism tended to free anti-Communists from a rigid position, too; "depolarization" worked both ways. In 1950–51 virtually all "liberals" backed the Korean War against Communist aggression. Fifteen years later they almost unanimously condemned the Indochina war as unwarranted on the part of the West.

ade of the '60s began with the first of many protest marches, organized by the C.N.D. in behalf of its demand for Britain unilaterally to abandon her nuclear weaponry. In the *New Left Review*, those impatient with the Labour Party's caution and pragmatism tried to discover new roads to socialism. The "establishment" came under attack from satirists. The new spirit was mocking, irreverent, and impatient.

If in a few years from such uncertain beginnings it reached a stage of near delirium in violent student uprisings, the causes lay as usual partly in the realm of ideas and partly in social circumstances. Among the latter must be included the revolution in higher education which sent far more students into institutions of higher learning, many of them new. In England, for example, the virtual monopoly of university education and of intellectual life by the two ancient universities, Oxford and Cambridge, with a place made for the University of London in certain subjects, had never been challenged and ensured the supremacy of a small intellectual elite steeped in the classical literary traditions of Western civilization. Now a considerable number of new universities served tens of thousands who would formerly never have gone to college.[5] The same situation, by and large, existed in all other European countries, as well as in the United States and other places. The new universities were taught by a kind of intellectual middle-class, less prestigious than Oxbridge, but more receptive to nontraditional studies: sociology flourished there in England, experiencing a remarkable boom in a land which heretofore had almost neglected it. The students were less subtle and perhaps less able but often intensely interested. It would perhaps not be unfair to say that the intellectual coinage underwent a certain debasement in such places; yet often they produced an atmosphere of great excitement. The immense expansion in numbers of university students clearly bore some relationship to student radicalism; students might complain of the mass effect, feeling unrecognized and "processed" rather than educated. At the University of Paris where the great student uprising took place in 1968, a critical situation due to dreadful overcrowding obviously existed. There may also have been an overproduction of degree recipients in such fields as sociology, leading to frustration.

But other factors entered also. A widespread *malaise* among the young at the sheer dullness of contemporary life lay behind their restless, often aimless protests. A spirit something like that of 1914 might

---

[5]In 1970 there were some 450,000 university students in Great Britain, with talk of another doubling in the next decade. A hundred years earlier, the most advanced country in the world in this respect, Germany, had but 14,000, with considerably fewer than this in Britain.

be detected; not that the young wanted this time to march off to war, for their protests were likely to be directed *against* war. But they craved excitement, demanded romance, and took to violence in their marches and protests. Their bitter complaints, directly vaguely against "the system," "the establishment," or other whopping abstractions, more often reproached the quality of life in a society ever more technological, ever more specialized, ever more organized. It was Max Weber's "iron cage" of "rationalization" that closed in on them; they echoed Ruskin's complaint about men being fragmented by the division of labor, while art and adventure and spontaneity disappeared from life. They looked for some Great Adventure. They faced a long list of exhausted options: no more wars, no more revolutions, no great crusades, no more great movements in the arts, no more undiscovered lands or exotic places.[6] Whether destined for the factory or the office, they found the prospects of work unexciting.

Whatever one's preferences in a list of the causes of the "youth rebellion"—and many would wish to include the factor of affluence, of enough wealth to permit the spoiled children of yesterday's bourgeoisie to indulge all their fantasies of a world without work—it is obvious that ideas entered in, and this is our direct concern here. Not all the new radicals were young, and of course not all the young were radical; to speak of the movement in this way is as misleading as to call 1914 a youth movement. Ideas were in the air, and the intellectually inclined young are especially receptive to new ideas. And no doubt some young people, as well as some older ones, always respond readily to revolutionary, "activist" slogans. But in fact there were special intellectual currents abroad in this period which shaped the contours of radical thought.

Of these, a kind of vulgarized existentialism was a major one. The austere social idealism of the older radicalism, which often went with an almost puritanical code of personal behavior,[7] gave place to a highly hedonistic one; everyone was to do as he wished. The sexual revolution accompanied the social. A much-discussed event of the year 1960 which posterity will very likely keep in memory as a major landmark of cul-

---

[6] Rather pathetically, the American "beat" poets managed to persuade themselves that places like Iowa and New Mexico were glamorous, as they bummed their way about the country. Hippies later took to the roads of Asia. The Americans sought to invest the Peace Corps with glamor, as young people went forth to remote villages of Africa or South America to render service.

[7] Even Nietzsche, Gide, and Shaw, prophets of the older immoralism or release from conventional morality, were quite concerned to make it clear that only the completely self-disciplined individual merited such release. Thus Shaw: "Without high gifts of reason and self-control: that is, without strong common sense, no man dares yet trust himself out of the school of authority."

tural history was the British court case which adjudged Lawrence's *Lady Chatterley's Lover* not obscene. Lawrence's use of four-letter words, like James Joyce's (which had received a kind of special exemption from the obscenity laws) was not intended simply for salacity, it hardly needs to be said. But the decision opened the floodgates and soon Anglo-Saxon bookstands were flooded with pornography. To say that the younger people ignored the principles of Christian sexual morality for the first time in history is obviously absurd; and sometimes it seemed one of the more laughable illusions of a generation of innocents that they first discovered the pleasures of sex. Still, permissiveness undoubtedly advanced another long step along a road it had been treading at least since the beginning of the century. The message of "do as you please" is as old as Rabelais; but never before had it been so widely accepted. A culture of "pot and porn" grew up in the zones where hippies dwelt, and was usually connected with the culture of social protest, militancy, and soon rock-throwing violence.

Existentialized Marxism

The existential message as it percolated down to the hippy level was plain: it meant not only that each individual should express himself in his own way but that any social authority, any external standards are bad. The leading respectable exponents of the new mixture of Marx and Sartre included, notably, the migratory sociologists, Herbert Marcuse and Theodor Adorno, both from Germany but with a penchant for California as a place of residence. The "thought" of the student movement, as expressed by the students themselves, whose exploits in riot-fomenting sometimes caused publishers to seek their rather incoherent writings, was quite primitive; it consisted of a few slogans and much vituperation. Marcuse was a professor/philosopher of mature years with impressive intellectual antecedents, though in some of his writings he celebrated obscenity, dirt, and drug-taking quite as emphatically, if more ponderously than more popular hippy prophets such as Timothy Leary. Possibly the most provocative point made by Dr. Marcuse was one already familiar in the time of Georges Sorel and even Michael Bakunin: the necessary revolution against capitalism cannot be led by the workers, for they have become a part of the system, seduced by capitalistic values, made into bourgeoisie. The revolution must be the work of those completely outside the system, such as students, young people, dropouts from society.

If this seemed to be a wide departure from Marx, the Marcusians justified it by pointing to the other Marx, as expressed in certain juvenile writings of the socialist sage which had remained unpublished and were only discovered among his manuscripts in recent years (by Russian scholars, working at the Marx-Engels Institute in Leningrad). These writings, of which the mature Marx was evidently not proud, discussed the moral condition of man in modern society much more than did his later ones. The Hegel of *The Phenomenology of Mind* also came into this picture. The other Marx and the other Hegel could be much more readily reconciled to an existential view. Marcuse added Freud to his formula, embracing the sexual revolution and invoking a strong if vague image of a hippy-existentialist utopia where, after the destruction of a vile capitalistic system, all would live freely as they wished in sexual and esthetic fulfillment. The Marcusian utopia differed greatly from older socialistic ones in being far less materialistic. No socialist heretofore had doubted that an end to poverty through expanded industrial production, which capitalism was held to inhibit, would be the final goal— preparing the way, no doubt, for a fuller life, yet the indispensable foundation for such a life. But Marcuse spoke of overdeveloped countries and too much production of goods, reflecting a fairly widespread disenchantment in the '60s with affluence, more and more products, the consumer society. He even rejoiced in hippydom's congenial relations with dirt ("bodies unsoiled by plastic cleanliness"). His ideal class seemed almost to be that which Marx had contemptuously dismissed as the *lumpenproletariat* (someone suggested that a better term today is the *lumpenbourgeoisie.*)

So, in place of Marx's "Workers of the World Unite! You have nothing to lose but your chains!", contemporary existentialized or hippy-ized revolutionaries seem to say "Outcasts of the world unite! You have nothing to lose but your jobs!" It is not surprising that all this, including student revolts for the right to use obscenities or just "for the hell of it," struck some as the ultimate degeneracy of a dying civilization. Nevertheless a powerful idealism seemed to be involved. The "great refusal" of which Marcuse wrote was a defiant rejection of the whole of modern society, because it is at bottom corrupting, "dehumanizing," soul-destroying. At times Marcuse seems to reject any kind of group organization, in the name of an extreme anarchism.

Boiled down to its essence, this chiliastic hatred of the great Babylon of the world, accompanied by ecstatic visions of a future perfect state, resembled nothing so much as early Christianity. And perhaps the children living in communes as hippies are engaged in bringing forth a second Jerusalem. Certainly many of them see visions and believe in signs and portents. They predict the end of the world and cultivate witchcraft. Such a strange variety of spiritual phenomena has not been seen since the age of the Reformation. The violent ones, who engage in rock-throwing and fire-bombing, are a small minority of these alienated and strangely innocent people who congregate in communities or travel gypsy-like around the world. Not all of them are politically radical. After all, the formal or rational part of the new radicalism's thought is threadbare indeed; its ideas are left over from the earlier nineteenth century, its slogans are simple-minded, its utopias as old as the primeval dream of a Golden Age. The spiritual ferment of recent years is a religious phenomenon, which may portend, as in the latter days of the Roman Empire, the decline and fall of a great civilization.

The politics of the New Left seemed unlikely to lead to anything definite or constructive. The romantic anarchism of its devotees ensures their futility as anything other than personal gestures. Within a year after its tremendous uprising of May, 1968 amazed the world, the French student movement had drifted into extreme fragmentation and had proved unable to create a lasting organization. It exemplified what Lenin once scornfully rejected as "left-wing infantilism." Indiscriminate acts of destruction, the strategy of the most activist wing of the revolutionaries, was a throwback to that most barren chapter of revolutionary history, the Russian terrorists of the 1870s. Beyond a blind inarticulate rage at the whole system, the new revolutionaries had no clear goal. Theirs was a failure of thought, a complete nihilism if ever one had existed. In this respect observers noted a certain kinship with fascism, though this was something New Leftists thought they despised. Perhaps the New Left was a dialectical synthesis of fascism and communism.

The Exhaustion of Modernism

The theme of nihilism might be pursued with reference to the exhaustion of other once vital movements or traditions. Widely noted in the 1960s was the crisis in the arts, with the apparent playing out of the "modernist" movement in a paroxysm of fads. While thousands of "little magazines" flourished, and public poetry readings testified to an urgently felt need, the net effect was aimlessness and sterility. The modernists—in the age of symbolists and expressionists, of Eliot, Yeats, Joyce, the surrealists, all that dazzling exhibition of virtuosity and audacity that lay between Rimbaud and Pound—had played with the fire of extreme subtlety and subjectivity—statements personal, elliptical, complex, multi-leveled. They were often aware that after them, almost nothing else could be except chaos. The way that they had chosen could go only so far and then it turned into a swamp. In the words of Stephen Spender, himself a great modern poet, "to go further would lead to a new and completer fragmentation, utter obscurity, form (or rather form-lessness) without end." Nietzsche had foreseen the "dissolution of art" once it had cut loose completely from the discipline of the classical rules and bounds. Rimbaud, Verlaine, the surrealists, and the dadaists did it once; but one cannot add to them, one can only repeat them in ever more violent and therefore feebler ways. The "little magazines" for the most part contain only obscene[8] echoes of the great age of European experimental literature and esthetic revolt. No doubt the gesture is soothing to the souls of the men and women who fling these notes of defiance at an obtuse world. But the notes have gone sour, and the gesture is so stale it can have no significance. When not highly derivative in form, aping Tzara, Apollinaire, etc., these writings tend to be form-less. The French have produced the antinovel. Others like to let computers write poems. The content of this literature is a kind of parody of the decadents; the theme is not so much decay as putrefaction. A critic has spoken of "the charnel house flavor" of William Burroughs's novel *Naked Lunch*, a bible of the bedraggled avant-garde of the 1960s. American beats and hippies write of drug addiction, and other degraded states. Nihilistic in form and content alike to the last degree of nothing-ness, this is literature not of revolt nor even of despair, it seems beyond despair. Writing of the contemporary avant-garde Ken Baynes remarks that "the artist's brave cry of freedom has turned into the shout of a buffoon."

If the arts offered less scope for Western man's spirit, the same could perhaps be said for science. A considerable chapter in the history of recent thought can be written around the theme indicated in C. P. Snow's widely read and discussed book of 1959, *The Two Cultures*. Sir Charles, a novelist of note as well as a public administrator with a keen interest in science, charged the entire literary-humanist camp with a disregard for and ignorance of science, as well as with a general irre-sponsibility toward all public affairs. There was a good deal of merit in his charge, though he overstated it. Since the dawn of modernism the novelist and poet had cultivated a domain of private sensibilities, scorn-ing the area of "normal" life where dwelt such hopelessly philistine souls as politicians and businessmen. (If they turned to politics, as in the 1930s, they hoped to revolutionize it completely and were quite un-realistic.) It was a function of their profound alienation from modern society. Science, needless to say, was one of the West's grand intellec-tual traditions, if not *the* grand tradition, and the realm of Galileo and Newton remained central through the Enlightenment and into the age of

---

[8]Quite literally, in the case of such elegantly titled California organs as *Fuck You* and *Horseshit*.

Darwin and Pasteur. Educated, enlightened people normally expected it to lead the march of progress toward a better, more decent life for all. Even if, like the socialists, they rejected the way modern industrial society is organized, they expected a better organization to release the beneficial effects of scientific technology. Marxism, and the example of Soviet Russia, helped promote the myth of science and technology as brave, clean helpful servants when brought under human control and given proper direction.

Now the myth of science appeared to fade as it was increasingly identified with the kind of society intellectuals hated. The technological society looked uncivilized as well as polluted. Science meant technology. Its crowning achievement of the '60s was a trip to the moon, much heralded and looked toward; but when it happened the thrill did not last. The real frontiers for contemporary man lie within the human heart, and must be crossed with the help of studies quite other than the rational science for which Western civilization had long been famous. Such was the burden of many a book and essay, which attacked the environmental crisis created by an excess of products and wastes upsetting the balance of nature and corrupting air and water. Here was an ambivalence: science went on, technology went on, not only because there was no way of stopping them but because many of the things they created could not be rejected. Gloom about ever relieving the poverty and hunger of the majority of the world's population, residing in Africa and Asia and South America, decreased in the later 1960s because of a triumph of applied science in the area of high-yield cereal grains. Not even intellectuals appeared to want to do without the comforts offered by modern technology. Yet there was undeniably a serious questioning of the values of "more and more," of material goods for their own sake, questions Carlyle and Ruskin had raised long before but which now spread widely throughout society.

Fragmentation and the Quest For Unity

The post-1945 climate of opinion might be summed up as a profound revulsion against all that came before, especially the immediate prewar period in its dogmatic and statist aspects; followed by a probing for new values, slogans, and modes of thought which have not yet emerged clearly; the leading discernible theme being a mistrust of all ideologies and absolutes, a concern for the individual existent person against abstractions and pressures to conform as well as against the awful power of the state; with social, economic, and political inquiry reflecting this mood in being concrete and piecemeal. In modern times

European thought is too complex to submit to any such summation without all kinds of qualifications, however.

Among the leading dilemmas of modern man is this factor of sheer size. It is not less a factor in the realm of ideas than it is in social life generally; in fact, it is above all a problem here. Consider the quantity of writing. It has been estimated that more books have been published in the last thirty years than in the entire preceding 490 or so since the birth of printing. A hundred thousand or so books are published each year in western Europe and the United States, not to count the thousands of periodicals. Scholarship and criticism have proliferated with the multiplication of university posts; a vast number of people have been brought somewhere near the region of serious thought and expression as mass higher education spreads. This region was, as recently as the earlier part of this century, inhabited by a small intellectual elite, numbered probably in the low thousands for western Europe. That number has now swelled to millions. Never were so many books read by so many. Encouraging, no doubt; and yet bringing with it, as the inevitable price of quantity, fragmentation, loss of unity, and intense specialization. "Literature today is fragmented. . . . Scholarship is fragmented too; so is life." Thus the recent (1968) lament of a distinguished British scholar.

Specialization, with technical competence in a high degree but compensating losses in range, depth, and linkage with other fields, is found wherever we look. It has infected philosophy itself, no longer queen of the intellect but largely content to be a specialized branch of experimental science. Economics, also, has fallen victim to specialization, as has sociology, in that the grand classical syntheses have been abandoned in favor of micro-analysis, the examination of particular situations rather than the whole of society. It would be impossible to find a branch of learning not afflicted with this sort of crisis, examined in a recent symposium called *Crisis in the Humanities.* There is far more knowledge; it is far less meaningful because less integrated. This dilemma has also appeared in other disciplines formerly more humanistic. Much literary criticism in recent times has spurned the historical, biographical, or moral aspects for close verbal or structural analysis of the work of literature itself—a sort of literary linguistic analysis. The branches of creative literature themselves have shown a similar pattern. A distinguished contemporary English literary critic (Graham Hough) has spoken of the enormous gains in "technical competence, sheer skill in handling the tools" in the last forty years or so—of the conquering, among other things, of a whole new realm, the unconscious—and yet accompanying this a "loss of authority," a loss also of range and substance, a tendency to deal with the "ripples on the surface" of life. The recent French novel, too, exhibits an almost dismaying variety of technical tricks, regarded as necessary to be up-to-date. Poetry too, of course, has become ultrasophisticated in technique—subtle, oblique, capable of saying anything and saying it stylishly, but finding nothing very memorable to say—consisting of private rather than public statements.

Though these generalizations, indicative of a triumph of technique over life, are subject to exceptions, they seem broadly descriptive of an important trend. Technique has brought precision, has eliminated much untidiness and cleared up errors, but it would seem to have entailed a loss of vitality, and to have fragmented thought and culture into unrelated pieces. Historical writing, too, often today takes the form of well-researched, technically accomplished studies, making use of archival material—the sacred emblem of the historian's guild—but lacking the literary skill, the grand manner, the sweep of older historians. George M. Trevelyan's eloquent plea, written in 1913, for Clio as essentially a literary muse, belonging to the humanities and not to the sciences, has scarcely prevailed; Trevelyan was *passé* before he died, hopelessly dilettantish by the standards of the Lewis Namier school in Great Britain. It is true that since 1900 historians have moved away from the positivistic conception of history as capable of yielding laws on the analogy of the physical sciences, a view then very strong. (Witness J. B. Bury, Fustel de Coulanges.) They have rather tended to follow the line indicated by the German Wilhelm Dilthey, or by Benedetto Croce the great Italian historian and philosopher, a position well expressed in R. G. Collingwood's book, *The Idea of History* (1946). On this view history is neither the handmaiden of science nor a branch of *belles-lettres*, but is autonomous, its function being to recreate the past from the perspective of present thought and in so doing clarify the present. "The science of the particular," its job is not to search for general laws, but to explore unique past experiences in depth, choosing the ones most relevant to present experience. Such a view corresponds roughly to the professional historian's instinctive idea of what he does when he writes history. It is a defensible one; but it opens the door to a great deal of aimless and not very important research done just for the sake of doing—because it is "there," meaning by "it" all too often some archival sources. Complaints about the "Ph.D. pestilence" which requires or encourages useless and graceless pedantry in the humanities as well as the social sciences, could be heard more frequently perhaps because of the institutional necessity of writing theses and dissertations, under conditions of contemporary mass education.

The urge to unify knowledge in the teeth of vast undigested quantities of it created a dilemma. In the east of Europe, the great Soviet State has conducted since 1917 an experiment in the monist or monolithic society built on a single ideology. There are advantages in having one faith, but also disadvantages. It is tidier, but it involves suppression, and in the long run one cannot achieve unity except at a terrible price in tyranny. This is the medieval experience all over again. In the modern world, it must in any case fail, as is indicated by the trend in the USSR since the death of Stalin. Those who reproach Western civilization for its chaotic lack of unity are undoubtedly right in part, but they may be forgetting that for the last several hundred years that civilization—modern European civilization—has been committed to pluralism and freedom. "Monolithic social ends," as Karl Popper writes, "would mean the death of freedom: of the freedom of thought, of the free search for truth, and with it, of the rationality and dignity of man." The case for European liberalism rests on the value of the "open society" as well as on the hatefulness of persecution for conscience's sake. It rests on the belief that only through the free inquiry of many minds working in many ways can we hope to find solutions to our manifold human problems, still so numerous as almost to stagger the mind. The retreat to an island of dogmatism enforced by the sword is a shallow, superficial, erroneous answer—really an abdication.

The divergence between Soviet and Western thought may be illustrated by some exchanges to be found in the *History of Mankind* published under the auspices of UNESCO (United Nations Educational Scientific and Cultural Organization). In the first volume, *Prehistory and the Beginnings of Civilization*, written by two British historians (1963), Soviet historians dissented frequently, the general grounds of their dissent being that the Western historians present history as "no more than a kaleidoscopic change of whimsical patterns with no inner consistency and no principle in their development" (page 508), and more particularly that they fail to put the facts in the Marxian framework of concepts and stages. (All societies must involve "exploitation" by a bad ruling class, all history must exhibit an evolution from slavery to feudalism to capitalism, etc.) The reply of Sir Leonard Woolley to Professor I. M. Diakonoff and his Russian colleagues was of course that to represent history as the latter desire would be to misrepresent it, since the facts exposed by empirical investigation reveal no such neat agreement with the Marxist categories. The frequent exchanges between Diakonoff and Woolley recorded in the notes for each chapter leave the impression of a doctrinaire *a priori* approach on the Russian side which Western historians could only regard as naive, but which the Russians obviously consider to be the only way of rendering history intelligible at all. (Purely factual matters were often in question, but clearly the bias or presuppositions of the historians helped decide what they thought the facts were.) And it must be admitted that the Soviet historians could have written a better organized, more lucid account than is contained in the more than 800 large pages of this volume, replete with suspended or uncertain judgments and revealing as it does the enormous complexity of ancient history. Their history would have been clearer; but it could not have passed critical scrutiny by the eyes of knowledgeable experts in the West.

The pluralism and sophistication of the Western intellect create difficulties, though they are a source of strength. The Western intellectual tradition is doubtless the most complex ever known. It is now an old roué of civilization, which has experienced everything and seen through all myths. It now finds it difficult to believe in anything; it tries, but it is too self-conscious, it knows that its faith will be a myth. Modern achievement in every field is marked by great technical mastery. But the specialist has taken over at the expense of a general culture; and amid a wealth of specialized techniques for unearthing scientific, factual knowledge, modern man has the greatest difficulties finding values. These are among the leading dilemmas of modern man, who struggles to integrate all his intellectual subcultures into something like a single culture, and to find something his logic will let him believe in. Contemporary culture lacks unity and lacks faith; yet in some degree men want and seek these things.

The postwar years witnessed some valiant attempts at integration of knowledge. Arnold J. Toynbee's vast tapestry of universal history with its sweeping claim to unearth the laws governing the rise and fall of civilization was not favorably received by most professional historians. Yet the literate public eagerly bought and read it, indicating a thirst for "philosophical" history, not assuaged by most historical writing today. With vast erudition and an appropriately grave and classical style, Toynbee set forth on the somewhat romantic quest of finding in history the secret of the sickness of Western civilization. He offered a study in comparative civilizations, identifying twenty-one different civilizations in human history and seeking to show the common pattern of their inception, growth, decline, and disintegration—some, on his view, having perished completely. A meditative if sometimes platitudinous style, a deeply spiritual outlook, an awareness of an amazing range of ideas as well as historic facts, lends to Toynbee's leisurely *Study of History* (altogether in twelve volumes, the substance of it abridged by D. S. Somervell in two volumes) a great appeal. His conclusions are not regarded by most of his competent critics as having much validity. "Laws" turn out to be truisms; there is doubt about the neat isolating of civilizations as separate units; comparisons mean little when stripped of Toynbeean rhetoric. Nevertheless the large amount of discussion aroused by Toynbee has been a stimulus to historical thinking. A landmark of our times, Toynbee's massive work testifies to the global perspective and to the technical resources of the modern historian—the historian of no previous generation could have assembled so much knowledge from all over the world—and to the perennial interest in the great question, whither mankind? But it has scarcely provided an answer.

In reality, Toynbee's opus was the product of his feeling that modern Europe had fallen into decay and was headed for death, a feeling aroused by World War I, intensified by the rise of Communism and Nazism and the depression of the 1930s, and seemingly confirmed by the truly suicidal violence of World War II. He turned to history to try to find an answer to the causes, and thus possibly the cure, of such declines and falls, just as Thucydides had done when faced with the suicide of Periclean Greece in the Peloponnesian War, and Machiavelli had done in the twilight of Renaissance Italy. When a sophisticated civilization falls on bad times it will produce brilliant diagnosis. But it is not clear that the diagnosis helps. Toynbee seems to know what qualities civilizations have when they are at their creative zenith, and what symptoms they exhibit when in trouble–not a difficult thing to describe. But in the end he can only exhort Western civilization to be more creative and cease having troubles. His scheme of science, purporting to show that many other civilizations have gone through similar patterns, and his effort to find useful laws of the secular movements of whole civilizations, are too vague and subjective to command assent or have much meaning. So Toynbee's masterpiece turned out to be less the scientific analysis he thought it to be than a kind of vast prose poem lamenting the sickness of a civilization. This is not to say it is useless; on the contrary, less as science than as rhetoric, it has worked on literally millions of minds. No other serious work of such length has been so widely read in our time. History can console us as well as inspire us.

Results of Specialization

Toynbee protested against too much narrow specialization, but fell afoul of specialists. Most historians seem content to plough well their own narrow furrow, each building his own separate tunnel to the past, as one historian has recently put it (J. H. Hexter). This is the tendency in all branches of knowledge. Martin Heidegger wrote in 1929, in one of his searching criticisms of modern civilization, that "the scientific fields are far apart. Their subjects are treated in fundamentally different ways. Today this hodgepodge of disciplines is held together only by the technical organization of the universities and faculties, and preserves what meaning it has only through the practical aims of the different branches." The modern American university is an excellent cultural mirror of this sprawling disunity.[9] Scientist-novelist C. P. Snow, in *The Two Cultures*, a book much discussed in England, drew attention to the gulf developing between scientists and humanists in an age of specialization, even in the English universities with their traditions of a broad liberal education.

Overspecialization is a particular danger because it may cut off that cross-fertilization of the disciplines that has so often proved stimulating in the past. Students of intellectual history are especially aware of those cases, in which Darwin received vital stimulation and critical ideas from Malthus, Kant from Rousseau, Kepler from Pythagorean mysticism, etc.[10] If the disciplines—or even worse, small sections within each discipline, as seems to be the case today—are cut off from each other and from a matrix of general ideas common to all, we have a formula for scientific desiccation. Our sciences as well as our general culture will dry up, humanity itself will shrivel, the human personality lose itself in a wilderness of jargon and pettiness. This is the fear, and it seems well-grounded. Gabriel Marcel (*The Philosophy of Existence*, Chapter 1) has pointed out that the individual in modern specialized society loses his human personality to become "an agglomeration of functions." This destruction of his sense of whole being seems to be what the existentialist psychotherapists (such as the German Binswanger) have in mind as the basic cause of neurosis and psychosis in the individual.

It may be noted that this complexity and specialization defeats the dreams of the individual's mental power and thus ends a long epoch in modern history. The realm of knowledge becomes far too vast for any one mind to grasp, even in the most general terms, and one gives up the quest, resigning oneself to being at the most a cog in some incomprehensible machine. Renaissance, Enlightenment, and romantic man all

---

[9]In this respect one might consider as significant what happened to the General Education program established at Harvard College in 1945 following the report published (and widely read) as *General Education in a Free Society*. The idea of this educational program was, in substance, to counteract specialization by giving to all students a small number of basic courses which would set forth in broad terms the common cultural heritage. In practice, the idea never worked, and in 1964 another Harvard committee confessed failure and in effect gave up the broad courses and common-heritage approach. Its justification for doing so was largely that existing academic patterns simply will not support the 1945 program. Good faculty is not interested in teaching the general courses; they are therefore neglected and badly taught, while the better professors put their energy into specialized research and teaching. This is at a great institution of learning which has long dedicated itself especially to the liberal arts and the humane studies.

[10]One may urge on behalf of intellectual history that it attempts to combat this cultural chaos of isolated fields, this "hodgepodge of disciplines," by putting the various areas of thought in a common context and seeing the relations between them. It is one of the very few academic disciplines today trying to perform this task, so desperately needed if our civilization is to recover its sanity and balance.

thought it possible to understand everything. In the sixteenth century, Walter Ralegh observed casually that he bought *every* book that was published! In the eighteenth, a Voltaire, a Hume, a Jefferson kept abreast of just about all branches of knowledge, also without impeding their numerous other activities. The last of those who still sought omniscience were the great nineteenth-century synthesizers, Hegel, Marx, and Spencer, but their schemes broke down. Synthesis is beyond the grasp of anyone today, evidently. Such virtuosi of erudition as Toynbee and Teilhard reach toward it, but even these are far from achieving it. This dream must be abandoned; and if so, the failure would seem to entail a fundamental alteration in Western man's outlook: a defeat for individualism, for rationalism in the older sense. The assault on what David Knowles calls "a single reasoned and intelligible explanation of the universe on the natural level, and a single analysis of man and his powers . . . valid for all men and final within its sphere" came under attack as early as the fourteenth century with the skepticism of Ockham, and was further eroded in the Reformation. And yet, as Knowles adds, this skepticism "was never wholly victorious, and never finally accepted": European man clung to his dramatic belief in an ultimate knowledge accessible to the enlightened mind. Doubtless both Hegelianism and Darwinism in their different ways undermined it; doubtless no one had ever really been omniscient; and yet the great Victorians did continue to believe in the unity of knowledge, and the individual's ability to grasp in a general way this unity. If we are driven to complete fragmentation, we are at the end of rational individualism. Perhaps we are at the end of personality, as well as philosophy—condemned to be interchangeable with computers, or to be intellectual drones who heap up useless knowledge.

Another consequence of overspecialization, or at least a related cultural phenomenon, is the gulf between the average man and the expert or adept. There is no audience, no common ground. The complexity and diversity of thought, breeding a situation in which a few experts in any area communicate only with each other, leaves a vacuum in the popular mind which must be filled largely by rubbish. While the popular market for fiction and nonfiction alike is mostly satisfied by low-quality journalism, serious thought and advanced expression go on among isolated and esoteric minorities. Cultural distance between popular and advanced thought has always existed and perhaps always will; but there have been cultures wherein a general consensus or forum was closer to a possibility than in the vast democratic nations of today. This is sometimes blamed on their being vast, or their being democratic; but the true culprit, in the main, would seem to be the intellectual fragmentation we have been discussing.

The truly appalling shoddiness and silliness of this popular culture —American television or the average run of movie—is responsible for the alienation, to the point of insanity, of many people sensitive to beauty and human dignity, as it is also the source of opinions about the "degradation of the democratic era" or the abject decadence of modern man. The truth is that democracy arrived at the same time as specialization, doubling the dimensions of the problem. To absorb and civilize the millions who had heretofore lived beneath civilization would have been a challenging enough task at best. But simultaneously civilization itself has encountered the crisis of modern complexity and skepticism, and above all, the fragmentation of which we have been speaking.

It is far from clear that democracy is *responsible* for cultural anarchy. It is certainly not responsible for the cultural degradation of the common man, for this of course preceded it; Tocqueville had observed that "the common people is more uncivilized in aristocratic countries than any others." Matthew Arnold, in his sane appraisal a century ago, pointed out that democracy represented a striving of the common folk after whatsoever the reigning society affirmed as valuable. When democracy came to Athenian Greeks, the common folk sought after wisdom. If it comes to a military barbarism, they will want to be plundering soldiers. In Japan they write *hokku* poems. If democracy comes to an acquisitive capitalism, the people want to acquire. Arnold at least distributed the blame equally: "At the very moment when democracy becomes less and less disposed to follow and to admire, aristocracy becomes less and less qualified to command and to captivate."[11] Those qualities of "lofty spirit, commanding character, exquisite culture" which Arnold thought the eighteenth-century aristocracy possessed had ceased to be evident. In brief, cultural failure must not be blamed altogether on the mass, but on society for not holding up high values as a beacon to it.

The Search for Values

Another major dilemma of modern man obviously is this need for life-giving values, which can evidently come only from some sort of religious faith (religious in the widest sense), while his heritage of skepticism prevents any such belief. This dilemma is substantially that expressed by a Shavian character who cried that "we have outgrown our religion, outgrown our political system, outgrown our strength of mind and character. The fatal word NOT has been miraculously inscribed in

---

[11]"Democracy," in *Mixed Essays*, 1879, first published 1861.

all our creeds."[12] "I've been looking for something to believe in," says Alan Squier in Robert Sherwood's *Petrified Forest* (1936). "I've been hoping to find something that's worth living for—and dying for." Modern poets, novelists, dramatists, philosophers, preachers have now and again found things worth living and dying for. They found it in the 1930s and 1940s in the struggle against Nazism, and after that possibly in the fight against Communism. These were negative crusades—against something evil that had appeared, something itself the result of modern spiritual illness—and it is not clear that they provided the basis for a positive structure of value. Plainly many men believe in and struggle for such things as social justice, racial equality, honest government, the elimination of extreme poverty, national self-government for peoples who do not have it, etc. The questions remain, freedom for what? (Georges Bernanos, *La liberté pour quoi faire?*, 1953). A higher standard of life to what end? Can liberty, equality, and democracy really be ends in themselves, or are they not rather the means through which men can achieve some goals and values of life? If so, does not achievement of the former without the latter lead only to an ignoble materialism, an affluent society with vulgar tastes, the spiritual deserts of suburbia so often seen today in the United States?

In this dilemma there are signs of a yearning to return to traditional creeds. The great Italian writer and former communist, Ignazio Silone, has declared that "the rediscovery of a Christian heritage in the revolution of our time remains the most important gain that has been made in these last years for the conscience of our generation" (1946). Both World Wars I and II quickened interest in religion. Silone joined the late W. H. Auden, the late T. S. Eliot, Graham Greene, the late François Mauriac, and many another distinguished elder statesman of the literary world in embracing a Christian creed, sometimes after having followed strange gods earlier.[13] This is a movement of the greatest significance. Others have been led to such exotic shores of faith as India and Japan in their search for a tenable religion for modern man; still others explore the possibility of a higher religious synthesis between East and West. Jung directed attention to the universal symbols or archetypes underlying all religious experience. Zaehner, Kerenyi, and others are engaged in a massive exploration of the domain of comparative religions. Never has there been greater interest in historical and theological studies of the Christian past. Outstanding in the Christian world in recent times has been the ecumenical movement, the quest for

[12]*Too True To Be Good*, 1934.
[13]For a recent rather startling example, see Malcolm Muggeridge, *Jesus Rediscovered* (1969).

unity. Breaching the walls between sects and churches erected in Reformation times (or earlier, in the case of the Greek-Roman schism) has made some progress, and given rise to searching reexamination of church history and doctrine. The recent pontificate of John XXIII in the Roman Catholic Church was epochal for its turn in this direction. Many exciting world conferences have made what seem promising gains for ecumenicalism.

Yet though these is keen interest in religion, there is little assurance of what religion it is we are to hold. If Christianity, it must evidently be radically "de-mythologized" or revised. Some of the dilemmas confronting a Christianity that wishes to adjust to the modern age have been illustrated by recent "secular theology" which in its earnest desire to get back in the swing of things has virtually bracketed out any Christian content. The position popularized in England by the Bishop of Woolwich (*Honest to God*) and elsewhere by all kinds of swinging, protestleading, guitar-playing and folk-singing clergymen prided itself on being liberated from anything specifically Christian in the way of formal creed or liturgy. Leaning on "situation ethics," the Church could bypass conventional Christian morality; it could even talk of atheist or religionless Christianity. Critics of the "Honest to Godders" wonder whether such sweeping concessions to secularism will not soon liquidate historic Christianity altogether. Laudable in their desire to make the church and its teaching "relevant" to contemporary man, these Christians find that they must abolish Christianity in order to do so.

A series of books titled "Religious Perspectives," issued by a leading American publisher, dedicating to "dealing with basic spiritual concerns in the hope of defining a doctrine of man," illustrates some of the uncertainties. It distinguishes religion from theology, defining the former as "the feelings and aspirations of men . . . a sense of the sacred and the transcendent." "*Religious Perspectives* is an effort launched by informed and learned world leaders to guide us toward the spiritual serenity which is nowhere found amidst the mechanical triumphs of the rocket century," a distinguished scientist and historian wrote in the prospectus. Men hope, somehow, for "spiritual serenity" (which reminds us of the Stoic's quest during the period of the decline of the Roman Empire in ancient times) or for "feelings and aspirations." Granted the need and the sincerity of those who express it, one wonders if this vague yearning can possibly bear fruit in real religion. The miscellaneous tracts which have appeared in the above-mentioned series, excellent as some are, do not encourage one to believe that a religious renaissance is upon us. This one example is not of course conclusive. There are without question many earnest Christians in the world today, and many others who have adopted Zen Buddhism or something similar with equal sincerity. But there also appear to be modern Western intellectuals who are shopping for a good myth, and who cannot really believe in any except as a pose.

As has previously been suggested, there is (it is alleged) a degree of moral nihilism about the dominant mode of academic philosophy in the Anglo-Saxon world. If existentialism urges us to believe in something, no matter what, just so we believe, logical positivism tells us that no sort of moral belief has any rational defense and so one belief is as good as another—or perhaps none at all is best. C. E. M. Joad, in his book *A Critique of Logical Positivism* (1950), made the point eloquently. No community can survive, he pointed out, without a vigorous belief that some things are wrong (killing, cruelty, lying, faithlessness, etc.), yet our philosophers tell us these cannot be shown to be wrong but are merely subjective expressions of emotional preference. Nor can any civilization be vigorous unless its members are energized to action by their conviction that to do something is important, whether this be painting pictures, building steel mills, or raising food; yet contemporary philosophy declares all values unverifiable and thus implies that they are hardly worth holding. "Communism and Fascism," Joad added, "are the natural by-products of skepticism and nihilism. Most men need a creed and there is nothing in the empirical world upon which a creed can be based." If this indictment of our philosophers is overdrawn, as doubtless it is, it yet contains some truth.

Philosophy such as that of the analytical school would seem to be in danger of suffering the same fate as that which overtook the medieval philosophers. "Thought divorced from life must always wither, and the philosopher of the fourteenth century withdrew more and more into his own world, in which definitions and conclusions were no longer controlled by all other kinds of human experiences. . . . Thought preyed upon itself, and suffered fragmentation." David Knowles's comment on the schoolmen might be applied with equal force to the contemporary academics. If so, it is suggestive of decadence and the end-of-an-age, despite the subtlety of contemporary philosophical analysis. The late Middle Ages had their subtle doctors, too, but they were swept aside in the revolution of Renaissance and Reformation.

The reply of the philosophers would be that it cannot be wrong to apply intelligence and reason to moral and political questions, where irrational nonsense has reigned. The philosophers really assert a value, at bottom; it is the value of rational, critical, analytical thought. Now few in the West are prepared to deny this value. With it, however, it becomes impossible to accept in the fullest sense—and religions are not much good if half-hearted—any religious affirmation of values. Modern Western man, at least at the top intellectual level, is ultrasophisticated and disabused. He can find nothing to believe in. Despairingly, he may try to believe in belief itself, telling himself that there is something heroic in making up values. This is the path of existentialism from Nietzsche to Sartre. Academic philosophy seems content to show how irrational the whole process of value-making is and dismiss it from the list of problems to be tackled by logic and reason. It is, at least, not *their* business.

Looked at in this light, contemporary thought might be seen as a study in frustration in which myths are set up for logical analysis to demolish. In one corner of the ring is the positivistic philosopher, descended from Hume and possessing all the keen-edged weapons of modern logic, prepared to knock down anything that can be said about values, purpose, God, etc. He will allow us to believe in nothing except observed facts. Seconding him are hosts of scientists and scientific naturalists. In the other corner appear all kinds of myths, some imported from the Orient or even from the primitive world, some dredged up from the European past, some newly created; often they are violent and irrational, and they seek to overcome the sharp jabs of the analysts by the sheer force of their affirmations. Desperately needing a religion, modern man cannot really believe in any.

Perhaps the last such article of belief was a belief in History itself, the natural process of human evolution, as having a plan and a goal, to which we might look for guidance. But, as we have noted, empirical investigation reveals no such clear pattern, and we can only affirm it by a blind act of faith. The moral bankruptcy of a naturalistic ethic, which tries to endow with absolute value what is supposed to happen next, has been revealed as much by the dogmatic Marxists as by the social Darwinists. Men still look to history for a clue to what they should believe. Thus the very intelligent Frenchman, Bertrand de Jouvenel: "If we look at the history of Man since the Stone Age, we find that men have always been altering their processes; this, then, pertains to our species; as a believer I must conclude that we were meant to do so and therefore that it is good." It may seem a doubtful argument; are we to imitate all that "pertains to our species," including war, torture, greed, corruption, exploitation? Any set of values ranged against these all-too-human traits must in the last analysis come from outside man himself, outside the bald record of what he has done. Where to find such values?

Amid desperate attempts to affirm a faith gratuitously, there remain those who insist that scientific truth must be the touchstone of any faith. British empiricism as represented by Lord Russell and others remained unconvinced of the merits of anything not founded on experimental verification and the critical reason. "As soon as it is held that any belief . . . is important for some other reason than that it is true, a whole host of evils is ready to spring up," Russell has remarked. And it is more than doubtful that he would regard the truths of Jung, of the existentialists, and of the crisis theologians as demonstrable. Julian Huxley, for his part, has spoken at various times of "scientific humanism," "evolutionary humanism," and just "humanism." The term suffered from considerable vagueness, but Huxley was clear enough about (a) his dislike of Christianity and other of the classic "religions," such as Buddhism, and (b) his conviction that Western man desperately needs some sort of substitute for religion, some kind of integrating and orienting idea-system, rooted in science yet able to supply values. This feeling bears some relationship to the Russian-American social theorist P. A. Sorokin's call for an "integral" philosophy, to combine the best of all of his alleged sociocultural modes, the idealist, sensate, and ideational—in other words to get the best of both the religious, philosophical, and scientific worlds. So Huxley's humanism comes to look very much like Comte's religion of humanity, as he abjures us in effect to worship human nature. In the view of existentialist and religious critics, Sir Julian's man-worship leads to those very totalitarian systems he most abhors, to Nazism and Communism, which are the fruits of godlessness and "titanism." But this vigorous scientist, who later became the first director of UNESCO, would say that only through the scientific reason can man find his way to sanity in an age of irrationality.

If religious need is, as C. E. M. Joad has written, "a product of man's consciousness of his loneliness and helplessness in an alien and indifferent universe," then this need has never been greater than it is today; for with all his technological apparatus modern man must realize as never before how frightening are the cosmic forces he confronts. Hopefully launching his rockets at the moon, he cannot but be aware, if he reflects, what strange and terrifying adventures may await him if he probes into the incalculable vastness of the universe with its other possible worlds. At home, he suffers from the paralyzing fear of a nuclear war that would cause the most ghastly suffering in his history, while he continues to be plagued by political conflicts suggesting that he has hardly advanced much in this area since Thucydides and Plato tried to fathom the causes and cure of war and civil strife. Moreover all his economic affluence has not given him happiness.

"The spirit of man in the present age has been under a gray pall of uncertainty, insecurity, skepticism," a well-known British philosophical writer, Lord Samuel, remarked a few years ago. In the present age, it has also exhibited unconquerable vitality, defying a hostile universe to assert new values, in a truly Promethean gesture. But there remains a deep schism in the soul of the West which it is hard to see being altogether cured, so long as it retains the knowledge and subtlety of which skepticism is the natural fruit. This dilemma has haunted the most sensitive and creative minds of the twentieth century. *The Castle*, Franz Kafka's symbolic novel, depicted modern man frantically and unsuccessfully searching for those who will tell him what to do and to be. This feeling lies behind the desperate evocation of the primitive (back to the Etruscans or the blond beasts) which some of the most profound moderns have so strangely attempted. Fascism, Nazism, and communism may be seen as equally desperate reactions against the cultural crisis of a civilization built on skepticism, on freedom to do—what?[14] And this dilemma may explain why intelligent non-Westerners have been puzzled by the West's apparent lack of faith in itself. (Dr. Malik, the Arab philosopher, remarked a few years ago that "the Western mind . . . has been softened and undermined from within and without. The effect of this softening has been for this mind to lost faith in itself. . . .")

Despite signs of revival and of a toughness that defies disaster, one must surely concede extensive evidence of decadence in contemporary Europe. The European world shows signs of having exhausted its usable traditions. Paradoxically, in the midst of so rich an inheritance it finds no gesture that gives satisfaction, but compulsively repeats stale ones that have lost their magic. Or it may decide simply that life is absurd, and celebrate its absurdity. The "theater of the absurd" and the novel of the absurd are prominent features on the recent literary scene. Avantgarde musical composers give up all attempts to shape a work of art and simply record "environmental sounds and noises," or permit each instrument of the orchestra to play what it wishes (John Cage). Painting and sculpture, in total disarray, are subject to outlandish fads which change virtually every month.

The more serious of recent attitudes toward thought and culture deplore any effort to render it meaningful as a whole. We have noted this trend in the case of phenomenology in philosophy and *chosisme* in the novel: concentration on the immediate and particular, the object or momentary mental state as such, with total rejection in something like horror of any attempt to build a system, formulate a total ideology, or even extract any larger significance from the object or experience itself. In a book about Ezra Pound (1964), the notable British poet and critic Donald Davie reproached the poets of Pound's generation for taking the whole of history and culture as their subject matter. One settles for

---

[14]Erich Fromm, *Escape From Freedom* (1941): freedom, so long striven for, turned to ashes in the mouth of modern man and brought a terrible loneliness, from which he flees, because of the absence of values. Lewis Mumford, *A Faith for Living* (1940): "Fascism . . . reveals certain obdurate truths about life itself which never entered the doctrines of those who believed in automatic progress." Robert S. Lynd, *Knowledge for What?* (1939): the source of fascism is "in the human soul, not in economics."

utter pluralism and lets it go at that. Perhaps we shall learn to do so and live happily in a world of immediate sensations. But without unity—or continuity—can culture long survive? Do we return to the primitive from which we sprang? If so, the whole process would no doubt begin all over again. With a Vichian roll of thunder, the historical cycle is renewed; "the world's great age begins anew."

A recent study of André Malraux by William Righter finds the clue to that extraordinary Frenchman in a restless search for a cause. In turn revolutionary, novelist, art critic, and politician, this modern Chateaubriand, child of Nietzsche, Spengler, and Pascal, with a sense of modern man's tragic predicament has tried to escape it by finding a worthy goal to pursue. Though he has tried many, it is not clear that Malraux ever settled on one, and so rather like baroque man he has simply been a man in movement. It would be possible, with Heraclitus and Montaigne, to rest content with an ephemeral and illusory world, seeing change itself as the only value. But European man obviously is not happy with such a solution; he must find some absolute. Yet he seems unable to do so.

The Next Stage?

Having pointed out some notable areas of tension afflicting our common civilization today—between technology and humanism, reason and faith—and some signs of decadence, it would be wrong not to add that every civilization confronts similar conflicts, along with others, and that Western civilization possesses terrific resources of vitality with which to encounter them. It is not amiss to include a tribute to Europe and the West. Coming home from a trip to the Orient in which he investigated aspects of Indian and Japanese thought, Arthur Koestler in his interesting book *The Lotus and the Robot* told how

> I started my journey in a sackcloth and ashes and came back rather proud of being a European.

With the return of confidence after being shaken badly by the two horrible fratricidal wars of this century, Europe is likely to return to the fountains of its own traditions more and more. Western civilization has revealed powers of renewal and regeneration many times before. Its history is a history of renaissances, of which *the* Renaissance, the postmedieval renewal based on rediscovery of the ancient classics, was only one. Battered by the terrific crisis of the Reformation, Europe came up with the scientific and intellectual renaissance of the seventeenth century, a renewal based on the creative use of older materials. Shaken by the French Revolution and its wars, Europe integrated this revolution into its traditional culture in the nineteenth century. Mass democracy, specialization, and industrial technology today present a challenge that Western civilization may be able to meet.

The somewhat tentative and inconclusive quality of this final chapter testifies principally to the historian's inevitable uncertainty in the present. Tomorrow is necessary to understand today. That is the very reason for writing history: with the passage of time, the past falls into perspective—into various perspectives, indeed—and events or ideas which then seemed chaotic reveal their meaning. The historian is at a loss to predict the future. "Historicisms" of the past which claimed that they had found the key to all history, past, present, and future, stand forever discredited; we can no longer believe in this particular brand of theology disguised as science. Evolution creates ever fresh forms which are outgrowths of the past but could not have been predicted; lucky guesses are possible, but systematic prediction and control is not. If one knew only the seed one could hardly foretell the plant. In history, too, we are in the position of not knowing what the final result, if there is any, will be. We can see where we have been, and from this suggest some possibilities for the future, but possibilities only. Of all people, indeed, the historian is probably most aware of diversity and contingency in man's affairs.

One guess, often risked today, which seems very nearly a certainty in a broad sense, is that the West must and inevitably will make fruitful contacts with non-Western peoples' including not only the richly developed Oriental civilizations but also peoples much closer to the primitive than ourselves. Asia and Africa have entered into history, and the world has taken on new dimensions for European man. A typical comment is this one by Mircea Eliade: "Western culture will be in danger of a decline into a sterilizing provincialism if it despises or neglects the dialogue with the other cultures. . . . The West will have to know and to understand the existential situations and the cultural universe of the non-Western peoples. . . . Furthermore, this confrontation with 'the others' helps Western man better to understand himself." The last point is an illustration of the familiar fact that we as individuals or as social units commonly define ourselves, in good part, through our relation to others and to a larger organism consisting of ourselves and these others.

Professor Eliade, a leading student of comparative religions, adds that some recent developments in Western thought have prepared us for this task. Depth psychology, including Jung's interest in the world of myth as related to the dynamism of the psyche, is one; and in general that discovery of the unconscious irrational which came to Europe in the age of Nietzsche and Freud, and of the Symbolists in art. *Myths, Dreams and Mysteries: The Encounter Between Contemporary Faiths and Archaic Realities* is the title of Eliade's book from which the above quotation came. Cultural anthropologists have been at work, ever since the later nineteenth century, probing the psychology of contemporary primitive man and suggesting theories of the role of myth and religion. A good deal of what Christian Europe and rationalist Europe formerly dismissed as simply superstitious nonsense now has become of deep interest, because it reveals the primordial workings of the human mind, and insofar as it probes the religious element, it can be of more than clinical interest. It is perhaps significant that one of the outstanding influences on French thought in recent years has come from a brilliant anthropologist, Claude Lévi-Strauss, whose highly sophisticated, technically accomplished analyses of primitive societies seem to offer deep insights into all human cultures.

This "dialogue between East and West," or between civilized and primitive, need not submerge Western civilization in a syncretic world culture, though it might. It could result in more sharply defining and discovering the West's own being, as effective dialogue can do. It might wake that old civilization up and save it from its weary skepticism. It can remove misunderstandings between civilizations thus helping to reduce conflicts and wars. There is a great deal of mixing and mingling going on today, as everyone knows. Americans assist in the founding of African universities; people from all over the world come to American, British, French, and Russian universities; thousands of scholars annually exploit the lavish subsidization of international intellectual exchange.

The outcome of all this is most problematical; but no one would deny that it must eventually entail some sort of a revolution in the mental outlook of all men. What sort, it is impossible to predict. Wyndham Lewis spoke of "cosmic man," denationalized and made into a common mold; he thought the Americans represented this process, having no particular national culture but being products of the modern machine age, and that the rest of the world would sooner or later be "Americanized." It is a fate many European intellectuals would regard as worse than death, yet there may be something in it. Their own lands are in fact being to a degree "Americanized," though this is not really Americanization at all but the penetration of modern technology and its by-products (business methods, etc.) and of cultural democracy.[15] (One of

[15]This concern has been underscored by the rapid industrialization of parts of Western Europe in quite recent years. Since 1946 Italy has been transformed from a predominantly agricultural country into an industrial power. A considerable technological modernization of France went on in the de Gaulle era.

the most widely read serious books of recent years in France was *The American Challenge*, by the brilliant politician-journalist Jacques Servan-Schreiber.) Neither machine technology nor democracy was invented by the Americans, they only arrived at their full fruition earliest in the United States. Television and the cinema are "cosmic" cultural forces, along with the business and industry of a world increasingly knit together commercially. The "international style" in architecture may be as depressing as most motion pictures made on the French Riviera by American producers using Italian actresses; it may be equally depressing to some to watch Tokyo change from a Japanese city to a kind of exotic imitation of New York. Fads for Zen or for African art may seem the shallow pretensions of pseudointellectuals. But all this happened once before in history, at the time of the Alexandrian and then Roman Empire. And perhaps out of this vast process of syncretization will emerge new civilizations, as Western Europe emerged from the decay of the ancient world.

At any rate this dialogue and this mixing go on, and must surely hold one of the keys to our future. The process underscores the radical change that is taking place in the world of ideas. It looks very much as though this is a critical stage in man's long journey, and that what comes next, perhaps in the next century, must decide the question of his future on earth.

Apart from such larger issues, there are many potentialities of thought that may be provisionally projected, and some are outgrowths of more familiar Western preoccupations. Though the old ideologies may be in disarray, the drive toward social reform and amelioration continues. There are many dreadfully urgent evils to be assailed. Things are drastically wrong with society, culture, and the economy. Poverty needs to be remedied, labor made more creative, leisure more rewarding, urban living less bleak. Automation and overpopulation challenge industrial society to adapt or choke to death on its own products.

The influence of Marx in a more sophisticated and perhaps fruitful way appears in recent sociology: the work of Raymond Aron in France, of Ralf Dahrendorf (*Class and Conflict in Industrial Society*), or the volumes of *Marxismus Studien* sent out from the University of Tübingen, edited by Dr. I. Fetscher, can be instanced. Marx is here corrected and expanded beyond the toleration of any dogmatic Marxian ideologist, but the problems to which he pointed and many of his concepts remain. Industrial society with its classes, conflicts, and frustrations is still after all fundamental to Western civilization. Despite what was said about the apparent poverty of New Left thought, this quest for fresh formulations will go on, making judicious use of old materials. The crisis consists in the decadence of nineteenth-century social ideologies which were apocalyptic religions, essentially romantic faiths embracing historicism, messianic expectations, total solutions, and total explanations. These myths have been seen through, and have proved disastrous failures. The task consists in harnessing social reform to a different vehicle. Can it be a neutral science, or is this a sterile notion?

Foreign policy is another area beset by myths and goblins, never really reduced to a rational science, and in grave need of much high-level conceptualization that must involve historian and political scientist. The public mind must then be educated to accept more sophisticated views and analyses. This involves a better journalism and a more highly educated public. The whole vast undertaking of making democracy work by adjusting a complex, mass society to the individual's understanding looms before us. The old Matthew Arnold-Alexis de Tocqueville questions still demand an answer: can democracy be intelligent, produce a higher culture, and solve its problems effectively?

The crisis of literature is the need to socialize the rebellious artist, the lonely individual and defier of conventions, alienated from society. A recent perceptive study of American literature bears the title *After Alienation*. Must the creative writer always stand in opposition to the crowd? If so, need he stand quite so far away? And *after* alienation, *after* estheticism, what indeed? The desperation of recent bohemian gestures, referred to above, suggests that this can hardly go on. The Baudelaire-Rimbaud effect was grand, but it cannot forever be repeated. The future of literature, like the future of religion, is an open and an urgent question.

It is wrapped up with the broader question of the future of culture itself. Quite a few European historians and intellectuals in the past century have evoked the picture of the traditional European culture, rooted in the classics and carried by a literate elite, being borne under by a tide of mass-men which has increasingly thinned and degraded the great traditions. It is a familiar picture, and from Kierkegaard and Nietzsche to Jaspers and Ortega y Gasset it has inspired poignant lament. Its implication that what has ruined modern man is democracy repels the socialist left; and insofar as it blames the decline on machinery and industrialization, it is obviously a vain lament. But the concern to preserve culture—conceived of broadly as a power of serious, sustained thinking within a context of accepted knowledge—against the modern barbarism of mass media and on the other hand overspecialization, must be the enduring mission of those whom Mr. Henry Mencken liked to call the "civilized minority"—the clerks, the intellectuals, the teachers, writers, and readers. On the one hand lie the comic book, the tabloid newspapers, advertising, paperback sex, the average television program, opening up horizons of mental degeneracy never before known, not even by primitive man who had more dignity and content in his myths than this. These things represent a negation of all the high ideals of life in favor of a kind of least common denominator of the consciousness; they reflect the condition of people cut off from contact with any accepted and orderly body of expression and learning.

On the other hand is a vision of mountain ranges, reaching back through the centuries, of the poets, philosophers, and great thinkers, ultimately back in the far distance to Plato, Aristotle, and Homer; nearer lie high peaks called Shakespeare, Milton, Montaigne, Rousseau, and an incredible number of other hills. It has now become too formidable a terrain to be entered for most people; perhaps it always was. But it constitutes the West's spiritual home. Today the citizens of this mighty realm live in mud huts on the plain nearby, fearing to enter the magic land that was their home. They seem to have lost the map.

Epilogue

By way of brief epilogue to a book already overly long, though far too short for its subject, it may be noted simply that ideas do live on. Madame Sevigné, celebrated seventeenth-century wit, once remarked that Cartesianism, like coffee, would prove a temporary fashion. She was wrong (doubly!). There have been temporary fashions often enough in the world of ideas, now largely forgotten; but even the most obscure left some stamp on the human race, and Madame Sevigné's ghastly error reminds us that some leave a very heavy impress indeed. They shape our civilization, it is not too much to say. At least they shape the way we conceive and describe it, which comes to very nearly the same thing. We can hardly escape them.

Taking stock of Western civilization after World War II, Georges Bernanos opined that its future would have to be Cartesian or Hegelian (perhaps, as E. Morot-Sir has rejoined, it must manage to combine the two). Others, like Sartre, declare that we cannot escape coming to terms with Marxism, the "unsurpassable" ideological statement for our age. Still others would suggest that it is the Enlightenment, especially as summed up by Rousseau, that must be digested or thoroughly regurgitated, the central problem of our civilization.

Without pausing to examine or explain such statements, we can surely see roughly what they mean and in what sense they are valid. Ideas sum up epochs, generalize whole realms of individual human experience. "Cartesianism" is shorthand for the challenge of technological power and a scientific culture; Hegelianism for nationalism and secular messianism; Marxism for the problem of creativity in an industrial age, etc. Ideas, the ones that survive, have their roots in social reality and express urgent human needs. They enable us to think about these needs and so to begin to meet them. As an aid to such thinking, they need to be studied with the utmost care, and by more people; for as John Locke said, "in truth the ideas and images in men's minds are the invisible powers that constantly govern them."

This is the realm of what Father Teilhard de Chardin has named the "noösphere," the realm of the mind and all its products. Here, as Julian Huxley has written, man finds "floating in this noösphere . . . for his taking, the daring speculations and aspiring ideals of men long dead, the organized knowledge of science, the hoary wisdom of the ancients, the creative imaginings of all the world's poets and artists"—all this and much more too. The organization of the noösphere, as both these great modern biologists suggest, is the great task of the future and one which has scarcely yet begun. Huxley has noted how much of the vast amount of knowledge presently being accumulated, in the various special branches of learning, is "lying around unused" because "not integrated into fruitful concepts and principles, not brought into relevance to human life and its problems" (*The Humanist Frame*, 1961).

If the most urgent task confronting man is the organization of his ideas so that they may be creatively used, and if these ideas indeed are "the invisible powers that govern men," then the systematic study of ideas, in relation to life, that is, the social and historical context, would seem to be not the least important of the many studies currently pursued. A great deal of work remains to be done.

Suggested Reading

General Works

Suggested general works at the broadest level include John H. Randall, Jr., *The Making of the Modern Mind* (1940) and *The Career of Philosophy* (2 vols., 1970); Meyrick H. Carré, *Phases of Thought in England* (1949); Frederick Copleston, *A History of Philosophy* (8 vols., 1950–1967); Franklin L. Baumer (ed.), *Main Currents of Western Thought* (3rd ed., 1970), an excellent selection of source readings. A recent textbook, *The Emergence of Liberal Humanism: An Intellectual History of Western Europe*, by W. H. Coates, J. S. Schapiro and H. V. White (2 vols., 1966–1970) may be compared with the older Harry Elmer Barnes, *Intellectual and Cultural History of the Western World* (3 vols., 1937), also J. Bronowski and B. Mazlish, *The Western Intellectual Tradition: Leonardo to Hegel* (1960). See also Friedrich Heer, *Intellectual History of Europe* (tr. 1966), and Philippe Wolff, *Histoire de la pensée européenne*, a multivolume French series of which the first volume was published in 1971. Also notable are distinguished histories of special areas of thought: for example, George H. Sabine, *A History of Political Theory* (3rd ed., 1961); Marcel Prélot, *Histoire des idées politiques*

(4th ed., 1970); Emory S. Bogardus, *The Development of Social Thought* (4th ed., 1960); Eduard Heimann, *History of Economic Doctrines* (1964); René Taton, *History of Science* (4 vols., 1964–1966); Gilbert Highet, *The Classical Tradition* (1967); R. G. Collingwood, *The Idea of History* (1946); Arnold Hauser, *Social History of Art* (4 vols., 1963); Nikolaus Pevsner, *An Outline of European Architecture* (7th ed., 1963); Donald Jay Grout, *A History of Western Music* (1960); René Wellek, *A History of Modern Criticism* (4 vols., 1955–1963); William Boyd, *The History of Western Education* (9th ed., 1968); Walter M. Horton, *Christian Theology* (1955). For general historical background, *The New Cambridge Modern History*, by various authors (12 vols., 1957–1968).

Chapter 1

Many of the works cited under *General Works* are valuable for obtaining an overview of the Western tradition prior to modern times, for example, the earlier portions of Baumer, Lovejoy, Highet, Randall's *Making of the Modern Mind*, and Carré. Herschel Baker, *The Image of Man: A Study of The Idea of Human Dignity in Classical Antiquity, the Middle Ages, and the Renaissance* (1947) is a book with breadth and flair. There are some excellent surveys of medieval philosophy, mostly not too technical, including Gordon Leff, *Medieval Thought* (1958); David Knowles, *The Evolution of Medieval Thought* (1962); Etienne Gilson, *History of Christian Philosophy in the Middle Ages* (1955), a classic; Armand A. Maurer, *Medieval Philosophy* (1962); Walter Ullmann, *A History of Political Thought in the Middle Ages* (1965); John B. Morrall, *Political Thought in Medieval Times* (1958); Thomas Gilby (ed.), *St. Thomas Aquinas: Philosophical Texts* (1960); Charles H. Haskins, *The Renaissance of the Twelfth Century* (1953); and J. Huizinga, *The Waning of the Middle Ages* (1924).

Paul O. Kristeller's *The Classics and Renaissance Thought* (1955), published in paperback as *Renaissance Thought*, is a masterful condensation of information about the recovery of knowledge in the later Middle Ages. See also his more recent *Renaissance Concepts of Man* (1973). Federico Chabod, *Machiavelli and the Renaissance* (1958) is the work of a great modern historian and contains a valuable bibliographical essay. G. de Santillana (ed.), *The Age of Adventure* (1956) begins the useful and inexpensive Mentor series of five volumes on the philosophers. Wallace K. Ferguson's *The Renaissance in Historical Thought* (1948) clarifies the question of this period's role in history. Volumes recently published on the Renaissance include some roundups of current scholarship and some symposia: Bernard O'Kelly (ed.), *The Renaissance Image of Man and His World* (1966); Charles H. Singleton (ed.), *Art, Science and History in the Renaissance* (1967); and Eric Cochrane (ed.), *The Late Italian Renaissance* (1970). In *Architectural Principles in the Age of Humanism* (1965), Rudolf Wittkower makes luminously clear the foundations of Western order in the arts. Roberto Weiss, *The Spread of Italian Humanism* (1964) is a helpful summary.

J. S. Whale, *The Protestant Tradition* (1955); Karl Holl, *The Cultural Significance of the Reformation* (1911, repr. 1959); H. Daniel-Rops, *The Counter-Reformation* (1962); and Owen Chadwick, *The Reformation* (Volume III of *The Pelican History of the Church*, 1964) provide varying views of the Reformation. George H. Williams, *The Radical Reformation* (1962) is a thorough treatment of its significant subject. Gordon Leff, *Heresy in the Later Middle Ages* (2 vols., 1967) provides necessary background for the Protestant revolt. A. G. Dickens, *The Counter-Reformation* (1969) comes from an outstanding Reformation scholar. Further light on the troubled sixteenth century is shed by Lucien Febvre, *Le Problème de l'Incroyance au XVIe Siècle* (1946); Richard H. Popkin, *History of Scepticism from Erasmus to Descartes* (1960); and Hiram Haydn, *The Counter-Renaissance* (1950).

J. B. Bamborough, *The Little World of Man* (1952) and C. S. Lewis, *The Discarded Image* (1964) are brilliant dissections of the premodern psychology and outlook. On the baroque style, Frederick B. Artz, *From the Renaissance to Romanticism: Trends in Style, Art, Literature and Music 1300–1800* (1962); Jean Rousset, *Circe et le Paon* (1953); Jacques Ehrmann, *Un Paradis désesperé: L'Amour et l'illusion dans "L'Astrée"* (1963); Imbrie Buffum, *Studies in the Baroque from Montaigne to Rotrou* (1957); and a quantity of art books, of which Victor L. Tapié, *The Age of Grandeur* (1960) may serve as a sample. Randall's *Career of Philosophy*, again, contains a splendid review of the medieval heritage feeding into the modern world. Carl J. Friedrich's *The Age of Baroque 1610–1660* (1952), in the *Rise of Modern Europe* series, is excellent historical background, as is Friedrich and Charles Blitzer, *The Age of Power* (1957).

Chapter 2

The history of science owes much to such pioneers as George Sarton, *Introduction to the History of Science* (1927–1948) and Lynn Thorndike, *History of Magic and Experimental Science* (1923–1941), authors of multivolume works which deal mainly with ancient and medieval science. Also a pioneer in calling attention to the medieval predecessors of modern science was the Frenchman Pierre Duhem, *Études sur Leonard de Vinci* (1906–1913), and other works. Among more recent studies, Otto Neugebauer, *The Exact Sciences in Antiquity* (2nd ed., 1958) and Marshall Clagett, *Greek Science in Antiquity* (1955) can serve as references for the scientific legacy of the ancient world. Nicole Oresme's *Le Livre du ciel et du monde* has been edited by Albert D. Menut and Alexander J. Denomy for the University of Wisconsin Publications in Medieval Science, general editor Marshall Clagett, a series which includes other notable documents. Edward Grant, *Physical Science in the Middle Ages* (1971) forms a part of the Wiley History of Science series. A. C. Crombie, *Medieval and Early Modern Science* (paperback title, 2 vols., 1952), is an excellent study that includes the seventeenth-century founders of modern science, making clear the essential continuity from medieval foundations. A splendid introduction for the general reader is Herbert Butterfield, *Origins of Modern Science* (rev. ed. 1962); somewhat more detailed but still within the range of the nonscientist is A. R. Hall, *The Scientific Revolution 1500–1800* (1954). Hall and others collaborate in the *Rise of Modern Science* series, of which the third volume, *From Galileo to Newton* (1963), is by Hall, the second by Marie Boas dealing with the Renaissance period. Volume II of René Taton's *History of Science* deals with *The Beginnings of Modern Science* (1964). Edward Rosen (ed.), *Three Copernican Treatises*, containing a valuable Copernicus bibliography, appeared in a revised edition in 1971. Marie Boas Hall, *Nature and Nature's Laws* (1970) is one of a documentary series on Western civilization. Brief but authoritative is I. B. Cohen, *The Birth of a New Physics* (1960).

No writer has so vividly placed Copernicus, Kepler, Brahe, and Galileo in the framework of history as has Arthur Koestler, *The Sleepwalkers* (1959). The leading biographer of Kepler is Max Caspar (1960). On Copernicus, there are A. Armitage, *Sun, Stand Thou Still* (1947) and T. S. Kuhn, *The Copernican Revolution* (1956), Kuhn being also the author of *The Structure of Scientific Revolutions* (1962). G. de Santillana's *The Crime of Galileo* (1955) is a scholarly examination of the famous trial. Add John G. Gade, *Life and Times of Tycho Brahe* (1947).

Works on the intellectual implications of the new science include Alexander Koyré, *From the Closed World to the Infinite Universe* (1957); E. A. Burtt, *Metaphysical Foundations of Modern Science* (1932); R. G. Collingwood, *The Idea of Nature* (1945), an essay which contrasts the seventeenth-century mechanistic view of nature with both the ancient and the nineteenth-century evolutionary outlooks. Basil Willey, *The Seventeenth-Century Background* (1934) stresses the new climate of opinion in its impact on literature, as does J. A. Mazzeo, *Renaissance and Revolution: Backgrounds to Seventeenth-Century English Literature* (1967). Alfred North Whitehead, *Science and the Modern World* (1925) is a classic by a great modern philosopher; E. J. Dijksterhuis, *The Mechanization of the World Picture* (1961) is rather duller but well documented. Such books as E. M. W. Tillyard, *The Elizabethan World Picture* (1952) along with the previously cited books by Bamborough and Lewis help to delineate the older view of man and nature against which revolution was taking place. Francis A. Yates, *Giordano Bruno and the Hermetic Tradition* (1964) examines an important figure, on whom Dorothea W. Singer has also written (1950). An interesting sidelight is John Dillenberger's *Protestant Thought and Natural Science* (1960).

Volume IV of Copleston's *History of Philosophy* (1959) covers Descartes to Leibniz, an admirable survey. Stuart Hampshire (ed.), *The Age of Reason*, Volume II of the Mentor series, presents selections from the philosophers with explanatory comments. *Descartes: Philosophical Writings*, edited by Elizabeth Anscombe and Thomas Geach (1954), with an introduction by Alexander Koyré and a useful bibliography, may be recommended from among the popular editions of the great Frenchman's writings. A. G. A. Balz, *Descartes and the Modern Mind* (1952, 1967); Leon Roth, *Descartes's Discourse* on *Method* (1937) and Norman Kemp Smith, *Studies in Cartesian Philosophy* (repr. 1962) may be selected from a large literature on him, to which a good guide is Gregor Sebba, *Bibliographia Cartesiana: A Critical Guide to the Descartes Literature 1800–1960* (1964). There are also numerous popular editions of the writings of Francis Bacon. A useful paperback is Benjamin Farrington, *The Philosophy of Francis Bacon* (1964). Fulton H. Anderson, *The Philosophy of Francis Bacon* (1948), and also *Francis Bacon, His Career and Thought* (1962), are by the leading Bacon scholar in this country.

Pascal's *Pensées* is available in the paperback edition edited and translated by J. M. Cohen, and Ernest Mortimer, *Blaise Pascal* (1957) is among those that have been written about Pascal—a sound brief study. H. Wolfson, *The Philosophy of Spinoza* (1957) and Beatrice K. Rome, *The Philosophy of Malebranche* (1964) deal with the other great philosophers of the Cartesian century; see also H. F. Hallett, *Benedict de Spinoza* (1957) or Stuart Hampshire, *Spinoza* (1954) in *The Penguin Philosophy Series*. S. H. Mellone, *The Dawn of Modern Thought* (1930) is brief and popular but good on Descartes and Spinoza. Other significant figures are covered in Ernst Cassirer, *The Platonic Renaissance in England* (English tr. 1953); F. J. Powicke, *The Cambridge Platonists* (1926); and Richard S. Westfall, *Science and Religion in Seventeenth-Century England* (1958). Leslie Stephens, *Hobbes* (repr. 1961) discusses the materialist, on whom see further under the next chapter. H. G. van Leewen, *The Problem of Certainty in English Thought 1630–1690* (1963) discusses some philosophical issues.

John Herivel, *The Background of Newton's Principia* (1966) makes use of new materials, some of which are reprinted in A. R. Hall (ed.), *Unpublished Scientific Papers of Isaac Newton* (1962). *Newton's Philosophy of Nature*, edited by H. S. Thayer (1953), is still a usable introduction. Frank E. Manuel, *A Portrait of Isaac Newton* (1968) is an important new biography. Alexander Koyré, *Newton Studies* (1965) comes from a veteran historian of science. Voltaire's *Elements of Sir Isaac Newton's Philosophy* has been translated and reprinted (1968). Cf. the modern commentary by I. Bernard Cohen, *Introduction to Newton's Principia* (1971). Ralph M. Blake, Edward H. Madden, and Curt J. Ducasse, *Theories of Scientific Method from the Renaissance through the Nineteenth Century* (1960) puts this subject in perspective. A. E. Bell, *Christian Huygens and the Development of Science* (1947) handles Newton's distinguished contemporary and critic. Among other scientists, there is *Robert Boyle and Seventeenth-Century Chemistry* (1958) by Marie Boas, also G. Whitteridge's *William Harvey and the Circulation of the Blood* (1971). Lester S. King, *The Growth of Medical Thought* (1963) covers this field capably.

Chapter 3

In addition to Morrall's and Ullmann's books on medieval political thought, already cited, there are numerous others on that subject among which might be singled out Ralph Lerner and Muhsin Mahdi (ed.), *Medieval*

Political Philosophy: A Sourcebook (1963). In view of their primary importance, Ernest Barker, *Greek Political Theory* (1918); A. E. Taylor, *Aristotle* (1919); and Aristotle's own *Politics* should be read. Closer to our period, Otto Gierke, *Natural Law and the Theory of Society 1500–1800* (1950) and J. W. Allen, *History of Political Thought in the Sixteenth Century* (1928, 1957) are classic studies. So is J. N. Figgis, *The Divine Right of Kings* (2nd ed., 1934). Leonard Krieger has recently remedied the relative neglect in the English world of a major figure in his *The Politics of Discretion: Pufendorf and the Acceptance of Natural Law* (1965). *The Political Works of Spinoza*, edited and translated by A. G. Wernham (1958), are relevant here.

Wilbur K. Jordan, *The Development of Religious Toleration in England* (4 vols., 1932–1940), is a magisterial work of which the first volume covers the sixteenth century and the last three the seventeenth down to 1660. Hugh Martin, *Puritanism and Richard Baxter* (1954) is an interesting little book dealing with a prominent figure. Joseph Lecler has two able volumes on *Toleration and the Reformation* (1960). Works on seventeenth-century France are W. J. Stankiewicz, *Politics and Religion in Seventeenth-Century France* (1961) and J. H. M. Salmon, *The French Wars of Religion in English Political Thought* (1959). Donald R. Kelley, *François Hotman: A Revolutionary's Ordeal* (1973) is an important contribution to understanding this important Huguenot political thinker. Henry Bertram Hill has recently edited a critical edition of *The Political Testament of Cardinal Richelieu* (1961). The great Puritan Revolution in England may be approached via P. Zagorin's excellent *A History of Political Thought in the Puritan Revolution* (1954) and Christopher Hill's stimulating *Puritanism and Revolution* (1958). Hill is also the author of *The Intellectual Origins of the English Revolution* (1964). On Puritanism generally, see Marshall M. Knappen, *Tudor Puritanism* (1939) and Alan Simpson, *Puritanism in Old and New England* (1958). William Haller, author of *The Rise of Puritanism* (1938), also was the editor of *Tracts on Liberty in the Puritan Revolution* (3 vols., 1934), partially reprinted in a recent paperback. J. G. A. Pocock presents a significant aspect of the question in *The Ancient Constitution and the Feudal Law: A Study of English Historical Thought in the Seventeenth Century* (1957). Z. S. Fink, *The Classical Republicans* (1945) traces some seventeenth-century political ideas back to their ancient roots. Norman Cohn, *The Pursuit of the Millenium* (1961), an uncommonly interesting book, traces the tradition of revolutionary messianism back into the Middle Ages and concludes with comments on its appearance in the era of Cromwell. Leo F. Solt, *Saints in Arms: Puritanism and Democracy in Cromwell's Armies* (1964) is another study in popular ideology. Further on Puritanism, B. R. White, *The English Separatist Tradition 1553–1620* (1971) and H. C. Porter, *Puritanism in Tudor England* (1970). The work of an older master, Rufus M. Jones, *Mysticism and Democracy in the English Commonwealth* (1932) has recently been reprinted. John F. H. New, *Anglican and Puritan: The Basis of Their Opposition 1558–1640* (1964) is a work of exemplary scholarship. P. G. Rogers, *The Fifth Monarchy Men* (1966) does justice to the Left; see also Arthur L. Morton, *The World of the Ranters* (1970), B. S. Capp, also on *The Fifth Monarchy Men* (1972), and Christopher

Hill's *The World Turned Upside Down* (1972). Lewis H. Berens, *The Diggers* (1961), and *The Works of Gerrard Winstanley*, edited by George H. Sabine (1941), cover the communist phase of the Revolution. On the Levellers C. Howard Shaw, *The Levellers* (1968) supplements Joseph Frank's 1955 book with the same title.

Works on individual figures include Charles Blitzer, *An Immortal Commonwealth: The Political Thought of James Harrington* (1960) and the older study of *Harrington and His Oceana* (1914) by H. F. Russell-Smith. Blitzer has also edited *The Political Writings of James Harrington* in paperback. On Hobbes, in addition to Leslie Stephen as cited earlier, see Leo Strauss, *The Political Philosophy of Hobbes* (1936); Howard Warrender, *The Political Philosophy of Hobbes* (1957); John Bowle, *Hobbes and His Critics* (1951), supplemented by Samuel Mintz, *The Hunting of Leviathan* (1962), and Richard Peters, *Hobbes* (1956). F. C. Hood, in *The Divine Politics of Thomas Hobbes* (1965) offered a reinterpretation of Hobbes as Christian rather than atheist; for further debate on this point see K. C. Brown, ed., *Hobbes Studies* (1965). Among later additions to the literature on Hobbes are M. M. Goldsmith, *Hobbes' Science of Politics* (1966), David P. Gauthier, *The Logic of Leviathan* (1969), and F. S. McNeilly, *The Anatomy of Leviathan* (1968). Hobbes's *Leviathan* is available in many editions; one of the best was issued by Oxford in 1947 under the editorship of Michael Oakeshott. Arthur Barker's *Milton and the Puritan Dilemma* (1942) and D. M. Wolfe, *Milton in the Puritan Revolution* (1941) are of considerable relevance and interest here. Maurice Cranston, *John Locke, A Biography* (1957) introduces the author of the *Two Treatises on Government*, which have often been reprinted but which should now be studied in the Cambridge edition of 1960 edited by Peter Laslett. Ernest Barker (ed.), *The Social Contract* (1962) is a convenient source for Locke, Hume, and Rousseau. Standard commentaries are J. B. Gough, *John Locke's Political Philosophy* (1950) and *The Social Contract* (1936); also Sterling P. Lamprecht, *The Moral and Political Philosophy of John Locke* (repr. 1962). See also C. B. Macpherson, *The Political Theory of Possessive Individualism: Hobbes and Locke* (1962), a Marxist interpretation; John M. Dunn, *The Political Thought of John Locke* (1969), stressing links to Calvinism; James L. Axtell (ed.), *Educational Writings of John Locke* (1968), an important dimension of Locke's influence. (Cf. Richard L. Greaves, *The Puritan Revolution and Educational Thought*, 1969). The third edition of Richard I. Aaron's *John Locke* was published in 1971. Other signs of the unflagging interest in Locke are M. V. C. Jeffreys, *John Locke: Prophet of Common Sense* (1967); M. Seliger, *The Liberal Politics of John Locke* (1969); and Willmoore Kendall, *John Locke and the Doctrine of Majority Rule* (1965) which has a somewhat controversial thesis.

Chapter 4

Albert Guérard, *The Life and Death of an Ideal: France in the Classical Age* (1957) and Jacques Boulenger, *The Seventeenth Century in France* (repr.

1963) are good popular introductions to the Age of Louis XIV, on which there is also Voltaire's old classic, and W. H. Lewis's popular *The Splendid Century* (1953) and *Sunset of the Splendid Century* (1955). L. M. Marsak, *Fontenelle and the Idea of Science in the French Enlightenment* (1959) discusses one of the great figures of the age. James E. King, in *Science and Rationalism in the Government of Louis XIV* (1949), argued that the Cartesian spirit affected internal political organization. Robert Shackleton has edited Fontenelle's *Entretiens sur les pluralités des mondes* and *Digression sur les anciens et les modernes* (1955) in one volume. Richard F. Jones, *Ancients and Moderns* (1936) dealt with the famous *querelle* mostly in its English phase, but related it to the French. Nigel Abercrombie, *The Origins of Jansenism* (1936) is a scholarly monograph on a leading issue of this age. *Bossuet* (1964) has recently received the attention he deserves, from E. E. Reynolds. Volume V of the always useful *New Cambridge Modern History* (1962) is especially good on cultural and intellectual aspects. Paul Hazard, *The Crisis of the European Conscience* (1935) explores the 1680–1715 period as a critical one in the history of thought. Lionel Rothkrug, *Opposition to Louis XIV: The Political and Social Origins of the French Enlightenment* (1965) develops a similar theme. *Pierre Bayle* has found a keen student in Elizabeth Labrousse, though her extended study on the pioneer of the Enlightenment must be read in French (2 vols., 1963–1964). Bayle's *Historical and Critical Dictionary* is available in paperback (ed. R. H. Popkin, 1965). Other treatments of the celebrated skeptic include the older Howard Robinson book, *Bayle the Sceptic* (1932); H. T. Mason, *Pierre Bayle and Voltaire* (1963); Walter Rex, *Essays on Pierre Bayle and Religious Controversy* (1965); Craig B. Brush, *Montaigne and Bayle: Variations on the Theme of Scepticism* (1966). In *The Political Thought of the Huguenots of the Dispersion* (1947), G. H. Dodge devoted attention as well to Bayle's colleague and critic Jurieu. In *The Downfall of Cartesianism 1673–1712* (1966), Richard A. Watson discusses the age's philosophical and scientific debates.

James H. Hanford (ed.), *A Restoration Reader* (1954) is a delightful introduction to its subject; Louis I. Bredvold, *The Intellectual Milieu of John Dryden* (1934) is a splendid study in ideas, to which might be added Bernard N. Schilling, *Dryden and the Conservative Myth* (1961) and G. R. Cragg, *Puritanism in the Period of the Great Persecution 1660–1688* (1957). The excellent Pelican series of *Guides to English Literature* (1963) edited by Boris Ford includes *From Dryden to Johnson*, Vol. 4 of the series, preceded by *From Donne to Marvell*. Locke's "Essay" is found in numerous editions; it is lucidly commented on by Isaiah Berlin in the third of the Mentor series, *The Age of Enlightenment* (1956). James Gibson, *John Locke's Theory of Knowledge and Its Historical Relations* (1960) and John W. Yolton, *John Locke and the Way of Ideas* (1956) are among the best books about the Essay in relation to its times. Copleston's fifth volume (1959) treats Hobbes, Locke, and Hume. Further on Locke as philosopher, Jonathan Bennett, *Locke, Berkeley, Hume: Central Themes* (1971) and Charles B. Martin (ed.), *Locke and Berkeley: A Collection of Critical Essays* (1960). Recently reprinted, Richard F. Jones et al., *The Seventeenth Century: Studies in the History of English*

Thought from Bacon to Pope (1965) is a useful volume. Richard B. Schlatter's *Social Ideas of Religious Leaders 1660–1688* (1940) and G. R. Cragg's *From Puritanism to the Age of Reason* (1950) are among the best books on the religious climate in this crucial period between fanaticism and moderation.

Among the most satisfactory treatments of Leibniz for the nonspecialist are R. W. Meyer, *Leibniz and the Seventeenth-Century Revolution* (English ed., 1952) and portions of S. Mellone's book cited previously, along with Herbert W. Carr, *Leibniz* (1929). Ruth Saw's volume in the Penguin series (1954) is a little more analytical; one might also consult Bertrand Russell's older *Critical Exposition of the Philosophy of Leibniz* (1937). William A. Barber, *Leibniz in France* (1960) and Y. Belaval, *Leibniz Critique de Descartes* (1960) are outstanding monographs, the one primarily historical and the other philosophical. A paperback edition of *Leibniz: Selections* (1959) has been edited by Philip Wiener. Richard A. Brooks, *Voltaire and Leibniz* (1964) shows the king of the eighteenth-century Enlightenment grappling with the ghost of Leibniz.

Chapter 5

J. S. Spink, *French Free Thought from Gassendi to Voltaire* (1960) and R. N. Stromberg, *Religious Liberalism in Eighteenth-Century England* (1954) deal with deists and other religious radicals; so do E. M. Wilbur, *A History of Unitarianism* (1945); Walter M. Merrill, *From Statesman to Philosopher: A Study in Bolingbroke's Deism* (1949); and more recently G. R. Cragg, *Reason and Authority in the Eighteenth Century* (1964). Cragg's *The Church and the Age of Reason* is volume IV of the Pelican History of the Church (1963). A more recent handling of Bolingbroke is *Viscount Bolingbroke, Tory Humanist* by Jeffrey Hart (1965). The classic study in its field was Leslie Stephen, *History of English Thought in the Eighteenth Century* (2 vols., 1902). Ernest C. Mossner, *Bishop Butler and the Age of Reason* (1936) and Alfred Owen Aldridge, *Shaftesbury and the Deist Manifesto* (1951) shed further light. Rosemary Z. Lauer, *The Mind of Voltaire* (1961) is an examination of the French master's deism, as are Norman L. Torrey, *Voltaire and the English Deists* (1950) and René Pomeau, *La Religion de Voltaire* (1956), while Peter Gay has edited Voltaire's *Philosophical Dictionary* (1962).

Of the innumerable other books about Voltaire, there is *Voltaire and Mme. du Chatelet* (1941), by the leading American Voltaire scholar Ira O. Wade, who has written several others, including most recently *The Intellectual Development of Voltaire* (1969). Thomas Kendrick, *The Lisbon Earthquake* (1956) and David Bien, *The Calas Affair* (1960) authoritatively examine celebrated episodes involving Voltaire. On the earthquake, too, there is an essay by Theodore Besterman in his *Voltaire Essays* (1962), Besterman being best known for his work as director of the Voltaire Institute at Geneva and editor of the exhaustive edition of Voltaire's letters. Besterman has published a single volume of *Select Letters of Voltaire* (1963). Popular editions include

The Portable Voltaire, edited by Ben Ray Redman. Peter Gay, *Voltaire's Politics* (1959) is a lively book; see also J. H. Brumfitt, *Voltaire: Historian* (1958); Constance Rowe, *Voltaire and the State* (1955). The older (1906) biography of Voltaire by Gustave Lanson has been translated with an introduction by Peter Gay (1960). More than ninety volumes now exist of the series *Studies in Voltaire and the Eighteenth Century*, published annually by the Voltaire Institute in Geneva; these are a rich source of knowledge about Voltaire and the Enlightenment in general. See again Richard Brooks, *Voltaire and Leibniz.*

To the substantial biography of Montesquieu by Robert Shackleton (1962) may be added Thomas L. Pangle, *Montesquieu's Philosophy of Liberalism* (1973). L. Althusser, *Montesquieu: La Politique et l'histoire* (1959) is a succinct outline of ideas. Werner Stark has studied Montesquieu as *Pioneer of the Sociology of Knowledge* (1960). Both *The Spirit of the Laws* and *Persian Letters* are available in inexpensive editions. Arthur A. Wilson, *Diderot* (1972) is a most informative and useful work; another excellent one on Diderot by a distinguished American scholar is Lester G. Crocker's *The Embattled Philosopher* (1954). A. Vartanian, *Diderot and Descartes* (1953) is a study in ideas. Jonathan Kemp, *Diderot: Interpreter of Nature* (1963) is a selection of his writings stressing his philosophical materialism. Ronald Grimsley, *Jean D'Alembert* (1963) is a thorough treatment of Diderot's fellow Encyclopedist. John Lough, *Essays on the Encyclopedia of Diderot and D'Alembert* (1969) is by a veteran scholar in this field. *The Encyclopedia: Selections*, edited by Stephen J. Grendzier (1967), provides excerpts from the famous reference work. The journal *Diderot Studies* has been appearing since 1950. Roland Mortier, *Diderot en Allemagne* (1954) is an admirably careful piece of research.

F. C. Green, *Jean-Jacques Rousseau: A Critical Study of His Life and Writings* (1955) is an admirable and usually reliable guide. Among the many who have tackled what Ernst Cassirer called *The Question of Jean-Jacques Rousseau* (1954) are E. H. Wright, *The Meaning of Rousseau* (1929); John W. Chapman, *Rousseau: Totalitarian or Liberal?* (1956); and J. J. Broome, *Rousseau: A Study of His Thought* (1963). The *Confessions* and *First and Second Discourses* have been printed in popular editions along with the much-published *Social Contract*. Ronald Grimsley's *Rousseau: A Study in Self-awareness* (1961) is a psychological approach. J. L. Talmon, *The Origins of Totalitarian Democracy* (1960) joins Wright in being quite sure that Rousseau was not a liberal, but Alfred Cobban, *Rousseau and the Modern State* (rev. ed., 1965) disagrees. Older works of scholarship include C. E. Vaughan on Rousseau's political writings (1915) and P. M. Masson on his religion (1914). Testifying to a stream of interest in the Genevan that shows no sign of drying up are recent works in French by J. S. Spink, R. Derathé, Oliver Krafft, François Jost, and Jean Guéhenno. The latter's admirable two-volume biography was translated into English in 1966. Lester Crocker engaged in the same enterprise, of which volume 1, covering the years 1712–1758, was published in 1968, and the second and final one in 1973. See also Crocker's

Rousseau's Social Contract: An Interpretive Essay (1968). To an already long list of those fascinated by the Genevan one should add Ronald Grimsley, *Rousseau and the Religious Quest* (1968) and Judith Shklar, *Men and Citizens: A Study of Rousseau's Social Theory* (1969). The *Correspondance Complète* of Rousseau, in 12 volumes, edited by R. A. Leigh, was published in the United States by the University of Wisconsin Press, 1965–1970.

Thomas L. Hankins has written *Jean D'Alembert: Science and the Enlightenment* (1970). On other *philosophes:* David W. Smith, *Helvetius: A Study in Persecution* (1965) adds to the earlier I. L. Horowitz, *Claude Helvetius* (1954); William H. Wickwar, *Baron D'Holbach* (1935); J. S. Schapiro, *Condorcet and the Rise of Liberalism* (repr. 1963); M. L. Perkins, *The Moral and Political Philosophy of the Abbe St. Pierre* (1959); Aram Vartanian, *La Mettrie's 'L'Homme Machine'* (1960), to which may be compared Leonora C. Rosenfield, *From Beast Machine to Man Machine* (1941). Another of the French school receives competent attention in Isabel F. Knight, *The Geometric Spirit: The Abbe de Condillac and the French Enlightenment* (1968). Convenient anthologies of the entire movement have been assembled by Frank E. Manuel, *The Enlightenment* (1963) and Lester G. Crocker, *The Age of Enlightenment* (1969). Among older works which attempted a survey of the whole Enlightenment, Kingsley Martin, *French Liberal Thought in the Eighteenth Century* (1954) and George R. Havens, *The Age of Ideas* (1955) both tended to be rather uncritically adulatory; see Vincent Buranelli's criticism of the latter, "Another Look at the Philosophes," *Journal of the History of Ideas*, January, 1957. A more ambitious recent work of scholarship which attempts a reassessment is Peter Gay's two-volume *The Enlightenment: An Interpretation* (1966, 1970). Preserved Smith, *A History of Modern Culture: The Enlightenment* (Vol. II, 1934) is somewhat dated but still a useful survey, while Paul Hazard, *European Thought in the Eighteenth Century* (1954) is comprehensive if rather superficial, and the recent book by Norman Hampson, *A Cultural History of the Enlightenment* (1968) is more social than intellectual. Earl R. Wasserman (ed.), *Aspects of the Eighteenth Century* (1965) contains essays by a number of distinguished scholars on subjects literary, artistic, and philosophical. Other recent books of interest include Reginald J. White, *The Anti-Philosophers* (1970); Franco Venturi, *Utopia and Reform in the Enlightenment* (1971); Ira Wade, *Intellectual Origins of the French Enlightenment* (1971).

Chapter 6

Bishop Berkeley, *Three Dialogues* and David Hume, *Inquiry concerning Human Understanding* are both available in various editions; also H. D. Aiken (ed.), *Hume's Moral and Political Philosophy* (1948) and Eugene Rotwen (ed.), *Hume's Writings on Economics* (1955). Berlin, *Age of Enlightenment* and Copleston's Volume V are again relevant. C. R. Morris, *Locke, Berkeley, Hume* (1931) is a convenient short survey; G. J. Warnock, *Berkeley*

(1954) and A. H. Basson, *Hume* (1954) are in the Pelican series. The biography by Ernest Mossner, *Life of David Hume* (1954) is superb. See also the following: John Wild, *George Berkeley, A Study of His Life and Philosophy* (1936); John B. Stewart, *The Moral and Political Philosophy of David Hume* (1964); L. A. Selby-Bigge (ed.), *The British Moralists* (1897); and, again, Leslie Stephen's basic study of English thought in the eighteenth century. In his *David Hume, Prophet of the Counter-Revolution* (1965), Laurence L. Bongie noted the wide influence of Hume's historical writings. John Laird has studied *Hume's Philosophy of Human Nature* (1967). Norman Kemp Smith and A. G. N. Flew are among other philosophers with recent books on Hume.

William Letwin, *The Origin of Scientific Economics* (1963) studies English economic thought from 1660 to 1776. E. Strauss, *Sir William Petty: Portrait of a Genius* (1954) singles out perhaps the greatest of the mercantilists. E. A. J. Johnson, *Predecessors of Adam Smith* (1937) is a justly celebrated older work. Ronald L. Meek, *The Economics of Physiocracy* (1963) reprints some of the literature of Quesnay's school; it should be supplemented if possible with the several volumes in French (between 1910 and 1959) by G. Weulersse, the most assiduous student of the Physiocrats. Herbert W. Schneider (ed.), Adam Smith's *Moral and Political Philosophy* (1948) might serve as an introduction to the thought of the pioneer economist, to be followed by a reading of his own often reprinted *The Wealth of Nations*. An excellent study is Gladys Bryson, *Man and Society: The Scottish Inquiry of the Eighteenth Century* (1945). Eli Ginzberg's elegant essay, *The House of Adam Smith* (1934) has been deservedly reprinted. Economic thought may be approached through a good general history such as H. T. Overton, *Social Ideals and Economic Theories from Quesnay to Keynes* (1962). That witty anticipation of the school of economic individualism, Bernard Mandeville's *Fable of the Bees*, has been issued in paperback (1962, ed. Irwin Primer). See also William L. Taylor, *Francis Hutcheson and David Hume as Predecessors of Adam Smith* (1965). R. L. Meek has recently translated and edited *Turgot on Progress, Sociology, and Economics* (1973).

Emile Durkheim, *Montesquieu and Rousseau* (repr. 1960) may be suggested for a stimulating approach to the birth of sociology. On eighteenth-century historical writing, in addition to Brumfitt on Voltaire as historian and passages in Collingwood's *Idea of History*, see J. B. Black, *The Art of History: Four Eighteenth-Century Historians* (1926, recently reprinted); Benedetto Croce, *The Philosophy of Giambattista Vico* (repr. 1964), one great historian-philosopher on another; and A. R. Caponigri, *Time and Idea: The Story of History in G. Vico* (1953). The most exhaustive treatment of Vico's thought and influence is contained in the book edited by G. Tagliacozzo and Hayden V. White, *Giambattista Vico: An International Symposium* (1969). The related theme of the idea of progress has brought forth a small library, headed by the older classic of J. B. Bury, *The Idea of Progress* (1920), and including such later additions as Henry Vyverberg, *Historical Pessimism in the French Enlightenment* (1958); Charles Frankel, *The Faith of Reason: The Idea of Progress in the French Enlightenment* (1948); Charles Vereker, *Eighteenth-*

Century Optimism (1967); Ernest L. Tuveson, *Millenium and Utopia: A Study of the Background of the Idea of Progress* (1949); and John Baillie, *The Belief in Progress* (1950).

A short reading list on the Enlightenment in other countries could include Richard Herr, *The Eighteenth-Century Revolution in Spain* (1958); J. Sarrailh, *L'Espagne Eclairée* (1957); A. P. Whitaker, *Latin America and the Enlightenment* (1961); W. H. Bruford, *Germany in the Eighteenth Century* (1935); G. P. Gooch, *Frederick the Great* (1947) and *Catherine the Great and Other Studies* (1954); and Eric W. Cochrane, *Tradition and Enlightenment in the Tuscan Academies* (1962). Allen McConnell, *A Russian Philosophe: Alexander Radishchev* (1965) and D. M. Lang, *Alexander Radishchev, The First Russian Radical* (1959) tell another part of the story of the Enlightenment in Russia, as also does Hans Rogger, *National Consciousness in Eighteenth-Century Russia* (1961), which argues that here, as in Italy and Germany, the Enlightenment helped develop a national spirit. Raphael Demos, "The Neo-Hellenic Enlightenment, 1750–1821," *Journal of the History of Ideas* (October, 1958) suggests the influence of English, French, and German *philosophes* on Greece. On microfilm, there is a dissertation by Isaac Eisenstein-Barzilay, *The Enlightenment and the Jews* (1955; Univ. Microfilm 55–177); and a good chapter in Joseph L. Blau, *The Story of Jewish Philosophy* (1962), which may now be supplemented by Arthur Hertzberg, *The French Enlightenment and the Jews* (1968); see also an essay by Paul H. Meyer, "The Attitude of the Enlightenment toward the Jew," in *Studies in Voltaire*, Volume XXVI (1963). Further on the German Enlightenment, see the treatment of its greatest figure by Henry E. Allison, *Lessing and the Enlightenment* (1966); also Edward Heier, *L. H. Nicolay and His Contemporaries* (1965). Franco Venturi's *Italy and the Enlightenment* (1972) fills a gap. Nigel Glendinning, *The Eighteenth Century* (1973), one of a six-volume history of Spanish literature (Benn), is especially useful on ideas.

Further on eighteenth-century England, Caroline Robbins's *The Eighteenth-Century Commonwealthmen* (1959) is a mine of information about lesser political writers; James L. Clifford (ed.), *Eighteenth-Century English Literature* (1959) contains engaging and informative essays on most of the major poets and novelists from Pope, Swift, and Addison to Fielding, Gray, and Johnson; A. R. Humphreys, *The Augustan World* (1954) is charming and knowledgeable. Basil Willey, *The Eighteenth-Century Background* (1953) stresses ideas in relation to literature. An impressive work of scholarship by James W. Johnson deals with *The Formation of English Neoclassical Thought* (1967). On Dr. Johnson, possibly the greatest figure of the English eighteenth century, see Donald J. Greene, *The Politics of Samuel Johnson* (1960) and Walter J. Bate, *The Achievement of Samuel Johnson* (1955).

This book is not directly concerned with the American Enlightenment, but Durard Echeverria, in *Mirage in the West* (1957) catches the image of the New World as seen in the French Enlightenment. See also A. Owen Aldridge's charming portrait, *Franklin and His French Contemporaries* (1957).

On certain other cosmopolitan aspects of Enlightenment taste and thought there are Elizabeth Souleyman, *The Vision of World Peace in Eighteenth-Century France* (1941); W. W. Appleton, *A Cycle of Cathay* (1957), on Chinese influence on English taste in the seventeenth and eighteenth centuries; cf. Basil Gray, *The French Image of China before and after Voltaire* (1964), one of the volumes of *Studies on Voltaire*, and Hugh Honour, *Chinoiserie* (1962). Also important are Emil Kaufmann, *Architecture in the Age of Reason* (1955), and Michael Levey, *Rococo to Revolution: Major Trends in Eighteenth-Century Painting* (1966). Helmut Hatzfeld's book on *The Rococo: Eroticism, Wit, and Elegance in European Literature* (1972) contributes to an understanding of this aristocratic spirit. Daniel Foxon, *Libertine Literature in England 1660–1745* (1961) explores aspects of Enlightenment eroticism on which the curious might want also to consult John Masters's gorgeously illustrated biography of *Casanova* (1969). Robert Darnton, *Mesmerism and the End of the Enlightenment in France* (1968) contributes greatly to an understanding of the antirationalist reaction of the 1780s, which he relates to the Revolution. Michael Foucalt's *Madness and Civilization* (tr. 1965) is a history of insanity in the age of reason, with fascinating revelations. The theme of *Irrationalism in the Eighteenth Century* is discussed in Volume 2 of the series Studies in Eighteenth Century Culture (1972), ed. Harold E. Pagliaro.

Evaluation and criticism of the Enlightenment might begin by comparing Alfred Cobban, *In Search of Humanity: The Role of the Enlightenment in Modern History* (1960) and Peter Gay, *The Party of Humanity: Studies in the French Enlightenment* (1964), both largely admiring, with L. G. Crocker, *An Age of Crisis: Man and World in Eighteenth-Century French Thought* (1959), along with its sequel, *Nature and Culture: Ethical Thought in the French Enlightenment* (1963). See also Gay's *The Enlightenment*, previously cited. William F. Church (ed.), *The Influence of the Enlightenment on the French Revolution* (1964) reprints a number of interesting reactions to the Enlightenment. Carl L. Becker's celebrated essay, *The Heavenly City of the Eighteenth-Century Philosophers* (1932) may be compared with the various comments on it in R. O. Rockwood (ed.), *Carl Becker's Heavenly City Revisited* (1958). Talmon's *Origins of Totalitarian Democracy*, previously cited, contains implicit adverse judgments on the main stream of eighteenth-century political thought, but has aroused opposition. Louis I. Bredvold's *The Brave New World of the Enlightenment* (1961) is a sensitive and polished essay by a literary scholar. Whitehead's *Science and the Modern World* (1926) includes some perceptive remarks. Geoffrey Clive, *The Romantic Enlightenment* (1960) is a striking reevaluation, in the sense of noting how much of the Age of Reason was emotional or sentimental, while Henry Vyverberg's already cited *Historical Pessimism in the French Enlightenment* similarly points to a strain of thought contrary to the dominant one. Shelby T. McCloy, *The Humanitarian Movement in Eighteenth-Century France* (1957) is inclined to credit many enlightened reforms to *philosophe* influence. In conclusion, perhaps

Ernst Cassirer's *The Philosophy of the Enlightenment* (English ed. 1951) is
still as good a summation as any; but cf. K. B. Price's criticism in *Journal of
the History of Ideas*, January, 1957.

Chapter 7

Church, *Influence of the Enlightenment on the French Revolution* and
Talmon, *Origins of Totalitarian Democracy*, already cited, provide insights
into the ideology of the French Revolution; see also Renée Waldinger, *Voltaire
and Reform in the Light of the French Revolution* (1959). Jacques Godechot,
La Pensée revolutionaire en France et en Europe 1780–1799 (1964) and *Le
Contre-revolution 1789–1804* (1961) are by the outstanding French historian
of the Revolution today; in English, one can consult such authorities as Crane
Brinton, *The Jacobins* (1930); and Paul H. Beik, *The French Revolution Seen
from the Right* (1956). Elizabeth Eisenstein, *The First Professional Revolutionary: Buonarroti* (1959) brings out the Revolution's socialist Left, on which
the classic study was probably Jean Jaurès's old *Histoire socialiste de la
revolution* (1901–1904). Paul Beik also has an essay on "The Meaning of
the Revolution" in Charles K. Warner (ed.), *From the Ancien Regime to the
Popular Front* (1969), on which theme see also Richard Cobb, *Reactions to
the French Revolution* (1972). Gita May, *Madame Roland and the Age of
Revolution* (1970) concerns a prominent revolutionary intellectual. Joan Mc-
Donald, *Rousseau and the French Revolution* (1965) explains how the revolutionaries used but distorted Jean-Jacques; a similar type of study is Raymond
O. Rockwood, "The Legend of Voltaire and the Cult of Revolution," in *Ideas
in History*, edited by Richard Herr and Harold T. Parker (1965). Alfred
Cobban has an essay on "The Enlightenment and the French Revolution" in
Wasserman, *Aspects of the Eighteenth Century*, previously cited, and has also
launched revisionist lines in his *Social Interpretation of the French Revolution* (1965).

The *Letters of Joseph Priestley in England and America, 1789–1802*,
edited by Frank Beckwith and W. H. Chaloner (1970) contains fascinating
material from one of the representative radicals of the revolutionary era, many
of whose writings are still in print. A. Owen Aldridge's *Man of Reason* (1959)
is an engaging biography of Tom Paine. Carl B. Cone, *The English Jacobins*
(1968) is outstanding in treating British reformers of the revolutionary era;
see also John W. Osborne's studies of *William Cobbett* (1966) and *John Cart-
wright* (1972), as well as Ian Christie's *Wilkes, Wyvill, and Reform* (1963).
Burke's *Reflections on the Revolution in France* and Tom Paine's *Rights of
Man* are often reprinted; see also A. Cobban (ed.), *The Debate on the French
Revolution* (1949). R. R. Fennessy has written about *Burke, Paine, and the
Rights of Man: A Difference of Political Opinion* (1963). The large and grow-
ing literature on Burke includes biographies by Philip Magnus, *Edmund Burke:
A Life* (1939) and Carl B. Cone, *Burke and the Nature of Politics* (2 vols.,
1957–1963); Charles Parkin, *The Moral Basis of Burke's Political Thought*

(1956); Francis Canavan, *The Political Reason of Edmund Burke* (1959); other studies by Peter Stanlis and Ross J. S. Hoffman. Stanlis has edited some essays by American Burke scholars under the title *The Relevance of Edmund Burke;* Hoffman with Paul Levack edited *Burke's Politics* (1949). A recent and useful introduction to Burke's political thought is Gerald W. Chapman, *Edmund Burke: The Practical Imagination* (1967). See also B. T. Wilkins, *The Problem of Burke's Political Philosophy* (1967). Burke's *Correspondence* in nine volumes has been edited and published at the University of Chicago under the direction of Thomas W. Copeland and others.

Another interesting book is Bernard N. Schilling, *Conservative England and the Case against Voltaire 1789–1800* (1959). Christopher Herold, (ed.), *The Mind of Napoleon* (1955) reveals the revolutionary emperor's often fascinating thought processes; a recent study of considerable interest is F. C. Healey, *Rousseau et Napoleon* (1957). Herold has also authored an engaging biography of Mme. de Staël, *Mistress to an Age* (1958). Equally delightful is the old H. N. Brailsford classic, *Shelley, Godwin, and Their Circle* (1913, often repr.). There is an exploration of *William Godwin and His World* by Rosalie Grylls (1953).

Kant's philosophy may be approached through Volume VI of Copleston's *History of Philosophy* (1960); Volume VII (1963) is from Fichte to Nietzsche. H. D. Aiken (ed.), *The Age of Ideology* (Mentor series Vol. IV, 1956) contains a brief introduction with selections from Kant. *The Critique of Pure Reason, The Critique of Practical Reason, Religion within the Limits of Reason Alone*, and others of Kant's writings are available in recent paperback reprints. Arnulf Zweig has edited *The Essential Kant* (1971). Lewis W. Beck, *Commentary on Kant's Critique of Practical Reason* (1960) and Norman Kemp Smith, *Kant's Critique of Pure Reason* (2nd ed., 1962) are expert guides. Hans Reiss has edited *Kant's Political Writings* (1970). Richard Kroner, *Kant's Weltanschauung* (1956) sees the philosopher in a broader framework; Leonard Krieger, *The German Idea of Freedom* (1957) finds the political influence of Kant less liberal than usually indicated. A symposium, *The Heritage of Kant*, edited by G. T. Whitney and D. F. Bowers (1962), can be recommended for the philosophically sophisticated. Among the numerous other books about the greatest of philosophers, H. J. Paton, *The Categorical Imperative: A Study in Kant's Moral Philosophy* (1967); Georges Viachos, *La Pensée politique de Kant* (1962), extremely lucid; and another symposium, Robert Paul Wolff (ed.), *Kant: A Collection of Critical Essays* (1968). Jonathan Bennett, *Kant's Analytic* (1967) is philosophically sophisticated. The outstanding work on Fichte for the intellectual historian is in French: Xavier Leon, *Fichte et son temps* (3 vols., 1922–1924, 1958). Fichte's *Addresses to the German Nation* have often been reprinted. Light on the setting of German thought in this great age comes from J. H. Bruford, *Culture and Society in Classical Weimar, 1775–1806* (1962) and Henri Brunschwig, *The Crisis of the Prussian State at the End of the Eighteenth Century and the Genesis of the Romantic Mentality* (1947), now translated into English.

Among other German worthies of the grand epoch, Herder found an outstanding American student in Robert T. Clark, *Herder, His Life and Thought* (1955) as well as in A. Gillies, *Herder* (1945) and more recently F. M. Barnard, *Herder's Social and Political Thought* (1965). Barnard has also edited *Herder on Society and Political Culture* (1969). René Wellek, *Kant in England* (1931) and John H. Muirhead, *Coleridge as Philosopher* (1938) reveal the effect of the German philosophy on the English; see also C. F. Harrold, *Carlyle and German Thought 1819–1834* (1963). George Boas, *French Philosophy of the Romantic Period* (1925), and Philip P. Hallie, *Maine de Biran: Reformer of Empiricism 1766–1824* (1959) are helpful on French philosophy.

Jacques Barzun in *Romanticism and the Modern Ego* (1944) (paperback edition titled *Classic, Romantic, and Modern*) provides a broadly cultural and historical introduction to the subject of romanticism. Northrop Frye (ed.), *Romanticism Reconsidered* (1963) contains essays in definition and reevaluation of which the one by René Wellek is a particularly useful survey of recent writings on the subject. Wellek also has several essays on romanticism in his *Confrontations* (1965). Lovejoy's celebrated essay is reprinted in his *Essays in the History of Ideas* (1948), but compare his treatment in *The Great Chain of Being*, pp. 228–314. Meyer H. Abrams, *The Mirror and the Lamp* (1953) is a perceptive literary study, as is also (despite some eccentricities) G. Wilson Knight's *The Starlit Dame* (1959). These, along with Frank Kermode, *The Romantic Image* (1957), may be singled out from a vast amount of work in literary criticism or exegesis, to which, as usual, the *Pelican Guide* (Vol. V, *From Blake to Byron*) is a good guide in English literature. Graham Hough, *The Romantic Poets* (1953) is a thoughtful summation by one of today's outstanding British critics. Maurice Bowra, *The Romantic Imagination* (1961) and F. L. Lucas, *The Decline and Fall of the Romantic Ideal* (1948) are dependable classics. Among other general treatments, Anthony Thorlby, *The Romantic Movement* (1966); H. G. Schenk, *The Mind of the European Romantics* (1966); Malcolm Elwin, *The First Romantics* (reprinted 1967); Morse Peckham, *Romanticism: The Culture of the Nineteenth Century* (1965); Northrop Frye, *A Study of English Romanticism* (1968); and Walter J. Bate, *From Classic to Romantic* (1946) are worth inclusion on any list for the general reader. Morris Bishop, ed., *A Romantic Storybook* (1971) is a delightful collection. Montague Summers, *The Gothic Quest: A History of the Gothic Novel* was reprinted in 1964. Cf. Robert Kiely, *The Romantic Novel in England* (1972). The endless number of more specialized studies include such regional examinations as E. Allison Peers, *A History of the Romantic Movement in Spain* (1940) and Roger Duhamel, *Aux sources du romantisme français* (1964). Max Dufner (ed.), *Romantics: Kleist, Novalis, Tieck, Schlegel* (1964) reprints some of the works of the Germans. Kathleen Coburn (ed.), *Inquiring Spirit* (1951) is a carefully selected and arranged introduction to the thought and expression of Samuel Taylor Coleridge, most philosophical of the English romantic poets; compare E. D. Hirsch, Jr., *Wordsworth and Schelling* (1960). J. D. Boulger, *Coleridge as Religious Thinker* (1961) and Richard B. Brandt, *The Philosophy of Schleiermacher* (1945) suggest the relationship between religion and romanticism. See also Raymond Schwab, *La Renaissance orientale* (1950). On political aspects, see Crane Brinton, *Political Thought of the English Romantics* (1926); John Colmer, *Coleridge, Critic of Society* (1959); R. Aris, *History of Political Thought in Germany from 1789 to 1815* (repr. 1965); H. S. Reiss (ed.), *Political Thought of the German Romantics 1793–1815* (1956); R. J. White (ed.), *Political Tracts of Wordsworth, Coleridge, and Shelly* (1953); Gerald McNiece, *Shelly and the Revolutionary Idea* (1969). André Maurois, *Chateaubriand* (1958) is a dazzling portrait of one of the greatest of romantic personalities, the same popular biographer having also limned George Sand and Alexander Dumas. Chateaubriand's *Memoirs* (*Memoirs d'Outre-tombe*) were edited in 1961 by Robert Baldick. Donald Davie in *The Heyday of Walter Scott* (1961) discusses the romanticism of "ancestral feeling" and collective ties, so different from the *Menschenhass* of the Byronic hero. Walter Friedlaender, *David to Delacroix* (1952) deals with romantic painting with attention to the social background. There are, finally, Howard Hugo (ed.), *The Portable Romantic Reader* (1957), and in the Heath *Problems* series, John B. Halsted (ed.), *Romanticism: Definition, Explanation, and Evaluation* (1965). Halsted has also edited the volume on *Romanticism* in the Harper Documentary History of Western Civilization series. The periodical *Studies in Romanticism* may be used to keep up with scholarship in the field.

Chapter 8

Studies of Burke and Coleridge, already cited, are applicable to the conservative ideology; general surveys, somewhat useful, are Russell Kirk, *The Conservative Mind: Burke to Santayana* (1953) and Réne Rémond, *The Right Wing in France from 1815 to de Gaulle* (English tr. 1965), as well as a recent compilation edited by Hans Rogger and Eugen Weber, *The European Right* (1965) and J. S. McClelland (ed.), *The French Right from De Maistre to Maurras* (1970). Bertier de Sauvigny, *Metternich and His Times* (1962) and Henry A. Kissinger, *A World Restored: Metternich, Castlereagh, and the Problems of Peace 1812–22* (1957) are concerned with the leading practical conservative creeds of the era of reaction. E. L. Woodward, *Three Studies in European Conservatism* (repr. 1963) and Douglas Johnson, *Guizot* (1963) look at other conservative statesmen. Works on Bonald, Maistre, and Savigny are surprisingly few in English, but recently Jack Lively has selected from *The Works of Joseph De Maistre* (1965), supplying a long introduction. John Morley's essay in his *Biographical Studies* (1923) remains useful on "The Champion of Social Reaction. See also R. A. Lebrun, *Throne and Altar: The Political and Religious Thought of Joseph De Maistre* (1965). The best French treatment is now that of Robert Triomphe (1968). On German conservative thought, in addition to Aris and Reiss, already cited, see Klaus Epstein, *The Genesis of German Conservatism 1770–1806* (1966). Additionally on Coleridge, David P. Calleo, *Coleridge and the Idea of the Modern State* (1966).

John Stuart Mill's essay *On Bentham and Coleridge* has been reprinted with an introduction by F. R. Leavis (1950). On the former Leslie Stephen,

The English Utilitarians (repr. 1950) still may be the best, though E. Halévy, *The Growth of Philosophical Radicalism* (repr. 1955) is more prolix, and there is a recent major work on Bentham by Mary P. Mack, the first volume of which, *Jeremy Bentham: An Odyssey of Ideas* (1962) carries the founder of the Utilitarian school down to 1792. Miss Mack has also made a convenient selection of his writings in *A Bentham Reader* (1969). D. J. Manning, *The Mind of Jeremy Bentham* (1968) is brief but incisive. Bentham's entire *Collected Works* are being published in a number of volumes at the University of London's Athlone Press, appropriately enough. Gertrude Himmelfarb has an important essay on Bentham in Richard Herr and Harold T. Parker (ed.), *Ideas in History* (1965), also an article on Bentham interpretation in *Journal of Modern History*, June, 1969. David P. Crook, *American Democracy in English Politics 1815–1850* (1965) interestingly reveals how far the example of the United States affected utilitarian thinking. Graham Wallas's classic biography of *Francis Place* (1919) affords insight into Radicals in action. John L. Clive, *Scotch Reviewers: The Edinburgh Review 1802–1815* (1957) provides a picture of the Radical intelligentsia, and incidentally carries on the study of "the Scottish inquiry." William C. Havard, *Henry Sidgwick and Later Utilitarian Philosophy* (1959) carries on the story of the Benthamite tradition in thought, while an interesting sidelight is Eric T. Stokes, *The English Utilitarians and India* (1959).

Harold Silver, *The Concept of Popular Education: A Study of Ideas and Social Movements in the Early Nineteenth Century* (1965) makes a contribution to a significant subject. Warren J. Samuels, *The Classical Theory of Economic Policy* (1966) is a useful study; further on the Political Economists, in addition to histories of economic thought previously cited, see Marc Blaug, *Ricardian Economics* (1958); Kenneth Smith, *The Malthusian Controversy* (1951); Lionel Robbins, *Robert Torrens and the Evolution of Classical Economics* (1958); and, in view of its modern importance, John Maynard Keynes's essay on Malthus (among other economists) in *Essays in Biography* (1951). Also Marian Bowley, *Nassau Senior and Classical Economics* (1968). R. K. Webb, *Harriet Martineau: A Radical Victorian* (1960) scrutinized the celebrated bluestocking who popularized the ideas of the Political Economists. The best study of *The Manchester School of Liberalism* is by William D. Grampp (1960), the author also of a two-volume survey of *Economic Liberalism*. Donald Read, *Cobden and Bright* (1968) is a recent well-researched appraisal of the twin stars in the Manchester constellation. In his readable *Victorian People*, Asa Briggs includes portraits of Bright as well as Robert Lowe and the celebrated Samuel Smiles. There is also a scholarly biography of John Bright by Herman Ausubel (1965). The advanced student of economics might explore the acute contemporary criticism of utilitarian assumptions offered by I. M. D. Little in *A Critique of Welfare Economics* (1956). The rejoinder of one who then rejected "the dismal science" is presented in W. F. Kennedy, *Humanist versus Economist: The Economic Thought of Samuel Taylor Coleridge* (1958).

On liberalism generally, see L. T. Hobhouse, *Liberalism* (1934); Harry

K. Girvetz, *From Wealth to Welfare: The Evolution of Liberalism* (1950); G. de Ruggiero, *History of European Liberalism* (English transl. 1959); and Harold J. Laski, *The Rise of Liberalism* (1936), a Marxist interpretation. George L. Cherry, *Early English Liberalism* (1962) is useful as background. For a later era, Robert L. Kelley, *The Transatlantic Persuasion: The Liberal-Democratic Mind in the Age of Gladstone* (1969). Walter M. Simon edited a collection of documents on *French Liberalism* (1972). A reasonably representative selection of classic writings was made by David Sidorsky in *The Liberal Tradition in European Thought* (1970). Charles E. Timberlake, *Essays on Russian Liberalism* (1972) shows us a different environment than the West. Jack Lively, *The Social and Political Thought of Alexis de Tocqueville* (1962) authoritatively considers the ideas of one of the great nineteenth-century liberals. Among others who have been keen students of Tocqueville in recent times are Edward T. Gargan, Marvin Zetterbaum, Seymour Drescher, and Irving M. Zeitlin. The French liberal *Prévost-Paradol* (1955) has been treated by Pierre Guiral. Richard H. Thomas, *Liberalism, Nationalism, and the German Intellectuals 1822–1847* (1951) is more restricted than the title suggests but offers revealing insights into some German circles.

G. D. H. Cole's multivolume *History of Socialist Thought* begins with a volume on *The Forerunners* (1953). Another comprehensive history is Carl Landauer, *European Socialism* (2 vols., 1960). Cf. George Lichtheim, *Origins of Socialism* (1969). The first three volumes of M. Leroy's monumental *Histoire des idées sociales en France* (Volume III was published in 1954, covering the 1848–1871 period) are a mine of information. Frank E. Manuel, *The New World of Henri Saint-Simon* (1956) is by an outstanding American intellectual historian; G. G. Iggers, *The Cult of Authority: Political Philosophy of the Saint-Simonians* (1958) ranks high among other studies of the great socialist pioneer; see also Emile Durkheim, *Socialism and Saint-Simon* (1958). Manuel's entertaining *Prophets of Paris* (1962) includes sketches of Fourier and Comte as well as Saint-Simon. There is less in English on Fourier, but N. Riasonovsky's *The Teaching of Charles Fourier* (1969) helps. Several recent editions of his writings, including the paperback *Harmonian Man*, (ed.) Mark Poster (1971), testify to interest in Fourier. Other books on the early socialists are Leo A. Loubère, *Louis Blanc* (1961), the life of a participant in politics as well as a framer of social ideas, one of the great nineteenth-century democratic socialists; and Henri Lubac, *The Un-Marxian Socialist: Proudhon* (1948), a more thorough study than the summary by J. Hampden Jackson in *Marx, Proudhon, and European Socialism* (1957). Also on the French anarchist, Alan Ritter, *The Political Thought of P.-J. Proudhon* (1969) and Robert L. Hoffman, *Revolutionary Justice: The Social and Political Theory of P.-J. Proudhon* (1972). Alan B. Spitzer, *The Revolutionary Theories of Blanqui* (1957), and Peter Stearns, *Lamennais: Priest and Revolutionary* (1968) deal with other French firebrands of the pre-1848 period. On Lamennais, pioneer of social Catholicism, see also Alex Vidler, *Prophecy and Papacy* (1954).

Biographers of Robert Owen include Frank Podmore and G. D. H. Cole, whose 1930 *Life* was recently reprinted; also Owen himself (*Life of Robert*

Owen, Written by Himself, 1857–58, also recently reprinted). But the best book on the Owenite movement now is J. F. C. Harrison's *Quest for the New Moral World: Robert Owen and the Owenites in Britain and America* (1969). Recent British interest in social history has brought forth a number of books about the Chartists, including reprints of some of their periodicals such as *The Red Republican, Democratic Review, Notes to the People, Poor Man's Guardian*. A. R. Schoyen, *The Chartist Challenge: Portrait of George Julian Harney* (1958), and Asa Briggs (ed.), *Chartist Studies* (1959) are good examples of recent Chartist scholarship. For additional references on the socialists see under chapter 10.

On Hegel, see Copleston's seventh volume (1963); J. N. Findlay, *Hegel: A Re-examination* (1957), which may be compared with the hostile Karl Popper, *The Open Society and Its Enemies: Hegel and Marx*, Vol. II (4th ed., 1962); Herbert Marcuse, *Reason and Revolution: Hegel and the Rise of Social Theory* (1941); and especially Walter A. Kaufmann, *Hegel: A Reinterpretation* (1965). A recent addition is Shlomo Avineri, *Hegel's Theory of the Modern State* (1973). Hegel's own writings are readily available in selections such as *Reason in History*, or Carl J. Friedrich (ed.), *The Philosophy of Hegel. Hegel's Political Writings* have been edited by Z. A. Pelczynski (1962). The influence of Hegel on Russia is reflected in Edward J. Brown, *Stankevich and His Moscow Circle* (1967). For the "young Hegelians" see Chapter 10.

D. O. Evans, *Social Romanticism in France 1830–1848* (1951) is a valuable little book; wider in range is the work of E. J. Hobsbawn, *The Age of Revolution 1789–1848* (1962). Jean Lhomme's *La Grande Bourgeoisie au pouvoir* (1960) is, for those who can read French, a work of originality and deep insight into the class that dominated this era. J. L. Talmon, *Political Messianism: The Romantic Phase* (1960) treats the whole pre-1848 ferment of social prophecy. Briefer is the appraisal of *1848: The Revolution of the Intellectuals* (1948) by one of the greatest of twentieth-century historians, Lewis Namier. One of the leading prophets of 1848 is capably handled by G. Salvemini, *Mazzini*. Mazzini's own intoxicating rhetoric communicates the spirit of 1848: see the Everyman's Library selection, *Duties of Man and Other Essays*. A recent study of much interest stressing social history is Robert W. Lougee, *Midcentury Revolution, 1848: Society and Revolution in France and Germany* (1972).

Chapter 9

On the Victorian era generally, Walter E. Houghton, *The Victorian Frame of Mind* (1957) rounds up a good deal of the age's thought while G. M. Young, *Victorian England: Portrait of an Age* (1936) is a classic. *Victorian Prose*, edited by Kenneth Allott, is Volume V of *The Pelican Book of English Prose* (1956). Gordon Haight has edited *The Portable Victorian Reader* (1972), an unusually good selection of readings. The crowded and brilliant Victorian intellectual scene can only partially be reflected in the following outstanding books: Mario Praz, *The Hero in Eclipse* (1956), a study of the Victorian novelists; Owen Chadwick, *The Mind of the Oxford Movement* (1960) and Geoffrey Faber, *The Oxford Apostles* (1936); Benjamin Lippincott, *Victorian Critics of Democracy* (repr. 1964); John Holloway, *The Victorian Sage* (1953); R. Robson, ed., *Ideas and Institutions of Victorian England* (1967); W. L. Burn, *The Age of Equipoise*, rich in content with much about ideas (1964); Gertrude Himmelfarb, *Victorian Minds* (1968) including essays on Acton, Disraeli, Mill, Leslie Stephen. Chadwick also has two volumes on *The Victorian Church* of which the first (1966) covers the years 1829–1860. Among numerous individual figures, *Walter Bagehot* (1959) has been edited by Norman St. John Stevas and described by Alastair Buchan, *The Spare Chancellor* (1960); his *The English Constitution* (1867) is available. Lionel Trilling, *Matthew Arnold* (1949) is perhaps the outstanding book on another eminent Victorian; a useful selection of Arnold's poetry and prose has been edited by John Bryson for the Reynard Library (Rupert Hart-Davis, 1954), which also has a Macaulay edited by G. M. Young. Among recent Arnold studies of interest are books by William A. Madden and Fred S. Walcott. Recent Ruskin anthologizing reflects the tremendous interest in this formerly underrated Victorian; there are volumes selected by Joan Evans, *The Lamp of Beauty* (1959), John D. Rosenberg, *The Genius of John Ruskin: Selections from His Writings* (1963), and Kenneth Clark, *Ruskin Today* (1964). Rosenberg has written one of the best books about Ruskin, *The Darkening Glass* (1961). G. M. Trevelyan, the famous historian, edited a one-volume *Thomas Carlyle* (1954). Among a spate of Dickens books commemorating the centenary of the death of the century's most popular novelist, Angus Wilson's *World of Dickens* (1970) deserves priority. On another great mid-Victorian, see Bernard J. Paris, *Experiment in Life: George Eliot's Quest for Values* (1965). W. H. Dunn's *James Anthony Froude* (2 vols., 1961–1964) presents a noted historian. One may keep up with the voluminous literature on Victorians through *The Pelican Guide to English Literature*, vol. 6 (*Dickens to Hardy*) and via the periodical *Victorian Studies*. There is also, recently, a useful bibliographical handbook, *Victorian England 1837–1901*, compiled by Josef L. Altholz (1970).

John Stuart Mill best introduces himself in the famous and oft-reprinted *Autobiography*, but a superb modern biography is that by Michael St. John Packe, *Life of John Stuart Mill* (1954). Karl Britton writes on Mill in the Penguin series (1953); a rather controversial interpretation is Maurice Cowling, *Mill and Liberalism* (1963). Valuable studies are R. K. P. Pankhurst, *The Saint-Simonians: Mill and Carlyle* (1957), Iris W. Mueller, *John Stuart Mill and French Thought* (1956), John M. Robson, *The Improvement of Mankind: The Social and Political Thought of J. S. Mill* (1968), and Joseph Hamburger, *Intellectuals in Politics: John Stuart Mill and the Philosophical Radicals* (1966). Edward Alexander has studied *Matthew Arnold and John Stuart Mill* (1965). Shirley Letwin, in *The Pursuit of Certainty* (1965) deals with Bentham and Mill along with David Hume and Beatrice Webb in a lineage of British rationalists. Of much value on Mill the economist is the recent Pedro Schwartz book, *The New Political Economy of John Stuart Mill* (1973). A good selection from Mill's political writings was made by editor Bernard Wishy under the title *Prefaces to Liberty* (1959). The complete works have been edited and published at the University of Toronto.

Mill himself wrote on *August Comte and Positivism*, an essay recently (1961) reprinted. Among recent scholars, D. G. Charlton, *Positivist Thought in France 1852–1870* (1959) deals with the second generation positivists in the heyday of the creed; Walter M. Simon, *European Positivism in the Nineteenth Century* (1963), a major work of scholarship, ranges far and deep in the positivist vein. Frank Manuel's *Prophets of Paris*, previously cited, has a chapter on Comte. So does Volume I of Raymond Aron's useful survey, *Main Currents in Sociological Thought* (1965). On Renan, see R. M. Chadburne, *Ernest Renan as Essayist* (1957) and H. W. Wardman, *Ernest Renan: A Critical Biography* (1964). The ideas of the statesman who ruled over this era in France may be read in Brison D. Gooch (ed.), *The Napoleonic Ideas* (1969). *Schopenhauer* is introduced by Patrick Gardiner in the Penguin series on philosophers (1963); his own writings are available in several editions, but perhaps the most readable are the *Essays*, translated by T. B. Saunders (Barnes & Noble, 1957).

Basil Willey, *More Nineteenth Century Studies: A Group of Honest Doubters* (1957) detects the influence of Comte but it was much overshadowed in England by that of Darwin. On the latter there is of course a large literature, including the very scholarly *Forerunners of Darwin* (1959), edited by Bentley Glass; Milton Millhauser, *Just before Darwin: Robert Chambers and His "Vestiges"* (1959); G. G. Gillispie, *Genesis and Geology* (1951); Loren Eiseley, *Darwin's Century* (1958); Gertrude Himmelfarb, *Darwin and the Darwinian Revolution* (1959), an extremely useful and attractive summary of the impact on ideas; John C. Greene, *The Death of Adam* (1961); David Hull, *Darwin and His Critics* (1973); and W. Irvine, *Apes, Angels, and Victorians* (1955). Essential as background is Arthur O. Lovejoy's classic *Great Chain of Being* (1936). Alvar Ellegard has carefully studied the reception of Darwin's theory in the British press 1859–1872 in his *Darwin and the General Reader* (1958). In addition to various editions of *The Origin of Species*, of great interest is Darwin's *Autobiography* which must be read in the 1958 edition, edited by Nora Barlow, the first complete one published. (See article by Maurice Mandelbaum, "Darwin's Religious Views," *Journal of the History of Ideas*, June, 1958.) *Darwin*, edited by Philip Appleman (1970) brings together a large amount of material spanning the whole Darwinian debate. For the influence of Darwin, see J. Herman Randall, Jr., "The Impact of Darwin on Philosophy," *Journal of the History of Ideas* (October, 1961); Walter J. Ong (ed.), *Darwin's Vision and Christian Perspectives* (1960); Basil Willey, *Darwin and Butler* (1960); L. J. Henkin, *Darwinism and the English Novel 1860–1910* (repr. 1963); and especially John Dewey, *The Influence of Darwin on Philosophy* (1960) and *Reconstruction in Philosophy* (1937).

Cyril Bibby, *T. H. Huxley: Scientist, Humanist, Educator* (1959), deals sympathetically with "Darwin's bulldog." Talcott Parsons (ed.), *Spencer's*

Study of Sociology (1961) may be used as an entrance to the thought of this Victorian oracle. There is an illuminating essay by Robert L. Caneiro introducing his editing of *The Evolution of Society: Selections from Herbert Spencer's Principles of Sociology* (1967), and another by Irving Goldman on "Evolution and Anthropology" in *Victorian Studies*, Sept., 1959, an issue devoted entirely to Darwinism; likewise an essay on "Varieties of Social Darwinism" in Himmelfarb's *Victorian Minds*. J. D. Y. Peel has edited *Herbert Spencer on Social Evolution* and has also written a study of *Herbert Spencer: Evolution of a Sociologist* (1971). See also J. W. Burrow, *Evolution and Society: A Study in Victorian Social Theory* (1966). Bernard Semmel's *Imperialism and Social Reform* (1960, 1968) deals with some versions of social Darwinism. See also Frank M. Turner, *Between Science and Religion: The Reaction to Scientific Naturalism in Late Victorian England* (1974).

Chapter 10

Robert Tucker has edited *The Marx-Engels Reader* (1972); among other readily available source readings T. B. Bottomore (ed.), *Early Writings of Karl Marx* (1963) is worth noting. Works about Marx are so numerous that the student may want to consult John Lachs, *Marxist Philosophy: A Bibliographical Guide* (1967). H. B. Mayo, *Introduction to Marxist Theory* (1960) supplies a systematic critique, as does H. B. Acton, *The Illusion of the Epoch* (1954) on basic philosophy; Z. Jordan, *The Evolution of Dialectical Materialism* (1967); and Karl Popper, *The Open Society*, II. R. G. Tucker, *Philosophy and Myth in Karl Marx* (1961) is now supplemented by his *The Marxian Revolutionary Idea* (1969). Of unusual quality in the crowded field are E. Kamenka, *Ethical Foundations of Marxism* (1962); Joan Robinson, *An Essay on Marxian Economics* (1966); S. Avineri, *The Social and Political Thought of Marx* (1969); Bertold Ollman, *Alienation in Marx's Conception of Man in Capitalist Society* (1971). One can profitably add to a shelf on Marxism the following: George Lichtheim, *Marxism: An Historical and Critical Study* (1961); A. Cornu, *The Origins of Marxian Thought* (1957); M. M. Bober, *Karl Marx's Interpretation of History* (2nd ed., 1948); R. N. Carew Hunt, *Marxism Past and Present* (1954); the essentially biographical studies of Marx by Franz Mehring, *Karl Marx* (1948); E. H. Carr, *Karl Marx, a Study in Fanaticism* (1935); and Isaiah Berlin, *Karl Marx, His Life and Environment* (3rd ed., 1963). But David McLellan, *Karl Marx, His Life and Thought* (1973) is much more up-to-date and is the most thorough study of the life of Marx; it also contains a good bibliography. Gustav Mayer has written the best life of Friedrich Engels (1935). Biographical material is also supplied by Oscar J. Hammen, *The Red '48-ers* (1968); Henry Collins and C. Abramsky, *Karl Marx and the British Labour Movement* (1965); C. Tsuzuki, *Life of Eleanor Marx* (1967). W. O. Henderson has a new *Life of Friedrich Engels* (1973). August Cornu is engaged on a monumental life of Marx in East Germany. The Russian translation of Marx's writings, prepared by the Marx-Lenin

Institute in Moscow, and its German counterpart, are the only complete editions available. Ernest Bloch's *On Karl Marx*, the work of a notable German philosopher-scholar, was translated in 1971. On the "Young Hegelians," see Isaiah Berlin, *Life and Opinions of Moses Hess* (1960); John Weiss, *Moses Hess, Utopian Socialist* (1960); E. Kamenka, *The Philosophy of Feuerbach* (1970); William J. Brazill, *The Young Hegelians* (1970); Sidney Hook, *From Hegel to Marx* (1950), and David McLellan, *The Young Hegelians and Karl Marx* (1969). Feuerbach's *The Essence of Christianity* has recently been reprinted.

While some later versions of Marxism are discussed in portions of the next chapter, we may conveniently mention here books on some disciples and followers of Marx: Peter Gay, *The Dilemma of Democratic Socialism: Bernstein's Challenge to Marx* (1952) and Eduard Bernstein, *Evolutionary Socialism* (1909) present the most important "revisionist" among the German socialists; Samuel H. Baron, *Plekhanov: The Father of Russian Marxism* (1963) and A. G. Meyer, *Leninism* (1957), a most perceptive essay, introduce the Russian school, to which one might add Donald W. Treadgold, *Lenin and His Rivals 1889–1906* (1955) and L. H. Haimson, *The Russian Marxists and the Origins of Bolshevism* (1955). Harvey Goldberg's fine life of *Jean Jaurès* (1962) and Aaron Noland, *The Founding of the French Socialist Party 1893–1905* (1956) are among the best books on the French socialists. See also George Lichtheim, *Marxism in Modern France* (1966). R. Hostetter, *The Italian Socialist Movement 1860–1882* (1960) is to be followed by another volume. G. D. H. Cole's two volumes on *The Second International* in his *History of Socialist Thought* (1956) are good. David Footman has written a life of Ferdinand Lassalle, Marx's early rival within German socialism under the title *Ferdinand Lassalle, Romantic Revolutionary* (1947). Several scholarly studies detail the story of the great German Social Democratic Party: R. P. Morgan, *The German Social Democrats 1864–1872* (1965); Vernon Lidtke, *The Outlawed Party*, covering the years 1878–1890 (1966); and Carl Schorske, *German Social Democracy 1905–1917* (1955). An able synthesis is Leslie Derfler, *Socialism since Marx* (1973).

On the anarchist rivals of Marx, to the older works by George Woodcock, *Anarchism* (1962) and James Joll, *The Anarchists* (1964) may now be added Leonard I. Krimerman (ed.), *Patterns of Anarchy* (1966); *Kropotkin: Selected Writings on Anarchy and Revolution*, edited by Martin A. Miller (1970); *Bakunin on Anarchy*, edited by Paul Avrich (1972), Avrich being the author also of an excellent work on *The Russian Anarchists* (1967). April Carter, *The Political Theory of Anarchism* (1971), and Robert Hoffman, *Anarchism* (1970) are general studies while David Stafford has written a significant study of Paul Brousse called *From Anarchism to Reformism* (1971). The master historian of French anarchism was Jean Maitron, *Histoire du mouvement anarchiste en France 1880–1914* (1951).

On other than Marxian socialism: A. M. MacBriar, *Fabian Socialism and English Politics 1884–1914* (1962) is the best work on its subject, but can be supplemented by Margaret Cole, *Story of Fabian Socialism* (1961); the Beatrice

Webb *Diaries* (Vol. I, 1952); and the reprinted *Fabian Essays* of 1887, the manifesto of the movement. S. Maccoby, *English Radicalism, 1886–1914* (1955) deals with left-wing liberals in the British Isles. T. H. Green has found a biographer in Melvin Richter, under the title *The Politics of Conscience* (1963). Cf. A. J. M. Milne, *The Social Philosophy of English Idealism* (1962). Further on British socialism: A. B. Ulam, *Philosophical Foundations of British Socialism* (1964); C. Tsuzuki, *H. M. Hyndman and British Socialism* (1961); J. W. Hulse, *Revolutionists in London: A Study of Five Unorthodox Socialists* (1970), including the great literary converts, William Morris and George Bernard Shaw. Charles A. Barker's excellent study of *Henry George* (1956) should be included in view of this American's extensive influence in Britain. An attractive biography of Beatrice Webb is that by Kitty Muggeridge and Ruth Adam (1967). Daniel Roberts, *Victorian Origins of the Welfare State* (1960) and Herman Ausubel, *In Hard Times: Reformers among the Late Victorians* (1960) are among a plethora of books in this area. A. R. Vidler, *A Century of Social Catholicism 1820–1920* (1964) and Josef L. Altholz, *The Liberal Catholic Movement in England 1848–1864* (1960) are among recent works on this subject in English; there is a considerable library in French, including a lengthy survey by Emmanuel Barbier, *Histoire du Catholicisme liberal et du Catholicisme social en France 1870–1914* (5 vols., 1924). Additionally on Christian socialism, Lillian P. Wallace, *Leo XIII and the Rise of Socialism* (1966); Peter D'Arcy Jones, *The Christian Socialist Revival in England* (1968), which recounts the end-of-the-century return to a movement begun at mid-century by Charles Kingsley, F. Maurice, J. M. Ludlow. Matthew H. Elbow, in *French Corporative Theory 1789–1948: A Chapter in the History of Ideas* (1953) has explored a significant body of Catholic social theory. In *The Responsible Society* (1966), S. T. Glass discusses guild socialism. Martin J. Wiener, *Between Two Worlds: The Political Thought of Graham Wallas* (1972) devotes attention to a British scholar and socialist. There have also been recent studies of G. D. H. Cole by L. P. Carpenter (1973), and R. H. Tawney by Ross Terrill (1973). A useful anthology is Frank Beasley, ed., *The Social and Political Thought of the British Labour Party* (1970). A few works on the celebrated Russian revolutionary movements: Eugene Lampert, *Studies in Rebellion* (1957), on the generation of Bakunin, Herzen, and Belinsky, and *Sons against Fathers: Studies in Russian Radicalism and Revolution* (1965) on the next generation; Martin Malia, *Alexander Herzen and the Birth of Russian Socialism* (1961); Philip Pomper, *The Russian Revolutionary Intelligentsia* (1970); A. Yarmolinsky (ed.), *Road to Revolution: A Century of Russian Radicalism* (1968). Pomper is author also of a work on *Peter Lavrov* (1973). A brilliant work of intellectual history, Franco Venturi's *Roots of Revolution* (1960) explores the Russian populist mentality, on which see also James H. Billington, *Mikhailovsky and Russian Populism* (1958); also Ronald Hingley, *The Nihilists* (1967); Jonathan Frankel (ed.), *V. Akimov and Dilemmas of Russian Marxism 1895–1903* (1969). There are other good studies of individual Russian revolutionary leaders, such as Tkachev and Chernyshevsky.

To put Marx in the perspective of other nineteenth-century "historicisms," see Herbert Butterfield, *Man on His Past* (1955); Hayden White, *Metahistory: The Historical Imagination in Nineteenth-Century Europe* (1974); Georg Iggers, *The German Conception of History* (1968); G. P. Gooch, *History and Historians in the Nineteenth Century* (1959); on specific historians, Gertrude Himmelfarb, *Lord Acton* (1952), and Theodore von Laue, *Ranke: The Formative Years* (1950). For a more extensive bibliography, see Paul K. Conkin and Roland N. Stromberg, *The Heritage and Challenge of History* (1971).

Chapter 11

Students of nineteenth-century nationalism include Hans Kohn, *The Idea of Nationalism* (1944), and *Pan-Slavism* (1953); Carlton J. H. Hayes, *The Historical Evolution of Modern Nationalism* (1931) and others including *Nationalism: A Religion* (1960); and Elie Kedourie, *Nationalism* (1960). M. B. Petrovich, *The Emergence of Russian Pan-Slavism 1856–1870* (1956); Frank Fadner, *Seventy Years of Pan-Slavism in Russia* (1962); and N. Riasonovsky, *Russia and the West in the Teaching of the Slavophiles* (1952) are more detailed studies of Russian nationalist ideologies; see also biographies of the important reactionary nationalist *Pobedonostsev* by Robert F. Byrnes (1968) and of the pan-Slav *Danilevsky* by Robert E. MacMaster (1967), and Leonard Schapiro, *Rationalism and Nationalism in Russian Nineteenth-Century Thought* (1967).

Among the better books on French nationalism is Eugen Weber, *The Nationalist Revival in France 1905–1914* (1959). Weber has also written on the *Action Française* (1962) while Robert Byrnes in *Anti-Semitism in Modern France* (1950) presented the anti-Dreyfusards. Mildred Wertheimer (1924) and, in German, Alfred Kruck (1954) have examined the pan-German League (*Alldeutscher Verband*), leading agent of extreme German nationalism. Salo W. Baron's *Modern Nationalism and Religion* (1947) was a stimulating group of lectures by a notable contemporary scholar. The interesting *Diaries* (1958) of Theodore Herzl throw light on the mind of the founder of modern Jewish nationalism. See also works listed under Chapter 12.

On Nietzsche see Walter Kaufmann, *Nietzsche* (1956), an excellent and sympathetic study; F. C. Lea, *The Tragic Philosopher* (1957, reprinted 1973), evocative and penetrating, conceivably the best book on Nietzsche; George A. Morgan, *What Nietzsche Means* (1943), one of the first to rescue Nietzsche from misunderstanding in the English-speaking world; William D. Williams, *Nietzsche and the French* (1952), a study in intellectual influences; Otto Manthey-Zorn, *Dionysus* (1956), a sensitive appreciation; R. J. Hollingdale, *Nietzsche: The Man and His Philosophy* (1965), a serviceable introduction. The older and somewhat hostile treatment by Crane Brinton has been reprinted. Two of the high priests of existentialism have written formidable works on Nietzsche: Karl Jaspers, *Nietzsche: An Introduction to the Understanding of His Philosophical Activity* (English tr. 1965) and Martin Heidegger,

Nietzsche (1961). Kaufmann edits *The Portable Nietzsche* (1954), a good selection from the often reprinted writings. Janko Lavrin's *Nietzsche: A Biographical Introduction* (1971) is just that. For the dedicated Nietzschean, Christopher Middleton, *Selected Letters of Friedrich Nietzsche* (1969). A critical analysis is Arthur Danto, *Nietzsche as Philosopher* (1967). The first volume of *Nietzsche-Studien* appeared in 1972 with a rich content of articles. Specialists will profit from the *International Nietzsche Bibliography* by H. W. Reichert and K. Schlechta. John R. Staude's study of *Max Scheler* (1965) ably presents a significant German disciple of Nietzsche; see also *Scheler: Selected Philosophical Essays*, ed. David A. Lachterman (1973). There was a full-length study of John Davidson by James B. Townsend in 1961. The English musical composer Frederick Delius was another Nietzschean, as his writings indicate. Of more than usual interest is the biography of *Frau Lou: Nietzsche's Wayward Disciple* by Rudolph Binion (1968), a rather speculative analysis of the girl Nietzsche wanted to marry. Patrick Bridgwater, *Nietzsche in Anglosaxony* (1972) traces the influence of Nietzsche on the English-speaking peoples. William J. McGrath's *Dionysian Art and Popular Politics in Austria* (1973) discovers the influence of Nietzsche and Wagner around 1900 on Marxian socialists and others.

L. L. Whyte, *The Unconscious before Freud* (1960) is a splendid work of scholarship. The vast literature on the founder of psychoanalysis must begin with Ernest Jones's three-volume *Life and Work of Sigmund Freud* (1953–1955), abridged in paperback edition (1956). Otherwise, a generally stimulating and high-quality symposium is Benjamin Nelson (ed.), *Freud and the Twentieth Century* (1957); J. A. C. Brown, *Freud and the Post-Freudians* (1961) is one of the best books; Frederick J. Hoffman, *Freudianism and the Literary Mind* (1957) is a distinguished essay. Stanley E. Hyman, *The Tangled Bank* (1962) discusses Darwin, Marx, and Freud, the last most effectively. Reuben Fine's *Freud* (1962) is "a critical reevaluation." Freud's writings are available in many editions, separately and in selections such as the Modern Library *Basic Writings* and John Rickman (ed.), *General Selection from the Works of Freud* (1957). From the recent large number of works about Freud, Vincent Brome, *Freud and His Early Circle* (1967); a new edition of Herbert Marcuse's *Eros and Civilization* (1966); Walter A. Stewart, *Psychoanalysis: The First Ten Years 1888–1898* (1967); Paul Roazen, *Freud's Political and Social Thought* (1968); Paul Ricoeur, *Freud and Philosophy* (tr. 1970); Jonathan Miller, ed., *Freud* (1972), a symposium rounding up many perspectives, some critical; Richard Wollheim, *Sigmund Freud* (1971), one of the Fontana/Viking "Modern Masters" series.

For Carl Jung, Frieda Fordham, *Introduction to Jung's Psychology* (1956); Joland Jacobi, *The Psychology of C. G. Jung* (1969); Avis M. Dry, *The Psychology of Jung* (1961); and the many writings of Jung himself, published in an edition of his collected works (18 volumes). More recent contributions to the understanding of Carl Jung include Charles B. Hanna, *The Face of the Deep: The Religious Ideas of Carl Jung* (1967); J. R. Singer, *Boundaries of the Soul: The Practice of Jung's Psychology* (1972); Edward

C. Whitmont, *The Symbolic Quest: Basic Concepts of Analytical Psychology* (1969); a selection, *C. G. Jung: Psychological Reflections*, edited by the distinguished Jung scholar Jolande Jacobi with R. F. C. Hull (1970). See also R. Hostie, *Religion and the Psychology of Jung* (1957).

Ian W. Alexander, *Bergson* (1957), one of the Bowes and Bowes series of *Studies in Modern European Literature and Thought*, is a concise introduction. Ben Ami Scharfstein, *The Roots of Bergson's Philosophy* (1943) finds many anticipations. Thomas Hanna (ed.), *The Bergsonian Heritage* (1962) is a recent reappraisal. A helpful short Bergson readings book is H. A. Larrabee (ed.), *Selections from Bergson* (1947). S. K. Kumar, *Bergson and the Stream of Consciousness Novel* (1963) and P. A. Y. Gunter (ed.), *Bergson and the Evolution of Physics* (1967) trace influences from the philosopher; see also M. Capek, *Bergson and Modern Physics* (1971) and J. J. Gallagher, *Morality in Evolution: The Moral Philosophy of Henri Bergson* (1970). Gerhard Masur, *Prophets of Yesterday* (1961) ranged widely over European literature and philosophy in the age of Freud, Jung, and Bergson.

The impact of the new physics can be discerned through the writings of the chief innovators themselves, for example, Max Planck, *The New Science* (1959), Albert Einstein, *The Meaning of Relativity* (5th ed., 1955), and Werner Heisenberg, *Physics and Philosophy* (1959). Successful in making the new concepts comprehensible and significant to the public were James Jeans, *The New Background of Science* (1934), *Physics and Philosophy* (1942), and Arthur Eddington, *Space, Time, and Gravitation* (1920). A more recent scholarly treatment is by the prolific science writer, George Gamow, *Thirty Years That Shook Physics*, a study of the quantum theory (1966). Lincoln Barnett, *The Universe and Dr. Einstein* (1948) is a familiar popularization. The growing interest in the history of recent scientific thought is reflected in L. Pearce Williams (ed.), *Relativity Theory: Its Origin and Impact on Modern Thought* (1965) and the annual series published by the University of Pennsylvania Press, Russell McCormmach (ed.), *Historical Studies in the Physical Sciences*, of which Volume II (1970) centers on relativity and quantum theory. From among many other books on the meaning of the new scientific revolution which extended into the 1920s, see Louis de Broglie, *Physics and Microphysics* (1955); Karl Heim, *The Transformation of the Scientific World View* (1953 in English tr.); C. E. M. Joad, *Philosophical Aspects of Modern Science* (1959); M. Capek, *The Philosophical Impact of Contemporary Physics* (1961). R. Harré (ed.), *Scientific Thought 1900–1960: A Selective Survey* (1969) is more broadly helpful. Arthur Koestler, *The Roots of Coincidence* (1972) has recently written brilliantly on the startling paradoxes of modern science.

Walter Kaufmann (ed.), *Religion from Tolstoy to Camus* (1961) is a convenient anthology. Other books illustrative of religious currents in the nineteenth century include B. M. G. Reardon (ed.), *Religious Thought in the Nineteenth Century* (1966), also an anthology; Owen Chadwick, *The Victorian Church*, Volume II, 1860–1901 (1970); Robert M. Grant, *A Short History of the Interpretation of the Bible* (1963), the Higher Criticism; Edward T. Gargan (ed.), *Leo XIII and the Modern World* (1961), the pope whose personality wrought a change in the Roman Catholic Church; J. H. Miller, *The Disappearance of God* (1963), the theme of dying faith traced in five nineteenth-century English writers; Adrien Dansette, *The Religious History of Modern France* (2 vols., 1961); S. R. Hopper (ed.), *Lift Up Your Eyes: The Religious Writings of Leo Tolstoy* (1960), the leading prophet of the age. In *The Bradlaugh Case* (1965), Walter L. Arnstein examines late Victorian atheism, on which see also some chapters in David Daiches, *Some Late Victorian Attitudes* (1969), and Warren S. Smith, *The London Heretics 1870–1914* (1967). The recent reprinting of Alfred W. Benn's *History of English Rationalism in the Nineteenth Century* (2 vols., 1906) makes available an older classic. Michele Ranchetti, *The Catholic Modernists* (1970) deals with the reform movement in the Church from 1864 to 1907, as does Lawrence F. Barmann, *Baron von Hügel and the Modernist Crisis in England* (1972). Donald Attwater, *Modern Christian Revolutionaries* (1947) is interesting. Jeanne Caron, *Le Sillon et la démocratie chrétienne* (Paris, 1967) has dealt thoroughly with a significant French school.

The enormous and revolutionary activity in literature and the arts can be partly apprehended through the following: Eugen Weber (ed.), *Paths to the Present* (1962), an anthology featuring literary movements; Enid Starkie, *From Gautier to Eliot* (1960, 1962), concerned with the French influence on British literature and shedding light on both; Arthur Symons, *The Symbolist Movement in Literature* (1919); and Edmund Wilson, *Axel's Castle* (1936), classic accounts of the literary revolution of the 1880's, to which can be added C. M. Bowra, *The Heritage of Symbolism* (1943), a thoughtful commentary, and Joseph Chiari, *Symbolism from Poe to Mallarmé* (1956); Mario Praz, *The Romantic Agony* (1954) which looks on the decadents with unfriendly but penetrating eyes; Graham Hough, *The Last Romantics;* David Daiches, *The Novel in the Modern World* (1939) and *Poetry in the Modern World* (1941); Holbrook Jackson, *The 1890's* (1913), a classic account of the Oscar Wilde-*Yellow Book* era in Britain; and, as a revelation of the social foundations of the literary revolt, C. Grana, *Bohemian versus Bourgeois: French Society and the French Man of Letters in the Nineteenth Century* (1964), on which see also Malcolm Easton, *Artist and Writer in Paris: The Bohemian Idea* (1964). Roger Shattuck, *The Banquet Years: The Arts in France 1885–1918* (1958) and H. M. Barzun, *Orpheus: Modern Culture and 1913 Renaissance* (1960) are valuable accounts of the prewar artistic scene. Roland N. Stromberg (ed.), *Realism, Naturalism, and Symbolism: Modes of Thought and Expression in Europe 1848–1914* (1968) supplies some documents. Studies of individual writers are too numerous to begin to cite, but a few may be mentioned as examples. F. W. J. Hemmings, *Zola* (1966) is by a leading authority on the outstanding naturalist. J. I. M. Stewart, *Eight Modern English Writers* (1963), Volume XII of the Oxford History of English Literature, chooses Hardy, Conrad, James, Shaw, Joyce, Yeats, Kipling, and D. H. Lawrence. Ernest J. Simmons, *Leo Tolstoy* (2 vols., 1960), is a scholarly life of the most famous of Russian writers; Richard Peace, *Dostoyevsky: An*

Examination of the Major Novels (1971) takes its place on a large shelf of studies of the most interesting of all novelists. André Billy, *The Goncourt Brothers* (1960) is unusually valuable for the literary life. Samuel Hynes, *The Edwardian Turn of Mind* (1968), a wise and witty book stressing the literati and intellectuals, may be compared with John A. Lester, *Journey through Despair: British Literary Culture 1880–1914* (1968), which stresses the anxieties of the age. Richard Ellman (ed.), *Edwardians and Late Victorians* (1960) also presents a gallery of major writers. An important group of French writers is treated in Richard M. Griffiths, *Reactionary Revolution: The Catholic Revival in French Literature 1870–1914* (1965). S. Nowell-Smith (ed.), *The Edwardian Age, 1901–1914* (1964) is far-ranging and includes literature, ideas, the press.

The other arts: John Rewald has written a scholarly *History of Impressionism* (1961) and also a book on *Post-Impressionism* (1956). John Golding, *Cubism: A History and Analysis, 1907–1914* (1968) and Vladimir Markov, *Russian Futurism* (1969) are good examples of monographs in the field of art history in this revolutionary age of painting. For a larger canvas, Herbert Read, *Concise History of Modern Painting* (1959) and Werner Hoffman, *Turning Points in Twentieth-Century Art* (1969). See further in the bibliography for the next chapter, carrying the revolution in the arts into the postwar years. H. H. Stuckenschmidt, *Twentieth-Century Music* (1969), and Wilfrid Mellers, *Caliban Reborn: Renewal in Twentieth-Century Music* (1967) are good introductions to their subject. Josef P. Hodin, *Modern Art and the Modern Mind* (1972), though a bit garrulous, has some interesting ideas.

For political and social thought, H. Stuart Hughes, *Consciousness and Society: European Social Thought 1890–1930* (1958) is generally useful. Michael Curtis, *Three against the Third Republic* (1959) ably and interestingly presents the outlook of Sorel, Maurras, and Barrès. Sorel is also the subject of a first-rate book by J. H. Meisel, *The Genesis of Georges Sorel* (1951) and one by I. L. Horowitz, *Radicalism and The Revolt against Reason* (1961). In *Fear of Power* (1967), Preston King compared Sorel with Proudhon and Tocqueville. Sorel's *Illusions of Progress*, ed. by J. and C. Stanley, was reprinted in 1970, his *Reflections on Violence* in 1961. On Barrès see now Robert Soucy, *Fascism in France: The Case of Maurice Barrès* (1973). Meisel has also edited Gaetano Mosca's *The Myth of the Ruling Class* (1958). That the Third Republic had at least a few intellectual defenders is indicated in J. A. Scott's *Republican Ideas and the Liberal Tradition in France 1870–1914* (1951), the chief of these being Charles Renouvier. Raymond Aron, *Main Currents of Sociological Thought*, Volume II (1967) covers Durkheim, Pareto, and Weber. Among many students drawn to Max Weber, deserving special note are the recent biography by Arthur Mitzman, *The Iron Cage* (1970); Reinhard Bendix, *Max Weber, An Intellectual Portrait* (1965), and Ilse Dronberger, *The Political Thought of Max Weber* (1971). Other recent Weber studies are by Julien Freund, Walter Runciman, and Karl Loewenstein. *From Max Weber* (1946), edited by C. Wright Mills and H. H. Garth is a fine selection from the great German sociologist. Vilfredo Pareto's magnum opus has been translated into English as *The Mind and Society*, reprinted in 1963; also available is a selection from Pareto edited by J. Lopreato. Kurt Wolff has edited Emile Durkheim's *Essays in Sociology and Philosophy* (1960) and also Georg Simmel's *Essays in Sociology* (1959). Durkheim is the subject of recent books by Robert Bierstadt (1966), Robert Nisbet (1965), Dominick LaCapra (1972), and Steven Lukes (1972). Anthony Giddens, in *Capitalism and Modern Social Theory* (1971) compares Weber and Durkheim with Marx.

Fritz Ringer, *The Decline of the German Mandarins* (1969) deals in part with the sociologists and "socialists of the chair." Much light on German political attitudes is shed by Harry F. Young's excellent biography of *Maximilien Harden* (1959), a noted German editor and publicist. The Italy of Pareto, Mosca, and Croce is capably chronicled in an excellent book by A. W. Salomone, *Italian Democracy in the Making 1900–1914: Italy in the Giolittian Era* (1960), as well as in portions of a recent book by John A. Thayer, *Italy and the Great War: Politics and Culture 1870–1914* (1964). Classics of political thought from this era, reprinted in popular editions, are Robert Michels, *Political Parties* (1915) and Graham Wallas, *Human Nature in Politics* (1908). Richard Mandell, *Paris 1900: The Great World's Fair* (1967) is an interesting study in the climate of opinion.

A significant area of political thought dealt with the question of imperialism. See A. P. Thornton, *The Imperial Idea and Its Enemies* (1959); Bernard Porter, *Critics of Empire* (1969); D. K. Fieldhouse (ed.), *Theory of Capitalist Imperialism* (1967), a selection of sources on this theme; Bernard Semmel, *Imperialism and Social Reform: English Social Reform Thought 1895–1914* (1960), which contains interesting chapters on the Darwinian imperialists Karl Pearson and Benjamin Kidd.

Chapter 12

Many works cited in the previous chapter bear on the mood of the intellectuals at the beginning of the war in 1914. Some additional ones: Walter Laqueur, *Young Germany* (1962) conveys the mood of the youth movement which affected the first days of the war. Peter Stansky (ed.), *The Left and War: The British Labour Party and World War I* (1969) contributes to an understanding of the socialist and workingclass abdication to war, as does Georges Haupt's book translated as *Socialism and the Great War: The Collapse of the Second International* (1972). An article by R. N. Stromberg, "The Intellectuals and the Coming of the War" in *Journal of European Studies*, July, 1973, attempts to analyze the several strains in the war spirit. See also J. D. Ellis, *French Socialists and the Problem of Peace 1904–1914* (1967). Hans Schmitt, *Charles Péguy, the Decline of an Idealist* (1967) views Péguy's turn to nationalism without sympathy. Christopher Hassall, *Rupert Brooke* (1964) is a good biography of the poet who symbolized the pro-war idealism of 1914. A good anthology of war writing is George Panichas (ed.), *Promise of Greatness* (1968); also Guy Chapman (ed.), *Vain Glory* (1968). Bernard

Bergonzi, *Heroes' Twilight* (1964) discusses the war literature. I. M. Parsons has edited a volume of war poetry as has Brian Gardner, *Up the Line to Death* (1965). *Lenin and the Bolsheviks: The Intellectual and Political History of the Triumph of Bolshevism in Russia* (1965) is by A. B. Ulam. *Lenin on Politics and Revolution* (1969) has been edited by James E. Connor. Helmut Gruber (ed.), *International Communism in the Era of Lenin: A Documentary History* (1967) is rich in contemporary materials. See also David Lane, *The Roots of Russian Communism* (1969). For postwar Communism and Socialism see under Chapter 13. Henry Winkler, *The League of Nations Movement in Great Britain 1914–1919* (1952) deals with an important wartime body of thought. W. W. Wagar, *H. G. Wells and the World State* (1961) provides an illuminating account of one man of letters heavily involved in this cause. D. A. Prater's *European of Yesterday: A Biography of Stefan Zweig* (1972) deals with a notable opponent of the war spirit.

In *Good Tidings: The Belief in Progress from Darwin to Marcuse* (1972), intellectual historian W. Warren Wagar also puts the post-1919 loss of hope in perspective. The neo-orthodox theology of Barth, Bultmann, Berdyaev, Tillich, and others may be approached through numerous editions of their writings, also via collections such as Leonhard Reinisch (ed.), *Theologians of Our Time* (1964), or the analyses in John Macquarrie (ed.), *Contemporary Religious Thinkers* (1968). See also Arnold Nash (ed.), *Protestant Thought in the Twentieth Century* (1951). H. Stuart Hughes, *Oswald Spengler: A Critical Estimate* (rev. ed., 1962) is a commentary on the author of *The Decline of the West* (repr. 1961), a most celebrated expression of war and postwar pessimism. Among Aldous Huxley's works, *Brave New World* (1932) has been reprinted along with his later comments, *Brave New World Revisited* (1958). Among other period pieces of the 1920s, J. Ortega y Gasset, *The Revolt of the Masses* (English ed., 1932) is a classic, while Montgomery Belgion, *Our Present Philosophy of Life* was a 1929 commentary; *The Long Weekend* (1941) by Robert Graves and Alan Hodge examined popular culture in Britain between the wars. Beatrice Webb's *Diaries*, Volume II, 1924–1932 (1956) edited by Margaret Cole are among the more interesting sources. Other documents of the times were Joseph Wood Krutch, *The Modern Temper*, and Freud's *Civilization and Its Discontents*, both published in the late '20s.

Needless to say there is a huge bibliography on the twentieth-century literary revolution. General works, such as Graham Hough, *Image and Experience: Studies in a Literary Revolution* (1960), Walter Allen, *The Modern Novel in Britain and America* (1964) (*Tradition and Dream*), and Germaine Bree and Margaret Guiton, *An Age of Fiction: The French Novel from Gide to Camus* (1958) may be supplemented by studies of specific literary movements, such as Maurice Nadeau, *History of Surrealism* (1965), Herbert S. Gershman, *The Surrealist Revolution in France* (1968), and Wallace Fowlie, *The Age of Surrealism* (1950), and then by the multitudinous works on individual authors. Among the latter such treatments as Mary Freeman, *D. H. Lawrence, A Study of His Ideas* (1960) are of greater interest to the intellectual historian than other types of literary criticism which often rigidly eschew the historical or intellectual approach. On Lawrence see also Harry T. Moore's engaging biography, *The Intelligent Heart* (1954), and perceptive analyses by H. M. Daleski, *The Forked Flame* (1966), Graham Hough, *The Dark Sun* (1956), and Eliseo Vivas, *D. H. Lawrence* (1960). Outstanding biographical-critical studies of modern masters include Richard Ellman, *Yeats: the Man and the Masks* (1948); George D. Painter's two-volume biography of *Marcel Proust* (1959, 1965); and, from among a host of Joyce studies, Richard M. Kain and Marvin Magalaner, *Joyce: The Man, the Work, the Reputation* (1965), and Frank Budgen, *James Joyce, The Making of 'Ulysses'* (1960). A volume in the paperback-published *Journal of Contemporary History* series, titled *Literature and Politics in the Twentieth Century*, edited by Walter Laqueur and George Mosse (1968) examines a number of authors from a historical standpoint. Hugh Kenner is the author of a recent major work, *The Pound Era* (1972); cf. Noel Stock's *Life of Ezra Pound* (1970), another major biography. Kenner is editor of the volume on T. S. Eliot in the "Critical Heritage" series, which reprints reviews of the writers showing how they looked to their contemporaries (volumes also on Lawrence, Joyce, Yeats, and others). The abundance of attention to major writers may be suggested by the appearance in the last few years of at least ten significant studies of Aldous Huxley, including books by John Atkins (1967), Peter Bowering (1968), Lawrence Brander (1970), Milton Birnbaum (1971), and Peter Firchow (1972). Major biographies have appeared of *Lytton Strachey*, by Michael Holroyd, and *Virginia Woolf* by Quentin Bell (1972). See also the latter's *Bloomsbury* (1968). In *The Master Builders* (1961) Peter Blake conveys the lives and times of the great modern architects. Peter Gay's *Weimar Culture* (1969) depicts the atmosphere in which many of them worked in the 1920s. John M. Brinnin's life of Gertrude Stein, *The Third Rose* (1959) takes us into the Parisian artistic world of the 1920s. Russian writers trying to adjust to an increasingly rigid tyranny are discussed in Robert A. Maguire, *Red Virgin Soil: Soviet Literature in the 1920's* (1968).

C. E. M. Joad, *Guide to Modern Thought* (1933) found modern physics, psychoanalysis, and Bergsonian vitalism among the doctrines most in need of explaining to the general public; references to these topics in Chapter 11 are therefore still relevant to the 1920s, as also are works on the modernist movement in the arts. The recent collection edited by C. B. Cox and A. E. Dyson, *The Twentieth-Century Mind* (1972) should be noted: Volume I covers 1900–1918 while Volume II relates to the interwar period.

Ernest Nolte, *Three Faces of Fascism* (tr. 1967) is a perceptive introduction to its subject. Nolte (ed.), *Theorien über den Faschismus* (1967) deserves translation also. A multitude of works on fascism and Nazism have appeared in recent years. Here are some: George L. Mosse, *The Crisis of German Ideology* (1964); Fritz Stern, *The Politics of Cultural Despair* (1961); Kurt von Klemperer, *Germany's New Conservatism* (1957); Peter Viereck, *Metapolitics: The Roots of the Nazi Mind* (rev. ed., 1961); *The Third Reich*, a 1955 UNESCO symposium (E. Vermeil *et al.*), all addressed to the debate about alleged traditional German affinities to Hitlerism. A whole library exists on

Hitler, of course. Of special value for our area is Eberhard Jäckel, *Hitler's Weltanschauung* (tr. 1972). Percy Schramm's introduction to the German edition of *Hitler's Table Talk* is valuable on the roots of the Führer's thought; see also Schramm material edited by Donald Detwiler under the title of *Hitler: The Man and the Military Leader* (1971). General studies on Hitler and Nazism include the standard biographies in English by Alan Bullock, in German by Karl Bracher and H. Heiber. Lewis Hertzman, *DNVP: Right-wing Opposition in the Weimar Republic 1918–1924* (1964) is an example of a well-researched monograph. Peter G. J. Pulzer, *The Rise of Political Anti-Semitism in Germany and Austria* (1965) reveals Austrian roots of Hitler's ideology, as do Andrew G. Whiteside, *Austrian National Socialism before 1918* (1962) and William A. Jenks, *Vienna and the Young Hitler* (1960). George L. Mosse's *Nazi Culture* is a unique record of the Nazi mind.

An excellent historical survey is Denis Mack Smith, *Italy: a Modern History* (1959). Not translated from the Italian, Renzo de Felice's three-volume biography of Mussolini, of which the first volume, *Mussolini il Rivoluzionaria 1883–1920* appeared in 1964, is the definitive work. Jack Roth's article "The Roots of Italian Fascism: Sorel and Sorelismo" in *Journal of Modern History*, March, 1967, sheds much light on the ideological roots of Mussolini's movement. H. S. Harris, *The Social Philosophy of Giovanni Gentile* (1960) examined the leading philosopher of Italian fascism. A. J. Gregor, *The Ideology of Fascism* (1969) is useful. Stanley G. Payne, *Falange* (1962) is an authoritative account of the Spanish variety of fascism. Charles F. Delzell has edited a collection of documents on *Mediterranean Fascism* (1969). A good many recent works address themselves to consideration of fascism as an international phenomenon, which it undoubtedly was. See among others Eugen Weber, *Varieties of Fascism* (1964); John Weiss, *The Fascist Tradition* (1967); W. Laqueur and George Mosse (ed.), *International Fascism 1920–1945* (1966); S. J. Woolf, ed., *European Fascism* (1968); Gilbert Allardyce (ed.), *The Place of Fascism in European History* (1973). Alastair Hamilton, *The Appeal of Fascism: A Study of Intellectuals and Fascism* (1971) is interesting but rather disappointingly thin. Additionally, Robert Benewick, *Political Violence and Public Order* (1969) and W. F. Mandle, *Anti-Semitism and the British Union of Fascists* (1968) are excellent on British fascism. M. D. Biddiss has studied *The Father of Racist Ideology*, the nineteenth-century Frenchman Gobineau (1970).

Chapter 13

Left-Wing Intellectuals between the Wars, edited by Laqueur and Mosse, is another of the Journal of Contemporary History volumes. The origins of the Communist parties out of elements of the older Left is the subject of a number of well-researched monographs including Walter Kendall, *The Revolutionary Movement in Britain 1900–1921* (1969); L. J. Macfarlane, *The British Communist Party: Its Origin and Development* (1966); Werner Angress, *The Stillborn Revolution* (1963), on the failure of Communist revolution in Germany 1920–1923; John M. Cammett, *Antonio Gramsci and the Origins of Italian Communism* (1967), dealing with a significant figure of twentieth century Marxist thought; Robert Wohl, *French Communism in the Making 1914–1924* (1966), also Annie Kriegel, *Aux origines du communisme francais* (1964). On the attraction of the intellectuals to Communism, a host of studies is headed by Neal Wood, *Communism and British Intellectuals* (1959) and David Caute, *Communism and the French Intellectuals* (1964), supplemented by such popular books as R. H. S. Crossman (ed.), *The God That Failed* (1950) and Raymond Aron, *The Opium of the Intellectuals* (1962). Caute has added *The Fellow Travellers* (1972). Martin Jay, in *The Dialectical Imagination* (1973) has provided exhaustive treatment of the Frankfurt group of German neo-Marxians which included Herbert Marcuse. George Lichtheim, *George Lukács* (1970) presents one of the more significant East European Marxist theoreticians of the interwar years. Among the more famous memoirs of ex-communists were Arthur Koestler's *Arrow in the Blue* (1952) and *The Invisible Writing* (1954); also George Orwell, in *Collected Essays* (1954) and *Homage to Catalonia* (1952). Such novels as Thomas Mann, *The Magic Mountain* (1930), Ignazio Silone, *Fontamara* (1934) and Koestler's *Darkness at Noon* (1941) provide deeper clues to this ideology-haunted decade than may be found in more formal histories. Among the latter, Volume V of G. D. H. Cole's *History of Socialist Thought* is *Socialism and Fascism 1931–1939* (1960). John T. Marcus, *French Socialism in the Crisis Years, 1933–1936* (1958) is a well-written account of the struggle with fascism and the emergence of the Popular Front, on which see especially Joel Colton's splendid biography of *Leon Blum: Humanist in Politics* (1966). See also Nathaniel Greene, *Crisis and Decline: The French Socialist Party in the Popular Front Era* (1969) and Daniel Brower, *The New Jacobins: The French Communists and the Popular Front* (1968), along with an article by Donald N. Baker, "The Socialist Party's Left Wing in France, 1921–1939," *Journal of Modern History*, March, 1971. Several books have looked at the Spanish Civil War in its relationship to European writers; among them, Stanley Weintraub, *The Last Great Cause* (1968) and J. M. Muste, *Say That We Saw Spain Die* (1966). *Beyond Marxism: The Faith and Works of Hendrik de Man* (1966), by Peter Dodge, is a monograph on an interesting deviant Marxist. Among further memoirs, Julian Trevelyan, *Indigo Days* (1857); Edward Upward, *In the Thirties* (1970); Kingsley Martin, *Editor* (1968); Simone Weil, *Selected Essays 1934–1943*, edited by R. Rees (1966); Victor Serge, *Memoirs of a Revolutionary 1901–1941* (London, 1965). Julian Symons, *The 1930's* (1960) is an evocative portrait of the mood of the decade. Bernard Zylstra, *From Pluralism to Collectivism: The Development of Laski's Political Thought* (1968) gives attention to a prominent British intellectual. G. L. S. Shackle, *The Years of High Theory* (1967) is relevant to the new economic thought of the 1930s, on which theme see also Michael Stewart, *Keynes and After* (1968). Other valuable treatments are Ben B. Seligman, *Main Currents in Modern Economics* (1962) and Claudio Napoleoni, *Economic Thought of the Twentieth Century* (1971).

Philosophy: Logical positivism and linguistic analysis can be studied in Viktor Kraft, *The Vienna Circle* (1953); J. O. Urmson, *Philosophical Analysis: Its Development between the Two World Wars* (1956); A. J. Ayer *et al., The Revolution in Philosophy* (1956); and Copleston, *Contemporary Philosophy* (1956), which divides its attention between the analytical and existential schools. I. M. Bochenski, *Contemporary European Philosophy* (1956) is also a sound and lucid guide. A. J. Ayer (ed.), *Logical Positivism* (1959) is a fairly technical symposium. R. J. Butler (ed.), *Analytical Philosophy* (1963, 1965) are volumes illustrating the trends of professional work. David Pears, *Ludwig Wittgenstein,* one of the Modern Master series (1969) and David Pole, *The Later Philosophy of Wittgenstein* (1959) are among a large number of works on the most important of the analytical philosophers. Richard Rorty (ed.), *The Linguistic Turn: Recent Essays in Philosophical Method* (1967) keeps up with more recent trends. See also J. L. Austin, *Philosophical Papers* (2nd edition, 1970). Shortcomings are noted by Patrima Bowles, *Is Metaphysics Possible?* (1965) and C. W. K. Mundle, *A Critique of Linguistic Philosophy* (1970). Bertrand Russell's fascinating *Autobiography* sheds light on the most colorful of twentieth-century philosophers, who died in 1970 at the age of 98; see also a biography by Alan Wood, and studies of Russell's philosophy by A. J. Ayer and by David F. Pears.

Existentialism has given rise to a battery of books. Among the earlier ones, H. J. Blackham, *Six Existentialist Thinkers* (1952) was one of the first and best, though rather compressed; Walter Kaufmann, *Existentialism from Dostoyevsky to Sartre* (1960); William Barrett, *Irrational Man* (1958), a popular book; Norman N. Greene, *Jean-Paul Sartre: The Existentialist Ethic* (1960). Martin Heidegger's *Existence and Being* (*Sein und Zeit,* 1927), Gabriel Marcel, *The Philosophy of Existence* (1949) and other writings, and Jean-Paul Sartre, *Being and Nothingness* (tr. 1956) are texts of the Fathers, along with the writings of Kierkegaard from which a selection was made by Lee H. Hollander (1960). Karl Jaspers, *Philosophy of Existence* has also been reprinted (1971). Philip Thody, *Jean-Paul Sartre* (1960) was an attractive presentation; Thody also wrote about Albert Camus, as did John Cruickshank in his *Albert Camus and the Literature of Revolt* (1960). Walter Lowrie was the foremost authority on Kierkegaard, through his *Short Life of Kierkegaard* (1951) and other works. David E. Roberts, *Existentialism and Religious Belief* (1963) suggests the relationship which many others have explored; for example, John Macquarrie, *An Existentialist Theology: A Comparison of Heidegger and Bultmann* (1955). Rudolf Bultmann, *Existence and Faith* (tr. 1960) is a collection of writings by the German scholar who exercised so great an influence on Protestant religious thought. William J. Richardson, *Heidegger* (1965) is a valiant survey of the existentialist in all his phases, by a Roman Catholic priest. The debate went on in F. H. Heinemann, *Existentialism and the Modern Predicament* (1954); J. von Rintelen, *Beyond Existentialism* (1961); Paul Roubiczek, *Existentialism: For and against* (1964). More recently, Frederick A. Olafson, *Principles and Persons: An Ethical Interpretation of Existentialism* (1967); Thomas Molnar, *Sartre: Ideologue of Our Time* (1968); Mary

Warnock, *Existentialism* (1970); D. G. Cooper and R. D. Laing (ed.), *Reason and Violence: A Decade of Sartre's Philosophy, 1960–1970* (2nd ed., 1971), also Robert D. Cummings (ed.), *The Philosophy of Jean-Paul Sartre* (1965); *Sartre: A Collection of Critical Essays*, edited by Mary Warnock (1971). Charles F. Wallraff has a discriminating work on Karl Jaspers (1970). Alden L. Fisher has made available in English *The Essential Writings of Merleau-Ponty* (1969), one of the major French thinkers. Paul Ilie has a book on the Spanish philosopher, *Unamuno: An Existential View of Self and Society* (1967). A useful paperback anthology is *The Existentialist Tradition: Selected Writings*, edited by N. Langiulli (1971).

Chapter 14

The following tracts for the times could help understand the immediate postwar years: Alfred J. Weber, *Abschied von der Bisherigen Geschichte*, translated as *Farewell to European History* (1946); Georges Bernanos, *La liberté pour quoi faire?* (1953), essays on the European spirit written 1946–1947; José Ortega y Gasset, *The Modern Theme* (tr. 1961); Gabriel Marcel, *Man against Mass Society* (1952); Judith N. Shklar, *After Utopia: the Decline of Political Faith* (1959); Hannah Arendt, *The Human Condition: A Study of the Central Dilemmas Facing Modern Man* (1958); Julian Huxley, *The Human Crisis* (1963); J. H. Plumb (ed.), *Crisis in the Humanities* (1964); R. Guardini, *The End of the Modern World* (1957); Adrienne Koch (ed.), *Philosophy for a Time of Crisis* (1959); Richard M. Weaver, *Visions of Order: The Cultural Crisis of Our Time* (1964); Jacques Ellul, *The Technological Society* (1964); Northrop Frye, *The Modern Century* (1967); Raymond Aron, *Progress and Disillusion* (1968). Such a list in the teeming present could go on endlessly. In a 1975 book, *After Everything: European Thought and Culture since 1945*, Roland N. Stromberg attempts to grapple with the richness and fragmentation of contemporary thought. A more general text is Maurice Crouzet, *The European Renaissance since 1945* (1970). T. R. Fyvel, *Intellectuals Today* (1968) is a jaundiced view. Lionel Trilling, in *The Liberal Imagination* (1950), *Beyond Culture* (1965), and *Mind in the Modern World* (1972) offers acute commentary on the culture of today. The *New Outline of Modern Knowledge*, edited by Alan Pryce-Jones in 1956, bravely tried to keep up with everything in one volume; a new edition is needed. Attention is called again to the Cox-Dyson *Twentieth-Century Mind*, Volume III covering the English years since 1945. Further on existentialism, and other philosophical trends: Edward N. Lee and Maurice Mandelbaum (ed.), *Phenomenology and Existentialism* (1967); Marvin Farber, *The Aims of Phenomenology* (1966); Colin Smith, *Contemporary French Philosophy* (1964); George L. Kline (ed.), *European Philosophy Today* (1965), covering some Spanish, Italian, and east European thinkers as well as Heidegger and Sartre.

An attempt to keep abreast of contemporary literature might consult books such as Maurice Nadeau, *The French Novel since the War* (1967); Peter Demetz, *Postwar German Literature: A Critical Introduction* (1970); Rubin

Rabinovitz, *The Reaction against Experiment in the English Novel 1950–1960* (1967); John Press, *A Map of English Verse* (1969). Press's more detailed study of poetry in the 1950's was titled *Rule and Energy* (1963). Cf. M. L. Rosenthal, *The New Poets* (1967); Martin Dodsworth (ed.), *The Survival of Poetry* (1970), among others. On the theater to Martin Esslin's *Theater of the Absurd* may be added Eric Bentley, *The Theater of Commitment* (1968), and John R. Taylor, *Anger and Afterward* (2nd ed. 1969), Edward Lucie-Smith, *Movements in Art since 1945* (1970) struggles manfully with an awkward subject. Cf. Gerald Woods, *Art without Boundaries 1950–1970* (1972).

Among a number of recent books on the fashionable topic of structuralism, Jean Piaget (ed.), *Structuralism, an Introduction* (1970) and Michael Lane (ed.), *Structuralism, a Reader* (1970). The Fontana Modern Masters series contains volumes on the following alleged leaders of recent thought: Camus, Wittgenstein, Che Guevara, Frantz Fanon, Herbert Marcuse, Claude Lévi-Strauss, Noam Chomsky, Wilhelm Reich, George Orwell, Marshall McLuhan, Joyce, Yeats, Gandhi—a list suggestive of the profusion and confusion of recent life. Orwell was an influential journalist of the postwar years whose *Collected Essays, Journalism and Letters*, Volume IV (1968) is an interesting document of the times. Guevara, Fanon, and Marcuse were of course fashionably radical ideologists of the 1960s. Political thought of a more traditional sort can be approached via Roy Pierce, *Contemporary French Political Thought* (1966). Paul A. Robinson, in *The Freudian Left* (1969) and Richard King, *The Party of Eros* (1972) treat a portion of New Left thought which is personalist, anarchist, and utopian. In *Marxism and the Existentialists* (1967), the prolific French sociologist Raymond Aron examined one type of neo-Marxism. Cf. Richard T. De George, *The New Marxism: Soviet and East European Marxism since 1956* (1968). Peter Reddaway supplied information about *Russia's Underground Intellectuals* (1970), as does D. Pospielovsky, *Soviet Dissent: 1964 to 1970* (1971). Erich Fromm (ed.), *Socialist Humanism* reprints eastern European revisionists, discussed in L. Labedz (ed.), *Revisionism: Essays in the History of Marxist Ideas* (1962). Several volumes in the series *New Theology*, edited by M. E. Marty and Don G. Peerman (1966–1969) kept up with recent currents of thought in a lively area. George W. Morgan, *The Human Predicament: Dissolution or Wholeness* (1968) and Christopher Booker, *The Neophiliacs* (1969) were striking comments on the current cultural scene. In *Left or Right: The Bogus Dilemma* (1969) economist Samuel Brittan suggested the irrelevancy of old ideologies.

Further on postwar political thought, W. J. Stankiewicz (ed.), *Political Thought since World War II* (1965); Hannah Arendt, *On Revolution* (1963); Kenneth Minogue, *The Liberal Mind* (1963); Stephen Spender, *The Year of the Young Rebels* (1969) and George Paloczi-Horvath, *Youth up in Arms* (1971), among an abundance of books on this subject; T. H. Rigby (ed.), *The Disintegrating Monolith: Pluralist Trends in the Communist World* (1967); Michael Oakeshott, *Rationalism in Politics and Other Essays* (1962), the conservative school; Chad Walsh, *From Utopia to Nightmare* (1962), an essay in disenchantment. H. Stuart Hughes, *The Obstructed Path* (1968) deals with French social thought between 1930 and 1960. Statements from the embattled ranks of radical youth included Tariq Ali (ed.), *New Revolutionaries* (1969).

C. P. Snow's *The Two Cultures and the Scientific Revolution* (1959) began a debate carried on by F. R. Leavis in his (with Michael Yudkin) *Two Cultures? The Significance of C. P. Snow* (1962) and in Snow's *The Two Cultures and a Second Look* (1965). See also Charles Davy, *Towards a Third Culture* (1965); Jacques Barzun, *Science: The Glorious Entertainment* (1964). On another theme of the age, Douglas A. Hughes (ed.), *Perspectives on Pornography* (1970). But the teeming productivity of the contemporary world, embracing dozens of huge academic industries, hundreds of more or less significant creative writers, all kinds of oddities and fads, and an abundance of political polemics defies the bibliographer. If any one periodical comes close to enabling the serious person to keep abreast of the world of ideas, it would be the London *Times Literary Supplement*, with its comprehensive and perceptive coverage of the realm of expression and its occasional special issues devoted entirely to some pertinent special theme.

Locating Additional Books and Articles

The foregoing bibliography being but a highly selective listing, any student doing a serious research paper must have recourse to bibliographical aids to assist him in locating books and articles on his subject, a need that becomes greater as the volume of publication grows. Reference has already been made to bibliographies and guides to further reading in various areas: the several volumes of the *Pelican Guide to English Literature: French Literature and Its Backgrounds*, edited by John Cruickshank, also in several volumes; to special bibliographies of Marxist philosophy, of Nietzsche (see under these subjects in the above bibliography); to periodicals such as *Studies in Romanticism* and *Victorian Studies* which publish bibliographies for their fields. A number of others will be mentioned here.

The five-volume bibliography, *English Literature 1600–1800*, edited by R. S. Crane and others, taken from the periodical *Philological Quarterly*, covers publications from the years 1926–1965; it is frequently annotated and goes beyond strictly literary studies. There is a similar *Bibliography of Studies in Victorian Literature*, based on *Modern Philology*, edited for the years 1932–1944 by William D. Templeman (1945), continued by Austin Wright for 1945–1954 (1956) and by R. C. Stack for the years 1955–1964 (1967). The *New Cambridge Bibliography of English Literature*, ed. George Watson, is being published in five volumes (1969–   ), replacing the older Cambridge Bibliography (5 vols., 1940; 1957 supplement), edited by F. W. Bateson. Bateson's handbook, *A Guide to English Literature* (2nd ed., 1968) remains useful. Annual bibliographies are supplied by the Modern Humanities Research Association, *Annual Bibliography of English Language and Literature* (1920–   ); the English Association (London), *The Year's Work in English*

Studies (1920–   ); and The Modern Language Association, *Annual Bibliography* (1955–   ). The Goldentree Bibliographies in Language and Literature, published by Appleton-Century-Crofts, have separate volumes for periods such as eighteenth-century, romantic, Victorian. A French standard is the annual *Bibliographie de la litterature française du moyen age à nos jours* (Armand Colin, Paris).

Josef L. Altholz, *Victorian England, 1837–1901: A Bibliographical Handbook*, mentioned earlier, is one of a series of such guides to the various periods of British history being published by Cambridge University Press for the Conference on British Studies, general editor Jean Hecht. *Changing Views of British History*, edited by Elizabeth C. Furber (1966) supplied surveys of writing about England since 1939 by historians expert in their fields. For French literature and culture, in addition to Cruickshank, R. L. Ritchie's *France: A Companion to French Studies* (5th ed., 1965) has now been replaced by the similarly titled volume edited by D. C. Charlton (1972). The German equivalent in this Methuen series is Malcolm Pasley (ed.), *Germany: A Companion to German Studies* (1972), which is the successor to Jethro Bithell. The French series, *Nouvelle Clio* (1963–   ) is bibliographically useful with numerous volumes on the various historical periods. *French Historical Studies* is a basic journal. The bibliographies published serially since 1955 by the French Institute of New York, including *French VI* for the nineteenth century and *French VII* for the twentieth are excellent for French thought and literature. The leading aid to the study of German history is Bruno Gebhardt (ed.), *Handbuch der Deutschen Geschichte* (9th ed., 4 vols., 1970). For some guidance in Russian intellectual history see the bibliography in Marc Raeff (ed.), *Russian Intellectual History: An Anthology* (1966). General problems of historical bibliography are discussed by a panel of experts in Dagmar H. Perman (ed.), *Bibliography and the Historian* (1968).

The periodical *Isis* prints every year a "Critical Bibliography of the History of Science and Its Cultural Influence"; in 1972 M. Whitrow edited a *Cumulative Bibliography from Isis*, covering the years 1913 to 1965. See also J. Agassi, *Towards an Historiography of Science* (1963), a special issue of the journal *History and Theory*, which also issues periodical bibliographies in the philosophy of history; and A. C. Crombie and M. A. Hoskin, *History of Science: An Annual Review of Literature, Research and Teaching* (1962–   ). *The Philosopher's Index* contains abstracts of articles; Richard T. De George, *A Guide to Philosophical Bibliography and Research*, published by Appleton-Century-Crofts (1971) is also helpful in this area. An *International Bibliography of the History of Religions* has been published annually since 1953 at Leiden. Other guides to current literature include the *International Bibliography of the Social Sciences* and the *International Bibliography of Political Science* published periodically by UNESCO; *Historical Abstracts*, and *Twentieth-Century Abstracts*, published by the Clio Press, an indispensable guide to the scholarly periodical literature for historians; similar abstracts for sociology and political science; and of course the more general guides to periodical literature, *Reader's Guide* and *International Index to Periodicals*.

An unusual special project is the *Wellesley Index to Victorian Periodicals,* edited by Walter E. Houghton, now in progress, two volumes thus far. Another is *Index Expressionismus,* edited by Paul Raabe.

A valuable research tool is Constance Winchell, *Guide to Reference Books* (8th edition, 1967); another is Jean K. Gates, *Guide to the Use of Books and Libraries.* The "How to Find Out" series from Pergamum Press is worth knowing about; for example, *How to Find Out in Philosophy and Psychology,* by Dietrich H. Borchardt (1968). The most valuable of research tools, perhaps, is the bibliography of bibliographies, which can guide you to a bibliography on the subject of your choice. See Theodore Besterman, *A World Bibliography of Bibliographies* (5 vols., 1965–1966); the periodical *Bibliographical Index: A Cumulative Bibliography of Bibliographies;* also Robert L. Collison, *Bibliographies, Subject and National: A Guide to Their Contents, Arrangements and Use* (3rd ed., 1968); and Richard A. Gray, *Serial Bibliographies in the Humanities and Social Sciences* (1969). John G. Barrow, *A Bibliography of Bibliographies in Religion* is an example of a more specialized bibliography of bibliographies. In addition, Wood Gray, *Historian's Handbook* (1964) and Helen J. Paulton, *The Historian's Handbook: A Descriptive Guide to Reference Books* (1972) may prove helpful.

In addition to journals mentioned, a few more of special revelance may be mentioned: the *Journal of the History of Ideas,* especially, the leading periodical for intellectual historians; *Journal of Modern History, Comparative Studies in Society and History, Past and Present, International Review of Social History, History and Theory, Clio* ("an interdisciplinary journal of literature, history, and the philosophy of history"), *Eighteenth-Century Studies, Journal of European Studies, Comparative Literature Studies, Journal of the History of Philosophy, Review of Politics;* others too numerous to mention.

Index

Morris, William, 348, 351, 404
Mosca, Gaetano, 439
Moseley, Oswald, 444
Mounier, Emmanuel, 395, 463
Mozart, Wolfgang A., 201
Müller, Adam, 255
Mun, Albert de, 359
music, 98, 189, 224, 401, 405, 436
Musset, Alfred de, 230, 235
Mussolini, Benito, 374, 413, 422, 423, 428,
436–39, 443

Namier, L. B., 477, 478, 494
Napier, John, 38
Napoleon I of France (Bonaparte) (1769–1821),
210–12, 214, 225, 234, 235, 239–40, 364,
366
Napoleon III of France, 264, 284–85, 294, 296,
300, 302, 349
nationalism, 185, 202, 213–15, 276, 337, 364–
69, 413, 473
nature, idea of, 43–46, 193, 231, 309–11, 316
Nazism (National Socialism), 373, 375, 380,
417, 422, 439–43, 456, 468, 473, 482, 501,
505
neo-classicism, 17–18, 27, 97–99, 109–11, 144,
165, 179, 188–93, 225, 229, 236, 237
Neo-Platonism, 8, 14, 44, 185, 232
Nerval, Gerald, 233
Neurath, Otto, 456
New Left, 485–490, 510
Newman, John Henry, Cardinal, 232, 292,
361
Newton, Isaac (1642–1727), 7, 11, 37, 41, 43,
46, 47, 53, 59–67, 108, 111, 118, 123, 133,
141, 174, 185, 188, 237, 387
Nicholas of Cusa, 33, 41
Niebuhr, Berthold, 270
Niebuhr, Reinhold, 429, 479
Nietzsche, Friedrich (1844–1900), 1, 5, 9, 198,
215, 316, 350, 363, 371–75, 396, 397–98,
401–2, 409, 415, 437, 440, 462, 480, 510
Nordau, Max, 403
Norris, John, 117
North, Dudley, 169
Novalis (Georg von Hardenburg), 224, 232

Oakeshott, Michael, 477
Oates, Titus, 90, 108
occultism, 394, 397
Ockham, William of, 9, 16–17, 18, 52, 105,
218
O'Connor, Feargus, 280
Oldenburg, Henry, 43
Ollivier, Emile, 302
Oratorians, 55
Oresme, Nicole de, 19, 32
Ortega y Gasset, José, 182, 389, 428, 510
Orwell, George, 449, 476, 478–79, 481, 484
Osborne, John, 485
Overton, Richard, 83–84

Owen, Robert (1771–1858), 260, 261–63, 266–
67, 330, 340
Owen, Wilfred, 423
Oxford Movement, 232

pacifism, 259, 395, 455–56
Padua, University of, 32, 73
Paine, Thomas, 183, 212
painting, 28–30, 189, 225, 404, 433, 435
Paley, William, 163, 252
Palissot, Charles, 195
Palladio, Andrea, 99, 109
pantheism, 56–67, 231
Papini, Giovanni, 383, 439
Paracelsus, Philippus, 41
Pareto, Vilfredo (1848–1923), 410–11, 437, 439
Parker, Henry, 81
Pascal, Blaise (1623–1662), 39, 41, 42, 45, 49,
58–59, 129, 218, 219
Pasteur, Louis, 302, 305
Pater, Walter, 4
Pattison, Mark, 317
Paul, St., 25
Pauli, Wolfgang, 119
Pavlov, Ivan, 460
Pearson, Karl, 368
Péguy, Charles (1873–1914), 359, 366, 383,
393, 396, 420
Pepys, Samuel, 107, 108
Perrault, Charles, 109
Pestalozzi, Johann, 183
Petty, William, 109, 169
phenomenology, 383, 482–83
Physiocrats, 144, 167–71, 184, 195, 256
Picard, Jean, 61
Picasso, Pablo (1881–1973), 405, 432, 450, 451
pietism, 102, 121
Pigou, Arthur, 254
Pisarev, Dimitri, 355
Pius IX, Pope, 392
Pius X, Pope, 392
Place, Francis, 251
Planck, Max, 388, 429
Plato and Platonism, 1, 8–9, 10–11, 24, 25, 33,
40, 45, 70, 103, 117, 153, 218, 260, 370,
371, 505 (*see also* Neo-Platonism)
Plekhanov, G. V., 355–56
Poe, Edgar Allen, 401
Political Economy, *see* economic ideas
Politiques, 24, 27, 75
Polybius, 85
Pompadour, Jeanne, Marquise de, 140, 141
Pope, Alexander (1688–1744), 111, 116, 120,
141, 142, 166, 179, 189, 223
Popper, Karl, 331, 336, 344, 477, 495
Populism, Russian, 355
positivism, 296–302, 360 (*see also* Logical
Positivism)
Pound, Ezra, 401, 425, 432, 506
Poussin, Nicolas, 29, 30, 99
pragmatism, 383
Prévost-Paradol, Lucien, 294
Prezzolini, Giuseppe, 383